lon

Thailand's Islands & Beaches

Bangkok
p54

Ko Chang & Eastern Seaboard
p100

Hua Hin & the Upper Gulf
p140

Ko Samui & the Lower Gulf
p173

Phuket & the Andaman Coast
p243

THIS EDITION WRITTEN AND RESEARCHED BY

Mark Beales, Austin Bush,
David Eimer, Damian Harper, Isabella Noble

PLAN YOUR TRIP

BY PAZAI40 /GETTY IMAGES ©

KO LIPE, P353

LONELY PLANET /GETTY IMAGES ©

PHUKET TOWN, P274

ON THE ROAD

Contents

UNDERSTAND

SURVIVAL GUIDE

SPECIAL FEATURES

Welcome to Thailand's Islands & Beaches

Golden-sand bays, lazily swaying cotton hammocks, castle-like karsts emerging from sapphire seas: southern Thailand's coasts make your dreams of tropical paradise come true.

Seductive Beaches

Thailand's beaches are legendary. Slender palms angle over pearlescent sand, warm turquoise seas conceal technicolour coral gardens, and beach parties beckon revellers. With two long coastlines and jungle-topped islands anchored in azure waters, Thailand embraces the hedonist and the hermit, the luxury lover and the budget-savvy traveller. Scale Krabi's sheer sea cliffs, dive amid whale sharks off Ko Tao and the Surin Islands, toe the curling tide alongside Trang's gypsy fishermen, stroll Ko Lipe's dusty-white sands, feast at Hua Hin's sizzling seafood stalls or delight in unparalleled luxury Phuket digs.

Hot & Spicy

Beaches may bring you to Thailand, but it's often the food that lures you back. Adored all over the world, Thai cuisine embodies Thai culture: generous and warm, outgoing and nuanced, refreshing and relaxed, delicate and colourful. With its tropical bounty, the varied national menu twirls around four fundamental flavours: spicy, sweet, salty, sour. And it's exquisitely hot and salty in the seafood-focused south. Dishes build on fresh local ingredients, from pungent lemongrass, juicy yellow mangoes and searing chillies to just-caught seafood, plump tofu and crispy fried chicken.

Local Smiles

Whether it's the glimmering eye of the meditative *wâi* (palms-together Thai greeting) or the joyful smirk of passers-by, it's hard not to be charmed by the Land of Smiles. Thailand has long been Southeast Asia's *mama-san*, inviting travellers from near and far to indulge in the kingdom's natural splendours. These days it isn't all perfectly paradisical, but its original charm can still be found amid the islands and beaches, where a heady mix of sparkling seascapes, limestone towers and equatorial sunshine provides the perfect backdrop to welcoming family-run resorts.

Outdoor Thrills

Thailand's natural beauty is even more intoxicating for the myriad ways it can be savoured. From white-knuckle jungle ziplines and river rafting to seaside horse rides and stand-up paddle boarding, Thailand's activities menu is as endlessly exhilarating as its culinary delights. Lovers of the outdoors can hike sultry jungles in Ko Chang and Khao Sok National Parks; kitesurf off Phuket, Krabi, Ko Samui and Hua Hin; yoga-up on Ko Lanta and Ko Samui; kayak past Ao Phang-Nga's limestone spires; rock climb Railay; and dive deep into the blue across the South. Post-adventure, let the region's brilliant masseuses twist and click you back into place.

Why I Love Thailand's Islands & Beaches

By Isabella Noble, Writer

It's oh-so-obvious why Thailand's islands and beaches have superstar travel status, but what I really adore about this region is how it caters so well to all kinds. Flashpacking couple? Four-strong family? All-night partygoer? Off-the-beaten-track adventurer? Whatever your travel style, the glossy sands and heavenly waters of Thailand's islands and beaches have you covered. On every visit, I love exploring serene wát, admiring the Sino-Portuguese architecture of Phuket Town, eating my body weight in *kôw pàt pak* (veg fried rice) and remembering that there's nothing like soft sand, tropical breezes and friendly smiles to soothe the soul.

For more about our writers, see page 448

Above: Ko Phi-Phi Leh (p324)

Thailand's Islands & Beaches

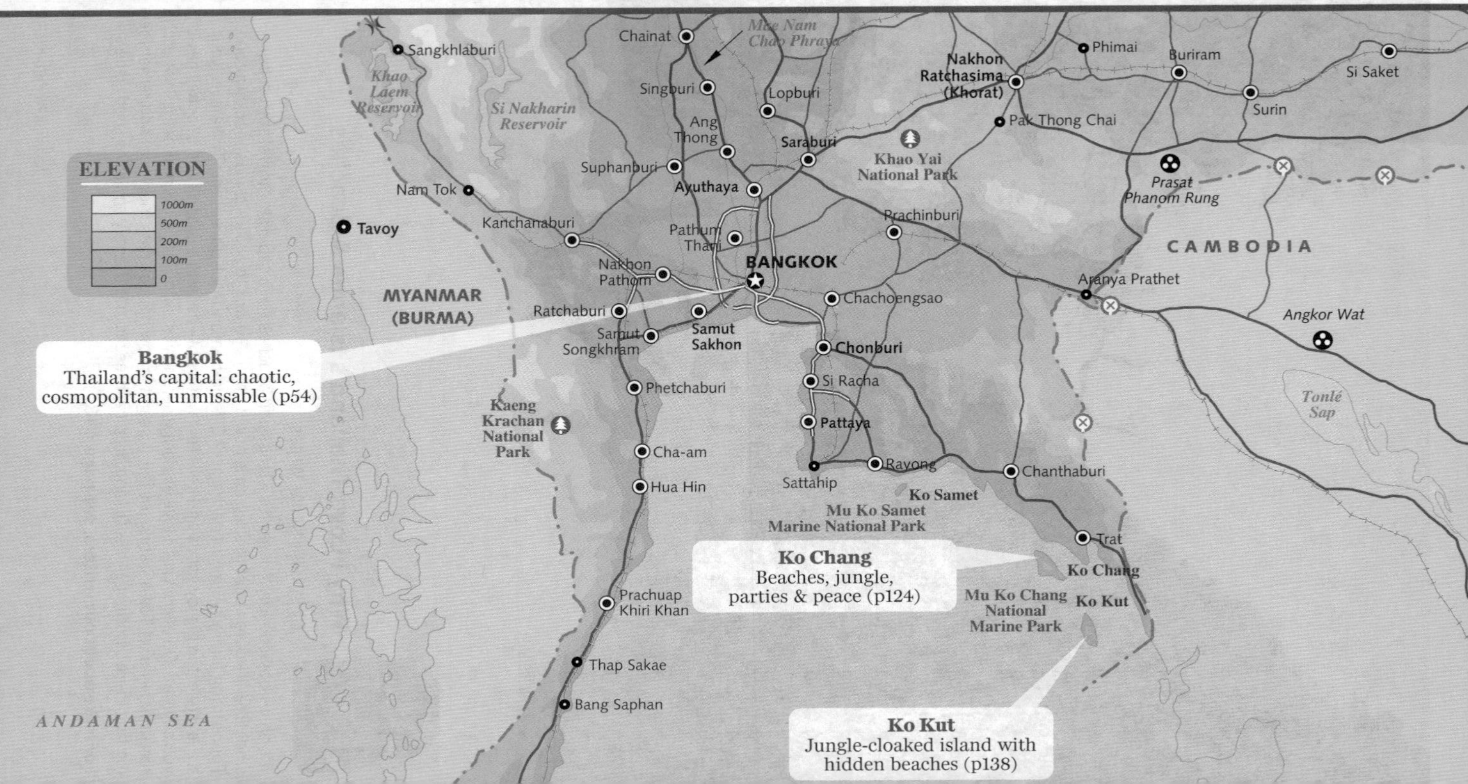

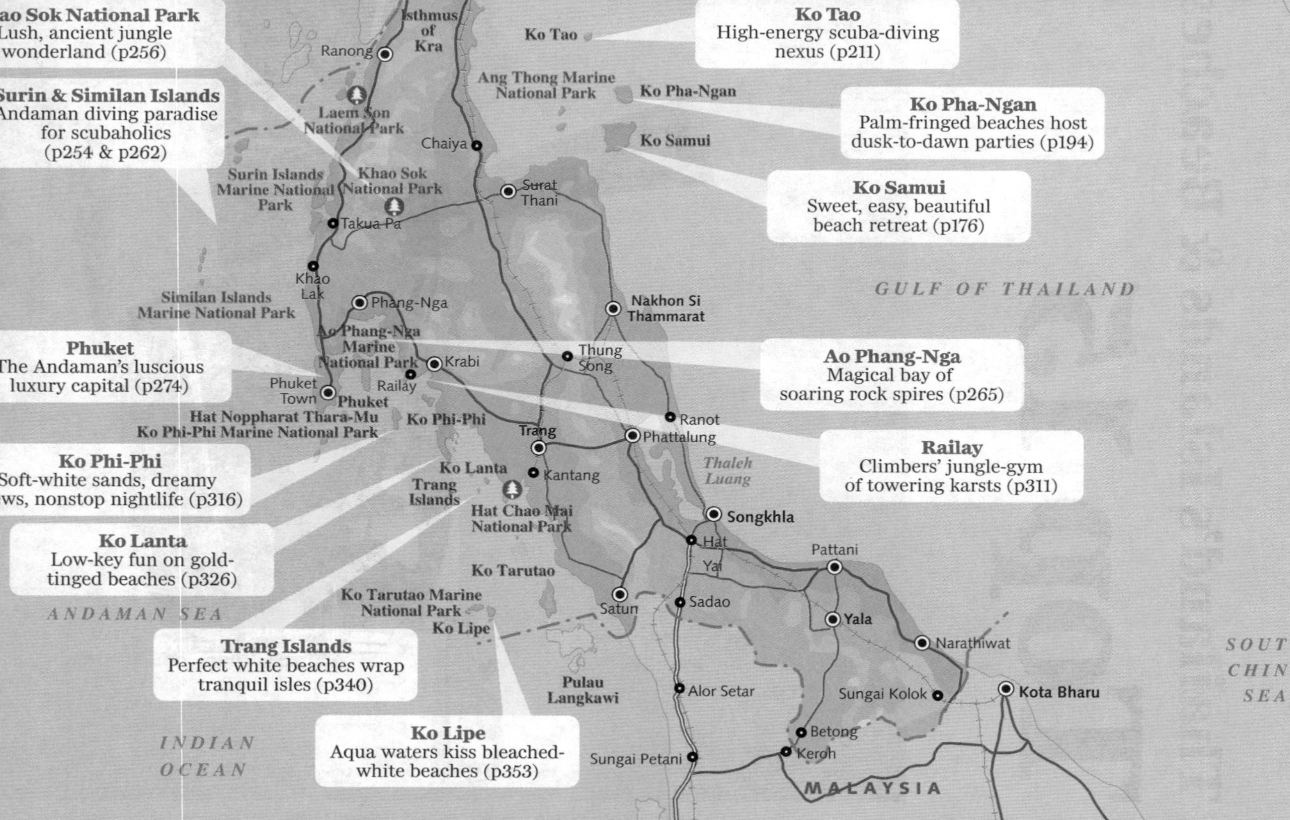
Khao Sok National Park
Lush, ancient jungle wonderland (p256)
Surin & Similan Islands
Andaman diving paradise for scubaholics (p254 & p262)
Phuket
The Andaman's luscious luxury capital (p274)
Ko Phi-Phi
Soft-white sands, dreamy views, nonstop nightlife (p316)
Ko Lanta
Low-key fun on gold-tinged beaches (p326)
Trang Islands
Perfect white beaches wrap tranquil isles (p340)
Ko Lipe
Aqua waters kiss bleached-white beaches (p353)
Ko Tao
High-energy scuba-diving nexus (p211)
Ko Pha-Ngan
Palm-fringed beaches host dusk-to-dawn parties (p194)
Ko Samui
Sweet, easy, beautiful beach retreat (p176)
Ao Phang-Nga
Magical bay of soaring rock spires (p265)
Railay
Climbers' jungle-gym of towering karsts (p311)
Isthmus of Kra
Ranong
Laem Son National Park
Chaiya
Surat Thani
Ko Tao
Ang Thong Marine National Park
Ko Pha-Ngan
Ko Samui
Surin Islands Marine National Park
Khao Sok National Park
Takua Pa
Khao Lak
Similan Islands Marine National Park
Phang-Nga
Ao Phang-Nga Marine National Park
Krabi
Railay
Phuket Town
Phuket
Hat Noppharat Thara-Mu Ko Phi-Phi Marine National Park
Ko Phi-Phi
Nakhon Si Thammarat
Thung Song
Ranot
Trang
Phattalung
Kantang
Ko Lanta
Trang Islands
Hat Chao Mai National Park
Thaleh Luang
Songkhla
Hat Yai
Ko Tarutao
Ko Tarutao Marine National Park
Ko Lipe
Satun
Sadao
Pattani
Yala
Narathiwat
GULF OF THAILAND
ANDAMAN SEA
INDIAN OCEAN
SOUTH CHINA SEA
Pulau Langkawi
Alor Setar
Sungai Kolok
Kota Bharu
Betong
Keroh
Sungai Petani
MALAYSIA

Thailand's Islands & Beaches Top 15

1

Trang Islands

1 The honeylike morning sun casts shadows across another green-cloaked isle rising out of the blue. All you can hear is the motor of the weather-beaten long-tail boat, adorned with multicoloured cloth bands that frame the scene. Your next island-hopping stop is that brilliantly white beach in the distance – one of many to explore, snorkel and hike from. It might be beach-chic Ko Ngai, shimmering Ko Kradan or popular Ko Muk, but the boat ride is so extraordinarily gorgeous that it's just as delightful as your dreamy Trang Islands (p340) destination. Below left: Long-tail boats, Ko Ngai (p340), Trang Islands

Railay

2 Whether you're an expert or have never grabbed a notch hole in your life, the Railay (p311) rock-climbing world will have you scrambling skywards with excitement. More than 700 bolted routes on limestone walls deliver unbeatable vistas across some of the world's most spectacular scenery – vertical rock spires draped in greenery, surrounded by crystalline sea and creamy beaches – and even the shortest jaunt guarantees thrills. Seasoned climbers stay for months. For the ultimate adventure, try deep-water soloing: climbs ending with a splash into the water below. When you're done, mellow reggae bars await. Below: Rock climber, Railay

ERIC PHAN-KIM / GETTY IMAGES ©

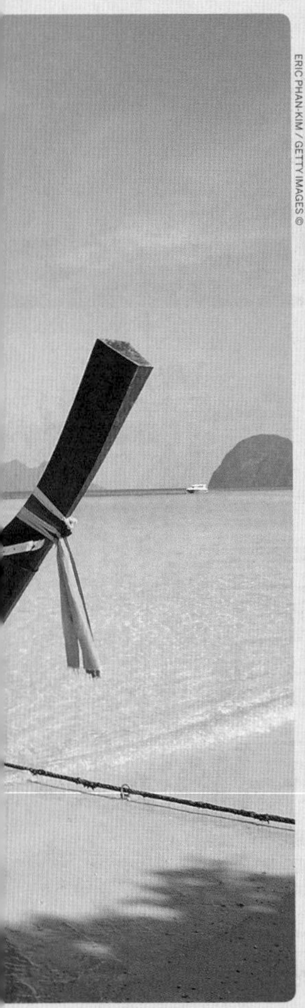

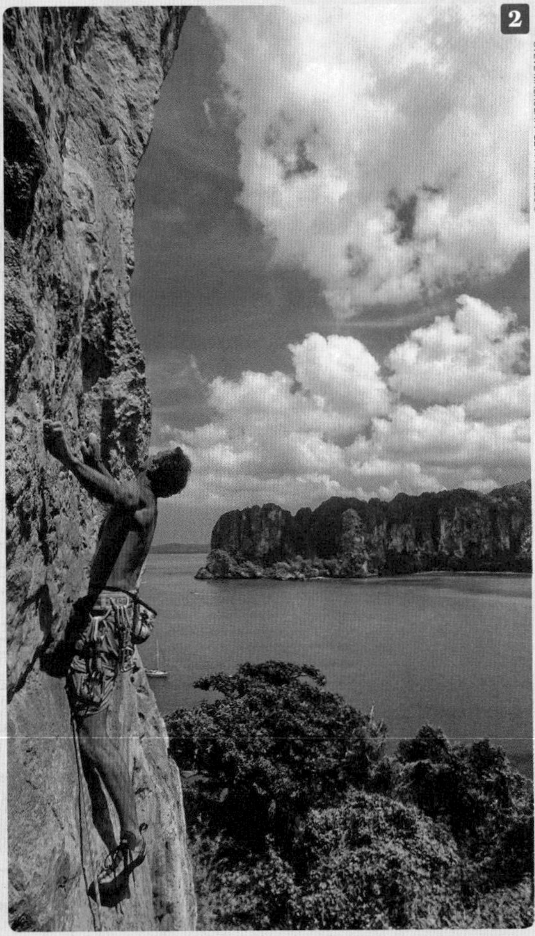

2

STEVE MACAULAY / GETTY IMAGES ©

Ko Kut

3 Thailand's fourth-largest island and eastern island frontier is an easygoing verdant canvas of dense jungle hemmed by pristine beaches – perfect for uninterrupted afternoons of sun worshipping or kayaking and snorkelling, and evenings blissfully free of throbbing sound systems. Although the topography of Ko Kut (p138) is similar to that of many other Thai islands, with rainforest and waterfalls hidden within, its location on the southern tip of the Ko Chang archipelago means that the coastal waters glimmer with a unique emerald tint. Below: Boat pier, Ko Kut

Ko Pha-Ngan

4 World-famous for its Full Moon Parties and all-night electronic madness, Ko Pha-Ngan (p194) long graduated from sleepy bohemian island to full-on attraction pulling in travellers of all types. The shanties are turning more boutique, so comfort seekers and families have an alternative to Ko Samui. And on the northern and eastern coasts, hammock hangers can still escape to feel like a modern-day castaway (a well-fed one, of course). Just offshore is one of the gulf's best dive sites, Sail Rock, which is visited by whale sharks. Right: Fishing village, Ko Pha-Ngan

Phuket

5 Forever loved for its luxury resorts, plush beach clubs, island-chic boutiques and Patong's after-hours hedonism, Phuket (p269) has many more attractions than the brochures suggest. Stroll past incense-cloaked shrines and beautiful restored Sino-Portugese buildings in Phuket Town, dig into local history in Thalang, hike the steamy jungles of Khao Phra Thaew Royal Wildlife & Forest Reserve, join a cooking class, go diving or try surfing or kitesurfing during low season. For beach lounging away from the buzz, head to northern beaches such as Hat Nai Thon or go south to Laem Phanwa. Left: Kitesurfing at Hat Kata (p284), Phuket

Ko Phi-Phi

6 One of Thailand's most instantly recognisable characters, Ko Phi-Phi (p316) deserves all the praise and criticism it receives. Stunning azure waters, salt-white beaches and soaring limestone cliffs make it ideal for diving, hiking, snorkelling, rock climbing or soaking up the scenery while you roast on the beach. After dark, Phi-Phi morphs into a hedonistic party haven, with electrifying fire dancers and energetic revellers swinging super-sweet cocktail buckets. Morning headaches are inevitable, but there are plenty of sandy stretches and island cruises to recover on until the next round.
Top: Fire dancing, Ko Phi-Phi

Ko Lanta

7 Even a short wander off the gorgeous tourist beaches of Ko Lanta (p326) is a ticket to a wonderland of friendly Muslim fishing villages, unexplored coves and gentle jungle scenery. Don't miss Ban Si Raya, with its century-old stilted houses and artsy shops, as you venture down the east coast that remains largely unaffected by the tourism industry thriving beyond it. For natural beauty, Mu Ko Lanta National Park is hard to beat, and there are plenty of caves and lovely blonde beaches en route. Add to this good diving and snorkelling, accessible yoga, and a chilled-out nightlife scene.

6

7

8

NICHOLAS PITT / GETTY IMAGES ©

9

10

KAMPEE PATISENA / GETTY IMAGES ©

Ko Samui

8 Eager to please, Ko Samui (p176) is a civilised beach-resort island for the holidaying masses, many of whom fly in and out, and rarely leave the confines of their resort to engage with the local culture. If you wish to venture beyond the resorts, seek out sleepier beaches and coves to the south and west, which recall Samui's old moniker, 'Coconut Island'. Swim in waterfalls, explore the thriving wellness scene with its myriad yoga, meditation and detox retreats, and stop by a temple or two. Above left: Belmond Napasai resort (p186), Mae Nam, Ko Samui

Ko Lipe

9 Lining south-coast Ko Lipe (p353), Hat Pattaya is a perfect arc of alabaster sand with long-tail boats bobbing in its azure bay and busy seafood barbecues and laid-back beach bars dotted along the foreshore. Soft, blonde Hat Sunrise is equally exquisite, stretching along the east coast until it curves at the sight of majestic Ko Adang across the blue. If you tire of these fabulous but busy beaches, take jungle-shrouded trails to wilder Hat Sunset and hidden swathes of sand. Offshore, stellar dive sites shine in the early monsoon.

Ko Tao

10 Thailand's diving headquarters, Ko Tao (p211) is still the cheapest and easiest spot in the region to learn how to strap on a tank and dive into the deep. The water is gentle and bathtub-warm, and the submarine visuals are not to be missed. Just offshore, scenic rocky coves and shallow coral reefs frequented by all manner of fish provide a snorkelling 'aperitif'. Ko Tao's small size means you can easily explore all of its jungly nooks and crannies when you need a break from diving. Above: Diving among anemones off Ko Tao

MICHAEL ZEGERS / GETTY IMAGES ©

Ko Chang

11 The rugged landscape of remote Ko Chang (p124) conceals some of Southeast Asia's best-preserved wilderness. Its craggy mountainous interior holds a real-life Jurassic Park of flora and fauna that stars exotic reptiles, colourful birds and lumbering elephants. The hills are cut with rivers and waterfalls, and plenty of guides are available to help you explore the abounding biodiversity on jungle hikes. Although developers have bagged all the attractive beachfront real estate and there's a lively party scene, sand-fringed nooks in the east and south still feel decidedly off the beaten path. Above left: Ao Khlong Prao beach (p124), Ko Chang

Khao Sok National Park

12 Escape inland to the steamy jungle-coated hills and low-slung valleys of the South's most beloved national park (p256) – the wettest region in Thailand. Roam dirt trails below verdant canopies thick with humidity to multi-level waterfalls, sky-reaching limestone towers and explorable caves, eyes permanently peeled for exotic local inhabitants that include bears, bats, gibbons, wild elephants, the odd tiger and the elusive *Rafflesia kerrii*, one of the planet's most pungent flowers. A one-of-a-kind Khao Sok highlight involves overnighting atop dramatic Chiaw Lan Lake in floating huts (pictured above).

Similan & Surin Islands

13 The world-renowne dive sites dotted below the glassy aqua seas of the Similan and Surin Islands (p254) are some of the top spots in Thailand to don a scuba mask and delve into the region's colour-bursting underwate world. Ko Bon is a worthy candidate favoured by giar manta rays, but the ultima prize is distant Richelieu Rock (p254). Accessible only to those who venture north towards Myanmar or a live-aboard diving trip, th horseshoe-shaped outcrop acts as a feeding station luring manta rays and wha sharks. Above: Diving with manta rays, Similan Islands

ιo Phang-Nga

14 While other visitors squeeze onto crowded speedboats for blurry impses of the spectacular limestone-ower-studded bay of Ao Phang-Nga ational Park (p266), early-morning sea-ayakers enjoy it in slow silence. Glide past ea caves inscribed with prehistoric rock t, picnic on secluded beaches, swim in lky water and, if you like, stay overnight n the stilted Muslim village clinging to Ko anyi. Yes, plenty of boats will whizz by, but ostly you'll just enjoy the music of your addle rippling through the water. At night-ll, become enchanted with the bay's famed oluminescence.

Bangkok

15 Setting aside a few days for Thailand's frenzied, cosmopolitan capital adds another dimension to your islands and beaches tour. Among its most atmospheric neighbourhoods, the artificial island of Ko Ratanakosin is the birthplace of modern Bangkok (p54) and home to the bulk of the city's must-see sights, such as Wat Pho and Wat Phra Kaew, with its stunning Emerald Buddha. And then there are sweaty street-side food markets, sultry skyscraper bars, shiny mega-malls and the colourful, cacophonous depths of the massive Chatuchak Weekend Market to explore. Bottom: Wat Phra Kaew (p57), Bangkok

14

15

Need to Know

For more information, see Survival Guide (p407)

Currency

Thai baht (B)

Language

Thai

Visas

Thirty-day visas for international air arrivals; 15-day visas at land borders; 60-day visas from a Thai consulate before leaving home.

Money

ATMs are widespread and charge a 150B to 180B foreign-account fee. Visa and MasterCard are accepted at upmarket establishments.

Mobile Phones

Thailand is on a GSM network; inexpensive prepaid SIM cards are available. Bangkok, major cities and the more populated islands have 4G.

Time

GMT/UTC plus seven hours.

When to Go

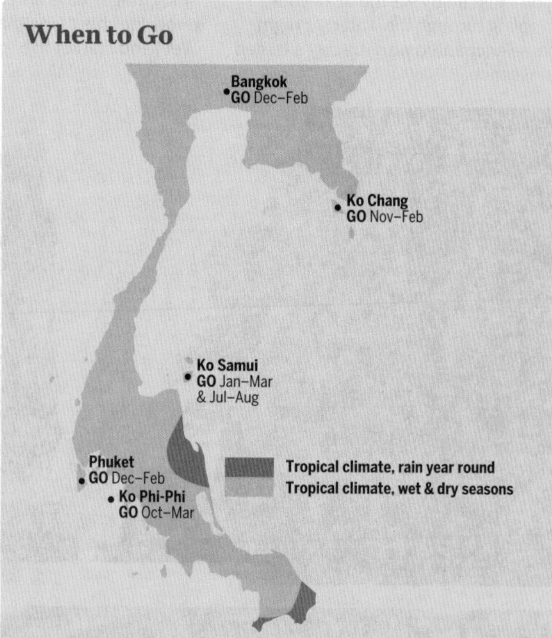

High Season
(Nov–Mar)

- A cool and dry season follows the monsoons, meaning the landscape is lush and temperatures are comfortable.
- Western Christmas and New Year's holidays bring crowds and inflated rates to the beaches.

Shoulder
(Apr–Jun)

- April, May and June are generally very hot and dry, with an average temperature of 30°C, but the sea breeze provides plenty of natural air-con.

Low Season
(Jul–Oct)

- The Andaman and gulf coasts take turns being pummelled by monsoon rains.
- Weather is generally favourable along the southern gulf in July and August.
- Some islands shut down and boats are limited during stormy weather.

Useful Websites

Tourism Authority of Thailand (TAT; www.tourismthailand.org) National tourism department covering info and special events.

Thaivisa (www.thaivisa.com) Expat site with useful forum.

Lonely Planet (www.lonelyplanet.com/thailand) Country profile and what to do and see.

Bangkok Post (www.bangkokpost.com) English-language daily newspaper.

Thai National Parks (www.dnp.go.th) Official site for all national-park reservations.

Important Numbers

Thailand country code	☎66
Emergency	☎191
International access codes (different service providers)	☎001, ☎007, ☎008, ☎009
Operator-assisted international calls	☎100
Tourist police	☎1155

Exchange Rates

Australia	A$1	26B
Canada	C$1	27B
China	Y10	54B
Euro zone	€1	38B
Japan	¥100	27B
Korea	100W	3B
New Zealand	NZ$1	23B
Russia	R10	6B
UK	£1	53B
USA	US$1	34B

For current exchange rates, visit www.xe.com.

Daily Costs

Budget: Less than 2000B

- Basic guesthouse room: 400B–1000B
- Market and street-stall meals: 40B–100B
- Small bottle of beer: 60B
- Mix of walking and public transport: 10B–200B

Midrange: 2000B–5000B

- Flashpacker guesthouse or midrange hotel room: 1000B–3000B
- Western lunches and seafood dinners: 150B–300B
- One-day snorkelling tour: 1500B
- Motorbike hire: 150B–250B

Top end: More than 5000B

- Boutique hotel room: from 3000B
- Fine dining: from 300B
- Private tours: from 2000B
- Car hire (per day): from 800B

Opening Hours

Opening hours vary, especially in more remote places where businesses open and close at whim. Shopping malls have banks that open late.

Banks 9.30am–3.30pm Monday to Friday

Bars 6pm-midnight

Clubs 8pm–2am

Government offices 8.30am–4.30pm Monday to Friday

Licensing hours Alcohol can be bought in shops from 11am–2pm and 5pm–midnight

Restaurants 10am–10pm

Shops 9am–6pm

Arriving in Thailand

Suvarnabhumi International Airport (Bangkok; p422)
Taxis (220B to 380B, plus 50B airport surcharge and tolls) take an hour to the city. Buses run to central Bangkok (24B to 35B, 5am to midnight). The airport rail link (45B, 30 minutes, 6am to midnight) local service runs to Phaya Thai station every 15 minutes; the express service (90B, 17 minutes) runs to Makkasan or Phaya Thai stations.

Don Mueang International Airport (Bangkok; p422)
Taxis (200B to 220B, plus 50B airport surcharge and tolls) take 30 minutes to one hour to the city. Buses take one to two hours to Th Khao San (35B), while shuttles run every 30 minutes (30B, 8.30am to 11pm) from the airport to Mo Chit BTS station (20 minutes) and Victory Monument (30 minutes). Trains run hourly to Hualamphong station (5B to 51B, 45 minutes) between 3.40am and 10.16pm.

Getting Around

Planes, trains, buses and boats whisk you south. Or fly directly to Phuket or Ko Samui from abroad rather than via Bangkok.

Air Lots of flights and destinations, but can be expensive.

Bus & minivan Lots of options, cheap and efficient.

Train Cheap and comfortable, but slower and less reliable than buses.

Boat Big, slow ferries to fast, private long-tails or flashy speedboats.

Rentals Vehicle hire in every town.

For much more on **getting around**, see p422

First Time

For more information, see Survival Guide (p407)

Checklist

- Make sure your passport is valid for at least six months.
- Inform your debit/credit card company of your travels.
- Visit the Thai consulate for a tourist visa for stays of more than 30 days.
- Organise travel insurance and diver's insurance.
- Check baggage restrictions.
- Visit the doctor for a check-up and medical clearance if you intend to go scuba diving.

What to Pack

- Thai phrasebook
- Power converter
- Waterproof sunscreen
- Mosquito repellent with DEET
- Anti-itch cream (for sandfly bites)
- Light, long-sleeve shirt
- Breathable pants
- Hat
- Sunglasses
- Comfortable sandals
- Torch/headlamp

Top Tips for Your Trip

- If you rent a vehicle (especially a jet ski), take pictures of it before use. This may shield you from the rife rental scam of accusing tourists of damaging already beat-up vehicles.
- If booking online, make sure you know exactly where your hotel is located. Many 'great deals' end up being out in the middle of nowhere. Pay upfront for as few nights as possible so you can leave without having to haggle your money back.
- Don't lose your cool, even in the most difficult situations. Thais greatly respect a 'cool heart', and shouting or anger will only escalate a situation, never to your benefit.
- Avoid conversations that involve the monarchy or politics.

What to Wear

Light, loose-fitting clothes will prove the most comfortable in the tropical heat throughout the year. Bring one reasonably warm jacket for the odd cool evening (or the blasting air-con on the plane). To visit temples, you will need shirts with long sleeves and full-length pants. While sandals are the way to go, you should bring one pair of good shoes for the occasional night out in the big cities (sandals are not permitted in many of Bangkok's sky bars, for example).

Sleeping

Outside high season only the most popular resorts need to be booked in advance. At this time of year, walk-in or call-in prices are cheaper than those you will find online.

- **Resorts** Range from villas with their own swimming pools and butlers to ageing shacks cooled by sea breezes.
- **Guesthouses** These are still prevalent, despite the growing number of resorts. They may lack amenities but come with low price tags and helpful service.
- **Hostels** The vast number of cheap guesthouses limits the demand for hostels, but some islands have dorms for as little as 200B a night.

Driving

Renting a motorbike or car to get around makes things convenient, but be wary. Driving on Thai roads can be a hazardous affair: jumping red lights, undertaking (passing on the kerb side of the slower vehicle) and driving on the wrong side of the road are just some of the dangers to watch out for. Make sure you have insurance to cover any medical bills.

For more information, see p425.

Bargaining

➡ **When to bargain** Bargaining forms the crux of almost any commercial interaction in Thailand. If you're purchasing something, it's best to buy in bulk – the more T-shirts you buy, the lower the price will go. Keep it light-hearted.

➡ **When not to bargain** You shouldn't bargain in restaurants, 7-Elevens and petrol stations. Don't haggle for a better price at a high-end hotel, though bargaining is fair game at most beach establishments.

Tipping

Tipping is not generally expected in Thailand. The exception is loose change from a large restaurant bill. Some restaurants add on a service charge.

Luxuriating in the waters of Ko Kut (p138)

Etiquette

The best way to win over the Thais is to smile – visible anger or arguing is embarrassing; the locals call this 'loss of face'. It is a criminal offence to disrespect the royal family; treat objects depicting the king (like money) with respect. Avoid touching anyone on the head and be careful where you point your feet; they're the lowest part of the body literally and metaphorically.

➡ **Temples** When visiting a temple, dress neatly and conservatively with shoulders to knees covered. Remove all footwear before entering. Sit with your feet tucked behind you, so they are not facing the Buddha image. Women may not touch monks or their belongings.

➡ **At the beach** Avoid public nudity; in fact, most Thais swim fully clothed. Away from the sand, men should wear shirts and women should wear clothing over swimwear.

Language

Don't speak Thai? In the main tourist areas, you won't need to. Bus drivers, market vendors and taxi drivers tend to know at least basic English. In small, less touristy towns, few people speak English and so it helps to know how to order food and count in Thai. With a few phrases, you'll be rewarded with grins and instant respect.

Thais have their own script, which tend to turn Westerners into illiterates. Street signs are always transliterated into English, but there is no standard system so spellings vary widely and confusingly.

What's New

Phuket Town Gets Hip

Phuket Town is now buzzing with arty cafes, affordable boutique guesthouses and atmospheric markets. The town's Sino-Portuguese architecture is another big draw for the island's culture capital.

Wreck Dives

Ko Phi-Phi has several new wreck dives, including a former Thai navy ship that was deliberately sunk as an artificial reef and is already swarming with fish. Three more erstwhile navy ships are now dive sites off Ao Nang.

Airport Expansion

U-tapao Airport, near Pattaya, is set for major expansion. Bangkok Air currently flies to Ko Samui and Phuket from U-tapao while Air Asia heads to Kuala Lumpur in Malaysia. Planned new routes will reach Thai provinces and Chinese cities. (p112)

Budget Flights

Snorkelling off Samui or immersing yourself in Ko Lanta's charismatic old town has never been simpler. Thailand's expanding array of budget airlines means routes are increasing while prices are dropping.

Visa Ease

Six-month, multiple-entry visas are now available to virtually all foreign visitors to Thailand. The 5000B visa will mean an end to the tiresome border-hops that long-stay travellers had to make. (p420)

Better Roads, Still No Airport

A new road to Than Sadet waterfall and an improved route to Thong Nai Pan make getting around Ko Pha-Ngan a breeze. Work on a planned airport is still ongoing.

On the Grid

Ko Chang's smaller neighbours, Ko Mak and Ko Kut, have just had a power boost. An underwater cable to both islands opened in August 2015, meaning they are now hooked up to the national grid. The result means no more reading-by-torch-light evenings when the power goes, and probably more development.

Smoother Samet

Ko Samet's remotest beaches are stunning places to sit and sip a cocktail. Reaching them is simple these days, as the former quagmire-like tracks have been replaced with proper roads.

Beach Bans

Authorities have attempted to tidy up Phuket beaches by bulldozing restaurants and banning sun loungers and umbrellas. Some traders inevitably pay little attention to such edicts and continue to offer a handful of beach mats and drinking areas.

For more recommendations and reviews, see lonelyplanet.com/thailand

If You Like...

Beautiful Beaches

Gone are the days of keeping paradise to yourself, but Thailand's beaches remain some of the most gorgeous on Earth.

Ko Kut Kilometres of unpopulated sand arc around lonely Ko Kut. Hat Khlong Chao is dreamy. (p138)

Trang Islands Waters in a million shades of turquoise fringe bleach-blonde beaches and limestone karsts across this alluring southern archipelago. (p340)

Ko Pha-Ngan The original beach-bum island hosts wild Full Moon Parties, plus hammock-hanging on northern beaches. (p194)

Ko Lipe Crystal-white sand entrances your inner beach addict on Hat Pattaya and Hat Sunrise. (p353)

Similan Islands Boulder-strewn, pearly-white beaches punctuate azure vistas, as sublime above water as below. (p262)

Fabulous Food

Street stalls spring up out of nowhere, night markets sizzle dinner, family restaurants deliver colourful traditional favourites and high-end fusion cuisine blends it all together.

Bangkok The entire spectrum of Thai eats, from noodle soup on the street to celebrity-chef-driven gastronomy. (p83)

Hua Hin Seafood meets a night market geared towards Thai tourists: crab curry, mussel omelettes, giant prawns. (p149)

Trang Famed for roast pork, dim sum and filtered-coffee shops, Trang hosts the Andaman Coast's star night market. (p336)

Phuket Town Classy, fantastic-value fusion Thai served in restored Sino-Portuguese buildings, and sensational street and market food. (p274)

Aziamendi A fine-dining dream, the South's favourite new fusion spot merges Basque and Thai ingredients and techniques. (p264)

Five-Star Pampering

Thailand's larger islands house some of the world's glitziest five-star properties (and some are surprisingly affordable).

Phuket A parade of upmarket accommodation graces Phuket's white-fringed coastline, such as exclusive east-coast **Point Yamu by Como**. (p303)

Ko Samui Samui blends smart villas with quiet seclusion, offering a private northern beach paradise to those craving comfort. (p176)

Bangkok Intense competition keeps prices low, so splurge on a capital luxury headliner like the **Siam Heritage**. (p81)

Hat Pakarang & Hat Bang Sak Close to diving-town Khao Lak, five-star lodgings such as the **Sarojin** (p261) are better value than nearby Phuket's picks.

Ko Yao Noi No one does sustainable luxury like the exquisitely private **Six Senses Hideaway** (p268) on this Andaman island.

Basic Beach Shacks

Though numbers are dwindling, there are still cheap beachside bungalows in Thailand with just a terrace, bed, cold shower and mosquito net.

Ko Phayam There's some development, but Ko Phayam revels in its barefoot-beach-shack vibe, embodied by **Aow Yai Bungalows**. (p251)

Ko Pha-Ngan Though things are moving upmarket, Ko Pha-Ngan still hosts some nooks that are mostly development-free, such as Chalok Lam. (p194)

Ko Wai Laze in **Ko Wai Paradise** bungalows on this fleck of white-sand in the Ko Chang Archipelago. (p135)

Ko Chang (Ranong) This beachy slice of jungle-clad hippiedom near the Myanmar border has been slow to change. (p249)

Bang Saphan Yai On upper gulf mainland, Bang Saphan Yai basks in back-to-Thai lifestyle and bamboo huts, like **Roytawan**. (p168)

Adventure Activities

Sure, Thailand has plenty of diving, but you'll find just as many blood-pumping thrills without strapping on a tank.

Rock climbing in Railay The Andaman's signature limestone towers peak dramatically in Railay. Join hundreds of climbers dangling up high. (p311)

Kitesurfing off Phuket (p272), **Krabi** (p310), **Ko Samui** (p180) **& Hua Hin** (p153) Steady winds and shallow waters make these ideal spots to tackle this increasingly popular sport.

Hiking in Khao Sok National Park Wind through jungled hills to gushing waterfalls, keeping your eyes open for unique local wildlife. (p257)

Sea kayaking in Ao Phang-Nga Paddle through glassy waters in kayak comfort, gazing up at jagged stone piercing the clouds above. (p265)

Top: Ko Similan Beach (p262)

Bottom: *Sà·dé* (satay) on a streetside grill

Month by Month

TOP EVENTS

Songkran, April

Loi Krathong, November

Full Moon Party, Monthly

Vegetarian Festival, October

HM the King's Birthday, December

January

The weather is cool and dry in Thailand, ushering in the peak tourist season when Europeans escape dreary winter weather.

Chinese New Year

Thais with Chinese ancestry celebrate the Chinese lunar new year (dates vary) with a full week of housecleaning and fireworks. Phuket, Bangkok and Pattaya all host citywide festivities, but in general Chinese New Year *(đrùt jeen)* is a family event.

February

Still in high-season swing, Thailand sees a bevy of northern hemispherites arrive for sun and fun.

Makha Bucha

One of three holy days marking significant moments of Buddha's life, Makha Bucha *(mah·ká boo·chah)* commemorates the day when 1250 *arhants* assembled to visit Buddha and received the principles of Buddhism; the festival falls on the full moon of the third lunar month. It is a public holiday.

March

The hot and dry season approaches, and the beaches start to empty out. The winds kick up swells, ushering in kite-flying and kiteboarding season. This is also Thailand's semester break, and students head out on sightseeing trips.

Golden Mango Season

Luscious, ripe mangoes come into season from March to June and are sliced before your eyes, packed in containers with sticky rice and accompanied with a sweet sauce.

Kite-Flying Festivals

During the windy season, colourful kites battle it out over the skies of Sanam Luang in Bangkok and elsewhere in the country.

Pattaya International Music Festival

Pattaya showcases pop and rock bands from across Asia at this free music event, attracting busloads of Bangkok university students.

April

Hot, dry weather sweeps across the land as the tourist season winds down, except for one last hurrah during Songkran. Make reservations well in advance since the whole country is on the move for this holiday.

Songkran

Thailand's traditional new year (mid-April) starts with morning visits to the temple. Afterwards everyone loads up their water guns and heads out to the streets for battle: water is thrown, catapulted and sprayed from roving commandos at targets both willing and unwilling.

May

Leading up to the rainy season, festivals encourage plentiful rains and bountiful harvests. This is an under-appreciated shoulder season with lower prices and fewer tourists, but it's still remorselessly hot.

Royal Ploughing Ceremony

This royal ceremony employs astrology and ancient Brahman rituals to kick off the rice-planting season. Sacred oxen are hitched to a wooden plough and part the ground of Sanam Luang in Bangkok. The ritual was revived in the 1960s by the king.

Visakha Bucha

Visakha Bucha, on the full moon of the sixth lunar month (May or June), is considered the date of the Buddha's birth, enlightenment and *parinibbana* (passing away). Activities are centred on the local wát, with candlelit processions, chanting and sermonising.

June

In some parts of the region, the rainy season is merely an afternoon shower, leaving the rest of the day for music and merriment.

Hua Hin Jazz Festival

Jazz groups descend on this royal retreat for a musical homage to the king, an accomplished jazz saxophonist and composer. Sometimes held in May.

July

With the start of the rainy season, the religious community and attendant festivals prepare for Buddhist Lent, a period of reflection and meditation.

Asanha Bucha

The full moon of the eighth lunar month commemorates Buddha's first sermon. Khao Phansaa, also called Buddhist Lent, begins the day after.

Khao Phansaa

Buddhist Lent (the first day of the waning moon in the eighth lunar month) is the traditional time for men to enter the monkhood and monks typically retreat inside the monastery for a period. During Khao Phansaa, worshippers make offerings to the temples and attend ordinations.

August

Overcast skies and daily showers mark the middle of the rainy season. The predictable rain just adds to the ever-present humidity.

HM the Queen's Birthday

The Thai Queen's Birthday (12 August) is a public holiday and national mother's day. In Bangkok, the day is marked with cultural displays along Th Ratchadamnoen and Sanam Luang.

October

Religious preparations for the end of the rainy season and the end of Buddhist Lent begin. The monsoons are reaching the finish line (in most of the country).

Ork Phansaa

The end of Buddhist Lent (three lunar months after Khao Phansaa) is followed by the *gà·tin* ceremony, in which new robes are given to monks by merit-makers.

Vegetarian Festival

The Vegetarian Festival is a holiday from meat taken for nine days (during the ninth lunar month) in adherence with Chinese Buddhist beliefs of mind and body purification. In Phuket the festival can turn extreme, with entranced marchers transforming themselves into human shish kebabs.

November

The cool, dry season has arrived and if you get here early enough, you'll beat the tourist crowds. The landscape is lush: perfect for hiking and waterfall-spotting.

Loi Krathong

Loi Krathong is celebrated on the first full moon of the 12th lunar month. The festival thanks the river goddess for providing life to the fields and forests, and asks for forgiveness. Origami-like boats made from banana leaves are set adrift on the country's waterways.

Top: Lanterns taking flight during Loi Krathong
Bottom: Thai dancers performing for Ork Phansaa

December

The peak of the tourist season has returned with fair skies and a holiday mood.

HM the King's Birthday

Honouring the king's birthday on 5 December, this public holiday hosts parades and merit-making events; it is also recognised as national father's day. Th Ratchadamnoen Klang in Bangkok is decorated with lights and regalia. Everyone wears pink shirts, pink being the colour associated with the monarchy.

SIMONLONG / GETTY IMAGES ©

Plan Your Trip
Itineraries

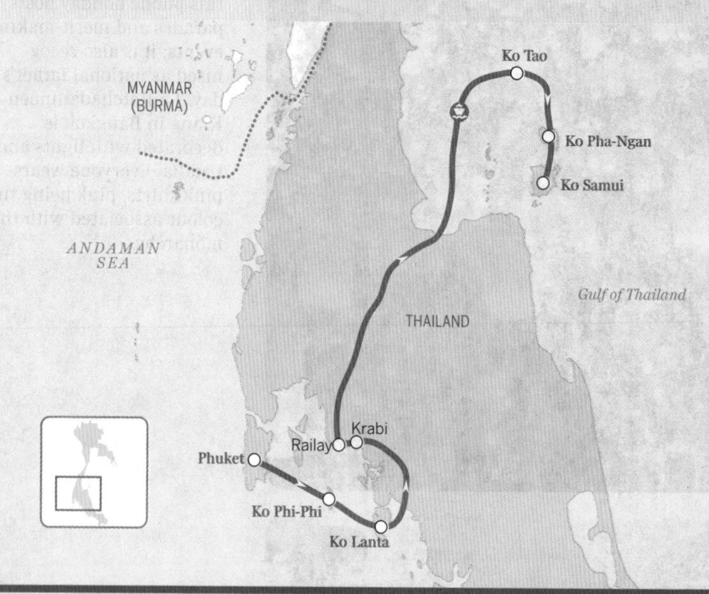

2 WEEKS Essential Islands & Beaches

Consider this the itinerary for the uninitiated, and what a warm welcome you'll receive. Flying directly to the islands either internationally or from Bangkok will save you about a day's worth of travel at either end, so decide what's more valuable to you: beach time or money.

Do not pass 'Go', do not collect $200, just head directly to **Phuket** and pick a beach from which to recover from jet lag for a day or two before starting your journey along one of the finest stretches of coastline in the world. Serious party-goers should base themselves in lively, if sleaze-tinged, Patong, while peace-seekers should consider the northern beaches, but there's a perfect seaside ambience for everyone on this huge island. For variety, Phuket Town brims with gorgeous, heritage Sino-Portuguese architecture.

Once the first stages of relaxation have set in, hop on a boat over to **Ko Phi-Phi** and join the legions of whisky-bucket-wielding backpackers as they sit in the soft sands of the island's signature hourglass bays, or take a boat to the quieter east side

Long-tail boats at Ko Phi-Phi (p316)

of the island. Soak in the beauty of this place for two days until taking another boat to **Ko Lanta**, with its flat vistas of tawny shoreline and lapping waves. Park yourself on the sand for a couple of days or rent a motorbike to tour the less touristed parts of this Muslim fishing island. Take a bus and boat combo to **Krabi** where you'll enjoy the craggy spires of stone in **Railay**, a rock climber's paradise with some of the most awesome beaches and sea views on the planet.

Then it's time to switch coasts to choose one or two of the gulf's triad of idyllic islands – dive-centric **Ko Tao**, lazy, lie-in-the-sun **Ko Pha-Ngan** and luxury-focused **Ko Samui** – for around five days before your flight out. If you're up for some serious partying, try to arrange your visit to coincide with Ko Pha-Ngan's notorious Full Moon Party, which comes roaring to life every month on the southeastern shore.

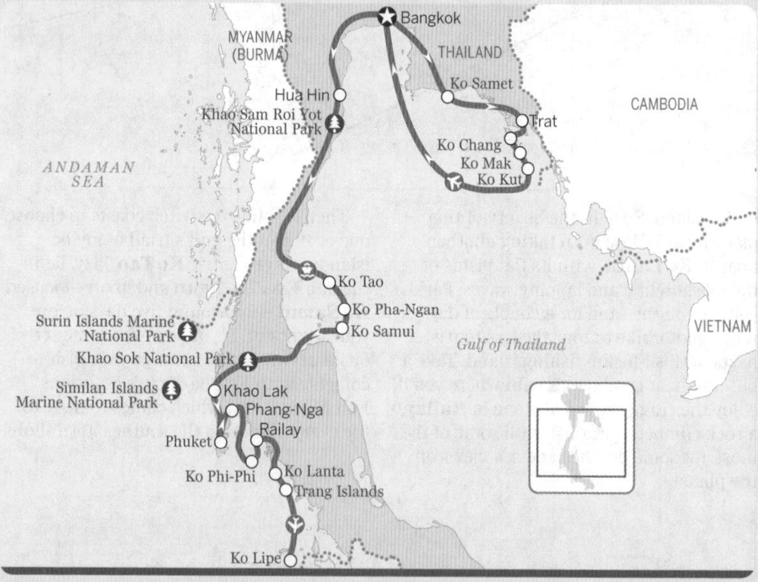

Bangkok
MYANMAR (BURMA)
THAILAND
Hua Hin
Khao Sam Roi Yot National Park
Ko Samet
Trat
CAMBODIA
Ko Chang
Ko Mak
Ko Kut
ANDAMAN SEA
Ko Tao
Ko Pha-Ngan
Ko Samui
Surin Islands Marine National Park
Khao Sok National Park
Gulf of Thailand
VIETNAM
Similan Islands Marine National Park
Khao Lak
Phang-Nga
Railay
Phuket
Ko Phi-Phi
Ko Lanta
Trang Islands
Ko Lipe

PREMIUM UIG / GETTY IMAGES ©

TBRADFORD / GETTY IMAGES ©

Top: Karst formations in Chiaw Lan Lake (p256), Khao Sok National Park
Bottom: Street food on display in Hua Hin (p149)

The Full Monty

A month, you say? This is not just any old beach trip; it allows enough time to sample a full range of southern Thailand's islands, beaches and jungle-clad parks.

Start your journey in Thailand's capital city, **Bangkok**, before heading south. Your first stop is beach-laden **Ko Samet**, where Bangkokians and expats let loose on weekends. Follow the coast to sleepy **Trat,** then hop on a boat for one of the Ko Chang archipelago's many islands. Hike the interior of jungle-topped **Ko Chang**, the largest and most developed island in the region. Hop over to flat but beachy **Ko Mak** or rugged **Ko Kut**. Next, backtrack by making your way to **Hua Hin**, the king's preferred holiday destination and home to a thriving local and expat scene with seafood markets and charming shanty piers. Hike the craggy hills of quiet **Khao Sam Roi Yot National Park** before making your way out to **Ko Tao** via Chumphon. Strap on your tank and dive with the fish below before moving over to **Ko Pha-Ngan** for some subdued beachside relaxing. **Ko Samui**, next door, offers a bit more variety and has a magical stash of holiday fodder to suit every budget and desire.

From Ko Samui stop in at **Khao Sok National Park** (via Surat Thani), known to be one of the oldest stretches of jungle in the world. Depending on how much time you have, take either a day trip or live-aboard diving excursion in **Khao Lak** to explore the diving treasures of the **Surin Islands** and **Similan Islands Marine National Parks**. Travel down the coast to **Phuket** and sample Thailand's finest iteration of luxury hospitality. Paddle around the majestic limestone islets of quiet **Phang-Nga**, then sleep beneath the ethereal crags of **Ko Phi-Phi** after a spirited evening (no pun intended) of beach dancing and fire twirling. Scale the stone towers of **Railay** next door, zoom around the flat tracts of land on mellowed-out **Ko Lanta**, then hop on a boat bound for the idyllic **Trang Islands** – paradise found. One last archipelago awaits those who travel further south towards the Malaysian border – **Ko Lipe** is the island of choice for those looking for stunning beaches with a fun, social vibe.

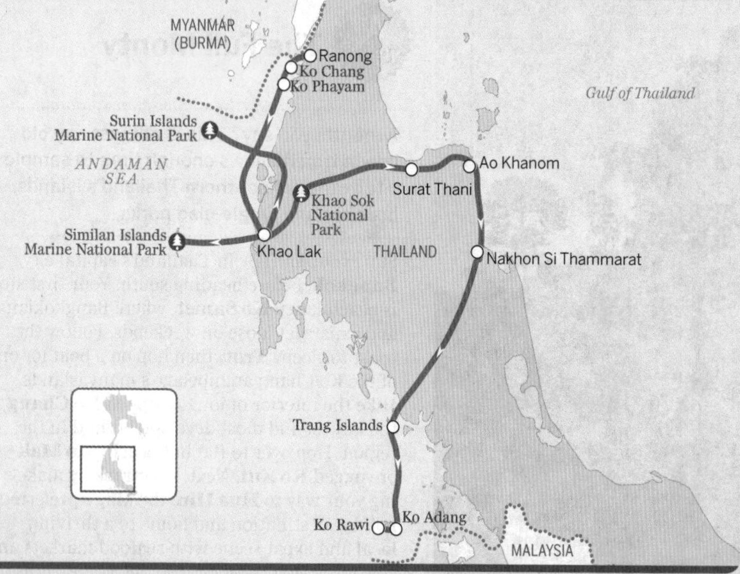

2 WEEKS Andaman Sea & the Gulf

Buck the travel trends and blaze your own trail through some of the lesser-known beaches and islands of southern Thailand, switching from west to east and back again.

Kick off in the bustling frontier town of **Ranong** on the eastern bank of the Sompaen River, a 45-minute boat ride from the Myanmar border, before sinking your tanned tootsies into the warm white sands of a beach on the sleepy, sparsely populated island of **Ko Phayam** nearby. Take more time out on no-frills 'Little' **Ko Chang** (not to be confused with the 'big' Ko Chang in Trat Province near Cambodia), a rustic getaway with a laid-back, easy-going vibe. You can trade some serious diver tips in **Khao Lak** further south and hop aboard a day diving and snorkelling excursion to the **Similan** and **Surin Islands** or push the boat out on a live-aboard for three to five days.

Back on mainland terra firma, flip coasts and zip east, halting in **Khao Sok National Park** to immerse yourself in some of the oldest rainforest jungle on the planet and hunt out one of the world's largest flowers, or go hiking, kayaking, rafting or boating. Don't overlook **Surat Thani** – a traditional Thai town with a large Thai-Chinese population and a scattering of colourful Chinese temples – on your way east. You'll find lazy beach days waiting once you reach the gulf's **Ao Khanom**, minus the pockets of overdevelopment and crowds on Ko Samui, Ko Pha-Ngan and Ko Tao. Hopefully the local pink dolphins will make an appearance.

Travel south to explore the rich cultural centre of **Nakhon Si Thammarat**, a likeable and historic city that is home to one of Thailand's most significant and sacred Buddhist temples. Head back to the Andaman coast to pick up where you left off, island-hopping. Take your pick from the lonely limestone specks of the **Trang Islands** – perhaps the allure of white sand-fringed **Ko Kradan**, sleepy **Ko Sukorn** or lush, wildlife-rich **Ko Libong** – then wander south for a camping excursion with the *chow lair* (sea gypsies) on whisper-quiet **Ko Adang** or **Ko Rawi** north of Ko Lipe.

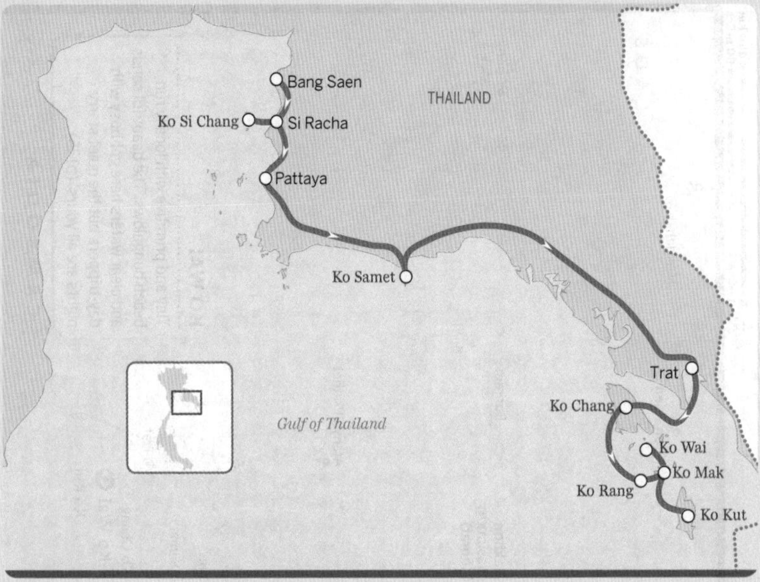

Eastern Island-Hop

Thailand's southern island strings are undoubtedly the kingdom's major treasures, but if you're pushed for time or Cambodia-bound, why not explore the eastern gulf?

This was once the lesser-visited island region of Thailand, but with their proximity to Bangkok, these islands, for the most part, are accessible and popular for beach-combing, diving, snorkelling, hiking and kayaking. The nearest stretch of sand to Bangkok, the beach and long promenade at **Bang Saen**, is a mere hour away from the capital (so gets busy at weekends), from where it's a short journey to the the seaside town of **Si Racha** and the nearby rocky island retreat of **Ko Si Chang**; the island's beaches aren't its strength, but it's great to explore.

Missing the supercharged beach scene and go-go bars of **Pattaya** is no loss – but consider taking your fill of its excellent international restaurant scene and admiring its astonishing temple-like Sanctuary of Truth. Join flashpackers on the gorgeous white-sand beaches and at the fire-juggling shows of slender and forested **Ko Samet**. Bangkokians let loose on big boisterous weekends but there's more than enough room to escape, journeying from cove to cove along the lovely coastal footpath. Despite its fame, the island remains attractively under-developed, and many of its sleeping options are still rustic and old-school.

Follow the coast along the mainland to sleepy **Trat** with its traditional charms, then hop on a boat for one of the Ko Chang archipelago's myriad islands. Hike the lush interior of rugged, jungle-topped **Ko Chang**, the largest and most developed island in the region, or pop yourself into a kayak to size up the island from the waves. Some excellent dive sites await the scuba inclined; choose between **Ko Rang**, Ko Yak, Ko Tong Lang and Ko Laun. Get further off the beaten track on secluded, pint-sized **Ko Mak** or go snorkelling in the crystal waters off reef-fringed **Ko Wai**. Hardcore Robinson Crusoes can go one step further on neighbouring, ultra-simple Ko Kham. Walk along the talcum-powder-soft sands of nightlife-free **Ko Kut** to round off your journey.

Off The Beaten Track: Thailand's Islands & Beaches

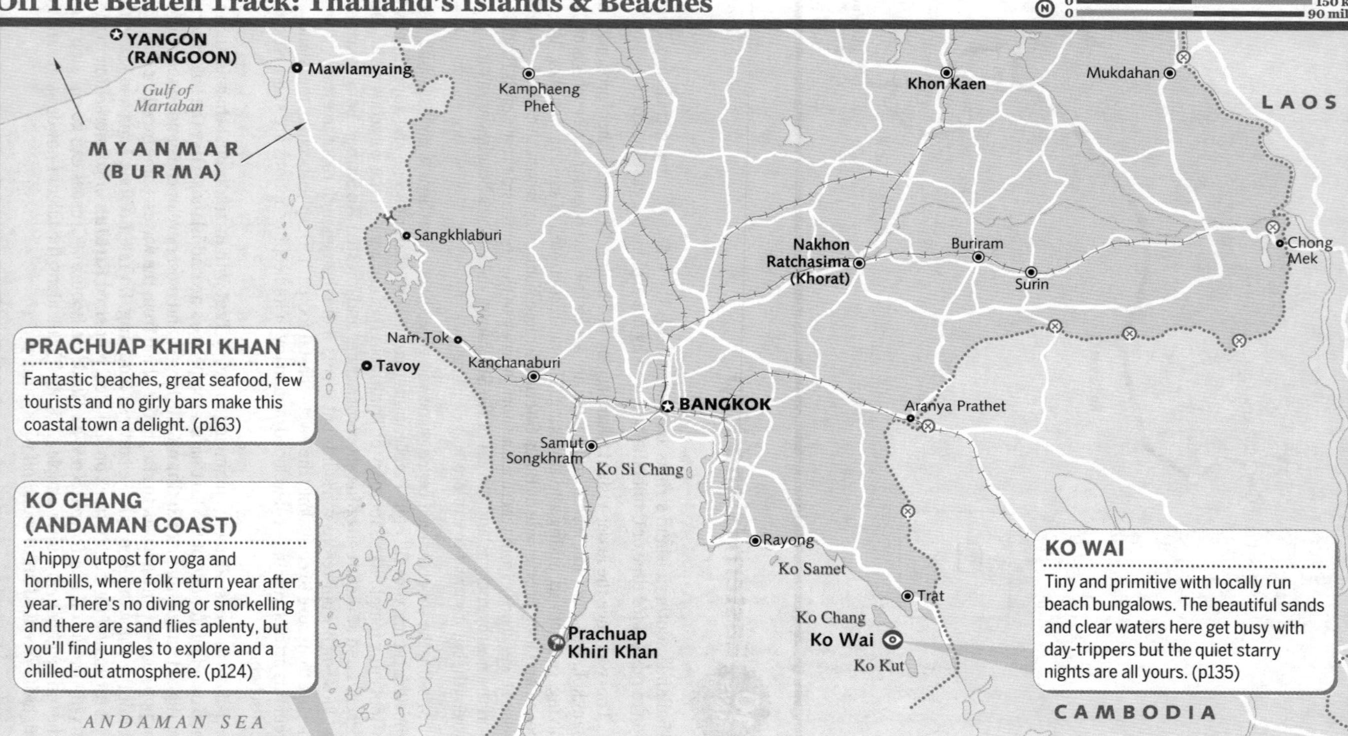

PRACHUAP KHIRI KHAN

Fantastic beaches, great seafood, few tourists and no girly bars make this coastal town a delight. (p163)

KO CHANG (ANDAMAN COAST)

A hippy outpost for yoga and hornbills, where folk return year after year. There's no diving or snorkelling and there are sand flies aplenty, but you'll find jungles to explore and a chilled-out atmosphere. (p124)

KO WAI

Tiny and primitive with locally run beach bungalows. The beautiful sands and clear waters here get busy with day-trippers but the quiet starry nights are all yours. (p135)

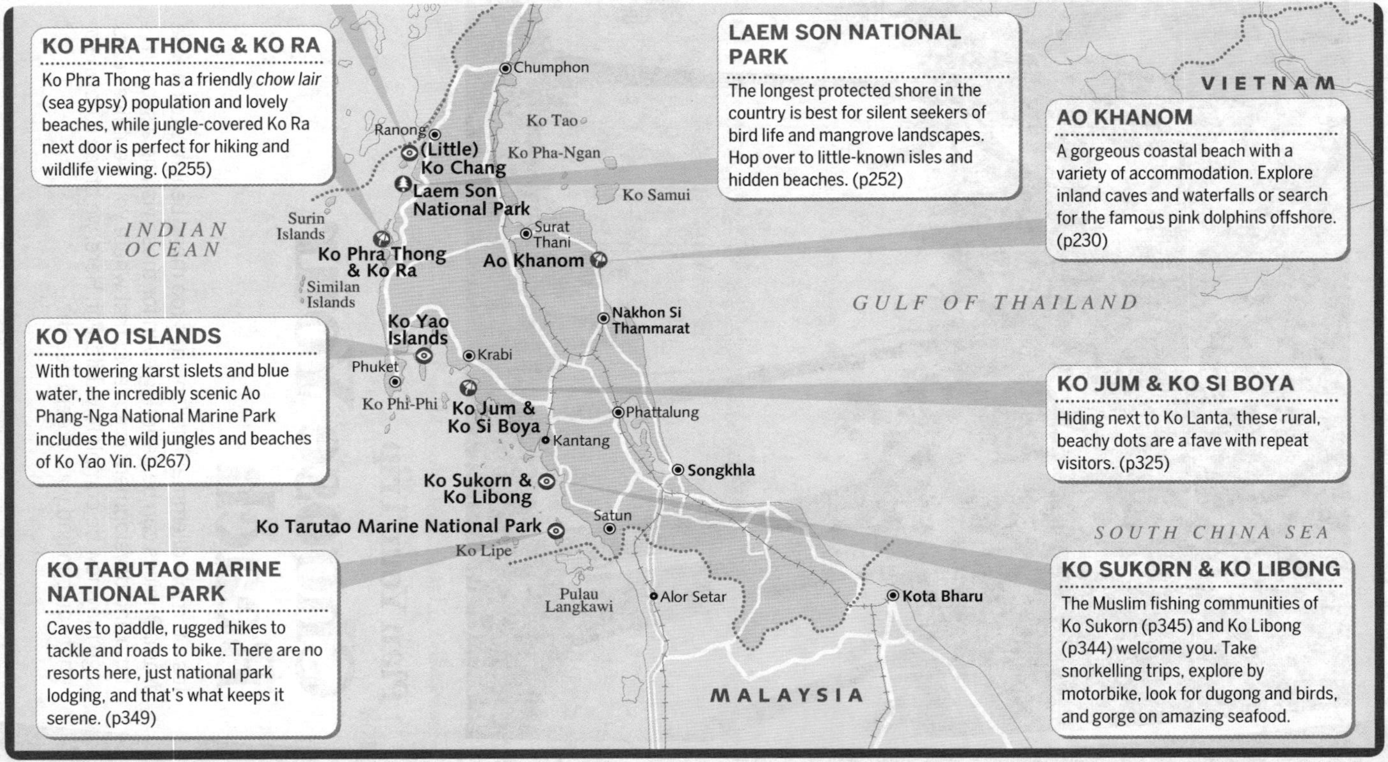

KO PHRA THONG & KO RA

Ko Phra Thong has a friendly *chow lair* (sea gypsy) population and lovely beaches, while jungle-covered Ko Ra next door is perfect for hiking and wildlife viewing. (p255)

LAEM SON NATIONAL PARK

The longest protected shore in the country is best for silent seekers of bird life and mangrove landscapes. Hop over to little-known isles and hidden beaches. (p252)

AO KHANOM

A gorgeous coastal beach with a variety of accommodation. Explore inland caves and waterfalls or search for the famous pink dolphins offshore. (p230)

KO YAO ISLANDS

With towering karst islets and blue water, the incredibly scenic Ao Phang-Nga National Marine Park includes the wild jungles and beaches of Ko Yao Yin. (p267)

KO JUM & KO SI BOYA

Hiding next to Ko Lanta, these rural, beachy dots are a fave with repeat visitors. (p325)

KO TARUTAO MARINE NATIONAL PARK

Caves to paddle, rugged hikes to tackle and roads to bike. There are no resorts here, just national park lodging, and that's what keeps it serene. (p349)

KO SUKORN & KO LIBONG

The Muslim fishing communities of Ko Sukorn (p345) and Ko Libong (p344) welcome you. Take snorkelling trips, explore by motorbike, look for dugong and birds, and gorge on amazing seafood.

Ko Yao Noi (p267), Ao Phang-

Plan Your Trip

Choose Your Beach

It's a terrible dilemma: Thailand has too many beaches to choose from. Choices can be daunting even for those visiting a second time and development is so rapid that where you went five years ago may now be completely different. Here, we break it down so that you can find your dream beach.

Best Beaches for...

Relaxation and Activities

Ko Mak Beach bar scene, explorably flat and vast expanses of sand.

Ko Phayam Bike back roads to empty beaches or parties.

Hat Mae Nam Quiet Ko Samui beach close to lots of action.

Ko Bulon Leh Chilled-out vibe but lots to do.

Local Culture

Ko Yao Noi Thai-Muslim fishing island with beautiful karst scenery.

Ko Sukorn Agricultural and fishing gem filled with mangroves and water buffalo.

Ko Phra Thong Look for rare orchids with *chow lair* (Moken; 'sea gypsies').

Hua Hin Mingle with middle-class Thais in this urban beach getaway.

Quick & Easy Access from Bangkok

Nowadays the closest beaches to Bangkok aren't necessarily the quickest and easiest to get to. There are international flights direct to Phuket and Ko Samui that allow you to skip the big city altogether, and flights from Bangkok (and some Southeast Asian countries) can shuttle you to several southern towns with ease.

If you don't want or can't afford to fly, but are still short on time, the closest beach island to Bangkok is Ko Samet (count on around four hours' total travel time) while the closest beach resorts are Bang Saen (one hour by bus) and Pattaya (1½ hours). The next-closest stops by land are the beach towns of Cha-am (2½ hours) and Hua Hin (three hours). It takes around six hours to get to Ko Chang, which beats the minimum of 10 hours to reach the lower gulf islands. If you're in a hurry and want to take the bus, anywhere on the Andaman Coast is not your best choice.

To Party or Not to Party

Where

A big percentage of travellers to southern Thailand aim to party, and the local tourism industry happily accommodates them with an array of thumping beach bars lining many of the main beaches.

Luckily, it's as easy to escape the revelry as it is to join in. The main party zones are well known to be just that. Anywhere you go that's not a major tourist enclave will have peace and quiet on offer.

The Girly-Bar Issue

Bangkok, Pattaya and Phuket are the capitals of push-up bras and 'hello meesta', while Hat Lamai on Ko Samui is the centre of this small universe in the lower gulf islands. Islands like Ko Chang and mid-sized towns such as Hat Yai and Ao Nang have small enclaves of questionable massage parlours and bars with the telltale pole dancer silhouette on the sign, but they won't be in your face. Smaller islands and towns will be clear of this sort of thing, at least on the surface.

Your Party Level

Level One: Dead Calm Surin and Similan Islands, Laem Son National Park, Hat Pak Meng and Hat Chang Lang

Level Two: A Flicker of Light Ko Tarutao, Ko Libong, Prachuap Khiri Khan

Level Three: There's a Bar Ko Yao Islands, Ao Khanom, Ko Kut

Level Four: Maybe a Few Bars Hat Khao Lak, Ko Muk, Ao Thong Nai Pan (Pha-Ngan)

Level Five: Easy to Find a Drink Hua Hin, Bo Phut (Samui), Ao Nang

Level Six: There's a Beach-Bar Scene Ko Mak, Ko Phayam, Railay

Choose your own Beach Adventure

How far will you travel to find your perfect beach? Pick a starting point based on your travel priorities, then fill in the blanks.

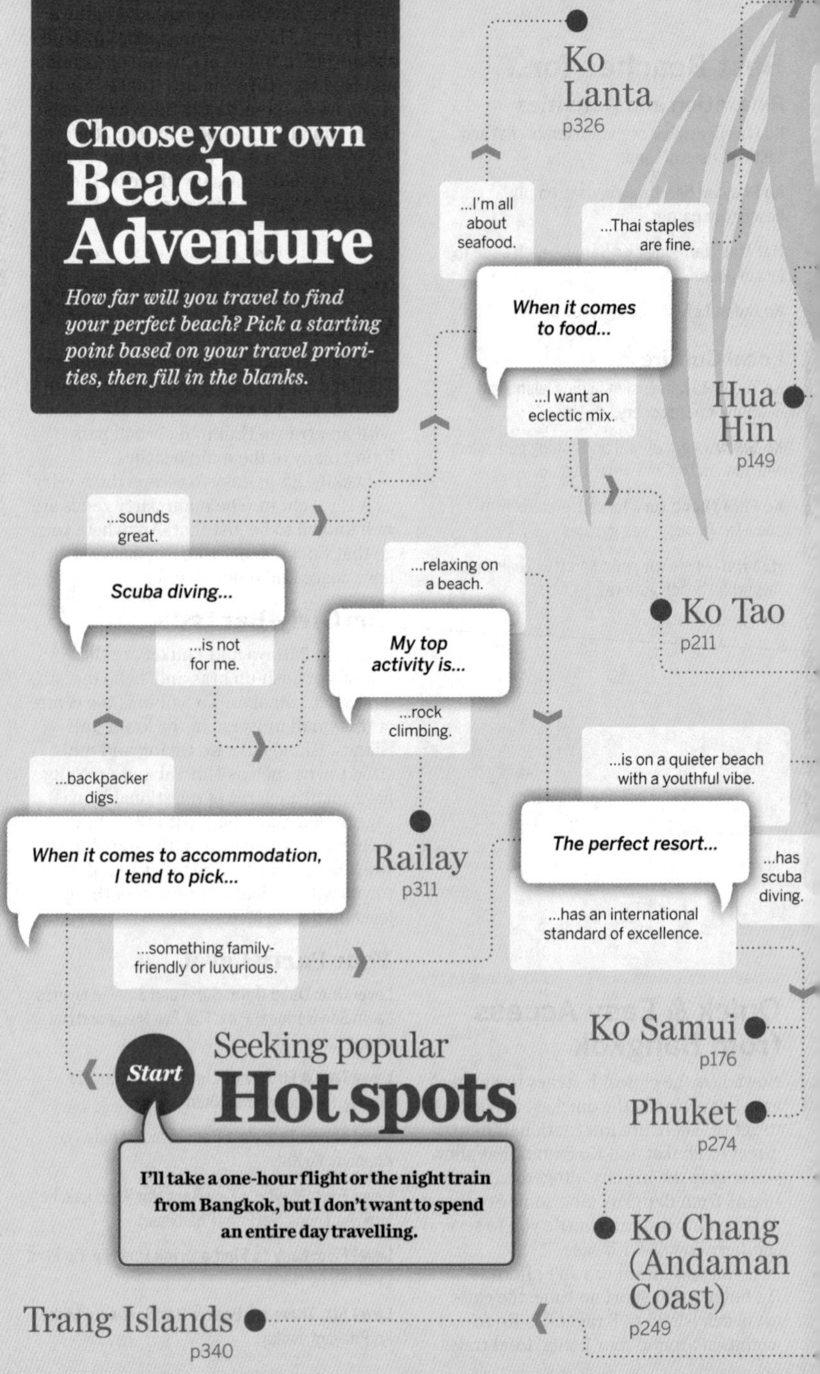

Start

Seeking popular Hot spots

I'll take a one-hour flight or the night train from Bangkok, but I don't want to spend an entire day travelling.

When it comes to accommodation, I tend to pick...

...backpacker digs.

...something family-friendly or luxurious.

Scuba diving...

...sounds great.

...is not for me.

When it comes to food...

...I'm all about seafood.

...Thai staples are fine.

...I want an eclectic mix.

My top activity is...

...relaxing on a beach.

...rock climbing.

The perfect resort...

...is on a quieter beach with a youthful vibe.

...has scuba diving.

...has an international standard of excellence.

Ko Lanta p326

Hua Hin p149

Ko Tao p211

Railay p311

Ko Samui p176

Phuket p274

Ko Chang (Andaman Coast) p249

Trang Islands p340

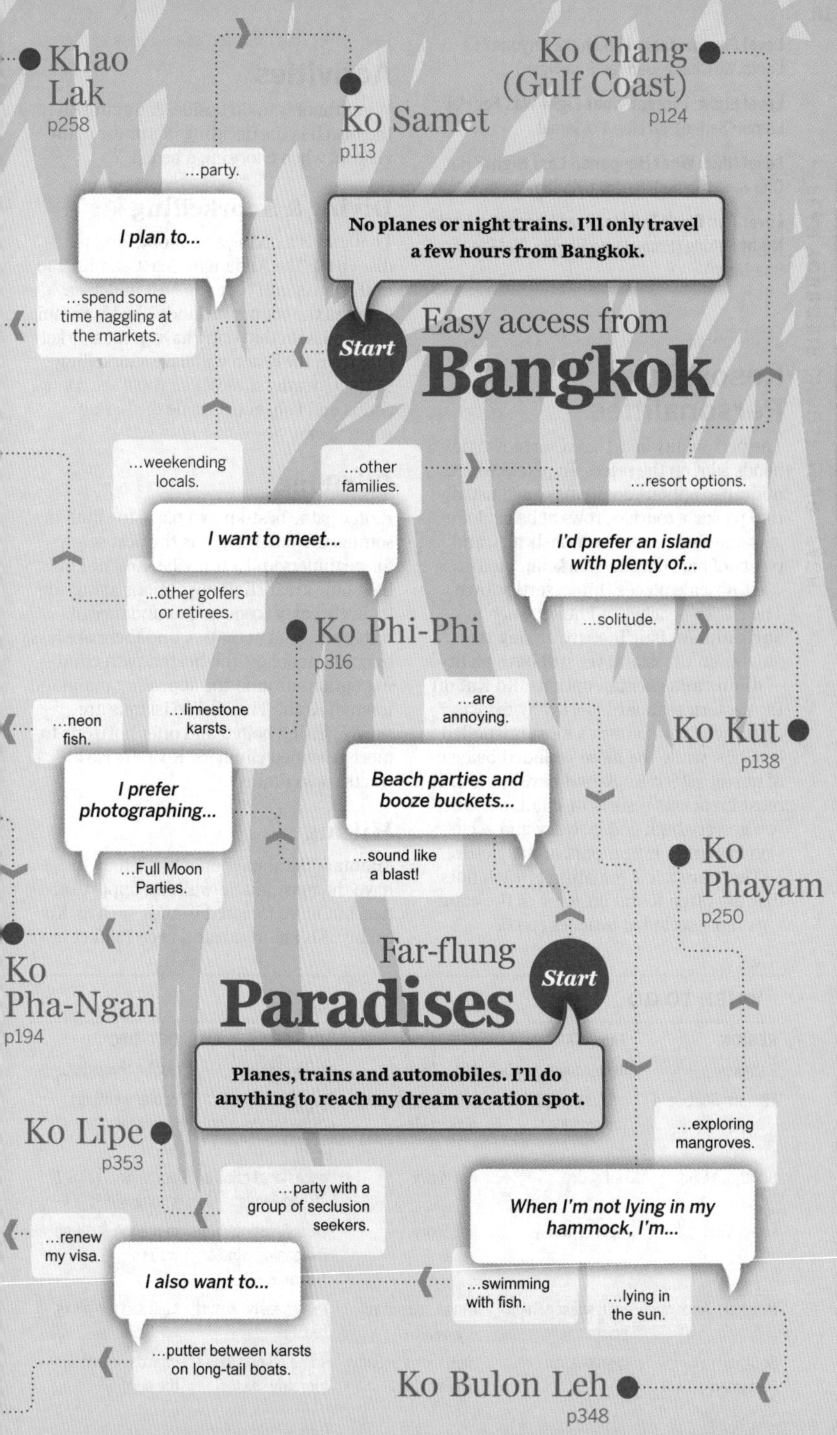
Easy access from
Bangkok
Start
No planes or night trains. I'll only travel a few hours from Bangkok.
I plan to...
...party.
...spend some time haggling at the markets.
Khao Lak
p258
Ko Samet
p113
Ko Chang (Gulf Coast)
p124
I want to meet...
...weekending locals.
...other families.
...other golfers or retirees.
I'd prefer an island with plenty of...
...resort options.
...solitude.
Ko Phi-Phi
p316
Ko Kut
p138
I prefer photographing...
...neon fish.
...limestone karsts.
...Full Moon Parties.
Beach parties and booze buckets...
...are annoying.
...sound like a blast!
Ko Phayam
p250
Ko Pha-Ngan
p194
Far-flung
Paradises
Start
Planes, trains and automobiles. I'll do anything to reach my dream vacation spot.
Ko Lipe
p353
When I'm not lying in my hammock, I'm...
...exploring mangroves.
...swimming with fish.
...lying in the sun.
I also want to...
...party with a group of seclusion seekers.
...renew my visa.
...putter between karsts on long-tail boats.
Ko Bulon Leh
p348

Level Seven: Magic Milkshake Anyone? Ko Lanta, Ko Chang, Ban Tai (Pha-Ngan)

Level Eight: I Forget What Eight Was For Hat Lamai (Samui), Ko Lipe, Ko Samet

Level Nine: What Happened Last Night? Hat Chaweng (Samui), Pattaya, Ko Tao

Level Ten: Don't Tell Me What Happened Last Night Patong (Phuket), Ko Phi-Phi, Hat Rin (Ko Pha-Ngan)

Resort-Town Personalities

The personality of a Thai resort town depends a lot on the prices. In places where midrange options dominate, you'll usually find package tourists, rows of beach loungers and umbrellas along the beach, and plenty of big boats for snorkelling tours.

At upscale places things settle down. The ritzier beaches of Phuket, such as Surin and Ao Ban Tao, are among the quieter on the island yet still have plenty of dining and cocktail options. Ko Kut off the eastern seaboard has lovely resorts on some of the country's most unspoiled beaches, while the more secluded beaches of northeastern Ko Samui have some of the most luxurious resorts in Thailand. Once you go very high end, privacy and seclusion become a bigger part of the picture.

There are a few remaining beach huts that are often found on some of the country's most secluded beaches (p32).

Activities

What there is to do besides lounging on the beach is the deciding factor for many visitors when choosing a beach.

Diving & Snorkelling

Thailand is a diving and snorkelling paradise (p41). The Andaman Coast and Ko Tao in the lower gulf have the best undersea views in the country. Islands like Ko Samui and Ko Lanta that don't have great snorkelling from the beach will have snorkelling tours to nearby sites where you'll see some corals and fish, and a turtle or shark if you're lucky.

Climbing

Railay is the best-known place to climb in southern Thailand; it has the best set-up for beginners and a fun vibe. Ko Phi-Phi has some great climbing options alongside its lively party scene and abundance of water and land activities, and there are less busy and more off-the-beaten-path climbing options around the appealing mainland town of Krabi. The Ko Yao islands are slowly getting bolted and offer horizons to more seasoned climbers. Ko Tao also attracts rock climbers.

Hiking

Mainland national parks like Khao Sok have the most jungle-walking opportunities, but more forested islands such as Ko Chang, Ko Pha-Ngan and even Phuket have

WHEN TO GO

REGION	JAN–MAR	APR–JUN	JUL–SEP	OCT–DEC
Bangkok	hotter towards Mar	hot & humid	rainy season	cooler towards Dec
Eastern Seaboard	peak season; thins towards Mar	rainy season begins in May	smaller islands close for the monsoon	cooler weather; low hotel rates
Southern Gulf	hot & dry	hot & dry	occasional rains & strong winds	occasional rains & strong winds
Lower Gulf	clear & sunny	hot & dry	clear & sunny, increasing wind & rain on Ko Tao	monsoon & rough waters
Northern Andaman	high season; high prices	fringe season with iffy weather	rainy season & surf season	high season picks up again
Southern Andaman	high season	monsoons usually begin in May	some resorts close for rainy season	crowds return with the sun

OVERVIEW OF THAILAND'S ISLANDS & BEACHES

BEACHES	PACKAGE TOURISTS	BACK-PACKERS	FAMILIES	PARTIES	DIVE/ SNORKEL	PERSONALITY
Ko Chang & Eastern Seaboard						
Ko Samet	✓	✓	✓	✓		pretty beach, easy getaway from Bangkok
Ko Chang	✓	✓	✓	✓	✓	international resort, jungle interior
Ko Wai		✓	✓		✓	primitive day tripper, deserted in the evening
Ko Mak	✓	✓	✓			mediocre beach, great vibe
Ko Kut	✓	✓	✓			lovely semi-developed island, great for solitude
Hua Hin & the Upper Gulf						
Hua Hin	✓	✓	✓			international resort, easy access to Bangkok
Pranburi & Around	✓		✓			quiet & close to Bangkok
Ban Krut			✓			low-key, popular with Thais
Bang Saphan Yai		✓	✓			cheap mainland beach
Ko Samui & the Lower Gulf						
Ko Samui	✓	✓	✓	✓		international resort for social beach-goers
Ko Pha-Ngan	✓	✓	✓	✓	✓	popular beaches, with boozy Hat Rin
Ko Tao	✓	✓	✓	✓	✓	dive schools galore
Ang Thong		✓	✓			gorgeous karst scenery
Ao Khanom		✓	✓			quiet, little known
Phuket & the Andaman Coast						
Ko Chang (Ranong)		✓	✓		✓	rustic
Ko Phayam		✓	✓			quiet, little known
Surin & Similan Islands			✓		✓	dive sites accessed by live-aboards
Ko Yao	✓	✓	✓			poor beaches but nice vibe, great scenery
Phuket	✓	✓	✓	✓	✓	international resort for social beach-goers
Ao Nang	✓	✓	✓		✓	touristy, close to Railay
Railay	✓	✓	✓			rock-climbing centre
Ko Phi-Phi	✓	✓		✓	✓	pretty party island
Ko Jum	✓	✓	✓			mediocre beach, nice vibe
Ko Lanta	✓	✓	✓		✓	emerging package scene
Trang Islands	✓	✓	✓		✓	Ko Ngai is good for kids
Ko Bulon Leh		✓	✓		✓	quiet, pretty beaches
Ko Tarutao		✓	✓			developing national park
Ko Lipe	✓	✓	✓	✓	✓	hot spot, good for visa runs
Ko Adang		✓			✓	popular with day trippers

SHARON LAPKIN / GETTY IMAGES ©

New Year's Eve fireworks, Ao Nang (p307)

great hiking, often to waterfalls or vistas looking across the blue sea.

Culture

For a taste of authentic Thai culture, head out of the main tourist zones to coastal towns like Trang, Surat Thani or Nakhon Si Thammarat, to lesser-known islands such as Ko Si Chang or Ko Sukorn, or to the less-visited parts of islands like the south coast of Ko Samui or the east coast of Ko Lanta. But even tourist central Patong or Ko Phi-Phi can give you a taste of what's beyond resort land, just by eating at food stalls and talking to the owners, smiling a lot and being open to interactions with locals.

Dangers

If renting a scooter or motorbike, you may not be insured. Insurance is not included in most rentals and your own insurance may not cover the cost of any accident. It is likely that you will be liable for medical expenses and repair or replacement costs for any damaged vehicle. If you don't have a Thai driving licence or an international driving licence, you will also be driving illegally (many rental outfits don't check). If you do rent, watch out for sand or grit on the road (especially if braking), drive slowly (under 40km/h), particularly after rain, and avoid alcohol.

Drownings are common. Pay attention to red- and yellow-flag warnings and be aware that many beaches do not have lifeguards. Also beware of rip tides, which can carry you out to sea. If caught in a rip tide in deep water, do not fight against it as you may rapidly, and dangerously, tire. It is more advisable to try to call for help, to go with the flow and conserve energy; the rip tide will take you further out to sea, but you should be able to swim back. Rip tide channels are quite narrow, so another technique is to gradually swim parallel to the shore when caught in a rip tide and you should escape it.

Signs on some beaches warn of box jellyfish, so check before swimming. Stings from box jellyfish can be fatal, and although there are few deaths, there were two fatalities in Ko Pha-Ngan waters in a 12-month period between 2014 and 2015.

Diving & Snorkelling

Whether it's your first plunge or your 50th, Thailand offers a diverse range of underwater experiences, with warm waters, abundant marine life and some of the planet's most beautiful dive sites, with reasonable prices to boot.

Diving & Snorkelling Lowdown

Best Places to Learn

Ko Tao Fantastic dive energy and scores of shallow dive sites sometimes visited by whale sharks. This is the best (and cheapest) place in Thailand to lose your scuba virginity. Sail Rock (closer to Ko Pha-Ngan) and Chumphon Pinnacle are the star sites.

Best Live-Aboards

Khao Lak The gateway to the Surin and Similan Islands. Explore the myriad dive sites on a live-aboard trip and check out Richelieu Rock – a stunning diving spot discovered by Jacques Cousteau.

Best Marine Life

Ko Lanta/Ko Phi-Phi Don Top spots for plenty of fish, recurrent visits by manta rays and the odd whale shark. Try the submerged pinnacles at Hin Daeng and Hin Muang, which are accessible from both sites.

Best Snorkelling

Ko Phi-Phi Has made a triumphant comeback after the tsunami, with loads of shimmering reefs. Ko Mai Phai and Ko Nok are great snorkelling spots, while Hin Bida and Ko Bida Nok are the local diving faves.

Diving

For the beginner through to the pro, Thailand has some of the most affordable, easily accessible and stunning diving in the world.

Planning Your Trip

The monsoon rains and peak tourist season are two factors determining when to go and which islands and beaches to pick. The severity of the rainy weather varies between seasons and coasts, and there are dry and wet microclimates as well.

When to Go

Generally speaking, the Gulf of Thailand has a year-round dive season, while the Andaman Coast has optimal diving conditions between December and April. In the Ko Chang archipelago, November to early May is the ideal season. Try to avoid the monsoon and rainy seasons.

December–February Days are mostly rain-free and under the waves you'll find a conglomeration of large pelagics at the feeding stations along the Andaman Coast.

April–June Along the gulf things are pretty quiet at this time, and the weather holds out nicely, allowing for good visibility underwater.

June–September The monsoon rains arrive on the Andaman Coast, some hotels shut down and boat travel can be interrupted by storms.

October–December The gulf coast bears the brunt of its rainy season during this period.

Pre-Booking

It is not necessary to pre-book diving excursions in Thailand unless you plan on doing a live-aboard up to the Surin Islands and Similan Islands Marine National Parks, as places on these boats are limited. Note, however, that rooms on Ko Pha-Ngan in the week up to and including the Full Moon Party sell out and rooms in Ko Tao can be stuffed in the days after the monthly shenanigans, so book early if diving then, or avoid.

Costs

Diving in Thailand is significantly cheaper than in most other nations. A 10-dive package goes for around 7000B to 12,000B on the more affordable beaches. Day-trip prices largely depend on how far the boat will travel, as petrol prices are at a premium. Figure on around 2500B for a day trip from Ko Pha-Ngan and up to 6000B for a trip out to Hin Daeng and Hin Muang from Ko Lanta.

Where to Dive

Thailand's coastal topography sits at the junction of two distinct oceanic zones – the Andaman waters wash in from the west, while the gulf coast draws its waters from the islands of Indonesia and the South China Sea.

WHALE SHARKS

The elusive whale shark – the largest fish in the sea – has a giant mouth that can measure about 2m wide (so just imagine how big their bodies are!) Don't worry: they are filter feeders, which means they mostly eat plankton, krill and other tiny organisms. Usually these gentle creatures gravitate towards submerged pinnacles. They often hang out at a site for several days before continuing on, so if rumours are flying around about a recent sighting, grab your snorkel gear and hit the high seas.

Diving the Andaman

When the weather is right, the Andaman Sea has some of the finest diving in Southeast Asia. Many would argue that the Andaman has better diving than the gulf, but this is mostly attributed to excellent visibility during the few months of favourable sea conditions. Over the last several years coral bleaching has been an issue; you'll encounter less of this around more remote sites like Richelieu Rock.

Exploring the Gulf

Sea conditions in the Gulf of Thailand are generally favourable throughout the year. The southwestern gulf coast has the finest diving spots, near the islands of Ko Tao and Ko Pha-Ngan. Pattaya, a quick two-hour hop from the Bangkok bustle, offers a few memorable dives as well, including a couple of wrecks. On the far eastern side of the coast, the Ko Chang archipelago has some pleasant scuba possibilities including several dive wrecks, although choppy seas limit the season to between November and May.

Safe Diving

Before You Dive

Before embarking on a scuba-diving trip, carefully consider the following points to ensure a safe and enjoyable experience:

- Ensure you feel comfortable diving and that you are very hydrated on days you dive.
- Remember that your last dive should be completed 24 hours before you fly. It is, however, fine to dive soon after arriving by air.
- Make sure your insurance policy covers diving injuries. If it doesn't, consider purchasing additional coverage via the website www.diversalertnetwork.org.
- Download and check through the medical health from PADI (www.padi.com), as there are some strict health requirements for diving.

Decompression Chambers

For the amount of diving occurring in Thailand, the kingdom has a surprisingly limited number of medical facilities dedicated to diving accidents.

Decompression (hyperbaric) chambers can be found at most major hubs, including Bangkok, Ko Samui, Pattaya and Phuket. Ko Tao does not have an emergency chamber – the nearest one is on Ko

Samui, a 90-minute speedboat journey away. Injured divers out of Khao Lak are generally rushed south to Phuket (about an hour away). We advise you to ask your operator of choice about the nearest chamber. Also, make sure there is an emergency supply of oxygen on your dive boat.

Coursework

Thailand is one of the best places in the world to learn how to dive. If you are looking for the best bang for your baht, we recommend getting certified on Ko Tao, where coursework starts at 9000B to 10,000B depending on the type of licence you receive. Beyond Ko Tao, there are plenty of places to get certified, though you're looking at an extra 3000B to 6000B for your Open Water Diver (OWD) certificate. Ko Pha-Ngan, Ko Phi-Phi, Khao Lak and Ko Lanta round out Thailand's top five places to learn to dive.

Live-Aboards

The live-aboard industry has been steadily growing in Thailand over the past 20-odd years. Most live-aboards are based out of Khao Lak, just north of Phuket on the Andaman Coast. These live-aboard excursions are all-inclusive (lodging on the boat, food, scuba gear, guides), varying in length from two to five nights. When it's low season on the Similan Islands off the Andaman Coast, a few live-aboards head to the Gulf to operate on dive sites around Koh Tao, Ang Thong Marine National Park and Koh Pha-Ngan.

Freediving

Freediving involves the diver submersing with a single breath (with no scuba gear or snorkel). Currently, one of the top spots to try this sport is on Ko Tao in the southern gulf, but freediving schools have also appeared on Ko Pha-Ngan and Ko Lanta. Beginner courses (usually two days of diving) cost around 5000B.

For more information on freediving, check out AIDA International (www.aidainternational.org) and CMAS (www.cmas.org).

Technical Diving

Often called tec diving, technical diving is an advanced type of scuba diving involving additional equipment and, most notably, a tank of mixed breathing gases to allow for deeper dives. Technical diving is often taken on as a recreational sport for those interested in exploring deep wrecks and caves.

Underwater caving has really taken off in recent years, and there are several operators on Ko Tao that offer one-day/one-night trips out to the submerged grottoes in Khao Sok National Park.

Snorkelling

Many islands, including the Trang island chain, Ko Tao, Ko Pha-Ngan, Ko Phi-Phi and the islands in the Ko Chang archipelago, have phenomenal snorkelling spots right offshore.

Tours

Many tour offices and dive operators offer snorkelling trips. Expect to pay between 500B and 1200B for a day trip depending on how far you travel. Often a snorkelling component is tied into larger day trips that take in pristine islands and kayaking too.

High-end excursions usually use fancy speedboats and expensive equipment, while cheaper deals tend to focus more on the social aspect of the trip, taking customers to so-so reefs.

On Your Own

Orchestrating your own snorkelling adventure is easy – there are loads of resorts and dive shops spread throughout Thailand's islands and beaches that rent out gear for 100B to 200B per hour. If you plan on snorkelling under your own steam, follow the same simple rules that you would for scuba diving:

- Bring a buddy with you.
- Don't go without a guide if you're not a confident swimmer, or are unsure how to handle rips.
- Let someone on land know that you are going snorkelling, just in case something happens to you and your buddy.
- Keep an eye out above water to make sure you're not swimming too far out.

Scuba diver and comb coral off Ko Phi-Phi (p316

Preserving Thailand's Reefs

Thailand's underwater kingdom is incredibly fragile and it's worth taking some time to educate yourself on responsible practices while you're visiting. Here are a few of the more important rules to follow, but this is by no means an exhaustive list.

- Whether on an island or in a boat, take all litter with you – even biodegradable material like apple cores – and dispose of it back on the mainland.
- Remember that it is an offence to damage or remove coral in marine parks.
- Don't touch or harass marine animals.
- Never rest or stand on coral because touching or walking on it will damage it. It can also cause some nasty cuts.
- Ensure that no equipment is dragging over the reef.
- If you're snorkelling (and especially if you are a beginner), practise your technique away from coral until you've mastered control in the water.
- Hire a wetsuit or rash vest rather than slathering on sunscreen, which can damage the reef.
- Watch where your fins are – try not to stir up sediment or disturb coral.
- Do not take any shells home with you – it's illegal.
- Remember that snorkelling is the best way to see whale sharks; divers' bubbles can annoy or confuse them.

Plan Your Trip
Eat Like a Local

Incendiary curries, oodles of noodles, fresh seafood and the tropical fruit you've been dreaming about – Thailand has it all. But what many visitors don't know is that by eating in guesthouse restaurants and tourist-frequented stalls they're often experiencing a Westernised version of Thai food. To experience and be inspired by the true flavours of Thailand, you should familiarise yourself with the dishes of Thailand's various regions and ethnic groups.

Food Experiences

Top Local Restaurants

➡ **Krua Apsorn** (p83) This award-winning Bangkok restaurant has a thick menu of decadent Bangkok- and central Thailand–style fare.

➡ **Jay Fai** (p85) Lauded Bangkok shophouse that specialises in seafood-heavy stir-fries that blur the line between Thai and Chinese cuisines.

➡ **Hua Hin Koti** (p157) The queue for a table stretches around the corner, so you know this Hua Hin restaurant is good.

➡ **Chowlay** (p134) True to its 'if it swims, we have it' motto, this pier restaurant in Ko Chang has an epic seafood menu and great bay views.

➡ **Fisherman's Restaurant** (p207) Book super early during the full moon. This romantic place right by the sea on Ko Pha-Ngan hits all the right notes, especially with its delectable Thai seafood and serene ambience.

➡ **Krua Thara** (p310) One of Thailand's very best seafood kitchens attracts domestic tourists from around the country to Krabi.

➡ **Krua Talay** (p233) A feast of flavour and texture, the seafood dishes at this excellent restaurant are one of the highlights of a visit to Nakhon Si Thammarat.

➡ **Suay** (p277) An outstanding Thai fusion menu at this Phuket restaurant blends seasonal,

The Year in Food

Summer (March to June)

Thailand's hot season is the best time of year for fruit. Durian, mangoes, mangosteen and lychees are all at their juicy peak during these months.

Rainy season (July to October)

One holiday to look out for during the rainy season is Thailand's annual Vegetarian Festival (typically held in late September or early October). The festival is particularly popular in places with large Chinese populations, such as Bangkok, Phuket Town and Trang.

Winter (November to January)

During Thailand's brief cool season, open-air beer halls, many serving spicy Thai drinking snacks, spring up in the country's larger cities.

local ingredients into elegantly creative concoctions such as mangosteen *sôm đam*.

➡ **In Town** (p166) Fantastic seafood and views of Prachuap Khiri Khan's awesome bay at this locals' favourite.

➡ **Mum Aroy** (p105) Discover why seafood on the eastern seaboard is so highly rated by cracking open some crabs and munching on prawns at this hugely popular Si Racha spot.

Cooking Courses

A standard one-day course usually features a shopping trip to a local market to choose ingredients, followed by preparation of curry pastes, soups, curries, salads and desserts.

➡ **Amita Thai Cooking Class** (p69) Bangkok.

➡ **Buchabun Art & Crafts Collection** (p154) Hua Hin.

➡ **Koh Chang Thai Cookery School** (p128) Ko Chang.

➡ **Samui Institute of Thai Culinary Arts** (p179) Ko Samui.

➡ **Suay Cooking School** (p276) Phuket.

Regional Specialities

Unlike the way it is often touted abroad, Thai food is anything but a single entity. It is made up of a vast repertoire of ingredients, cooking techniques and dishes that can often pinpoint a particular province, or even a town.

Bangkok & Central Thai Cuisine

In Bangkok, geography, the influence of the royal palace and the country's main minorities – Chinese and Muslims – have all served to shape the local cuisine.

The people of central Thailand are fond of sweet/savoury flavours, and many dishes include freshwater fish, pork, coconut milk and palm sugar – common ingredients in the central Thai plains. Because of the region's proximity to the Gulf of Thailand, central Thai eateries, particularly those in Bangkok, also serve a wide variety of seafood. Chinese labourers and vendors introduced a huge variety of noodle and wok-fried dishes to central Thailand as far back as 200 years ago.

Must-eat central Thai and Bangkok dishes include the following:

➡ **Pàt tai** Thin rice noodles stir-fried with dried and/or fresh shrimp, bean sprouts, tofu, egg and seasonings, traditionally served with lime halves and a few stalks of Chinese chives and a sliced banana flower.

➡ **Yam ƀlah dùk foo** Fried shredded catfish, chilli and peanuts served with a sweet/tart mango dressing.

➡ **Đôm yam** Lemongrass, kaffir lime leaf and lime juice give this soup its characteristic tang; fresh chillies or an oily chilli paste provide it with its legendary sting.

➡ **Yen đah foh** Combining a slightly sweet crimson-coloured broth with a variety of meatballs, cubes of coagulated chicken or pork blood and crispy greens, *yen đah foh* is probably both the most intimidating and popular noodle dish in Bangkok.

➡ **Gaang sôm** Central Thailand's famous 'sour soup' often includes freshwater fish, vegetables and/or herbs, and a thick, tart broth.

➡ **Gŏo·ay đěe·o reu·a** Known as boat noodles because they were previously served from small boats along the canals of central Thailand, these intense pork- or beef-based bowls are among the most full-flavoured of Thai noodle dishes.

Southern Thai Cuisine

Don't say we didn't warn you: southern Thai cooking is undoubtedly the spiciest regional cooking style in a land of spicy regional cuisines. The food of Thailand's southern provinces also tends to be very salty, and seafood, not surprisingly, plays an important role. Dishes range from fresh fish that is grilled or added to soups to pickled or fermented fish served as sauces or condiments.

Two of the principal crops in the south are coconuts and cashews, both of which find their way into a variety of dishes. In addition to these, southern Thais love their greens, and nearly every meal is accompanied by a platter of fresh herbs and veggies, and a spicy 'dip' of shrimp paste, chillies, garlic and lime.

Dishes you are likely to come across in southern Thailand include the following:

➡ **Gaang đai ƀlah** An intensely spicy and salty curry that includes *đai ƀlah* (salted fish kidney); much tastier than it sounds.

Cooking class at Samui Institute of Thai Culinary Arts (p179), Ko Samui

➡ **Gaang sôm** Known as *gaang lĕu·ang* (yellow curry) in central Thailand, this sour/spicy soup gets its orange hue from the liberal use of turmeric, a root commonly used in southern Thai cooking.

➡ **Gài tôrt hàht yài** The famous deep-fried chicken from the town of Hat Yai gets its rich flavour from a marinade containing dried spices.

➡ **Kà·nŏm jeen nám yah** This dish of thin rice noodles served with a spicy curry-like sauce is always accompanied by a tray of fresh vegetables and herbs.

➡ **Kôo·a glîng** Minced meat fried with a fiery curry paste is a southern staple.

➡ **Kôw yam** A popular breakfast, this dish includes rice topped with sliced herbs, bean sprouts, dried prawns, toasted coconut and powdered red chilli, served with a sour/sweet fish-based sauce.

➡ **Pàt sà·dor** This popular stir-fry of 'stink beans' with shrimp, garlic, chillies and shrimp paste is both pungent and spicy.

Ethnic Specialities

In addition to geography, the country's predominant minorities – Muslims and the Chinese – have had different but profound influences on the local cuisine.

Islamic World–Influenced Cuisine

Muslims are thought to have first visited Thailand during the late 14th century. Along with the Quran, they brought with them a cuisine based on meat and dried spice from their homelands in India and the Middle East. Nearly 700 years later, the impact of this culinary commerce can still be felt.

While some dishes influenced by the Islamic world – such as *ro·đi*, a fried bread similar to the Indian *paratha* – have changed little, if at all, others such as *gaang mát·sà·màn* are a unique blend of Thai, Indian and Middle Eastern cooking styles and ingredients. In more recent years, additional Islamic World–influenced dishes have arrived via contact with Thailand's neighbour to the south, Malaysia.

Common Thai dishes influenced by the Islamic world include the following:

➡ **Gaang mát·sà·màn** 'Muslim curry' is a rich coconut milk–based dish, which, unlike most Thai curries, gets much of its flavour from dried spices. As with many Islamic World–influenced Thai dishes, there is an emphasis on the sweet.

➡ **Kôw mòk** Biryani, a dish found across the Muslim world, also has a foothold in Thailand. Here the dish is typically made with chicken and is served with a sweet and sour dipping sauce and a bowl of chicken broth.

➡ **Má·đà·bà** Known as *murtabak* in Malaysia and Indonesia, these are *ro·đi* that have been stuffed with a savoury or sometimes sweet filling and fried until crispy.

➡ **Sà·đé (satay)** The savoury peanut-based dipping sauce served with these grilled skewers of meat is often mistakenly associated with Thai cooking.

➡ **Sà·làt kàak** Literally 'Muslim salad' (*kàak* is a somewhat derogatory word used to describe people or things of South Asian and/or Muslim origin), this dish combines iceberg lettuce, chunks of firm tofu, cucumber, hard-boiled egg and tomato, all topped with a sweet peanut sauce.

➡ **Súp hăhng woo·a** Oxtail soup, possibly a Malay contribution, is even richer and often more sour than the 'Buddhist' Thai *đôm yam*.

Sah•lah•ɓow (Chinese-style steamed buns)

Thai-Chinese Cuisine

Immigrants from southern China have been influencing Thai cuisine for centuries, and it was Chinese labourers and vendors who most likely introduced the wok and several varieties of noodle dishes to Thailand.

Thai-Chinese dishes you're likely to run across include the following:

➡ **Bà·mèe** Chinese-style wheat and egg noodles are typically served with slices of barbecued pork, a handful of greens and/or wontons.

➡ **Gŏo·ay đěe•o kôo·a gài** Wide rice noodles fried with little more than egg, chicken, squid and garlic oil; a popular dish in Bangkok's Chinatown.

➡ **Kôw kăh mŏo** Braised pork leg served over rice, often with sides of greens and a hard-boiled egg, is the epitome of the Chinese-style one-dish meal.

➡ **Kôw man gài** Chicken rice, originally from the Chinese island of Hainan, is now found in just about every corner of Thailand.

➡ **Sah•lah•ɓow** Chinese-style steamed buns are a favourite at old-school Chinese-style coffeeshops across Thailand.

Travel with Children

Thais are serious 'cute' connoisseurs and exotic-looking foreign children rank higher on their adorable meter than stuffed animals and fluffy dogs. Children are instant celebrities and attract almost paparazzi-like attention. Older kids get less of this but will revel in the sandy beaches and warm water.

Thailand for Kids

Babies do surprisingly well with their new-found stardom. If you've got a babe in arms, food vendors will often offer to hold the child while you eat, taking the child for a brief stroll to visit the other vendors.

At a certain age, kids develop stranger anxiety, which doesn't mix well with the Thai passion for children. For the preschool set, who are becoming self-conscious but still have major cute quotient, we recommend sticking to tourist centres instead of trotting off to far-flung places where foreigners, especially children, will attract too much attention.

To smooth out the usual road bumps of dragging children from place to place, check out Lonely Planet's *Travel with Children,* which contains useful advice with a focus on travel in developing countries.

Children's Highlights

Outdoors

➡ **Swimming** Of Thailand's many kid-friendly destinations, children will especially love the beaches, as most are shallow, gentle bays good for beginner swimmers. Be aware of rips, however, and treat all **sea-related warnings**

Best Regions for Kids

Ko Samui & the Lower Gulf

Older children can strap on a mask and snorkel Ko Tao without worry. Ko Samui's northern beaches and Ko Pha-Ngan's north and eastern beaches are popular with toddlers, while Hat Chaweng appeals to older kids.

Phuket & the Northern Andaman Coast

As well as the beach, Phuket has amusements galore, but steer clear of the Patong party scene.

Ko Phi-Phi & the Southern Andaman Coast

Ko Lanta has long stretches of beach with mellow surf, while the Trang Islands offer peaceful sands and easy swimming.

Ko Chang & the Eastern Seaboard

Shallow seas are kind to young swimmers and low evening tides make for good beachcombing. Older children will like the interior jungle, elephant interactions and mangrove kayaking.

Hua Hin & the Upper Gulf

Hua Hin has a long sandy coastline and hillside temples for monkey spotting. Phetchaburi's cave temples often deliver a bat sighting. Ban Krut and Bang Saphan Yai are very casual.

(p40) with the utmost seriousness, including checking flag colours.

➡ **Resorts** Many of the beach resorts, such as Phuket and Ko Chang, also have wildlife encounters, waterfall spotting and waterfall swimming, and organised water sports ideal for children aged six years and older. Wherever you take the kids, however, remember that many forms of elephant tourism are associated with animal-welfare issues.

➡ **Older Kids** Look out for rock climbing, kayaking, ziplining, scuba diving and freediving for kids searching for more exciting and exhilarating options.

Urban

➡ **Construction** Bangkok is great fun for those in awe of construction sites: the city is filled with cranes, jackhammers and concrete-pouring trucks.

➡ **Skytrain** Then there's the above-ground Skytrain and shopping malls complete with escalators (a preschool favourite).

➡ **Shopping** The city's immense shopping options will appeal to tweens and teens.

Other

➡ **Overnight Train** Kids on a train kick might like the fun of an overnight journey. They can walk around on the train and they're assigned the lower sleeping berths with views of the stations.

➡ **Temples** These can be engaging places for children. Some of the forested temples have resident monkeys and cave shrines. Merit-making at a Buddhist temple is surprisingly kid-friendly – there's the burning joss sticks, the bowing in front of the Buddha and the rubbing of gold leaf on the central image. Most temples also have a fortune-telling area, where you shake a bamboo container until a numbered stick falls out, with the number corresponding to a printed fortune.

Planning & Practicalities

➡ Child-safety seats for cars, high chairs in restaurants and nappy-changing facilities in public restrooms are virtually nonexistent. Parents will have to be resourceful in seeking out substitutes, or follow the example of Thai families (holding smaller children on their laps).

➡ Baby formula and nappies (diapers) are available at minimarkets and 7-Elevens in larger towns and cities, but sizes are usually small, smaller and smallish. If your kid wears size three or larger, head to Tesco Lotus, Big C or Tops Market stores. Nappy-rash cream is sold at pharmacies.

➡ Thailand's footpaths are often too crowded to push a pram. Opt for a lightweight, compact umbrella stroller that can squeeze past the fire hydrant and the mango cart and that can be folded up and thrown in a túk-túk. A baby pack is also useful, but make sure that the child's head doesn't sit higher than yours: there are lots of hanging obstacles poised at forehead level.

Eating with Kids

Dining with children, particularly with infants, in Thailand is a liberating experience as the Thais are so fond of kids. Take it for granted that your babies will be fawned over, played with and, more often than not, carried around by restaurant waitstaff. Regard this as a much-deserved break, not to mention a bit of free cultural exposure.

Because much Thai food is so spicy, there is an entire art devoted to ordering 'safe' dishes for children, and the vast majority of Thai kitchens are more than willing to oblige.

In general, Thai children don't start to eat spicy food until primary school. Before then they seemingly survive on rice and jelly snacks. Other kid-friendly meals include chicken in all its nonspicy permutations – *gài yâhng* (grilled chicken), *gài tôrt* (fried chicken) and *gài pàt mét má•môo•ang* (chicken stir-fried with cashew nuts) – as well as *kài jee•o* (Thai-style omelette). Another mild option is *kôw man gài* (Hainanese chicken rice).

Health & Safety

For the most part parents needn't worry too much about health concerns, although a few ground rules (such as regular hand washing) can head off potential medical problems. In particular:

➡ Children should be warned not to play with animals (from dogs to monkeys), as rabies is relatively common in Thailand.

➡ Mosquito bites often leave big welts on children. If your child is bitten, there is a variety of locally produced balms that can reduce swelling and itching. All the usual health precautions apply.

Regions at a Glance

Bangkok

Culture/History
Food
Nightlife

Classic Siam

Once a show of strength after the devastating 1765–67 war with Burma (now Myanmar), Bangkok's royal Buddhist temples are now both national pilgrimage sites and fabulous, intriguing displays of classical art and architecture.

Open-Air Dining

For adventurous foodies who can live without white tablecloths, there's probably no better dining destination than Bangkok. And until you've eaten on the capital's streets, your just-sizzled noodles mingling with your sweat amid a cloud of exhaust fumes, you haven't actually eaten Thai food.

Rooftop Bars

In Bangkok, nobody seems to mind if you slap the odd bar on top of a skyscraper. Indeed, the city has become associated with elegant open-air rooftop bars, with venues offering views that range from riverside to hyper-urban.

p54

Ko Chang & the Eastern Seaboard

Beaches
Diving
Small Towns

A Herd of Islands

Ko Chang has jungles and party animals, Ko Mak boasts a laid-back island vibe, and Ko Kut has some of the prettiest views you'll ever see. There are easy transport connections between these three islands.

Wrecks & Reefs

It may not compare with those further south, but new wrecks and coral banks make this a worthy region to blow bubbles. Finely preserved reefs cluster around uninhabited Ko Rang, while the purposely sunk *HTMS Chang* lies in wait off Ko Chang.

Provincial Prominence

The eastern seaboard's small towns include trendy Bang Saen; charming Chanthaburi, famous for a weekend gem market; and Trat, a transit link to Ko Chang. These provincial towns delight with their ordinariness and a middle-class prosperity that is not found on the islands.

p100

Hua Hin & the Upper Gulf

Culture/History
Coastal Scenery
Food

Royal Coast

Thai kings escaped from Bangkok's stifling climate to Hua Hin, and modern Bangkokians follow in their footsteps, touring the historic hilltop palace and cave shrines. The region's coastline is long, inviting and nowhere near as crowded as Thailand's other resort areas.

Surf & Turf

Little Prachuap Khiri Khan has stunning karst panoramas dotted with bobbing fishing boats, while Hua Hin and Phetchaburi boast atmospheric shophouse districts dating from the time when parts of Thailand's coast were settled by Chinese merchants.

Southern Seafood

Some of Thailand's most authentic southern seafood lies in wait along the upper gulf coast, which caters more to Thai tourists. Get ready for an explosion of tastes amid the affordable markets and seafood eateries of Prachuap Khiri Khan and Chumphon.

p140

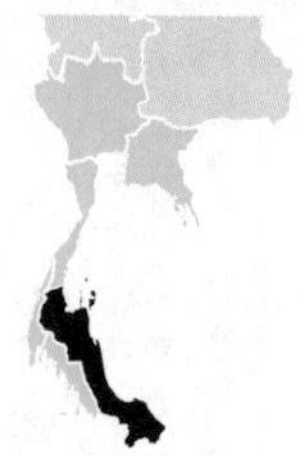

Ko Samui & the Lower Gulf

Beaches
Diving
Nightlife

Island Life

On the classic gulf trail, Ko Pha-Ngan's beachy layabout vibe stands strong, while professional Ko Samui caters to international tastes, high-end tendencies and active holidaymakers. A day-trip dreamboat, stunning limestone Ang Thong Marine National Park juts out of azure seas.

Diving Ko Tao

With warm gentle seas, shallow bays, year-round activity and masses of dive schools that keep prices wallet-friendly, Ko Tao remains one of the world's top places to master the art of scuba diving. Just offshore are snorkelling points that make fish-spotting easy and fun.

Full Moon Fun

The biggest and boldest of Thailand's beach parties bursts into action once a month on Hat Rin Nok on Ko Pha-Ngan. Prepare for fire twirling, thumping bass, neon body paint, sickly sweet booze buckets and absolutely no sleep.

p173

Phuket & the Andaman Coast

Beaches
Diving
Food

Spectacular Sands

Fringed by lush sloping jungle and twinkling turquoise sea, the white strand lining Ko Ngai's east coast in the Trang Islands is only the most marvellous example of hundreds of beautiful blonde beaches sprinkled along the Andaman Coast.

Under the Sea

Big fish, beautiful corals, sparkling aqua water – stellar diving and snorkelling sites orbit the renowned Similan and Surin Islands. Hop on a live-aboard to cavort with manta rays and the occasional whale shark at Richelieu Rock and Ko Bon.

To Market

Trang, Krabi, Ranong, Phuket Town and Satun have fantastic night markets where you can feast on perfect noodles, fragrant rice, bubbling curries, grilled fish, fresh juices or spicy salads. Beachside barbecues on the region's islands sizzle up the day's catch to steal the show.

p243

On the Road

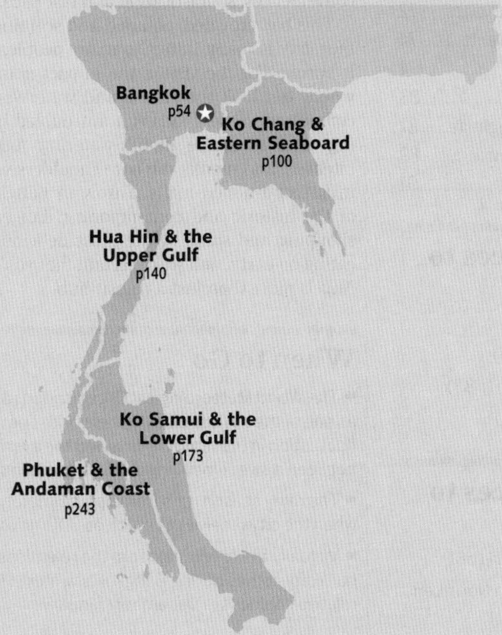

Bangkok
p54

Ko Chang & Eastern Seaboard
p100

Hua Hin & the Upper Gulf
p140

Ko Samui & the Lower Gulf
p173

Phuket & the Andaman Coast
p243

Bangkok

Includes ➡

Best Places to Eat

- ➡ nahm (p86)
- ➡ Eat Me (p86)
- ➡ Krua Apsorn (p83)
- ➡ Jay Fai (p85)

Best Places to Stay

- ➡ AriyasomVilla (p81)
- ➡ Phra-Nakorn Norn-Len (p82)
- ➡ Siam Heritage (p81)
- ➡ Bangkok Tree House (p82)
- ➡ Lamphu Treehouse (p76)

Why Go?

If all you want to do is kick back on a beach, Bangkok might seem like a transit burden full of concrete towers instead of palm trees. But it's shockingly easy to succumb to Bangkok's conveniences, sophistication and fast pace.

This big, crowded, polluted and seemingly chaotic Asian megacity is many things to many people, but no one calls it boring. For the visitor, the impact is immediate. Everywhere you look the streets and waterways are alive with commuters. School kids run untroubled by the heat, smiling vendors create mouth-watering food in push-away kitchens, and monks rub bare shoulders with businessmen in air-conditioned malls. Throw in Bangkok's unique mix of the historic and contemporary, dangerously appealing shopping and some of the most delicious and best-value eating on earth, and we're certain that you'll find the City of Angels more than just a transit hub.

When to Go

➡ The World Meteorological Organisation rates Bangkok as one of the hottest cities in the world. There's very little fluctuation in the temperature, and the average high sways between a sweat-inducing 32°C and a stifling 34°C.

➡ The rainy season runs from approximately May to October, when the city receives as much as 300mm of rain a month.

➡ Virtually the only break from the relentless heat and humidity comes during Bangkok's winter, a few weeks of relative coolness in December/January.

Bangkok Highlights

❶ Basking in the glow of all that gold at **Wat Phra Kaew & Grand Palace** (p57).

❷ Taking in the immense Buddha statue at **Wat Pho** (p57).

❸ Skipping between sightseeing spots on a cruise of **Thonburi's canals** (p57).

❹ Encountering the best of Thai architecture and artwork at **Jim Thompson House** (p66).

❺ Burning baht at **Chatuchak Weekend Market** (p93).

❻ Learning to make authentic Thai dishes at one of Bangkok's cooking schools, such as **Amita Thai Cooking Class** (p69).

❼ Toasting the stars and the twinkling skyscraper lights at **Moon Bar** (p91) or one of the city's other rooftop bars.

❽ Being blissfully pounded into submission at one of Bangkok's terrific-value Thai massage centres, such as **Health Land** (p69).

History

Now the centre of government and culture in Thailand, Bangkok was a historical miracle during a time of turmoil. Following the fall of Ayuthaya in 1767, the kingdom fractured into competing forces, from which General Taksin emerged as a decisive unifier. He established his base in Thonburi, on the western bank of Mae Nam Chao Phraya (Chao Phraya River), a convenient location for sea trade from the Gulf of Thailand. Taksin proved more of a military strategist than a popular ruler. He was later deposed by another important military general, Chao Phraya Chakri, who in 1782 moved the capital across the river to a more defensible location in anticipation of a Burmese attack. The succession of his son in 1809 established the present-day royal dynasty, and Chao Phraya Chakri is referred to as Rama I.

Court officials envisioned the new capital as a resurrected Ayuthaya, complete with an island district (Ko Ratanakosin) carved out of the swampland and cradling the royal court (the Grand Palace) and a temple to the auspicious Emerald Buddha (Wat Phra Kaew). The emerging city, which was encircled by a thick wall, was filled with stilt and floating houses ideally adapted to seasonal flooding.

Modernity came to the capital in the late 19th century as European aesthetics and technologies filtered east. During the reigns of Rama IV (King Mongkut; r 1851–68) and Rama V (King Chulalongkorn; r 1868–1910), Bangkok received its first paved road (Th Charoen Krung, formerly known as New Road) and a new royal district (Dusit) styled after European palaces.

Bangkok was still a gangly town when soldiers from the American war in Vietnam came to rest and relax in the city's go-go bars and brothels. It wasn't until the boom years of the 1980s and 1990s that Bangkok exploded into a fully fledged metropolis crowded with hulking skyscrapers and an endless spill of concrete that gobbled up rice paddies and green space. The city's extravagant tastes were soon tamed by the 1997 economic meltdown, the effects of which can still be seen in the numerous half-built skyscrapers. Nearly two decades later, many of these still exist, but they are becoming increasingly obscured behind a modern public-transport system and the seemingly endless high-rise condos and vast glass-fronted mega-malls that have come to define the Bangkok of today.

Sights

Thailand's islands and beaches are not particularly well stocked with traditional Thai 'sights', so it's well worth taking in a few while you're in Bangkok.

Ko Ratanakosin, Banglamphu & Thonburi เกาะรัตนโกสินทร์/บางลำพู/ธนบุรี

Most of Bangkok's must-see sights are in compact, walkable Ko Ratanakosin, the former royal district.

Next door, Banglamphu is a study in extremes, encompassing both the most characteristically old-school-Bangkok part of town as well as Th Khao San, a brash, neon-lit decompression zone for international backpackers.

Directly across the river from Banglamphu is Thonburi, which served a brief tenure as the Thai capital after the fall of Ayuthaya. It's calm enough on the west bank of the Mae Nam Chao Phraya to seem like another province.

BANGKOK IN...

One Day

Get up as early as you can and take the **Chao Phraya Express Boat** (p72) to Chang Pier to explore the temples and museums of **Ko Ratanakosin** (p56), then lunch in **Banglamphu** (p83).

After freshening up, gain a new perspective on Bangkok with sunset cocktails at one of the city's **rooftop bars** (p91), followed by an upscale Thai dinner at **nahm** (p86) or **Bo.lan** (p87).

Two Days

Allow the BTS (Skytrain) to whisk you to various **shopping** (p91) destinations in central Bangkok and to **Jim Thompson House** (p66), breaking for lunch at one of the city's **food courts**. Wrap up the daylight hours with a **traditional Thai massage** (p69). Then work off those calories at the city's **nightclubs** (p87).

Three Days

Spend a day at **Chatuchak Weekend Market** (p93) or, if it's a weekday, enrol in a **cooking school** (p69). Unwind by bumping to a retro-Thai DJ set at **Studio Lam** (p88) or rocking to traditional Thai music at **Tep Bar** (p88).

Four Days

Take the MRT (Metro) to **Chinatown** (p85) for bustling markets and for some of the city's best street food. Cap the evening off by bar-hopping in **Banglamphu** (p87).

DON'T MISS

EXPLORING THONBURI'S CANALS

Bangkok was formerly criss-crossed by an advanced network of *klorng* (also spelt *khlong*), artificial canals that inhabitants used both for transport and to ship goods. Today, cars and motorcycles have superseded boats, and the majority of Bangkok's canals have been filled in and covered by roads, or are fetid and drying up. Yet a peek into the watery Bangkok of yesteryear can still be had west of Mae Nam Chao Phraya, in Thonburi.

Thonburi's network of canals and river tributaries still carries a motley fleet of watercraft, from paddle canoes to rice barges. Homes, trading houses and temples are built on stilts with front doors opening out to the water. **Khlong Bangkok Noi** is lined with greenery and historic temples; smaller **Khlong Mon** is largely residential. **Khlong Bangkok Yai** was in fact the original course of the river until a canal was built to expedite transits.

Today, long-tail boats that ply these and other Thonburi canals are available for charter at Chang Pier and Tien Pier, both on Ko Ratanakosin. Trips generally traverse Khlong Bangkok Noi and Khlong Mon, taking in the Royal Barges National Museum, Wat Arun and a riverside temple with fish feeding. Longer trips diverge into Khlong Bangkok Yai, and can include a visit to an orchid farm. On weekends, you have the option of visiting the **Taling Chan Floating Market** (ตลาดน้ำตลิ่งชัน; Map p78; Khlong Bangkok Noi, Thonburi; ⌚7am-4pm Sat & Sun; S Wongwian Yai exit 3 & taxi). However, it's worth pointing out that to actually disembark and explore any of these sights, the most common tour of one hour (1000B, up to six people) is simply not enough time; you'll most likely need 1½ or two hours (1300/1500B). Most operators have set tour routes, but if you have a specific destination in mind, you can request it. Tours are generally conducted from 8am to 5pm.

★Wat Phra Kaew & Grand Palace — BUDDHIST TEMPLE

(วัดพระแก้ว, พระบรมมหาราชวัง; Map p60; Th Na Phra Lan; admission 500B; ⌚8.30am-3.30pm; Chang Pier, Maharaj Pier, Phra Chan Tai Pier) FREE Also known as the Temple of the Emerald Buddha, **Wat Phra Kaew** is the colloquial name of the vast, fairy-tale compound that also includes the former residence of the Thai monarch, the Grand Palace.

This ground was consecrated in 1782, the first year of Bangkok rule, and is today Bangkok's biggest tourist attraction and a pilgrimage destination for devout Buddhists and nationalists. The 94.5-hectare grounds encompass more than 100 buildings that represent 200 years of royal history and architectural experimentation.

Housed in a fantastically decorated *bòht* (ordination hall), the **Emerald Buddha** is the temple's primary attraction.

Except for an anteroom here and there, the buildings of the **Grand Palace** are now put to use by the king only for certain ceremonial occasions, such as Coronation Day, and are largely off-limits to visitors. Formerly, Thai kings housed their huge harems in the inner palace area, which was guarded by combat-trained female sentries. Outer palace buildings that visitors can view include **Borombhiman Hall**, a French-inspired structure that served as a residence for Rama VI (King Vajiravudh; r 1910–25). The building to the west is **Amarindra Hall** (open from Monday to Friday), originally a hall of justice and more recently used for coronation ceremonies; it's the only palace building that tourists are generally allowed to enter. The largest of the palace buildings is the **Chakri Mahaprasat**, the Grand Palace Hall. Last is the Ratanakosin-style **Dusit Hall**, which initially served as a venue for royal audiences and later as a royal funerary hall.

Guides can be hired at the ticket kiosk; ignore offers from anyone outside. An audio guide can be rented for 200B for two hours.

Admission for the complex includes entrance to **Dusit Palace Park** (p66), which includes Vimanmaek Teak Mansion and Abhisek Dusit Throne Hall.

★Wat Pho — BUDDHIST TEMPLE

(วัดโพธิ์/วัดพระเชตุพน, Wat Phra Chetuphon; Map p60; Th Sanam Chai; admission 100B; ⌚8.30am-6.30pm; Tien Pier) You'll find (slightly) fewer tourists here than at Wat Phra Kaew, but Wat Pho is our fave among Bangkok's biggest sights. In fact, the compound incorporates a host of superlatives: the city's largest reclining Buddha, the largest collection of Buddha images in Thailand and the country's earliest centre for public education.

Almost too big for its shelter is Wat Pho's highlight, the impressive **Reclining Buddha**.

Wat Phra Kaew & Grand Palace

EXPLORE BANGKOK'S PREMIER MONUMENTS TO RELIGION AND REGENCY

The first area tourists enter is the Buddhist temple compound generally referred to as Wat Phra Kaew. A covered walkway surrounds the area, the inner walls of which are decorated with the **murals of the *Ramakian*** 1 and 2. Originally painted during the reign of Rama I (r 1782–1809), the murals, which depict the Hindu epic the *Ramayana*, span 178 panels that describe the struggles of Rama to rescue his kidnapped wife, Sita.

After taking in the story, pass through one of the gateways guarded by ***yaksha*** 3 to the inner compound. The most important structure here is the ***bòht*, or ordination hall** 4, which houses the **Emerald Buddha** 5.

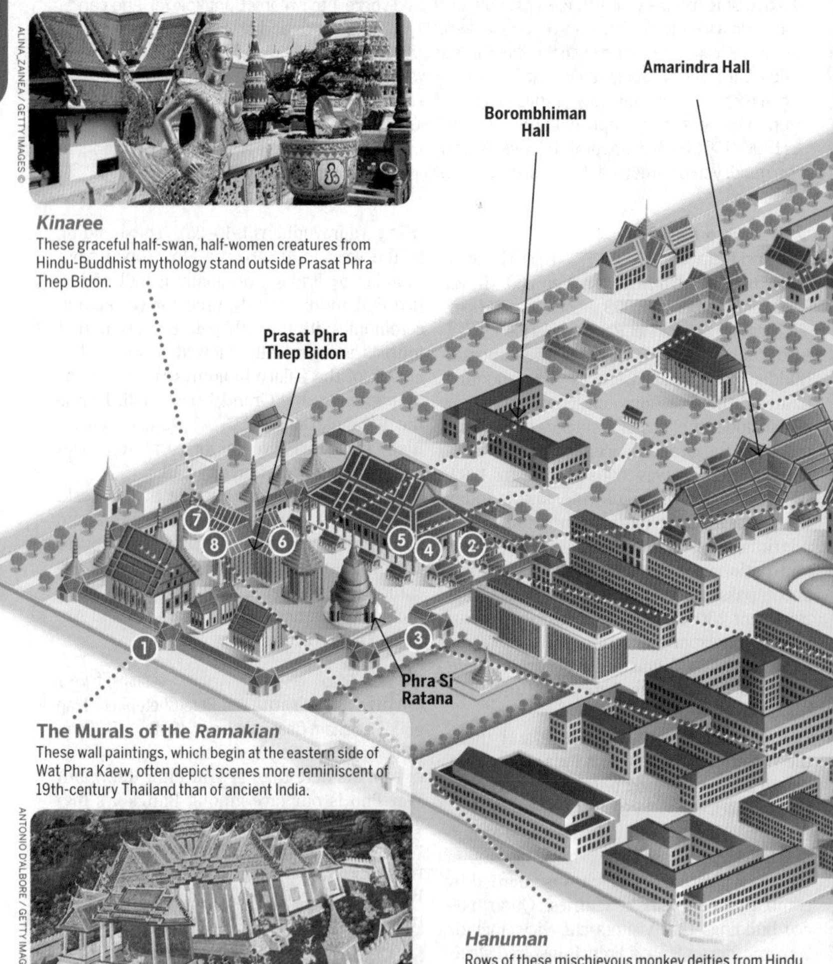

Kinaree
These graceful half-swan, half-women creatures from Hindu-Buddhist mythology stand outside Prasat Phra Thep Bidon.

The Murals of the *Ramakian*
These wall paintings, which begin at the eastern side of Wat Phra Kaew, often depict scenes more reminiscent of 19th-century Thailand than of ancient India.

Hanuman
Rows of these mischievous monkey deities from Hindu mythology appear to support the lower levels of two small *chedi* near Prasat Phra Thep Bidon.

Head east to the so-called Upper Terrace, an elevated area home to the **spires of the three primary *chedi*** 6. The middle structure, Phra Mondop, is used to house Buddhist manuscripts. This area is also home to several of Wat Phra Kaew's noteworthy mythical beings, including beckoning ***kinaree*** 7 and several grimacing **Hanuman** 8.

Proceed through the western gate to the compound known as the Grand Palace. Few of the buildings here are open to the public. The most noteworthy structure is **Chakri Mahaprasat** 9. Built in 1882, the exterior of the hall is a unique blend of Western and traditional Thai architecture.

The Three Spires
The elaborate seven-tiered roof of Phra Mondop, the Khmer-style peak of Prasat Phra Thep Bidon, and the gilded Phra Si Ratana *chedi* are the tallest structures in the compound.

THANT ZAW WAI / GETTY IMAGES ©

Emerald Buddha
Despite the name, this diminutive statue (it's only 66cm tall) is actually carved from nephrite, a type of jade.

ALEXEY STIOP / GETTY IMAGES ©

The Death of Thotsakan
The panels progress clockwise, culminating at the western edge of the compound with the death of Thotsakan, Sita's kidnapper, and his elaborate funeral procession.

Chakri Mahaprasat
This structure is sometimes referred to as *fa·ràng sài chá·dah* (Westerner in a Thai crown) because each wing is topped by a *mon·dòp*: a spire representing a Thai adaptation of a Hindu shrine.

DESIGN PICS / GETTY IMAGES ©

9

Dusit Hall

***Bòht* (Ordination Hall)**
This structure is an early example of the Ratanakosin school of architecture, which combines traditional stylistic holdovers from Ayuthaya along with more modern touches from China and the West.

Yaksha
Each entrance to the Wat Phra Kaew compound is watched over by a pair of vigilant and enormous *yaksha*, ogres or giants from Hindu mythology.

ZZVET / GETTY IMAGES ©

Ko Ratanakosin, Banglamphu & Thonburi

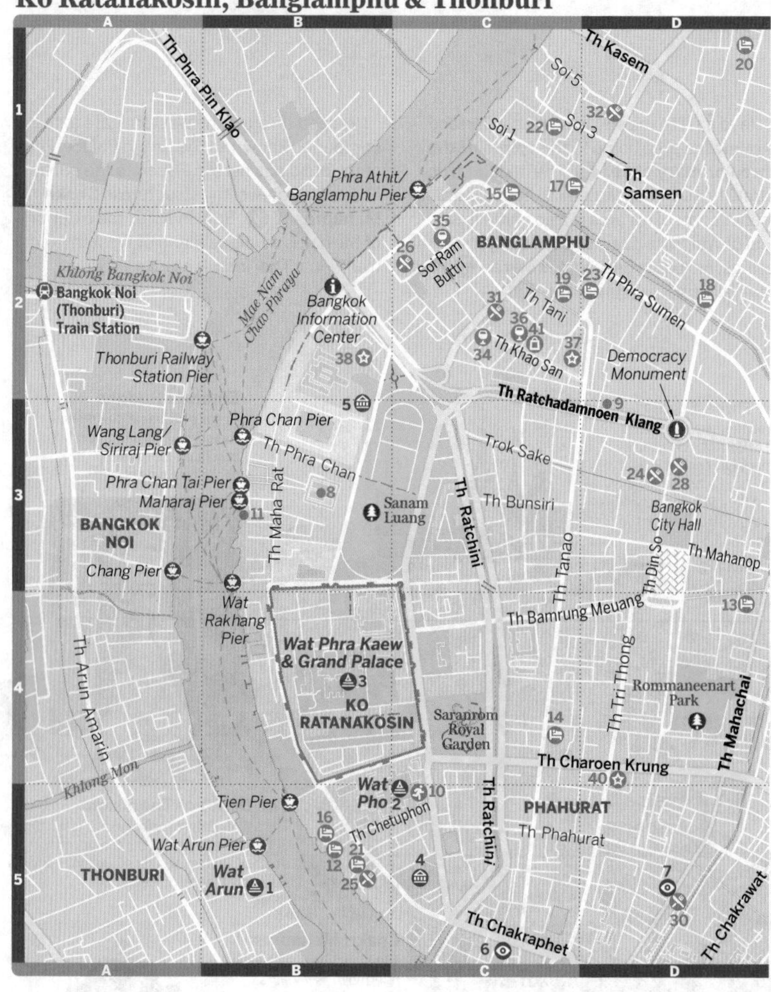

The rambling grounds of Wat Pho cover 8 hectares, with the major tourist sites occupying the northern side of Th Chetuphon and the monastic facilities found on the southern side. The temple compound is also the national headquarters for the teaching and preservation of traditional Thai medicine, including Thai massage, a mandate legislated by Rama III when the tradition was in danger of extinction. The famous massage school has two **massage pavilions** (Map p60; Wat Pho, Th Sanam Chai; Thai massage per hr 420B; ⏲9am-6pm; ⛴Tien Pier) located within the temple area and additional rooms within the **training facility** (Map p60; ☎02 622 3551; www.watpomassage.com; 392/32-33 Soi Phen Phat; lessons from 2500B, Thai massage per hour 420B; ⏲lessons 9am-4pm, massage 9am-6pm; ⛴Tien Pier) outside the temple.

★Wat Arun — BUDDHIST TEMPLE

(วัดอรุณฯ; Map p60; www.watarun.net; off Th Arun Amarin; admission 50B; ⏲8am-6pm; ⛴cross-river ferry from Tien Pier) After the fall of Ayuthaya, King Taksin ceremoniously clinched control here on the site of a local shrine and established a royal palace and a temple to house the Emerald Buddha. The temple was re-

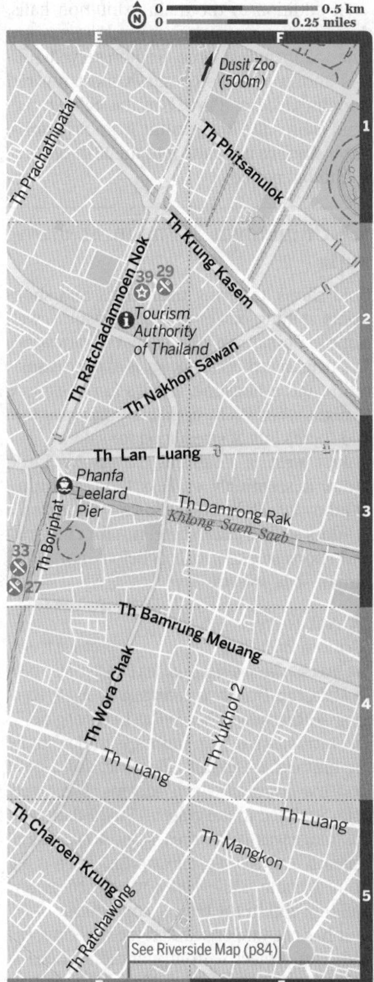

named after the Indian god of dawn (Aruna) and in honour of the literal and symbolic founding of a new Ayuthaya.

At the time of research, the spire of Wat Arun was closed until 2016 due to renovation. Visitors can enter the compound, but cannot climb the tower.

It wasn't until the capital and the Emerald Buddha were moved to Bangkok that Wat Arun received its most prominent characteristic: the 82m-high *brahng* (Khmer-style tower). The tower's construction was started during the first half of the 19th century by Rama II and later completed by Rama III. Not

Ko Ratanakosin, Banglamphu & Thonburi

Top Sights
1 Wat Arun B5
2 Wat Pho C5
3 Wat Phra Kaew & Grand Palace B4

Sights
4 Museum of Siam C5
5 National Museum B3
6 Pak Khlong Talat C5
7 Phahurat D5

Activities, Courses & Tours
8 Center Meditation Wat Mahadhatu B3
Chetawan Traditional Massage School .... (see 21)
9 Grasshopper Adventures D3
10 Massage Pavilions C5
11 Muay Thai Lab B3
National Museum Tours .... (see 5)

Sleeping
12 Arun Residence B5
13 Chern D4
14 Feung Nakorn Balcony C4
15 Fortville Guesthouse C1
16 Inn A Day B5
17 Khaosan Immjai C1
18 Lamphu Treehouse D2
19 NapPark Hostel C2
20 Phra-Nakorn Norn-Len D1
21 Royal Tha Tien Village B5
22 Sam Sen Sam Place C1
23 Suneta Hostel Khaosan D2

Eating
24 Arawy Vegetarian Food D3
25 Err B5
26 Hemlock C2
27 Jay Fai E3
28 Krua Apsorn D3
29 Likhit Kai Yang E2
May Kaidee's .... (see 17)
30 Royal India D5
31 Shoshana C2
32 Thamna D1
33 Thip Samai E3

Drinking & Nightlife
34 Hippie de Bar C2
35 Madame Musur C2
Roof .... (see 16)
36 The Club C2

Entertainment
37 Brick Bar C2
38 National Theatre B2
39 Ratchadamnoen Stadium E2
40 Sala Chalermkrung D4

Shopping
41 Thanon Khao San Market C2

apparent from a distance are the ornate floral **mosaics** made from broken, multihued Chinese porcelain, a common temple ornamentation in the early Ratanakosin period, when Chinese ships calling at the port of Bangkok discarded tonnes of old porcelain as ballast.

Also worth an inspection is the interior of the *bòht*. The main Buddha image is said to have been designed by Rama II (King Phraphutthaloetla Naphalai; r 1809–24) himself. The **murals** date from the reign of Rama V (King Chulalongkorn; r 1868–1910); particularly impressive is one that depicts Prince Siddhartha encountering examples of birth, old age, sickness and death outside his palace walls, an experience that led him to abandon the worldly life. The ashes of Rama II are interred in the base of the Buddha image.

Frequent cross-river ferries run over to Wat Arun from Tien Pier (3B).

National Museum MUSEUM

(พิพิธภัณฑสถานแห่งชาติ; Map p60; 4 Th Na Phra That; admission 200B; 9am-4pm Wed-Sun; Chang Pier, Maharaj Pier, Phra Chan Tai Pier) Often touted as Southeast Asia's biggest museum, Thailand's National Museum is home to an impressive, albeit occasionally dusty, collection of items, best appreciated on one of the museum's twice-weekly guided **tours** (Map p60; National Museum, 4 Th Na Phra That; free with museum admission; 9.30am Wed & Thu; Chang Pier, Maharaj Pier).

Most of the museum's structures were built in 1782 as the palace of Rama I's viceroy, Prince Wang Na. Rama V turned it into a museum in 1874, and today there are three permanent exhibitions spread out over several buildings. At the time of research some of the exhibition halls were being renovated.

The **history wing** has made impressive bounds towards contemporary curatorial aesthetics with a succinct chronology of prehistoric, Sukhothai-, Ayuthaya- and Bangkok-era events and figures. Gems include King Ramkamhaeng's inscribed stone pillar, said to be the oldest record of Thai writing (although this has been contested); King Taksin's throne; the Rama V section; and the screening of a movie about Rama VII, *The Magic Ring*.

The **decorative arts and ethnology exhibit** seems to cover every possible handicraft: traditional musical instruments, ceramics, clothing and textiles, woodcarving, regalia and weaponry. The **archaeology and art history wing** has exhibits ranging from prehistoric to the Bangkok period.

In addition to the main exhibition halls, the **Bhuddhaisawan (Phutthaisawan) Chapel** includes some well-preserved murals and one of the country's most revered Buddha images, Phra Phuttha Sihing. Legend claims the image came from Sri Lanka, but historians attribute it to the 13th-century Sukhothai period.

Chinatown & Phahurat เยาวราช/พาหุรัด

Gold shops, towering neon signs and shopfronts spilling out onto the sidewalk – welcome to Chinatown (also known as Yaowarat). The neighbourhood's energy is at once exhilarating and exhausting, and it's fun to explore at night when it's lit up like a Christmas tree and there's lots of street food for sale.

Just west is Phahurat, Bangkok's Little India: a seemingly endless bazaar uniting flamboyant Bollywood fabric, photogenic vendors selling *paan* (betel nut for chewing) and shops stocked with delicious northern-Indian-style sweets.

★ **Wat Traimit (Golden Buddha)** BUDDHIST TEMPLE

(วัดไตรมิตร, Temple of the Golden Buddha; Map p84; Th Mittaphap Thai-China; admission 40B; 8am-5pm; Ratchawong Pier, M Hua Lamphong exit 1) The attraction at Wat Traimit is undoubtedly the impressive 3m-tall, 5.5-tonne, **solid-gold Buddha image**, which gleams like, well, gold. Sculpted in the graceful Sukhothai style, the image was 'discovered' some 40 years ago beneath a stucco/plaster exterior, when it fell from a crane while being moved to a new building within the temple compound.

It has been theorised that the covering was added to protect it from marauding hordes, either during the late Sukhothai period or later in the Ayuthaya period when the city was under siege by the Burmese. The temple itself is said to date from the early 13th century.

Donations and a constant flow of tourists have proven profitable, and the statue is now housed in a new four-storey marble structure. The 2nd floor of the building is home to the **Phra Buddha Maha Suwanna Patimakorn Exhibition** (Map p84; Th Mittaphap Thai-China; admission 100B; 8am-4pm Tue-Sun; Ratchawong Pier, M Hua Lamphong exit 1), which has exhibits on how the statue was made, discovered and came to arrive at its current home, while the 3rd floor is home to the **Yaowarat Chinatown Heritage Center** (Map p84; Th Mittaphap Thai-China; admission 100B;

OFF THE BEATEN TRACK

MARKETS AS SIGHTS

Even if you don't have a shopping list, several of Bangkok's produce and wholesale markets are well worth a visit. Here are some of our favourites:

➜ **Pak Khlong Talat** (ปากคลองตลาด, Flower Market; Map p60; Th Chakkaraphet; ⏲24hr; ⛴Pak Klong Taladd Pier, Saphan Phut/Memorial Bridge Pier) This sprawling wholesale flower market has become a tourist attraction in its own right. The endless piles of delicate orchids, rows of roses and stacks of button carnations are a sight to see, and the shirtless porters wheeling blazing piles of colour set the place in motion. The best time to come is late at night, when the goods arrive from upcountry.

➜ **Or Tor Kor Market** (องค์กรตลาดเพื่อเกษตรกร; Map p78; Th Kamphaengphet 1; ⏲8am-6pm; Ⓜ Kamphaeng Phet exit 3) Or Tor Kor is Bangkok's highest-quality fruit and agricultural market, and taking in the toddler-sized mangoes and dozens of pots full of curries amounts to culinary trainspotting. To get here, take the MRT to Kamphaeng Phet station and exit on the side opposite Chatuchak (the exit says 'Marketing Organization for Farmers').

➜ **Nonthaburi Market** (ตลาดนนทบุรี; Map p78; Tha Nam Nonthaburi, Nonthaburi; ⏲5-9am; ⛴Nonthaburi Pier) Exotic fruits, towers of dried chillies, smoky grills and the city's few remaining rickshaws form a very un-Bangkok backdrop at this expansive and atmospheric produce market. Come early, though, as most vendors are gone by 9am. To get to the market, take the Chao Phraya Express boat to Nonthaburi Pier, the northernmost stop for most lines. The market is a two-minute walk east along the main road from the pier.

➜ **Khlong Toey Market** (ตลาดคลองเตย; Map p70; cnr Th Ratchadaphisek & Th Phra Ram IV; ⏲5-10am; Ⓜ Khlong Toei exit 1) This wholesale market, one of the city's largest, is inevitably the origin of many of the meals you'll eat during your stay in Bangkok. Get there early and bring a camera – although some corners of the market can't exactly be described as photogenic, the stacks of durians and cheery fishmongers make great happy snaps.

⏲8am-4pm Tue-Sun; ⛴Ratchawong Pier, Ⓜ Hua Lamphong exit 1), a small but engaging museum with multimedia exhibits on the history of Bangkok's Chinatown and its residents.

Talat Mai MARKET
(ตลาดใหม่; Map p84; Soi Yaowarat 6/Charoen Krung 16; ⏲6am-6pm; ⛴Ratchawong Pier, Ⓜ Hua Lamphong exit 1 & taxi) With nearly two centuries of commerce under its belt, New Market is no longer an entirely accurate name for this strip of commerce. Regardless, this is Bangkok's, if not Thailand's, most Chinese market, and the dried goods, seasonings, spices and sauces will be familiar to anyone who's ever spent time in China. Even if you're not interested in food, the hectic atmosphere (be on guard for motorcycles squeezing between shoppers) and exotic sights and smells culminate in something of a surreal sensory experience.

Phahurat NEIGHBOURHOOD
(พาหุรัด; Map p60; Th Chakkaraphet; ⏲9am-5pm; ⛴Saphan Phut/Memorial Bridge Pier, Pak Klong Taladd Pier) Heaps of South Asian traders set up shop in Bangkok's small but bustling Little India, where everything from Bollywood movies to bindis is sold by enthusiastic, small-time traders. It's a great area to just wander through, stopping for masala chai and a Punjabi sweet as you go.

The bulk of the action unfolds along unmarked Soi ATM, which runs alongside the large India Emporium shopping centre.

The emphasis is on cloth, and Phahurat proffers boisterously coloured textiles, traditional Thai dance costumes, tiaras, sequins, wigs and other accessories to make you look like a cross-dresser, a *mŏr lam* (Thai country music) performer, or both. Amid the spectacle of colour there are also good deals on machine-made textiles and children's clothes.

⊙ Siam Square สยามสแควร์

Commerce, mainly in the form of multistorey mega-malls, forms the main attraction in this part of town, but there are a couple of sights that don't involve credit cards.

Wat Pho

A WALK THROUGH THE BIG BUDDHAS OF WAT PHO

The logical starting place is the main *wi·hăhn* (sanctuary), home to Wat Pho's centrepiece, the immense **Reclining Buddha** ❶. Apart from its huge size, note the **mother-of-pearl inlays** ❷ on the soles of the statue's feet. The interior walls of the *wí·hăhn* are covered with murals depicting previous lives of the Buddha, and along the south side of the structure are 108 bronze monk bowls; for 20B you can buy 108 coins, each of which is dropped in a bowl for good luck.

Exit the *wí·hăhn* and head east via the two **stone giants** ❸ who guard the gateway to the rest of the compound. Directly south of these are the four towering **royal *chedi*** ❹.

Continue east, passing through two consecutive **galleries of Buddha**

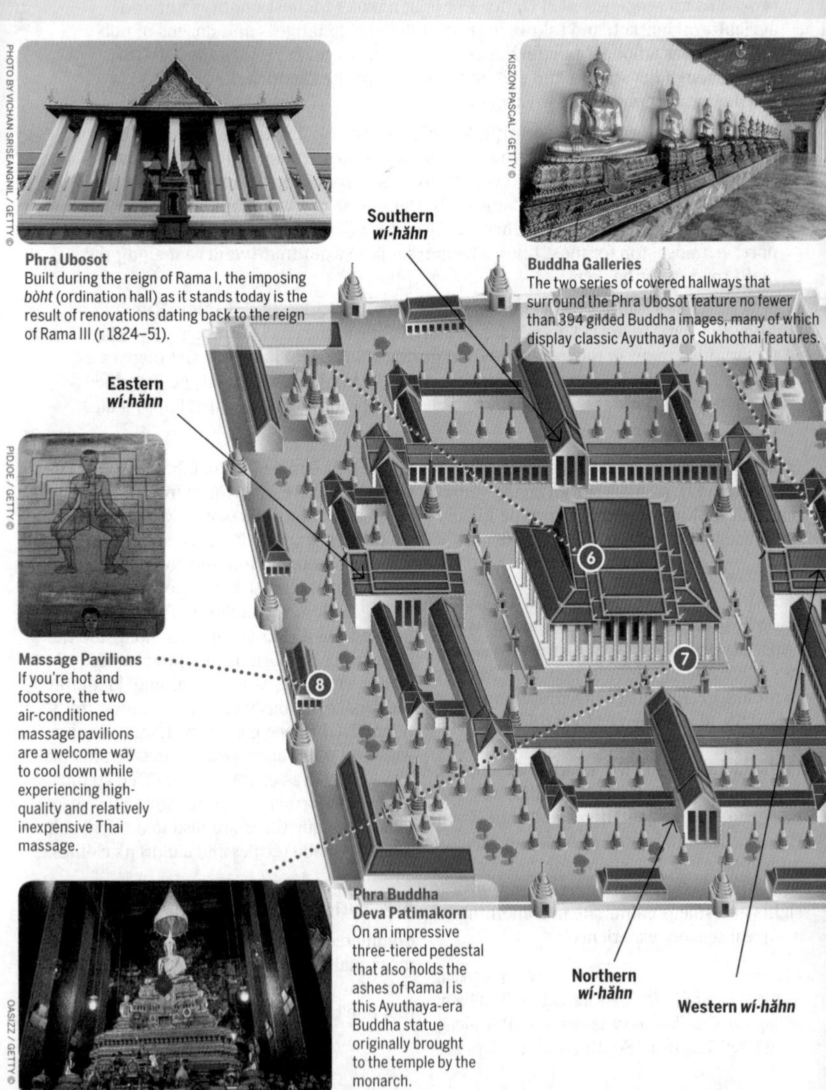

Phra Ubosot
Built during the reign of Rama I, the imposing *bòht* (ordination hall) as it stands today is the result of renovations dating back to the reign of Rama III (r 1824–51).

Buddha Galleries
The two series of covered hallways that surround the Phra Ubosot feature no fewer than 394 gilded Buddha images, many of which display classic Ayuthaya or Sukhothai features.

Massage Pavilions
If you're hot and footsore, the two air-conditioned massage pavilions are a welcome way to cool down while experiencing high-quality and relatively inexpensive Thai massage.

Phra Buddha Deva Patimakorn
On an impressive three-tiered pedestal that also holds the ashes of Rama I is this Ayuthaya-era Buddha statue originally brought to the temple by the monarch.

statues ❺ linking four *wí·hăhn*, two of which contain notable Sukhothai-era Buddha statues; these comprise the exterior of **Phra Ubosot** ❻, the immense ordination hall that is Wat Pho's second-most noteworthy structure. The base of the building is surrounded by bas-relief inscriptions, and inside is the notable Buddha statue, **Phra Buddha Deva Patimakorn** ❼.

Wat Pho is often referred to as Thailand's first university, a tradition that continues today in an associated traditional Thai medicine school and, at the compound's eastern extent, two **massage pavilions** ❽.

Interspersed throughout the eastern half of the compound are several additional minor *chedi* and rock gardens.

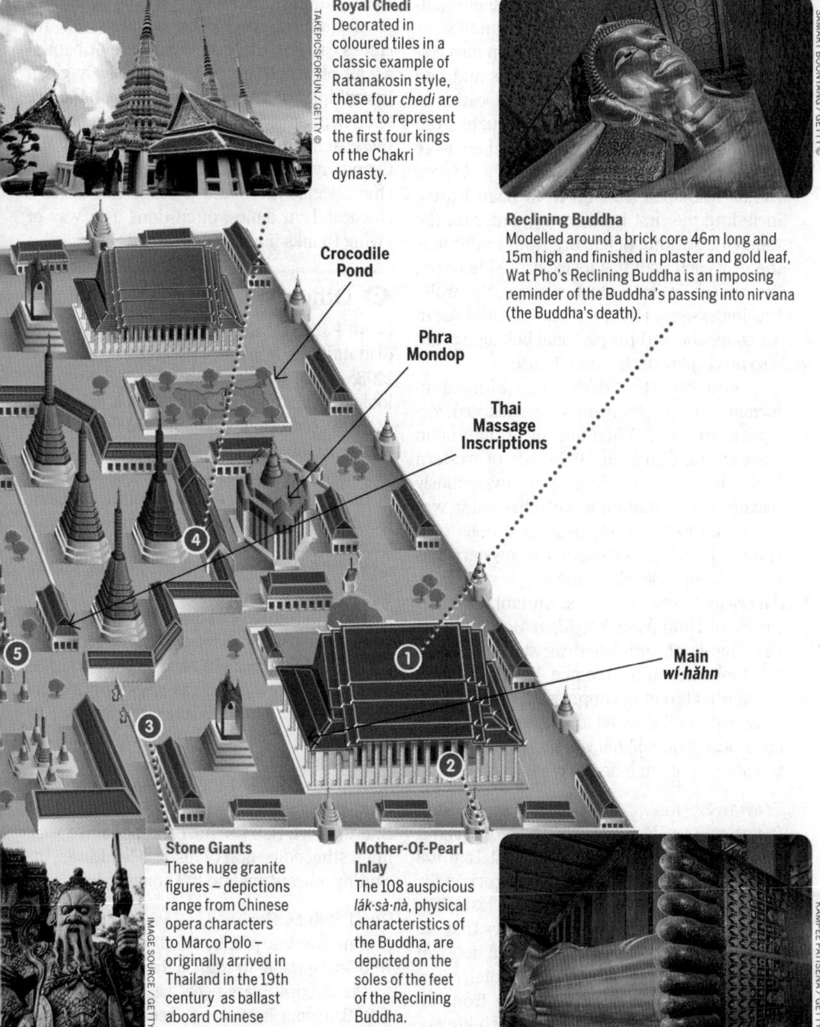

Royal Chedi
Decorated in coloured tiles in a classic example of Ratanakosin style, these four *chedi* are meant to represent the first four kings of the Chakri dynasty.

Reclining Buddha
Modelled around a brick core 46m long and 15m high and finished in plaster and gold leaf, Wat Pho's Reclining Buddha is an imposing reminder of the Buddha's passing into nirvana (the Buddha's death).

Stone Giants
These huge granite figures – depictions range from Chinese opera characters to Marco Polo – originally arrived in Thailand in the 19th century as ballast aboard Chinese junks.

Mother-Of-Pearl Inlay
The 108 auspicious *lák·sà·nà*, physical characteristics of the Buddha, are depicted on the soles of the feet of the Reclining Buddha.

★ **Jim Thompson House** HISTORIC BUILDING
(Map p74; www.jimthompsonhouse.com; 6 Soi Kasem San 2; adult/student 150/100B; 9am-6pm, compulsory tours every 20 min; klorng boat to Sapan Hua Chang Pier, National Stadium exit 1) This jungly compound is the former home of the eponymous American silk entrepreneur and art collector. Born in Delaware in 1906, Thompson briefly served in the Office of Strategic Services (the forerunner of the CIA) in Thailand during WWII. He settled in Bangkok after the war, when his neighbours' handmade silk caught his eye and piqued his business sense; he sent samples to fashion houses in Milan, London and Paris, gradually building a steady worldwide clientele.

In addition to textiles, Thompson also collected parts of derelict Thai homes and had them reassembled in their current location in 1959. Some of the homes were brought from the old royal capital of Ayuthaya; others were pulled down and floated across the *klorng* (canal; also spelt *khlong*) from Baan Khrua, including the first building you enter on the tour. One striking departure from tradition is the way each wall has its exterior side facing the house's interior, thus exposing the wall's bracing system. His small but splendid Asian art collection and his personal belongings are also on display in the main house.

Thompson's story doesn't end with his informal reign as Bangkok's best-adapted foreigner, however. While out for an afternoon walk in the Cameron Highlands of western Malaysia in 1967, Thompson mysteriously disappeared. That same year his sister was murdered in the USA, fuelling various conspiracy theories. Although the mystery has never been solved, evidence revealed by American journalist Joshua Kurlantzick in his profile of Thompson, *The Ideal Man,* suggests that the vocal anti-American stance Thompson took later in his life may have made him a potential target of suppression by the CIA.

Beware well-dressed touts near the Thompson house who will tell you it is closed and try to haul you off on a dodgy buying spree.

Erawan Shrine MONUMENT
(ศาลพระพรหม; Map p74; cnr Th Ratchadamri & Th Phloen Chit; 6am-11pm; Chit Lom exit 8) FREE The Erawan Shrine was originally built in 1956 as something of a last-ditch effort to end a string of misfortunes that occurred during the construction of a hotel, at that time known as the Erawan Hotel.

After several incidents ranging from injured construction workers to the sinking of a ship carrying marble for the hotel, a Brahmin priest was consulted. Since the hotel was to be named after the elephant escort of Indra in Hindu mythology, the priest determined that Erawan required a passenger, and suggested it be that of Lord Brahma. A statue was built and, lo and behold, the misfortunes miraculously ended.

Although the original Erawan Hotel was demolished in 1987, the shrine still exists, and today remains an important place of pilgrimage for Thais, particularly those in need of some material assistance. Those making a wish from the statue should ideally come between 7am and 8am, or 7pm and 8pm, and should offer a specific list of items that includes candles, incense, sugar cane or bananas, all of which are almost exclusively given in multiples of seven. Particularly popular are teak elephants, with money from the sale of these items donated to a charity run by the Grand Hyatt Erawan. And as the tourist brochures depict, it is also possible to charter a classical Thai dance, often done as a way of giving thanks if a wish is granted.

Other Areas

Suan Pakkad Palace Museum MUSEUM
(วังสวนผักกาด; Map p78; Th Si Ayuthaya; admission 100B; 9am-4pm; Phaya Thai exit 4) An overlooked treasure, Suan Pakkad is a collection of eight traditional wooden Thai houses that was once the residence of Princess Chumbon of Nakhon Sawan and before that a lettuce farm – hence the name. Within the stilt buildings are displays of art, antiques and furnishings, and the landscaped grounds are a peaceful oasis complete with ducks, swans and a semi-enclosed garden.

The diminutive **Lacquer Pavilion**, at the back of the complex, dates from the Ayuthaya period and features gold-leaf *Jataka* and *Ramayana* murals, as well as scenes from daily Ayuthaya life. The building originally sat in a monastery compound on Mae Nam Chao Phraya, just south of Ayuthaya. Larger residential structures at the front of the complex contain displays of Khmer-style Hindu and Buddhist art, Ban Chiang ceramics and a very interesting collection of historic **Buddhas**, including a beautiful late U Thong–style image.

Dusit Palace Park MUSEUM, HISTORIC SITE
(วังสวนดุสิต; Map p78; bounded by Th Ratchawithi, Th U Thong Nai & Th Nakhon Ratchasima; admission for all Dusit Palace sights adult/child 100/20B; 9.30am-4pm Tue-Sun; Thewet Pier, Phaya

TOUGH TIMES AT THE ERAWAN SHRINE

One of the more cliched tourist images of Bangkok is that of elaborately dressed classical Thai dancers performing at the Hindu shrine in front of the Grand Hyatt Erawan Hotel. Although not a fabrication, as with many things in Thailand, there is great deal hidden behind the serene facade.

After 50 years of largely benign existence, the Erawan Shrine became a point of focus when, just after midnight on 21 March 2006, 27-year-old Thanakorn Pakdeepol, a man with a history of mental illness and depression, destroyed the highly revered, gilded plaster image of Brahma with a hammer. Thanakorn was almost immediately attacked and beaten to death by two Thai rubbish collectors in the vicinity. Although the government ordered a swift restoration of the statue, the incident became a galvanising omen for the protest movement opposing then Prime Minister Thaksin Shinawatra, which was in full swing at the time. At a rally the following day, protest leader Sondhi Limthongkul suggested that the prime minister had masterminded the image's destruction in order to replace the deity with a 'dark force'. Rumours spreading through the capital claimed that Thaksin had hired Cambodian shamans to put spells on Thanakorn so that he would perform the unspeakable deed. In response, Thanakorn's father was quoted as saying that Sondhi was 'the biggest liar I have ever seen'. Thaksin, when asked to comment on Sondhi's accusations, simply replied, 'That's insane.' A new statue, which incorporated pieces of the previous one, was installed a month later, and Thaksin has remained in exile since 2008.

In 2010, the Ratchaprasong Intersection, where the shrine is located, became the main gathering point for anti-government Red Shirt protesters, who occupied the area for several months. Images of the predominately lower class, rural protesters camped out in front of the Ratchaprasong's luxury storefronts became a media staple. When the Red Shirts were forcibly cleared out by the military on 19 May, five people were killed and fleeing protesters set fire to the nearby CentralWorld mall.

CentralWorld was renovated in 2012, but a year later Ratchaprasong Intersection again became a major protest site, this time occupied by opponents of Thaksin's sister, then Prime Minister Yingluck Shinawatra. The protests were known colloquially as Shutdown Bangkok (complete with protest merchandise featuring the computer-shutdown icon), and this time images of the largely middle- and upper-class urban protesters in front of malls drew comparisons rather than contrasts. On 20 May 2014, the Thai Army declared martial law and took over the government in a coup d'état, leading the protesters to disperse.

Yet undoubtedly the most significant event in the shrine's history came on the evening of 17 August 2015, when a bomb planted in the Erawan Shrine compound exploded, killing 20 and injuring more than 100 people. Prime Minister Prayut Chan-o-cha described the apparent act of terrorism as the 'worst incident that has ever happened' in Thailand. At press time, two suspects had been arrested, although their nationalities and motives remain unknown.

Why so much turmoil associated with a shrine that most believe to have positive powers? Some feel that the Erawan Shrine sits on land that carries long-standing, and potentially conflicting supernatural powers. Others feel that the area is currently spiritually overcrowded, as other nearby structures also have their own, potentially competing, Hindu shrines. What's certain is that in Thailand politics, faith, fortune and tragedy are often linked.

Thai exit 2 & taxi) Following his first European tour in 1897, Rama V (King Chulalongkorn; r 1868–1910) returned with visions of European castles and set about transforming these styles into a uniquely Thai expression, today's Dusit Palace Park. These days, the current king has yet another home (in Hua Hin) and this complex now holds a house museum and other cultural collections.

Because this is royal property, visitors should wear shirts with sleeves and long pants (no capri pants) or long skirts.

Originally constructed on Ko Si Chang in 1868 and moved to the present site in 1910, **Vimanmek Teak Mansion** (Map p78; Dusit Palace Park, Th Ratchawithi; adult/child 100/20B, or free with Grand Palace ticket; 9.30am-4pm Tue-Sun; Thewet Pier, Phaya Thai exit 2 & taxi) contains 81 rooms, halls and anterooms, and

Silom & Sathon

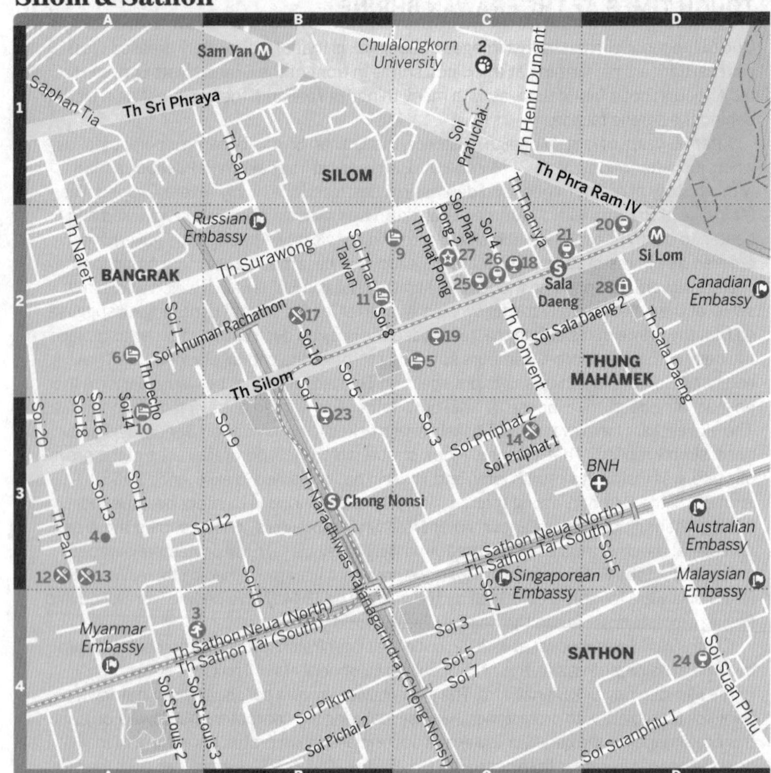

is said to be the world's largest golden-teak building, allegedly built without the use of a single nail. The mansion was the first permanent building on the Dusit Palace grounds, and served as Rama V's residence in the early 1900s. The interior of the mansion contains various personal effects of the king and a treasure trove of early Ratanakosin-era art objects and antiques. Compulsory tours (in English) leave every 30 minutes between 9.45am and 3.15pm, and last about an hour.

The nearby **Ancient Cloth Museum** (Map p78; Dusit Palace Park, Th Ratchawithi; adult/child 100/20B, or free with Grand Palace ticket; 9.30am-4pm Tue-Sun; Thewet Pier, S Phaya Thai exit 2 & taxi) presents a beautiful collection of traditional silks and cottons that make up the royal cloth collection, although at the time of research it was closed for renovations.

Originally built as a throne hall for Rama V in 1904, the smaller **Abhisek Dusit Throne Hall** (Map p78; Dusit Palace Park, Th Ratchawithi; adult/child 100/20B, or free with Grand Palace ticket; 9.30am-4pm Tue-Sun; Thewet Pier, S Phaya Thai exit 2 & taxi) is typical of the finer architecture of the era. Victorian-influenced gingerbread architecture and Moorish porticoes blend to create a striking and distinctly Thai exterior. The hall houses an excellent display of regional handiwork crafted by members of the Promotion of Supplementary Occupations & Related Techniques (Support) foundation, a charity organisation sponsored by Queen Sirikit.

Near the Th U Thong Nai entrance, two large stables that once housed three white elephants – animals whose auspicious albinism automatically make them crown property – now form the **Royal Thai Elephant Museum** (Map p78; Dusit Palace Park, Th Ratchawithi; adult/child 100/20B, or free with Grand Palace ticket; 9.30am-4pm; Thewet Pier, S Phaya Thai exit 2 & taxi). One of the structures contains artefacts

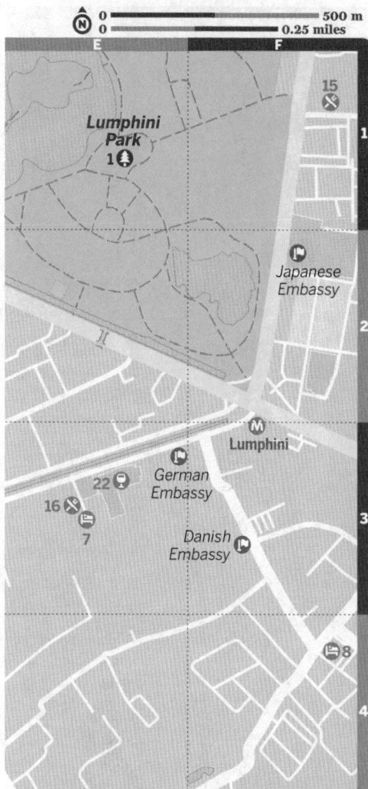

Silom & Sathon

and photos outlining the importance of elephants in Thai history and explaining their various rankings according to physical characteristics. The second stable holds a life-sized model of the king's first royal white elephant. Draped in royal vestments, the statue is more or less treated as a shrine by the visiting Thai public.

Activities

Health Land MASSAGE
(Map p68; ☎02 637 8883; www.healthlandspa.com; 120 Th Sathon Neua/North; 2hr massage 500B; ⏲9am-11pm; S Surasak exit 3) This, the main branch of a long-standing Thai massage mini-empire, offers good-value, no-nonsense massage and spa treatments in a tidy environment.

Asia Herb Association SPA
(Map p70; ☎02 261 7401; www.asiaherbassociation.com; 33/1 Soi 24, Th Sukhumvit; Thai massage per hr 500B, Thai massage with herbal compress 1½hr 1100B; ⏲9am-2am; S Phrom Phong exit 4) With multiple branches along Th Sukhumvit, this Japanese-owned chain specialises in massage using *Ъrà·kóp* (traditional Thai herbal compresses) filled with 18 different herbs.

Courses

★ **Amita Thai Cooking Class** COOKING COURSE
(Map p78; ☎02 466 8966; www.amitathaicooking.com; 162/17 Soi 14, Th Wutthakat, Thonburi; 3000B; ⏲lessons 9.30am-1pm Thu-Tue; klorng boat from Maharaj Pier) One of Bangkok's most charming cooking schools is held in this canalside

Sukhumvit

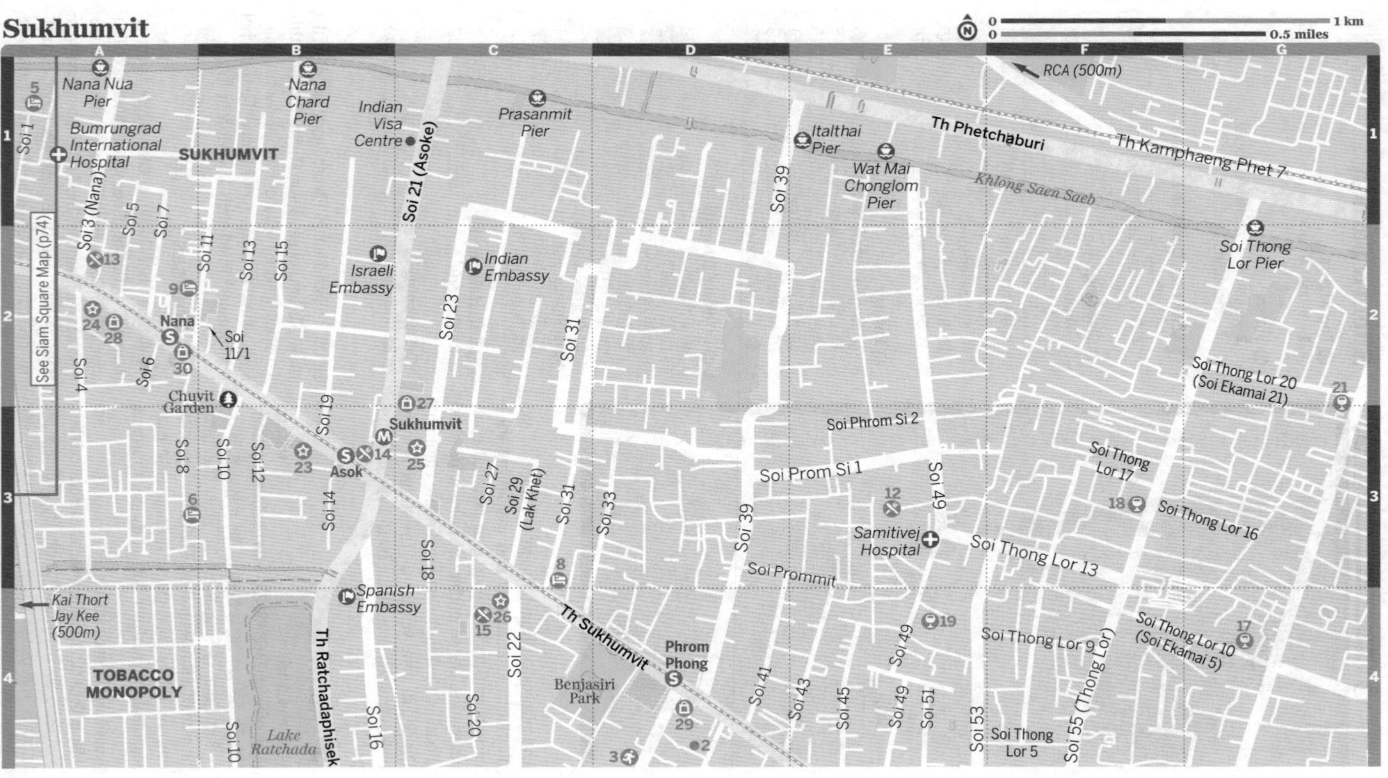
0.5 miles
1 km
Nana Nua Pier
Nana Chard Pier
Indian Visa Centre
Prasanmit Pier
RCA (500m)
Th Phetchaburi
Th Kamphaeng Phet 7
Khlong Saen Saeb
Italthai Pier
Wat Mai Chonglom Pier
Soi Thong Lor Pier
Soi 1
Bumrungrad International Hospital
SUKHUMVIT
Soi 21 (Asoke)
Soi 39
Soi 3 (Nana)
Soi 5
Soi 7
Soi 11
Soi 13
Soi 15
Israeli Embassy
Indian Embassy
See Siam Square Map (p74)
Nana
Soi 11/1
Soi 23
Soi 31
Soi 4
Soi 6
Chuvit Garden
Soi 19
Sukhumvit
Soi Thong Lor 20 (Soi Ekamai 21)
Soi Phrom Si 2
Soi 8
Soi 10
Soi 12
Asok
Soi Prom Si 1
Soi 49
Soi Thong Lor 17
Soi 14
Soi 27
Soi 29 (Lak Khet)
Soi 33
Soi 39
Samitivej Hospital
Soi Thong Lor 16
Soi Thong Lor 13
Soi 18
Soi Prommit
Kai Thort Jay Kee (500m)
Spanish Embassy
Th Sukhumvit
Soi Thong Lor 9
Soi Thong Lor 10 (Soi Ekamai 5)
TOBACCO MONOPOLY
Th Ratchadaphisek
Soi 22
Phrom Phong
Soi 55 (Thong Lor)
Benjasiri Park
Soi 41
Soi 43
Soi 45
Soi 51
Soi 53
Soi 10
Lake Ratchada
Soi 16
Soi 20
Soi Thong Lor 5

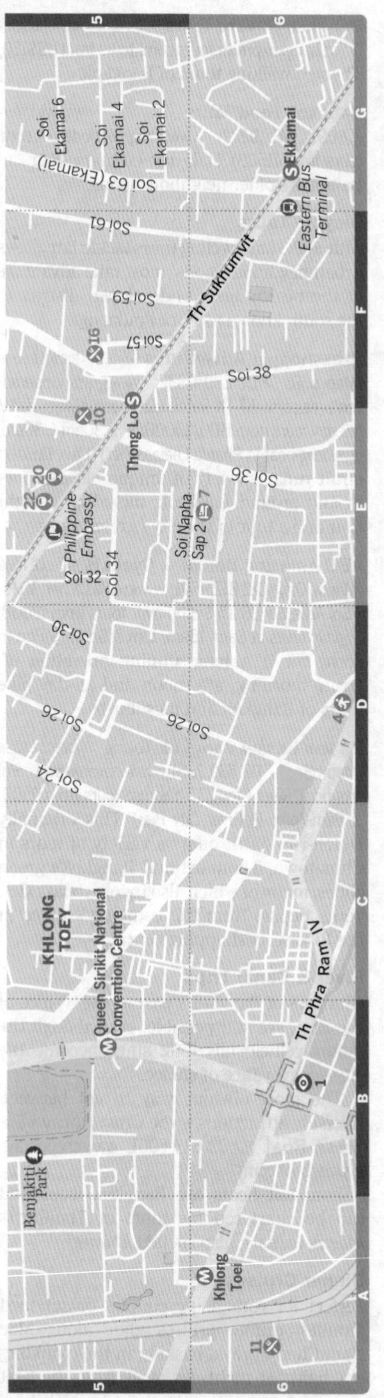

Sukhumvit

Sights

1 Khlong Toey Market B6

Activities, Courses & Tours

2 ABC Amazing Bangkok Cyclists D4
3 Asia Herb Association D4
4 Fun-arium D6

Sleeping

5 AriyasomVilla A1
6 FU House Hostel A3
7 Napa Place E6
8 S-Box C3
9 Suk 11 .... A2

Eating

10 Bo.lan E5
11 Issaya Siamese Club A6
Jidori-Ya Kenzou .... (see 2)
12 Klang Soi Restaurant E3
13 Nasir Al-Masri A2
14 Pier 21 .... B3
15 Saras C4
16 Soul Food Mahanakorn F5

Drinking & Nightlife

17 Arena 10 .... G4
18 Badmotel F3
Demo .... (see 17)
Funky Villa .... (see 17)
19 Grease E4
20 Studio Lam E5
21 Tuba G2
22 WTF E5

Entertainment

23 Living Room B3
24 Nana Entertainment Plaza A2
25 Soi Cowboy C3
26 Titanium C4

Shopping

27 Dive Indeed C2
28 Nickermann's A2
29 Planet Scuba D4
30 Raja's Fashions A2

house in Thonburi. Taught by the delightfully enthusiastic Piyawadi 'Tam' Jantrupon, a course here includes a romp through the garden and instruction in four dishes. The fee covers transport, which in this case takes the form of a boat ride from Maharaj Pier.

Helping Hands COOKING COURSE

(☎080 434 8686; www.cookingwithpoo.com; 1500B; ⊙lessons 8.30am-1pm) This popular cooking course was started by a native of Khlong Toey's slums and is held in her neighbourhood. Courses, which must be booked in advance, span three dishes and include a visit to Khlong Toey Market and transport to and from Emporium Shopping Centre.

Silom Thai Cooking School COOKING COURSE
(Map p68; ☎084 726 5669; www.bangkokthaicooking.com; 68 Soi 13, Th Silom; courses 1000B; ⏱lessons 9am-1pm, 1.40-5.30pm & 6-9pm; S Chong Nonsi exit 3) Spread over two simple but charming facilities; lessons at Silom Thai Cooking School include a visit to a local market and instruction for six dishes in four hours, making it the best bang for your baht. Hotel pick-up in central Bangkok is available.

Muay Thai Lab MARTIAL ARTS
(Map p60; ☎02 024 1326; www.muaythailab.net; 2nd fl, Maharaj Pier, Th Maha Rat; lessons from 990B; ⏱11am-8pm; ⛴Maharaj Pier, Chang Pier, Phra Chan Tai Pier) Muay Thai Lab is a new, impressive one-stop centre for everything related to Thai boxing. Start in the lobby, which has free displays on the history and culture of Thai boxing and a small shop stocked with both souvenirs and gear, before heading to the open-air rooftop gym, which looks over Mae Nam Chao Phraya.

Drop-ins are encouraged to join the introductory lessons, which take place from 11am to 3pm daily; the fee includes clothing and equipment, access to a locker and showers, and a towel.

Center Meditation Wat Mahadhatu MEDITATION
(Map p60; ☎02 223 3813, 02 222 6011; Section 5, Wat Mahathat, Th Maha Rat; donations accepted; ⏱lessons 7am, 1pm & 6pm; ⛴Chang Pier, Maharaj Pier, Phra Chan Tai Pier) Located within Wat Mahathat, this small centre offers informal daily meditation classes. Taught by English-speaking Prasuputh Chainikom (Kosalo), classes last three hours. Longer periods of study, which include accommodation and food, can be arranged, but students are expected to follow a strict regimen of conduct.

☞ Tours

If you're not travelling with a group but would like a guide, or some guidance in investigating a more specific side of the city, recommended outfits include the following:

Tour With Tong GUIDED TOUR
(☎081 835 0240; www.tourwithtong.com; tours from 1000B) Established outfit whose guides conduct tours in and around Bangkok.

Bangkok Private Tours WALKING TOUR
(www.bangkokprivatetours.com; tours from US$150) Themed walking tours of Bangkok.

Bangkok Food Tours WALKING TOUR
(☎095 943 9222; www.bangkokfoodtours.com; tours from 1150B) Half-day culinary tours of Bangkok's older neighbourhoods.

Bicycle Tours

Although some cycling tours tackle Bangkok's urban neighbourhoods, most take advantage of the nearby lush, undeveloped district to the south known as Phra Pradaeng.

Grasshopper Adventures BICYCLE TOUR
(Map p60; ☎02 280 0832; www.grasshopperadventures.com; 57 Th Ratchadamnoen Klang; half-/full-day tours from 1100/1600B; ⏱8.30am-6.30pm; ⛴klorng boat to Phanfa Leelard Pier) This lauded outfit runs a variety of unique bicycle tours in and around Bangkok, including a night tour and a tour of the city's green zones.

ABC Amazing Bangkok Cyclists BICYCLE TOUR
(Map p70; ☎081 812 9641; www.realasia.net; 10/5-7 Soi Aree, Soi 26, Th Sukhumvit; tours from 1300B; ⏱daily tours at 8am, 10am, 1pm & 6pm; S Phrom Phong exit 4) A long-running operation offering morning, afternoon and all-day bike tours of Bangkok and its suburbs.

Co van Kessel Bangkok Tours BICYCLE TOUR
(Map p84; ☎02 639 7351; www.covankessel.com; ground fl, River City, 23 Th Yotha; tours from 950B; ⏱6am-7pm; ⛴River City Pier) This originally Dutch-run outfit offers a variety of tours in Chinatown, Thonburi and Bangkok's green zones, many of which also involve boat rides. Tours depart from the company's office in the River City shopping centre.

River & Canal Trips

Glimpses of Bangkok's past as the 'Venice of the East' are still possible, even though the motor vehicle has long since become the city's conveyance of choice.

The most obvious way to get between riverside attractions is the **Chao Phraya Express Boat** (☎02 623 6001; www.chaophrayaexpressboat.com).

Long-tail boats are Bangkok icons and can be chartered for tours of Thonburi's *klorng* (canals; also spelled *khlong*).

Dinner Cruises

Perfect for romancing couples or subdued families, dinner cruises glide along Mae Nam Chao Phraya, basking in the twinkling city lights at night, far away from the heat

BANGKOK FOR CHILDREN

There aren't a whole lot of attractions in Bangkok meant to appeal directly to the little ones, but there's no lack of locals willing to provide attention. The website www.bangkok.com/kids has an excellent spread of things to do for kids, and www.bambiweb.org is a useful resource for parents of young children in Bangkok.

Kid-Friendly Museums

Although not specifically child-targeted, the **Museum of Siam** (สถาบันพิพิธภัณฑ์การเรียนรู้แห่งชาติ; Map p60; www.museumsiam.org; Th Maha Rat; admission 300B; ⏲10am-6pm Tue-Sun; 👪; ⛴Tien Pier) has lots of interactive exhibits that will appeal to children.

Outside town, **Ancient City** (เมืองโบราณ, Muang Boran; www.ancientcitygroup.net/ancientsiam/en; 296/1 Th Sukhumvit, Samut Prakan; adult/child 9am-4pm 700/350B, 4-7pm 350/175B; ⏲9am-7pm; S Bearing exit 1) recreates Thailand's most famous monuments. They're linked by bicycle paths and were practically built for being climbed on.

Play Centres & Parks

For kid-specific play centres, consider **Fun-arium** (Map p70; ☎02 665 6555; www.funarium.co.th; 111/1 Soi 26, Th Sukhumvit; admission 110-320B; ⏲9am-6pm Mon-Thu, to 7pm Fri-Sun; S Phrom Phong exit 1 & taxi), central Bangkok's largest; or the impressive **KidZania** (Map p74; ☎02 683 1888; www.bangkok.kidzania.com/en; 5th fl, Siam Paragon, 991/1 Th Phra Ram I; adult 425-500B, child 425-1000B; ⏲10am-5pm Mon-Fri, 10.30am-8pm Sat & Sun; S Siam exits 3 & 5).

Lumphini Park (สวนลุมพินี; Map p68; bounded by Th Sarasin, Th Phra Ram IV, Th Witthayu/Wireless Rd & Th Ratchadamri; ⏲4.30am-9pm; 👪; M Lumphini exit 3, Si Lom exit 1, S Sala Daeng exit 3, Ratchadamri exit 2) is a trusty ally in the cool hours of the morning and evening for kite-flying (during February and March) as well as for stretching the legs and lungs.

Rainy-Day Fun

MBK Center (p91) and **Siam Paragon** (p92) both have bowling alleys to keep the older ones occupied. **Krung Sri IMAX** (Map p74; ☎02 129 4635; www.majorcineplex.com/en/cinema/paragon-cineplex/; 5th fl, Siam Paragon, 991/1 Th Phra Ram I; tickets 250-1200B; S Siam exits 3 & 5) screens special-effects versions of Hollywood action flicks and nature features.

Zoos & Animals

Dusit Zoo (สวนสัตว์ดุสิต (เขาดิน); Map p78; www.dusitzoo.org; Th Ratchawithi; adult/child 150/70B; ⏲8am-6pm; ⛴Thewet Pier, S Phaya Thai exit 3 & taxi) covers 19 hectares with caged exhibits of more than 300 mammals, 200 reptiles and 800 birds, including relatively rare native species such as banteng, gaur, serow and some rhinoceros. There are shady grounds plus a lake in the centre with paddleboats for hire and a small children's playground.

A massive underwater world has been recreated at the **Siam Ocean World** (p92) shopping-centre aquarium.

Nearby, kids can view lethal snakes becoming reluctant altruists at the adjacent antivenin-producing snake farm, **Queen Saovabha Memorial Institute** (สถานเสาวภา, Snake Farm; Map p68; cnr Th Phra Ram IV & Th Henri Dunant; adult/child 200/50B; ⏲9.30am-3.30pm Mon-Fri, to 1pm Sat & Sun; 👪; M Si Lom exit 1, S Sala Daeng exit 3).

and noise of town. Cruises range from downhome to sophisticated, but the food generally ranges from mediocre to forgettable.

A good one-stop centre for all your dinner-cruise needs is the **River City Boat Tour Check-In Center** (Map p84; www.rivercity.co.th; ground fl, River City, 23 Th Yotha; ⏲10am-10pm; ⛴Si Phraya/River City Pier, or shuttle boat from Sathon/Central Pier), where tickets can be purchased for the following outfits:

Wan Fah DINNER CRUISE
(Map p84; ☎02 622 7657; www.wanfah.in.th/eng/dinner; 1300B; ⏲cruise 7-9pm; ⛴Si Phraya/River City Pier) Dinner cruise along Mae Nam Chao Phraya.

White Orchid DINNER CRUISE
(Map p84; ☎02 438 8228; www.thairivercruise.com; 1400B; ⏲cruise 7.20-9.45pm; ⛴Si Phraya/River City Pier) Dinner cruise along Mae Nam Chao Phraya.

Siam Square

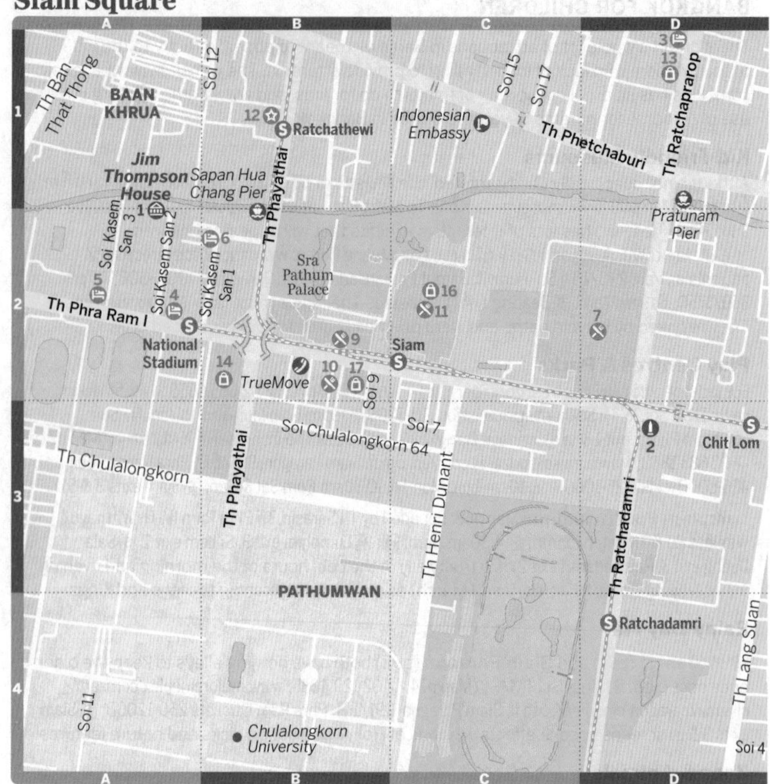

Festivals & Events

In addition to the national holidays, there's always something going on in Bangkok. Many Thai holidays are based on the lunar calendar, which varies year to year, so check the website of **TAT** (Tourism Authority of Thailand; www.tourismthailand.org) or the Bangkok Information Center (p94) for exact dates.

Chinese New Year CULTURAL

(Jan or Feb) Thai-Chinese celebrate the lunar New Year with a week of housecleaning, lion dances and fireworks. Most festivities centre on Chinatown. Dates vary.

Songkran CULTURAL

(mid-Apr) The celebration of the Thai New Year has morphed into a water war with high-powered water guns and water balloons being launched at suspecting and unsuspecting participants. The most intense water battles take place on Th Khao San.

Vegetarian Festival FOOD

(Sep or Oct) A 10-day Chinese-Buddhist festival wheels out yellow-bannered streetside vendors serving meatless meals. The greatest concentration of vendors is found in Chinatown. Dates vary.

Loi Krathong CULTURAL

(early Nov) A beautiful festival where, on the night of the full moon, lotus-shaped boats made of banana leaf and containing a lit candle are set adrift on Mae Nam Chao Phraya.

King's Birthday/Father's Day CULTURAL

(5 Dec) Locals celebrate their monarch's birthday with lots of parades and fireworks.

Sleeping

At first glance, deciding where to lay your head in Bangkok appears an insurmountable task – there are countless hotels in virtually every corner of this sprawling city.

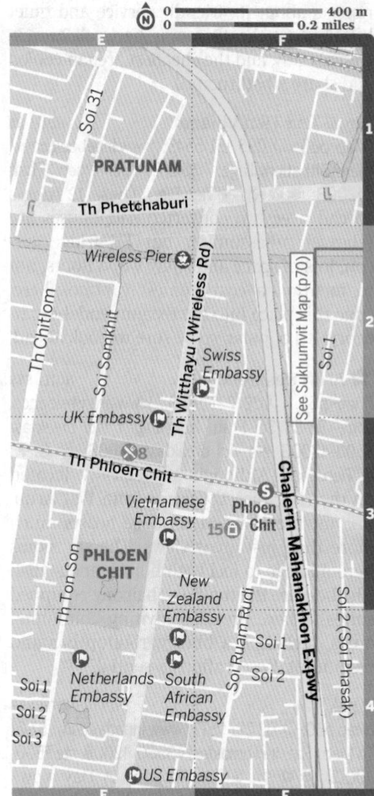

Siam Square

Top Sights
1 Jim Thompson House A2

Sights
2 Erawan Shrine D3
Siam Ocean World .... (see 16)

Activities, Courses & Tours
KidZania .... (see 16)

Sleeping
3 Indra Regent Hotel D1
4 Lub*d A2
5 Siam@Siam A2
6 Wendy House B2

Eating
7 Din Tai Fung D2
8 Eathai E3
9 Food Republic B2
Gourmet Paradise .... (see 16)
10 Koko B2
MBK Food Island .... (see 14)
11 Nuer Koo C2

Entertainment
Krung Sri IMAX .... (see 16)
Paragon Cineplex .... (see 16)
12 Playhouse Magical Cabaret B1

Shopping
13 Baiyoke Garment Center D1
14 MBK Center B2
15 Pinky Tailors F3
16 Siam Paragon C2
17 Siam Square B2

Making the job slightly easier is the fact that where you stay is largely determined by your budget. Banglamphu and the tourist ghetto of Th Khao San still hold the bulk of Bangkok's budget accommodation, although the downside is that it can be difficult to get to other parts of town. Cheap rooms are also available around lower Th Sukhumvit, although you'll have to put up with sex tourists and touts. Chinatown also has its share of hotels in this category.

Those willing to spend a bit more can consider staying in 'downtown' Bangkok. Both Th Sukhumvit and Th Silom have solid midrange options, typically within walking distance of the BTS or MRT. The sois opposite the National Stadium, near Siam Sq, have some good budget/midrange options, and have the benefit of being close to the BTS.

Upper Sukhumvit is home to many of Bangkok's boutique and designer hotels. The city's most legendary luxury hotels are largely found along the riverside near Th Silom.

Ko Ratanakosin, Banglamphu & Thonburi

★Chern HOSTEL $

(Map p60; ☎02 621 1133; www.chernbangkok.com; 17 Soi Ratchasak; dm 400B, r 1400-1900B; ❄@📶; ⛴klorng boat to Phanfa Leelard Pier) The vast, open spaces and white, overexposed tones of this hostel converge in an almost afterlife-like feel. The eight-bed dorms are above average, but we particularly like the private rooms, which, equipped with attractively minimalist touches, a vast desk, TV, safe, fridge and heaps of space, are a steal at this price.

Fortville Guesthouse HOTEL $

(Map p60; ☎02 282 3932; www.fortvilleguesthouse.com; 9 Th Phra Sumen; r 870-1120B; ❄@📶; ⛴Phra Athit/Banglamphu Pier) With an exterior that combines elements of a modern church and/or castle, and an interior that relies on mirrors and industrial themes, the design concept of this hotel – undergoing a renovation at the time of research – is tough to pin down. The rooms themselves are stylishly minimalist, and the more expensive ones include perks such as a fridge and balcony.

Khaosan Immjai HOSTEL $

(Map p60; 02 629 3088; www.khaosanimmjai.com; 240 Soi 1, Th Samsen; dm incl breakfast 350-420B; ; Phra Athit/Banglamphu Pier) There's nothing flashy or exceptional about this hostel. But a homely feel and positive feedback edge it into the recommendable column. Dorms, ranging from four to 14 beds, are clean, done out in pastel tones and have ample natural light. There's access to lots of convenient amenities (washing machines, computers, etc), although none are free.

★ **Lamphu Treehouse** HOTEL $$

(Map p60; 02 282 0991; www.lamphutreehotel.com; 155 Wanchat Bridge, off Th Prachathipatai; incl breakfast r 1650-2500B, ste 3500-4500B; ; klorng boat to Phanfa Leelard Pier) Despite the name, this attractive midranger has its feet firmly on land, and as such represents brilliant value. The wood-panelled rooms are attractive and inviting, and the rooftop bar, pool, internet cafe, restaurant and quiet canal-side location ensure that you may never feel the need to leave. An annexe a couple of blocks away increases your odds of snagging an elusive reservation.

★ **Feung Nakorn Balcony** HOTEL $$

(Map p60; 02 622 1100; www.feungnakorn.com; 125 Th Fuang Nakhon; incl breakfast dm 700B, r 1650B, ste 2100-4700B; ; Saphan Phut/Memorial Bridge Pier, Pak Klong Taladd Pier) Located in a former school, the 42 rooms here surround an inviting garden courtyard and are generally large, bright and cheery. Amenities such as a free minibar, safe and flat-screen TV are standard, and the hotel has a quiet and secluded location away from the strip, with capable staff. A charming and inviting (if not particularly great-value) place to stay.

★ **Sam Sen Sam Place** GUESTHOUSE $$

(Map p60; 02 628 7067; www.samsensam.com; 48 Soi 3, Th Samsen; r incl breakfast 590-2400B; ; Thewet Pier) One of the homeliest places in this area, if not Bangkok, this colourful, refurbished antique villa gets glowing reports about its friendly service and quiet location. Of the 18 rooms here, all are extremely tidy, and the cheapest are fan-cooled and share a bathroom.

Royal Tha Tien Village HOTEL $$

(Map p60; 095 151 5545; www.facebook.com/theroyalthatienvillage; 392/29 Soi Phen Phat; r 1200B; ; Tien Pier) These 12 rooms spread over two converted shophouses are relatively unassuming, but TV, fridge, air-con, lots of space and shiny wood floors, not to mention a cosy homestay atmosphere, edge this place into the recommendable category. It's popular, so be sure to book ahead.

★ **Arun Residence** HOTEL $$$

(Map p60; 02 221 9158; www.arunresidence.com; 36-38 Soi Pratu Nokyung; r incl breakfast 3500-4200B, ste incl breakfast 5800B; ; Tien Pier) Although strategically located on the river directly across from Wat Arun, this multilevel wooden house boasts much more than just great views. The six rooms here manage to feel both homey and stylish (the best are the top-floor, balcony-equipped suites). There are also inviting communal areas, including a library, rooftop bar and restaurant. Reservations essential.

Inn A Day HOTEL $$$

(Map p60; 02 221 0577; www.innaday.com; 57-61 Th Maha Rat; incl breakfast r 3500-4200B, ste 7500-9000B; ; Tien Pier) Inn A Day wows with its hyper-cool retro/industrial theme (the hotel is located in a former sugar factory) and its location (it towers over the river and Wat Arun). The 11 rooms aren't huge, but they include unique touches such as clear neon shower stalls, while the top-floor suites have two levels and huge clawfoot tubs.

Chinatown & Phahurat

Siam Classic GUESTHOUSE $

(Map p84; 02 639 6363; 336/10 Trok Chalong Krung; r incl breakfast 450-1200B; ; Ratchawong Pier, M Hua Lamphong exit 1) The rooms here don't include much furniture, and the cheapest don't include air-con or en suite bathrooms, but an effort has been made at making them feel comfortable, tidy and even a bit stylish. An inviting ground-floor communal area encourages meeting and chatting, and the whole place exudes a welcoming homestay vibe.

BANGKOK'S BEST HOSTELS

If you're on a shoestring budget, Bangkok has heaps of options for you, ranging from hi-tech, pod-like dorm beds in a brand-new hostel to cosy bunk beds in a converted Chinatown shophouse. (If you decide that you need a bit more privacy, nearly all of Bangkok's hostels also offer private rooms.) And best of all, at the places listed here, we found the bathrooms to be clean and convenient, and sharing will hardly feel like a compromise. Some of our picks:

➡ **Lub*d** (Map p74; ☎ 02 634 7999; www.siamsquare.lubd.com; Th Phra Ram I; dm 590B, r 1550-2000B; ❄ @ 📶; Ⓢ National Stadium exit 1) The title is a play on the Thai *làp dee*, meaning 'sleep well', but the fun atmosphere here might make you want to stay up all night. It has an inviting communal area stocked with games and a bar, and thoughtful facilities ranging from washing machines to a theatre room. If this one's full, there's another **branch** (Map p68; ☎ 02 634 7999; www.silom.lubd.com; 4 Th Decho; dm 550-600B, r 1250-1900B; ❄ @ 📶; Ⓢ Chong Nonsi exit 2) just off Th Silom.

➡ **Silom Art Hostel** (Map p68; ☎ 02 635 8070; www.silomarthostel.com; 198/19-22 Soi 14, Th Silom; dm 380-450B, r 1200B; ❄ @ 📶; Ⓢ Chong Nonsi exit 3) Quirky, artsy, bright and fun, Silom Art Hostel combines recycled materials, bizarre furnishings and colourful kitsch to arrive at a hostel that's quite unlike anywhere else in town. But it's not all about style: beds and rooms are functional and comfortable, and share clean bathrooms and appealing communal areas.

➡ **Loftel 22** (Map p84; www.loftel22bangkok.com; 952 Soi 22, Th Charoen Krung; dm 350B, r 900-1350B; ❄ @ 📶; ⛴ Marine Department Pier, Ⓜ Hua Lamphong exit 1) Stylish, inviting dorms and private rooms (all with shared bathrooms) have been coaxed out of these two adjoining shophouses. Friendly service and a location in one of Chinatown's most atmospheric corners round out the package.

➡ **NapPark Hostel** (Map p60; ☎ 02 282 2324; www.nappark.com; 5 Th Tani; dm 440-650B; ❄ @ 📶; ⛴ Phra Athit/Banglamphu Pier) This popular hostel features dorm rooms of various sizes, the smallest and most expensive of which boasts six pod-like beds outfitted with power points, mini-TV, reading lamp and wi-fi. Cultural-based activities and inviting communal areas mean you may not get the chance to plug in.

➡ **Saphaipae** (Map p84; ☎ 02 238 2322; www.saphaipae.com; 35 Th Surasak; incl breakfast dm 450B, r 1000-1600B; ❄ @ 📶; Ⓢ Surasak exit 1) The bright colours, chunky furnishings and bold murals in the lobby of this new hostel give it the vibe of a day-care centre for travellers – a feel that continues through to the playful communal areas and rooms. Dorms and rooms are thoughtful and well-equipped. It has heaps of useful travel resources and facilities.

➡ **Suneta Hostel Khaosan** (Map p60; ☎ 02 629 0150; www.sunetahostel.com; 209-211 Th Kraisi; dm incl breakfast 490-590B, r incl breakfast 1180B; ❄ @ 📶; ⛴ Phra Athit/Banglamphu Pier) Suneta is a standout, with a pleasant, low-key atmosphere; a unique, retro-themed design (some of the dorm rooms resemble sleeping-car carriages); a location just off the main drag; and friendly service.

➡ **Yim Huai Khwang Hostel** (Map p78; ☎ 02 118 6038; www.yimhuaikhwang.com; 70 Th Pracha Rat Bamphen; incl breakfast dm 450-550B, r 1556-3000B; ❄ 📶; Ⓜ Huay Khwang exit 1) A new suburban hostel decked out in an eclectic, colourful fashion, with dorm rooms ranging in size from four to six comfortable, hi-tech bunk beds. Yes, it's far from any sights, but is very close to the MRT.

➡ **S1 Hostel** (Map p68; ☎ 02 679 7777; www.facebook.com/S1hostelBangkok; 35/1-4 Soi Ngam Du Phli; dm 330-380B, r 700-1300B; ❄ @ 📶; Ⓜ Lumphini exit 1) A huge new hostel with dorm beds decked out in a simple yet attractive primary-colour scheme. A host of facilities (laundry, kitchen, rooftop garden) and a convenient location within walking distance of the MRT make it great value.

Greater Bangkok

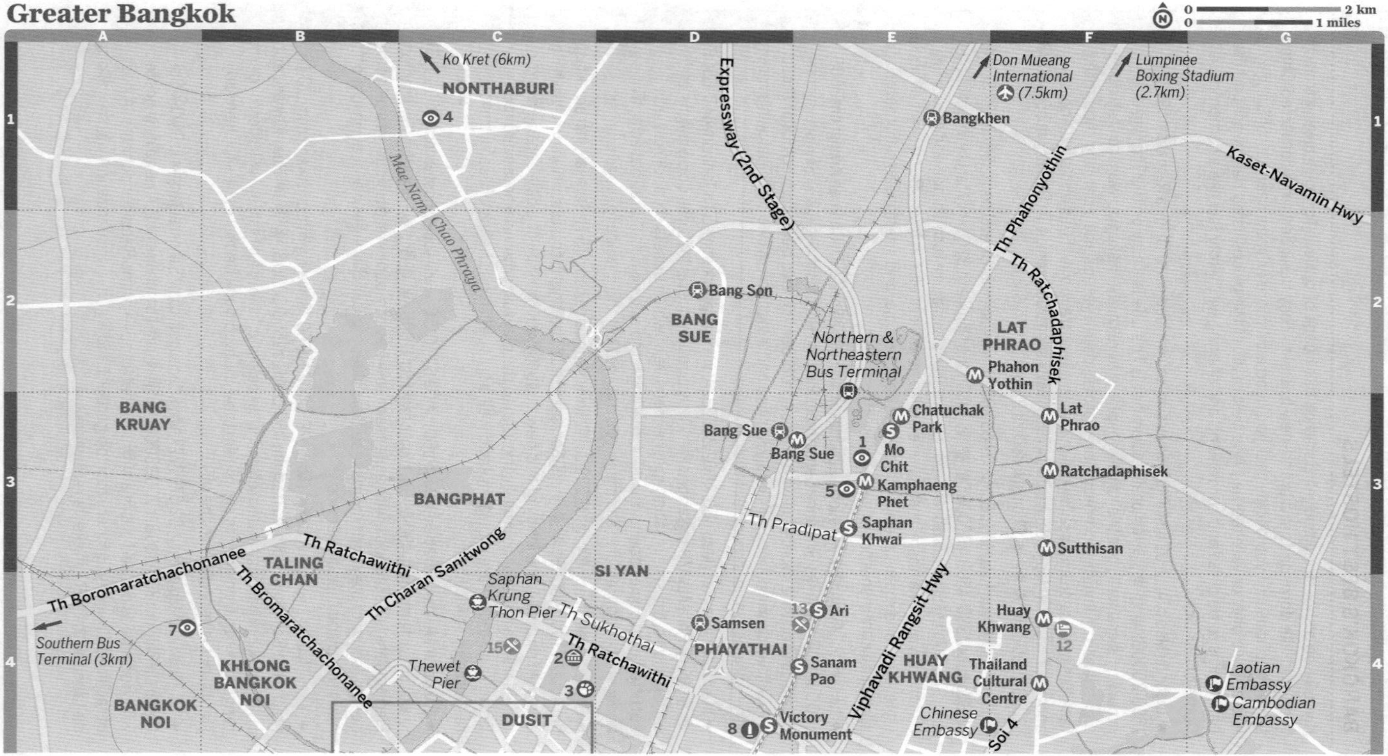

0 — 2 km
0 — 1 miles

Ko Kret (6km)
NONTHABURI
4
Mae Nam Chao Phraya
Expressway (2nd Stage)
Don Mueang International (7.5km)
Lumpinee Boxing Stadium (2.7km)
Bangkhen
Kaset-Navamin Hwy
Th Phahonyothin
Th Ratchadaphisek
Bang Son
BANG SUE
Northern & Northeastern Bus Terminal
LAT PHRAO
Phahon Yothin
Lat Phrao
Chatuchak Park
Mo Chit
1
Bang Sue
Bang Sue
5
Kamphaeng Phet
Ratchadaphisek
BANG KRUAY
BANGPHAT
Th Pradipat
Saphan Khwai
Sutthisan
Th Ratchawithi
Th Charan Sanitwong
Th Boromaratchachonanee
TALING CHAN
SI YAN
Th Bromaratchachonanee
Saphan Krung Thon Pier
Th Sukhothai
Th Ratchawithi
13
Ari
Samsen
PHAYATHAI
Viphavadi Rangsit Hwy
Huay Khwang
12
7
Southern Bus Terminal (3km)
KHLONG BANGKOK NOI
BANGKOK NOI
15
Thewet Pier
2
3
DUSIT
Sanam Pao
HUAY KHWANG
Thailand Cultural Centre
Laotian Embassy
Cambodian Embassy
8
Victory Monument
Chinese Embassy
Soi 4

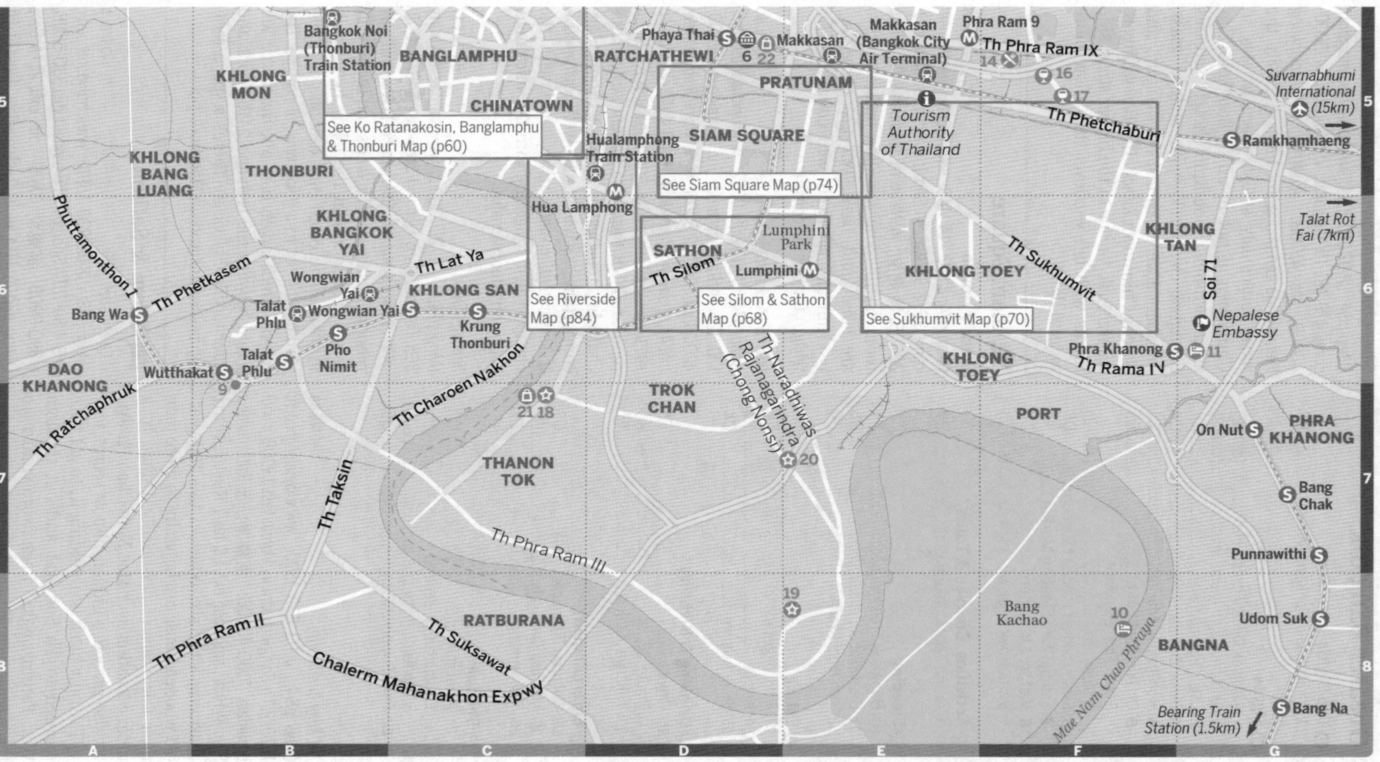
Bangkok Noi (Thonburi) Train Station
BANGLAMPHU
KHLONG MON
CHINATOWN
See Ko Ratanakosin, Banglamphu & Thonburi Map (p60)
KHLONG BANG LUANG
THONBURI
RATCHATHEWI
Phaya Thai
6
22
Makkasan
Makkasan (Bangkok City Air Terminal)
Phra Ram 9
Th Phra Ram IX
14
16
17
PRATUNAM
Tourism Authority of Thailand
Th Phetchaburi
Suvarnabhumi International (15km)
Ramkhamhaeng
Hualamphong Train Station
SIAM SQUARE
See Siam Square Map (p74)
Hua Lamphong
Talat Rot Fai (7km)
Phuttamonthon 1
KHLONG BANGKOK YAI
Lumphini Park
SATHON
Th Lat Ya
Th Silom
Lumphini
KHLONG TOEY
Th Sukhumvit
KHLONG TAN
Soi 71
Th Phetkasem
Wongwian Yai
KHLONG SAN
See Riverside Map (p84)
See Silom & Sathon Map (p68)
See Sukhumvit Map (p70)
Nepalese Embassy
Bang Wa
Talat Phlu
Wongwian Yai
Krung Thonburi
Pho Nimit
Th Naradhiwas Rajanagarindra (Chong Nonsi)
KHLONG TOEY
Phra Khanong
11
Th Rama IV
DAO KHANONG
Wutthakat
Talat Phlu
9
Th Charoen Nakhon
21
18
TROK CHAN
PORT
Th Ratchaphruk
On Nut
PHRA KHANONG
20
THANON TOK
Th Taksin
Bang Chak
Th Phra Ram III
Punnawithi
19
RATBURANA
Bang Kachao
10
Udom Suk
Th Phra Ram II
Th Suksawat
BANGNA
Chalerm Mahanakhon Expwy
Mae Nam Chao Phraya
Bearing Train Station (1.5km)
Bang Na
A
B
C
D
E
F
G
5
6
7
8

Greater Bangkok

★**Loy La Long** HOTEL $$
(Map p84; ☎02 639 1390; www.loylalong.com; 1620/2 Th Songwat; dm incl breakfast 1300B, r incl breakfast 2100-4000B; ❄@📶; ⛴Ratchawong Pier, Ⓜ Hua Lamphong exit 1 & taxi) Rustic, retro, charming – the six rooms in this 100-year-old wooden house can lay claim to more than their fair share of personality. United by a unique location over Mae Nam Chao Phraya, it's also privy to a hidden, almost secret, feel.

The only hitch is in finding it; to get here proceed to Th Songwat and cut through Wat Patumkongka Rachaworawiharn to the river.

Shanghai Mansion HOTEL $$$
(Map p84; ☎02 221 2121; www.shanghaimansion.com; 479-481 Th Yaowarat; incl breakfast r 3000-4000B, ste 4500B; ❄@📶; ⛴Ratchawong Pier, Ⓜ Hua Lamphong exit 1 & taxi) Easily the most consciously stylish place to stay in Chinatown, if not in all of Bangkok. This award-winning boutique hotel screams Shanghai circa 1935 with stained glass, an abundance of lamps, bold colours and cheeky Chinatown kitsch. If you're willing to splurge, ask for one of the bigger street-side rooms with tall windows that allow more natural light.

Siam Square

Wendy House HOSTEL $
(Map p74; ☎02 214 1149; www.wendyguesthouse.com; 36/2 Soi Kasem San 1; r incl breakfast 750-2000B; ❄@📶; Ⓢ National Stadium exit 1) The rooms at this long-standing budget option are small and basic, but are exceedingly clean and relatively well equipped (TV, fridge) for this price range.

Indra Regent Hotel HOTEL $$
(Map p74; ☎02 208 0022; www.indrahotel.com; 120/126 Th Ratchaprarop; incl breakfast r 2500-4200B, ste 5000-12,500B; ❄📶🏊; Ⓢ Ratchathewi exit 4) A classic Bangkok hotel dating back to 1971, nearly half of its 500 rooms have been renovated, but the Indra Regent still retains charming touches of its past. Rooms are comfortable, spacious and well equipped – if somewhat conservative – and with the cheapest just squeezing into the midrange, represent decent value.

Siam@Siam HOTEL $$$
(Map p74; ☎02 217 3000; www.siamatsiam.com; 865 Th Phra Ram I; r incl breakfast 5467-9200B; ❄@📶🏊; Ⓢ National Stadium exit 1) A seemingly random mishmash of colours and industrial/recycled materials in the lobby here result in a style one could only describe as 'junkyard chic' – but in a good way, of course. The rooms, which largely continue the theme, are found between the 14th and 24th floors, and offer terrific city views. There's a spa, a rooftop restaurant and an 11th-floor pool.

Silom & Sathon

HQ Hostel HOSTEL $
(Map p68; ☎02 233 1598; www.hqhostel.com; 5/3-4 Soi 3, Th Silom; incl breakfast dm 330-520B, r 890-990B; ❄@📶; Ⓜ Si Lom exit 2, Ⓢ Sala Daeng exit 2) HQ is a flashpacker hostel in

the polished-concrete-and-industrial-style mould. It includes four- to 10-bed dorms, a few private rooms (some with en suite bathroom) and inviting communal areas in a narrow multistorey building in the middle of Bangkok's financial district.

★Smile Society HOTEL $$

(Map p68; ☎081 442 5800, 081 444 1596; www.smilesocietyhostel.com; 30/3-4 Soi 6, Th Silom; incl breakfast dm 420B, r 900-1880B; ❄@📶; M Si Lom exit 2, S Sala Daeng exit 1) Part boutique, part hostel, this four-storey shophouse combines small but comfortable and well-equipped rooms and dorms with spotless shared bathrooms. A central location, overwhelmingly positive guest feedback, and helpful, English-speaking staff are other perks. And a new and virtually identical annexe next door helps with spillover as Smile Society gains more fans.

Amber HOTEL $$

(Map p68; ☎02 635 7272; www.amberboutiquesilom.com; 200 Soi 14, Th Silom; r incl breakfast 1650-2150B; ❄📶; S Chong Nonsi exit 3) Spanning design themes such as Moroccan, Sino-Portuguese and Modern, it's easy to assume that Amber might emphasise style over comfort. But nothing here is flashy or overwrought, and what you'll get are 19 excellent-value, spacious rooms with lots of amenities and natural light in a quiet location.

★Siam Heritage HOTEL $$$

(Map p68; ☎02 353 6101; www.thesiamheritage.com; 115/1 Th Surawong; incl breakfast r 4900-5700B, ste 7000-13,500B; ❄@📶🏊; M Si Lom exit 2, S Sala Daeng exit 1) Tucked off busy Th Surawong, this hotel overflows with homey Thai charm – probably because the owners also live in the same building. The 73 rooms are decked out in silk and dark woods with classy design touches and thoughtful amenities. There's an inviting rooftop garden/pool/spa, and it's all cared for by a team of professional, accommodating staff. Highly recommended.

★Metropolitan by COMO HOTEL $$$

(Map p68; ☎02 625 3333; www.comohotels.com/metropolitanbangkok; 27 Th Sathon Tai/South; incl breakfast r 4500-6500B, ste 7500-40,000B; ❄@📶🏊; M Lumphini exit 2) The exterior of Bangkok's former YMCA has changed relatively little, but a peek inside reveals one of the city's sleekest, sexiest hotels. A 2014 renovation has all 171 rooms looking better than ever in striking tones of black, white and yellow. It's worth noting that the City rooms tend to feel a bit tight, while in contrast the two-storey penthouse suites are like small homes.

Sukhumvit

FU House Hostel HOSTEL $

(Map p70; ☎098 654 5505; www.fuhousehostel.com; 77 Soi 8, Th Sukhumvit; incl breakfast dm 500B, r 1650B; ❄📶; S Nana exit 4) Great for a quiet, low-key stay is this two-storey wooden villa on a residential street. Choose between attractive bunk beds in one of two spacious, private-feeling dorms, or rooms with en suite bathrooms.

Suk 11 HOSTEL $

(Map p70; ☎02 253 5927; www.suk11.com; 1/33 Soi 11, Th Sukhumvit; r incl breakfast 535-1712B; ❄@📶; S Nana exit 3) Extremely well run and equally popular, this rustic guesthouse is an oasis of woods and greenery in the urban jungle that is Th Sukhumvit. The rooms are basic, clean and comfy, if a bit dark, while the cheapest of them share bathrooms. Although the building holds nearly 70 rooms, you'll still need to book at least two weeks ahead.

Napa Place HOTEL $$

(Map p70; ☎02 661 5525; www.napaplace.com; 11/3 Soi Napha Sap 2; incl breakfast r 2200-3100B, ste 3400-4100B; ❄@📶; S Thong Lo exit 2) Hidden in the confines of a typical Bangkok urban compound is what must be the city's homeliest accommodation. The 12 expansive rooms have been decorated with dark woods from the family's former lumber business and light-brown cloths from the hands of Thai weavers, while the cosy communal areas might not be much different from the suburban living room you grew up in.

S-Box HOTEL $$

(Map p70; ☎02 262 0991; www.sboxhotel.com; 4 Soi 31, Th Sukhumvit; r incl breakfast 1000-2524B; ❄@📶; S Phrom Phong exit 5) The name says it all: the rooms here are little more than boxes – albeit attractive, modern boxes with stylish furniture and practical amenities. The cheapest are pod-like and lack natural light, while the more expensive have floor-to-ceiling windows.

★AriyasomVilla HOTEL $$$

(Map p70; ☎02 254 8880; www.ariyasom.com; 65 Soi 1, Th Sukhumvit; r incl breakfast 6650-14,750B; ❄@📶🏊; S Phloen Chit exit 3) Located at the end of Soi 1 behind a wall of tropical greenery, this beautifully renovated 1940s-era villa is

WORTH A TRIP

KO KRET

If you can't wait to see an island but aren't yet ready to head south, consider a visit to **Ko Kret**. An artificial 'island', it was created 300 years ago when a canal was dug to shorten an oxbow bend in Mae Nam Chao Phraya. Today, Ko Kret is a popular weekend getaway, known for its hand-thrown terracotta pots and its busy weekend market.

A 6km paved path circles the island, and can be easily completed on foot or by bicycle, the latter available for hire from Ko Kret's main pier (40B per day). Alternatively, it's possible to charter a longtail boat for up to 10 people for 500B; the typical island tour stops at a batik workshop, a sweets factory and, on weekends, a floating market.

Ko Kret's most identifiable landmark is the curiously leaning stupa at **Wat Poramai Yikawat** (วัดปรมัยยิกาวาส; Ko Kret, Nonthaburi; 9am-5pm; river-crossing ferry from Wat Sanam Neua) FREE. From here, go in either direction to find both abandoned kilns and working pottery centres on the island's east and north coasts. Yet even more prevalent than temples or pottery is food. On weekends, droves of Thais flock to Ko Kret to eat deep-fried savoury snacks and Thai-style sweets. Arrive on a weekday and the eating options are much fewer, but you'll have the island to yourself.

Ko Kret is in Nonthaburi, about 15km north of central Bangkok. To get there, take bus 166 from the Victory Monument or a taxi to Pak Kret, before boarding the cross-river ferry (2B, from 5am to 9pm) that leaves from Wat Sanam Neua.

one of the worst-kept accommodation secrets in Bangkok. The 24 rooms are spacious and meticulously outfitted with thoughtful Thai design touches and sumptuous, beautiful antique furniture. There's also a spa and an inviting tropical pool. Book well in advance.

Other Areas

The following hotels lie outside our neat neighbourhood designations, so they require a little more effort to reach. This also means that they tend to be located in less hectic parts of the city, perfect for those who'd rather not stay in the thick of it.

Accommodation is also available near Bangkok's two airports.

Glur Bangkok HOSTEL $

(Map p84; 02 630 5595; www.glurbangkok.com; 45 Soi 50, Th Charoen Krung; incl breakfast dm 400-650B, r 800-1200B; ; Sathon/Central Pier, S Saphan Taksin exit 1) A narrow shophouse with three attractive and comfy eight-bed dorms. Space is limited, but Glur makes the most of it with fun and functional communal areas, including a ground-floor cafe.

Swan Hotel HOTEL $$

(Map p84; 02 235 9271; www.swanhotelbkk.com; 31 Soi 36/Rue de Brest, Th Charoen Krung; r incl breakfast 1200-2000B; ; Oriental Pier) The 1960s-era furnishings date this classic Bangkok hotel despite relatively recent renovations. But the rooms are airy and virtually spotless, and the antiquated setting provides the Swan with a fun, groovy vibe – particular around the pool area.

Beat Hotel HOTEL $$

(Map p78; 02 178 0077; www.beathotelbangkok.com; 69/1 Th Sukhumvit; r incl breakfast 2000-2500B; ; S Phra Khanong exit 3) This new, art-themed hotel has a vibrant, youthful vibe that kicks off in the lobby. The 54 rooms continue this feeling, ranging in design from those with colourful floor-to-ceiling wall art to others painted in a monochromatic bold hue. It's worth shelling out for the super-huge Deluxe rooms.

★ **Phra-Nakorn Norn-Len** HOTEL $$$

(Map p60; 02 628 8188; www.phranakorn-nornlen.com; 46 Soi Thewet 1; r incl breakfast 2200-4200B; ; Thewet Pier) Set in an enclosed garden compound decorated like the Bangkok of yesteryear, this bright and cheery hotel is a fun and atmospheric, if not necessarily stupendous-value, place to stay. Although the 31 rooms are attractively furnished with antiques and paintings, it's worth noting that they don't include TV or in-room wi-fi, a fact made up for by daily activities, massage and endless opportunities for peaceful relaxing.

★ **Bangkok Tree House** HOTEL $$$

(Map p78; 082 995 1150; www.bangkoktreehouse.com; near Wat Bang Na Nork, Phrapradaeng; bungalow incl breakfast 6000-10,000B; ; S Bang Na exit 2 & taxi) The 12 multilevel bungalows here are stylishly sculpted from sustainable and recycled materials, giving it the feel of a sophisticated, eco-friendly summer camp. Thoughtful amenities include private computers equipped with movies, free mobile phone and bicycle use, and free ice cream. Significant online discounts are available.

The Bangkok Tree House is located in the lush green zone known as the Phrapradaeng Peninsula. To get here, take the BTS to Bang Na and then a taxi for the short ride to the pier at Wat Bang Na Nork. From there, take the river-crossing ferry (4B, 5am to 9.30pm), and continue by motorcycle taxi (10B) or on foot (call ahead for directions).

Mandarin Oriental HOTEL $$$
(Map p84; 02 659 9000; www.mandarinoriental.com; 48 Soi 40/Oriental, Th Charoen Krung; incl breakfast r 14,150-30,000B/ ste 26,700-160,000B; ; Oriental Pier, or hotel shuttle boat from Sathon/Central Pier) For the true Bangkok experience, a stay at this grand old riverside hotel is a must. The majority of rooms are in the modern and recently refurbished New Wing, but we prefer the old-world ambience of the Garden and Authors' Wings, the latter of which was undergoing a significant renovation at the time of research.

Eating

Nowhere else is the Thai reverence for food more evident than in Bangkok. The city's odour is a unique blend of noodle stall and car exhaust, and in certain parts of town, restaurants appear to form the majority of businesses, typically flanked by street-side hawker stalls and mobile snack vendors. Because of this obsession with eating, and because much of the food served at Thailand's beaches and islands is modified for foreigners, Bangkok is the ideal place to dig into the real deal.

Ko Ratanakosin, Banglamphu & Thonburi

Ko Ratanakosin, Bangkok's royal district, has an abundance of sights but a relative dearth of restaurants – a pity considering the potential riverfront views. Fortunately, neighbouring Banglamphu is one of the city's most famous eating areas, where decades-old restaurants and legendary hawkers line the streets.

Thip Samai CENTRAL THAI $
(Map p60; 313 Th Mahachai; mains 50-250B; 5pm-2am; klorng boat to Phanfa Leelard Pier) Brace yourself – you should be aware that the fried noodles sold from carts along Th Khao San have little to do with the dish known as *pàt tai*. Luckily, less than a five-minute túk-túk ride away lies Thip Samai, home to some of the most legendary fried noodles in town. Note that Thip Samai is closed on alternate Wednesdays.

★**Krua Apsorn** THAI $$
(Map p60; www.kruaapsorn.com; Th Din So; mains 80-400B; 10.30am-8pm Mon-Sat; ; klorng boat to Phanfa Leelard Pier) This homely dining room is a favourite of members of the Thai royal family and restaurant critics alike. Just about all of the central and southern Thai dishes are tasty, but regulars never miss the chance to order the decadent 'stir-fried crab with yellow chilli' or the *tortilla Española*–like 'omelette with crab'.

There's another branch on Th Samsen in **Thewet & Dusit** (Map p78; www.kruaapsorn.com; 503-505 Th Samsen; mains 80-400B; 10.30am-7.30pm Mon-Fri, to 6pm Sat; ; Thewet Pier).

★**Likhit Kai Yang** NORTHEASTERN THAI $$
(Map p60; off Th Ratchadamnoen Nok, no roman-script sign; mains 50-280B; 9am-9pm; ; Thewet Pier, S Phaya Thai exit 3 & taxi) Located just behind Ratchadamnoen Stadium (avoid the grotty branch directly adjacent to the stadium), this decades-old restaurant is where locals come for a northeastern-Thai-style meal before a Thai boxing match. The friendly English-speaking owner will steer you through the ordering process, but don't miss the deliciously herbal, eponymous 'charcoal roasted chicken'. The restaurant has no English-language sign; look for the huge yellow banner.

Err THAI $$
(Map p60; www.errbkk.com; off Th Maha Rat; dishes 65-360B; 11am-late Tue-Sun; ; Tien Pier) Think of all those different smoky, spicy, crispy, meaty bites you've encountered on the street. Now imagine them assembled in one funky, retro-themed locale, and coupled with tasty Thai-themed cocktails and domestic

> **DAY OFF**
>
> Fans of street food be forewarned that all of Bangkok's stalls close on Monday for compulsory street cleaning (the results of which are never entirely evident come Tuesday morning). If you happen to be in the city on this day, take advantage of the lull to visit one of the city's upscale hotel restaurants, which virtually never close.

Riverside

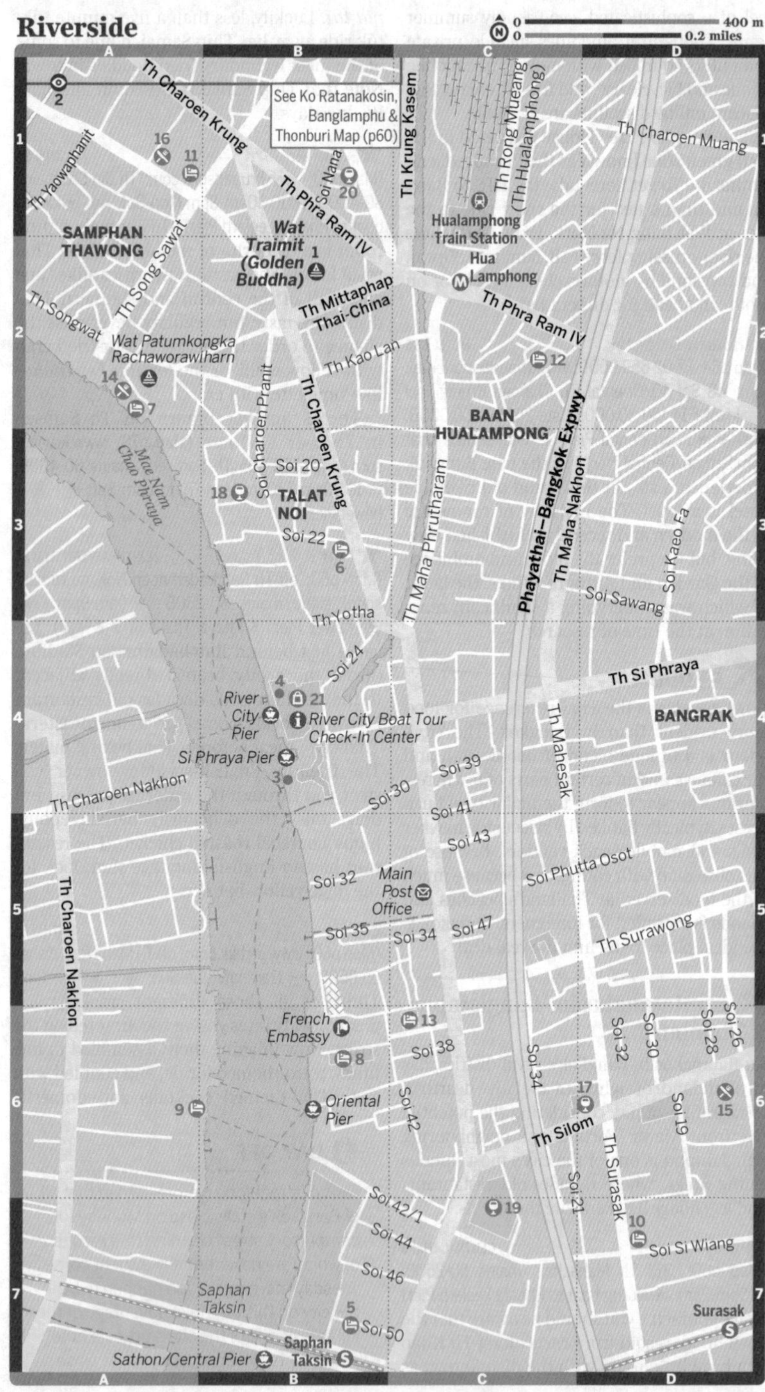
0 — 400 m
0 — 0.2 miles
See Ko Ratanakosin, Banglamphu & Thonburi Map (p60)
Th Charoen Krung
Th Yaowaphanit
SAMPHAN THAWONG
Th Song Sawat
Th Songwat
Wat Patumkongka Rachaworawiharn
Soi Nana
Th Phra Ram IV
Wat Traimit (Golden Buddha)
Th Mittaphap Thai-China
Th Krung Kasem
Th Rong Mueang (Th Hualamphong)
Hualamphong Train Station
Hua Lamphong
Th Charoen Muang
Th Phra Ram IV
Th Kao Lan
Soi Charoen Pranit
Mae Nam Chao Phraya
BAAN HUALAMPONG
Soi 20
TALAT NOI
Soi 22
Th Maha Phrutharam
Phayathai–Bangkok Expwy
Th Maha Nakhon
Soi Kaeo Fa
Soi Sawang
Th Yotha
Soi 24
Th Si Phraya
River City Pier
River City Boat Tour Check-In Center
BANGRAK
Si Phraya Pier
Th Charoen Nakhon
Soi 39
Soi 30
Soi 41
Th Mahesak
Soi 43
Soi 32
Main Post Office
Soi Phutta Osot
Soi 35
Soi 34
Soi 47
Th Surawong
Th Charoen Nakhon
French Embassy
Soi 38
Soi 32
Soi 30
Soi 28
Soi 26
Soi 34
Oriental Pier
Soi 42
Th Silom
Soi 19
Th Surasak
Soi 21
Soi 42/1
Soi 44
Soi Si Wiang
Soi 46
Saphan Taksin
Soi 50
Surasak
Sathon/Central Pier
Saphan Taksin
A B C D
1 2 3 4 5 6 7
1 2 3 4 5 6 7 8 9 10 11 12 13 14 15 16 17 18 19 20 21

Riverside

Top Sights
1 Wat Traimit (Golden Buddha).............B2

Sights
Phra Buddha Maha Suwanna Patimakorn Exhibition................(see 1)
2 Talat Mai A1
Yaowarat Chinatown Heritage Center..........................(see 1)

Activities, Courses & Tours
Co van Kessel Bangkok Tours .... (see 21)
3 Wan Fah B4
4 White Orchid...B4

Sleeping
5 Glur Bangkok...B7
6 Loftel 22 ....B3
7 Loy La Long A2
8 Mandarin Oriental...................................B6
9 Peninsula Hotel......................................A6
10 Saphaipae...D7
11 Shanghai Mansion A1
12 Siam Classic C2
13 Swan Hotel.. C6

Eating
14 Samsara...A2
15 Taling Pling D6
16 Thanon Phadungdao Seafood Stalls.. A1

Drinking & Nightlife
17 Maggie Choo's....................................... D6
18 River Vibe...B3
19 Sky Bar C7
20 Tep Bar... B1

Shopping
21 River City...B4

microbrews. If Err (a Thai colloquialism for agreement) seems too good to be true, we empathise, but insist that it's true.

Shoshana ISRAELI $$
(Map p60; 88 Th Chakraphatdi Phong; mains 70-240B; 10am-midnight; ; Phra Athit/Banglamphu Pier) One of Khao San's longest-running Israeli restaurants, Shoshana resembles your grandparents' living room right down to the tacky wall art and plastic placemats. Feel safe in ordering anything deep-fried – they do an excellent job of it – and don't miss the deliciously garlicky eggplant dip.

★ **Jay Fai** CENTRAL THAI $$$
(Map p60; 327 Th Mahachai; mains 180-1000B; 3pm-2am Mon-Sat; klorng boat to Phanfa Leelard Pier) You wouldn't think so by looking at her bare-bones dining room, but Jay Fai is known far and wide for serving Bangkok's most expensive *pàt kêe mow* ('drunkard's noodles'; wide rice noodles fried with seafood and Thai herbs).

Jay Fai is located in a virtually unmarked shophouse on Th Mahachai, directly across from a 7-Eleven.

Chinatown & Phahurat

When you mention Chinatown, most Bangkokians immediately dream of street food.

On the western side of the neighbourhood is Phahurat, Bangkok's Little India, filled with small Indian and Nepali restaurants tucked into the tiny soi off Th Chakkaraphet.

Samsara JAPANESE, THAI $$
(Map p84; Soi Khang Wat Pathum Khongkha; mains 110-320B; 4pm-midnight Tue-Thu, to 1am Fri-Sun; ; Ratchawong Pier, M Hua Lamphong exit 1 & taxi) Combining Japanese and Thai dishes, Belgian beers and an artfully ramshackle atmosphere, Samsara is easily Chinatown's most eclectic place to eat. It's also very tasty, and the generous riverside breezes and views simply add to the package.

The restaurant is at the end of tiny Soi Khang Wat Pathum Khongkha, just west of the temple of the same name.

Thanon Phadungdao Seafood Stalls THAI $$
(Map p84; cnr Th Phadungdao & Th Yaowarat; mains 100-600B; 4pm-midnight Tue-Sun; Ratchawong Pier, M Hua Lamphong exit 1 & taxi) After sunset, these two opposing open-air restaurants – each of which claims to be the original – become a culinary train wreck of outdoor barbecues, screaming staff, iced seafood trays and messy sidewalk seating. True, the vast majority of diners are foreign tourists, but this has little impact on the cheerful setting, the fun experience and the cheap bill.

Royal India INDIAN $$
(Map p60; 392/1 Th Chakkaraphet; mains 70-350B; 10am-10pm; ; Saphan Phut/Memorial Bridge Pier, Pak Klong Taladd Pier) Yes, we're aware that this hole-in-the-wall has been in every edition of our guide since the beginning, but after all these years it's still the most reliable place to eat in Bangkok's Little India. Try any of the delicious breads or rich curries, and don't forget to finish with a homemade Punjabi sweet.

Siam Square

If you find yourself hungry in this part of central Bangkok, you're largely at the mercy of shopping-mall food courts and chain restaurants. However, this is still Thailand, and if you can ignore the prefabricated atmosphere, the food can often be quite good.

Nuer Koo CHINESE-THAI $

(Map p74; 4th fl, Siam Paragon, 991/1 Th Phra Ram I; mains 85-970B; ⊙11.30am-9.15pm; ❄; S Siam exits 3 & 5) Is this the future of the noodle stall? Mall-bound Nuer Koo does a luxe version of the formerly humble bowl of beef noodles. Choose your cut of beef (including Kobe beef from Japan), enjoy the rich broth and cool air-con, and quickly forget about the good old days.

Kai Thort Jay Kee NORTHEASTERN THAI $$

(Polo Fried Chicken; Map p68; 137/1-3 Soi Sanam Khli/Polo; mains 50-350B; ⊙11am-9pm; ❄; M Lumphini exit 3) Although the *sôm·đam*, sticky rice and *lâhp* of this former street stall give the impression of a northeastern-Thai-style eatery, the restaurant's namesake deep-fried bird is more southern in origin. Regardless, smothered in a thick layer of crispy deep-fried garlic, it is none other than a truly Bangkok experience.

Din Tai Fung CHINESE $$

(Map p74; 7th fl, CentralWorld, Th Ratchadamri; dishes 65-315B; ⊙11am-10pm; ❄✍; S Chit Lom exit 9 to Sky Walk, Siam exit 6 to Sky Walk) Most come to this lauded Taiwanese chain for the *xiao long bao,* broth-filled 'soup' dumplings. And so should you. But the other northern-Chinese-style dishes are just as good, and justify exploring the more remote regions of the menu.

Silom & Sathon

Th Silom has a bit of everything, from old-school Thai to some of the city's best upscale international dining.

Soi 10 Food Centres THAI $

(Map p68; Soi 10, Th Silom; mains 20-60B; ⊙8am-3pm Mon-Fri; M Si Lom exit 2, S Sala Daeng exit 1) These two adjacent hangar-like buildings tucked behind Soi 10 are the main lunchtime fuelling stations for the area's office staff. Choices range from southern-style *kôw gaang* (point-and-choose curries ladled over rice) to just about every incarnation of Thai noodle.

Taling Pling THAI $$

(Map p84; Baan Silom, Soi 19, Th Silom; mains 110-275B; ⊙11am-10pm; ❄✍; S Surasak exit 3) Don't be fooled by the flashy interior; long-standing Taling Pling continues to serve a thick menu of homely, full-flavoured Thai dishes. It's a good starting point for rich, southern and central Thai fare such as *gaang kôo·a* (crabmeat curry with wild betel leaves), with tasty pies and cakes and refreshing drinks rounding out the choices.

★nahm THAI $$$

(Map p68; ☎02 625 3388; www.comohotels.com/metropolitanbangkok/dining/nahm; ground fl, Metropolitan Hotel, 27 Th Sathon Tai/South; set lunch/dinner 550-1500/2300B, dishes 280-750B; ⊙noon-2pm Mon-Fri, 7-10.30pm daily; ❄; M Lumphini exit 2) Australian chef-author David Thompson is the man behind one of Bangkok's – and if you believe the critics, the world's – best Thai restaurants. Using ancient cookbooks as his inspiration, Thompson has given life to previously extinct dishes with exotic descriptions such as 'smoked fish curry with prawns, chicken livers, cockles, chillies and black pepper'.

Dinner is best approached via the multi-course set meal, while lunch means *kà·nŏm jeen*, thin rice noodles served with curries.

If you're expecting bland, gentrified Thai food meant for foreigners, prepare to be disappointed. Reservations recommended.

★Eat Me INTERNATIONAL $$$

(Map p68; ☎02 238 0931; www.eatmerestaurant.com; Soi Phiphat 2; mains 275-1400B; ⊙3pm-1am; ❄✍; M Si Lom exit 2, S Sala Daeng exit 2) With descriptions like 'charred witlof and mozzarella salad with preserved lemon and dry aged Cecina beef', the dishes may sound all over the map or perhaps somewhat pretentious, but they're actually just plain tasty. A casual yet sophisticated atmosphere, excellent cocktails, a handsome wine list, and some of the city's best desserts also make this one of our favourite places in Bangkok to dine.

Sukhumvit

This seemingly endless ribbon of a road is where to go if, for the duration of a meal, you wish to forget that you're in Thailand.

Klang Soi Restaurant THAI $

(Map p70; Soi 49/9 Th Sukhumvit; mains 80-250B; ⊙11am-2.30pm & 5-10pm Tue-Sun; ❄; S Phrom Phong exit 3 & taxi) If you had a Thai grandma who lived in the Sukhumvit area, this is where she'd eat. The mimeographed menu spans old-school specialties from central and southern Thailand, as well as a few Western dishes.

Located at the end of Soi 49/9, in the Racquet Club complex.

★ Jidori-Ya Kenzou JAPANESE $$$

(Map p70; off Soi 26, Th Sukhumvit; dishes 60-350B; ⌚5pm-midnight Mon-Sat; ❄; Ⓢ Phrom Phong exit 4) This cosy Japanese restaurant does excellent tofu dishes, delicious salads, and even excellent desserts; basically everything here is above average, but the highlight is the smoky, perfectly seasoned chicken skewers.

Nasir Al-Masri MIDDLE EASTERN $$$

(Map p70; 4/6 Soi 3/1, Th Sukhumvit; mains 160-370B; ⌚24hr; ❄ ✍; Ⓢ Nana exit 1) One of several Middle Eastern restaurants on Soi 3/1, Nasir Al-Masri is easily recognisable by its floor-to-ceiling stainless steel 'theme'. Middle Eastern food often means meat, meat and more meat, but the menu here also includes several delicious vegie-based *mezze* (small dishes).

Bo.lan THAI $$$

(Map p70; ☎02 260 2962; www.bolan.co.th; 24 Soi 53, Th Sukhumvit; set meals 980-2680B; ⌚noon-2.30pm & 7-10.30pm Thu-Sun, 11.30am-10.30pm Tue & Wed; ❄ ✍; Ⓢ Thong Lo exit 1) Upscale Thai is often more garnish than flavour, but Bo.lan has proven to be the exception. Bo and Dylan (Bo.lan is a play on words that also means 'ancient') take a scholarly approach to Thai cuisine, and generous set meals featuring full-flavoured Thai dishes are the results of this tuition (à la carte is not available; meat-free meals are). Reservations recommended.

Soul Food Mahanakorn THAI $$$

(Map p70; ☎02 714 7708; www.soulfoodmahanakorn.com; 56/10 Soi 55/Thong Lor, Th Sukhumvit; mains 140-300B; ⌚5.30pm-midnight; ❄ ✍; Ⓢ Thong Lo exit 3) Soul Food gets its interminable buzz from its dual nature as both an inviting restaurant – the menu spans tasty interpretations of rustic Thai dishes – and a bar serving deliciously boozy, Thai-influenced cocktails. Reservations recommended.

Drinking & Nightlife

Bangkok's bar scene is notably legendary and, well, justifiably infamous. But if you ask us, it gets insufficient credit for its diversity. A drink in Bangkok can mean sweaty bottles of Singha at a roadside table or a cocktail crafted by a Swedish mixologist in a themed den, or just about anything in between. The official closing time for most bars is midnight.

Bangkok's nightclub scene is similarly diverse, yet fickle as a ripe mango, and that really fun disco you found on your last trip three years ago is most likely history today. To find out what is going on when you're in town, check listings rag *BK* (www.bk.asia-city.com) or the *Bangkok Post* Friday supplement, *Guru*. Don't even think about showing up before 11pm, and always bring ID. Most clubs close at 2am.

Ko Ratanakosin, Banglamphu & Thonburi

Romantic riverside drinking dominates the bar scene in Ko Ratanakosin, while rowdy Th Khao San is one of the city's best areas for a night out.

Hippie de Bar BAR

(Map p60; www.facebook.com/hippie.debar; 46 Th Khao San; ⌚3pm-2am; ⛴ Phra Athit/Banglamphu Pier) Our vote for Banglamphu's best bar, Hippie boasts a funky retro vibe and indoor and outdoor seating, all set to the type of indie/pop soundtrack that you're unlikely to hear elsewhere in town. Despite being located on Th Khao San, there are surprisingly few foreign faces, and it's a great place to make some new Thai friends.

Madame Musur BAR

(Map p60; 41 Soi Ram Buttri; ⌚8am-1am; ⛴ Phra Athit/Banglamphu Pier) Saving you the trip north to Pai, Madame Musur pulls off that elusive combination of 'northern Thailand meets *The Beach* meets Th Khao San'. It's a fun place to chat, drink and people-watch, and it's also not a bad place to eat, with a short menu of northern Thai dishes priced from 100B to 200B.

The Club CLUB

(Map p60; www.facebook.com/theclubkhaosanbkk; 123 Th Khao San; admission Fri & Sat 120B; ⌚9pm-2am; ⛴ Phra Athit/Banglamphu Pier) Located right in the middle of Th Khao San, this cavernlike dance hall hosts a good mix of locals and backpackers; check the Facebook page for upcoming events and guest DJs.

Chinatown & Phahurat

Other than a few new bars on Soi Nana, there's little in the realm of non-dodgy nightlife in Bangkok's Chinatown. Instead, fuel up on street eats here first, then head to nearby Banglamphu or Silom for drinks.

★Tep Bar BAR

(Map p84; www.facebook.com/TEPBAR; 69-71 Soi Nana; 5pm-midnight Tue-Sun; M Hua Lamphong exit 1) We never expected to find a bar this sophisticated – yet this fun – in Chinatown. Tep does it with a Thai-tinged, contemporary interior, tasty signature cocktails, Thai drinking snacks, and raucous live Thai music performances Friday to Sunday.

Silom & Sathon

Lower Silom is Bangkok's gaybourhood, but the area as a whole has several fun bars and dance clubs for all comers.

Smalls BAR

(Map p68; 186/3 Soi Suan Phlu; 8.30pm-late; M Lumphini exit 2 & taxi) The kind of new bar that feels like it's been here forever, Smalls combines a cheekily decadent interior, an inviting rooftop and live music on Thursdays and Fridays. The eclectic house cocktails are strong, if sweet, and bar snacks range from rillettes to quesadillas.

Namsaah Bottling Trust BAR

(Map p68; www.namsaah.com; 401 Soi 7, Th Silom; 5pm-2am; M Si Lom exit 2, S Sala Daeng exit 2) Namsaah is all about twists. From its home (a former mansion incongruously painted hot pink and with in a dark, clubby vibe), to the cocktails (classics with a tweak or two) and the bar snacks and dishes (think *pàt tai* with foie gras), everything's a little bit off in just the right way.

Tapas Room CLUB

(Map p68; 114/17-18 Soi 4, Th Silom; admission 100B; 7pm-2am; M Si Lom exit 2, S Sala Daeng exit 1) Although it sits staunchly at the front of Bangkok's pinkest street, this long-standing two-level disco manages to bring in just about everybody. Come from Thursday to Saturday, when the combination of DJs and live percussion brings the body count to critical level.

Maggie Choo's BAR

(Map p84; www.facebook.com/maggiechoos; basement, Novotel Bangkok Fenix Silom, 320 Th Silom; 7.30pm-2am Sun-Thu, to 3am Fri & Sat; S Surasak exit 1) A former bank vault with a Chinatown-opium-den vibe, secret passageways and lounging women in silk dresses. With all this going on, it's easy to forget that Maggie Choo's is actually a bar, although you'll be reminded by the creative and somewhat sweet cocktails, and a crowd that blends selfie-snapping locals and curious tourists.

Sukhumvit

This long street is home to Bangkok's most sophisticated bars and clubs.

★WTF BAR

(Map p70; www.wtfbangkok.com; 7 Soi 51, Th Sukhumvit; 6pm-1am Tue-Sun; ; S Thong Lo exit 3) Wonderful Thai Friendship (what did you think it stood for?) is a funky and friendly neighbourhood bar that also packs in a gallery space. Arty locals and resident foreigners come for the old-school cocktails, live music and DJ events, poetry readings, art exhibitions and tasty bar snacks. And we, like them, give WTF our vote for Bangkok's best bar.

Tuba BAR

(Map p70; www.facebook.com/tubabkk; 34 Room 11-12 A, Soi Thong Lor 20/Soi Ekamai 21; 11am-2am; S Ekkamai exit 1 & taxi) Part storage room for over-the-top vintage furniture, part restaurant, part friendly local boozer; this quirky bar certainly doesn't lack in diversity – nor fun. Indulge in a whole bottle (they'll keep it for you if you don't finish it) and don't miss the moreish chicken wings or the delicious deep-fried *lâhp* (a tart/spicy salad of minced meat).

Badmotel BAR

(Map p70; www.facebook.com/badmotel; 331/4-5 Soi 55/Thong Lor, Th Sukhumvit; 5pm-1am; S Thong Lo exit 3 & taxi) Badmotel blends the modern and the kitschy, the cosmopolitan and the Thai, in a way that has struck a nerve among Bangkok hipsters. This is manifested in drinks that combine rum with Hale's Blue Boy, a Thai childhood drink staple, and bar snacks such as *naam prìk ong* (a northern Thai-style dip), here served with pappadams.

Studio Lam BAR

(Map p70; www.facebook.com/studiolambangkok; Soi 51, Th Sukhumvit; 6pm-1am Tue-Sun; S Thong Lo exit 3) This new venue is an extension of uberhip record label ZudRangMa, with a Jamaican-style sound system custom-built for world and retro-Thai DJ sets and the occasional live show. Thai-influenced signature drinks bring Studio Lam to the present day.

Grease CLUB

(Map p70; www.greasebangkok.com; 46/12 Soi 49, Th Sukhumvit; 6pm-2am Mon-Sat; S Phrom Phong exit 3 & taxi) Bangkok's youngest-feeling, hottest nightclub is also one of its biggest – you could get lost here in the four floors of dining venues, lounges and dance floors.

LGBT BANGKOK

Bangkok is so gay it makes San Francisco look like rural Texas. With out-and-open nightspots and annual pride events, the city's homosexual community enjoys an unprecedented amount of tolerance considering attitudes in the rest of the region. It should be mentioned, however, that recent years have seen a sharp rise in HIV and other STDs among gay men in Bangkok; when in town, be sure to play it safe.

Local listings mags such as *BK* (www.bk.asia-city.com) can point you in the direction of the bars and clubs that are hot when you're in town. The Lesbian Guide to Bangkok (www.bangkoklesbian.com) is the only English-language tracker of the lesbian scene.

Lower Th Silom is Bangkok's unofficial gaybourhood, and highlights include tiny Soi 2, which is lined with dance clubs such as **DJ Station** (Map p68; www.dj-station.com; 8/6-8 Soi 2, Th Silom; admission from 150B; 10pm-2am; M Si Lom exit 2, S Sala Daeng exit 1), the busiest and arguably most famous gay nightclub in Thailand, if not Asia. Virtually next door is Soi 2/1, where bars like **G.O.D** (Guys on Display; Soi 2/1, Th Silom; admission 300B; 11pm-late; M Si Lom exit 2, S Sala Daeng exit 1) are not averse to a little shirtless dancing. A more casual scene is found on Soi 4, home to longstanding street-side bars **Balcony** (Map p68; www.balconypub.com; 86-88 Soi 4, Th Silom; 5.30pm-2am; ; M Si Lom exit 2, S Sala Daeng exit 1) and **Telephone Pub** (Map p68; www.telephonepub.com; 114/11-13 Soi 4, Th Silom; 6pm-1am; ; M Si Lom exit 2, S Sala Daeng exit 1).

Arena 10 CLUB
(Map p70; Soi Thong Lor 10/Soi Ekamai 5; S Ekkamai exit 2 & taxi) This open-air entertainment zone is the destination of choice for Bangkok's young and beautiful – for the moment at least. **Demo** (Map p70; www.facebook.com/demobangkok; Arena 10, Soi Thong Lor 10/Soi Ekamai 5; 9pm-2am; S Ekkamai exit 2 & taxi) combines blasting beats and a NYC warehouse vibe, while **Funky Villa** (Map p70; www.facebook.com/funkyvillabkk; Arena 10, Soi Thong Lor 10/Soi Ekamai 5; 7pm-2am; S Ekkamai exit 2 & taxi), with its outdoor seating and Top 40 soundtrack, is more chilled.

There's a 400B entrance fee for foreigners on Friday and Saturday.

☆ Entertainment

Shame on you if you find yourself bored in Bangkok. And even more shame if you think the only entertainment options involve the word 'go-go'. Nowadays Bangkok's nightlife is as diverse as that of virtually any modern city.

Gà·teu·i Cabaret

Over the last few years, *gà·teu·i* (transgender women; also spelt *kathoey*) cabaret has emerged to become a staple of the Bangkok tourist circuit. **Calypso Bangkok** (Map p78; 02 688 1415; www.calypsocabaret.com; Asiatique, Soi 72-76, Th Charoen Krung; adult/child 900/600B; show times 8.15pm & 9.45pm; shuttle ferry from Sathon/Central Pier), **Mambo Cabaret** (Map p78; 02 294 7381; 59/28 Yannawa Tat Mai; tickets 800-1000B; show times 7.15pm & 8.30pm; S Chong Nonsi exit 2 & taxi) and **Playhouse Theater Cabaret** (Map p74; 02 215 0571; www.playhousethailand.com; 5 Ratchadapisek Rd, Chompol Sub-District, Chatuchak; adult/child 1200/600B; show times 7pm & 8.20pm; S Ratchathewi exit 1) host choreographed stage shows featuring Broadway high kicks and lip-synched pop tunes.

Go-Go Bars

Although technically illegal, prostitution is fully 'out' in Bangkok, and the influence of organised crime and healthy kickbacks mean that it will be a long while before the existing laws are ever enforced. Yet, despite the image presented by much of the Western media, the underlying atmosphere of Bangkok's red-light districts is not necessarily one of illicitness and exploitation (although these do inevitably exist), but rather an aura of tackiness and boredom.

Patpong (Map p68; Th Phat Phong & Soi Phat Phong 2; 4pm-2am; M Si Lom exit 2, S Sala Daeng exit 1), arguably one of the world's most infamous red-light districts, earned its notoriety during the 1980s for its wild sex shows involving everything from ping-pong balls to razors to midgets on motorbikes. Today it is more of a circus for curious spectators than sexual deviants. These days, **Soi Cowboy** (Map p70; Soi Cowboy; 4pm-2am; M Sukhumvit exit 2, S Asok exit 3) and **Nana Entertainment Plaza** (Map p70; Soi 4, Th Sukhumvit; 4pm-2am; S Nana exit 2) are the real scenes of sex for hire.

Live Music

Music is an essential element of a Thai night out, and just about every pub has a house band. For the most part this means perky Thai pop covers or tired international standards (if you've left town without having heard a live version of *Hotel California*, you haven't really been to Bangkok), but an increasing number of places are starting to deviate from the norm with quirky bands and performances.

★Brick Bar LIVE MUSIC
(Map p60; www.brickbarkhaosan.com; basement, Buddy Lodge, 265 Th Khao San; admission Sat & Sun 150B; ⏲8pm-1.30am; ⛴Phra Athit/Banglamphu Pier) This basement pub, one of our fave destinations in Bangkok for live music, hosts a nightly revolving cast of bands for an almost exclusively Thai crowd – many of whom will end the night dancing on the tables. Brick Bar can get infamously packed, so be sure to get there early.

Living Room LIVE MUSIC
(Map p70; ☎02 649 8888; www.thelivingroomatbangkok.com/en; Level 1, Sheraton Grande Sukhumvit, 250 Th Sukhumvit; ⏲6pm-midnight; Ⓜ Sukhumvit exit 3, Ⓢ Asok exit 2) Don't let looks deceive you: every night this bland hotel lounge transforms into the city's best venue for live jazz. True to the name, there's comfy, sofa-based seating, all of it within earshot of the music. Enquire ahead of time to see which sax master or hide-hitter is in town.

Tawandang German Brewery LIVE MUSIC
(Map p78; www.tawandang.co.th; cnr Th Phra Ram III & Th Narathiwat Ratchanakharin/Th Chong Nonsi; ⏲5pm-1am; Ⓢ Chong Nonsi exit 2 & taxi) It's Oktoberfest all year round at this hangar-sized music hall. The Thai-German food is tasty, the house-made brews are entirely potable, and the nightly stage shows make singing along a necessity. Music starts at 8.30pm.

Titanium LIVE MUSIC
(Map p70; www.titaniumbangkok.com; 2/30 Soi 22, Th Sukhumvit; ⏲8pm-1am; Ⓢ Phrom Phong exit 6) Many come to this cheesy 'ice bar' for the chill, the skimpily dressed working girls and the flavoured vodka, but we come for Unicorn, the all-female house band, who rock the house every night from 9.30pm to 12.30am.

Thai Boxing (Moo·ay tai)

Thai boxing's best of the best fight it out at Bangkok's two boxing venues: **Lumpinee Boxing Stadium** (☎02 282 3141; www.muaythailumpinee.net/en; 6 Th Ramintra; tickets 3rd-class/2nd-class/ringside 1000/1500/2000B; Ⓜ Chatuchak Park exit 2 & taxi, Ⓢ Mo Chit exit 3 & taxi) and **Ratchadamnoen Stadium** (Map p60; off Th Ratchadamnoen Nok; tickets 3rd-class/2nd-class/ringside 1000/1500/2000B; ⛴Thewet Pier, Ⓢ Phaya Thai exit 3 & taxi). You'll note that tickets are not cheap, and these prices are exponentially more than what Thais pay. To add insult to injury, the inflated price offers no special service or seating, and at Ratchadamnoen Stadium foreigners are sometimes corralled into an area with an obstructed view. As long as you are mentally prepared for the financial jabs from the promoters, you'll be better prepared to enjoy the real fight.

Fights are held throughout the week, alternating between the two stadiums. Ratchadamnoen, Bangkok's oldest and most venerable venue, hosts matches on Monday, Wednesday and Thursday from 6.30pm to around 11pm, and Sunday at 3pm and 6.30pm. Lumpinee, in a new building far north of the city centre, hosts matches on Tuesdays and Fridays from 6.30pm to 11pm, and on Saturdays from 4pm to 8.30pm and 9pm to 12.30am. There is a total of eight to 10 fights of five rounds apiece. The stadiums don't usually fill up until the main events, which normally start around 8pm or 9pm.

Traditional Arts

National Theatre THEATRE
(Map p60; ☎02 224 1342; 2 Th Ratchini; tickets 60-100B; ⛴Chang Pier, Maharaj Pier, Phra Chan Tai Pier) The National Theatre holds performances of *kŏhn* (masked dance-drama based on stories from the *Ramakian*) at 2pm on the first and second Sundays of the month from January to September, and *lá·kon* (Thai dance-dramas) at 2pm on the first and second Sundays of the month from October to December. Tickets go on sale an hour before performances begin.

Sala Chalermkrung THEATRE
(Map p60; ☎02 222 0434; www.salachalermkrung.com; 66 Th Charoen Krung; tickets 800-1200B; ⏲shows 7.30pm Thu & Fri; ⛴Saphan Phut/Memorial Bridge Pier, Ⓜ Hua Lamphong exit 1 & taxi) This Art Deco Bangkok landmark, a former cinema dating to 1933, is one of the few remaining places *kŏhn* can be witnessed. The traditional Thai dance-drama is enhanced here by laser graphics, high-tech audio and English subtitles. Concerts and other events are also held; check the website for details.

DON'T MISS

BANGKOK'S BEST ROOFTOP BARS

In previous years, Bangkok's rooftop bars were largely the realm of well-heeled tourists, but nowadays they comprise a diverse spread, with options ranging from basic to formal. Yet it's worth noting that nearly all of Bangkok's hotel-based rooftop bars have strictly enforced dress codes barring access to those wearing shorts and/or sandals.

➡ **Moon Bar** (Map p68; www.banyantree.com/en/web/banyantree/ap-thailand-bangkok/vertigo-and-moon-bar; 61st fl, Banyan Tree Hotel, 21/100 Th Sathon Tai/South; 5pm-1am; M Lumphini exit 2) An alarmingly short barrier at this rooftop bar is all that separates one from the street, 61 floors down. Located on top of the Banyan Tree Hotel, Moon Bar claims to be among the highest al fresco bars in the world.

➡ **River Vibe** (Map p84; 8th fl, River View Guesthouse, off Soi Charoen Phanit; 7.30-11pm; Marine Department Pier, M Hua Lamphong exit 1 & taxi) Can't afford the overpriced cocktails at Bangkok's upscale rooftop bars? The excellent river views from the top of this guesthouse will hardly feel like a compromise.

➡ **Cloud 47** (Map p68; https://www.facebook.com/thecloud47; 47th fl, United Center, 323 Th Silom ; 5pm-1am; M Si Lom exit 2, S Sala Daeng exit 2) If you like a bit of elbow room in your bar/restaurants – say, enough to hold a cricket match – consider this rooftopper. Spread out and enjoy live music and a location in the middle of the city's financial district, where there are impressively tall buildings in just about every direction.

➡ **Sky Bar** (Map p84; www.lebua.com/sky-bar; 63rd fl, State Tower, 1055 Th Silom; 6pm-1am; Sathon/Central Pier, S Saphan Taksin exit 3) Descend the Hollywood-like staircase to emerge at this bar that juts out over the Bangkok skyline and Mae Nam Chao Phraya. Scenes from *The Hangover Part II* were filmed here, and while it doesn't come cheap, the bar's 'hangovertini' cocktail is actually quite drinkable.

➡ **Roof** (Map p60; www.salaresorts.com/rattanakosin; 5th fl, Sala Rattanakosin, 39 Th Maha Rat; 5pm-midnight Mon-Thu, to 1am Fri-Sun; Tien Pier) Although not as lofty as the others, the riverside Roof has upped the stakes for sunset views of Wat Arun – if you can see the temple at all through the wall of selfie-snapping tourists. Be sure to get there early for a good seat.

Shopping

Welcome to a true buyer's market. Home to one of the world's largest outdoor markets, numerous giant upscale malls, and sidewalk-clogging bazaars on nearly every street, it's impossible not to be awed by the amount of commerce in Bangkok. However, despite the apparent scope and variety, Bangkok really excels in one area when it comes to shopping: cheap stuff. Although luxury items and brand names are available in Bangkok, prices are high, and you'll find much better deals at online warehouses in the US or bargain-basement sales in Hong Kong. Ceramics, dirt-cheap T-shirts, fabric, Asian knick-knackery and, yes, if you can deal with the guilt, pirated items, are Bangkok's bargains.

Shopping Centres

Bangkok may be crowded and polluted, but its malls are modern oases of order. They're also downright frigid, and Sunday afternoons see a significant part of Bangkok's population crowding indoors to escape the heat.

★ MBK Center SHOPPING CENTRE
(Map p74; www.mbk-center.com; cnr Th Phra Ram I & Th Phayathai; 10am-10pm; S National Stadium exit 4) This colossal shopping mall underwent an extensive renovation in 2015 and is set to retain its role as one of Bangkok's top attractions. On any given weekend half of Bangkok's residents (and most of its tourists) can be found here combing through a seemingly inexhaustible range of small stalls and shops that span a whopping eight floors.

MBK is Bangkok's cheapest place to buy mobile phones and accessories (4th floor). It's also one of the better places to stock up on camera gear (ground floor and 5th floor), and the expansive food court (6th floor) is one of the best in town.

★ Siam Square SHOPPING CENTRE
(Map p74; Th Phra Ram I; 11am-9pm; S Siam exits 2, 4 & 6) This open-air shopping zone is

ground zero for teenage culture in Bangkok. Pop music blares out of tinny speakers, and gangs of hipsters in various costumes ricochet between fast-food restaurants and closet-sized boutiques. It's a great place to pick up labels and designs you're guaranteed not to find anywhere else, though most outfits require a barely there waistline.

River City ANTIQUES

(Map p84; www.rivercity.co.th; 23 Th Yotha; ⏲10am-10pm; Si Phraya/River City Pier, or shuttle boat from Sathon/Central Pier) Several upscale art and antique shops occupy the 3rd and 4th floors of this riverside mall, but, as with many antique stores in Bangkok, the vast majority of pieces appear to come from Myanmar and, to a lesser extent, Cambodia.

A free shuttle boat to River City departs from Sathon/Central Pier every 30 minutes from 10am to 8pm.

Siam Paragon SHOPPING CENTRE

(Map p74; www.siamparagon.co.th; 991/1 Th Phra Ram I; ⏲10am-10pm; S Siam exits 3 & 5) As much air-conditioned urban park as it is a shopping centre, Siam Paragon is home to **Siam Ocean World** (สยามโอเชี่ยนเวิร์ล; Map p74; www.siamoceanworld.com; basement, Siam Paragon, 991/1 Th Phra Ram I; adult/child from 990/790B; ⏲10am-9pm; S Siam exits 3 & 5), **Paragon Cineplex** (Map p74; ☎02 129 4635; www.paragoncineplex.com; 5th fl, Siam Paragon, 991/1 Th Phra Ram I; S Siam exits 3 & 5) and Gourmet Paradise (p88), a huge basement-level food court. Then there are the shops; on the 3rd floor is Kinokuniya, Thailand's largest English-language bookstore.

ONE NIGHT IN BANGKOK… IS NOT ENOUGH TO HAVE A SUIT MADE

Many tourists arrive in Bangkok with the notion of getting clothes custom-tailored at a bargain price, which is entirely possible. Prices are almost always lower than what you'd pay at home, but common scams ranging from commission-hungry túk-túk (pronounced *đúk đúk*) drivers to shoddy workmanship and inferior fabrics make bespoke tailoring in Bangkok a potentially disappointing investment. To maximise your chances of walking away feeling (and looking) good, read on…

➡ **You get what you pay for** If you sign up for a suit, two pants, two shirts and a tie, with a silk sarong thrown in for US$169 (a very popular offer in Bangkok), the chances are it will look and fit like a sub-US$200 wardrobe.

➡ **Have a good idea of what you want** If it's a suit you're after, should it be single- or double-breasted? How many buttons? What style trousers? Of course, if you have no idea then the tailor will be more than happy to advise.

➡ **Set aside a week to get clothes tailored** Shirts and trousers can often be turned around in 48 hours or less with only one fitting, but no matter what a tailor may tell you, it takes more than one and often more than two fittings to create a good suit. Any tailor who can sew your order in less than 24 hours should be treated with caution.

Reputable tailors include the following:

➡ **Pinky Tailors** (Map p74; www.pinkytailor.com; 888/40 Mahatun Plaza, Th Phloen Chit; ⏲10am-7pm Mon-Sat; S Phloen Chit exits 2 & 4) Custom-made shirts and suit jackets have been Mr Pinky's speciality for more than three decades. Located behind the Mahatun Building.

➡ **July** (Map p68; ☎02 233 0171; www.julytailor.com; 30/6 Th Sala Daeng; ⏲9am-6pm Mon-Sat; M Si Lom exit 2, S Sala Daeng exit 4) Tailor to Thailand's royalty and elite alike. The suits here don't come cheap and the cuts can be somewhat conservative, but the quality is unsurpassed.

➡ **Raja's Fashions** (Map p70; ☎02 253 8379; www.rajasfashions.com; 160/1 Th Sukhumvit; ⏲10.30am-8pm Mon-Sat; S Nana exit 4) One of Bangkok's more famous tailors, Raja's gets a mixed bag of reviews, but the majority swear by the service and quality.

➡ **Nickermann's** (Map p70; ☎02 252 6682; www.nickermanns.net; basement, Landmark Hotel, 138 Th Sukhumvit; ⏲10am-8.30pm Mon-Sat, noon-6pm Sun; S Nana exit 2) Corporate ladies rave about Nickermann's tailor-made power suits: pants and jackets that suit curves and busts. Formal ball gowns are another area of expertise.

Markets

Although air-conditioned malls have better PR departments, open-air markets are the true face of commercial Bangkok, and are where you'll find the best bargains.

Chatuchak Weekend Market MARKET
(ตลาดนัดจตุจักร, Talat Nat Jatujak; Map p78; www.chatuchak.org; Th Phahonyothin; ⌚9am-6pm Sat & Sun; Ⓜ Chatuchak Park exit 1, Kamphaeng Phet exits 1 & 2, Ⓢ Mo Chit exit 1) Among the largest markets in the world, Chatuchak seems to unite everything buyable, from used vintage sneakers to baby squirrels. Plan to spend a full day here, as there's plenty to see, do and buy. But come early, ideally around 10am, to beat the crowds and the heat.

★ **Thanon Khao San Market** SOUVENIRS
(Map p60; Th Khao San; ⌚10am-midnight; ⛴ Phra Athit/Banglamphu Pier) The main guesthouse strip in Banglamphu is a day-and-night bazaar peddling all the backpacker 'essentials': foul-mouthed T-shirts, bootleg MP3s, hemp clothing, fake student ID cards, knock-off designer wear, selfie sticks, orange juice and, of course, those croaking wooden frogs.

Talat Rot Fai MARKET
(ตลาดรถไฟ; www.facebook.com/taradrodfi; Soi 51, Th Srinakharin; ⌚6pm-1am Thu-Sun; Ⓢ Udom Suk exit 2 & taxi) The emphasis at this night market is on the retro, from vintage clothes to kitschy antiques. And with stalls and food trucks, VW-van-based bars and land-bound pubs, and even a few hipster barber shops, it's also much more than just a shopping destination.

If this isn't enough vintage for you, consider the recently opened and slightly smaller (yet more convenient to reach) Talat Rot Fai 2, on Th Ratchadaphisek. To get here, take the MRT to Thailand Cultural Centre and walk through the Esplanade mall.

Asiatique MARKET
(Map p78; www.thaiasiatique.com; Soi 72-76, Th Charoen Krung; ⌚4-11pm; ⛴ shuttle boat from Sathon/Central Pier) One of Bangkok's more popular night markets, Asiatique takes the form of warehouses of commerce next to Mae Nam Chao Phraya. Expect clothing, handicrafts, souvenirs and quite a few dining and drinking venues.

To get here, take one of the frequent, free shuttle boats from Sathon/Central Pier that run from 4pm to 11.30pm.

Baiyoke Garment Center CLOTHING
(Map p74; cnr Th Phetchaburi & Th Ratchaprarop; ⌚10am-10pm; ⛴ klorng boat to Pratunam Pier, Ⓢ Ratchathewi exit 4) This rabbit warren of stalls is the undisputed epicentre of Bangkok's garment district. The vendors spill from the covered market area to dozens of nearby shops selling similarly cheap T-shirts, bags and other no-brand clothing items.

Scuba-Diving Supplies

Most of Bangkok's dive shops are located around Th Sukhumvit.

Dive Indeed SCUBA-DIVING SUPPLIES
(Map p70; ☎02 2665 7471; www.diveindeed.com; 14/2 Soi 21 (Asoke), Th Sukhumvit; ⌚11am-7pm Mon-Sat; Ⓜ Sukhumvit exit 2, Ⓢ Asok exit 3)

Dive Supply SCUBA-DIVING SUPPLIES
(Map p78; ☎02 2354 4815; www.divesupply.com; 457/4 Th Si Ayuthaya; ⌚11am-7.30pm Tue-Sat; Ⓢ Phaya Thai exit 4)

Planet Scuba SCUBA-DIVING SUPPLIES
(Map p70; ☎02 2261 4412; www.planetscuba.net; 666 Th Sukhumvit; ⌚10am-8pm Mon Sat, 11am-6pm Sun; Ⓢ Phrom Phong exit 4)

ℹ Information

EMERGENCY

If you have a medical emergency and need an ambulance, contact the hospitals listed below. In case of a police or safety issue, contact emergency services.

Police (☎191) The police contact number functions as the de facto universal emergency number in Thailand, and can also be used to call an ambulance or report a fire.

Tourist Police (☎24hr hotline 1155) The best way to deal with most problems requiring police (usually a rip-off or theft) is to contact the tourist police, who are used to dealing with foreigners and can be very helpful in cases of arrest.

INTERNET & TELEPHONE ACCESS

The ubiquity of smartphones has meant that internet cafes are an almost extinct species in Bangkok, although you can still find a couple in touristy areas such as Th Khao San.

Wi-fi, provided mostly free of charge, is ubiquitous around Bangkok, especially in mall-based cafes and restaurants.

TrueMove (Map p74; www.truemove.com; Soi 2, Siam Sq; ⌚7am-10pm; Ⓢ Siam exit 4) A convenient place to take care of your communication needs in the centre of Bangkok, this multifloor centre has high-speed internet computers equipped with Skype, sells phones and mobile subscriptions, and can also provide information on city-wide wi-fi for computers and phones.

MEDIA

Daily newspapers are available at streetside newsagents. Monthly magazines are available in most bookstores.

Bangkok 101 (www.bangkok101.com) A tourist-friendly listings magazine.

Bangkok Post (www.bangkokpost.com) Bangkok's leading English-language newspaper.

BK (www.bk.asia-city.com) Online version of Bangkok's best listings magazine.

Nation (www.nationmultimedia.com) English-language daily with a heavy focus on business.

MEDICAL SERVICES

Thanks to its high standard of hospital care, Bangkok is fast becoming a destination for medical tourists shopping for more affordable dental check-ups, elective surgery and cosmetic procedures. Pharmacists (chemists) throughout the city can diagnose and treat most minor ailments (Bangkok belly, sinus and skin infections etc).

The following hospitals offer 24-hour emergency services, and the numbers given should be contacted if you need an ambulance or immediate medical attention.

BNH (Map p68; ☎02 686 2700; www.bnhhospital.com; 9 Th Convent; Ⓜ Si Lom exit 2, Ⓢ Sala Daeng exit 2) Modern, centrally located hospital.

Bumrungrad International Hospital (Map p70; ☎02 667 1000; www.bumrungrad.com/thailandhospital; 33 Soi 3, Th Sukhumvit; Ⓢ Phloen Chit exit 3) An internationally accredited hospital.

Samitivej Hospital (Map p70; ☎02 022 2222; www.samitivejhospitals.com; 133 Soi 49, Th Sukhumvit; Ⓢ Phrom Phong exit 3 & taxi) Modern hospital in Bangkok.

MONEY

Regular bank hours in Bangkok are generally 8.30am to 3.30pm, although branches in busy areas and shopping malls are open later. ATMs are common in all areas of the city. Many Thai banks also have currency-exchange bureaus; there are also exchange desks within eyeshot of most tourist areas. Go to 7-Eleven shops or other reputable places to break 1000B bills; don't expect a vendor or taxi to be able to change a bill 500B or larger.

POST

Main Post Office (Map p84; ☎02 233 1050; Th Charoen Krung; ⏲8am-8pm Mon-Fri, to 1pm Sat & Sun; ⛴ Oriental Pier) Bangkok's main post office.

TOILETS

Public toilets in Bangkok are few and far between and your best bet is to head for a shopping centre, fast-food restaurant or, our favourite, a luxury hotel (just waltz in as if you're staying there). Shopping centres might charge 2B to 5B for a visit; some newer shopping centres have toilets for the disabled. Despite what you'll hear, squat toilets are a dying breed in Bangkok.

TOURIST INFORMATION

Official tourist offices distribute maps, brochures and advice on sights and activities. Some private travel agencies incorporate elements of the official national tourism organisation name (Tourism Authority of Thailand; TAT) into their own name to mislead tourists.

Bangkok Information Center (Map p60; ☎02 225 7612-4; www.bangkoktourist.com; 17/1 Th Phra Athit; ⏲9am-7pm Mon-Fri, to 5pm Sat & Sun; ⛴ Phra Athit/Banglamphu Pier) City-specific tourism office providing maps, brochures and directions. Kiosks and booths are found around town; look for the green-on-white symbol of a mahout on an elephant.

Tourism Authority of Thailand (TAT; ☎call centre 1672; www.tourismthailand.org) Head office (TAT; Map p78; ☎02 250 5500; 1600 Th Phetchaburi Tat Mai; ⏲8.30am-4.30pm; Ⓜ Phetchaburi exit 2); Banglamphu (TAT; Map p60; ☎02 283 1500; cnr Th Ratchadamnoen Nok & Th Chakraphatdi Phong; ⏲8.30am-4.30pm; ⛴ klorng boat Phanfa Leelard Pier); Suvarnabhumi International Airport (TAT; ☎02 134 0040; 2nd fl, btwn Gates 2 & 5, Suvarnabhumi International Airport; ⏲24hr).

Getting There & Away

Bangkok is Thailand's undisputed transportation hub. A huge and growing number of domestic air routes, convenient and modern buses, and a reliable and comprehensive train network mean that getting to just about any of the country's beachy destinations is a snap.

AIR

Bangkok has two airports. **Suvarnabhumi International Airport** (p422), 30km east of central Bangkok, began commercial international and domestic service in 2006. The airport's name is pronounced *sù·wan·ná·poom*, and it inherited the airport code (BKK) previously used by the old airport at Don Mueang. The airport website has real-time details of arrivals and departures.

Bangkok's former international and domestic **Don Mueang International Airport** (p422), 25km north of central Bangkok, was retired from commercial service in September 2006, only to reopen later as Bangkok's de-facto budget hub.

The following airlines operate domestic routes to Thailand's islands and beaches:

Air Asia (☎02 515 9999; www.airasia.com) Don Mueang to Hat Yai, Krabi, Nakhon Si Thammarat, Narathiwat, Phuket, Surat Thani and Trang.

COMMON BANGKOK SCAMS

Commit these classic rip-offs to memory and join us in our ongoing crusade to outsmart Bangkok's crafty scam artists.

➡ **Closed today** Ignore any 'friendly' local who tells you an attraction is closed for a Buddhist holiday or for cleaning. These are set-ups for trips to a bogus gem sale.

➡ **Túk-túk rides for 10B** Say goodbye to your day's itinerary if you climb aboard this ubiquitous scam. These alleged 'tours' bypass all the sights and instead cruise to all the fly-by-night gem and tailor shops that pay commissions.

➡ **Flat-fare taxi ride** Flatly refuse any driver who quotes a flat fare (usually between 100B and 150B for in-town destinations), which will usually be three times more expensive than the reasonable meter rate. Walking beyond the tourist area will usually help in finding an honest driver.

➡ **Tourist buses to the south** On the long journey south, well-organised and connected thieves have hours to comb through your bags, breaking into (and later resealing) locked bags, searching through hiding places and stealing credit cards, electronics and even toiletries. This scam has been running for years but is easy to avoid simply by carrying valuables with you on the bus.

➡ **Friendly strangers** Be wary of smartly dressed men who approach you asking where you're from and where you're going. Their opening gambit is usually followed with: 'Ah, my son/daughter is studying at university in (your city)' – they seem to have an encyclopaedic knowledge of major universities. As the tourist authorities here pointed out, this sort of behaviour is out of character for Thais and should be treated with suspicion.

Bangkok Airways (☎1771; www.bangkokairways.com) Suvarnabhumi to Krabi, Pattaya, Phuket, Ko Samui and Trat.

Happy Air (☎02 216 5151; www.happyair.co.th) Suvarnabhumi to Chumphon and Ranong.

Kan Air (☎02 551 6111; www.kanairlines.com) Don Mueang to Hua Hin.

Nok Air (☎1318; www.nokair.com) Don Mueang to Chumphon, Hat Yai, Krabi, Nakhon Si Thammarat, Phuket, Ranong, Surat Thani and Trang.

Orient Thai (☎02 229 4100; www.flyorient-thai.com/en/home) Don Muang to Phuket.

Solar Air (☎02 535 2456; www.solarair.co.th) Don Muang to Chumphon.

Thai Lion Air (☎02 529 9999; www.lionairthai.com) Don Mueang to Hat Yai, Krabi, Nakhon Si Thammarat, Phuket and Surat Thani.

Thai Smile (☎02 118 8888; www.thaismileair.com) Don Mueang to Phuket; Suvarnabhumi to Hat Yai, Phuket, Narathiwat and Surat Thani.

BUS

Bangkok has three main bus terminals – two of which are an inconvenient distance from the centre of the city – and a terminal at the public transport centre at Suvarnabhumi International Airport with a few inter-provincial departures.

For long-distance journeys to popular tourist destinations it is advisable to buy tickets directly from the bus companies at the bus stations, rather than through travel agents in tourist centres such as Th Khao San.

Eastern Bus Terminal (Map p70; ☎02 391 2504; Soi 40, Th Sukhumvit; Ⓢ Ekkamai exit 2) The departure point for buses to Pattaya, Rayong, Chanthaburi and other points east. Most people call it *sà·tăh·nee èk·gà·mai* (Ekamai station). It's near the Ekkamai BTS station.

Southern Bus Terminal (Sai Tai Mai; ☎02 422 4444, call centre 1490; Th Boromaratchachonanee) The city's southern bus terminal lies a long way west of the centre of Bangkok. Commonly called *săi đâi mài*, it's among the more pleasant and orderly in the country, and serves as the departure point for all buses south of Bangkok.

Northern & Northeastern Bus Terminal (Mo Chit; Map p78; ☎northeastern routes 02 936 2852, ext 602/605, northern routes 02 936 2841, ext 325/614; Th Kamphaeng Phet; Ⓜ Kamphaeng Phet exit 1 & taxi, Ⓢ Mo Chit exit 3 & taxi) Located just north of Chatuchak Park, this hectic bus station is also commonly called *kŏn sòng mŏr chít* (Mo Chit station) – not to be confused with Mo Chit BTS station. Buses depart from here for all northern and northeastern destinations, as well as international destinations including Pakse (Laos), Phnom Penh (Cambodia), Siem Reap (Cambodia) and Vientiane (Laos).

Suvarnabhumi Public Transport Centre (☎02 134 4099; Suvarnabhumi Airport) Located 3km from Suvarnabhumi International Airport, this terminal has relatively frequent departures to points east and northeast including Chanthaburi, Ko Chang, Pattaya and Trat. It can be reached from the airport by a free shuttle bus.

TRAIN

Hua Lamphong Train Station (☎02 220 4334, call centre 1690; www.railway.co.th; off Th Phra Ram IV; Ⓜ Hua Lamphong exit 2) Hualamphong is the terminus for the main rail services to the south, north, northeast and east.

Hualamphong has the following services: showers, mailing centre, luggage storage, cafes and food courts. To get there from Sukhumvit take the MRT to the Hua Lamphong stop. From western points (Banglamphu, Thewet), take bus 53.

Getting Around

Bangkok's rush-hour traffic is the stuff of nightmares, and seemingly random acts of gridlock can impede even the shortest trip, any day, any time. If it's an option, going by river, canal or BTS/MRT is always the best choice; otherwise, assume a 45-minute journey for most outings.

A good, up-to-date resource for public transportation in Bangkok is www.transitbangkok.com.

TO/FROM THE AIRPORT

Bangkok is served by two airports; the vast majority of flights are out of Suvarnabhumi International Airport, while the budget airlines operate out of Don Muang International Airport. If you need to transfer between the two, pencil in *at least* an hour, as the two airports are at opposite ends of town. Minivans run between the two airports from 5.30am to 5pm (50B).

Suvarnabhumi International Airport

The following transport options leave directly from the Suvarnabhumi terminal to in-town destinations: metered taxis, hotel limousines, airport rail link, private vehicles and some minivans.

Airport Rail Link (☎call centre 1690; www.srtet.co.th)This service connects Suvarnabhumi International Airport and the BTS (Skytrain) stop at Phaya Thai (45B, 30 minutes, from 6am to midnight) and the MRT (Metro) stop at Phetchaburi (45B, 25 minutes, from 6am to midnight). The Airport Rail Link is on floor B1 of Suvarnabhumi International Airport.

Bus & Minivan A public transport centre is 3km from the airport and includes a bus terminal with buses to a handful of provinces, and inner-city-bound buses and minivans. A free airport shuttle connects the transport centre with the passenger terminals. Bus lines for city-bound tourists include line 551 to BTS Victory Monument station (40B, frequent from 5am to 10pm) and 552 to BTS On Nut (20B, frequent from 5am to 10pm). From these points, you can continue by public transport or taxi to your hotel.

Relatively frequent minivans to Don Muang International Airport wait on floor 1, outside door 8 (50B, 40 minutes, from 5.30am to 5pm).

From town, you can take the BTS to On Nut, then from near the market entrance opposite Tesco Lotus, take minivan 552 (20B, frequent from 5am to 10pm); BTS to Udom Suk, then bus A3 (30B, frequent from 6am to 8.30pm); or BTS to Victory Monument, then one of the infrequent minivans to Suvarnabhumi International Airport (40B, from 5am to 8pm).

Taxi As you exit the terminal, ignore the touts and all the signs pointing you to overpriced 'official airport taxis'; instead, descend to floor 1 to join the generally fast-moving queue for a public taxi. Cabs booked through these desks should always use their meter, but they often try their luck, so insist by saying, 'Meter, please'. Toll charges (paid by the passengers) vary between 25B and 70B. Note also that there's an additional 50B surcharge added to all fares departing from the airport, payable directly to the driver.

Don Muang International Airport

Bus & Minivan From outside the arrivals hall, there are two airport bus lines from Don Muang: A1 makes a stop at BTS Mo Chit (30B, frequent from 7.30am to 11.30pm); while the less frequent A2 makes stops at BTS Mo Chit and BTS Victory Monument (30B, every 30 minutes from 7.30am to 11.30pm).

Relatively frequent minivans also departing from outside the arrivals hall link Don Muang international Airport and Suvarnabhumi international Airport (50B, one hour, from 5.30am to 5pm).

Public buses stop on the highway in front of the airport. Useful lines include 29, with a stop at Victory Monument BTS station before terminating at Hualamphong Train Station (24 hours); line 59, with a stop near Th Khao San (24 hours); and line 538, stopping at Victory Monument BTS station (4am to 10pm); fares are approximately 23B.

Taxi As at Suvarnabhumi, public taxis leave from outside the arrivals hall and there is a 50B airport charge added to the meter fare.

Train The walkway that crosses from the airport to the Amari Airport Hotel also provides access to Don Muang train station, which has trains to Hualamphong Train Station every one to 1½ hours from 4am to 11.30am and then roughly every hour from 2pm to 9.30pm (5B to 10B).

BOAT

Once the city's dominant form of transport, public boats still survive along the mighty Mae Nam Chao Phraya and on a few interior *klorng*.

Canal Routes

Canal taxi boats run along Khlong Saen Saep (Banglamphu to Ramkhamhaeng). They are an easy way to get from Banglamphu to Jim

MINIVANS TO/FROM BANGKOK

Privately run minivans, called *rót đôo*, are a fast and relatively comfortable way to get between Bangkok and its neighbouring provinces. Minivans bound for a number of destinations wait at various points around the **Victory Monument** (อนุสาวรีย์ชัย; Map p78; cnr Th Ratchawithi & Th Phayathai; ⏲24hr; Ⓢ Victory Monument exit 2).

DESTINATION	COST (B)	DURATION	FREQUENCY
Ban Phe (for Ko Samet)	200	3hr	hourly 6am-8pm
Chanthaburi	200	3hr	hourly 5.30am-6pm
Hua Hin	180	3hr	every 45min 5am-8pm
Pattaya	150	2hr	hourly 6am-8pm
Phetchaburi	100	2hr	every 45min 5.15am-8pm
Southern Bus Terminal	35	20min	every 30min 8am-9pm

Thompson House and the Siam Sq shopping centres – get off at **Sapan Hua Chang Pier** (Map p74; Th Phayathai; Ⓢ Siam exit 1) for both. You can get to other points further east along Th Sukhumvit after a mandatory change of boat at **Pratunam Pier** (Map p74). These boats are mostly used by daily commuters and pull into the piers for just a few seconds – jump straight on or you'll be left behind. Fares range from 9B to 19B. Boats run from 5.30am to 7.15pm from Mondays to Fridays, from 6am to 6.30pm on Saturdays, and from 6am to 6pm on Sundays.

River Routes

Chao Phraya Express Boat (p72) operates the main ferry service along Mae Nam Chao Phraya. The main pier is known as Tha Sathon, Saphan Taksin or sometimes Central Pier, and connects to the BTS at Saphan Taksin station.

Boats run from 6am to 8pm. You can buy tickets (10B to 40B) at the pier or on board; hold on to your ticket as proof of purchase (they are occasionally checked).

The most common boats are the orange-flagged express boats. These run between Wat Rajsingkorn, south of Bangkok, to Nonthaburi, north, stopping at most major piers (15B, frequent from 6am to 7pm). A blue-flagged tourist boat (40B, every 30 minutes from 9.30am to 5pm) with barely comprehensible English-language commentary runs from **Sathon/Central Pier** (Map p84; cnr Th Sathon Tai/South & Th Charoen Krung) to **Phra Athit/Banglamphu Pier** (Map p60; off Th Phra Athit) with stops at eight major sightseeing piers. Vendors at Sathon/Central Pier tout a 150B all-day pass, but unless you plan on doing a lot of boat travel, it's not great value.

Cross-River Boats

There are also flat-bottomed cross-river ferries that connect Thonburi and Bangkok. These piers are usually next door to Chao Phraya Express Boat piers, cost 3B per crossing and run from approximately 7am to 7pm.

BTS & MRT

The elevated **BTS** (☎02 617 6000, tourist information 02 617 7341; www.bts.co.th), also known as the Skytrain (*rót fai fáh*), whisks you through 'new' Bangkok (Silom, Sukhumvit and Siam Sq). The interchange between the two lines is at Siam station. Trains run frequently from 6am to 11.45pm. Fares range from 15B to 52B, or 140B for a one-day pass. Most ticket machines only accept coins, but change is available at the information booths.

Bangkok's **MRT** (☎02 354 2000; www.bangkokmetro.co.th) or Metro is helpful for people staying in the Sukhumvit or Silom area who want to reach the train station at Hualamphong. Fares cost from 16B to 42B, or 120B for a one-day pass. The trains run frequently from 6am to midnight.

BUS

The city's public bus system is operated by **Bangkok Mass Transit Authority** (☎02 246 0973, call centre 1348; www.bmta.co.th). As the routes are not always clear, and with Bangkok taxis being such a good deal, you'd really have to be pinching pennies to rely on buses as a way to get around Bangkok. However, if you're determined, fares for air-con bus range from 10B to 23B, and fares for fan-cooled buses start at 6.50B. Most of the bus lines run between 5am and 10pm or 11pm, except for the 'all-night' buses, which run from 3am or 4am to midmorning. You'll most likely require the help of thinknet's *Bangkok Bus Guide*, a map available at Bangkok bookshops.

MOTORCYCLE TAXI

The backdrop of modern Bangkok, teams of cheeky, numbered and vested motorcycle-taxi drivers can be found at the end of just about every long street. A ride to the end *(sùt soy)* or mouth *(Ъàhk soy)* of an average soi usually costs 10B to 15B. Longer journeys should be negotiated in advance, and can range from 20B to 100B.

TAXI

Although many first-time visitors are hesitant to use them, in general Bangkok's taxis are new and spacious and the drivers are courteous and helpful, making them an excellent way to get around.

All taxis are required to use their meters, which start at 35B. Fares to most places within central Bangkok cost 60B to 90B. Freeway tolls – 25B to 70B depending on where you start – must be paid by the passenger. **Taxi Radio** (☎1681; www.taxiradio.co.th) and other 24-hour 'phone-a-cab' services are available for 20B above the metered fare.

App-based alternatives to the traditional taxis operating in Bangkok include All Thai Taxi (www.allthaitaxi.com), Easy Taxi (www.easytaxi.com/th) and Uber (www.uber.com/cities/bangkok).

TRANSPORT TO/FROM BANGKOK

The following table shows travel times and costs to Thailand's most popular beach and island destinations. For more detailed information, be sure to refer to the Getting There & Away information of your specific destination.

DESTINATION	AIR	BUS	MINIVAN	TRAIN
Chumphon	from 1534B; 70min; 5.40am & 5.25pm	337-524B; 7hr; frequent 7am-9.30pm (from Southern Bus Terminal)	N/A	10 departures 8.05am-10.50pm
Hat Yai	from 1440B; 1½hr; frequent departures daily (from Don Mueang International Airport); 1900B; 1½hr; 5 departures daily (from Suvarnabhumi International Airport)	514-1028B; 13hr; frequent 2-9.15pm (from Southern Bus Terminal)	N/A	259-1590B; 12-15hr; 6 departures 1-10.40pm
Khao Lak	see to Phuket	549-896B; 12hr; 7.30pm & 8pm (from Southern Bus Terminal)	N/A	N/A
Ko Lipe	N/A	662B; 13hr; 7am & 6.30pm (from Southern Bus Terminal to La-Ngu)	N/A	N/A
Ko Pha-Ngan	see to Chumphon, Ko Samui or Surat Thani	see to Chumphon, Ko Samui or Surat Thani	N/A	N/A
Ko Phi-Phi	see to Krabi or Phuket	see to Krabi or Phuket	N/A	N/A
Ko Samet	N/A	220B; 4hr; frequent departures 7am-6.30pm (from Eastern Bus Terminal to Ban Phe)	200B; 3hr; hourly 6am-8pm (from Victory Monument)	N/A
Ko Samui	from 3600B; 65min; frequent departures daily (from Suvarnabhumi International Airport)	813B; 12hr; 7.15am & every 30min 7-8.30pm (from Southern Bus Terminal to Don Sak)	N/A	N/A
Ko Tao	see to Chumphon, Ko Samui or Surat Thani	see to Chumphon, Ko Samui or Surat Thani	N/A	see to Chumphon, Ko Samui or Surat Thani

TÚK-TÚK

A ride on Thailand's emblematic three-wheeled vehicle is an experience particularly sought after by new arrivals, but it only takes a few seconds to realise that most foreigners are too tall to see anything beyond the low-slung roof.

Túk-túk drivers also have a knack for smelling crisp bills and can potentially take you and your wallet far away from your desired destination. Beware of drivers who offer to take you on a sightseeing tour for 10B or 20B – it's a touting scheme (see p95). A short trip on a túk-túk will cost at least 60B.

DESTINATION	AIR	BUS	MINIVAN	TRAIN
Krabi	1190B; 1½hr; 10 departures daily (from Don Mueang International Airport); from 1590B; 1½hr; 6 departures daily (from Suvarnabhumi International Airport)	569-886B; 12hr; every 30min 6pm-8pm (from Southern Bus Terminal)	N/A	N/A
Phuket	from 1400B; 75min; frequent departures daily (from Don Mueang Airport); from 1790B; 75min; frequent departures daily (from Suvarnabhumi International Airport)	482-938B; 12-15hr; every 30min 7.30am-8.20pm (from Southern Bus Terminal)	N/A	N/A
Surat Thani	from 880B; 70min; frequent departures daily (from Don Mueang International Airport); from 2000B; 70min; 2 departures daily (from Suvarnabhumi International Airport)	470-731B; 9hr; 7.15am & every 30min 7-8.30pm (from Southern Bus Terminal)	N/A	217-1379B; 12hr; 10 departures 8.05am-10.50pm (to Phun Phin)
Trang	1100B; 1½hr; 6 departures daily (from Don Mueang International Airport)	599-932B; 12hr; 7am & every 30min 6-7.30pm (from Southern Bus Terminal)	N/A	245-1480B; 15hr; 5.05pm & 6.30pm
Trat (for Ko Chang)	from 2550B; 1hr; 3 departures daily (from Suvarnabhumi International Airport)	48-275B; 5½hr; frequent 4-9.45am (from Eastern Bus Terminal); 243B; 6hr; 5 departures 7.30am-10pm (from Northern & Northeastern Bus Terminal)	300B; 5hr; hourly 5am-5pm (from Victory Monument); 300B; 5hr; hourly 9am-5pm (from Northern & Northeastern Bus Terminal)	N/A

Ko Chang & Eastern Seaboard

Best Places to Eat

- ➡ Relax (p101)
- ➡ Glass House (p110)
- ➡ Jep's Restaurant (p117)
- ➡ Chanthorn Phochana (p120)
- ➡ Pan & David Restaurant (p106)

Best Places to Stay

- ➡ Bann Makok (p139)
- ➡ Rabbit Resort (p110)
- ➡ Samed Pavilion Resort (p115)
- ➡ Baan Luang Rajamaitri (p120)
- ➡ Koh Chang Sea Hut (p131)

Why Go?

Two islands – Ko Samet and Ko Chang – are the magnets that draw travellers to the eastern seaboard. The mainland has plenty of its own attractions, though, from international resorts like Pattaya to the charismatic, old-world charm of Chanthaburi.

Ko Samet, the nearest major island to Bangkok, is a flash-packer fave where visitors sip from vodka buckets and admire the fire jugglers or head for the quieter southern coves. Further down the coast is Ko Chang, Thailand's second-largest island. Spend your days diving, chilling on the west-coast beaches or hiking through dense jungle – then recover in time to experience the island's vibrant party scene.

Fewer travellers make it to Bang Saen, though its hip sea-front restaurants and long beach make it worth a stopover. Less serene is the raucous resort of Pattaya, with its hedonistic nightlife, numerous attractions and some of the best international cuisine in the kingdom.

When to Go

➡ The best time to visit is the end of the rainy season (usually around November) but before the start of high season (December to March) when the weather is cool, the landscape green and rates reasonable. Peak season on Ko Chang is the Christmas and New Year holiday period. Crowds thin in March, the start of the hot season.

➡ The rainy season runs from May to October, though there are often days or weeks with no rain at all. A few businesses on Ko Chang close, and Ko Kut, Ko Mak and Ko Wai go into hibernation with many places shut. Your best bet during monsoon is Ko Samet, which enjoys its own microclimate and stays relatively dry.

Bang Saen บางแสน

POP 42, 843

As the closest beach to Bangkok, Bang Saen is a weekend favourite for those wanting to escape city life. Recent renovations to the beachfront and a slew of new boutique hotels have boosted its popularity. During the day, the 4km-long promenade is packed with tandem bicycles and seafood stalls. By night, the string of hip restaurants and bars facing the sea draw a student crowd.

Sights & Activities

Khao Sam Muk HILL
(เขาสามมุข, Monkey Mountain) Hundreds of rhesus monkeys with greedy eyes and quick hands live on this small hill (avoid feeding them, as this just makes them more aggressive). Local folklore says the hill is named after a girl who took her life here after a doomed romance.

Wang Saen Suk BUDDHIST TEMPLE
(วังแสนสุข, Temple of Happiness; Soi 19, Sai 2; 8am-6pm) FREE Despite its name, this site contains gruesome Dante-esque statues of sinners being eternally punished. Half-human, half-animal creatures surround two huge figures by the entrance. On the flip side, there are statues depicting Thai fairy tales and more righteous behaviour. A nearby pond has giant catfish and turtles that can be fed (10B).

Mangrove Forest Conservation Centre FOREST
(038 398268; Ang Sila; 8.30am-3.30pm) FREE This forest is such a well-kept secret, many locals don't even know it's here. A 2km-long wooden walkway gives access to the mangrove forest, which is mostly shaded. Look out for the crabs, cockles and mudfish. The forest is 3km north of Ang Sila's daily fish market, also worth exploring. Ang Sila is 6km north of Bang Saen.

Wihahn Tepsatit Pra Gitichairloem CHINESE TEMPLE
(วิหารเทพสถิตพระกิติเฉลิม; Ang Sila; 8am-5pm; P) FREE Created to mark the king's 72nd birthday, this four-storey Chinese temple is filled with intricate paintings and magnificent sculptures. Locals regularly come to make merit, and temple volunteers are happy to explain the rituals if you want to make your own offerings. The temple is on the main road in Ang Sila.

Flight of the Gibbon ZIPLINING
(089 970 5511; www.treetopasia.com; tours from 3000B) This zipline course extends 3km via 26 platforms through the forest canopy of Khao Kheow Open Zoo. It is an all-day tour with additional add-on activities, like a jungle obstacle course and a visit to the neighbouring zoo.

Sleeping

Suk Jai Guesthouse GUESTHOUSE $
(086 839 1688; Soi 1, Bang Saen Sai 1; r 500B;) The rooms may be functional rather than fancy but you will be on the beach in only a few steps. There is no English sign so look for the red-and-white-tiled wall.

Bangsaen Heritage Hotel HOTEL $$$
(038 399899; www.bs-heritagehotel.com; 50 Sai 1; r incl breakfast 2942-11,181B;) A sign of Bang Saen's recent growth comes in the form of this beautiful resort, which fuses traditional Thai design with modern twists.

Eating & Drinking

Summer's Corner CAFE $
(193/25 Th Long Had Bang Saen; dishes 100-150B; 10am-10pm;) Students from the local uni are regulars here thanks to cheery staff, creative dishes and cool decor.

Relax THAI $$
(Th Rob Khao Sum Muk; dishes 150-300B; 4pm-midnight) Aptly named, Relax lets its customers sit on the beach, sipping beer, listening to live music and snacking on grilled squid.

Getting There & Away

Minivans and buses leave from either side of Th Sukhumvit, close to the main turn off into Bang Saen. Red *sŏrng·tăa·ou* (passenger pick-up trucks) go to Si Racha (15B, 20 minutes, 5.30am to 9pm).

DESTINATION	BUS	MINIVAN
Bangkok's Eastern Bus Terminal (Ekamai)	83B; 1hr; hourly	
Bangkok's Northern Bus Terminal (Mo Chit)	95B; 1½hr; hourly	120B; 1½hr; hourly; 5am-8.30pm
Bangkok Suvarnabhumi International Airport	110B; 1hr; hourly	
Victory Monument (Bangkok)	110B; 1½ hr; hourly	
Ban Phe (for Ko Samet)		180B; 2hr; 8am-5pm

Ko Chang & Eastern Seaboard Highlights

1 Snorkelling and jungle trekking on **Ko Chang** (p124).

2 Floating the day away on the crystalline waters of **Ko Kut** (p138).

3 Swimming with the fishes in the gin-clear coves of **Ko Wai** (p135).

4 Cove-hopping on pretty **Ko Samet** (p113).

5 Strolling through the old waterfront community in **Chanthaburi** (p118).

6 Riding a tandem bike along the shady promenade in **Bang Saen** (p101).

7 Kicking back in the atmospheric wooden shophouse quarter of **Trat** (p121).

8 Escaping Bangkok's bustle with a day trip to peaceful **Ko Si Chang** (p106) and a layover in **Si Racha** (p104).

9 Admiring the modern masterpiece of Pattaya's **Sanctuary of Truth** (p107), an elaborately carved testament to the artistry of Buddhism and Hinduism.

10 Dining on seafood beside the sea everywhere – the principal reason Thais travel to the beach.

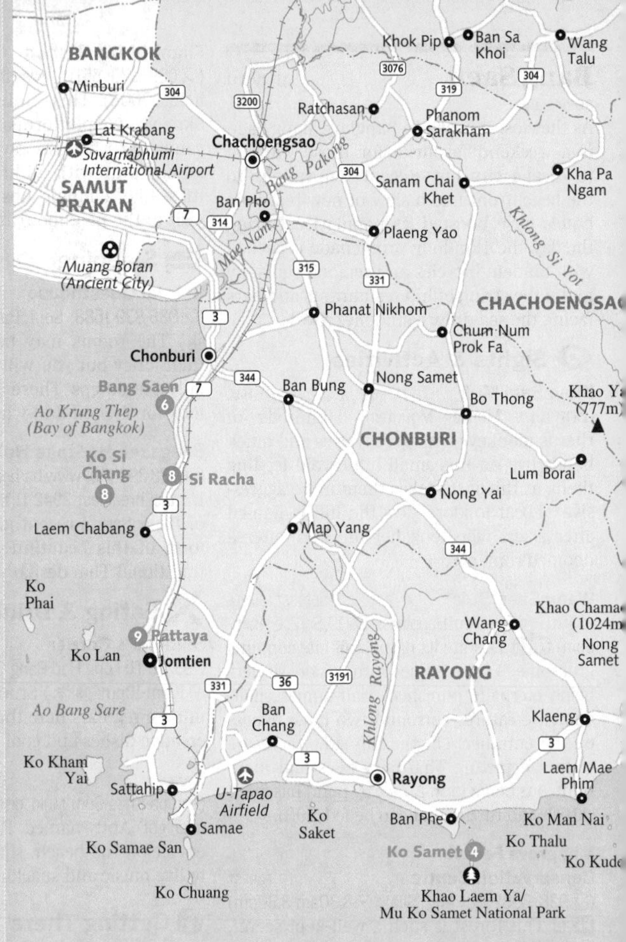

Lam
Prachinburi
Sa Kaew
Watthana Nakhon
Huay Jot
Sai Yoi
Khao Chakan
Ang Sila
Non Mak Mun
Aranya Prathet
Poipet
CAMBODIA
Sai Diaw
Non Sao-Eh
Sisophon
Khlong Hat
Khao Takrup (660m)
Wang Mai
Khao Daeng
Thun Khanan
CHANTHABURI
Tamun
Battambang
Khao Soi Dao Nua (1566m)
Pung Ngon
Nong Chek Soi
Takra
Ban Pakard
Psar Pruhm
Khao Chamao/ Khao Wong National Park
Khao Khitchakut National Park
Pong Nam Ron
Pailin
Si Yaek Kong Din
Nong Khla
Makham
Ban Pa-Ah
Tha Mai
5 Chanthaburi
Chang Thun
Nam Tok Phlio National Park
Nong Sii
Laem Sadet
Chao Lao
Ta Chalap
Chak Yai
Laem Sing
Khlung
Pong
Dan Chumpon
Laem Ko Proet
Tha Chot
TRAT
CAMBODIA
Trat
7
Ban Noen Sung
Bang Kradan
Laem Muang
Laem Ngop
Ao Trat
Tha Sen
Laem Sok
1 Ko Chang
Mu Ko Chang National Marine Park
Hat Mai Rut
Ko Wai 3
Ko Kradat
Ko Mak
Ko Ran
Khlong Yai
Ko Mai Si
2 Ko Kut
Hat Lek
Krong Koh Kong
348
33
317
3395
3
3157
3159
3271
3156
318

Si Racha

ศรีราชา

POP 80,088

Si Racha (pronounced 'see-ra-cha') is an unlikely blend of traditional and modern. Colourful, creaking fishing boats and squid rigs are still moored here, but these days they share the water with giant container ships from the nearby port of Laem Chabang.

Sushi restaurants and karaoke bars cater for the hundreds of Japanese employees who work at nearby industrial estates, giving the town centre a Little Tokyo vibe. The heart of Si Racha is the seafront health park.

Sights

Si Racha's attractions are limited, but the town centre makes for a pleasant stroll.

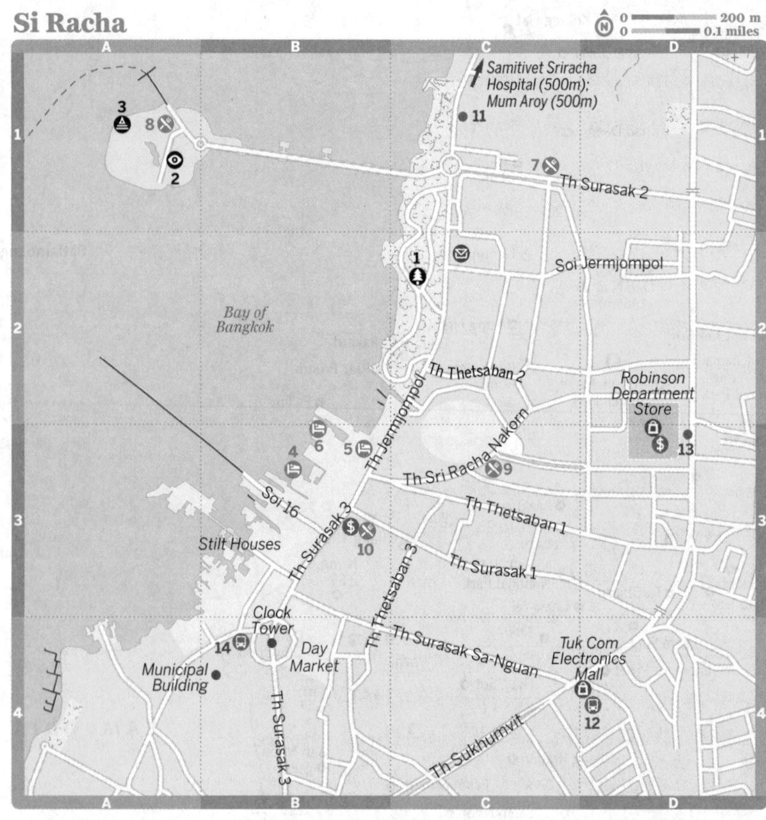

Si Racha

Sights
1 Health Park C2
2 Ko Loi A1
3 Thai-Chinese Temple A1

Sleeping
4 Samchai B3
5 Seaview Sriracha Hotel B3
6 Siriwatana Hotel B3

Eating
7 California Steak C1
8 Ko Loi Seafood Stalls A1
9 Lahp Ubon C3
10 My One B3

Information
11 Immigration Office C1

Transport
12 Buses to Bangkok D4
13 Minivans to Bangkok D3
14 Sŏrng·tăa·ou to Pattaya & Bang Saen B4

Ko Loi ISLAND

This island has a **Thai-Chinese temple** and a sunset viewing area. Below the temple is a pond, where huge turtles can be fed squid (10B). This is also where you can catch the ferry to Ko Si Chang.

Health Park PARK

Locals fill this well-maintained municipal park every evening to practise yoga, tai chi and skateboarding. The park includes a coffee shop, jogging track and play equipment.

Sleeping

The most authentic (read: basic) places to stay are the wooden hotels on the piers.

Samchai HOTEL $

(038 311800; Soi 10, Th Jermjompol; r 350-900B;) This pier hotel has rustic rooms and good sea views. Cheaper rooms are fan-only.

Siriwatana Hotel HOTEL $

(038 311037; 35 Soi Siriwatana, Th Jermjompol; r 200-380B;) Locals reckon this guesthouse on stilts has been here for almost a century. Get a sea view by looking straight ahead – or down through the wooden slats.

Seaview Sriracha Hotel HOTEL $$

(038319000; seaview_hotel@hotmail.com; 50-54 Th Jermjompol; r incl breakfast 990-1900B;) Rooms are large and comfortable; try to score one at the back for sea views.

Eating

Unsurprisingly, Si Racha is famous for its seafood. You can try it Thai-, Japanese- or Korean-style.

Ko Loi Seafood Stalls SEAFOOD $

(dishes 40-160B; 10am-9pm) On the Ko Loi jetty, these spots specialise in fresh seafood.

Lahp Ubon NORTHEASTERN THAI $

(Th Si Racha Nakorn; dishes 20-80B; 10am-10pm) An Isan place with yummy *nám đòk mŏo* (spicy pork salad).

My One VIETNAMESE $

(14/10 Th Surasak 1; dishes 50-160B; 9am-9pm) This simple Thai-Vietnamese restaurant has a variety of fresh, healthy dishes, including (non-fried) spring rolls and salads.

Mum Aroy SEAFOOD $$

(Soi 8, Th Jermjompol; dishes 60-420B; 11am-10pm) Mum Aroy ('delicious corner') is *the* place to enjoy a seafood meal with views of the squid rigs. It is north of the town; turn left at Samitivet Sriracha Hospital and look for the tank with the 2m fish out front.

California Steak STEAK $$

(4/3-4 Th Surasak 2; mains 200-300B; 5.30pm-midnight) This stylish steakhouse has a good range of pizzas and imported meats.

Information

Immigration Office (038 312571; 3/1 Th Jermjompol; 8.30am-4.30pm)

Krung Thai Bank (cnr Th Surasak 1 & Th Jermjompol; 8.30am-3.30pm) ATM and exchange.

Post Office (Th Jermjompol; 8.30am-4.30pm Mon-Fri, 8.30am-12.30pm Sat) The post office is opposite the Health Park.

Samitivet Sriracha Hospital (038 324111; Soi 8, Th Jermjompol)

Getting There & Around

Minivans leave from Th Sukhumvit (Hwy 3) by Robinson Department Store and buses and minivans leave from the nearby IT mall, Tuk Com.

White *sŏrng·tăa·ou* leave from near the clock tower for Pattaya's Naklua market (40B, 45 minutes, 6am to 6pm); red *sŏrng·tăa·ou* go to Bang Saen (15B, 20 minutes, 6am to 6pm). Motorbike taxis zip around town for a cost of about 30B to 40B.

TRANSPORT TO/FROM SI RACHA

DESTINATION	BUS	MINIVAN	TRAIN
Bangkok's Eastern Bus Terminal (Ekamai)	94B; 1½hr; hourly; 5am-8pm		
Bangkok's Northern Bus Terminal (Mo Chit)	97B; 2hr; hourly; 5am-7.30pm		
Bangkok Suvarnabhumi International Airport	110B; 1hr; hourly; 5.10am-8pm		
Pattaya		40B; 30min; frequent	
Victory Monument (Bangkok)		100B; 1½hr; every 30min; 5am-8pm	
Bangkok Hualamphong			28B; 3hr; 2.52pm daily

Ko Si Chang เกาะสีชัง

POP 4,975

Once a royal beach retreat, Ko Si Chang has a fishing village atmosphere and enough attractions to make it a decent day's excursion from Si Racha, or an overnight stop for those who want to chill out. It gets busier at weekends, when Bangkok Thais come to eat seafood, pose in front of the sea and make merit at the local temples.

Sights

Phra Chudadhut Palace HISTORIC SITE

(9am-5pm Tue-Sun) FREE This former royal palace was used by Rama V (King Chulalongkorn) over the summer months, but was abandoned when the French briefly occupied the island in 1893. The main throne hall – a magnificent golden teak structure known as Vimanmek Teak Mansion – was moved to Bangkok in 1910. What's left are Victorian-style buildings set in gardenlike grounds.

Ruen Vadhana and Ruen Mai Rim Talay contain historical displays about the king's visits to the island and his public works programs, including a lecture to the local people on Western tea parties. Up the hill is Wat Atsadang Khanimit, a temple with Gothic-style windows that contains a small, consecrated chamber where Rama V used to meditate. The Buddha image inside was fashioned more than 50 years ago by a local monk. Nearby is a stone outcrop wrapped in holy cloth, called Bell Rock because it rings like a bell when struck.

San Jao Phaw Khao Yai CHINESE TEMPLE

FREE The most imposing sight on the island, this ornate Chinese temple dates back to the days when Chinese traders anchored in the sheltered waters. During Chinese New Year in February, the island is overrun with Chinese tourists. There are shrine caves, multiple platforms and a good view of the ocean. It's north of the main town.

Wat Tham Yai Phrik BUDDHIST TEMPLE

(วัดถ้ำยายปริก; www.watthamyaiprig.com; donations appreciated; 5am-6pm) FREE This Buddhist monastery is built around several meditation caves running into the island's central limestone ridge and offers fine views from its hilltop *chedi* (stupa). Monks and *mâa chee* (nuns) from across Thailand come to take advantage of the caves' peaceful environment. Someone is usually around to give informal tours and talk about Buddhism.

The body of a former nun is displayed in a small room within the grounds, a reminder of the impermanence of earthly life. Accommodation is available for those taking a meditation course.

Hat Tham Phang BEACH

On the southwest side of the island, Hat Tham Phang (Fallen Cave Beach) is the only sandy beach on the island. You can hire kayaks and there's deckchair and umbrella rental. Snorkelling is possible around the northern section.

Activities

Several locals run **snorkelling** trips to nearby Ko Khang Khao (Bat Island), which has a good beach, or you can take a speedboat (400B) there from the main pier. **Kayaks** are available (200B per hour) on Hat Tham Phang. You can paddle to Ko Khang Khao in 45 minutes.

Sichang Healing House MASSAGE

(081 572 7840; off Th Makham Thaew) The charming, English-speaking owner of this leafy haven offers a range of excellent massages (300B to 600B). She also sells homemade health products and has modest bamboo rooms for rent (300B).

Sleeping & Eating

There are a smattering of guesthouses and homestays on the island, as well as restaurants specialising in seafood.

Charlie's Bungalows GUESTHOUSE $$

(085 191 3863; www.kosichang.net; Th Makham Thaew; r 1000-1100B;) Bright, fresh, all-white bungalows set around a garden. All come with TVs and DVD players. Friendly and helpful staff. Book ahead at weekends and public holidays.

★ **Pan & David Restaurant** INTERNATIONAL, THAI $$

(038 216629; www.ko-sichang.com; 167 Mu 3, Th Makham Thaew; dishes 120-440B; 8.30am-10pm) With free-range chicken, homemade ice cream, a reasonable wine list and excellent Thai dishes, you can't go wrong here. It also has rooms available (750B to 1800B), which include converted fishing boats.

Pa Noi Rim Tahng SEAFOOD $$

(Th Makham Thaew; 100-350B; 11am-9pm) This eat-on-the-street restaurant is a favourite with locals thanks to its great seafood options. Look for the blue tables and umbrellas.

Information

The island's one small settlement faces the mainland and is the terminus for the ferry. A bumpy road network links the village with the other sights.

Pan & David's website (www.ko-sichang.com) is an excellent source of local information.

Kasikornbank (99/12 Th Atsadang; 8.30am-3.30pm) Has an ATM and exchange facilities.

Post Office (Th Atsadang; 8.30am-4.30pm Mon-Fri, 8.30am-12.30pm Sat) Near the pier.

Getting There & Around

Boats to Ko Si Chang leave hourly 7am to 8pm from the jetty of Ko Loi (p105) in Si Racha (one way 50B, 45 minutes). From Ko Si Chang boats shuttle back hourly from 6am to 7pm.

Motorbike taxis wait at the pier and will take you anywhere for 30B to 50B, and souped-up sǎhm·lór (also spelt sǎamláw) do tours of the main spots for 250B.

Motorbikes are available to rent on the pier (250B per day, 80B hourly).

Pattaya พัทยา

POP 192,372

If you long for quiet beaches and hammocks swaying in the breeze, make a sharp U-turn before arriving in Pattaya. The city's reputation as a sex capital is well deserved, with hundreds of beer bars, go-go clubs and massage parlours. But Pattaya does perennially try to lose its sex tag and many of its 10 million annual visitors instead come for the mega shopping centres and amenities. Pattaya is also home to a growing number of cultural and action-packed attractions and international restaurants.

The city is built around **Ao Pattaya**, a wide, crescent-shaped bay that was one of Thailand's first beach resorts in the 1960s when American GIs came for some R&R. North Pattaya (Pattaya Neua) is a more upmarket area while Pattaya South (Pattaya Tai) remains the nightlife hub.

To the south of Pattaya, **Jomtien** is a resort with a gay-friendly beach at Hat Dongtan, while to the north **Naklua** is also quieter, with some top-end resorts at Wong Amat.

The best beaches in the area are on **Ko Samae San**, a tiny island with good snorkelling, and the navy-run **Hat Nahng Ram**, both 35km south of Pattaya.

Sights & Activities

Sanctuary of Truth MONUMENT

(ปราสาทสัจธรรม; 038 367229; www.sanctuaryoftruth.com; 206/2 Mu 5, Soi Naklua 12; adult/child 500/250B; 8am-6pm) Made entirely of wood (without any metal nails) and commanding a celestial view of the ocean, the Sanctuary of Truth is best described as a visionary environment: part art installation, religious shrine and cultural monument. Constructed in four wings dedicated to Thai, Khmer, Chinese and Indian religious iconography, its architecture and setting is impressive.

The ornate temple-like complex was conceived by Lek Viriyaphant, a Thai millionaire who spent his fortune on this and other heritage projects (such as Ancient City near Bangkok) that revived and preserved ancient building techniques and architecture in danger of extinction. In this case, the building continues to support hand-hewn woodworking skills as it's been under construction since 1981 and still isn't finished.

PATTAYA FOR CHILDREN

Pattaya has lots to offer younger visitors, from water parks to family-friendly farms.

Cartoon Network Amazone (038 237797; www.cartoonnetworkamazone.com; 888 Mu 8, Th Sukhumvit; adult/child 1290/890B; 10am-6pm;) The world's first Cartoon Network–themed water park includes a surfing arena, a 1km-long river and the chance to meet Ben 10.

Greta Farm (092 634 7979; www.gretafarm.com; 68/5 Mu 3, Th Wat Yarn; 7am-11pm;) Goats, horses and cows are the star attractions at this children's farm, which also includes archery, a fun park and rope bridges.

Underwater World (038 756879; www.underwaterworldpattaya.com; 22/22 Mu 11, Th Sukhumvit; adult/child 500/300B; 9am-6pm;) The area's largest aquarium is particularly child-friendly, with touch pools and koi feeding sessions.

Art in Paradise (038 424500; www.artinparadise.co.th; 78/34 Mu 9, Th Pattaya Sai 2; adult/child 400/200B; 9am-9pm;) Thais come here for the ultimate selfie as they pose amid 3D paintings of dinosaurs, waterfalls and, bizarrely, an elephant on a toilet.

Pattaya & Naklua

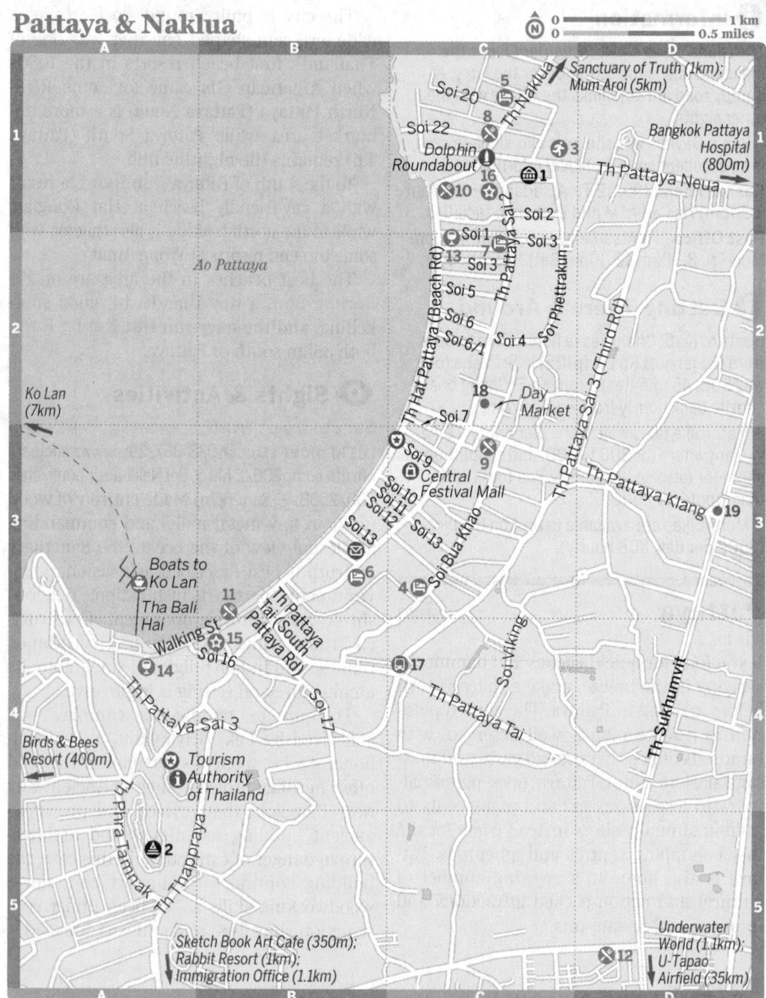

Every part of the 105m-tall building is covered with wood carvings of Hindu and Buddhist gods and goddesses.

Compulsory tours are led through the building every 30 minutes. Thai dancing is at 11.30am and 3.30pm. Motorcycle taxis can be hired from Pattaya for 50B to 70B. The sanctuary is 1km down Soi 12 off Th Naklua, about 3km from the centre of town.

Anek Kusala Sala (Viharn Sien) MUSEUM
(อเนกกุศลศาลา / วิหารเซียน); ☎038 235250; off Th Sukhumvit; admission 50B; ⏰8am-5pm) A popular stop for tour groups, this museum contains more than 300 impressive pieces of Chinese artwork, mainly bronze and brass statues depicting historical figures as well as Buddhist, Confucian and Taoist deities. Founded by Sa-nga Kulkobkiat, a Thai national who grew up in China, the museum was intended as a friendship-building project between the two countries.

The 1st floor is a crowded pavilion of Chinese immortals, from Pangu, the cosmic giant, to Guan Yin, the goddess of mercy. The 2nd-floor terrace is the museum's most dramatic, with larger-than-life-sized statues of Shaolin monks depicting different martial-arts poses.

Pattaya & Naklua

Sights
1 Art in Paradise C1
2 Khao Phra Tamnak A5

Activities, Courses & Tours
3 Fairtex Sports Club C1

Sleeping
4 Asia BackPackers C3
5 Garden Lodge Hotel C1
6 Nag's Head B3
7 Siam@Siam C2

Eating
8 La Baguette C1
9 Leng Kee C3
10 Mantra C1
11 Nang Nual B3
12 Thepprasit Market D5

Drinking & Nightlife
13 Gulliver's C2
14 Lima Lima A4

Entertainment
15 Blues Factory B4
16 Tiffany's C1

Transport
17 35 Group C4
18 Bangkok Airways C2
19 Minivans to Bangkok D3

Nearby is a touching collection of daily life statues that visitors place 1B coins on.

The museum is 16km south of Pattaya; take a Pattaya–Sattahip *sŏrng·tăa·ou* (25B) to the Wat Yangsangwaram turn-off. Hire a passing motorbike to go the final 5km to the museum. Ask the driver to stick around, as getting a lift back is hard to find. Private transport is 1500B.

Ko Lan ISLAND
(เกาะล้าน) Day trippers head for this small island, 7km offshore from central Pattaya. On weekends, its five beaches entertain 5000 visitors and the sea is busy with banana boats and other marine merriment. Ferries leave Pattaya's Bali Hai pier (30B, 45 minutes, five daily) at the southern end of Walking St. The last boat back from Ko Lan is at 6pm.

Khao Phra Tamnak BUDDHIST SITE
(เขาพระตำหนัก; dawn-dusk) A giant golden Buddha sits atop this forested hill between Jomtien and south Pattaya. The serene Buddha figure of Wat Phra Yai dates back to when Pattaya was a small fishing village. On a neighbouring hill is **Monument Park**, which offers great sunset views of Ao Pattaya. You can walk here from the southern end of Walking St.

Fairtex Sports Club HEALTH & FITNESS
(038 253888; www.fairtexpattaya.com; 179/185-212 Mu 5, Th Pattaya Neua; per session 800B) Burnt-out professionals, martial-arts fans and adventurous athletes head to this resort-style sports camp for training in *moo·ay tai* (Thai boxing; also spelt *muay Thai*) and a sweat-inducing vacation. Accommodation packages are available and use of the club's pool and other sports facilities are included.

Festivals & Events

Pattaya International Music Festival MUSIC
(www.pattayamusicfest.com) In mid-March, Pattaya's oceanfront esplanade is transformed into an outdoor concert venue for three days of live music. Local musicians, as well as bands from across Asia, take to the stages to perform everything from hip-hop to rock.

Sleeping

Rooms around central or south Pattaya tend to be cheaper but closer to the noisy nightlife. North Pattaya and parts of Naklua host the signature hotels, while Soi Bua Khao and Jomtien have budget options.

Jomtien Hostel HOSTEL $
(038 233416; www.jomtienhostel.com; Mu 12, Hat Jomtien; dm/r 280/550B;) Clean dorms with good bedding, 200m from the beach. Lockers are available.

Asia BackPackers HOSTEL $
(038 420528; www.asia-backpackers.com; 420/162 Mu 9, Soi Bua Khao; r 330B;) One of the few dorms in the heart of Pattaya, this no-frills place is a welcome alternative to the myriad guesthouses. Lockers are available.

Nag's Head GUESTHOUSE $
(038 425274; nagshead_pattaya@yahoo.co.th; 485/15 Th Pattaya Sai 2; r 700B;) Clean rooms and friendly staff make this a good budget option. Try and score a room away from the road.

Garden Lodge Hotel HOTEL $$
(038 429109; www.gardenlodgepattaya.net; cnr Soi 20 & Th Naklua; r 1350-3000B;) A favourite among German tourists; the rooms

PATTAYA – EXPAT CENTRAL

No other Thai city has a reputation like Pattaya's. Ever since the first US servicemen started arriving in the 1960s for some R&R, hedonism has been a permanent guest. Beer bars, go-go clubs and massage parlours are omnipresent, with thousands of prostitutes working in the city.

While Pattaya is known for sleaze, there is another side to the city. Thousands of expats from numerous countries live here, making it Thailand's only truly international city after Bangkok. Many are attracted to the resort by the quality of life, relatively low cost of living and amenities – the area has some of Thailand's finest golf courses.

Many Brits have businesses here, there is a thriving Arab community centred around Soi 16 at the south end of Walking St, and Naklua is popular with the German crowd. As a result of such diversity, there are specialist shops offering everything from South American coffee to French cheese.

It is thought that around 40,000 foreigners live in Pattaya, with many more spending part of the year here. Those numbers are likely to rise as rapid development continues; an underground tunnel to the seafront is the latest venture and new high-rise condos pop up every month to meet demand.

here are old-fashioned but surrounded by landscaped gardens and a swimming pool.

★Rabbit Resort HOTEL $$$
(☎038 251730; www.rabbitresort.com; Hat Dongtan; r incl breakfast 5000-10,990B; ❄@📶🏊) Rabbit Resort has stylish and secluded bungalows and villas that showcase Thai design and art, all set in beachfront forest hidden between Jomtien and Pattaya Tai. With two pools (one designed for families) and superb service, the resort is an excellent option.

Birds & Bees Resort HOTEL $$$
(☎038 250556; www.cabbagesandcondoms.co.th; Soi 4, Th Phra Tamnak; r 2000-12,000B; ❄@📶🏊) 🍃 A tropical garden resort with two pools and good-sized rooms. The resort helps fund the work of the PDA, a rural development charity run by social campaigner Mechai Viravaidya. Cheaper rooms have no views.

Siam@Siam HOTEL $$$
(☎038 930600; www.siamatpattaya.com; 390 Mu 9, Th Pattaya Sai 2; r incl breakfast 6250-15,000B; ❄@📶🏊) Merging contemporary design with recycled materials and vibrant colours, Siam@Siam ticks every box. A rooftop restaurant, infinity pool and, ingeniously, a bar made from secondhand jeeps and túk-túks (pronounced *đúk đúks*) are some of the highlights. Rates are often flexible.

Eating

Pattaya has an eclectic range of quality international and Thai restaurants, but there are still plenty of markets and street stalls for baht-watchers.

Thepprasit Market MARKET $
(cnr Th Thepprasit & Th Sukhumvit; dishes 30-80B; ⏲4-10pm Fri-Sun) As well as intriguing knick-knacks and endless clothes stalls, this thriving weekend market has a great range of smoothies, noodles and Thai snacks.

Leng Kee CHINESE-THAI $
(Th Pattaya Klang; dishes 100-300B; ⏲24hr) Duck dishes rule the roost in this well-established Thai-Chinese restaurant, though the seafood dishes are also tasty.

★Glass House THAI $$
(☎038255922; www.glasshouse-pattaya.com; 5/22 Mu 2, Jomtien; dishes 170-380B; ⏲11am-midnight) Diners at this all-white beachfront spot plunge their toes into the warm sand as waiters deliver seafood, pizza and steak.

Mum Aroi THAI $$
(☎038 223252; 83/4 Soi 4, Th Naklua; dishes 150-420B; ⏲11am-11pm) This long-established restaurant is perched beside the sea in the fishing-village end of Naklua. Old fishing boats sit marooned offshore and crisp sea breezes envelop diners as they devour fantastic Thai food. Try *sôm·đam Ъoo* (spicy papaya salad with crab) and *Ъlah mèuk nêung ma-now* (squid steamed in lime juice).

Nang Nual SEAFOOD $$
(☎038 428478; Walking St; dishes 180-500B; ⏲11am-midnight) One of Pattaya's most famous seafood restaurants spreads across both sides of Walking St. The massive range

of dishes (including plenty of Western options) is good, and the fish are all on display.

Bang Sare THAI $$
(dishes 100-300B; ⌚11am-11pm) Around 20km south of Pattaya is Bang Sare, a developing resort with a long strip of sand and some trendy, tasty international and Thai restaurants and cafes. It gets busy at weekends.

Rimpa Lapin THAI $$
(☎038 235515; www.rimpa-lapin.com; Hat Jomtien; dishes 150-400B; ⌚2pm-midnight) With spectacular views looking back over the entire Pattaya bay, this clifftop restaurant conjures up excellent Thai fushion food. Reservations are needed around sunset. Private transport is required to get here.

Sketch Book Art Cafe INTERNATIONAL, THAI $$
(478/938 Mu 12, Th Tha Phraya; dishes 90-365B; ⌚8am-10pm) This gorgeous, leafy art cafe offers pleasant respite from the normal Pattaya vibe. It's surrounded by a sprawling garden, and the restaurant's walls are covered with the owner's artwork. Smoothies are lush and the Thai food is fresh.

La Baguette BAKERY $$
(☎038 421707; 164/1 Mu 5, Th Naklua; dishes 160-290B; ⌚8am-midnight) This stylish cafe has excellent salads, yummy crêpes and lots of coffee and tea options. Make a reservation if visiting at the weekend.

Mantra INTERNATIONAL $$$
(☎038 429591; Th Hat Pattaya; dishes 160-1240B; ⌚6-11.30pm) One of Pattaya's top restaurants, Mantra is fun even if you can only afford a classy cocktail (from 180B). The menu combines Japanese, Thai and Western dishes. The 1690B Sunday brunch is legendary among locals.

Drinking & Nightlife

Despite the profusion of identikit beer bars, there are still some good places for a no-strings-attached drink.

Gulliver's BAR
(Th Hat Pattaya; beers from 85B; ⌚3pm-2am) The neocolonial facade belies the sports bar inside. There are lots of screens for watching English Premier League football.

Lima Lima CLUB
(Walking St; ⌚10pm-5am) International DJs sometimes, and a mix of Western and local party-goers. Entry is 200B.

☆ Entertainment

Tiffany's THEATRE
(☎038 421700; www.tiffany-show.co.th; 464 Th Pattaya Sai 2; admission 800-1200B; ⌚6pm, 7.30pm & 9pm) Family-friendly ladyboy show featuring lots of sequins, satin and songs, aimed largely at Chinese tour groups.

Blues Factory LIVE MUSIC
(Soi Lucky Star, Walking St; ⌚10pm-2am) New management now runs this long-established live music venue, but the same rock and soul classics are still belted out nightly.

ℹ Information

DANGERS & ANNOYANCES

Most problems in Pattaya are alcohol-induced, especially bad driving and fights. Leave valuables in your room to be on the safe side. Avoid renting jet-skis as scams involving fictional damage are common.

EMERGENCY

Tourist Police (☎emergency 1155; tourist@police.go.th) The head office is beside the Tourism Authority of Thailand office on Th Phra Tamnak, with police boxes along Pattaya and Jomtien beaches.

IMMIGRATION

Immigration Office (☎038 252750; Soi 5, Hat Jomtien; ⌚8.30am-4.30pm)

MEDIA

Pattaya Mail (www.pattayamail.com) is one of the city's English-language weekly newspapers. Pattaya One (www.pattayaone.net) offers an intriguing insight into the darker side of the city.

MEDICAL SERVICES

Bangkok Pattaya Hospital (☎038 259999; www.bangkokpattayahospital.com; 301 Mu 6, Th Sukhumvit, Naklua; ⌚24hr) For first-class health care.

MONEY

There are banks and ATMs throughout the city.

POST

Post Office (Soi 13/2, Th Pattaya Sai 2; ⌚8.30am-4.30pm Mon-Fri, 8.30am-12.30pm Sat)

TOURIST INFORMATION

Tourism Authority of Thailand (TAT; ☎038 428750; tatchon@tat.or.th; 609 Th Phra Tamnak; ⌚8.30am-4.30pm) Located at the northwestern edge of Rama IX Park. Helpful staff have brochures and maps.

TRANSPORT TO/FROM PATTAYA

DESTINATION	BUS	MINIVAN	TRAIN	AIR
Bangkok's Eastern Bus Terminal (Ekamai)	119B; 2hr; every 30min; 4.30am-11pm	130B; 2hr; frequent		
Bangkok's Northern Bus Terminal (Mo Chit)	128B; 2½hr; every 40min; 4.30am-9pm	150B; 2½hr; frequent		
Bangkok's Southern Bus Terminal	119B; 3hr; every 2hr; 6am-6.30pm	150B; 2½hr; hourly		
Bangkok Suvarnabhumi International Airport	250B; 2hr; 7 daily; 6pm-7pm	120B; 2hr; frequent		
Bangkok Hualamphong		150B; 3½hr; 1 daily		
Aranya Prathet (for Cambodia)		260B; 5hr; hourly; 4am-6pm		
Ko Samet		160B; 1hr; hourly		
Rayong		100B; 1½hr; frequent		
Si Racha		40B; 50min; frequent	5B; 1¼hr; 1 daily	
Ko Samui				from 3890B; 1hr; daily
Phuket				from 2650B; 1½hr; daily

Getting There & Away

Pattaya's airport is **U-Tapao Airfield** (☎038 245595; www.utapao.com), 33km south of town. **Bangkok Airways** (☎038 412382; www.bangkokair.com; 179/85-212 Th Pattaya Sai 2) and **Air Asia** (www.airasia.com) fly from here.

The main bus station is on Th Pattaya Neua.

Minivans heading north to Bangkok leave from the corner of Th Sukhumvit and Th Pattaya Klang. Minivans heading for the Cambodian border leave from the junction of Th Sukhumvit and Th Pattaya Tai. The **35 Group** (☎080 070 3341; cnr Th Pattaya 3 & Th Pattaya Tai) has minivans for Ko Chang (550B), Ko Mak (750B) and Ko Kut (800B).

Pattaya Train Station (☎038 429285) is off Th Sukhumvit south of town.

Getting Around

Locally known as 'baht buses', *sŏrng·tăa·ou* do a loop along the major roads; just hop on and pay 10B when you get off. If you are going all the way to or from Naklua, you will have to change vehicles at the dolphin roundabout in Pattaya Neua. Baht buses run to the bus station from the dolphin roundabout as well. If you are going further afield, you can charter a baht bus; establish the price beforehand. Motorbikes can be hired for 200B a day.

Rayong & Ban Phe ระยอง/บ้านเพ

POP 106,737 / 17,116

You are most likely to transit through these towns en route to Ko Samet. Rayong has frequent bus connections to elsewhere and the little port of Ban Phe has ferry services to Ko Samet. Blue *sŏrng·tăa·ou* link the two towns (25B, 45 minutes, every 15 minutes).

Sleeping

Rayong President Hotel HOTEL $
(☎038 611307; www.rayongpresidenthotel.com; off Th Sukhumvit, Rayong; d/tw 400-500/550B; ❄📶) From the bus station, cross to the other side of Th Sukhumvit and walk right. Look for a Siam Commercial Bank on the corner and turn left.

Christie's Guesthouse GUESTHOUSE $
(☎038 651976; www.christiesbanphe.com; 280/92 Soi 1, Ban Phe; r 600B; ❄📶) Christie's is a comfortable place near the pier if you need a room, a meal or a book.

Eating

★**Tamnanpar** THAI $$
(www.tamnanpar-rayong.com; 167/6 Mu 7, Ban Phe; dishes 150-300B; ⏲10am-10pm) It is worth making a detour to experience this rainforest-style restaurant's incredible food and, ahem, award-winning bathrooms. There is also a waterpark on-site (adult/child 200/100B).

Getting There & Away

Minivans from Rayong's bus station go to Bangkok's eastern (Ekamai) and northern (Mo Chit) bus terminals (both 160B, 3½ hours, hourly, 4.40am to 8pm), as well as Suvarnabhumi International Airport (160B, 3½ hours, hourly, 5am to 8pm).

There are minivans to Pattaya (80B, 1½ hours, frequent), Chanthaburi (120B, two hours, frequent) and Trat (200B, three hours, frequent).

Buses opposite Ban Phe's Nuanthip pier go to/from Ekamai (166B, four hours, every two hours, 7am to 6pm).

Ban Phe also has minivan services to Laem Ngop for boats to Ko Chang (250B, three hours, three daily), Pattaya (200B, two hours, hourly) and Bangkok's Victory Monument (200B, four hours, every 40 minutes).

There are boats to/from Ko Samet (p117).

Ko Samet เกาะเสม็ด

Once the doyen of backpacker destinations, today Ko Samet shares its charms with a wider audience. The sandy shores, cosy coves and aquamarine waters attract ferry-loads of Bangkokians looking to party each weekend, while tour groups pack out many resorts. Fire-juggling shows and beach barbecues are nightly events on the northern beaches, but the southern parts of the island are far more secluded and sedate.

Despite being the closest major island to Bangkok, Ko Samet remains surprisingly underdeveloped, with a thick jungle interior crouching beside the low-rise hotels.

Sights & Activities

On some islands you beach-hop, but on Ko Samet you cove-hop. The coastal footpath traverses rocky headlands, cicada-serenaded forests and one stunning bay after another, where the mood becomes successively more mellow the further south you go.

Hat Sai Kaew BEACH

(หาดทรายแก้ว) In the island's northeastern corner, Hat Sai Kaew is the island's widest, whitest and wildest stretch of sand. Sunbathers, sarong-sellers, speedboats, jet-skis and restaurants take up almost every inch of space. At night, the scene is rambunctious, with parties and karaoke sessions.

Ao Hin Khok & Ao Phai BEACH

(อ่าวหินโคก/อ่าวไผ่) Less frenetic than their northern neighbour of Hat Sai Kaew, Ao Hin Khok and Ao Phai are two gorgeous bays separated by rocky headlands. The crowd here tends to be younger and more stylish than the tour groups who gather in Hat Sai Kaew; these two beaches are the traditional backpacker party centres of the island.

> **BYPASSING BANGKOK**
>
> An expanding network of bus and minivan services now connects the eastern seaboard with Suvarnabhumi International Airport, meaning that you don't have to transit through Bangkok for a flight arrival or departure. This is especially alluring to winter-weary visitors eager to reach a beach fast. Ko Samet is the closest prettiest beach to the airport and its southeastern beaches are serene enough for honeymooners. From the airport bus terminal, check the schedule for Rayong-bound buses and then catch a *sŏrng·tăa·ou* to reach the ferry pier to Ko Samet.

Ao Phutsa (Ao Tub Tim) BEACH

(อ่าวพุทรา / อ่าวทับทิม) South of Ao Hin Khok and Ao Phai is wide and sandy Ao Phutsa (Ao Tub Tim), a favourite for solitude seekers, families and couples who need access to 'civilisation' but not much else.

Ao Wong Deuan BEACH

(อ่าววงเดือน) Ao Wong Deuan, meaning 'crescent moon bay', is Samet's second-busiest beach, with a range of resorts and more modest guesthouses.

Ao Thian BEACH

(อ่าวเทียน) Ao Thian (Candlelight Beach), is punctuated by big boulders that shelter small sandy spots, creating a castaway ambience. It remains one of Samet's most easy-going beaches and is deliciously lonely on weekdays. On weekends, Bangkok university students serenade the stars with all-night guitar sessions.

Ao Wai BEACH

(อ่าวหวาย) Ao Wai is a lovely beach far removed from everything else (though in reality it is only 2km from Ao Thian).

Ao Prao BEACH

On the west coast, Ao Prao (Coconut Beach) is worth a visit for a sundowner cocktail, but the small beach is outsized by resorts that promise (but don't deliver) solitude.

Tours

Ko Samet, along with nine neighbouring islands, is part of the Khao Laem Ya/Mu Ko Samet National Park. While there is some development on the other islands, most visitors come for day trips. **Ko Kudee** has a

Ko Samet

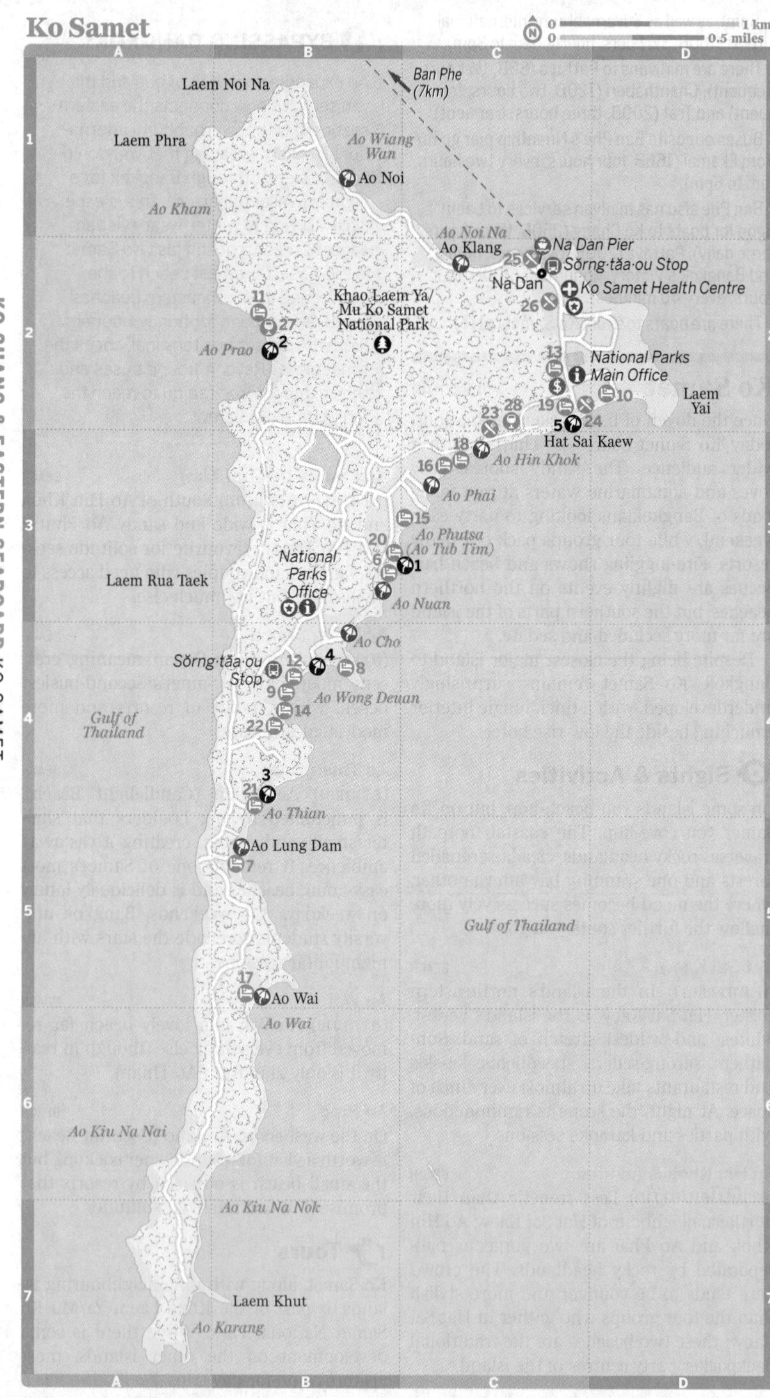
0 1 km
0 0.5 miles
Ban Phe (7km)
Laem Noi Na
Laem Phra
Ao Wiang Wan
Ao Noi
Ao Kham
Ao Noi Na
Ao Klang
Na Dan Pier
Sŏrng·tăa·ou Stop
Na Dan
Ko Samet Health Centre
Khao Laem Ya/ Mu Ko Samet National Park
Ao Prao
National Parks Main Office
Laem Yai
Hat Sai Kaew
Ao Hin Khok
Ao Phai
Ao Phutsa (Ao Tub Tim)
National Parks Office
Laem Rua Taek
Ao Nuan
Ao Cho
Sŏrng·tăa·ou Stop
Ao Wong Deuan
Gulf of Thailand
Ao Thian
Ao Lung Dam
Gulf of Thailand
Ao Wai
Ao Wai
Ao Kiu Na Nai
Ao Kiu Na Nok
Laem Khut
Ao Karang

Ko Samet

Sights

1	Ao Phutsa (Ao Tub Tim)	C3
2	Ao Prao	B2
3	Ao Thian	B4
4	Ao Wong Deuan	B4
5	Hat Sai Kaew	C2

Sleeping

6	Ao Nuan Bungalows	B3
7	Apache	B5
	Ban Thai Sang Thain	(see 21)
8	Blue Sky	B4
9	La Lune Beach Resort	B4
10	Laem Yai Hut Resort	D2
11	Lima Coco Resort	B2
12	Malibu Garden Resort	B4
13	Mossman House	C2
14	Nice & Easy	B4
15	Pudsa Bungalow	C3
16	Samed Pavilion Resort	C3
17	Samet Ville Resort	B5
18	Silver Sand	C3
19	Sinsamut	C2
20	Tubtim Resort	B3
21	Viking Holiday Resort	B4
22	Vongdeuan Resort	B4

Eating

23	Jep's Restaurant	C2
24	Ploy	C2
25	Rabeang Baan	C2
26	Red Ginger	C2
	Sea Breeze	(see 18)

Drinking & Nightlife

27	Ao Prao Resort	B2
	Baywatch Bar	(see 9)
28	Naga Bar	C2

small, pretty sandy stretch, clear water for decent snorkelling and a nice little hiking trail. Ko Man Nai is home to the **Rayong Turtle Conservation Centre**, which is a breeding place for endangered sea turtles, and has a small visitor centre.

Agents for boat tours can be found on the popular beaches and have a couple of different trips on offer (from 500B per person).

Sleeping

Though resorts are replacing bungalows, much of Ko Samet's accommodation is still simple and old-fashioned. There are a handful of sub-700B fan rooms remaining. Look for low season and weekday discounts.

A word of caution to early risers: Hat Sai Kaew, Ao Hin Khok, Ao Phai and Ao Wong Deuan are the most popular beaches and host well-amplified night-time parties.

Hat Sai Kaew

Mossman House GUESTHOUSE $
(038 644017; r 800-1300B;) On the main street, just before the national park ticket office, is this sound guesthouse, with large, comfortable rooms and leafy grounds. Choose a spot at the back for some quiet.

Sinsamut GUESTHOUSE $$
(038 644134; www.sinsamutkohsamed.com; r 1100-2500B;) This former grungy guesthouse is now a shiny boutique sleep, with bright, cheery rooms and an upstairs garden area. Check for discounts.

Laem Yai Hut Resort BUNGALOW $$
(038 644282; r 1500-2500B;) A colourful collection of 15 bungalows scattered around a shady garden on the north end of the beach. The tatty outside appearance belies the interior's modern bathrooms and soft bedding.

Ao Hin Khok & Ao Phai

★ **Samed Pavilion Resort** BOUTIQUE HOTEL $$$
(038 644420; www.samedpavilionresort.com; Ao Phai; r incl breakfast 3500-5500B;) This gorgeous boutique resort has 85 elegant, spacious rooms set around a pool.

Silver Sand HOTEL $$$
(038 644300; www.silversandsamed.com; Ao Phai; r incl breakfast 2200-4000B;) An expanding empire, Silver Sand is a mini-resort, complete with bar, restaurant and shops. It's a little impersonal but the rooms are flashpacker quality and set on a super strip of beach.

Ao Phutsa & Ao Nuan

Ao Nuan Bungalows BUNGALOW $$
(081 781 4875; bungalow fan/air-con 800-1200/1500-3000B;) Ao Nuan is Samet's one remaining bohemian bay, with no internet and access only via a dirt track. Guests hang in hammocks outside their wooden bungalows here or chill in the attached restaurant. Tents are also available (450B).

Tubtim Resort HOTEL $$
(038 644025; www.tubtimresort.com; Ao Phutsa; r incl breakfast 800-3800B;) A well-organised place with great, nightly barbecues and a range of solid, spacious bungalows of varying quality close to the beach.

Pudsa Bungalow BUNGALOW $$

(☎038 644030; Ao Phutsa; bungalow with fan/air-con 800/1700B; ❄📶) Fan rooms are showing their age, but the air-con ones come with a balcony and better bedding. Check out the strange stone sculptures on the beach.

Ao Wong Deuan & Ao Thian (Candlelight Beach)

Ferry services run between Ao Wong Deuan and Ban Phe (140B return), with increased services at the weekend. To get to Ao Thian, catch a ferry to Ao Wong Deuan and walk south over the headland. It is also a quick walk from here to the west coast – look for the marked trail on Ao Thian.

Blue Sky BUNGALOW $

(☎089 936 0842; Ao Wong Deuan; r 600-1200B; ❄) A rare budget spot on Ao Wong Deuan, Blue Sky has beaten-up bungalows set on a rocky headland.

Apache GUESTHOUSE $

(☎081 452 9472; Ao Thian; r 800-1500B; ❄) Apache's eclectic, quirky decorations add character to this super-chilled spot. Bungalows are basic but adequate. Apache's restaurant on stilts is worth a look.

Nice & Easy HOTEL $$

(☎038 644370; www.niceandeasysamed.com; Ao Wong Deuan; r 1200-2500B; ❄📶) As the name suggests, this is a very amiable place, with comfortable, modern bungalows set around a garden behind the beach.

Viking Holiday Resort HOTEL $$

(☎038 644353; thammaraksa@hotmail.com; Ao Thian; r incl breakfast 1200-2000B; ❄📶) About as developed as things get around here, Viking has homely rooms. Staff are helpful and friendly. Cheaper rooms are fan-only.

BEACH ADMISSION FEE

Ko Samet is part of the Mu Ko Samet National Park and charges all visitors an entrance fee (adult/child 200/100B) upon arrival. If you can prove that you live and work in Thailand, it will only cost you 40B, the price Thais pay. The fee is collected at the national parks office; *sŏrng·tăa·ou* from the pier will stop at the gates for payment. Hold on to your ticket for later inspections. There is a 20B fee when using Na Dan pier.

Ban Thai Sang Thain HOTEL $$

(☎081 305 9408; www.banthaisangthain.com; Ao Thian; r 1700-3000B; ❄📶) Thai travellers stay in many of the pavilion-style rooms in this traditional, all-wood resort. Rooms are functional rather than fab. Few staff speak English.

Malibu Garden Resort GUESTHOUSE $$

(☎038 427277; www.malibu-samet.com; Ao Wong Deuan; r incl breakfast 1950-3400B; 📶🏊) Set just behind the main row of beach resorts, Malibu has clean, nondescript rooms, but gets bonus points for having a pool. Staff are helpful and friendly.

La Lune Beach Resort RESORT $$$

(☎in Bangkok 02 260 3592; www.lalunebeachresort.com; Ao Wong Deuan; r incl breakfast 2500-3200B; ❄📶🏊) Meet the new face of Samet. Stylish, chic resorts like this are becoming more common – and this is the best of the bunch. The 40 rooms, all with a soft brown-and-white theme, face a central pool. Rates vary so check for discounts.

Vongdeuan Resort HOTEL $$$

(☎038 644171; www.vongdeuan.com; Ao Wong Deuan; r incl breakfast 2700-4900B; ❄📶🏊) This sprawling resort with its garden-like setting occupies much of the southern part of Ao Wong Deuan. Popular with families and efficiently run, the smart bungalows come with the best bathrooms in this part of the world.

Ao Wai

Ao Wai is a 2km walk from Ao Thian or it can be reached from Ban Phe by chartered speedboat.

Samet Ville Resort HOTEL $$$

(☎038 651682; www.sametvilleresort.com; r incl breakfast 1400-6500B; ❄📶🏊) Spread over two bays – Ao Wai and Ao Hin Kleang – this leafy, 4½-hectare resort is as secluded as it is soporific. The rooms, of which there are several types, are all a few steps from the excellent beach.

Ao Prao

Lima Coco Resort RESORT $$$

(☎in Bangkok 02 129 1140; www.limasamed.com; r incl breakfast 2590-7290B; ❄📶🏊) Ao Prao, on Samet's west coast, has three fancy resorts. Lima Coco is the least ostentatious of these, with bright, whitewashed rooms, energetic staff and beachside massages.

Eating

Most hotels and guesthouses have restaurants that moonlight as bars after sunset. The food and service won't blow you away, but there aren't many alternatives. Nightly beach barbecues, starring all manner of seafood, are an island favourite. There are cheapie Thai places in Na Dan.

Jep's Restaurant INTERNATIONAL $
(Ao Hin Khok; mains 60-150B; 7am-11pm) Canopied by the branches of an arching tree decorated with pendant lights, this pretty place does a wide range of international, and some Thai, dishes. Leave room for dessert.

Rabeang Baan THAI $
(Na Dan; dishes 70-120B; 8am-9pm) By the ferry terminal, this spot has good enough food to make you forget you have to leave the island. It is busier at lunch than dinner.

Red Ginger INTERNATIONAL, THAI $$
(Na Dan; dishes 120-320B; 11am-11pm) A small but select menu of the French-Canadian chef's favourite dishes star at this atmospheric eatery between the pier and Hat Sai Kaew. Good salads, great oven-baked ribs, and some Thai food.

Sea Breeze SEAFOOD $$
(Ao Phai; dishes 80-500B; 11am-11pm) Appropriately named: you can dine on a wide range of seafood right on Ao Phai's pretty beach. There's some Western food on the menu too.

Ploy SEAFOOD $$
(Hat Sai Kaew; dishes 50-400B; 11am-11pm) Before heading to the island's only nightclub, right next door, crunch down on some crab and lobster at this lively restaurant. The menu is epic and the accompanying bar is constantly busy.

Drinking & Nightlife

On weekends, Ko Samet is a boisterous night-owl with tour groups crooning away on karaoke machines and the young ones slurping down beer and buckets to a techno beat. There is usually a crowd on Hat Sai Kaew, Ao Hin Khok, Ao Phai and Ao Wong Deuan.

Ao Prao Resort BAR
(Ao Prao; drinks from 90B; sunset-midnight;) On the sunset-side of the island, this is a lovely sea-view restaurant perfect for a sundowner. You will need private transport to reach it.

LOCAL KNOWLEDGE

A MONSTER WELCOME

The imposing statue of a topless female giant at Na Dan pier is impossible to miss. She is an allusion to Ko Samet's most famous son, the poet Sunthorn Phu and his famous story *Phra Aphaimani*. In the tale, a prince is exiled to an undersea kingdom ruled by the lovesick female giant. A mermaid helps the prince escape to Ko Samet, where he defeats the giant by playing a magical flute.

Baywatch Bar BAR
(Ao Wong Deuan; beers from 80B; sunset-late) A good spot for after-dark beach-gazing, with a fun crowd and strong cocktails.

Naga Bar BAR
(Ao Hin Khok; beers from 70B; sunset-late) This busy beachfront bar is covered in Day-Glo art and run by a friendly bunch of locals who offer good music, lots of whisky and vodka/Red Bull buckets.

Information

There are many ATMs on Ko Samet, including those near the Na Dan pier, Ao Wong Deuan and Ao Thian.

Ko Samet Health Centre (038 644123; 24hr) On the main road between Na Dan and Hat Sai Kaew.

National Parks Main Office (btwn Na Dan & Hat Sai Kaew; sunrise-sunset) Has another office at Ao Wong Deuan.

Police Station (1155) On the main road between Na Dan and Hat Sai Kaew. There's a substation at Ao Wong Deuan.

Getting There & Away

Ko Samet is accessed via the mainland piers in Ban Phe. There are many piers each used by different ferry companies, but they all charge the same fares (one way/return 70/100B, 40 minutes, hourly, 8am to 5pm) and dock at Na Dan, the main pier on Ko Samet. The last boat back to the mainland leaves at 6pm.

If you are staying at Ao Wong Deuan or further south, catch a ferry from the mainland directly to the beach (one way/return 90/140B, one hour, three daily departures).

Speedboats charge 200B to 500B one way and will drop you at the beach of your choice, but only leave when they have enough passengers.

Getting Around

Ko Samet's small size makes it a great place to explore on foot. A network of roads connects most of the island.

Green *sŏrng·tăa·ou* meet boats at the pier and provide drop-offs at the various beaches (10B to 70B, depending on the beach and number of passengers). Chartering one costs 100B to 400B.

You can rent motorcycles nearly everywhere along the northern half of the island for 300B per day. Newly improved roads mean that ATVs have bitten the dust.

Chanthaburi จันทบุรี

POP 121,549

Chanthaburi is proof all that glitters is not gold. Here, gems do the sparkling, with precious stones ranging from sapphires to emeralds traded every weekend in a bustling street market. Nearby, wonderfully restored waterfront buildings are evidence of how the Chinese, French and Vietnamese have influenced life – and architecture – here.

Vietnamese Christians fled persecution from Cochin China (southern Vietnam) in the 19th century and came to Chanthaburi. More Vietnamese arrived in the 1920s and 1940s as they fled French rule, then a third wave in 1975 after the communist takeover of southern Vietnam. The French occupied Chanthaburi from 1893 to 1905 due to a dispute over the border between Siam and Indochina.

Head south for 25km, past the numerous salt fields, to find the quiet coastal towns of **Laem Sing** and **Chao Lao**. The latter has good beaches and accommodation.

GETTING TO CAMBODIA: BAN PAKARD TO PSAR PRUHM

Getting to the Border In Chanthaburi, **minivans** (092 037 6266) depart from a stop across the river from the River Guest House to Ban Pakard/Pong Nam Ron (150B, 1½ hours, 10am, 11am, 6.30pm).

At the Border This is a far less busy and more pleasant crossing than Poipet further north. You need a passport photo and US$20 for the visa fee.

Moving On Hop on a motorbike taxi to Pailin in Cambodia. From there, you can catch frequent shared taxis (US$5 per person, 1½ hours) to scenic Battambang. After that, you can move on to Siem Reap by boat, or Phnom Penh by bus.

Sights & Activities

★Chantaboon Waterfront Community HISTORIC SITE

(Th Sukhaphiban) Hugging the banks of Mae Nam Chanthaburi is this charismatic part of town, filled with restored houses and elderly residents sitting around reminiscing about their Chanthaburi tales with each other. The **Learning House** (081 945 5761; 10am-4.30pm Sat & Sun) displays neighbourhood photos, paintings and architectural designs, including upstairs drawings of intricate ventilation panels that feature Chinese characters and French fleurs-de-lis.

Around 300 years ago, farmers and merchants started trading alongside the river, which provided easy transport links. Later, Chinese and Vietnamese traders and refugees came to the area. Today, the 1km-long street scene still includes many private homes, but the art galleries, coffee shops and snack stalls entice visiting Thais at weekends.

Gem Market MARKET

(ตลาดพลอย; Th Si Chan & Trok Kachang; 9am-6pm Fri-Sun) Every weekend, the normally quiet streets that are near Th Si Chan (Gem Road) burst into life as gem traders arrive to bustle and bargain. Incongruously humble considering the value of commodities on offer, people cluster around makeshift tables examining small piles of unset stones.

Buying and selling is not for the uninitiated, but it is a fascinating glimpse at a trade that has taken place here for decades. In the hills surrounding Chanthaburi, several sapphire and ruby mines once supplied the palace with fine ornaments prior to the mid-19th century when the mines were developed into commercial operations by Shan (Burmese) traders. These days, locally mined gems are of inferior international quality but the resourceful Chanthaburi traders roam the globe acquiring precious and semi-precious stones, which are in turn traded to other globetrotters.

The last remaining mine in the area is **Khao Phloi Waen**, 6km from town, which is famous locally for its 'Mekong Whiskey' yellow-coloured sapphire.

Cathedral CHURCH

(dawn-dusk) FREE Thailand's largest cathedral, situated on the east bank of Mae Nam Chanthaburi, started life as a modest chapel in 1711. Since then there have been four

Chanthaburi

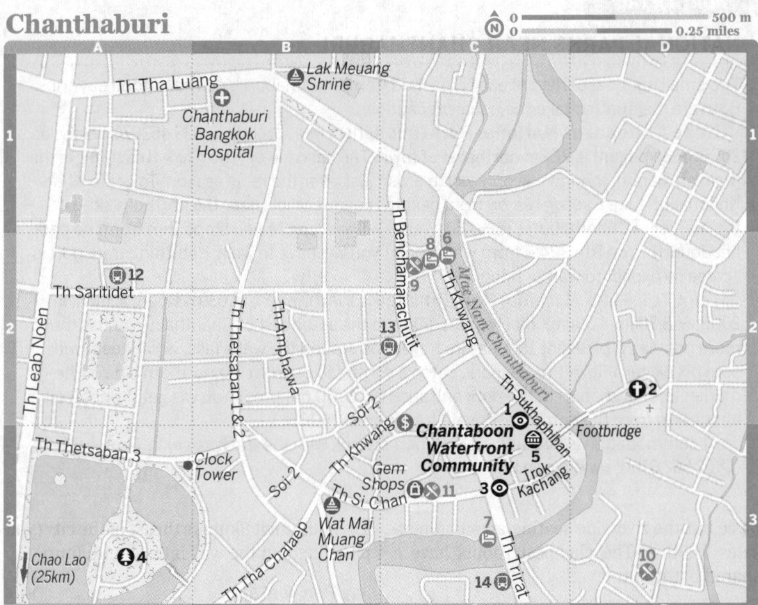

Chanthaburi

Top Sights
1 Chantaboon Waterfront Community ... C2

Sights
2 Cathedral ... D2
3 Gem Market ... C3
4 King Taksin Park ... A3
5 Learning House ... C3

Sleeping
6 Baan Luang Rajamaitri ... C2
7 River Guest House ... C3
8 Tamajun Hotel ... C2

Eating
9 Chanthorn Phochana ... C2
10 Jay Pen Yentafo ... D3
11 Muslim Restaurant ... C3

Transport
12 Bus Station & Minivans ... A2
13 Minivan Stop ... C2
14 Minivans to Ban Pakard/Pong Nam Ron ... C3

reconstructions and the current Gothic-style structure includes stained-glass windows. The statue of the Virgin Mary at the front is bedecked with more than 200,000 sapphires – a fitting link between religion and the city's famous gem trade. Cross a footbridge to access the Chantaboon Waterfront Community.

King Taksin Park PARK

(สวนสาธารณะสมเด็จพระเจ้าตากสิน; Th Tha Chalaep; ⏲dawn-dusk) The town's main oasis is filled with joggers and picnicking families. It is a pleasant spot to visit for an evening stroll.

Festivals & Events

Fruit Festival FOOD

Held at the end of May or beginning of June, Chanthaburi's annual fruit festival is a great opportunity to sample the region's superb produce, especially rambutans, mangosteens and the ever-pungent durian.

Sleeping

Several boutique and budget spots can be found near Th Sukhaphiban.

River Guest House HOTEL $

(☎039 328211; 3/5-8 Th Si Chan; r 190-490B; ❄@☜) Rooms are tiny and the beds are

WORTH A TRIP

NATIONAL PARKS NEAR CHANTHABURI

Two small national parks are easily reached from Chanthaburi, and make good day trips. Both are malarial, so take the usual precautions.

Khao Khitchakut National Park (อุทยานแห่งชาติเขาคิชฌกูฏ; ☎039 452074; admission 200B; ⏰6am-6pm) is 28km northeast of town. The cascade of **Nam Tok Krathing** is the main attraction, though it is only worth a visit just after the rainy season. To get to Khao Khitchakut, take a *sŏrng·tăa·ou* from next to the post office, near the northern side of the market in Chanthaburi (35B, 45 minutes). The *sŏrng·tăa·ou* stops 1km from the park headquarters on Rte 3249, from which point you will have to walk. Returning transport is scarce so expect to wait or hitch.

Nam Tok Phlio National Park (อุทยานแหง่ ชาติน้ำตกพลิ้ว; ☎039 434528; admission 200B; ⏰8.30am-4.30pm), off Hwy 3, is 14km to the southeast of Chanthaburi and is much more popular. A pleasant 1km nature trail loops around the waterfalls, which teem with soro brook carp. To get to the park, catch a *sŏrng·tăa·ou* from the northern side of the market in Chanthaburi to the park entrance (50B, 30 minutes). You will get dropped off about 1km from the entrance. Private transport is 1500B.

Accommodation is available at both parks; book with the **park reservation system** (☎02 562 0760; www.dnp.go.th).

basic but the riverside seating area compensates for this. The cheapest rooms have a shared bathroom.

★ **Baan Luang Rajamaitri** HISTORIC HOTEL $$
(☎039 322037; www.baanluangrajamaitri.com; 252 Th Sukhaphiban; r incl breakfast 1100-2650B; ❄📶) Named after a local philanthropist, this expertly restored hotel has elegant rooms.

Tamajun Hotel BOUTIQUE HOTEL $$
(☎039 311977; www.tamajunhotel.com; 248 Th Sukhaphiban; r incl breakfast 1500-1800B; ❄📶) From the fake grass on the stairs to the individually themed rooms, Tamajun has a fun, retro-chic feel. Riverside rooms come with a shared balcony and there's a good on-site restaurant. Weekday rates are 15% cheaper.

Eating & Drinking

Fruit Stalls FRUIT STALL $
(Th Sukhumvit; fruit 40-80B; ⏰8am-9pm; 🖉) Chanthaburi is famed for its fruit. You can taste why at the various fruit stalls that line Th Sukhumvit 8km northeast of the city (you pass them on the way into Chanthaburi).

Jay Pen Yentafo THAI $
(Wat Phai Lom; noodles 100B; ⏰9am-3.30pm) Pink-coloured noodle soup combined with crab has given this temple restaurant a great reputation with locals.

Muslim Restaurant INDIAN, THAI $
(☎081 353 5174; cnr Soi 4, Th Si Chan; dishes 50-80B; ⏰9.30am-6pm) Run by Thai Muslims, this tiny place has excellent *paratha*, *biryani*, curries and chai tea.

Chanthorn Phochana THAI $$
(102/5-8 Th Benchamarachutit; dishes 100-200B; ⏰9am-9pm) A great place to try local specialities; the *chamung* leaves with pork and Chanthaburi crab noodles are particularly good.

Information

Banks with change facilities and ATMs can be found across town.

Bank of Ayudhya (Th Khwang; ⏰8.30am-3.30pm)

TRANSPORT TO/FROM CHANTHABURI

DESTINATION	BUS	MINIVAN
Bangkok's Eastern Bus Terminal (Ekamai)	198B; 4hr; 25 daily	
Bangkok's Northern Bus Terminal (Mo Chit)	205B; 4hr; 2 daily	
Khorat	279B; 4hr; every 2 hours	
Sa Kaew	145B; 2hr; every 2 hours	
Rayong		120B; 2hr; hourly
Trat		70B; 1hr; frequent

Chanthaburi Bangkok Hospital (☎039 319888; Th Tha Luang; ⏲24hr) Part of the Bangkok group; handles emergencies.

Getting There & Around

Chanthaburi's bus station is west of the river. Minivans leave from the bus station. Motorbike taxis charge 30B to 40B for trips around town.

Trat

ตราด

POP 21,590

Trat is a major transit point for Ko Chang and coastal Cambodia, with underappreciated old-world charm. The guesthouse neighbourhood occupies a wooden shophouse district, bisected by winding sois and filled with Thai street life: children riding bikes, housewives running errands and small businesses selling trinkets and necessities.

Trat's signature product is a medicinal herbal oil (known as *nám·man lĕu·ang*), touted as a remedy for everything from arthritis to bug bites and available at local pharmacies. It is produced by resident Mae Ang-Ki (Somthawin Pasananon), using a secret pharmaceutical recipe that has been handed down through her Chinese-Thai family for generations.

Sights

One booming business in Trat is **swiftlet farming**. Walk down Th Lak Meuang and you will see that the top floors of shophouses have been converted into nesting sites for birds that produce the edible nests considered a Chinese delicacy. Swiflets' nests were quite rare (and expensive) in the past because they were only harvested from precipitous sea caves by trained, daring climbers. In the 1990s, entrepreneurs figured out how to replicate the cave atmosphere in multistorey shophouses and the business has become a key operation in Trat.

Indoor Market MARKET

The indoor market sprawls east from Th Sukhumvit to Th Tat Mai and has a little bit of everything, especially all the things that you forgot to pack. Without really noticing the difference you will stumble upon the **day market** (Th Tat Mai; ⏲6-11am), selling fresh fruit, vegetables and takeaway food.

Sleeping

Trat has many budget hotels in traditional wooden houses on and around Th Thana Charoen.

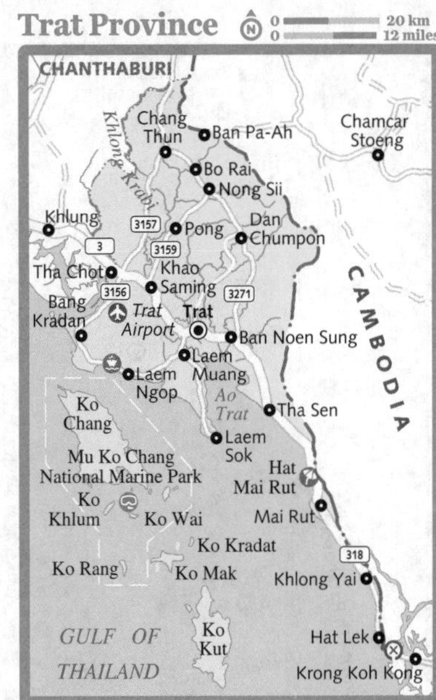

★Ban Jai Dee Guest House GUESTHOUSE $

(☎083 589 0839; banjaideehouse@yahoo.com; 6 Th Chaimongkol; r 200B; 📶) This relaxed traditional wooden house has simple rooms with shared bathrooms (hot-water showers). Paintings and objets d'art made by the artistically inclined owners decorate the common spaces. Booking ahead is essential. Ask the owner, Serge, for travel advice.

Garden Guest House GUESTHOUSE $

(☎087 019 3111; 87/1 Th Sukhumvit; r 150-400B; 📶) A charming, elderly lady runs this guesthouse, though it feels more like a homestay as she makes such an effort. Bedding is of varying quality, so check first. All but one of the 10 rooms have shared bathrooms.

Orchid GUESTHOUSE $

(☎039 530474; orchidguesthouse@gmail.com; 92 Th Lak Meuang; r 150-500B; ❄📶) Big, slightly battered rooms in a house with a large garden. The cheapest rooms are fan-only and share bathrooms. The laid-back owner sometimes opens her attached restaurant, which serves good pizzas.

Pop Guest House GUESTHOUSE $

(☎039 512392; popgoodguesthouse@hotmail.com; 1/1 Th Thana Charoen; r 150-600B; ❄@📶)

Trat

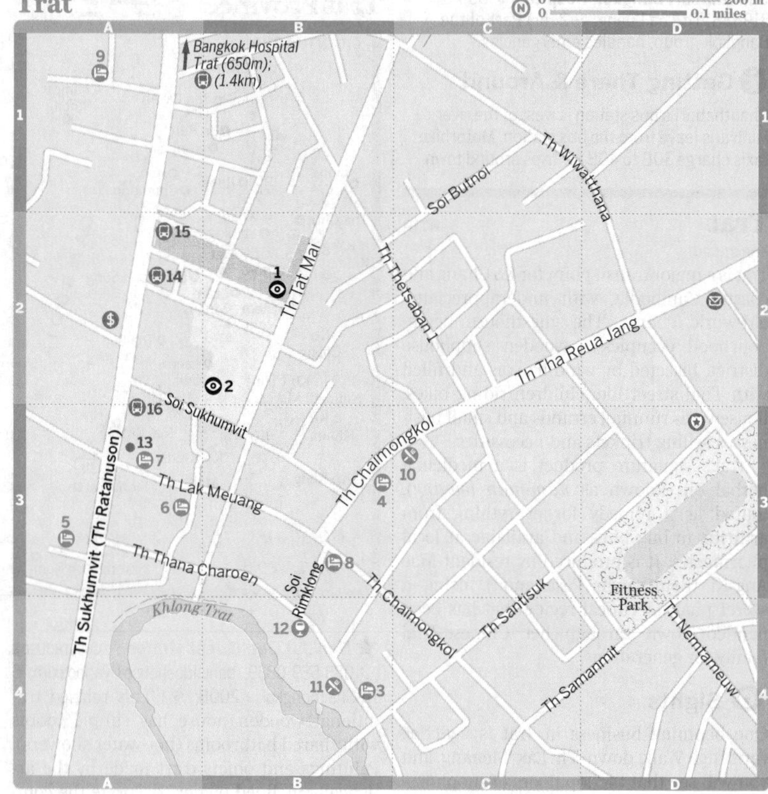

Trat

Sights

1 Day Market B2
2 Indoor Market B2

Sleeping

3 Artist's Place B4
4 Ban Jai Dee Guest House B3
5 Garden Guest House A3
6 Orchid A3
7 Pop Guest House A3
8 Rimklong Boutique Hotel B3
9 Trat Center Hotel A1

Eating

10 No Name Steak & Pasta C3
11 Pier 112 .... B4

Drinking & Nightlife

12 Cafe Oscar B4

Transport

13 Family Tour A3
14 Minivans to Chanthaburi A2
15 Sŏrng·tăa·ou to Bus Station & Laem Ngop A2
16 Sŏrng·tăa·ou to Tha Centrepoint & Th Thammachat (Laem Ngop) A3

Pop, which has two neighbouring locations, comes with somewhat uninspiring rooms in lots of guises. The staff are not particularly friendly but the restaurant is good. Cheaper rooms are fan-only.

Artist's Place GUESTHOUSE $$

(☎082 469 1900; pier.112@hotmail.com; 132/1 Th Thana Charoen; r incl breakfast 800-1100B; ❄️📶) The individually decorated rooms, and pieces of art dotted around the adjoining garden, come courtesy of the owner, Mr Phukhao.

Trat Center Hotel HOTEL $$
(☎039 531234; www.tratcenterhotel.com; 45/65 Th Tasaban 5; r incl breakfast 900B;) Spotless, modern rooms with comfy beds at this decent midrange option. It is a five-minute walk north of the day market.

Rimklong Boutique Hotel BOUTIQUE HOTEL $$
(☎039 523388; soirimklong@hotmail.co.th; 194 Th Lak Meuang; r 1000B;) Trat's only boutique hotel has five bright, airy rooms. There's a pleasant cafe attached.

Eating & Drinking

Trat is all about market eating: head to the day market on Th Tat Mai for *gah·faa bohrahn* (ancient coffee), the night market (which is in the same location from 5pm to 9pm) or the indoor market for lunchtime noodles. Food stalls line Th Sukhumvit at night.

No Name Steak & Pasta INTERNATIONAL, THAI $
(61-65 Th Chaimongkol; dishes 50-120B; 8am-9pm Sun-Fri) Restaurant serving Thai and Western classics, plus sandwiches. It makes for a good coffee/smoothie stop, too.

Pier 112 THAI $$
(132/1 Th Thana Charoen; dishes 80-250B; 10.30am-10.30pm;) Good range of vegetarian dishes, as well as reliable curries.

Cafe Oscar BAR
(Th Thana Charoen; beers from 50B; 9am-1am) An eclectic crew of locals and expats gather at this corner bar, with wooden furniture and a retro 1970s and '80s soundtrack. In low season it opens in the evening only.

Information

Th Sukhumvit runs through town, though it is often called Th Ratanuson.

Trat Map (www.tratmap.com) is a useful online directory of businesses and attractions in Trat.

Bangkok Hospital Trat (☎039 532735; www.bangkokhospital.com; 376 Mu 2, Th Sukhumvit; 24hr) Located 400m north of the town centre.

Krung Thai Bank (Th Sukhumvit; 8.30am-3.30pm) Has an ATM and exchange facilities.

Police Station (☎1155; cnr Th Santisuk & Th Wiwatthana) A short walk from Trat's centre.

Post Office (Th Tha Reua Jang; 8.30am-4.30pm Mon-Fri, 8.30am-12.30pm Sat) East of Trat's commercial centre.

Getting There & Around

Trat's bus station is 2km out of town. Minivans leave from points along Th Sukhumvit. **Family Tour** (☎081 940 7380; cnr Th Sukhumvit & Th Lak Meuang) has minivans to Bangkok's Victory Monument and northern bus terminal (Mo Chit).

The three piers that handle boat traffic to Ko Chang, Ko Kut, Ko Mak and Ko Wai are located in Laem Ngop, about 30km southwest of Trat. For boat transport details to the islands, see those sections of each island.

Sŏrng·tăa·ou to Laem Ngop and the piers (60B per person for six passengers, 200B for the whole vehicle, 40 minutes) leave from Th Sukhumvit, just past the market.

Bangkok Airways (☎Trat airport 039 5516545, in Bangkok 02 265 5555; www.bangkokair.com) operates flights from the airport, which is 40km from town. Taxis to Trat are a rip-off at 600B; try to hail a *sŏrng·tăa·ou*.

Motorbike taxis charge 20B to 30B for local hops.

Motorbikes can be rented for 200B a day along Th Sukhumvit near the guesthouse area.

TRANSPORT TO/FROM TRAT

DESTINATION	BUS	MINIVAN	AIR
Bangkok Suvarnabhumi International Airport	261B; 5-6hr; 5 daily		from 2550B; 1hr; 2 daily
Bangkok's Eastern Bus Terminal (Ekamai)	254B; 5hr; 17 daily	270B; 4hr; every 2hr; 8.30am-4.30pm	
Bangkok's Northern Bus Terminal (Mo Chit)	261B; 5-6hr; 4 daily	270B; 4hr; every 2hr; 8.30am-4.30pm	
Chanthaburi	70B; 1hr; every 2hr; 8.15am-6pm	70B; 50min; frequent; 6am-6pm	
Hat Lek (for Cambodia)		120B; 1½hr; hourly; 5am-6pm	
Pattaya		300B; 3½hr; every 2hr; 8am-6pm	
Rayong/Ban Phe (for Ko Samet)		200B; 2½hr; every 2hr; 8am-6pm	

GETTING TO CAMBODIA: HAT LEK TO KRONG KOH KONG

Getting to the Border From Trat, the closest Thailand–Cambodia crossing is from Hat Lek to the Cambodian town of Krong Koh Kong. Minivans run to Hat Lek hourly from 5am to 6pm (120B, 1½ hours) from Trat's bus station.

At the Border This is the most expensive place to cross into Cambodia from Thailand. Visas are a steep 1500B (they are US$20 at other crossings) and payment is only accepted in baht. You will need a passport photo too. Avoid anyone who says you require a 'medical certificate' or other paperwork. The border closes at 8pm.

Moving On Take a taxi (US$10) or *moto* (US$3) to Koh Kong where you can catch onward transport to Sihanoukville (four hours, one or two departures per day) and Phnom Penh (five hours, two or three departures until 11.30am).

Thai visas can be renewed here, but visas at land borders have been shortened to 15 days.

Ko Chang เกาะช้าง

POP 12,346

With steep, jungle-covered peaks, picturesque Ko Chang (Elephant Island) retains its remote and rugged spirit – despite attempts to transform it into a package-tour destination. Sweeping bays are sprinkled along the west coast; most have super-fine sand, some have pebbles. What it lacks in sand it makes up for in an unlikely combination: accessible wilderness with a thriving party scene. Convenient forays into a verdant jungle or underwater coral gardens can be enthusiastically toasted at one of Lonely Beach's many beer and bucket parties.

Because of its relative remoteness, it is only in the past decade or so that tourists – and 24-hour electricity – have arrived. Today, it is still a slog to get here, but the resorts are now busy with Chinese package tourists, Cambodian-bound backpackers and beach-hopping couples funnelling through to more remote islands in the Mu Ko Chang National Marine Park. Along the populous west coast are virtual mini-towns with a standard of living that has outpaced the island's infrastructure. For a taste of old-school Chang, head to the southeastern villages and mangrove forests of Ban Salak Phet and Ban Salak Kok.

Sights

Although Thailand's second-largest island has accelerated into the modern world with some understandable growing pains, Ko Chang still has tropically hued seas, critter-filled jungles and a variety of water sports for athletic beach bums.

West Coast

The west coast is by far the most developed part of Ko Chang, thanks to its beaches and bays. Public *sŏrng·tăa·ou* make beach-hopping easy and affordable. Some beaches are rocky, so it's worth bringing swim boots for children. Most of the time the seas are shallow and gentle but be wary of rips during storms and the rainy season (May to October).

Hat Sai Khao BEACH
(หาดทรายขาว) The longest, most luxurious stretch of sand on the island is packed with package-tour hotels and serious sunbathers. Head to the north section of the beach to find the more secluded backpacker spot. Along the main road, the village is busy and brash – but comes with all the necessary amenities.

Hat Kai Mook BEACH
(หาดไข่มุก) The name means 'pearl beach', although the 'pearls' here are just large pebbles that pack the shore and culminate in fish-friendly headlands. Swimming and sunbathing are out but there's good snorkelling.

Ao Khlong Prao BEACH
(อ่าวคลองพร้าว) Khlong Prao's beach is a pretty sweep of sand pinned between hulking mountainous headlands and bisected by two estuaries. At low tide, beachcombers stroll the rippled sand eyeing the critters left naked by the receding water. Sprawling luxury resorts dominate here and the primary pastime is sunbathing by the pool, as high tide gobbles up much of the beach.

With hired transport, you can head in to the interior of the island to do some waterfall-spotting. The island's biggest is **Nam Tok Khlong Plu**, a three-tiered cascade with a swimmable pool. It is reached via a 600m jungle path.

Hat Kaibae BEACH
(หาดไก่แบ้) A companion beach to Khlong Prao, Hat Kaibae is a good spot for families and thirty-something couples. A slim strip of sand unfurls around an island-dotted bay far enough removed from the package-tour scene that you'll feel independent. There is kayaking to the outlying island and low tide provides hours of beachcombing.

Lonely Beach BEACH
The last thing you'll be here is lonely, as this is Ko Chang's backpacker enclave and the liveliest place to be after dark. Here, vodka buckets are passed around and the speakers turned up. The beach has pebbles at the southern tip but the rest is sandy.

Tree Top Adventure Park PARK
(www.treetopadventurepark.com; Bailan Bay; 950B; 9am-5pm) Swing through the jungle like Tarzan, walk the rope bridges, or ride the ziplines, flying skateboards and bicycles at this popular attraction. Close to Bailan Bay, this is a two-hour adventure. Add on 150B for transport there and back. All tour agencies around Ko Chang can book it.

Ban Bang Bao VILLAGE
(บ้านบางเบ้า) The villagers of Bang Bao, a former fishing community built in the traditional fashion of interconnected piers, have swapped their nets for renting out portions of their homes to souvenir shops and restaurants.

At first glance, Bang Bao may look like a tourist trap, but the traders who pack the pier generally offer quality, locally made produce. Walk to the far end to see a white lighthouse and boats bound for the nearby islands. Unless you are staying in one of the pier's guesthouses, get going before dark as it can be hard to find a taxi back.

Hat Khlong Kloi BEACH
At the eastern end of Ao Bang Bao, Khlong Kloi is a sandy beach that feels a lot like a secret though there are other people here, as well as all the requisite amenities (beer, food, fruit, massage) and a few guesthouses. You'll need private transport to get out here.

Northern Interior

Ko Chang's mountainous interior is predominately protected as a national park. The forest is lush and alive with wildlife and threaded by silver-hued waterfalls.

Ban Kwan Chang ELEPHANT INTERACTION
(บ้านควาญช้าง; 087 811 3599; chaitientong@yahoo.com; tours 800-1300B; 8am-5pm) Tours ranging from 30 minutes to one hour (800/1300B) that involve feeding, bathing and riding a pachyderm are offered in a beautiful forested setting home to 10 rescued female elephants. Owner Pittaya Homkrailas is a well-regarded conservation enthusiast who works to preserve a humane relationship between the elephant and mahout, but it's worth considering the animal welfare issues involved with elephant rides before choosing that particular option.

Transport is included in the price. Be sure to apply mozzie spray.

East Coast

The east coast is still peaceful and undeveloped, filled with undulating hills of coconut and palm trees and low-key fishing villages in the far south. You will need private transport to explore this charming coast of scenic bays and mangrove forests.

Nam Tok Than Mayom WATERFALL
(น้ำตกธารมะยม; park fee 200B; 8am-5pm) A series of three falls along the stream of

WORTH A TRIP

HAT MAI RUT

If you are going through coastal withdrawal, the sliver of Trat province that extends southeast towards Cambodia is fringed by sandy beaches. One of the easiest beaches to reach is **Hat Mai Rut**, roughly halfway between Trat and the border crossing of Hat Lek. Nearby is a traditional fishing village filled with colourful wooden boats and the sights and smells of a small-scale industry carried on by generations of families. **Mairood Resort** (089 841 4858; 28 Mu 6; r from 1950B;) is a lovely spot to stay overnight, with cottages by the sea and in the mangroves.

You can get to Hat Mai Rut from the Trat bus station via Hat Lek–bound *sŏrng·tăa·ou*. The resort is 3km from the Km 53 highway marker.

Ko Chang

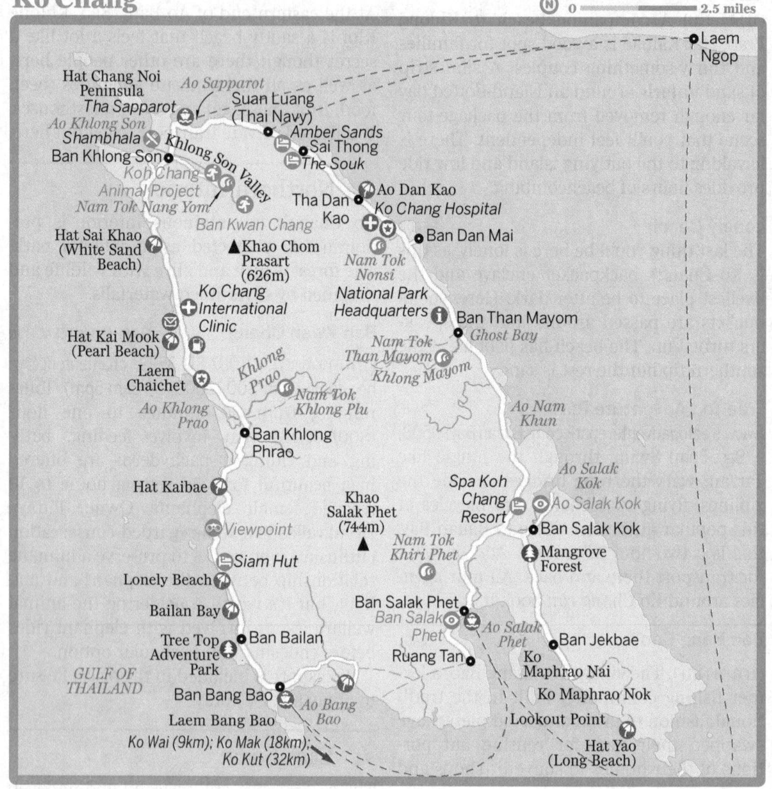

Khlong Mayom can be reached via the park office near Tha Than Mayom. The view from the top is superb and nearby there are inscribed stones bearing the initials of Rama V, Rama VI and Rama VII.

Ao Salak Kok BAY

(อ่าวสลักคอก) The dense tangle of mangroves here are protected by a group of fisherfolk who recognise their ecological importance. Mangroves are the ocean's nurseries, fostering the next generation of marine species, as well as resident birds and crustaceans, and this bay is now Ko Chang's prime ecotourism site.

Villagers, working in conjunction with Khun Pittaya, of Ban Kwan Chang elephant park, operate an award-winning program to preserve the environment and traditional way of life. They rent kayaks through the Salak Kok Kayak Station and run an affiliated restaurant.

Ban Salak Phet VILLAGE

(บ้านสลักเพชร) To discover what Ko Chang was like before the tourists came, visit Ban Salak Phet, in the far southeastern corner. This sleepy community is full of fishing boats and yawning dogs who stretch out on the roadside; it also provides access to some good treks.

Most visitors come for the seafood restaurants or to cruise the lonely byways for a secluded beach. Beyond the commercial heart of the village is **Ao Salak Phet**, a beautiful blue bay serenely guarded by humpbacked islands.

Nam Tok Khiri Phet WATERFALL

(น้ำตกคีรีเพชร) This small waterfall, 2km from Ban Salak Phet, is a 15-minute walk from the road and rewards you with a deep plunge pool. It is usually less crowded than many of the larger falls and is easily reached if you are in the neighbourhood of Ao Salak Phet.

Activities

Kayaking

Ko Chang cuts an impressive and heroic profile when viewed from the sea aboard a kayak. The water is generally calm and offshore islands provide a paddling destination that is closer than the horizon. Most hotels rent open-top kayaks (from 300B per day) that are convenient for near-shore outings and noncommittal kayakers. Some provide them for free.

KayakChang KAYAKING
(☎087 673 1753; www.kayakchang.com; Emerald Cove Resort, Khlong Prao; kayak per day from 2000B) For experienced paddlers, KayakChang rents high-end, closed-top kayaks that handle better and travel faster. They also lead multiday trips (from 4500B) to other islands in the archipelago.

Salak Kok Kayak Station KAYAKING
(☎087 748 9497; kayak rental per hr 200B) On the east side of the island, explore the mangrove swamps of Ao Salak Kok while supporting an award-winning ecotour program. Salak Kok Kayak Station rents self-guided kayaks and is a village work project designed to promote tourism without affecting the traditional way of life. They can also help arrange wooden-boat trips with a guide (200B), village homestays and hiking tours.

Hiking

Ko Chang isn't just about the beaches. The island has a well-developed trekking scene, with inland routes that lead to lush forests filled with birds, monkeys and flora. A handful of English-speaking guides grew up near the jungle and are happy to share their secrets **Mr Tan** (tantrekking@hotmail.com; ☎089 645 2019) from **Evolution Tour** (☎039 557078; www.evolutiontour.com) has family-friendly hikes and more challenging eight-hour mountain treks. **Mr Raht** (kohchang_trekking@yahoo.com; ☎086 155 5693) leads one-day jungle treks around the southern and eastern parts of the island. Overnight camping can also be arranged. Treks range from 450B to 1500B.

Koh Chang Trekking HIKING
(☎081 588 3324) Birdwatchers should contact Koh Chang Trekking, which runs one- and two-day trips (950B to 1800B) into Mu Ko Chang National Marine Park and hikes to the top of Khao Chom Prasat, two nearby rocky-tipped peaks. Prices are for a group of four people.

Volunteering

Koh Chang Animal Project VOLUNTEERING
(☎089 042 2347; www.kohchanganimalproject.org; Ban Khlong Son; ⌚9am-5.30pm Mon-Sat) Abused, injured or abandoned animals receive medical care and refuge at this nonprofit centre. With local people it also works on general veterinarian services and spaying and neutering. Volunteers and donations are welcome. Travelling vets and vet nurses often drop by, while non-vets are needed to help with numerous odd jobs. Call to make an appointment.

Most *sŏrng·tăa·ou* drivers know how to get here; say you are going to 'Ban Lisa' (Lisa's House) in Khlong Son. If you have a bike, turn off the main road in Ban Khlong Son at 7-Eleven; the project is 1.5km down the road.

Massage

Sima Massage MASSAGE
(☎081 489 5171; Khlong Prao; massage per hr 250-400B; ⌚8am-10pm) On the main road and next to KaTi Culinary (p134), Sima is regarded by locals as the best massage on the island – quite an accolade in a place where a massage is easier to find than a 7-Eleven.

KO CHANG IN...

Three Days

Lie on the beach, rotate your body and repeat, with occasional forays into the ocean. Do this until you get bored, then rouse yourself out of your sun-induced stupor to explore the island. Do a **day hike** through the jungle or view the island from aboard a **kayak**. Catch a *sŏrng·tăa·ou* to **Ban Bang Bao** (p125) for lunch or an early dinner, followed by souvenir shopping. The next day rent a motorbike and explore the mangrove forest and fishing villages of the **east coast** (p125).

One Week

Migrate to the nearby islands of **Ko Wai** (p135) or **Ko Kut** (p138) for powder-soft sands, or devote a day or two giving back to the island by lending a hand at the **Koh Chang Animal Project** (p127).

DON'T MISS

DIVING & SNORKELLING KO CHANG

The dive sites near Ko Chang offer a variety of coral, fish and beginner-friendly shallow waters.

The seamounts off the southern tip of the island within the Mu Ko Chang National Marine Park are reached within a 30-minute cruise. Popular spots include **Hin Luk Bat** and **Hin Rap**, rocky, coral-encrusted seamounts with depths of around 18m to 20m. These are havens for schooling fish and some turtles. In 2013, near Hin Rap, a 30m gunship was deliberately sunk and now lies on its side.

By far the most pristine diving in the area is around **Ko Rang**, an uninhabited island protected from fishing by its marine park status. Visibility here is much better than near Ko Chang and averages between 10m and 20m. Everyone's favourite dive is **Hin Gadeng** – spectacular rock pinnacles with coral visible to around 28m. On the eastern side of Ko Rang, **Hin Kuak Maa** (also known as Three Finger Reef) is another top dive spot and is home to a coral-encrusted wall sloping from 2m to 14m and attracting swarms of marine life.

Ko Yak, **Ko Tong Lang** and **Ko Laun** are shallow dives perfect for both beginners and advanced divers. These small rocky islands can be circumnavigated and have lots of coral, schooling fish, puffer fish, morays, barracuda, rays and the occasional turtle.

About 7km offshore from Ban Bang Bao there's a popular dive to the wreck of the **HTMS Chang**, a 100m-long former Thai naval vessel purposely sunk in 2012 to form an artifical reef that now sits 30m beneath the surface.

Reef-fringed **Ko Wai** features a good variety of colourful hard and soft corals and is great for snorkelling. It is a popular day-tripping island but has simple overnight accommodation for more alone time with the reef.

The snorkelling on **Ko Mak** is not as good, but the island offers some decent dives even if the reefs don't see as many fish as elsewhere.

One-day diving trips start at 2900B. PADI Open Water certification costs 14,500B per person. Many dive shops remain open during the rainy season (May to October) but visibility and sea conditions are poor. The following are recommended dive operators:

BB Divers (☎039 558040; www.bbdivers.com) In Bang Bao with branches in Lonely Beach, Khlong Prao and Hat Sai Khao, plus outposts on Ko Kut and Ko Wai (high season only).

Lonely Beach Divers (☎080 619 0704; www.lonelybeachdivers.com) Operating out of Lonely Beach, this place offers multilingual instructors.

Courses

Koh Chang Thai Cookery School COOKING COURSE
(☎039 557243; Blue Lagoon Bungalows, Khlong Prao) Break up your lazy days with classes designed to enhance mind and body. Classes are typically five hours, include a market tour and cost 1500B per person; book ahead. Slices, dices and sautés are performed in a shady open-air kitchen beside the estuary.

Sleeping

Ko Chang's package-tour industry has distorted accommodation pricing. In general, rates have risen while quality has not, partly because hotels catering to group tours are guaranteed occupancy and don't have to maintain standards to woo repeat visitors or walk-ins. There is also a lot of copy-cat pricing, giving value-oriented visitors little choice.

During the wet season (May to October) rates drop precipitously. Consider booking ahead and shopping for online discounts during peak season (November to March), weekends and holidays.

On the west coast, Lonely Beach is the best budget option, Hat Kaibae is the best-value option and Hat Sai Khao is the most overpriced. A few accommodation options exist on the east coast at Ao Salak Kok and Ao Dan Kao.

Hat Sai Khao

The island's prettiest beach is also its most expensive. The northern and southern extremities have some budget and midrange options worth considering if you need proximity to the finest sand. The southern end of the beach is rocky and lacks sand during high tide. There's a backpacker enclave north of KC Grande Resort accessible only via the beach.

Independent Bo's GUESTHOUSE $
(r 300-800B;) The closest this beach gets to bohemian is this eclectic range of rooms that cling to the cliff. Quirky signs and a wi-fi ban in the bar add to the hippie feel. All the fan-only bungalows are different so prices vary. No reservations (and no children).

Starbeach Bungalows GUESTHOUSE $
(084 345 1079; www.starbeach-kohchang.com; bungalows 500-750B;) Ramshackle in appearance, the simple fan-only bungalows wind up the hillside and are solid enough. You are close to the prime part of the beach.

Arunee Resort GUESTHOUSE $$
(086 111 9600; aruneeresorttour@hotmail.com; r incl breakfast fan/air-con 500/1500B;) Recent renovations mean the super-cheap rooms have been replaced by bright and breezy ones. Arunee is set back from the main road and is a 50m-walk to the beach.

Rock Sand Resort GUESTHOUSE $$
(084 781 0550; www.rocksand-resort.com; r 750-3500B;) Touting itself as a flashpacker destination, this place is not really a resort. But the sea-view rooms are decent and come with shared balconies. Cheaper rooms are plain. Be prepared to wade here at high tide.

Paddy's Palms Resort HOTEL $$
(039 619083; www.paddyspalmspub.com; r incl breakfast 1100-1300B;) It may be a bit of a walk to the beach, but Paddy's compensates with a pool/jacuzzi, smart rooms and an excellent sports bar at the front.

Sai Khao Inn GUESTHOUSE $$
(081 570 1380; r 1200-1800B;) A quiet garden setting on the interior side of the road and reasonable value in the land of resorts, Sai Khao Inn has a little bit of everything – bungalows on stilts and more ordinary rooms. It's up an alley off the main road.

Keereeelé HOTEL $$
(039 551285; keeree_ele@hotmail.com; r incl breakfast 2200-2600B;) This multi-storey hotel has modern and comfortable rooms, some of which have views of the verdant mountains behind. Beds are raised off the floor Chinese-style. The hotel is on the interior side of the road, with the beach 300m away. The name means 'elephant mountain', in case you wondered.

Apple Beachfront Resort HOTEL $$
(039 551228; applebeachfrontresort@gmail.com; r incl breakfast 2800B;) Employing lots of natural materials, Apple has neat, simple rooms facing the sea or a large terraced pool area.

Ao Khlong Prao

Ao Khlong Prao is dominated by high-end resorts, with just a few budget spots peppered in between. There are a handful of cheapies on the main road that are within walking distance to the beach.

★**Blue Lagoon Bungalows** GUESTHOUSE $$
(039 557243; www.kohchang-bungalows-bluelagoon.com; r 500-1800B;) Set beside a scenic estuary, Blue Lagoon has a variety of bungalows and rooms, or you can rent a tent (250B). A wooden walkway leads to the beach. Check out the larger family room, which was made using elephant dung. The staff, who are excelent, provide numerous activities, including yoga and cookery classes.

Lin Bungalow BUNGALOW $$
(084 120 1483; r 1500B;) A good mid-range choice, with 10 sturdy and sizeable bungalows right on the beach.

Baan Rim Nam GUESTHOUSE $$
(087 005 8575; www.iamkohchang.com; r 1300-1900B;) This converted fisherman's

DON'T FEED THE ANIMALS

On many of the around-the-island boat tours, operators amaze their guests with a stop at a rocky cliff to feed the wild monkeys. It seems innocent enough, and even entertaining, but there's an unfortunate consequence. The animals become dependent on this food source and when the boats don't come as often during the low season the young and vulnerable ones are ill-equipped to forage in the forest.

The same goes for the dive or boat trips that feed the fish leftover lunches, or bread bought on the pier specifically for this purpose. It might be a fantastic way to see a school of brilliantly coloured fish, but they then forsake the coral reefs for an easier meal, and without the daily grooming efforts of the fish the coral is soon overgrown with algae and will eventually suffocate.

NATIONAL PARK STATUS

Some areas of Ko Chang are protected and maintained as part of the Mu Ko Chang National Marine Park. Conservation efforts are a bit haphazard, but you will be required to pay a 200B park entrance fee when visiting some of the waterfalls (the waterfall reviews mention this fee where it applies). **National Park headquarters** (☎039 555080; Ban Than Mayom; ⊙8am-5pm) is on the eastern side of the island near Nam Tok Than Mayom.

Nudity and topless sunbathing are forbidden by law in Mu Ko Chang National Marine Park; this includes all beaches on Ko Chang, Ko Kut, Ko Mak and Ko Wai.

house sits over a mangrove-lined river and comes with cool, airy rooms. The English owner is well-informed about the island and keen to help. Free kayaks are provided – the beach is a three-minute paddle away.

Magic Resort BUNGALOW **$$**
(☎039 557074; www.magicresortkohchang.co.th; r incl breakfast 1300-2500B; ❄📶) Once a thriving backpacker commune, the magic here has faded a tad, but the basic beachside bungalows and neat chill-all-day garden are still popular. Wi-fi is limited to the reception area.

Sofia Garden Resort HOTEL **$$**
(☎080 095 1095; www.sofiagardenresort.net; r 1690-2200B; ❄📶🏊) Good price for the comfort factor, and there's a Finnish sauna as well as the pool, but the rooms are slightly dated and there is no direct beach access.

Keereeta Resort GUESTHOUSE **$$**
(☎039 551304; keeree_ta@hotmail.com; Hat Kai Mook; r incl breakfast 1900-2300B; ❄📶🏊) Rooms here have an extra splash of style, with warm colours and arty touches. Massage pavilions are right by the pool. The resort is just north of Ao Khlong Prao.

Aana HOTEL **$$$**
(☎039 551137; www.aanaresort.com; r 3500-6500B; ❄@📶🏊) Private villas perch prettily above the forest and Khlong Prao, kayaking distance from the beach. The cheaper rooms are a little faded for the price.

The Dewa RESORT **$$$**
(☎039 557339; www.thedewakohchang.com; r incl breakfast 7000-20,000B; ❄@📶🏊) Everything about the Dewa, the top luxury pad in these parts, is chic, from the dark-bottomed 700-sq-metre pool to the contemporary Thai-style rooms that Jim Thompson would have been proud of.

Hat Kaibae

Hat Kaibae has some of the island's best variety of accommodation, from boutique hotels to budget huts and midrange bungalows. The trade-off is that the beach is only sandy in parts.

Porn's Bungalows BUNGALOW **$**
(☎080 613 9266; www.pornsbungalows-kohchang.com; r 600-1500B) Very chilled spot at the far western end of the beach, with a popular on-site restaurant. All of the wooden bungalows are fan-only. The 1000B beachfront bungalows are a great deal.

KB Resort HOTEL **$$**
(☎039 557125; www.kbresort.com; r incl breakfast 2300-5000B; ❄@📶🏊) Yellow bungalows have cheery bathrooms and pose peacefully beside the sea.

Kai Bae Hut Resort HOTEL **$$**
(☎081 862 8426; www.kaibaehutresort.com; r incl breakfast 900-2500B; ❄📶) Sprawling across a scenic stretch of beach, Kai Bae Hut has a variety of lodging options – slightly worn fan huts, fancier concrete bungalows and modern hotel-style rooms. A large open-air restaurant fires up nightly barbecues and there's plenty of room for free-ranging kids. Cheaper rooms have fans.

Garden Resort HOTEL **$$**
(☎039 557260; www.gardenresortkohchang.com; r incl breakfast 2200-4500B; ❄@📶🏊) On the interior side of the main road, Garden Resort has large, clean bungalows dotted either side of a shady pathway that leads to a swimming pool. The bar and restaurant at the front are popular hang-outs. A sandy stretch of beach is 150m away.

The Chill RESORT **$$$**
(☎039 552555; www.thechillresort.com; r incl breakfast 5250-14,400B; ❄@📶🏊) Cleverly designed, with all ground-floor rooms opening onto one of three pools, the Chill has contemporary, bright rooms and bags of facilities. Popular with families.

Lonely Beach

A backpacker fave, Lonely Beach is one of the cheapest places to sleep on the island, though budget spots smack on the beach are harder to find. Having been ignored by the flashy resorts, the streets are filled with grungy bars and cheap guesthouses rather than spas and salons.

★ **BB World of Tapas** HOSTEL $
(089 504 0543; www.bbworldoftapas.com; dm 200B, r with fan 500-600B;) Much like tapas, you get a little taste of everything here. The on-site dive school, gym, eclectic tapas menu and a chill-out zone make it a great spot to meet fellow travellers. One of the only dorms within reach of the beach.

Siam Hut GUESTHOUSE $
(039 619012; www.siamhutkohchang.com; r 480-680B;) Part Ibiza and part Full Moon, Siam Hut is party central on Lonely Beach. Backpackers are attracted by the cheap wooden huts that sit next to one of the few sandy strips around here. Wi-fi is available by reception.

Paradise Cottage HOTEL $
(081 773 9337; y_yinggg@hotmail.com; r fan/air-con 500/800-1200B;) With house music as a backdrop, hammock-clad pavilions facing the sea and comfy rooms, Paradise Cottage is tailor-made for flashpackers. At low tide a sandbank just beyond the rocks can be reached.

Little Eden GUESTHOUSE $
(084 867 7459; www.littleedenkohchang.com; r 700-1100B;) There are 15 bungalows here, all connected by an intricate series of wooden walkways. Rooms are quite spacious with surprisingly good bathrooms. Pleasant communal area and staff.

KLKL Hostel GUESTHOUSE $
(083 088 3808; r 600-1200B;) Not a true hostel as there are no dorms here. Instead, you get pleasant blue, green and pink rooms at reasonable prices. Cheaper rooms are fan-only, but all have hot water. Wi-fi is only in the bar area.

Oasis Bungalows GUESTHOUSE $$
(081 721 2547; www.oasis-kohchang.com; r 450-1400B;) Literally the top place in Lonely Beach – largely due to its location on the peak of a hill – Oasis has great sea views, and the scene from its 12m-tall treehouse is even more impressive. Run by a friendly Dutch couple, Oasis has roomy, midrange bungalows. Cheaper rooms are fan-only.

It's a five-minute walk to the beach.

Warapura Resort HOTEL $$
(039 558123; r 1900-4500B;) Warapura has a collection of adorable cottages tucked in between the village and a mangrove beach. The large, oceanfront pool is perfect for people who would rather gaze at the ocean than frolic in it.

Lonely Beach Resort BUNGALOW $$
(081 279 5120; www.lonelybeach.net; r 900-1300B;) The bungalows here slope downhill amid a leafy garden. They're plain but a good size and comfortable enough. The attached restaurant is a bizarre, albeit tasty, mix of Danish and Thai dishes.

Ban Bang Bao

Despite its touristy veneer, Ban Bang Bao is still a charming place to stay. Accommodation options are mainly converted pier houses overlooking the sea, with easy access to departing inter-island ferries. Daytime transport to a swimmable beach is possible thanks to the steady flow of day trippers, or Khlong Kloi beach is just to the east. Night owls should either hire a motorbike or stay elsewhere, as *sŏrng·tăa·ou* become rare and expensive after dinnertime.

Bang Bao Cliff Cottage GUESTHOUSE $
(085 904 6706; www.cliff-cottage.com; r 600-1200B;) Partially hidden on a verdant hillside west of the pier are a few dozen simple thatch huts overlooking a rocky cove. Most have sea views and a couple offer spectacular vistas. Scubadawgs dive school has a base here. Tents are available in the high season.

★ **Koh Chang Sea Hut** HOTEL $$
(081 285 0570; www.kohchang-seahut.com; r incl breakfast 2800B;) Set at the far end of Bang Bao pier, this collection of luxurious bungalows and rooms offers near-panoramic views of the bay. Each bungalow is surrounded by a private deck where breakfast is served. Free kayaking.

Buddha View GUESTHOUSE $$
(039 558157; www.thebuddhaview.com; r 600-1400B;) Swish pier guesthouse popular with Bangkokians. There are only seven thoughtfully designed, all-wood rooms, four

of which come with private bathrooms. The restaurant is excellent too.

El Greco GUESTHOUSE $$
(☎086 843 8417; www.elgreco-kohchang.com; r 1200-1400B;) There are clean rooms, slightly hard beds and great views at this simple guesthouse half-way along Bang Bao pier. The on-site Greek restaurant is worth a look.

Nirvana HOTEL $$$
(☎039 558061; www.nirvanakohchang.com; r incl breakfast 3000-4700B;) Super-deluxe, Balinese-style bungalows hidden away on a rocky, jungle-filled peninsula. Spacious rooms feature stone bathrooms and retro pop posters. This is about as removed from everything else on the island as possible, though there is a shuttle bus to Bang Bao if civilisation is required. The adjacent beach is not swimmable.

Northern Interior & East Coast

The northern and eastern parts of the island are less developed than the west coast and more isolated. You will need your own transport and maybe even a posse not to feel lonely out here, but you'll be rewarded with a quieter, calmer experience.

Jungle Way GUESTHOUSE $
(☎089 247 3161; Khlong Son Valley; r 200-500B) Set deep in the forest, accessible via a rope bridge, is this wonderful jungle hideaway. Owner and local expert Khun Ann can arrange treks from here. The fan-only bungalows are simple but adequate and the on-site restaurant is good.

Jungle Way's Facebook page is updated regularly.

The Souk GUESTHOUSE $$
(☎081 553 3194; www.thesoukkohchang.com; Ao Dan Kao; r fan/air-con 900/1500-2200B;) This cool spot has reasonably priced bungalows that are decked out with pop art. There are lots of chill-out spaces and a low-key, open-deck restaurant and cocktail bar, just in front of the red-sand beach. Air-con rooms include breakfast.

Amber Sands HOTEL $$$
(☎039 586177; www.ambersandsbeachresort.com; Ao Dan Kao; r 2800-4250B;) Sandwiched between mangroves and a quiet red-sand beach, Amber Sands has smart bungalows and great sea views. The location feels a world away but it is only 15 minutes from the pier. Closes August to mid-October.

Spa Koh Chang Resort HOTEL $$$
(☎080 964 7614; www.thespakohchang.com; Ao Salak Kok; r incl breakfast 2136-3657B;) Specialising in health-care packages, including fasting, yoga and meditation, this resort has lush, peaceful surroundings that almost touch the bay's mangrove forests. Elegantly decorated bungalows scramble up a flower-filled hillside providing a peaceful getaway for some quality 'me' time. The restaurant has vegan and vegie options. No beach access.

Eating & Drinking

Virtually all of the island's accommodation choices have attached restaurants with adequate but not outstanding fare. Parties abound on the beaches and range from the more mature, restrained scene on Hat Sai Khao, to the younger and more frenetic on Lonely Beach.

West Coast

Porn's Bungalows Restaurant THAI $
(Hat Kaibae; dishes 80-180B; ⏲11am-11pm) This laid-back, dark-wood restaurant is the quintessential beachside lounge. Great barbecue. Feel free to have your drinks out-size your meal and don't worry about dressing up for dinner.

Nid's Kitchen THAI $
(nidkitchen@hotmail.com; Khlong Prao; dishes 50-150B; ⏲6-10pm) Nid's creates all the Thai standards like a wok wizard in a hut festooned with rasta imagery. Equally fine for a drink or three.

★**Barrio Bonito** MEXICAN $$
(Hat Kaibae; dishes 160-250B; ⏲5-10.30pm) Fab fajitas and cracking cocktails are served by a charming French-Mexican couple at this roadside spot in the middle of Kaibae. Authentic food and stylish surroundings.

★**Phu-Talay** SEAFOOD $$
(☎039 551300; Khlong Prao; dishes 100-320B; ⏲10am-10pm) There is a cute, homely feel at this wooden-floored, blue-and-white-decorated place perched over the lagoon. There's a sensible menu of Ko Chang classics (lots of fish) and it's far more reasonably priced than many other seafood places.

Oodie's Place INTERNATIONAL-THAI $$
(☎039 551193; Hat Sai Khao; dishes 80-390B; ⏰11am-midnight) Local musician Oodie runs a nicely diverse operation with excellent French food, tasty Thai specialities and live music from 10pm. After all these years, it is still beloved by expats.

Baanta THAI $$
(Khlong Prao; dishes 120-250B; ⏰noon-10pm; 📶) Baanta is run by the same folk who have the ultra-posh Panviman Resort, and the dishes here are both excellent in terms of quality and value. Expect Thai standards plus some modern twists.

Saffron on the Sea THAI $$
(☎039 551253; Hat Kai Mook; dishes 120-350B; ⏰8am-10pm; 📶) Owned by an arty escapee from Bangkok, this friendly boutique hotel has a generous portion of oceanfront dining and a relaxed, romantic atmosphere. All the Thai dishes are prepared in the island style, more sweet than spicy.

Jea Eaw THAI $$
(Khlong Prao; dishes 120-300B; ⏰10am-9pm) Locals fill this simple, open-air restaurant every evening due to the big flavours and prolific menu options. The prawns are recommended.

GETTING TO CAMBODIA: ARANYA PRATHET TO POIPET

Getting to the Border The easiest way to get from Bangkok to Siem Reap overland is the direct bus departing from the Northern (Mo Chit) Bus Terminal. The through-service bus trips sold on Th Khao San and elsewhere in Bangkok seem cheap and convenient, but they haven't been nicknamed 'scam buses' for nothing, and if using them you will be most likely hassled and ripped off, often quite aggressively.

If you choose to do it in stages (much cheaper than the direct Mo Chit bus), you can get from Bangkok to the border town of Aranya Prathet (aka Aran) by bus from Mo Chit, by bus or minivan from the Eastern (Ekamai) Bus Terminal, by bus from Suvarnabhumi International Airport bus station, by minivan from Victory Monument or by 3rd-class train (only the 5.55am departure will get you there early enough, at 11.35am, to reach Siem Reap the same day) from Hualamphong. Aran also has bus services about every one or two hours from other cities in the area including Khorat, Surin and Chanthaburi. All minivans, plus some buses, go all the way to the Rong Kluea Market next to the border, so there's no need to stop in Aranya Prathet city. Otherwise, you'll need to take a *sŏrng·tăa·ou* (15B), motorcycle taxi (60B) or túk-túk (pronounced *đúk đúk*; 80B) the final 7km to the border.

At the Border The border is open 7am to 8pm daily. There are many persistent scammers on the Thai side trying to get you to buy your Cambodia visa through them, but no matter what they might tell you, there's absolutely no good reason to get visas anywhere except the border. Buying them elsewhere costs more and takes longer. Don't even show your passport to anyone before you reach Thai immigration and don't change money.

After getting stamped out of Thailand – a straightforward process – follow the throng to Cambodian immigration and find the 'Visa on Arrival' sign if you don't already have a visa. Weekday mornings you might finish everything in 10 to 20 minutes, but if you arrive after noon it could take an hour or more. Weekends and holidays, when many Thais arrive to gamble and foreign workers do visa runs, are also busy. You will probably be offered the opportunity to pay a 'special VIP fee' of 200B to jump to the front of the queue. You will almost certainly be asked to pay another small 'fee', which will be called a 'stamping' or 'overtime' fee. You should refuse, though doing so might mean you have to wait a few extra minutes.

Moving On There are frequent buses and share taxis from Poipet to Siem Reap along a good sealed road from the main bus station, which is about 1km away (2000r by motorcycle taxi) around the main market, one block north of Canadia Bank off NH5. Poipet also has a second 'international' bus station 9km east of town where prices are double and which is only used by uninformed or gullible foreigners who get swept into the free shuttle that takes travellers out there. Lonely Planet's *Cambodia* guide has full details for travel on this side of the border.

Paul's Restaurant EUROPEAN $$
(039 551499; Hat Sai Khao; dishes 160-280B; 5-10pm) Great-value German and other European dishes are served up at this clifftop restaurant, along with side orders of sarcasm from the entertaining owner.

Magic Garden THAI $$
(039 558027; Lonely Beach; dishes 100-220B; 9am-midnight;) The hippest place on Lonely Beach to have a smoothie or vodka bucket, as travellers swap tales or catch up on some reading. The menu covers Thai and Western standards.

Chowlay SEAFOOD $$
(Ban Bang Bao; dishes 100-450B; 10am-midnight) 'If it swims, we have it', goes its motto, and this pier restaurant does indeed have a huge seafood menu as well as great bay views.

KaTi Culinary THAI $$
(081 903 0408; Khlong Prao; dishes 130-290B; 11am-3pm & 6-10pm) Seafood, a few Isan dishes and the famous homemade curry sauce are the best bets here. The menu features creative smoothies, featuring lychee, lemon and peppermint, and there's a children's menu.

Northern Interior & East Coast

Blues Blues Restaurant THAI $
(Ban Khlong Son; dishes 70-150B; 10am-9pm) Through the green screen of tropical plants is an arty stir-fry hut that is beloved for its expertise, efficiency and economy. The owner's delicate watercolour paintings are on display too. Take the road to Ban Kwan Chang; it's 600m ahead on the right.

Jungle Way Restaurant THAI $
(089 247 3161; Ban Khlong Son; dishes 70-120B; 7am-9pm;) Enjoy the natural setting and home-style cooking of this guesthouse restaurant. Meal preparation takes a leisurely pace so climb up to the elevated wildlife-viewing platform to spot some jungle creatures while the wok is sizzling.

★ **Shambhala** EUROPEAN $$
(Siam Royal View, Hat Chang Noi; dishes 120-390B; 1-9pm Thu-Tue) Perched at the top of the island, this poolside restaurant comes with some of the cheapest cocktails around and quality Thai/international dishes, including great risotto. Perfect for a sundowner.

Information

DANGERS & ANNOYANCES

Take extreme care when driving between Ban Khlong Son south to Hat Sai Khao, as the road is steep and treacherous, with several hairpin turns. There are mud slides and poor conditions during storms. If you do rent a motorbike, ride carefully between Hat Kaibae and Lonely Beach, especially in the rainy season. Wear protective clothing when riding on a motorcycle.

The police conduct regular drug raids on the island's accommodation. If you get caught with narcotics, you could face heavy fines or imprisonment.

Be aware of the cheap minibus tickets from Siem Reap to Ko Chang; these usually involve some sort of time- and money-wasting commission scam.

Ko Chang is considered a low-risk malarial zone, meaning that liberal use of mosquito repellent is probably an adequate precaution.

EMERGENCY

Police Station (039 586191; Ban Dan Mai)
Tourist Police Office (1155) Based north of Ban Khlong Prao. Also has smaller police boxes that are located in Hat Sai Khao and Hat Kaibae.

MEDICAL SERVICES

Bang Bao Health Centre (039 558086; Ban Bang Bao; 8.30am-4pm) For the basics.
Ko Chang Hospital (039 586096; Ban Dan Mai) Public hospital with a good reputation and affordably priced care; south of the ferry terminal.
Ko Chang International Clinic (039 551555; Hat Sai Khao; 24hr) Related to the Bangkok Hospital Group; accepts most health insurances and has expensive rates.

MONEY

There are banks with ATMs and exchange facilities along all the west-coast beaches.

POST

Ko Chang Post Office (039 551240; 9am-5pm) At the far southern end of Hat Sai Khao.

TOURIST INFORMATION

The free magazine *Koh Chang Guide* (www.koh-chang-guide.com) is widely available on the island and has handy beach maps.

The comprehensive website I Am Koh Chang (www.iamkohchang.com) is a labour of love from an irreverent Brit living on the island. It's jam-packed with opinion and information.

TRANSPORT TO/FROM KO CHANG

ORIGIN	DESTINATION	SPEEDBOAT	BUS
Bangkok's Eastern Bus Terminal (Ekamai)	Tha Thammachat		263B; 6hr; 2 daily
Tha Centrepoint (Laem Ngop)	Ko Chang	80B; 40min; hourly; 6am-7pm	
Tha Thammachat (Laem Ngop)	Ko Chang	80B; 30min; every 45min; 6.30am-7pm	
Ko Chang	Ko Kut	900B; 5hr; 2 daily	
Ko Chang	Ko Mak	600B; 2hr; 1 daily	
Ko Chang	Ko Wai	400B; 15 min; 2 daily	
Ko Chang	Bangkok Suvarnabhumi International Airport		263B; 5hr; 2pm

Getting There & Away

Whether starting from Bangkok or Cambodia, it is an all-day haul to reach Ko Chang.

Ferries from the mainland (Laem Ngop) leave from either Tha Thammachat, operated by **Koh Chang Ferry** (☎039 555188), or Tha Centrepoint with **Centrepoint Ferry** (☎039 538196). Boats from Tha Thammachat arrive at Tha Sapparot; Centrepoint ferries at a pier down the road.

Bang Bao Boat (☎039 558046; www.kohchangbangbaoboat.com) is the inter-island ferry that connects Ko Chang with Ko Mak, Ko Kut and Ko Wai during the high season. Boats leave from Bang Bao in the southwest of the island.

Speedboats travel between the islands during high season.

It is possible to go to and from Ko Chang from Bangkok's Eastern (Ekamai) bus terminal and Bangkok's Suvaranabhumi International Airport, via Chanthaburi and Trat.

Getting Around

Shared *sŏrng·tăa·ou* meet arriving boats to shuttle passengers to the various beaches (Hat Sai Khao 100B, Khlong Prao 150B and Lonely Beach 200B). Hops between neighbouring beaches range from 50B to 200B but prices rise dramatically after dark, when it can cost 500B to travel from Bang Bao to Hat Sai Khao.

Motorbikes can be hired from 200B per day. Ko Chang's hilly and winding roads are dangerous; make sure the bike is in good working order.

Ko Wai เกาะหวาย

Stunning Ko Wai is teensy and primitive, but endowed with gin-clear waters, excellent coral reefs for snorkelling and a handsome view across to Ko Chang. Expect to share the bulk of your afternoons with day trippers but have the remainder of your time in peace.

Most bungalows close from May to September when seas are rough and flooding is common.

Sleeping

Good Feeling BUNGALOW **$**
(☎081 850 3410; r 400-500B) There are 12 wooden bungalows here, all but one with private bathroom, spread out along a rocky headland interspersed with private, sandy coves. Good snorkelling nearby.

Ko Wai Paradise BUNGALOW **$**
(☎081 762 2548; r 300-800B) Simple wooden bungalows on a postcard-perfect beach. You'll share the coral out front with day trippers.

Grand Mar Hut GUESTHOUSE **$**
(☎081 841 3011; r 400-600B) On the rocky northeastern tip of the island is this basic and remote place; speedboat operators know it by the nearby bay of Ao Yai Ma.

Ko Wai Pakarang GUESTHOUSE **$$**
(☎084 113 8946; kohwaipakarang@hotmail.com; r fan/air-con 600-1200/2200-2500B; ❄@☎) Wooden and concrete bungalows, with an OK attached restaurant and helpful, English-speaking staff. Only the top-price rooms have air-con.

Koh Wai Beach Resort HOTEL **$$$**
(☎081 306 4053; www.kohwaibeachresort.com; r incl breakfast 2100-5900B; ❄☎) Upscale collection of spacious bungalows that are equipped with all the mod cons just a few steps from the beach and on the southern side of the island.

SPEEDBOAT TRANSPORT FROM KO WAI

DESTINATION	FARE (ONE WAY)	DURATION	FREQUENCY
Ko Chang	400B	15min	3 daily
Ko Kut	700B	1hr	3 daily
Ko Mak	300B	45min	3 daily
Laem Ngop (mainland pier)	450B	30min	4 daily

Getting There & Around

Boats will drop you off at the nearest pier to your guesthouse; otherwise you'll have to walk 15 to 30 minutes along a narrow forest trail.

Bang Bao Boat (www.kohchangbangbaoboat.com) is the archipelago's inter-island ferry, running a daily loop from Ko Chang to Ko Kut. Boats depart Ko Chang at 9.30am and noon and arrive at Ko Wai (one way 400B, 30 minutes) then continue on to Ko Mak (one way 600B, one hour) and Ko Kut (900B, two hours).

Ko Mak

เกาะหมาก

Little Ko Mak measures only 16 sq km and doesn't have any speeding traffic, wall-to-wall development, noisy beer bars or crowded beaches. The palm-fringed bays are bathed by gently lapping water and there's a relaxed vibe. But Ko Mak is not destined for island superstardom: the interior is a utilitarian landscape of coconut and rubber plantations and sand flies are a pain on some beaches.

Visiting the island is easier in the high season (December to March); during the low season (May to September) many boats stop running and bungalow operations wind down. A new underwater electricity cable means Ko Mak and Ko Kut now have 24-hour power.

Sights & Activities

The best beach on the island is **Ao Pra** in the west, but it is undeveloped and hard to reach. For now, swimming and beach strolling are best on the northwestern bay of **Ao Suan Yai**, which is a wide arc of sand and looking-glass-clear water that gets fewer sand flies than the southern beaches. It is easily accessible by bicycle or motorbike if you stay elsewhere.

Offshore is **Ko Kham**, a private island that was sold in 2008 for a reported 200 million baht. It used to be a popular day-trippers' beach; today work is slowly ongoing to create a luxury resort.

Koh Mak Divers DIVING
(☎083 297 7724; www.kohmakdivers.com; dive trips from 2400B) Koh Mak Divers runs dive trips to the Mu Ko Chang National Marine Park, about 45 minutes away.

Sleeping & Eating

Most budget guesthouses are on Ao Khao, a decent strip of sand on the southwestern side of the island, while the resorts sprawl out on the more scenic northwestern bay of Ao Suan Yai.

There are a handful of family-run restaurants on the main road between Monkey Island and Makathanee Resort. If you feel like a journey, use a meal or a sundowner as an excuse to explore different bays.

Koh Mak Cottage BUNGALOW $
(☎081 910 2723; www.kohmakcottage.com; Ao Khao; r 500B; @) Koh Mak has 19 small and rustic bungalows. No frills, but you are right on the beach. Wi-fi is only near reception.

Monkey Island GUESTHOUSE $$
(☎085 389 0949; www.monkeyislandkohmak.com; Ao Khao; r 600-4000B; @) The troop leader of guesthouses, Monkey Island has earthen or wooden bungalows in three creatively named models – Baboon, Chimpanzee and Gorilla – with various amenities. All have fun design touches and the hip restaurant does respectable Thai cuisine in a leisurely fashion. There's also a small children's pool. Rooms over 1500B come with air-con and breakfast.

Baan Chailay GUESTHOUSE $$
(☎080 101 4763; www.baanchailay.com; Ao Khao; r incl breakfast 1000-1600B;) A cross between a homestay and a guesthouse, you can stay in bungalows on the beach, or rooms in the family house at this friendly place at the eastern, less busy, end of Ao Khao. Foodies will appreciate the beach barbecues and bakery.

Makathanee Resort
HOTEL $$

(☎087 802 7575; www.makathaneekohmak.com; Ao Khao; r incl breakfast 1200-5500B; ❄📶🏊) Floor-to-ceiling windows are open to sea views in these plush bungalows, which have deliciously soft mattresses and lots of breathing room. Some rooms are in a hotel block; the cheapest of these don't have a view but do offer great value. Professional service, and kayaks for rent (400B per day).

Baan Koh Mak
BUNGALOW $$

(☎089 895 7592; www.baan-koh-mak.com; Ao Khao; r 1690-3990B; ❄📶) Each of the 18 white bungalows here comes with heaps of natural light and arty features. Wi-fi is available at the restaurant.

Ao Kao Resort
GUESTHOUSE $$

(☎083 152 6564; www.aokaoresort.com; Ao Khao; r 2500-3000B; ❄📶) 🍃 In a pretty crook of the bay, Ao Kao has an assortment of Thai-style bungalows, all with balconies and easy beach access. Amenities include a range of sports options and a massage pavilion. Ao Kao Resort also gets kudos for its ecofriendly projects, which include solar panels and energy-saving schemes. Wi-fi is in the restaurant only.

Lazy Day Resort
BUNGALOW $$

(☎081 882 4002; www.kohmaklazyday.com; r incl breakfast 2500-2700B; ❄📶) This professionally run operation has a dozen big bungalows stationed around an attractive garden.

Koh Mak Resort
HOTEL $$$

(☎039 501013; www.kohmakresort.com; Ao Suan Yai; r incl breakfast 2800-6800B; ❄📶🏊) A speedboat from Laem Ngop (450B) takes guests directly to this all-encompassing resort. Once they've arrived, they get to stay in pretty, white beachfront bungalows that offer lots of natural light. Services include kayak rentals and cookery classes.

Ko Mak & Ko Kut

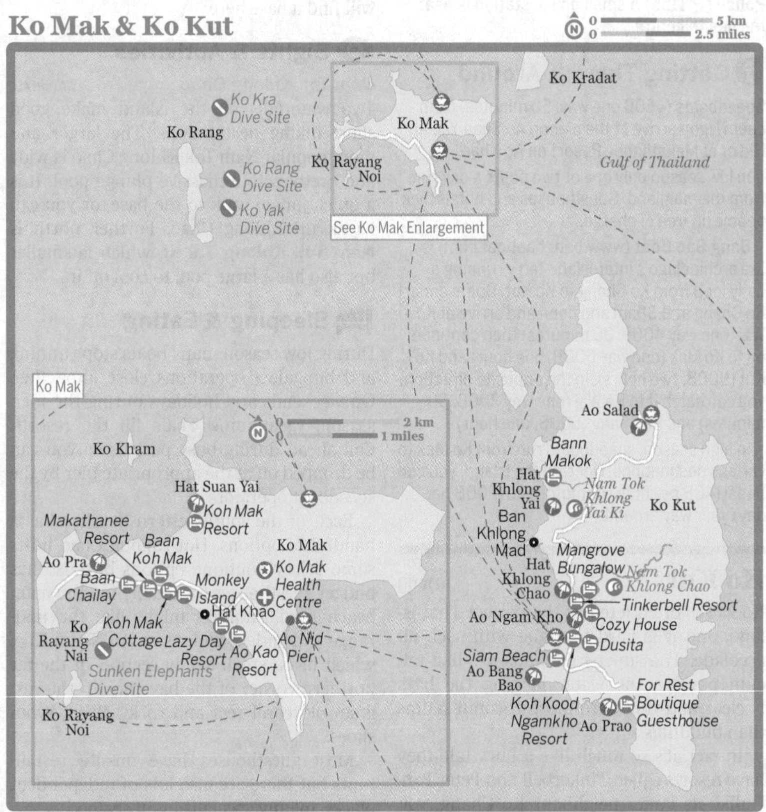

SPEEDBOAT TRANSPORT FROM KO MAK

DESTINATION	FARE (ONE WAY)	DURATION	FREQUENCY
Ko Chang	600B	45min	3 daily
Ko Kut	400B	45min	2 daily
Ko Wai	300B	30min	3 daily
Laem Ngop (mainland pier)	450B	1hr	2 daily

Information

There are no banks or ATMs on the island, so stock up on cash before visiting.

Ball's Cafe (081 925 6591; Ao Khao; 8am-9pm;) Khun Ball runs his internet cafe, coffee shop and information centre in a spot just behind Baan Koh Mak; he's an active island promoter and runs www.kohmak.com as well as environmental initiatives.

Ko Mak Health Centre (8.30am-4.30pm) Can handle basic first-aid emergencies and illnesses. It is on the cross-island road near Ao Nid Pier.

Police (1155) A small police station is near the health centre.

Getting There & Around

Speedboats (450B one way, 50 minutes) from Laem Ngop arrive at the pier on Ao Suan Yai, Ao Nid or at Makathanee Resort on Ao Khao.

In low season only one or two boats a day run from the mainland. Guesthouses and hotels pick people up free of charge.

Bang Bao Boat (www.bangbaoboat.com) is the archipelago's inter-island ferry running a daily loop from Ko Chang to Ko Kut. Boats depart Ko Chang at 9.30am and noon and arrive at Ko Wai (one way 400B, 30 minutes) then continue on to Ko Mak (one way 600B, one hour) and Ko Kut (900B, two hours). In the opposite direction, you can catch it to Ko Wai (one way 300B, 30 minutes) and Ko Chang (600B, one hour).

In high season, speedboats run from Ko Mak to various destinations. Once on the island, you can pedal (40B per hour) or motorbike (200B per day) your way around.

Ko Kut เกาะกูด

Ko Kut is often feted as the perfect Thai island, and it is hard to argue with such an accolade. The super-soft sands are like talcum powder, the water lapping the bays is clear and there are more coconut palms than buildings.

In fact, it's so much like a fairy tale they have resorts called Tinkerbell and Peter Pan. Unlike its larger neighbour Ko Chang, you can forget about any nightlife, traffic or noise – this is where you come to do almost nothing. If you can be roused from your hammock, kayaking and snorkelling are the main activities (nearby Ko Rang is particularly good for fish gazing).

Half as big as Ko Chang and the fourth-largest island in Thailand, Ko Kut (also known as Koh Kood) has long been the domain of package-tour resorts and a seclusion-seeking elite. But the island is becoming more egalitarian, and independent travellers, especially families and couples, will find a base here.

Sights & Activities

Nam Tok Khlong Chao WATERFALL

Two waterfalls on the island make good short hiking destinations. The larger and more popular Nam Tok Khlong Chao is wide and pretty with a massive plunge pool. It is a quick jungle walk to the base, or you can kayak up Khlong Chao. Further north is **Nam Tok Khlong Yai Ki**, which is smaller but also has a large pool to cool off in.

Sleeping & Eating

During low season many boats stop running and bungalow operations close altogether. On weekends and holidays during the high season, vacationing Thais fill the resorts. Call ahead during busy periods so you can be dropped off at the appropriate pier by the speedboat operators.

Each of the southwestern beaches has a handful of options. Hat Khlong Chao hosts some pricey boutique options but also has budget guesthouses tucked behind the main beach road. Families might like the mid-range and budget options on Ao Ngam Kho, which has a small sandy section in the far northern corner of the bay, though the rest is an old coral reef and rocky. Bring swim shoes.

Most guesthouses have on-site restaurants but there are also lots of independent places, mainly specialising in seafood.

Cozy House GUESTHOUSE **$**
(☎089 094 3650; www.kohkoodcozy.com; Khlong Yai; r incl breakfast 600-1200B; ❄📶) The go-to place for backpackers, Cozy is a 10-minute walk from delightful Hat Khlong Yai. There are cheap and cheerful fan rooms or more comfortable wooden bungalows with air-con.

Mangrove Bungalow BUNGALOW **$**
(☎089 936 2093; www.kohkood-mangrove.com; Ban Khlong Chao; r incl breakfast with fan/air-con 700-1000/1500B; ❄📶) With a mangrove forest on one side and the beach a short walk away, this collection of wooden bungalows is immersed in nature. Khlong Chao waterfall is a 20-minute kayak, and short walk, away. Rooms are clean and neat. Wi-fi is by reception only.

Koh Kood Ngamkho Resort BUNGALOW **$$**
(☎081 825 7076; www.kohkood-ngamkho.com; Ao Ngam Kho; r incl breakfast with fan/air-con 1000/1500-2000B; ❄📶) One of the best budget-by-the-beach options. Agreeably rustic huts perch on a forested hillside over a reasonable beach. They rent kayaks (250B per day) and there's a good restaurant, where you keep your own tab.

For Rest Boutique Guesthouse HOTEL **$$**
(☎084 524 4321; www.kohkoodboutiquehouse.com; Ao Prao; r incl breakfast 1200-2500B; ❄📶) Almost at the southernmost point of the island is this secluded, peaceful hotel that was converted from two traditional houses on stilts. Reservations are required. Closed low season (May to September).

Dusita HOTEL **$$**
(☎081 707 4546; www.dusitakohkood.net; Ao Ngam Kho; r 1490-3890B; ❄) Justifiably popular with families, whose children can run wild in the huge oceanfront garden. For everyone else, well-spaced-out, slightly dated bungalows provide a perfect retreat from the real world.

Siam Beach BUNGALOW **$$**
(☎084 332 0788; www.siambeachkohkood.net; Ao Bang Bao; r incl breakfast 1400-2500B; ❄@📶) The bungalows on stilts may not be outstanding, but you do get to gaze at one beautiful beach from your room. The cheaper fan rooms are a good deal. Wi-fi is in the lobby area only.

★**Bann Makok** HOTEL **$$$**
(☎081 643 9488; www.bannmakok.com; Khlong Yai Ki; r incl breakfast 3200-3800B; ❄@📶) 🍃 This boutique hotel, tucked into the mangroves, uses recycled timbers painted in vintage colours to create a maze of eight rooms that resembles a traditional pier fishing village. Common decks and reading nooks provide peaceful spaces to listen to birdsong or get lost in a book.

Tinkerbell Resort HOTEL **$$$**
(☎081 826 1188; www.tinkerbellresort.com; Hat Khlong Chao; r incl breakfast 9900-12,000B; ❄@📶🏊) Natural materials, like bamboo privacy fences and thatched roof villas, sew this resort seamlessly into the landscape. The terracotta-coloured bungalows open right onto a postcard-perfect beach; the villas behind come with plunge pools. The bar is a great spot for a sundowner. Expect 40% discounts in low season.

ℹ Information

There is now one ATM on Ko Kut (though when we visited it didn't contain money). Major resorts can exchange money. A small **hospital** (☎039 525748; ⏰8.30am-4.30pm) at Ban Khlong Mad can handle minor emergencies. The **police station** (☎039 525741) is nearby. Almost all hotels and guesthouses have wi-fi.

ℹ Getting There & Around

Ko Kut is accessible from the mainland pier of Laem Sok, 22km southeast of Trat, the nearest bus transfer point.

Koh Kood Princess (☎086 126 7860; www.kohkoodprincess.com) runs an air-con boat (one way 350B, one daily, one hour 40 minutes) that docks at Ao Salad, in the northeastern corner of the island. There's free land transfer on your arrival to the island's main beaches. **Boonsiri** (☎085 921 0111; www.boonsiriferry.com) has a catamaran (one way 500B, twice daily, 1½ hours) that runs from Laem Sok to Ao Salad.

Speedboats make the crossing to/from Laem Sok (one way 500B, 1½ hours) during high season and will drop you off at your hotel's pier.

Bang Bao Boat (www.bangbaoboat.com) is the archipelago's inter-island ferry running a daily loop from Ko Chang to Ko Kut. Boats depart Ko Chang at 9.30am and noon and arrive at Ko Wai (one way 400B, 30 minutes) then continue on to Ko Mak (one way 600B, one hour) and Ko Kut (900B, two hours).

Ko Kut's roads are steep, which rules out renting a push bike unless you are a champion cyclist. Motorbikes can be rented for 300B per day.

Hua Hin & the Upper Gulf

Includes ➡

Best Places to Eat

➡ Rang Yen Garden (p148)
➡ Hua Hin Koti (p157)
➡ Prikhorm (p171)
➡ In Town (p166)
➡ Rabieng Rim Nam (p145)

Best Places to Stay

➡ Baan Bayan (p156)
➡ Brassiere Beach (p161)
➡ Away Hua Hin (p161)
➡ House 73 (p165)
➡ Pattana Guest House (p155)

Why Go?

The upper gulf has long been the favoured playground of the Thai elite. Following in the footsteps of the royal family – every Thai king from Rama IV on has spent his summers at a variety of regal holiday homes here – they in turn have inspired countless domestic tourists to flock to this stretch of coast in pursuit of fun and fine seafood.

A winning combination of outdoor activities and culture is on offer here, with historic sites, national parks and long sandy beaches ideal for swimming all an easy hop from Bangkok. Increasing numbers of foreign travellers are also drawn here, by the twin delights of an unspoiled coastline and the relaxed pace of provincial life. There's not much diving or snorkelling, but kiteboarders will be in paradise as this part of the gulf is by far the best place in Thailand to ride the wind.

When to Go

➡ The best time to visit is during the hot and dry season (February to June). From July to October (southwest monsoon) and October to January (northeast monsoon) there is occasional rain and strong winds, but the region tends to stay drier than the rest of the country because of a geographic anomaly.

➡ During stormy periods, jellyfish are often carried close to shore, making swimming hazardous. Thais get around this by swimming fully clothed.

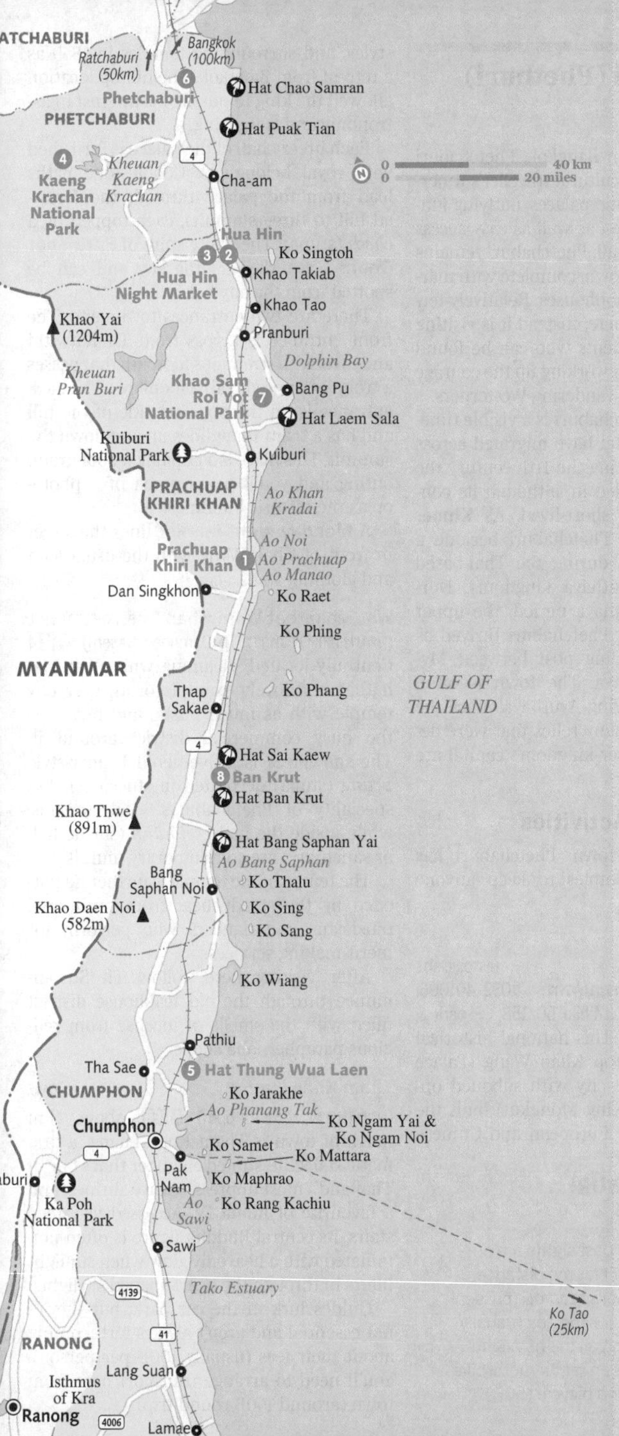

Hua Hin & the Upper Gulf Highlights

1. Motorcycling between curvaceous bays and limestone peaks in **Prachuap Khiri Khan** (p163).
2. Strolling the long blond coastline of **Hua Hin** (p149) dotted with wave-jumping kiteboarders.
3. Eating and shopping (and eating some more) at Hua Hin's **night market** (p156).
4. Escaping into the depths of **Kaeng Krachan National Park** (p146) and spotting gibbons and wild elephants.
5. Stepping off the backpacker trail on laid-back **Hat Thung Wua Laen** (p169).
6. Exploring the hilltop palace and underground caves, while dodging monkeys, in **Phetchaburi** (p142).
7. Making the pilgrimage to see the illuminated cave shrine of Tham Phraya Nakhon at **Khao Sam Roi Yot National Park** (p161).
8. Finding your own secluded strip of sand to laze on at **Ban Krut** (p167).

Phetchaburi (Phetburi)

เพชรบุรี

POP 23,235

An easy escape from Bangkok, Phetchaburi should be on every cultural traveller's itinerary. It has temples and palaces, outlying jungles and cave shrines, as well as easy access to the coast. Best of all, Phetchaburi remains a sleepy provincial town, complete with markets and old teak shophouses. Relatively few foreigners make it here; instead it is visiting groups of Thai students who can be found touring the sites and working up the courage to say 'hello' to any wandering Westerners.

Historically, Phetchaburi is a visible timeline of kingdoms that have migrated across Southeast Asia. During the 11th century the Khmer empire settled in, although its control was relatively short-lived. As Khmer power diminished, Phetchaburi became a strategic royal fort during the Thai-based Sukhothai and Ayuthaya kingdoms. During the stable Ayuthaya period, the upper gulf flourished and Phetchaburi thrived as a 17th-century trading post between Myanmar and Ayuthaya. The town is often referred to as a 'Living Ayuthaya', since the equivalent of the many relics that were destroyed in the former kingdom's capital are still intact here.

Sights & Activities

For such a small town, Phetchaburi has enough historic temples to keep anyone busy for the day.

Phra Nakhon Khiri Historical Park HISTORIC SITE

(อุทยานประวัติศาสตร์พระนครคีรี; ☎032 401006; 150B, tram return adult/child 50/15B; ⏲park & tram 8.30am-4.30pm) This national historical park sits regally atop Khao Wang (Palace Hill), surveying the city with subdued opulence. Rama IV (King Mongkut) built the palace, in a mix of European and Chinese styles, and surrounding temples in 1859 as a retreat from Bangkok. The hilltop location allowed the king to pursue his interest in astronomy and stargazing.

Each breezy hall of the palace is furnished with royal belongings. Cobblestone paths lead from the palace through the forested hill to three summits, each topped by a *chedi* (stupa). The white spire of **Phra That Chom Phet** skewers the sky and can be spotted from the city below.

There are two entrances to the site. The front entrance is across from Th Ratwithi and involves a strenuous footpath that passes a troop of unpredictable monkeys. The back entrance is on the opposite side of the hill and has a **tram** that glides up and down the summit. This place is a popular school-group outing and you'll be as much of a photo-op as the historic buildings.

A **Monday night market** lines the street in front of Khao Wang with the usual food and clothing stalls.

PHETCHABURI SIGHTSEEING

Some of the city's best sights are outside town, but don't let the distance deter you. Hire a *sŏrng·tăa·ou* (passenger pick-up truck) for the day (usually around 500B) to hit all the highlights. Alternatively, you can rent a motorbike (200B to 300B) or a bicycle (50B).

Wat Mahathat Worawihan BUDDHIST TEMPLE

(วัดมหาธาตุวรวิหาร; Th Damnoen Kasem) FREE Centrally located, gleaming white Wat Mahathat is a lovely example of an everyday temple with as much hustle and bustle as the busy commercial district around it. The showpiece is a five-tiered Khmer-style *prang* (stupa) decorated in stucco relief, a speciality of Phetchaburi's local artisans, while inside the main *wí·hăhn* (shrine hall or sanctuary) are contemporary murals.

The tempo of the temple is further heightened by the steady beat from traditional musicians and dancers who perform for merit-making services.

After visiting here, follow Th Suwanmunee through the old teakhouse district filled with the smells of incense from religious paraphernalia shops.

Tham Khao Luang CAVE

(ถ้ำเขาหลวง; ⏲8am-6pm) FREE About 4km north of town is Tham Khao Luang, a dramatic stalactite-stuffed chamber that's one of Thailand's most impressive cave shrines, and a favourite of Rama IV. Accessed via steep stairs, its central Buddha figure is often illuminated with a heavenly glow when sunlight filters in through the heart-shaped skylight.

Guides lurk in the car park, but they're not essential and aren't always forthcoming about their fees (usually 100B per person). You'll need to arrange transport here from town (around 150B round-trip).

At the opposite end of the chamber are a row of sitting Buddhas casting shadows on the undulating cavern wall.

The story is that Rama IV built the stone gate that separates the main chamber from a second chamber as a security measure for a couple who once lived in the cave. A figure of a prostrate body in the third chamber is said to represent the cycle of life and death but it hasn't experienced a peaceful resting place as bandits destroyed much of it in search of hidden treasures. Deeper in the cave is supposedly a rock formation that looks like Christ on the cross, but our eyes couldn't spot it. (Thais are especially imaginative at spotting familiar forms in cave stalactites.)

Around the entrance to the cave you'll meet brazen monkeys looking for handouts.

Phra Ram Ratchaniwet HISTORIC SITE
(พระรามราชนิเวศน์; ☎032 428083; Ban Peun Palace; admission 50B; ⏰8.30am-4.30pm Mon-Fri) An incredible art nouveau creation, construction of this elegant summer palace began in 1910 at the behest of Rama V (who died just after the project was started). It was designed by German architects, who used the opportunity to showcase contemporary design innovations; inside there are spacious sun-drenched rooms decorated with exquisite glazed tiles, stained glass, parquet floors and plenty of wrought-iron details.

The palace is on a military base 1km south of town; you may be required to show your passport.

While the structure is typical of Thailand in the early 20th century, a period that saw a local passion for erecting European-style buildings in an effort to keep up with the 'modern' architecture of Thailand's colonised neighbours, the scale of the palace is impressive. Check out the double-spiral staircase, which provides a classic debutante's debut, and the state-of-the-art, for the time, personal bathroom of the king.

Wat Kamphaeng Laeng BUDDHIST TEMPLE
(วัดกำแพงแลง; Th Phokarang) FREE A wonderful 12th-century remnant of the time when the Angkor (Khmer) kingdom stretched from present-day Cambodia all the way to the Malay peninsula, this ancient and once-ornate shrine was originally Hindu before Thailand's conversion to Buddhism. There is one intact sanctuary, flanked by two smaller shrines and crumbling sandstone walls, making for intriguing photo opportunities.

MONKEY BUSINESS

Phetchaburi is full of macaque monkeys who know no shame or fear. Having once just congregated on Khao Wang (Palace Hill), they have now spread to the surrounding streets, as well as to the road leading to Tham Khao Luang. There, they lurk by food stands, or eye up passing pedestrians as potential mugging victims. These apes love plastic bags – regarding them as a signal that you are carrying food – so be wary about displaying them. Keep a tight hold on camera bags too. Above all, don't feed or bait the monkeys. They do bite.

Tham Khao Bandai-It CAVE
(ถ้ำเขาบันไดอิฐ; donation appreciated; ⏰9am-4pm) This hillside monastery, 2km west of town, sprawls through several large caverns converted into Buddha shrines and meditation rooms. English-speaking guides (100B tip appreciated) lead tours, mainly as a precaution against the monkeys. One cavern contains a population of bats, and guides will instruct you not to look up with your mouth open (a good rule for everyday life).

Hat Puak Tian BEACH
(หาดปึกเตียน) On weekends locals come to this dark-sands beach, 20km southeast of Phetchaburi and famed for its role in Thai literature, to eat seafood and frolic in the surf. You'll need private transport to get here.

The beach is mentioned in the Thai epic poem *Phra Aphaimani,* written by Sunthorn Phu. A partially submerged statue of a giant woman standing offshore with an outstretched hand and a forlorn expression depicts a character from the poem who disguised herself as a beautiful temptress to win the love of the hero and imprison him on this beach. But he discovers her treachery (and her true ugliness) and with the help of a mermaid escapes to Ko Samet (which has nicer beaches so maybe he was onto something).

Festivals & Events

Phra Nakhon Khiri Fair CULTURAL
Centred on Khao Wang, this provincial-style celebration lasts nine days and takes place in late March and early April. Phra Nakhon Khiri is festooned with lights, there are traditional dance performances, craft and food displays, and a beauty contest.

Phetchaburi (Phetburi)

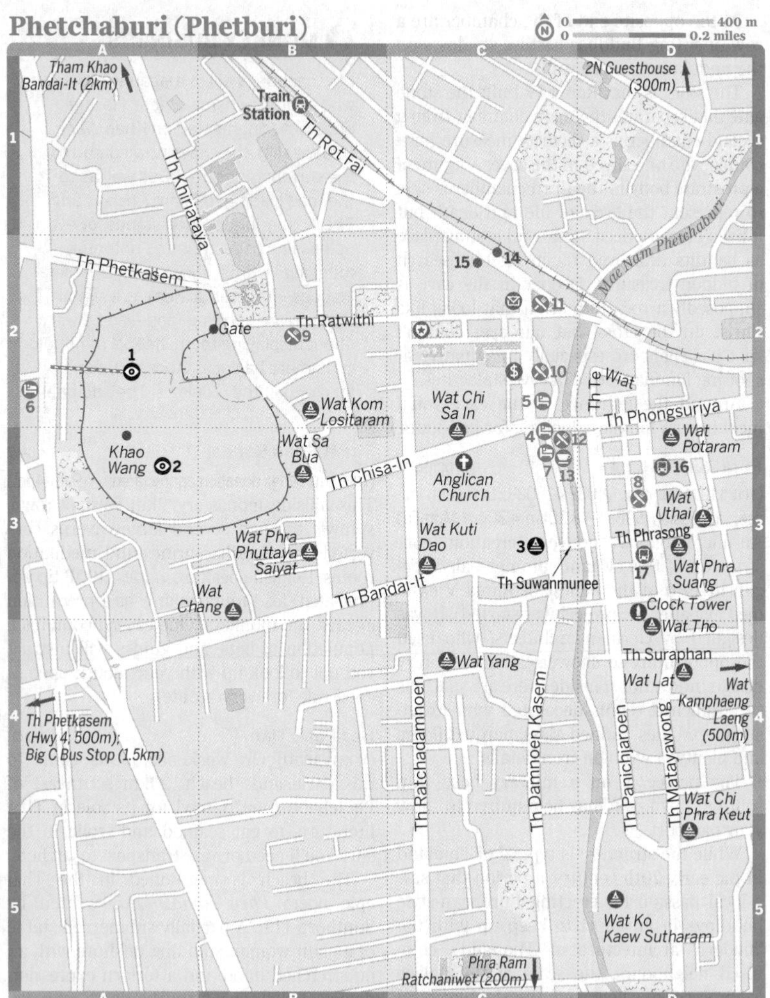

Sleeping

Once bereft of guesthouses, Phetchaburi's accommodation options have improved in recent years. But there aren't many places, so it's worth booking ahead, especially in high season (November to March).

2N Guesthouse GUESTHOUSE $
(081 817 1134; two_nguesthouse@hotmail.com; 98/3 Mu 2, Tambol Bankoom; d & tw 580B;) In a secluded location away from the centre of town, the six rooms here are big and bright and come with small balconies. The friendly staff are a solid source of information and they offer free pick-ups and bicycles.

Sabaidee Resort GUESTHOUSE $
(086 344 4418; sabai2505@gmail.com; 65-67 Th Klongkrachang; r 250-500B;) Basic but well-kept bungalows and rooms, some fan-only and all with shared bathrooms, are set around a small garden. There's a communal terrace overlooking the river that's a decent spot for a sundowner. The pleasant staff can arrange Thai cooking classes, and bikes (50B) and scooters (300B) can be hired.

Phetchaburi (Phetburi)

J.J. Home GUESTHOUSE $
(☎081 880 9286; a.sirapassorn@hotmail.com; 2 Th Chisa-In; r 300-500B; ❄📶) On both sides of the road, the rooms here are clean and a decent deal. The more expensive options have private bathrooms, air-con and shared balconies.

White Monkey GUESTHOUSE $$
(☎032 898238; whitemonkey.guesthouse@gmail.com; 78/7 Th Klongkrachang; r 600-1000B; ❄📶) New, if pricey, guesthouse with bright, spacious, spick-and-span rooms (the more expensive have air-con and private bathrooms), a fine communal terrace and helpful English-speaking staff who can organise trips in the area.

Sun Hotel HOTEL $$
(☎032 401000; www.sunhotelthailand.com; 43/33 Soi Phetkasem; r 950B; ❄@📶) Sitting opposite the back entrance to Phra Nakhon Khiri, the Sun Hotel has professional staff and large, modern but uninspiring rooms. There's a pleasant cafe downstairs and you can rent bikes for 20B per hour.

Eating & Drinking

Surrounded by palm sugar plantations, Phetchaburi is famous for its sweet concoctions, including *kà·nŏm môr gaang* (egg custard) and the various 'golden' desserts made from egg yolks to portend good fortune. Nearby fruit orchards produce refreshingly aromatic *chom·pôo Phet* (Phetchaburi rose apple), pineapples and golden bananas.

★**Rabieng Rim Nam** INTERNATIONAL, THAI $
(☎032 425707; 1 Th Chisa-In; dishes 50-100B; ⏲8am-midnight; 📶) This riverside restaurant serves up terrific food in an agreeable atmosphere and the English-speaking owner is a fount of tourist information. The affiliated guesthouse has a few run-down but bearable rooms (120B), all with shared bathrooms.

Jek Meng THAI $
(www.jekmeng-noodle.com; 85 Th Ratwithi; dishes 50-100B; ⏲7am-5pm) A cut above your average hole-in-the-wall joint, you can get curries and dumplings here, as well as fried rice and noodles. It's opposite the Shell petrol station. Look for the black-and-white checked tablecloths.

Ne & Nal THAI $
(Th Damnoen Kasem; dishes 30-50B; ⏲8am-4pm) Great slow-cooked soups in claypots are the signature dishes at this casual place. Their *gŏo·ay đĕe·o gài* (chicken noodles) comes southern style with a chicken drumstick.

Night Market MARKET $
(Th Ratwithi; ⏲4-10pm) Big and bustling from the late afternoon, head to this market for all the standard Thai fast-food favourites and decent barbecue.

Day Market MARKET $
(⏲6am-6pm) A good spot for watching people, the day market, north of the clock tower, has food stalls on the perimeter serving the usual noodle dishes as well as specialities such as *kà·nŏm jeen tôrt man* (thin noodles with fried spicy fishcake) and the hot-season favourite *kôw châa pét·bù·ree* (moist chilled rice served with sweetmeats).

Pagoda Cafe CAFE
(95 Th Klongkrachang; tea/coffee from 35B; ⏲9am-6pm Tue-Sun; 📶) A hip cafe that draws lots of students and makes a wonderful

TRANSPORT TO/FROM PHETCHABURI

DESTINATION	BUS	MINIVAN	TRAIN
Bangkok Hualamphong			34-84B; 3-4hr; 11 daily; 1.51am-4.46pm
Bangkok Southern Bus Terminal	120B; 2-3hr; frequent	100B; 2hr; hourly; 4.30am-5pm	
Bangkok Victory Monument		100B; 2hr; every 45min; 4.30am-8pm	
Cha-am (from Th Matayawong)	30B; 45min; frequent		20-30B; 1hr; 3 daily
Hua Hin (from Th Matayawong)	40B; 1½ hr; frequent		13-34B; 2hr; 11 daily; 1.51am-4.46pm
Kaeng Krachan National Park		100B; 1hr; hourly; 8.30am-5pm	

air-conditioned retreat away from the afternoon sun.

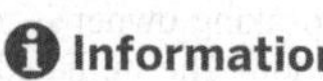

Information

There's no formal information source in town, but all the guesthouses can provide up-to-date travel tips.

Main Post Office (cnr Th Ratwithi & Th Damnoen Kasem; ⌚8.30am-4.30pm Mon-Fri, 9am-noon Sat)

Police Station (☎032 425500; Th Ratwithi) Near the intersection of Th Ratchadamnoen.

Siam Commercial Bank (2 Th Damnoen Kasem; ⌚9.30am-3.30pm Mon-Fri) You can change money here and it has an ATM (as do other nearby banks).

Getting There & Away

Air-conditioned buses to Bangkok's southern bus terminal leave from opposite the Big C department store on Th Phetkasem outside town. Southbound buses and minivans stop outside Big C. Motorcycle taxis await and charge 50B to take you into town.

Minivans to Bangkok (Victory Monument and the southern bus terminal) and Kaeng Krachan National Park leave from close to the night market.

Ordinary buses to Cha-am and Hua Hin stop in town near Th Matayawong.

Frequent rail services run to/from Bangkok's Hualamphong station. Fares vary depending on the train and class.

Getting Around

Motorcycle taxis go anywhere in the town centre for 30B to 40B. *Sŏrng·tăa·ou* (passenger pick-up trucks) cost about the same. It's a 20-minute walk (1km) from the train station to the town centre.

All the guesthouses hire out bicycles (50B per day) and motorbikes (200B to 300B per day).

Kaeng Krachan National Park อุทยานแห่งชาติแก่งกระจาน

Wake to an eerie symphony of gibbon calls as the early morning mist hangs limply above the forest canopy. Hike through lush forests in search of elephant herds and other wildlife at the communal watering holes. Or sweat through your clothes as you summit the park's highest peak. At 3000 sq km, Thailand's largest **national park** (☎032 459291; www.dnp.go.th; 300B; ⌚visitors centre 8.30am-4.30pm) is surprisingly close to civilisation but shelters an intense tangle of wilderness that sees relatively few tourists. Two rivers (Mae Nam Phetchaburi and Mae Nam Pranburi), a large lake and abundant rainfall keep the place green year-round. Animal life is prolific and includes wild elephants, deer, gibbons, boars, dusky langurs and wild cattle.

This park also occupies an interesting, overlapping biozone for birds as the southernmost spot for northern species and the northernmost for southern species. There are about 400 species of birds, including hornbills, as well as pheasants and other ground dwellers.

Activities

Hiking is the best way to explore the park. Most of the trails are signed and branch off the main road. The **Nam Tok Tho Thip** trail starts at the Km 36 marker and continues for 4km to an 18-tiered waterfall. **Phanoen Thung** (1112m) is the park's highest point and can be summited via a 6km hike that starts at the Km 27 marker. Note that most trails, including the one to Phanoen Thung, are closed during the rainy season (August to October).

The twin waterfalls of **Pa La-U Yai** and **Pa La-U Noi** in the southern section of the park are popular with day trippers on tours from Hua Hin and stay open in the rainy season, when they are in full flow. It's also possible to organise mountain biking in the park from Hua Hin.

Tourist infrastructure in Kaeng Krachan is somewhat limited and the roads can be rough. The park rangers can help arrange camping-gear rental, food and transport, which you'll need to go deep into the park where the wildlife is. There are crowds on weekends and holidays but weekdays should be mostly free of people. The best months to visit are between November and April.

Sleeping & Eating

There are various **bungalows** (☎02 562 0760; www.dnp.go.th/parkreserve; bungalows from 1200B) within the park, mainly near the reservoir. These sleep from four to six people and are simple affairs with fans and fridges. There are also **campsites** (per person 60-90B), including a pleasant grassy one near the reservoir at the visitors centre, and a modest restaurant. Tents can be rented at the visitors centre. Bear in mind that you can't stay overnight during the rainy season and that the campsites and bungalows are a fair distance from where the animals roam.

A&B Bungalows BUNGALOW **$$**
(☎089 891 2328; bungalow for 2 people 1000B; ❄📶) On the road out to the Kaeng Krachan National Park entrance, about 3.5km before reaching the visitors centre, this family-run place is popular with birdwatching groups. There's an attached restaurant that can provide you with a packed lunch.

Getting There & Away

Kaeng Krachan is 52km southwest of Phetchaburi, with the southern edge of the park 35km from Hua Hin. If you have your own vehicle, drive 20km south from Phetchaburi on Hwy 4 to the town of Tha Yang. Turn right (west) and after 38km you'll reach the visitors centre. You use the same access road from Tha Yang if coming south from Hua Hin.

You can also reach the park by **minivan** (☎089 231 5810; one way 100B; ⏲hourly 8.30am-5.30pm) from Phetchaburi. Alternatively you can catch a *sŏrng·tăa·ou* (80B, 1½ hours, 6am to 2pm) from Phetchaburi (near the clock tower) to the village of Ban Kaeng Krachan, 4km before the park. From the village, you can charter transport to the park. You can also hire your own *sŏrng·tăa·ou* all the way to the park; expect to pay around 1500B for the return trip.

Minivan tours also operate from Hua Hin.

Cha-am ชะอำ

POP 35,581

Cheap and cheerful Cha-am is a popular beach getaway for working-class families and Bangkok students. On weekends and public holidays, neon-painted buses (called '*chor ching cha*'), their sound systems pumping, deliver groups of holidaymakers. It is a very Thai-style beach party, with eating and drinking marathons held around umbrella-shaded beach chairs and tables. Entertainment is provided by the banana boats that zip back and forth, eventually making a final jack-knife turn that throws the passengers into the sea. Applause and giggles usually follow from the beachside audience.

Cha-am doesn't see many foreigners; visitors are usually older Europeans who winter here instead of more expensive Hua Hin. And there are even fewer swimsuits on display as most Thais frolic in the ocean in T-shirts and shorts. But Cha-am's beach is long, wide and sandy, the grey-blue water is clean and calm, the seafood is superb, the people-watching entertaining and the prices are some of the most affordable anywhere on the coast.

Festivals & Events

Crab Festival FOOD
(⏲Feb) In February, Cha-am celebrates one of its local marine delicacies: blue crabs. Food stalls, concerts and lots of neon turn the beachfront into a pedestrian party.

Gin Hoy, Do Nok, Tuk Meuk FOOD
(⏲Sep) You really can do it all at this annual festival held in September. The English translation means 'Eat Shellfish, Watch Birds, Catch Squid' and is a catchy slogan for all of Cha-am's local attractions and fishing traditions. Mainly it is a food festival showcasing a variety of shellfish but there are also birdwatching events at nearby sanctuaries and squid-fishing demonstrations.

Cha'am International Kite Festival SPORTS
(⏲Mar) Every March, kites from around Thailand and the world take to the skies over the beach for two days.

Sleeping

Cha-am has two basic types of accommodation: hotels along the beach road (Th Ruamjit) and more expensive 'condotel' developments (condominiums with a kitchen and operating under a rental program). Expect a discount on posted rates for weekday stays. For guesthouses, head to Soi 1 North off Th Ruamjit (the beach road) or raucous Soi Bus Station, a few hundred metres south of Soi 1 North.

The northern end of the beach (Long Beach) has a wider, blonder strip of sand and is the most crowded. Th Narathip divides the beach into north and south and the sois off Th Ruamjit are numbered in ascending order in both directions from this intersection.

Pa Ka Ma GUESTHOUSE $$
(032 433504; Soi 1 North, Th Ruamjit; r 600-1200B;) The best of the Soi 1 guesthouses: attractively designed and with better bathrooms than its competitors. Comfy beds, and the honeymoon suite has an attractive terrace. Not much English spoken.

Charlie House GUESTHOUSE $$
(032 433799; www.charlie-chaam.com; 241/60-61, Soi 1 North, Th Ruamjit; r 650-800B;) This quiet place boasts a lime-green lobby and modern, comfortable rooms, although the bathrooms are cramped. Don't confuse it with the institutional Charlie Place or Charlie TV on the same soi.

Cha-am Mathong Guesthouse GUESTHOUSE $$
(081 550 2947; www.chaammathong.com; 263/47-48 Th Ruamjit; r 600-700B;) No frills here, but the rooms are clean and you're right across from the beach. Better rooms have sea views and small balconies. The attached restaurant does brisk business during the day.

Baan Pantai Resort HOTEL $$$
(032 433111; www.baanpantai.com; 247/58 Th Ruamjit; r from 2000B;) Rather more upmarket than most hotels in Cha-am, this family-friendly place has a huge pool, a small fitness centre and the beach is just across the road. Rooms are big with great beds and all come with terraces.

Eating

From your deck chair you can wave down vendors selling seafood, or order from the many nearby beachfront restaurants and they'll deliver. At the far northern end of the beach, seafood restaurants with reasonable prices can be found at the fishing pier. There's also a large night market on Th Narathip close to the train station.

★ **Rang Yen Garden** THAI $
(032 471267; 259/40 Th Ruamjit; dishes 60-180B; 11am-10pm Nov-Apr) This lush garden restaurant is a cosy and friendly spot to feel at home after a day of feeling like a foreigner. It serves up Thai favourites and is only open in the high season.

Hello Restaurant INTERNATIONAL, THAI $$
(Soi Bus Station, Th Ruamjit; dishes from 155B; 10am-10pm;) The French chef here turns

ANIMAL ENCOUNTERS

Modern sensibilities have turned away from circus-like animal attractions but many well-intentioned animal lovers curious to see Thailand's iconic creatures (such as elephants, tigers and monkeys) unwittingly contribute to an industry that is poorly regulated and exploitative. Wild animals are often trapped and then disfigured to make them less dangerous (tigers sometimes have their claws and teeth removed), they are acquired as pets and then neglected or inhumanely confined, or abandoned when they are too sick or infirm to work.

Wildlife Friends Foundation Thailand runs a **wildlife rescue centre** (032 458135; www.wfft.org; Wat Khao Luk Chang), 35km northwest of Cha-am, that adopts and cares for abused and abandoned animals. Most of these animals are creatures that can't return to the wild due to injuries or lack of survival skills. The centre cares for 400 animals, including bears, tigers, gibbons, macaques, loris and birds. There is also an affiliated elephant rescue program that buys and shelters animals being used to beg on the streets.

The centre offers a **full access tour** (1800B per person) that introduces the animals and discusses their rescue histories. The tour includes a visit with the elephants (but no rides are offered) and hotel transfer from Hua Hin or Cha-am.

Those looking for a more intimate connection with the animals can volunteer to help at the centre. An average day could involve chopping vegetables to feed sun bears, cleaning enclosures and rowing out to the gibbon islands with a daily meal. Volunteers are required to stay a minimum of one week and have to make a compulsory donation (from US$455/16,152B) to the centre. Contact the centre or visit the website (www.wildlifevolunteer.org) for details.

TRANSPORT TO/FROM CHA-AM

DESTINATION	BUS	MINIVAN	TRAIN
Bangkok Hualamphong			40-90B; 4½hr; 4.55am & 2.33pm daily
Bangkok Southern Bus Terminal	155B; 3hr; frequent	160B; 2½hr; hourly; 7am-6pm	
Bangkok Victory Monument		160B; 2½hr; every 30min; 7am-6.30pm	
Hua Hin	25B; 45min; frequent	40B; 30min; frequent	30-40B; 1½hr; 2 daily
Phetchaburi	30B; 45min; frequent	50B; 30min; frequent	20-30B; 1hr; 3 daily

out high-quality international dishes, as well as Thai standards and lots of seafood.

Bella Pizza ITALIAN, THAI **$$**
(032 470980; 328/19 Th Nongjiang; pizzas from 175B; 4-11pm) Located at the southern end of town (but they deliver), this popular, Italian-run pizza place has a large, quiet outdoor terrace. Thai food is on offer as well.

Information

Phetkasem Hwy runs through Cha-am's busy town centre, which is about 1km away from the beach. The town centre is where you'll find the main bus stop, banks, the main post office, an outdoor market and the train station.

There are plenty of banks along Th Ruamjit with ATMs and exchange services.

Only Chaam (www.onlychaam.com) is a useful online blog and website about visiting Cha-am.

Post Office (Th Ruamjit; 8.30am-4.40pm Mon-Fri, 9am-noon Sat) On the main beach strip.

Tourism Authority of Thailand (TAT; 032 471005; tatphet@tat.or.th; 500/51 Th Phetkasem; 8.30am-4.30pm) On Phetkasem Hwy, 500m south of town. The staff speak good English.

Getting There & Away

Buses stop on Phetkasem Hwy at the intersection with Th Narathip. Frequent buses run to/from Bangkok, Phetchaburi and Hua Hin.

Minivans to Bangkok's Victory Monument and Bangkok's southern bus terminal leave from Soi Bus Station, in between Th Ruamjit and Th Chao Lay. Other minivan destinations include Hua Hin and Phetchaburi. A private taxi to Hua Hin costs 500B.

The **train station** (Th Narathip) is west of Phetkasem Hwy. From Bangkok's Hualamphong station trains go to Cha-am and continue on to Hua Hin. Note that Cha-am is listed in the timetable only in Thai as 'Ban Cha-am'.

Getting Around

From the city centre to the beach it's a quick motorcycle ride (40B). Some drivers may try to take you to hotels that offer commissions instead of the one you requested.

You can hire motorcycles for 200B per day all along Th Ruamjit. Bicycles are a good way to get around and are available everywhere for 20B per hour or 80B per day.

Hua Hin หัวหิน

POP 59,369

Thailand's original beach resort is no palm-fringed castaway island and arguably is the better for it. Instead, it is a delightful mix of city and sea with a cosmopolitan ambience, lively markets, tasty street eats, long beaches and a fully functional infrastructure.

Hua Hin traces its aristocratic roots to the 1920s when Rama VI (King Vajiravudh) and Rama VII (King Prajadhipok) built summer residences here to escape Bangkok's stifling climate. The most famous of the two is **Phra Ratchawang Klai Kangwon** (Far from Worries Palace), 3km north of town and still a royal residence today; it's so poetically named that Thais often invoke it as a city slogan. Rama VII's endorsement of Hua Hin and the construction of the southern railway made the town *the* place to be for Thai nobility who built their own summer residences beside the sea.

In the 1980s, luxury hotels started moving in and foreign tourists began arriving in numbers. Today, all the international hotel chains have properties in Hua Hin, and a growing number of wealthy expats retire to the condominiums that dot the town. Middle-class and high-society Thais from Bangkok swoop in on weekends, making parts of the city look a lot like upper Sukhumvit.

There's a lot of money swirling around but because this is a bustling Thai town, seafood is plentiful and affordable, there's cheap public transport for beach-hopping and it takes a lot less effort (and money) to get here from Bangkok than to the southern islands.

Hua Hin

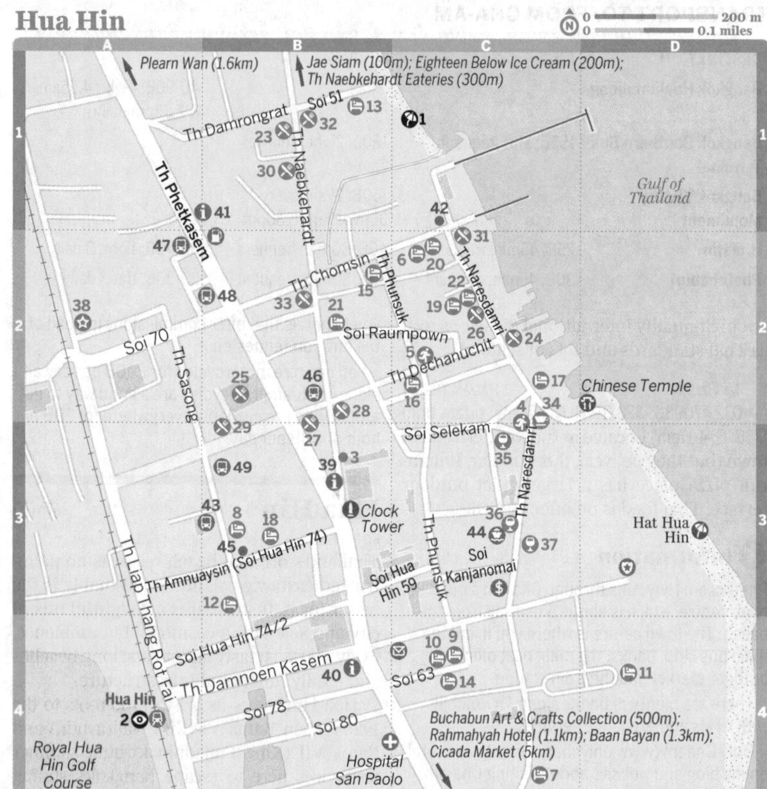

Sights

The city's beaches are numerous, wide and long; swimming is safe, and Hua Hin continues to enjoy some of the peninsula's driest weather. During the rainy season (July to September) watch out for jellyfish.

Hua Hin Town เมืองหัวหิน

A former fishing village, Hua Hin town retains links with its past with an old teak shophouse district bisected by narrow sois, pier houses that have been converted into restaurants and guesthouses, and a busy pier still in use today. South of the harbour is a rocky headland that inspired the name 'Hua Hin', which means 'Stone Head'. In the commercial heart are busy markets and shops selling all the things you forgot to pack.

Hat Hua Hin BEACH

(หาดหัวหิน; public access via eastern end of Th Damnoen Kasem) When viewed from the main public entrance, Hua Hin's beach is a pleasant but not stunning stretch of sand punctuated by round, smooth boulders. Don't be dismayed; this is the people-watching spot. If you're after swimming and sunbathing continue south where the sand is a fine white powder and the sea a calm grey-green.

The 5km beach stretches to a Buddha-adorned headland (Khao Takiab). The north end is where Thais come to photograph their friends wading ankle-deep in the sea and pony rides are offered to anyone standing still. Further south, resort towers rather than coconut trees line the interior of the beach, but that's a minor distraction if you're splashing around in the surf. Access roads lead to Th Phetkasem, where you can catch a green *sŏrng·tăa·ou* back to town.

Hua Hin Train Station HISTORIC SITE

(สถานีรถไฟหัวหิน; Th Liap Thang Rot Fai) An iconic piece of local architecture, the red-and-white pavilion that sits beside Hua

Hua Hin

Sights
1 Hat Hua Hin....C1
Hat Hua Hin Neua....(see 1)
2 Hua Hin Train Station....A4

Activities, Courses & Tours
3 Hua Hin Adventure Tour....B3
4 Hua Hin Golf Centre....C2
5 Thai Thai Massage....C2

Sleeping
6 Baan Chalelarn Hotel....C2
7 Baan Laksasubha....C4
8 Baan Manthana....B3
9 Baan Oum-or Hotel....C4
10 Ban Somboon....C4
11 Centara Grand Resort & Villas....D4
12 Euro-Hua Hin City Hotel YHA....B3
Fulay Guesthouse....(see 17)
13 Green Gallery....B1
14 Hotel Alley....C4
15 King's Home....B2
16 Love Sea House....C2
17 Mod....C2
18 My Place Hua Hin....B3
19 Pattana Guest House....C2
20 Tai Tai Guest House....C2
21 Tong-Mee House....B2
22 Victor Guest House....C2

Eating
23 Baan Tuayen Icy Beans....B1
24 Chaolay....C2
25 Chatchai Market....B2
26 Cool Breeze....C2
27 Hua Hin Koti....B3
28 Jek Pia Coffeeshop....B2
29 Night Market....B3
30 Ratama....B1
31 Sang Thai Restaurant....C2
32 Sôm·dam Stand....B1
33 Thanon Chomsin Food Stalls....B2

Drinking & Nightlife
34 Coffee Club....C2
35 El Murphy's Mexican Grill & Steakhouse....C3
36 Lounge Bar....C3
37 Mai Tai Cocktail & Beer Garden....C3

Entertainment
38 Bang Bar....A2

Information
39 Municipal Tourist Information Office....B3
40 Municipal Tourist Information Office....B4
41 Tourism Authority of Thailand....B1
42 Tuk Tours....C1

Transport
Air-con Buses to Bangkok....(see 43)
43 Bangkok Bus Office....B3
44 Lomprayah....C3
45 Minivans to Bangkok....B3
46 Minivans to Bangkok....B2
47 Minivans to Bangkok's Victory Monument....A2
48 Ordinary Buses to Phetchaburi & Cha-am....B2
49 Sŏrng·tăa·ou to Khao Takiab & Buses to Pranburi....B3

Hin's train station once served as the royal waiting room during Rama VI's reign. By cutting the journey time from Bangkok to a mere four hours, it was the arrival of the railway that made Hua Hin a tourist destination for the Bangkok-based monarchy and the city's elite. One hundred years later and even speeding minivan drivers fuelled by energy drinks can't do it much quicker.

North Hua Hin

The summer residences of the royal family and minor nobility dot the coast northwards from Hua Hin's fishing pier towards Cha-am.

Hat Hua Hin Neua BEACH
(หาดหัวหินเหนือ; North Hua Hin Beach; grounds 5.30-7.30am & 4-7pm) While the northern end of Hua Hin's beach is not its most spectacular section, it is lined with genteel Thai-Victorian garden estates bestowed with ocean-inspired names such as 'Listening to the Sea House'. The current king's palace lies about 3km north of town but visitors are only allowed on the **grounds** (passport ID required).

There are public access paths to the beach off Th Naebkehardt. On weekends, Th Naebkehardt is the preferred getaway for Bangkokians, some of whom still summer in the old-fashioned residences while others come to dine in the houses that have been converted into restaurants.

Plearn Wan NOTABLE BUILDING
(เพลินวาน; 032 520311; www.plearnwan.com; Th Phetkasem btwn Soi 38 & Soi 40; 9am-9pm) As much an art installation as a commercial enterprise, Plearn Wan is a recreation of the old-fashioned shophouses that once occupied the Thai-Chinese neighbourhoods of Bangkok and Hua Hin. There's a pharmacy selling

NEW ATTITUDES TOWARDS WINE

Common wisdom will tell you that tasty wine grapes don't grow alongside coconut trees. But advances in plant sciences and a global palette for wines has ushered in the geographic experiment dubbed New Latitude Wines, produced from grapes grown outside the traditional 30- to 50-degree parallels.

The New Latitudes' main challenge is to replicate the wine-producing grapes' preferred climate as best as possible. That means introducing a false dormancy or winter period through pruning, regulated irrigation and companion planting of grasses to prevent soil loss during the rainy season. If you're familiar with viticulture in the Old World, you'll be shocked to see all the cultivation rules Thai vineyards successfully break.

Wine experts have yet to crown a New Latitude that surpasses the grande dames, but they do fill a local niche. Siam Winery, the parent company of **Hua Hin Hills Vineyard**, aims to produce wines that pair with the complex flavours of Thai food. The vineyard grows colombard, chenin blanc, muscat, shiraz and sangiovese grapes, among others, and typically the citrus-leaning whites are a refreshing complement to the fireworks of most Thai dishes.

A wine drinker's palette is often altered in a hot climate. The thinner wines produced in Thailand tend to have a more satisfying effect than the bold chewy reds that pair well with a chilly spring day. Drinking red wine in Thailand has always been a challenge because the heat turns otherwise leathery notes straight into vinegar. To counteract the tropical factor, break yet another wine rule and chill reds in the refrigerator to replicate 'cellar' temperature as close as possible.

(well actually displaying) roots and powders that Thai grandmothers once used, as well as music and clothes stores.

Phra Ratchaniwet Mrigadayavan HISTORIC SITE
(พระราชนิเวศนมฤคทายวัน; ☎032 508443; admission 50B; ⏲8.30am-4pm Thu-Tue) With a breezy seaside location 12km north of Hua Hin, this summer palace was built in 1924 during the reign of Rama VI. Set in a beautiful garden with statuesque trees and stunning sea views, it's a series of interlinked teak houses with tall, shuttered windows and patterned fretwork built upon stilts forming a shaded ground-level boardwalk.

The functional but elegant style of the palace was a result of Rama VI suffering from rheumatoid arthritis; the court's Italian architect designed it to maximise air circulation and make the most of the seaside location. There's not a huge amount to see (a small selection of royal photos is on display), but it's a tranquil spot and Thais flock here to pay their respects.

The palace is within the grounds of Camp Rama VI, a military base, and you may need to show ID (passport). It is easiest to get here with private transport but you can also catch a Hua Hin–Cha-am bus and ask to be dropped off opposite the camp's front gate. Motorcycle taxis are sometimes waiting to take you the remaining 2km. As this is a royal palace, legs and arms should be covered, otherwise you'll be given a sarong-like garment to hide your limbs.

Inland from Hua Hin

Baan Silapin GALLERY
(บ้านศิลปิน; ☎032534830; www.huahinartistvillage.wordpress.com; Th Hua Hin-Pa Lu-U; art classes per hr adult/child 150/100B; ⏲10am-5pm Tue-Sun) Local painter Tawee Kase-ngam established this artist collective in a shady grove 4km west of Th Phetkasem. The galleries and studio spaces showcase the works of 19 artists, many of whom opted out of Bangkok's fast-paced art world in favour of Hua Hin's more relaxed atmosphere and scenic landscape of mountains and sea.

There are rotating exhibitions, while clay huts shelter the playful sculptures. **Art classes** are available for adults on Tuesday and Thursday and for children on Saturday.

Hua Hin Hills Vineyard VINEYARD
(ไร่องุ่นหัวหินฮิลล์ วินยาร์ด; ☎081 701 0222; www.huahinhillsvineyard.com; Th Hua Hin-Pa Lu-U; vineyard tour 1700-2400B, wine tasting 3 glasses 290B; ⏲9am-7pm) This vineyard is nestled in a scenic mountain valley 45km west of Hua Hin. The loamy sand and slate soil feeds Rhone grape varieties that are used in their Monsoon Valley wine label. There are daily **vineyard tours** from 1700B, including wine, an excellent

three-course meal and return transport. Alternatively, you can just do the **wine tasting**.

The most expensive tour also includes the completely unnecessary option of an elephant ride. There's also a *pétanque* course, mountain biking and the picturesque Sala Wine Bar & Bistro.

A vineyard shuttle leaves the affiliated **Hua Hin Hills Wine Cellar store** (☎032 511497; 2F Villa Market, Th Phetkasem) at 10.30am and 3pm and returns at 1.30pm and 6pm; a return ticket is 300B.

Khao Takiab เขาตะเกียบ

About 7km south of Hua Hin, Monumental Chopstick Mountain guards the southern end of Hua Hin beach and is adorned with a giant standing Buddha. Atop the 272m mountain is **Wat Khao Lat**, a Thai-Chinese temple, and many resident monkeys who are not to be trusted – but the views are great. On the southern side of Khao Takiab is **Suan Son Pradipath** (Sea Pine Garden), a muddy beach maintained by the army and popular with weekending Thais. Green *sŏrng·tăa·ou* go all the way from Hua Hin to Khao Takiab village, where you'll find loads of simple Thai eateries serving fish straight off the fishing boats that dock here.

The nearby **Cicada Market** (Th Phetkasem; dishes 45-120B; ⏱4-11pm Fri & Sat, 4-10pm Sun) hosts lots of outdoor food stalls at the weekend and is a pleasant, mellow spot with live music from 7pm. It's just before Khao Takiab on the left-hand side of the road. You can catch a green *sŏrng·tăa·ou* (20B, 6am to 9pm) from Hua Hin's night market; a hired túk-túk (pronounced *đúk đúk;* motorised three-wheeled taxi) will cost 150B one-way.

Activities

With nine courses scattered around its environs, Hua Hin continues to be an international and domestic golfing destination.

Cycling is a scenic and affordable option for touring Hua Hin's outlying attractions, especially since hiring a taxi to cover the same ground is ridiculously expensive. Don't be spooked by the busy thoroughfares; there are plenty of quiet byways where you can enjoy the scenery.

Kiteboarders flock to Hua Hin for the strong winds that blow almost all year round.

Kiteboarding Asia KITEBOARDING
(☎081 591 4593; www.kiteboardingasia.com; 143/8 Soi 75/1, Th Phetkasem, South Hua Hin; 3-day beginner course 11,000B) This long-established company operates three beachside shops that rent kiteboarding equipment and offer lessons. The three-day introductory course teaches beginners the physical mechanics of the sport, and the instructor recommends newbies come when the winds are blowing from the southeast (January to March) and the sea is less choppy.

Hua Hin Golf Centre GOLF
(☎032 530476; www.huahingolf.com; Th Selakam; ⏱noon-9pm) The friendly staff at this pro shop can steer you to the most affordable, well-maintained courses where the monkeys won't try to run off with your balls. The company also organises golf tours and rents sets of clubs (500B to 700B per day).

KITE CRAZY

Adding to the beauty of Hua Hin's beach are the kiteboarders flying and jumping above the ocean. Hua Hin is Thailand's kiteboarding, or kitesurfing, capital, blessed with strong, gusty winds, shallow water and a long, long beach off which to practise your moves.

From here down to Pranburi the winds blow from the northeast October to December, and then from the southeast January to May: perfect for kitesurfing. Even during the May to October rainy season there are plenty of days when the wind is fine for taking to the waves. In fact, this stretch of coast is so good for kiteboarding that Hua Hin hosted the Kiteboarding World Cup in 2010.

This is also the best place in Thailand to learn how to kiteboard, with a number of schools in Hua Hin offering tuition. After three days with them you can be leaping into the air too. The schools also cater for more advanced students, and you can qualify as an instructor here as well.

But if you prefer to stay on the ground while flying a kite, then check out the **Hua Hin International Kite Festival**. Staged every two years in March 12km north of town at the Rama VI military base, it's a chance to see stunt kiters in action, as well as kites of every conceivable size and colour.

SEVEN KINGS

If anyone needed further proof of Thailand's devotion to its monarchy, then the seven giant statues of the country's most revered kings newly erected in Ratchaphakdi Park outside Hua Hin are compelling evidence. Standing 14m high and weighing in at 30 tonnes each, the bronze statues tower over the park.

Cast in different foundries in central Thailand, the statues held up traffic for weeks as they were transported south to Hua Hin in convoys of flat-bed trucks that stretched for up to 200m.

The seven kings are Ramkhamhaeng, Naresuan, Narai, Taksin, Buddha Yodfa Chulalok, Mongkut and Chulalongkorn. Their statues will be the centrepiece of the 700-million-baht park located close to Klai Kangwon Palace, where the current king spends his summers, and are funded by the fiercely patriotic military.

With the army running Thailand since a May 2014 coup, the new park is symbolic of the way the military see the monarchy as central to Thailand's national identity. The kings have been carefully chosen to represent the most glorious periods of Thai history, and to hammer home the idea that only under the monarchy can the country prosper.

Black Mountain Golf Course GOLF

(☎032 618666; www.bmghuahin.com; green fees from 1800B, caddy 300B) The best course in Hua Hin, and one that has hosted Asian PGA tournaments. About 10km west of Hua Hin, its 18 holes are carved out of jungle and an old pineapple plantation and it retains some natural creeks as water hazards.

Thai Thai Massage MASSAGE

(20/1 Th Dechanuchit; massage from 250B; ⊙10am-11pm) There are luxury spas inside all the posh hotels, however if you want something less pricey but still a cut above the average, the trained and friendly masseuses at this respectable place get excellent feedback.

Courses

Thai Cooking Course Hua Hin COOKING COURSE

(☎081 572 3805; www.thai-cookingcourse.com; 19/95 Th Phetkasem; courses 1500B) Aspiring chefs should sign up for a one-day cooking class here that includes a market visit and recipe book. The course runs only if there are a minimum of three people.

Tours

There are many travel agencies in town offering day trips to nearby national parks. Unless you're in a group, you may have to wait until enough people sign up for the trip of your choice.

Hua Hin Adventure Tour ADVENTURE TOUR

(☎095 493 6942, 032 530314; www.huahinadventuretour.com; 69/7 Th Naebkehardt) Hua Hin Adventure Tour offers active excursions, including kayaking trips in the Khao Sam Roi Yot National Park and mountain biking in Kaeng Krachan National Park.

Hua Hin Bike Tours CYCLING

(☎081 173 4469; www.huahinbiketours.com; 15/120 Th Phetkasem btwn Soi 27 & 29; tours from 2000B) A husband-and-wife team operates this cycling company that leads day-long and multiday tours to a variety of attractions in and around Hua Hin. Pedal to the Hua Hin Hills Vineyard for some well-earned refreshment, tour the coastal byways south of Hua Hin, or ride among the limestone mountains of Khao Sam Roi Yot National Park.

They also rent premium bicycles (500B per day) for independent cyclists and can recommend routes. The same couple lead long-distance charity and corporate bike tours across Thailand; visit the parent company **Tour de Asia** (www.tourdeasia.org) for more information.

Festivals & Events

King's Cup Elephant Polo Tournament CULTURAL

(⊙Aug & Sep) This annual polo tournament involving pachyderms instead of ponies takes place in late August and early September. While this event raises money for elephant-welfare issues, it must be noted that using elephants for the purpose of entertainment, as this popular event does, is an elephant welfare issue in itself. For some background on the subject, see p148.

Hua Hin Jazz Festival JAZZ

(⊙Aug) In honour of the king's personal interest in the genre, the city that hosts royal getaways also hosts an annual jazz festival featuring Thai and international performers. All events are free.

Sleeping

Most budget and midrange options are in the old shophouse district. It is an atmospheric setting with cheap food nearby but you'll have to 'commute' to the beach, either by walking to north Hat Hua Hin (best at low tide) or catching a *sŏrng·tăa·ou* a couple of kilometres to the southern end of Hat Hua Hin.

The top-end options are beachfront resorts sprawling south from the Sofitel. All the international brands have a presence in Hua Hin but we've only listed special local options for a more intimate experience.

Hua Hin Town

Victor Guest House GUESTHOUSE $
(032 511564; victorguesthouse@gmail.com; 60 Th Naresdamri; r 390-1290B;) Popular with both Thais and foreigners, this efficient guesthouse has solid rooms, a small garden and a central location. Helpful staff and a good source of travel tips.

Fulay Guesthouse GUESTHOUSE $
(032 513145; www.fulayhuahin.net; 110/1 Th Naresdamri; r 550-1050B;) With the waves crashing underneath and the floorboards creaking, this is a fine old-school pier guesthouse. Rooms aren't huge, but the beds are good and the bathrooms are OK.

Euro-Hua Hin City Hotel YHA HOSTEL $
(032 513130; www.huahineurohotel.com; 5/15 Th Sasong; r 250-1600B;) Some dorms are fan-only, all are old-fashioned and it feels a tad institutional, but the price is right for Hua Hin and the staff are friendly. The private rooms are sizeable, if overpriced. Add 50B to these prices if you don't belong to HI. It's off the road; look for the sign.

★ **Pattana Guest House** GUESTHOUSE $$
(032 513393; 52 Th Naresdamri; r 990B;) Located in a simple teak house tucked away down a soi, this recently remodelled guesthouse features a lovely, peaceful garden. All rooms are two-storey, with bathrooms and a small living room downstairs.

King's Home GUESTHOUSE $$
(089 052 0490; huahinkingshome@gmail.com; off Th Phunsuk; r 600-1400B;) Family-run guesthouse with loads of character; it's crammed with antiques and artefacts from the owners' travels across Southeast Asia. Decent-sized rooms, and it even has a small splash pool out back. They get a lot of repeat guests, which says it all.

Baan Chalelarn Hotel HOTEL $$
(032 531288; www.chalelarnhotel.com; 11 Th Chomsin; r 1000-1800B;) Chalelarn has a lobby with wooden floors, while the 12 big rooms are equipped with king-size beds. Verandahs and breakfast are part of the perks.

Baan Oum-or Hotel HOTEL $$
(081 944 9390; baan_oum-or@hotmail.com; 77/18-19 Soi 63, Th Phetkasem; r 800-1200B;) Rooms here are big and bright. There are only six of them so book ahead.

Love Sea House GUESTHOUSE $$
(080 079 0922; siamozohlie@hotmail.com; 35 Th Dechanuchit; r 700-1200B;) Pleasant, family-run guesthouse decked out in fresh blue and white colours. Clean, good-sized rooms and a handy location.

Tai Tai Guest House GUESTHOUSE $$
(032 512891; Kallaya_Lasen@hotmail.com; 1/8 Th Chomsin; r 700-900B;) Large rooms with excellent beds, mermaid murals and OK bathrooms. The more expensive rooms have verandahs and a bit of road noise. There's a cosy communal roof terrace.

Tong-Mee House GUESTHOUSE $$
(032530725; tongmeehuahin@hotmail.com; 1 Soi Raumpown, Th Naebkehardt; r 600-1000B;) Hidden in a quiet residential soi, this long-running guesthouse has cosy and clean rooms with balconies. Book ahead.

Mod GUESTHOUSE $$
(032 512296; www.modguesthouse.com; Th Naresdamri; r 600-800B;) Refurbished and now more comfortable (better beds) than most pier guesthouses, the more expensive rooms here come with air-con and sea views. A few cheaper rooms lack windows and are fan-only.

Ban Somboon GUESTHOUSE $$
(032 511538; www.baansomboon.com; 13/4 Soi Hua Hin 63, Th Phetkasem; r 700B;) With family photos decorating the walls and a compact garden, this place on a very quiet centrally located soi is like staying at your favourite Thai auntie's house.

Hotel Alley HOTEL $$
(032 511787; www.hotelalleyhuahin.com; 13/5 Soi Hua Hin 63, Th Phetkasem; r 1300-1600B;) Hotel Alley is tucked away down a quiet soi,

with spacious and modern rooms decorated in pastel colours. Most have balconies and breakfast is included.

Baan Manthana HOTEL $$
(☎032 514223; www.manthanahouse.com; 24/10 Th Sasong; r 900-2500B; ❄📶🏊) With three separate wings, there's always space here even during public holidays. Rooms are comfortable and proper-sized and some have balconies. There's a small pool, too.

My Place Hua Hin HOTEL $$$
(☎032 514111; www.myplacehuahin.com; 17 Th Amnuaysin, Th Phetkasem; r 1850-4500B; ❄@📶🏊) A smart, amiable and efficient place in the heart of the city with stylish, good-sized rooms that qualify it for boutique status. There's a rooftop swimming pool.

Hua Hin Beaches

Rahmahyah Hotel GUESTHOUSE $$
(☎032 532106; Rahmahyah@yahoo.co.uk; 113/10 Soi Hua Hin 67, Th Phetkasem, South Hua Hin; r 800-1300B; ❄📶🏊) Across the street from Market Village, about 1km south of town, is a small guesthouse enclave tucked between the high-end resorts, with beach access. The Rahmahyah is the best of the bunch with clean, functional rooms. Guests can use the communal swimming pool opposite. Book ahead here.

★**Baan Bayan** HOTEL $$$
(☎032 533540; www.baanbayanresort.com; 119 Th Phetkasem, South Hua Hin; r 3500-21,000B; ❄📶🏊) A beautiful teak house built in the early 20th century, Baan Bayan is perfect for travellers seeking a luxury experience without the overkill of a big resort. Airy, high-ceilinged rooms, attentive staff and the location is absolute beachfront.

Baan Laksasubha HOTEL $$$
(☎032 514525; www.baanlaksasubha.com; Th 53/7 Naresdamri; r 3675-11,525B; ❄📶🏊) At this petite resort owned by a scion of the royal family there are 16 much-in-demand cottages on offer. The decor is crisp and subdued, meandering garden paths lead to the beach and there's a dedicated kids' room with toys and books. The taxi drivers will understand you better if you say 'baan lak-su-pah'.

Green Gallery HOTEL $$$
(☎032 530487; www.greenhuahin.com; 3/1 Soi Hua Hin 51, Th Naebkehardt, North Hua Hin; r 2650-12,980B; ❄📶🏊) As cute as candy, this small hotel occupies a converted colonial-style beach house that was once the vacation home of a princess and is very popular with upmarket Thais. Every room is individually decorated in a quirky, arty style. The attached restaurant is recommended.

Centara Grand Resort & Villas HOTEL $$$
(☎032 512021; www.centarahotelsresorts.com; 1 Th Damnoen Kasem; r 3720-9450B; ❄@📶🏊) The historic Railway Hotel, Hua Hin's first seaside hotel, has been restored to world-class levels. Fantastic grounds, great pool, beach access, huge rooms, many restaurants and super-smooth staff.

G Resort & Mall HOTEL $$$
(☎032 515199; www.ghuahin.com; 250/201 Th Phetkasem; r 2400-5900B; ❄📶🏊) A resort and shopping centre all in one: a combo designed to appeal to Asian tourists but also attracts a fair few Westerners. It has big, modern rooms with vast beds and decent balconies. Huge pool and the beach is a 200m walk away.

Eating

Jek Pia Coffeeshop THAI $
(51/6 Th Dechanuchit; dishes from 50B; ⏲6.30am-1.20pm & 5.30-8.30pm) More than just a coffeeshop, this 50-year-old restaurant is a culinary destination specialising in an extensive array of stir-fried seafood dishes. It's wildly popular with the locals – be prepared to queue for a table – and they stick rigidly to their serving hours; get here after 7.30pm and you won't be able to order.

Night Market MARKET $
(Th Dechanuchit btwn Th Phetkasem & Th Sasong; dishes from 50B; ⏲5pm-midnight) An attraction that rivals the beach, Hua Hin's night market mixes food and clothes and draws in both locals and visitors. Lobsters and king prawns appeal to the big spenders but the fare at stir-fry stalls is just as tasty. Try *pàt pǒng gà·rèe Ъoo* (crab curry), *gûng tôrt* (fried shrimp) and *hǒy tôrt* (fried mussel omelette).

Thanon Chomsin Food Stalls FOOD STALL $
(cnr Th Chomsin & Th Naebkehardt; dishes 35-45B; ⏲9am-9pm) If you're after 100% authentic eats, check out the food stalls congregated at this popular lunch corner. Though the setting is humble, Thais are fastidious eaters and use a fork (or their fingers with a pinch of *kôw nĕe·o*) to remove the meat from the bones of *gài tôrt* (fried chicken) rather than putting teeth directly to flesh.

WEEKENDS EATING WITH BANGKOK'S THAIS

On weekends, a different kind of tidal system occurs in Hua Hin. Bangkok professionals flow in, filling up hotels and restaurants on Th Naebkehardt, washing over the night market or crowding into nightclubs. And then come Sunday they clog the roadways heading north, obeying the pull of the upcoming work week.

Their presence is so pronounced that there is an irresistible urge to join them. And because of restaurant features on Thai TV or in food magazines, everyone goes to the same places. So don your designer sunglasses and elbow your way to a table at one of these popular spots in North Hua Hin:

Sôm·đam Stand (Th Naebkehardt; dishes from 35B; ⌚10am-2pm) Across from Iammeuang Hotel is a *sôm·đam* stand that easily wipes out the country's supply of green papayas in one weekend. Great grilled chicken too.

Baan Tuayen Icy Beans (Th Naebkehardt; dishes from 55B; ⌚7am-10pm) New hipster hang-out that draws the crowds with three different menus for breakfast, lunch and dinner. The green curry with simmered pork is famous already, as are the red bean smoothies.

Eighteen Below Ice Cream (Th Naebkehardt; ice cream from 55B; ⌚11am-5pm Wed-Mon) At the end of the road behind Baan Talay Chine Hotel, this gourmet ice-cream shop is run by a trained chef and specialises in rich and creamy flavours.

Ratama (12/10 Th Naebkehardt; dishes from 120B; ⌚10am-10pm) Visiting high-society Thais like the menu here that runs from simple noodle dishes to great, spicy seafood curries. If you're feeling very Thai, go for the hot and sour chicken-feet soup.

Jae Siam (Th Naebkehardt; dishes from 35B; ⌚9am-10pm) Cruise by this open-air noodle shop, just before the Evergreen Hotel, where Hua Hin civil servants pack in on weekdays and Bangkokians come on weekends. The shop is famous for *gŏo·ay đĕe·o mŏo đŭn* (stewed pork noodles) and *gŏo·ay đĕe·o gài đŭn* (stewed chicken noodles).

Chatchai Market MARKET **$**
(Th Phetkasem; dishes from 35B; ⌚daylight hours) The city's day market resides in an historic building built in 1926 with a distinctive seven-eaved roof in honour of Rama VII. There are the usual market refreshments: morning vendors selling *ɓah·tôrng·gŏh* (Chinese-style doughnuts) and *gah·faa boh·rahn* (ancient-style coffee spiked with sweetened condensed milk); as well as all-day noodles with freshly made wontons, and the full assortment of fresh fruit.

★**Hua Hin Koti** CHINESE, THAI **$$**
(☎032 511252; 16/1 Th Dechanuchit; dishes from 120B; ⌚noon-10pm) Across from the night market, this Thai-Chinese restaurant is a national culinary luminary. Thais adore the fried crab balls, while foreigners swoon over *đôm yam gûng* (shrimp soup with lemon grass). And everyone loves the spicy seafood salad *(yam tá-lair)* and deep-fried fish with ginger.

Sang Thai Restaurant SEAFOOD **$$**
(Th Naresdamri; dishes from 150B; ⌚10am-11pm) One of a number of long-established pier-side restaurants, Sang Thai is a Hua Hin institution and a massive operation. There's a vast choice of seafood housed in giant tanks awaiting your decision. You can eat very well for not much, or spend lots if you want to feast on prime lobster.

Chaolay SEAFOOD **$$**
(15 Th Naresdamri; dishes from 150B; ⌚10am-10pm) An atmospheric old-time pier restaurant and always busy. There's a big open kitchen on the ground floor enabling you to see the chefs preparing your seafood selection. Ascend the stairs to find a table.

Cool Breeze MEDITERRANEAN **$$**
(62 Th Naresdamri; tapas from 70B; ⌚11am-11pm; 📶) Popular tapas joint spread over two floors. The daily set lunch (260B) is a good deal. Decent wine list and an amiable spot for a drink as well.

🍷 Drinking & Entertainment

Drinking destinations in Hua Hin are stuck in a time warp of sports bars or hostess bars – and sometimes you can't tell the difference. Try the posh hotels if you want something more sophisticated.

Mai Tai Cocktail & Beer Garden BAR
(33/12 Th Naresdamri; beers from 70B, cocktails from 129B; ⏰noon-1am; 📶) Cheap and convivial and it always gets a crowd. Grab a table on the outdoor terrace for a pre-dinner drink.

El Murphy's Mexican Grill & Steakhouse BAR
(25 Soi Selakam, Th Phunsuk; beers from 90B, cocktails from 180B; ⏰7am-1.30am) Every sports bar needs a gimmick and this busy spot marries Mexico and Ireland. There's a big menu, live music and a pleasant vibe, although the beers aren't cheap.

Lounge Bar COCKTAIL BAR
(156 Th Naresdamri; cocktails from 150B; ⏰10am-midnight; 📶) Upmarket for a Hua Hin bar, this place has reasonably priced cocktails and outdoor seating to watch the world go by. During the day it's fine for a coffee stop.

Coffee Club CAFE
(130/2 Th Naresdamri; coffee from 90B, sandwiches from 180B; ⏰7am-10.30pm Mon-Thu, 7am-11pm Fri-Sun; 📶) This Starbucks-esque cafe serves many varieties of coffee and tea, as well as solid Western breakfasts, hefty sandwiches, salads and classic Thai dishes.

Bang Bar LIVE MUSIC
(Th Liap Thang Rot Fai) North of Soi 70 along Railway Rd are a string of Thai music bars, nearly all foreigner-free. This one stays packed to the early hours, with rotating singers and bands.

ℹ Information

EMERGENCY

Tourist Police (☎032 515995; Th Damnoen Kasem) At the eastern end of the street.

INTERNET ACCESS

Wi-fi is available all over Hua Hin, in guesthouses and cafes.

MEDICAL SERVICES

Bangkok Hospital Hua Hin (☎032 616800; www.bangkokhospital.com/huahin; Th Phetkasem btwn Soi Hua Hin 94 & 106) An outpost of the well-regarded hospital chain; it's in South Hua Hin.

Hospital San Paolo (☎032 532576; 222 Th Phetkasem) Just south of town with emergency facilities.

MONEY

There are exchange booths and ATMs all over town.

POST

Main Post Office (Th Damnoen Kasem; ⏰8.30am-4.30pm Mon-Fri, 9am-noon Sat)

TOURIST INFORMATION

Municipal Tourist Information Office (☎032 511047; cnr Th Phetkasem & Th Damnoen Kasem; ⏰8.30am-4.30pm Mon-Fri) Provides maps and information about Hua Hin. There's another branch (☎032 522797; Th Naebkehardt; ⏰9am-7.30pm Mon-Fri, 9.30am-5pm Sat & Sun) near the clock tower.

Tourism Authority of Thailand (TAT; ☎032 513885; 39/4 Th Phetkasem; ⏰8.30am-4.30pm) Staff here speak English and are quite helpful; the office is north of town near Soi Hua Hin 70.

TRAVEL AGENCIES

Tuk Tours (☎032 514281; www.tuktours.com; 2/1 Th Chomsin; ⏰9am-6pm) Helpful, no-pressure place that can book activities and transport all around Thailand.

USEFUL WEBSITES

Hua Hin Today (www.huahintoday.com) Expat-published newspaper.

Tourism Hua Hin (www.tourismhuahin.com) A cursory intro to the city with a good rundown on the outlying area.

ℹ Getting There & Away

The **airport** (www.huahinairport.com) is 6km north of town, but only has charter services.

Hua Hin's **long-distance bus station** (Th Phetkasem btwn Soi Hua Hin 94 & 98) is located south of town and has services that go to Chiang Mai, Prachuap Khiri Khan, Phuket, Surat Thani and Ubon Ratchathani. Buses to Bangkok leave from a bus company's in-town **office** (Th Sasong), near the night market. Buses to Bangkok Suvarnabhumi International Airport leave from the long-distance bus station.

Ordinary buses depart from north of the market on Th Phetkasem, and destinations include Cha-am and Phetchaburi.

Lomprayah offers a bus-boat combination from Hua Hin to Ko Tao (1050B, seven to eight hours, 8.30am), as well as to Ko Pha-Ngan (1300B, nine hours, 8.30am) and Ko Samui (1400B, 10 hours, 8.30am).

Minivans go to Bangkok's southern bus terminal and Victory Monument. They leave from near the night market and from an office that is situated on the corner of Th Phetkasem and Th Chomsin.

There are frequent trains running to/from Bangkok's Hualamphong station and other stations on the southern railway line.

TRANSPORT TO/FROM HUA HIN

DESTINATION	BUS	MINIVAN	TRAIN
Bangkok Hualamphong			44-622B; 4-6hr; 13 daily; 12.45am-4.01pm
Bangkok Southern Bus Terminal	180B; 4½hr; 8 daily; 3am-9pm		
Bangkok Suvarnabhumi International Airport	294B; 5hr; 7 daily; 6am-6pm		
Bangkok Victory Monument		180B; 4hr; every 30min; 6am-7pm	
Cha-am	25B; 40min; frequent		20-30B; 2 daily
Chiang Mai	813B; 12hr; 3 daily; 8am, 5.30pm & 6pm		
Phetchaburi	40B; 1½hr; frequent		30-40B; 12 daily
Phuket	1011B; 9-10hr; 2 daily; 10am & 9pm		
Surat Thani	787B; 7-8hr; 2 daily; 10am & 10pm		
Ubon Ratchathani	695B; 13hr; 1 daily; 6pm		

Getting Around

Green *sŏrng·tăa·ou* depart from the corner of Th Sasong & Th Dechanuchit, near the night market, and travel south on Th Phetkasem to Khao Takiab (20B). Pranburi-bound buses (20B) depart from the same stop.

Túk-túk fares in Hua Hin are outrageous and start at a whopping 100B and barely budge from there. Motorcycle taxis are much more reasonable (40B to 50B) for short hops.

Motorcycles (200B to 300B per day) and bicycles (50B to 100B per day) can be hired from shops on Th Damnoen Kasem and Th Chomsin. **Thai Rent A Car** (☎02 737 8888; www.thairentacar.com) is a professional car-rental agency with competitive prices, a well-maintained fleet and hotel drop-offs.

Hua Hin to Pranburi

South of Hua Hin are a series of beaches framed by dramatic headlands that make great day trips when Hua Hin beach feels too urban.

Hat Khao Tao หาดเขาเต่า

About 13km south of Hua Hin, a barely inhabited beach stretches several kilometres south from Khao Takiab to Khao Tao (Turtle Mountain). It's far quieter and less developed than Hua Hin's beach: there are no high-rises, no beach chairs, no sarong sellers and no horseback riders.

The mountain has a sprawling temple dedicated to almost every imaginable deity: Buddha, Guan Yin (Chinese goddess of Mercy), Vishnu and even the Thai kings. Follow the trail towards the oceanfront to hike up to the Buddha on the hill.

To get here, take a Pranburi-bound bus from Hua Hin and ask to be dropped off at the turn-off for Khao Tao (20B); a motorbike taxi can take you to the temple (20B). A motorbike from Hua Hin will cost 200B one way. Return transport is rare, though you can always walk or flag down a ride as people are usually coming and going from the temple.

Hat Sai Noi หาดทรายน้อย

About 20km south of Hua Hin, a scenic cove, Hat Sai Noi, drops off quickly into the sea, providing a rare opportunity for deep-water swimming. Mostly patronised by Thais, nearby are all the amenities: simple seafood restaurants and even small guesthouses. For ideal seclusion, come on a weekday. The beach is south of Khao Tao on a lovely road that passes a reservoir and is lined with bougainvillea and limestone cliffs. To get there take a Pranburi-bound bus from Hua Hin and ask to be dropped off at the turn-off for Khao Tao (20B); then ask a motorcycle taxi to take you to Hat Sai Noi (60B). Getting back to the highway will be difficult but enquire at one of the restaurants for assistance.

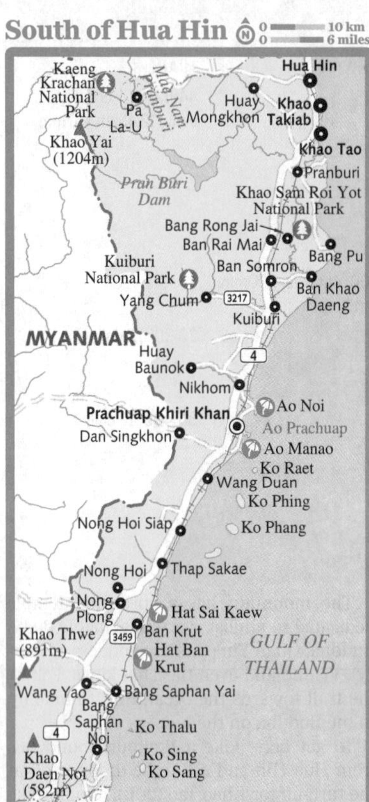

Pranburi & Around

POP 24,789

Continuing along the highway south from Hua Hin leads to the country 'suburb' of Pranburi district, which has become a popular coastal alternative for Bangkok Thais. Ever-more popular, some even go so far as to call it the 'Thai Riviera'. Locally, the fishing village and nearby beaches are known by a more humble name: **Pak Nam Pran** (mouth of the Pranburi River), which designates its geographic location only.

A coastal road separates a string of small villa-style resorts, and an increasing number of condo developments, from the beach. With each successive rainy season, the ocean claims more sand and a breakwater is being constructed along parts of the coastline. Since most of the visitors are Thai, the disappearing beach is of minor consequence. Instead, most domestic tourists come for sea views and the village's primary product: dried squid. Every morning the squid boats dock in the river, unload their catch and begin the process of sun-drying. It is a pungent but interesting affair with large drying racks spread out across town.

Bordering the river is an extensive mangrove forest, protected by the **Pranburi Forest Park** (☎032 621608). Within the park is a wooden walkway that explores the mangroves from the perspective of a mud-dweller, and a sea-pine-lined beach and accommodation facilities. The park also offers boat trips along the river and small canals.

The coastal road provides a pleasant trip to **Khao Kalok** (Skull Mountain), a mammoth headland that shelters a beautiful bay on the southern side. This southern beach is wide and sandy and far removed from the hubbub of Hua Hin and even from Pak Nam Pran for that matter, though it does get busy on weekends. Lazing along this stretch are several secluded boutique resorts that are ideal for honeymooners, or anyone looking to escape the crowds without travelling too far from civilisation.

The next southern bay is often called **Dolphin Bay**, because of the seasonal visits (February to May) from bottlenose dolphins and finless porpoise. Sculpted, jungle-covered islands sit scenically offshore and the beach is a lovely, wide strip of powdery sand. This area is a family favourite because the resorts are value-oriented, traffic is minimal and nightlife is nonexistent. You're also a few kilometres from the northern entrance to Khao Sam Roi Yot National Park.

Sleeping & Eating

It is mainly high-end here but not all of the beach resorts earn the price tag so be discerning when making online reservations for places not listed below. That said, this area has some of the best seaside boutique hotels in Thailand, making it a fine place to splash out.

Beach House GUESTHOUSE **$$**
(☎087 164 6307; karl@beachhousepranburi.com; Pak Nam Pran; r 700-1200B; ❄📶🏊) One of the cheapest options around, this affable, English-run guesthouse has comfortable, decent-sized rooms. It caters mainly to young kiteboarders; you can learn to kitesurf here and the wind is as good, if not better, than Hua Hin. The attached restaurant does a decent Sunday roast lunch.

★ Away Hua Hin HOTEL $$$
(☎089 144 6833; www.away-huahin.com; south of Khao Kalok; r 4500-6000B; ❄📶🏊) A boutique resort without pretence, and one of the more affordable in the area, its seven antique teak houses have been transported to this coastal patch of paradise and outfitted with huge, comfy beds and swish bathrooms.

The amiable owners, a Thai-Australian family, set a homey mood where breakfast is enjoyed at a common table in the 'big' house, providing instant camaraderie. Some villas offer extreme privacy while others accommodate families. The beach is just across the road.

★ Brassiere Beach HOTEL $$$
(☎032 630554; www.brassierebeach.com; Dolphin Bay; r 3000-9000B; ❄📶🏊) A delicious combination of privacy and personality; these 12 stucco villas abut the mountains of Khao Sam Roi Yot National Park and face a secluded beach, 100m from the nearest paved road. The rooms have an uncluttered Spanish colonial feel, some with roof decks and most with open-air showers. Ideal for people who want to leave the world behind for a while.

La a natu Bed & Bakery HOTEL $$$
(☎032 689941; www.laanatu.com; south of Khao Kalok; r 4488-15,888B; ❄📶🏊) Turning the Thai rice village into a luxury living experience is what La a natu does, and it does it with panache. The thatched roof villas rising on stilts have rounded modern corners and a Flintstones-esque playfulness to their design.

Each villa is private but evocative of traditional rustic lifestyles, with living quarters on the ground floor and often steep, ladderlike stairs leading to the sleeping area. Great food on offer too, and then there's the semi-private beach right on your doorstep.

Dolphin Bay Resort HOTEL $$$
(☎032 559333; www.dolphinbayresort.com; Dolphin Bay; r 1690-13,680B; ❄@📶🏊) The resort that defined Dolphin Bay as a family-friendly retreat offers a low-key holiday camp ambience with a variety of standard-issue, value-oriented bungalows and apartments, as well as a few very expensive ones. The grounds are large enough for kids to roam safely, there are two big pools and there's a great sandy beach opposite.

Palm Beach Resort & Hotel HOTEL $$$
(☎085 921 5533; www.palm-beachresort.com; Pak Nam Pran; r 2000-3000B; ❄📶🏊) Right by the beach and newly renovated, the 10 spacious rooms here are tastefully furnished and very comfortable. The staff are pleasant.

Khao Kalok Restaurant THAI $$
(Khao Kalok; dishes 90-300B; ⏰11am-10pm) At the southern base of the mountain, this open-air restaurant provides a front-row view of the moored fishing boats. Tasty dishes, like *gaang kĕe·o wăhn* (green curry), *Ƅlah mèuk gà·prow* (squid stir-fried with basil) and even the standard *pàt pàk roo·am* (stir-fried vegetables) arrive at a leisurely pace.

ℹ Getting There & Around

Pranburi is 35km south of Hua Hin and accessible by ordinary bus from Hua Hin's night market (20B). You'll be dropped off on the highway where you can catch a *sŏrng·tăa·ou* to Pak Nam Pran.

There is also a minivan service from Bangkok's Victory Monument to Pranburi (200B); if you're going to Dolphin Bay (sometimes referred to as Khao Sam Roi Yot Beach), you'll have to negotiate an additional fare with the driver (usually 100B).

If you want to explore the area, you'll need to rent a motorbike as public transport isn't an option.

Khao Sam Roi Yot National Park อุทยานแห่งชาติเขาสามร้อยยอด

Towering limestone outcrops form a rocky jigsaw-puzzled landscape at this 98-sq-km **park** (☎032 821568; www.dnp.go.th; adult/child 200/100B), whose name means Three Hundred Mountain Peaks. There are also caves, beaches and coastal marshlands to explore for outdoor enthusiasts and birdwatchers.

With its proximity to Hua Hin, the park is well travelled by day trippers and contains a mix of public conservation land and private shrimp farms, so don't come expecting remote virgin territory.

Rama IV and a large entourage of Thai and European guests came here on 18 August 1868 to see a total solar eclipse (apparently predicted by the monarch himself) and to enjoy a feast prepared by a French chef. Two months later the king died from malaria, contracted from mosquito bites inflicted here. Today the risk of malaria in the park is low but the mosquitoes can be pesky, especially during the rainy season.

The **Khao Daeng Visitors Centre** in the southern end of the park has the largest collection of tourist information and English-speaking rangers. Maps are handed out at the entrance gates.

Travel agencies in Hua Hin run day trips to the park. Hua Hin Bike Tours (p154) offers cycling and hiking tours.

Sights & Activities

The maps provided at the park checkpoints are often in Thai. The following sites are listed in geographical order from north to south.

Tham Kaew CAVE

(ถ้ำแก้ว) Tham Kaew is a series of underground chambers and narrow passageways accessed by a steep scramble 128m up the mountain. It's not a popular stop, even though the stalactites and limestone formations here glitter with calcite crystals (hence the cave's name, 'Jewel Cave'). You can hire lamps from the booth at the footpath's entrance. The path can be slippery and dangerous.

Tham Phraya Nakhon & Hat Laem Sala CAVE

(ถ้ำพระยานคร/หาดแหลมศาลา) The park's most-visited attraction is this revered cave sheltering a royal *săh·lah* (meeting hall; often spelled *sala*) built for Rama V in 1890 that is often bathed in streams of light. It's accessed via a walking trail from the picturesque sandy beach of **Hat Laem Sala**, flanked on three sides by limestone hills and casuarinas.

The beach hosts a small visitors centre, restaurant, bungalows and campsites. The cave trail is 450m long and is steep, rocky and at times wet, so don't come in your flip-flops. Once there you'll find two large caverns with sinkholes – the meeting hall is the second of the two.

Reaching Laem Sala requires alternative travel since there is no road connection. It is reached by boat from Bang Pu (400B return), which sits beachfront from the turn-off from Tham Kaew. Alternatively, you can follow the steep footpath from Bang Pu for a 20-minute hike to the beach.

Tham Sai CAVE

(ถ้ำไทร) Sitting at the end of a 280m hillside trail, Tham Sai features a large single cavern filled with stalactites and stalagmites. Be careful of steep drop-offs inside and slippery footings. Usually, only more adventurous types undertake this cave. Villagers rent out lamps near the cave mouth. It is just north of Hat Sam Phraya.

Hat Sam Phraya BEACH

(หาดสามพระยา) This shady casuarina-lined beach is about 1km long and is a pleasant stop for a swim after a sweaty hike. There is a restaurant and toilets.

Khao Daeng HIKING

(เขาแดง) The turn-off to the trail winds through towering mountains promising a rewarding hike. The 30-minute steep trail that leads to the top of Khao Daeng delivers spectacular views of limestone cliffs against a jagged coastline.

Khlong Khao Daeng BIRDWATCHING

(คลองเขาแดง) You can hire a boat at Wat Khao Daeng for a cruise (500B, 50 minutes) along the canal in the morning or afternoon. Before heading out, chat with your prospective guide to see how well they speak English. Better guides will know the English names of common waterfowl and point them out to you.

Thung Sam Roi Yot BIRDWATCHING

(ทุ่งสามร้อยยอด) The country's largest freshwater marsh is recognised as a natural treasure and provides an important habitat for songbirds, waterbirds, amphibians and other wetland species. It sits in the western

BIRDS OF A FEATHER

At the intersection of the East Asian and Australian migration routes, Khao Sam Roi Yot National Park is home to as many as 300 migratory and resident bird species, including yellow bitterns, cinnamon bitterns, purple swamp hens, water rails, ruddy-breasted crakes, bronze-winged jacanas, grey herons, painted storks, whistling ducks, spotted eagles and black-headed ibises. The park is one of only two places in the country where the purple heron breeds.

Waterfowl are most commonly seen in the cool season from November to March. The birds come from as far as Siberia, China and northern Europe to winter here. Common places for birdwatchers are the Mangrove Centre, Khlong Khao Daeng and even some of the beaches.

Thai Birding (www.thaibirding.com) provides more in-depth information about the park's bird species and where to spot them.

WORTH A TRIP

WHERE THE ELEPHANTS ARE

Want to see herds of wild elephants enjoying an evening bath surrounded by the sounds of the jungle? Although urbanised Thailand seems hundreds of kilometres away from such a natural state, **Kuiburi National Park** (☎032 646292; Hwy 3217; adult/child 200/100B), southwest of Khao Sam Roi Yot National Park, shelters one of the country's largest herds of wild elephants (around 230 of them). The park provides an important habitat link between the rugged Myanmar border and Kaeng Krachan National Park, forming one of the largest intact forest tracts in Southeast Asia. The herds can frequently be found bathing at the watering ponds near the Pa Yang substation, which is equipped with wildlife-viewing platforms. You'll also likely spot barking deer, wild cattle and the inevitable monkeys.

Trekking and elephant-spotting tours include English-speaking guides and transport and can be arranged through the park headquarters.

Bungalow **accommodation** (☎02 562 0760; www.dnp.th.go/parkreserve; bungalows 1800B) is available for overnight stays with advance reservations.

corner of the park accessible from Hwy 4 (Th Phetkasem) at the Km 275.6 marker; hold on to your entrance-fee ticket to avoid having to pay again.

Mangrove Walk WALKING
Located behind the visitors centre in the southern end of the park is a 900m wooden boardwalk that circumnavigates a mangrove swamp popular for birdwatching and crab spotting. There are guides available for hire from the centre depending on availability and English-language skills.

Sleeping & Eating

There are private resorts within 4km of the park at Dolphin Bay.

National Parks Department CAMPGROUND $$
(☎02 562 0760; www.dnp.go.th/parkreserve; tent sites 160-225B, visitors centre bungalows 1200-1400B, Hat Laem Sala bungalows 1600-3000B) The National Parks Department hires out bungalows (sleeping up to six people) at Hat Laem Sala and at the visitors centre; advance reservations are required. You can pitch a tent at campsites near the Khao Daeng viewpoint, Hat Laem Sala or Hat Sam Phraya. There are basic restaurants at all these locations, as well as lots of monkeys.

Getting There & Away

The park is around 40km south of Hua Hin, and best visited by vehicle. There are two main entrances into the park. The turn-off for the northern entrance is at Km 256 marker on Hwy 4 (Th Phetkasem). The southern entrance is off the Km 286.5 marker.

If there's a group of you, a taxi from Hua Hin is 1500B return. You can also visit on day tours from there. Alternatively, you can catch a minivan from Bangkok's Victory Monument to Pranburi (200B) and then hire a motorcycle to tour the park independently. You can also negotiate with the minivan driver to drop you off at the entrance to the park but then you won't have transport inside.

Prachuap Khiri Khan ประจวบคีรีขันธ์

POP 33,521

A sleepy seaside town, Prachuap Khiri Khan is a delightfully relaxed place; one of the real jewels of this part of Thailand. The broad bay is a tropical blue punctuated by bobbing fishing boats and there are tremendous beaches close by, all overlooked by honeycombed limestone mountains – scenery that you usually have to travel to the southern Andaman to find.

In recent years, foreigners have discovered Prachuap's charms and begun defecting from the overdeveloped Samui archipelago. Families especially are flocking here. But their numbers are still small compared to better-known destinations, leaving plenty of room on the beaches, at the hilltop temples and the many excellent seafood restaurants.

Sights & Activities

Khao Chong Krajok VIEWPOINT
(เขาช่องกระจก) At the northern end of town, Khao Chong Krajok ('Mirror Tunnel Mountain', so named for the mountain-side hole that seemingly reflects the sky) provides a beloved Prachuap tradition: climbing to the **temple** at the top, dodging ill-behaved monkeys and enjoying a view of the coastline.

Prachuap Khiri Khan

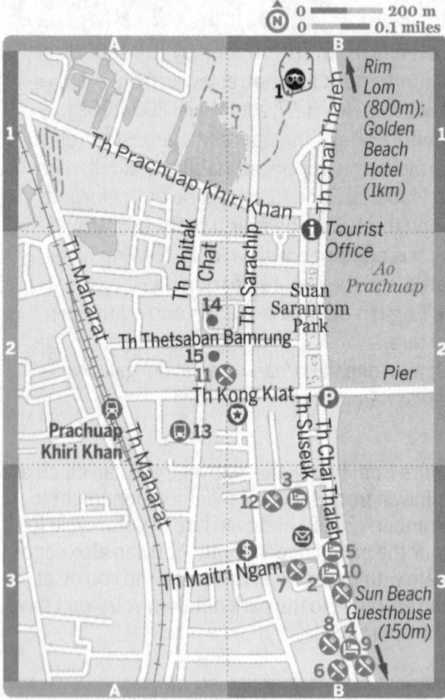

Prachuap Khiri Khan

Sights
1 Khao Chong Krajok B1

Sleeping
2 House 73 .... B3
3 Maggie's Homestay B3
4 Prachuap Beach Hotel B3
5 Thur Hostel B3

Eating
6 Ciao Pizza B3
7 Day Market B3
8 Grandma's B3
9 In Town B3
10 Longmug-Paa Lord B3
11 Night Market A2
12 Suan Krua B3

Drinking & Nightlife
Top Deck .... (see 5)

Transport
13 Air-con Buses to Hua Hin, Cha-am, Phetchaburi & Bangkok A2
14 Minivans to Ban Krut, Bang Saphan Yai & Chumphon A2
15 Minivans to Hua Hin & Bangkok A2

A long flight of stairs leads to a mountaintop temple established by Rama VI. From here there are perfect views of the town and the bay and even the border with Myanmar, just 12km away.

Don't bring food, drink or plastic bags with you as the monkeys will assume they're prizes worth having.

Ao Prachuap BAY

(อ่าวประจวบ) The town's crowning feature is Ao Prachuap (Prachuap Bay), a gracefully curving bay outlined by an oceanfront esplanade. In the cool hours of the morning and evening, locals run, shuffle or promenade along this route enjoying the ocean breezes and sea music.

On Friday and Saturday evenings, the esplanade hosts a Walking Street market, selling food, souvenirs and clothes.

North of Khao Chong Krajok, just over the bridge, the bay stretches peacefully to a toothy mountain that's less-visited than its in-town counterpart. There is a good, long sandy beach here running parallel with the road that only sees people on weekends, making it a fine place to idle and beachcomb. At the far northern end is a traditional fishing village and a pier where colourfully painted wooden trawlers tie up after a day or night at sea.

Wat Ao Noi BUDDHIST TEMPLE

(วัดอ่าวน้อย) FREE From Ao Prachuap, follow the coastal road 8km north as it skirts through the fishing village to reach this beautiful teak temple that straddles two bays (Ao Noi and Ao Khan Kradai). Limestone mountains pose photogenically in the background, while a dramatic nine-headed *naga* (mythical serpent) protects the temple's exterior. Inside are unique bas-relief murals depicting the *Jataka* (stories of Buddha's previous lives).

The temple grounds are forested with a variety of fruit trees (jackfruit, pomegranate, mango and rose apple) and a lotus pond filled with ravenous fish, eager to be fed by merit-makers. You'll catch an unpleasant odour nearby indicating that the temple is in the business of raising swiftlets for the profitable edible-bird's-nest industry; the punishment for stealing nests or eggs is severe (five years' imprisonment and 500,000B).

A craggy limestone mountain (Khao Khan Kradai) shelters the temple from the coast and contains a locally famous cave temple, known as Tham Phra Nawn (Sleeping Buddha Cave). The cave is accessible via a concrete trail that leads up and around the side of the hill, providing scenic views of Ao Khan Kradai and the foothills beyond. It is blissfully quiet and the forested hill is dotted with blooming cacti clinging to the craggy rocks. Inside the cave is a small cavern leading to a larger one that contains the eponymous reclining Buddha. If you have a torch (flashlight) you can proceed to a larger second chamber also containing Buddha images.

Ao Manao SWIMMING
(อ่าวมะนาว) On weekends, locals head to Ao Manao, an island-dotted bay 4km south of town ringed by a clean sandy beach. It is within Wing 5 of a Thai Air Force base and each and every week the beach is given a military-grade clean up.

There are the usual beach amenities: a restaurant as well as beach chairs, umbrellas and inner tubes for hire. En route to the beach you'll pass Thailand's Top Guns relaxing on a nearby golf course and driving range. You enter the base through a checkpoint on Th Suseuk from town; you may need to show your passport. The beach closes at 8pm.

Sleeping

There are an increasing number of oceanfront options, ranging from guesthouses to hotels, but with Prachuap becoming more popular, it's worth booking ahead. A number of homestays are scattered on and off Th Suseuk: look for the signs.

In Town

Thur Hostel HOSTEL $
(☎096 047 5622; Thurhostel@gmail.com; 58 Th Chai Thaleh; dm 350B, r 600-1000B; ❄📶) A hostel right on the oceanfront that has small but well-maintained dorms with good, thick mattresses. The most expensive rooms have terraces with fine sea views.

Maggie's Homestay GUESTHOUSE $
(☎087 597 9720; 5 Soi Tampramuk; r 180-550B; ❄@📶) In the old-school backpacker tradition, owner Maggie oversees an eclectic collection of travellers who call her house home. Rooms in a converted traditional house mostly have shared bathrooms and range from the very basic to the comfortable, and there's a shady garden and shared kitchen facilities.

★**House 73** GUESTHOUSE $$
(☎086 046 3923; www.facebook.com/house73prachuab/info; 73 Th Suseuk; r 800-1300B; ❄📶) Lovingly designed to within an inch of its life, this modernist boutique guesthouse is the most eye-catching building in town. There are only four (big) rooms here, all painted in pastel colours, with huge beds. There's a communal lounge and, best of all, a fantastic roof terrace with commanding views across the bay.

Sun Beach Guesthouse GUESTHOUSE $$
(☎032 604770; www.sunbeach-guesthouse.com; 160 Th Chai Thaleh; r 700-1000B; ❄@📶🏊) With hotel amenities and guesthouse hospitality, Sun Beach is a superb midranger. Its neo-classical styling and bright-yellow paint liven things up, while the rooms are super-clean and come with large verandahs. Book ahead.

Prachuap Beach Hotel HOTEL $$
(☎032 601288; www.prachuapbeach.com; 123 Th Suseuk; r 700-1300B; ❄📶) Crisp white linens and modern, comfortable rooms at this multistorey number. One side has fabulous sea views, while the other has decent, though not exciting, mountain views.

Out of Town

Natural Home GUESTHOUSE $
(☎032 602082; 149-151 Th Suanson; r 300-400B; ❄📶) About 1km north of town, these bungalows are simple, but you are right across the

PRACHUAP KHIRI KHAN IN WORLD WAR II

Prachuap, and specifically Ao Manao, was one of seven points on the gulf coast where Japanese troops landed on 8 December 1941 during their invasion of Thailand. The Air Force base at Ao Manao was the site of fierce skirmishes, with the Japanese unable to capture it until the Thai government ordered its soldiers to stop fighting as an armistice had been arranged.

Several street names around town refer to that time, such as Phithak Chat (Defend Country), Salachip (Sacrifice Life) and Suseuk (Fight Battle), and an annual memorial service commemorates the soldiers and civilians who died in the battle.

road from Ao Prachuap's beach. The cheapest rooms are fan-only. Pleasant, English-speaking staff and a talkative parrot at reception.

Aow Noi Sea View HOTEL $$
(032 604440; www.aownoiseaview.com; Ao Noi; r 800-900B;) North of town and close to the pier where fishing boats tie up, this secluded three-storey hotel has Ao Noi beach on its doorstep. Rooms with balconies are spacious, if a little old-fashioned.

Golden Beach Hotel HOTEL $$
(032 601626; www.goldenbeachprachuap.com; 113-115 Th Suanson; r 800B;) A comfortable midrange option opposite Ao Prachuap's beach, and a decent deal these days for a sea view. The rooms are clean and sizeable.

Eating & Drinking

Restaurants in Prachuap are cheap and offer excellent seafood, while Western dishes are popping up more frequently. The **day market** (Th Maitri Ngam; daylight hours) is the place to get pineapples fresh from the orchards; ask the vendor to cut it for you. The **night market** (Th Kong Kiat; 5-9pm) is small and has the usual stir-fry stalls.

Suan Krua VEGETARIAN $
(Soi Tampramuk; dishes from 35B; 6.30am-3pm;) Super vegetarian, buffet-style eatery. Choose from an array of dishes, but they go fast and then the place shuts. Arrive here promptly and with an appetite.

Grandma's CAFE $
(081 743 9737; 238 Th Suseuk; dishes from 35B, coffee from 30B; 7.30am-7pm;) Cool cafe on the ground floor of a renovated 80-year-old traditional wooden house. Run by artists, it's a good spot for breakfast, or a coffee or smoothie break. There are also three tastefully decorated rooms for rent here (from 690B).

★In Town THAI $$
(118 Th Chai Thaleh; dishes from 80B; 3-10pm) Now the go-to place for discerning locals, here you can eat outside while gazing at the bay. Great range of fresh seafood on display – barracuda, tuna, crab and shellfish – so you can point and pick, and they will tone down the spices if you ask.

Rim Lom SEAFOOD $$
(5 Th Suanson; dishes 90-190B; 10am-10pm) Popular with the locals, the *pàt pǒng gà·rèe Ѣoo* (crab curry) comes with big chunks of sweet crab meat and the *yam tá-lair* (seafood salad) is spicy and zesty. It's 200m past the bridge on the left and right opposite Ao Prachuap beach.

Longmug-Paa Lord THAI $$
(Th Chai Thaleh; dishes from 100B; noon-10pm) Another open-air spot with great bay views that gets busy once the sun goes down. Choose from the wide selection of seafood on display.

Ciao Pizza ITALIAN $$
(Th Suseuk; pizzas from 180B; 10am-2pm & 4-10pm) Ciao Pizza is Italian-owned; come here for pizzas, homemade pasta and gelato, as well as fresh bread baked daily and a take-away selection of cheese, sausage and salami.

Top Deck BAR
(53 Th Chai Thaleh; beers from 60B, cocktails from 130B; 1pm-midnight Thu-Tue;) Prachuap is an early-to-bed town, but at the Top Deck

TRANSPORT TO/FROM PRACHUAP KHIRI KHAN

DESTINATION	BUS	MINIVAN	TRAIN
Ban Krut	70B; 1½hr; hourly	90B; 1hr; hourly; 6am-5pm	13B; 1 daily
Bang Saphan Yai	60B; 2hr; hourly	100B; 1½hr; hourly; 6am-5pm	16B; 8 daily
Bangkok Hualamphong			168-455B; 7-8hr; 8 daily; 12.14am-11.35pm
Bangkok Southern Bus Terminal	200B; 6-7hr; 3 daily; 9am, 12.30pm & 1am	220B; 5-6hr; hourly; 7am-5pm	
Bangkok Victory Monument		220B; 6hr; hourly; 6am-5pm	
Cha-am		120B; 2hr; hourly; 6am-5pm	14B; 2hr; 1 daily
Hua Hin		80B; 1½hr; hourly; 6am-5pm	19B; 1hr; 8 daily
Phetchaburi		150B; 3hr; hourly; 6am-5pm	32B; 3hr; 8 daily

WORTH A TRIP

DAN SINGKHON BORDER MARKET

A mere 12km southwest of Prachuap Khiri Khan is the Myanmar border and at the time of research there were persistent rumours that the frontier would be open for foreigners to cross in the very near future. If that is the case – and check before you try it – you'll need to have arranged a Myanmar visa beforehand.

In the meantime, you can still visit the town of Dan Singkhon on the Thai side of the border. Once a strategic military point, Dan Singkhon now hosts a lively **market** known for its many bargains.

Beginning at dawn on Saturday mornings, locals from Myanmar appear from a bend in the road just beyond the checkpoint, pushing handcarts piled high with the usual trinkets, market goods and plants. Short-term tourists might be befuddled as to what will fit in a suitcase, but locals and expats make frequent buying trips here for orchids, the market's speciality, and hardwood furniture. Even if you come to window-shop, the market has a festive vibe, with music blaring, colourful umbrellas lining the road and thatched 'sales booths' hidden under palms. You'll need to arrive well before noon to enjoy it, as the market closes at midday.

To get to Dan Singkhon from Prachuap Khiri Khan with your own vehicle, head south on Hwy 4. After several kilometres you'll see a sign for Dan Singkhon; from there head west about 15km to reach the border.

you can sip a libation until late while gazing out at the winking lights of the fishing boats in the bay. Also does Thai and Western comfort food (from 120B).

Information

Bangkok Bank (cnr Th Maitri Ngam & Th Sarachip; ⌚9.30am-3.30pm Mon-Fri)

Police Station (Th Kong Kiat) Just west of Th Sarachip.

Post Office (cnr Th Maitri Ngam & Th Suseuk; ⌚8.30am-4.30pm Mon-Fri, 9am-noon Sat)

Tourist Office (☎032 611491; Th Chai Thaleh; ⌚8.30am-4.30pm) At the northern end of town. The staff speak English and are very helpful.

Getting There & Away

Three air-conditioned buses run daily to Bangkok's southern terminal from Th Phitak Chat. Buses also leave from here for Ban Krut and Bang Saphan Yai.

Minivans leave from the corner of Th Thetsaban Bamrung and Th Phitak Chat.

Long-distance buses to southern destinations (such as Phuket and Krabi) stop at the new bus station, 2km northwest of town on the main highway; motorcycle taxis will take you for 40B to 50B.

The train station is on Th Maharat; there are frequent services to/from Bangkok.

Getting Around

Prachuap is small enough to get around on foot, but you can hop on a motorcycle taxi for 30B. A bike to Ao Noi and Ao Manao is 100B to 150B.

You can hire motorbikes for 250B per day and bicycles for 50B; the roads in the area are good and it's a great way to see the surrounding beaches.

Ban Krut & Bang Saphan Yai บ้านกรูด/บางสะพานใหญ่

POP 4198 / 15,134

What a nice surprise to find these lovely, low-key beaches (80km to 100km south of Prachuap Khiri Khan, respectively) so close to civilisation yet so bucolic. Dusk falls softly through the coconut trees and the crystalline blue sea laps at a long sandy coastline. No high-rises, no late-night bars and no speeding traffic to distract you from a serious regimen of reading, swimming, eating and biking.

Although both beaches are pleasantly subdued, they are also well known to Thais. Ban Krut, in particular, hosts bus tours as well as weekending families. During the week you'll have the beaches largely to yourself and a few long-tail boats.

Check out the websites Ban Krut Info (www.bankrutinfo.com) and Bang Saphan Guide (www.bangsaphanguide.com) for local information on the area.

Sights & Activities

Ban Krut is divided into two beaches by a temple-topped headland. To the north is **Hat Sai Kaew**, which is remote and private with only a few resorts in between a lot of jungle. To the south is **Hat Ban Krut**, with a string of bungalow-style resorts and restaurants sitting opposite the beach. Both are golden-sand beaches with clear, calm water but Hat Ban Krut is more social and developed (you'll find ATMs here) and easier to get around without private transport.

Bang Saphan Yai, 20km south of Ban Krut, fits that most famous beach cliché: it is Thailand 15 years ago before pool villas and package tourists pushed out all the beach bums. Once you settle into a simple beachfront hut, you probably won't need any shoes and the days will just melt away. Islands off the coast, including **Ko Thalu** and **Ko Sing**, offer good **snorkelling** and **diving** from the end of January to mid-May.

Sleeping & Eating

Ban Krut

You'll struggle to find true budget options here, but if you visit on a weekday you should secure a discount. In Hat Ban Krut, bicycles (100B per day) and motorcycles (300B per day) can be hired to run errands in town, and most accommodation options arrange snorkelling trips to nearby islands. If you stay in Hat Sai Kaew you'll need private transport.

NaNa Chart Baan Krut HOTEL $$
(☎032 695525; www.thailandhostel.com; 123 Th Ban Krut-Kohktahom; r 700-4800B; ❄📶🏊) Technically it is a hostel – although there are no dorms – but NaNa Chart easily qualifies as a resort with a variety of rooms and bungalows on a barely inhabited, superb stretch of beach. The cheapest are wooden huts with fans, while the ritzy beachfront ones have all the mod cons.

The resort caters to large groups so expect some company at peak times; in low season (May to September) it's much quieter. Hostel members receive discounted rates.

Proud Thai Beach Resort GUESTHOUSE $$
(☎089 682 4484; www.proudthairesort.com; Hat Ban Krut; r 800-1200B; ❄📶) Eight well-maintained bungalows in a flower-filled garden, all with terraces. Prices rise at weekends and on public holidays, when you should book ahead.

Bayview Beach Resort HOTEL $$$
(☎032 695566; www.bayviewbeachresort.com; Hat Ban Krut; r 1600-5000B; ❄📶🏊) A great choice for families and popular with Bangkok Thais at the weekend, Bayview has handsome bungalows with large verandahs amid shady grounds. There's a beachside pool and a kid-friendly wading pool as well as a small playground. The resort also offers snorkelling and diving trips and rents kayaks and bikes.

Kasama's Pizza ITALIAN $$
(Hat Ban Krut; pizza from 190B; ⏰7.30am-11pm Fri-Wed; 📶) Has substantial, succulent baguettes (from 100B) for beach-snacking, and it's fine for breakfast or a New York–style pizza in the evening.

Bang Saphan Yai

The beach is 6km south of the town of Bang Saphan Yai. It's not as idyllic a strip of sand as Ban Krut, but there's both budget accommodation and high-end pool villas here. Walk north of the Why Not Bar for the cheaper places.

Roytawan GUESTHOUSE $
(☎087 670 8943; Hat Bang Saphan Yai; r from 300B; 📶) Smack dab on the beach, this laid-back, bare-bones operation is run by a friendly local Muslim family. The bungalows are simple (fan-only) but adequate and the resident roosters kindly sleep until daybreak. There's wi-fi in the attached restaurant.

Suan Luang Resort GUESTHOUSE $
(☎032 691663; www.suanluangresort.com; Hat Bang Saphan Yai; bungalows 480-680B; ❄📶) Family-run Suan Luang is the most professional of the guesthouses, with rustic wooden bungalows that are arranged around an interior garden, although it's located 700m from the beach. The air-con bungalows are a big step up from the fan rooms. The excellent restaurant serves Thai and French food, and motorbikes are available for rent (250B per day).

Coral Hotel HOTEL $$$
(☎032 817121; www.coral-hotel.com; Hat Bang Saphan Yai; r 2640-7705B; ❄📶🏊) Catering mostly to French tourists – the restaurant is decent – this upmarket hotel is right on the beach and has all the resort amenities, including organised diving and snorkelling tours and Thai cooking classes. The tastefully decorated rooms are very comfortable and the pool is big.

Getting There & Around

Public transport is either nonexistent or limited. When booking transport, don't confuse Bang Saphan Yai with Bang Saphan Noi, which is a fishing village 15km further south.

From Bangkok's southern terminal buses go to Bang Saphan Yai (275B, hourly, six hours).

Frequent minivans run from Prachuap Khiri Khan to Ban Krut (90B) and Bang Saphan Yai (100B). Most minivans to Ban Krut will stop on the highway, a 100B motorbike ride from the beach.

Many seasoned visitors prefer to take the train for closer proximity to the beaches, although trains in this region are increasingly prone to delays. Six trains run to Ban Krut daily from Bangkok's Hualamphong station (265B to 615B, five to seven hours): the 08.05am train gets in at 1.07pm and is the best option. The train station is also handy if you are continuing south to Chumphon to catch the ferry to Ko Tao.

A motorcycle taxi from town to Bang Saphan Yai is 70B. Talk to your hotel or guesthouse about arranging transport back to town for your onward travel.

Chumphon

ชุมพร

POP 33,516

A transit town funnelling travellers to and from Ko Tao or westwards to Ranong or Phuket, Chumphon is also where the south of Thailand starts proper; Muslim headscarves are a common sight here.

While there's not a lot to do while you wait for your ferry, there's good seafood in town and the surrounding beaches are great places to step off the backpacker bandwagon for a few days. **Hat Thung Wua Laen** (15km north of town) is an excellent beach with plenty of traveller amenities and during the week you'll have it mostly to yourself.

For a transit hub, Chumphon is surprisingly unconsolidated: the main bus station and piers for boats to Ko Tao, Ko Samui and Ko Pha-Ngan are some distance from town. But travel agencies and all guesthouses can book tickets, provide timetables and point you to the right bus stop.

Festivals & Events

Chumphon Marine Festival CULTURAL

(Mar) Normally held in mid-March, Hat Thung Wua Laen hosts a variety of sea-related events – boat and fishing trips, diving and snorkelling – as well as exhibitions and beach displays.

Chumphon Traditional Boat Race CULTURAL

(Oct) To mark the end of Buddhist Lent in October (Ork Phansaa), traditional long-tail boats race each other on the Mae Nam Lang Suan (Lang Suan River), about 60km south of Chumphon. Other merit-making activities coincide with the festival.

Sleeping

As most people overnighting in Chumphon are backpackers, accommodation is priced accordingly. Th Tha Taphao is the local Th Khao San, with many guesthouses and travel agencies.

★ **Suda Guest House** GUESTHOUSE $

(080 144 2079; 8 Soi Sala Daeng 3; r 200-650B;) Suda, the friendly English-speaking owner, maintains her impeccable standards with six rooms, all with wooden floors and a few nice touches that you wouldn't expect for the price. It's very popular so phone ahead. Suda can also book tickets and rents motorbikes (200B to 300B).

Salsa Hostel HOSTEL $

(077 505005; www.salsachumphon.com; 25/42 Th Krom Luang Chumphon; dm 280-300B, d 650-750B;) Helpful hostel (the owner speaks good English) with cramped but bright, clean and modern dorms. The private rooms are big and comfortable, even if they are overpriced for this town.

Fame Guest House GUESTHOUSE $

(077 571077; www.chumphon-kohtao.com; 188/20-21 Th Sala Daeng; r 150-300B;) A *fa·ràng* (Westerner) depot, Fame does a little bit of everything, from providing basic rooms for people overnighting to booking tickets and renting motorbikes. The attached restaurant is a key backpacker hang-out, and offers a decent and wide range of Thai, Indian and Western food.

View Resort BUNGALOW $$

(077 560214; Hat Thung Wua Laen; r 700-1000B;) Sleepy bungalow operation outside town that's right on the beach. Bungalows aren't big and come with severely slanted roofs, but they're comfortable enough, and the attached restaurant is pretty good.

Chumphon Gardens Hotel HOTEL $$

(077 506888; www.chumphongarden.com; 66/1 Th Tha Taphao; r 590-750B;) Sports a 1970s-style design but has large, comfortable rooms and the bathrooms are a cut above the local competition.

Chumphon

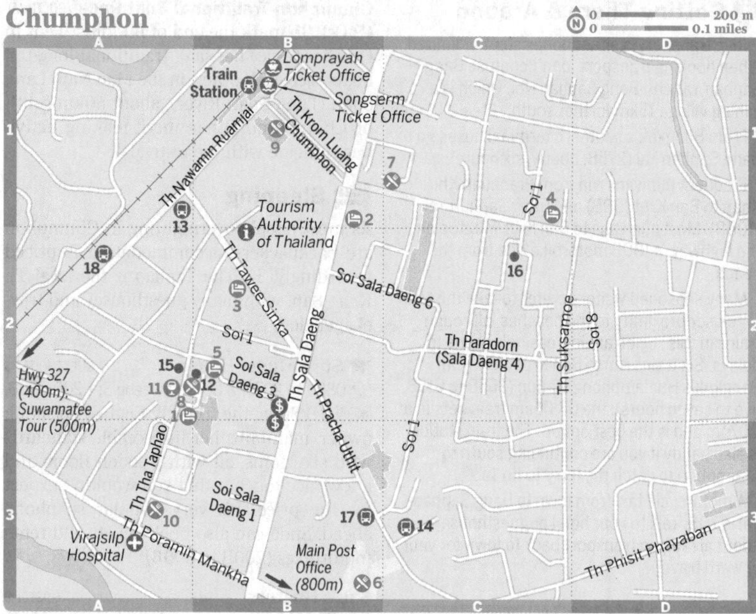

Chumphon

Sleeping

1	Chumphon Gardens Hotel	A2
2	Fame Guest House	B1
3	Morakot Hotel	B2
4	Salsa Hostel	C1
5	Suda Guest House	B2

Eating

6	Day Market	B3
7	Night Market	C1
8	OK Restaurant	A2
9	Papa Seafood	B1
10	Prikhorm	A3

Drinking & Nightlife

11	Farang Bar	A2

Information

12	New Infinity Travel	B2

Transport

13	Buses to Hat Yai	A1
14	Choke Anan Tour	C3
15	Minivans to Ranong	A2
16	Minivans to Surat Thani, Bang Saphan Yai & Prachuap Khiri Khan	C2
17	Sŏrng·tăa·ou to Hat Thung Wua Laen	B3
18	Sŏrng·tăa·ou to Main Bus Terminal	A2

Morakot Hotel HOTEL $$
(077 502999; www.morakothotel.com; 102-112 Th Tawee Sinka; r 490-890B;) Spread across two buildings: the newer wing houses the better and more expensive rooms, but the older wing is acceptable for the price.

Chumphon Cabana Resort & Diving Centre HOTEL $$$
(077 560245; www.chumphoncabanaresort.com; Hat Thung Wua Laen; r 1850-2500B;) The most pleasant resort on the beach, despite the rather plain bungalows, Chumphon Cabana is ecofriendly, with the owner using traditional methods in an effort to be as green as possible. The grounds are devoted to raising the resort's own food with rice fields, hydroponic vegetable gardens and a chicken farm, while waste water is recycled through water-hyacinth ponds.

Even if you don't stay here, the home-grown food at **Rabieng Talay**, the resort's affiliated restaurant, is worth a try.

Eating & Drinking

Chumphon's **night market** (Th Krom Luang Chumphon; ⏲4-11pm) is excellent, with a big variety of food options and good people-watching. There is also a **day market** (⏲6am-4pm) on Th Pracha Uthit, while Th Sala Daeng and Th Pracha Uthit are both lined with hole-in-the-wall noodle joints.

OK Restaurant THAI $

(Th Tha Taphao; buffet 119B; ⏲4-9pm) A new, open-air buffet-style restaurant where you can eat as much you like for the price. Unsurprisingly, it gets busy in the early evening.

Papa Seafood SEAFOOD $

(2-2/1 Th Krom Luang Chumphon; dishes from 70B; ⏲8am-4am; 📶) There's a huge display of seafood on offer at this big, open-air place that sometimes features live music; it's good without being exceptional. Foreigner-friendly, but many locals come here too. Next door is the affiliated club Papa 2000, where you can dance off dinner.

Pirates Terrace INTERNATIONAL, THAI $

(Hat Thung Wua Laen; dishes from 80B; ⏲7.30am-10pm; 📶) Opposite the beach, this is a popular spot for breakfast, a daytime coffee, or a drink in the evening. The menu mixes Thai classics with pizza and pasta. They can also book tickets and rent motorbikes for 200B a day.

★ **Prikhorm** SOUTHERN THAI $$

(32 Th Tha Taphao; dishes 150-450B; ⏲11am-11pm) The place where the locals come for fiery and delicious southern Thai cuisine. Their *gaang sôm* is a superbly spicy and flavoursome fish curry, but all the dishes are delicious.

Farang Bar BAR

(☎077 501003; www.farangbarchumphon.com; 69/36 Th Tha Taphao; beers from 80B; ⏲11am-midnight; 📶) An agreeable hang-out for expat English teachers and passing travellers, the Farang Bar is an easy place to while away a few hours over a drink. The menu mixes Thai and Western dishes; the local ones are better. It closes in the depths of low season (July and August).

Information

There are banks along Th Sala Daeng with exchange facilities and ATMs.

Bangkok Bank (Th Sala Daeng; ⏲9.30am-3.30pm Mon-Fri) Has an ATM.

Main Post Office (Th Poramin Mankha; ⏲8.30am-4.30pm Mon-Fri, 9am-noon Sat) In the southeastern part of town.

New Infinity Travel (☎077 570176; 68/2 Th Tha Taphao; ⏲8am-10pm; 📶) A great travel agency with knowledgable and friendly staff. It's also the only secondhand bookshop in town.

Tourism Authority of Thailand (TAT; ☎077 501831; 111/11-12 Th Tawee Sinka; ⏲8.30am-4.30pm) Hands out maps and brochures but you're likely to get better information from your guesthouse.

Virajsilp Hospital (☎077 503238; Th Poramin Mankha) Privately owned; handles emergencies.

Getting There & Away

Boats leave from different piers; bus transfer is sometimes included in the ticket price. Otherwise, you pay an extra 100B for transport to the pier.

BOAT

You have a number of boat options for getting to Ko Tao, though departure times are limited to mainly morning and night. Most ticket prices include pier transfer. If you buy a combination ticket, make sure you have a ticket for both the bus and the boat.

Car Ferry A comfortable ride with bunk or mattress options available on board.

Lomprayah Catamaran (☎077 558214; www.lomprayah.com; ⏲5am-9pm) The best and most popular bus-boat combination; it leaves from Tha Tummakam, 25km from town. The ticket office is beside Chumphon train station.**Songserm Express Boat** (☎077 506205; www.songserm-expressboat.com; ⏲9am-8pm) Faster, morning option leaving from Tha Talaysub, about 10km from town, but the company has a reputation for being poorly organised and not providing promised free transport into town if you are coming from the islands. The ticket office doesn't seem to open often; book tickets through guesthouses.

BUS

The main bus terminal is on the highway, an inconvenient 16km from Chumphon. To get there you can catch a *sŏrng·tăa·ou* (50B) from Th Nawamin Ruamjai. You'll have to haggle with the opportunistic taxi drivers for night transit to/from the station; no matter what they tell you, it shouldn't cost more than 200B.

There are several in-town bus stops to save you a trip out to the main bus station. **Choke Anan Tour** (☎077 511757; soi off Th Pracha Uthit), in the centre of town, has departures to Bangkok, Phuket and Ranong. **Suwannatee Tour** (☎077 504901), 700m southwest of the train station, serves Bangkok, Phetchaburi and Prachuap Khiri Khan. Buses to Hat Yai depart from near the petrol station on Th Nawamin Ruamjai.

TRANSPORT TO/FROM CHUMPHON

DESTINATION	BOAT	BUS	MINIVAN	TRAIN	AIR
Bang Saphan Yai			120B; 2hr; 1 daily; 2pm	20B; 2hr; 2 daily; 7am & 12.46pm	
Bangkok Don Mueang Airport					from 1720B; 1hr; 2 daily (Nok Air)
Bangkok Hualamphong				192-690B; 8hr; 11 daily	
Bangkok Southern Bus Terminal		300-591B; 8hr; 11 daily			
Hat Yai		400B; 7hr; 4 daily		269-652B, 6 hr; 7 daily	
Ko Pha-Ngan (Lomprayah)	1000B; 3¼hr; 2 daily; 7am & 1pm				
Ko Pha-Ngan (Songserm)	900B; 5½hr; 1 daily; 7am				
Ko Samui (Lomprayah)	1100B; 4½hr; 2 daily; 7am & 1pm				
Ko Samui (Songserm)	1000B; 6hr; 1 daily; 7am				
Ko Tao (car ferry)	400B; 6hr; 1 daily; 11pm Mon-Sat				
Ko Tao (Lomprayah)	600B; 1½hr; 2 daily; 7am & 1pm				
Ko Tao (Songserm)	500B; 3hr; 1 daily; 7am				
Phetchaburi		362B; 6hr; 5 daily		58-545B; 6-7hr; 11 daily	
Phuket		350B; 3½hr; 2 daily			
Prachuap Khiri Khan			180B; 4hr; 1 daily; 3pm	84B; 3-4hr; 10 daily	
Ranong		120B; 2½hr; 4 daily	120B; 2hr; frequent		
Surat Thani			170B; 3hr; hourly; 6am-5pm	100B; 2-3 hr; 12 daily	

All minivans for Surat Thani, Bang Saphan Yai and Prachuap Khiri Khan leave from the unnamed soi opposite Salsa Hostel.

TRAIN

There are frequent services to/from Bangkok (192B to 690B, 11 daily, eight hours).

Getting Around

Sŏrng·tăa·ou (40B per trip) and motorcycle taxis (20B to 30B per trip) can be taken around town. Yellow *sŏrng·tăa·ou* to Hat Thung Wua Laen cost 30B.

Motorcycles can be rented at travel agencies and guesthouses from 200B per day.

Ko Samui & the Lower Gulf

Includes ➡

Best Places to Eat

- Dining On The Rocks (p190)
- Chez François (p190)
- Pepenero (p188)
- Fisherman's Restaurant (p207)
- Baraccuda (p222)

Best Places to Stay

- Six Senses Samui (p184)
- Divine Comedie (p202)
- View Point Resort (p220)
- Place (p217)
- Sanctuary (p206)

Why Go?

The Lower Gulf features Thailand's ultimate island trifecta: Ko Samui, Ko Pha-Ngan and Ko Tao. This family of spectacular islands lures millions of tourists every year with their powder-soft sands and emerald waters. Ko Samui is the oldest sibling, who has made it big. Here, high-class resorts operate with Swiss efficiency as uniformed butlers cater to every whim. Ko Pha-Ngan is the slacker middle child with tangled dreadlocks and a penchant for hammock-lazing and all-night parties. Meanwhile Ko Tao is the outdoorsy, fun-loving kid with plenty of spirit and spunk – the island specialises in high-adrenalin activities, including world-class diving and snorkelling.

The mainland coast beyond the islands sees few foreign visitors, but is more authentic Thailand and in many ways more culturally enjoyable for that. From the pink dolphins and waterfalls of sleepy Ao Khanom to the Thai Muslim flavours of beach strolling Songkhla, this region will convince any naysayer that Thailand still holds a bevy of off-the-beaten-track wonders.

When to Go

- February to April celebrates endless sunshine after the monsoon rains have cleared.
- June to August, conveniently coinciding with the northern hemisphere's summer holidays, are among the most inviting months, with relatively short drizzle spells.
- October to December is when torrential monsoon rains rattle hot-tin roofs, and room rates drop significantly to lure optimistic beach goers.

Ko Samui & the Lower Gulf Highlights

1. Finding Nemo in the technicolour kingdom off **Ko Tao** (p211).
2. Paddling to the hidden bleach-blonde beaches of **Ang Thong Marine National Park** (p226).
3. Stringing up a cotton hammock and toeing the curling tide along a secluded beach on **Ko Pha-Ngan** (p194).
4. Enjoying five-star international cuisine and sipping fancy sunset cocktails on **Ko Samui** (p176).
5. Joining the masses of party pilgrims and trancing the night away at the **Full Moon Party** (p199) at Hat Rin on Ko Pha-Ngan.

0 100 km
0 60 miles

Chumphon
Pak Nam
Ao Chumphon
CHUMPHON
Laem Riu
Isthmus of Kra
1 Ko Tao
Chong Tao
Ang Thong Marine National Park
2
Ko Pha-Ngan
3
5 Hat Rin
Chong Pha-Ngan
4 Ko Samui
Ko Phaluai
Laem Sui
41
Chaiya
Ao Ban Don
Don Sak
Chong Samui
Khanom
7 Ao Khanom
Hin Lat Falls
Surat Thani
401
Phun Phin
401
Sichon
Khao Sok National Park (30km)
NAKHON SI THAMMARAT
SURAT THANI
Khao Luang National Park
Khao Luang (1835m)
401
Laem Talumphuk
41
Nakhon Si Thammarat
Lan Saka
Khiriwong
KRABI
Thung Song

6 Savouring steaming street-stall seafood on the sands of **Songkhla** (p234).

7 Spotting elusive pink dolphins gliding along the shores of **Ao Khanom** (p230).

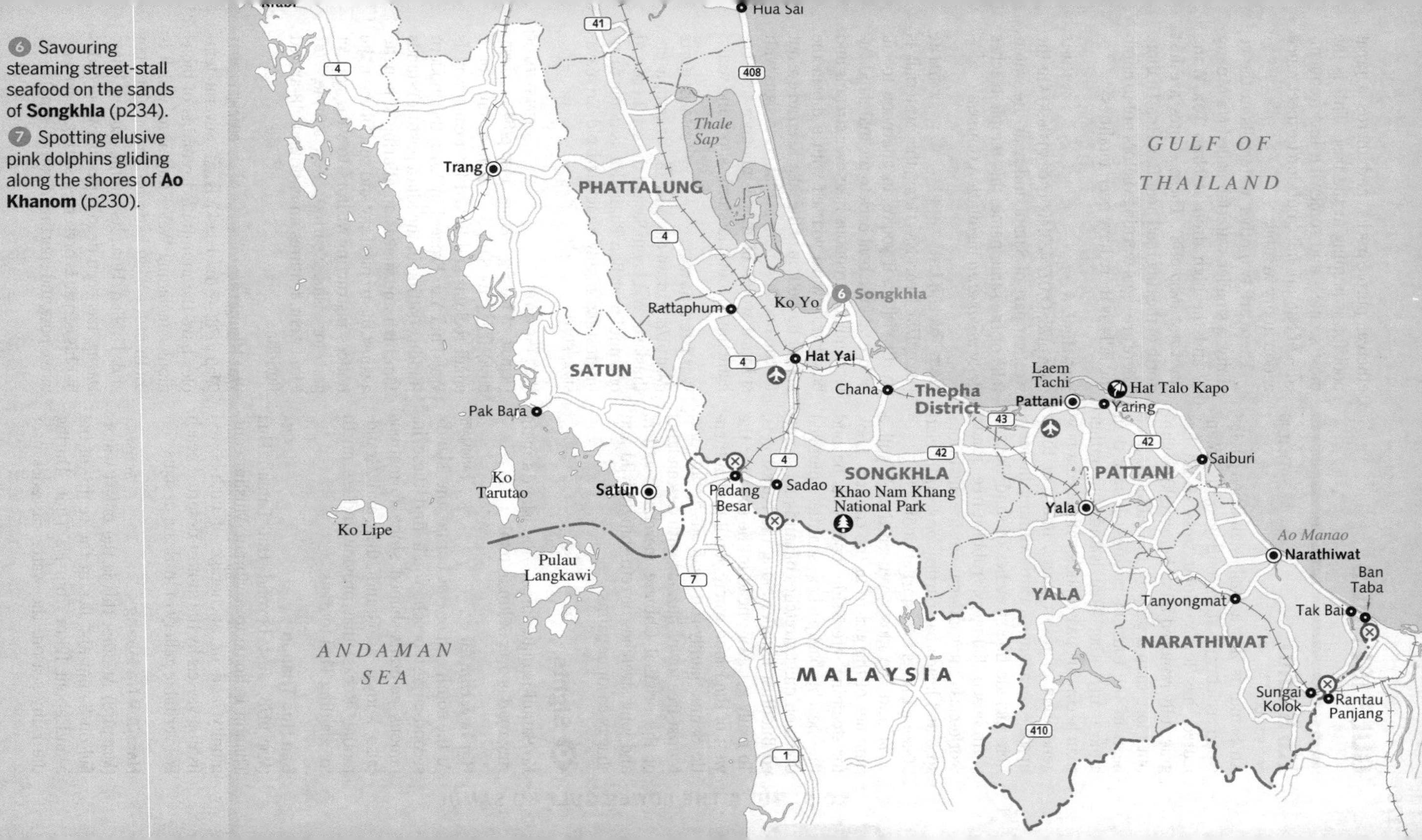

GULF ISLANDS

Ko Samui เกาะสมุย

POP 50,000

Ko Samui is like a well-established Hollywood celebrity: she's outrageously manicured, has lovely blond tresses and has gracefully removed all of her wrinkles without more than a peep in the tabloids. She's been in the tourism business longer than almost any other Thai island, but rather than becoming passé, she's embraced a new generation of resort goers, many of them upscale. Academy Award–winning holidays here include fine stretches of sand clogged with beach loungers, rubbish-free roads, world-class international cuisine, luxurious spas and beach bar parties for scantily clad 20-somethings that start at noon.

Behind the glossy veneer there's still a glimmer of the girl from the country. Look for steaming street-side food stalls beyond the beach, backpacker shanties plunked down on quiet stretches of sand and secreted Buddhist temples along the backstreets. To really get away, head to the south or the west of the island where you'll find authentic Samui family-run seafood restaurants, tourist-free towns buzzing with descendants of the original Chinese merchant settlers and long stretches of refreshingly wild and shaggy coconut palms.

Sights

Ko Samui is quite large – the island's main ring road is over 50km in total.

Hin-Ta & Hin-Yai LANDMARK

At the south end of **Hat Lamai**, the island's second-largest beach, you'll find these infamous genitalia-shaped stone formations (also known as Grandfather and Grandmother Rocks) that provide endless mirth for giggling Thai tourists.

Ban Hua Thanon AREA

(Map p178) Just beyond Hat Lamai, Hua Thanon is home to a vibrant Muslim community, and its anchorage of high-bowed fishing vessels by the almost deserted beach is a veritable gallery of intricate designs.

Nam Tok Na Muang WATERFALL

(Map p178) At 30m, this is the tallest waterfall on Samui and lies in the centre of the island about 12km from Na Thon. During the rainy season, the water cascades over ethereal purple rocks, and there's a great pool for swimming at the base. This is the most scenic – and somewhat less frequented – of Samui's falls, but don't expect much action in dry weather.

There are two other waterfalls in the vicinity: a smaller waterfall called **Na Muang 2**, and the high drop at **Nam Tok Wang Saotong** (Map p178). These chutes are just north of the ring road near Ban Hua Thanon. There are signs warning visitors not to climb the falls as there have been fatalities.

Wat Hin Lat TEMPLE

(Map p178; ☎077 423146; ⊙dawn-dusk) On the western part of Samui and near the waterfalls of the same name, this temple teaches daily *vipassana* meditation courses.

Nam Tok Hin Lat WATERFALL

(Map p178) Near Na Thon, this waterfall is worth visiting if you've an afternoon to kill before taking a boat back to the mainland. After a mildly strenuous hike over streams and boulders, reward yourself with a dip in the pool at the bottom of the falls. Keep an eye out for the Buddhist temple that posts signs with spiritual words of moral guidance and enlightenment, but take sturdy shoes and water.

Wat Laem Saw BUDDHIST TEMPLE

(Map p178; ⊙dawn-dusk) FREE For temple enthusiasts, Wat Laem Saw, at the southern end of Samui near Ban Phang Ka, is home to an interesting, highly venerated old Srivijaya-style stupa.

Wat Phra Yai BUDDHIST TEMPLE

(Temple of the Big Buddha; Map p184; ⊙dawn-dusk) FREE At Samui's northern end, on a small rocky island linked by a causeway, is Wat Phra Yai. Erected in 1972, the modern Buddha (sitting in the Mara posture) stands 15m high and makes an alluring silhouette against the tropical sky and sea. Observe the notices instructing visitors to wear correct garb for visits. Nearby, a new temple, **Wat Plai Laem**, features an enormous 18-armed Buddha.

Wat Khunaram BUDDHIST TEMPLE

(Map p178; ⊙dawn-dusk) FREE Several temples have the mummified remains of pious monks, including Wak Khunaram, which is south of Rte 4169 between Th Ban Thurian and Th Ban Hua. Its monk, Luang Phaw Daeng, has been dead for over two decades but his corpse is preserved sitting in a meditative pose and sporting a pair of sunglasses.

GULF ISLANDS IN...

One Week

After coming to terms with the fact that you only have a week to explore these idyllic islands, start on one of **Ko Pha-Ngan's** secluded western beaches or journey east to live out your ultimate castaway fantasies. For the second half of the week choose between partying in **Hat Rin**, pampering on **Ko Samui** or diving off little **Ko Tao**.

Two Weeks

Start on **Ko Tao** with a 3½-day Open Water certification course, or sign up for a few fun dives. Slide over to **Ko Pha-Ngan** and soak up the sociable vibe in party-prone Hat Rin. Then, grab a long-tail and make your way to one of the island's hidden coves for a few days of detoxing and quiet contemplation. **Ko Samui** is next on the agenda. Try **Bo Phut** for boutique sleeps or live it up like a rock star on Chaweng or Choeng Mon beach. And, if you have time, do a day trip to **Ang Thong National Marine Park**.

One Month

Follow the two-week itinerary at a more relaxed pace, infusing many extra beach-book-and-blanket days on all three islands. Be sure to plan your schedule around the Full Moon Party, which takes place at Hat Rin's Sunrise Beach on **Ko Pha-Ngan**.

Wat Samret BUDDHIST TEMPLE
(Map p178; dawn-dusk) FREE At Wat Samret, near Th Ban Hua, you can see a typical Mandalay sitting Buddha carved from solid marble – a common sight in India and northern Thailand, but not so common in the south.

Activities

Ko Samui is an excellent choice for families travelling with kids as there are many activities especially geared to the little ones.

Blue Stars KAYAKING, SNORKELLING
(Map p182; 077 300615; www.bluestars.info; Hat Chaweng; kayak & snorkelling tours adult/child 2500/1600B) There are many choices for snorkelling and kayak tours to Ang Thong Marine National Park, but Blue Stars has the best reputation and the coolest boat. Even if you don't go with this company, don't miss taking a trip to these islands.

Football Golf GOLF
(Map p178; 089 771 7498; www.samuifootballgolf.com; adult/child 730/350B; 9am-6.30pm) At Hat Choeng Mon there's a curious hybrid called 'football golf' where you 'putt' your football into a rubbish-bin-sized hole. It's great for the kids and each game comes with a complimentary soft drink. It's a par 69.

Koh Samui Rum RUM TASTING
(Map p178; www.rum-distillery.com; Ban Bang Kao; tasting shots 50-75B; 9am-6pm) The only rum distillery in Thailand produces Caribbean agricole style (distilled from fresh, fermented sugar cane juice) in a variety of all natural flavours, including a delectable coconut rum obtained from soaking coconut meat in the rum for several months. There's a video about the production process, a tasting area, an excellent French and Thai restaurant and a shop in beautiful palm-shaded surrounds.

Aquapark WATER PARK
(Map p182; www.aquaparkchaweng.com; Hat Chaweng; hourly/half-day/full-day 300/500/700B; 10am-6pm) Let the kids loose on these gigantic green, climbable, slip-off-able and all-around-fun inflatables (including a UFO, an iceberg climbing wall and trampolines) anchored to a corded-off area of Ao Chaweng. All participants are required to wear life jackets. Meanwhile you can lounge on the beach and watch, or join them as many parents do.

Coco Splash Waterpark WATER PARK
(www.samuiwaterpark.com; Ban Lamai; admission over/under 1.3m 490/390B; 10.30am-5.30pm) Kids under 10 will love this small park of fun painted concrete water slides. Towel hire is 60B (200B deposit) and there's mediocre food available. Note that if you're planning on watching the kids and not going in the water yourself, you get in for free.

Samui Dog & Cat Rescue Centre VOLUNTEERING
(Map p182; 077 413490; www.samuidog.org; Soi 3, Chaweng Beach Rd; 9am-6pm) Donations of time and/or money are hugely appreciated at the aptly named Samui Dog & Cat Rescue

Ko Samui

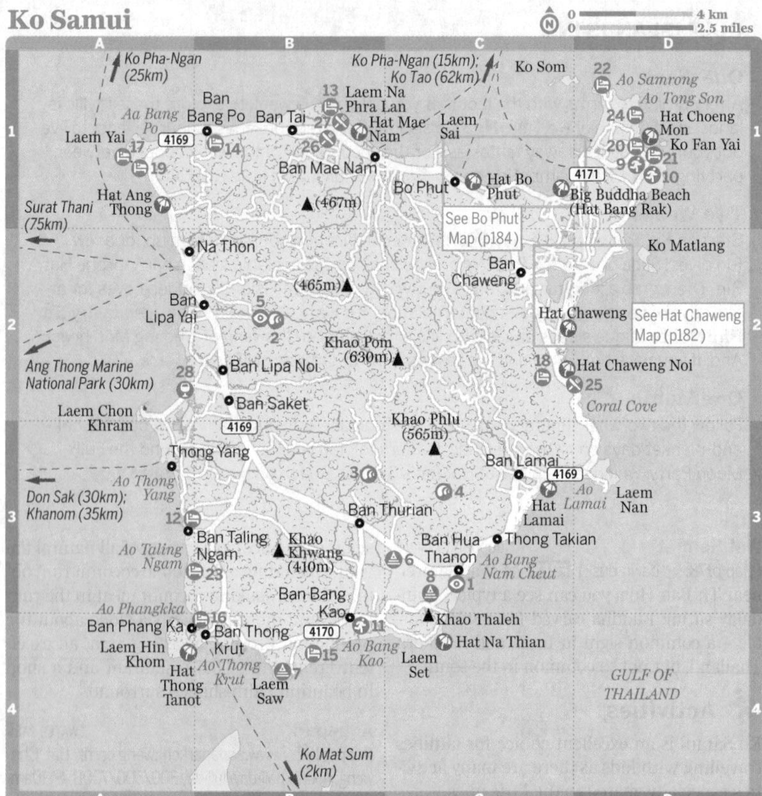

Centre. Volunteers are always needed to take care of the animals at their kennel/clinic in Ban Taling Ngam (but not at the smaller Hat Chaweng branch). Call the centre for volunteering details or swing by for additional info. Check the website for directions.

The organisation has played an integral role in keeping the island's dog population under control through an active spaying and neutering program. The centre also vaccinates dogs against rabies.

Diving

If you're serious about diving, head to Ko Tao and base yourself there. If you're short on time and don't want to leave Samui, there are plenty of operators who will take you to the same dive sites (at a greater fee, of course). Try to book with a company that has its own boat (or leases a boat) – it's slightly more expensive, but you'll be glad you did it. Companies without boats often shuttle divers on the passenger catamaran to Ko Tao, where you board a second boat to reach your dive site. These trips are arduous, meal-less and rather impersonal.

Certification courses tend to be twice as expensive on Ko Samui as they are on Ko Tao, due largely to use of extra petrol, since tiny Tao is significantly closer to the preferred diving locations. You'll spend between 14,000B and 22,000B on an Open Water certification, and figure on between 4500B and 6200B for a diving day trip including two dives, depending on the location of the site.

Ko Samui's hyperbaric chamber is at Big Buddha Beach (Hat Bang Rak).

100 Degrees East DIVING
(☎077 425936; www.100degreeseast.com; Hat Bang Rak; ⏲9am-6.30pm Dec-Oct) Highly recommended, with a dedicated team.

Ko Samui

Discovery Dive Centre DIVING
(Map p182; 077 300656; www.discoverydivers.com; Chaweng Beach Rd, Amari Palm Reef Resort; courses 5900-17,400B; 11am-11pm) This popular office offers dive courses from beginner to professional as well as dive trips and snorkelling.

Spas & Yoga

Competition between Samui's five-star accommodation is fierce, meaning spas are of the highest calibre. For top-notch pampering, try the spa at Anantara (p185) in Bo Phut, or the Hideaway Spa at the Six Senses Samui (p184). The Spa Resort (p183) in Lamai is the island's original health destination, and is still known for its effective 'clean me out' fasting regime.

Samahita Retreat YOGA, SPA
(077 920090; www.samahitaretreat.com; Laem Saw Beach; retreats around €840) Secreted away along the southern shores, Samahita Retreat has state-of-the-art facilities and a dedicated team of trainers for the growing band of therapeutic holidaymakers, wellness seekers and detoxers. Accommodation is in a comfy apartment block up the street while yoga studios, wellness centres and a health food restaurant sit calmly along the shore.

Tamarind Springs MASSAGE
(077 424221; www.tamarindsprings.com) Tucked away in a location far from the beach within a silent coconut-palm plantation, Tamarind's small collection of villas and massage studios is seamlessly incorporated into nature: some have granite boulders built into the walls and floors, while others offer private ponds or creative outdoor baths.

Absolute Sanctuary YOGA, SPA
(Map p178; 077 601190; www.absolutesanctuary.com; Choeng Mon) Detox, spa, yoga, pilates and lifestyle packages, in a Moroccan-inspired setting.

Courses

Samui Institute of Thai Culinary Arts COOKING COURSE
(SITCA; Map p182; 077 413172; http://sitca.com; Hat Chaweng; 1-day course 1850B) For Thai cooking skills, SITCA is the place to do it, with daily Thai-cooking classes and courses in the aristocratic Thai art of carving fruits and vegetables into intricate floral designs. Lunchtime classes begin at 11am, while dinner starts at 4pm (both are three-hour courses with three or more dishes).

Included is a tutorial about procuring ingredients in your home country. Of course you get to eat your projects, and can even invite a friend along for the meal. Complimentary DVDs with Thai cooking instruction are also available so you can practise at home.

Lamai Muay Thai Camp THAI BOXING
(087 082 6970; www.lamaimuaythaicamp.com; 82/2 Moo3, Lamai; 1-day/1-week training sessions 300/1500B; 7am-8pm) The island's best *moo·ay tai* (also spelt *muay Thai*) training (best for the seriously serious) is at this place,

which caters to beginners as well as those wanting to hone their skills. There's also a well-equipped gym for boxers and nonboxers who want to up their fitness levels.

Kiteboarding Asia KITEBOARDING
(☎083 643 1627; www.kiteboardingasia.com; 1-/3-day courses 4000/11,000B; ⌚9am-6pm) This pro place will get you kitesurfing on flat shallow water. The Na Thon location on the west side is for December to March winds (another in Hua Thanon in the south of the island is for April to October gusts).

Mind Your Language LANGUAGE COURSE
(☎077 960103; www.mindyourlanguagethailand.com) With lessons from 600B per hour, this accessible and professional language school in Lamai can gear you up with classes in Thai. There's another branch in Bo Phut.

Sleeping

The island's array of sleeping options is overwhelming. If you're looking to splurge, there is definitely no shortage of top-end resorts sporting exclusive bungalows, pampering spas, private infinity pools and top-notch dining. Bo Phut, on the island's northern coast, has an attractive collection of boutique lodging – the perfect choice for midrange travellers. Backpack-lugging visitors may have to look a little harder, but budget digs pop up periodically along all of the island's beaches.

Most visitors pre-book their resort, but outside peak season most midrange and budget places offer discounted walk-in rates equal or better to what you'll find online.

Private villa services have become popular in recent years; www.gosamuivillas.com is a good place to book the luxury variety.

Hat Chaweng

Busy, commercial Chaweng is packed wall-to-wall with every level of accommodation from cheap backpacker pads advertised with cardboard signs to futuristic villas with private swimming pools – and these might be just across the street from each other. There's little charm here, though: the northern half of the beach is the biggest party zone and nearby resorts are in ear-shot of the thumping bass pumping from Ark Bar at the centre of it all. If you're hoping for early nights, pick a resort near the southern half of the beach or bring earplugs. Bristling with selfie sticks and an assault course of low-hanging street signs that will clobber anyone over six foot, Chaweng Beach Road is crowded with souvenir shop owners, ads for wet T-shirt competitions, tattoo parlours and Heath Ledger *Joker* acrylic portraits, as jets roar overhead. Lamai is much quieter, less intense and altogether more pleasant.

Lucky Mother GUESTHOUSE $
(Map p182; ☎077 230931; 60 Moo 2; r & bungalows 800-1500B; ❄📶) The action-filled beachfront location, clean, bright rooms and popular bar out front that's prime for mingling with your toes in the sand all get the thumbs up. If you want a Chaweng beach location, it's a great deal (though some staff members could be friendlier).

P Chaweng HOTEL $
(Map p182; ☎077 230684; r from 600B, f 1000B; ❄@📶) At the end of a road off the main drag, this vine-covered cheapie has clean, pink-tiled rooms and wood-floored family rooms in two blocks, all decked out with air-con, hot water, TVs and fridges. It's a 10-minute walk to the bar zone and not particularly hip, but good luck finding a better room in the area for this price.

Queen Boutique Place HOTEL $
(Map p182; ☎077 413148; queensamui@yahoo.com; r 700-1500B; ❄@📶) With welcoming and well-mannered staff, the Queen serves up boutique sleeps at backpacker prices. Rooms are clean and well-equipped (with air-con, TVs and DVD players) and garner style points for colourful throw pillows, but the cheapest are boxy and windowless.

Pott Guesthouse GUESTHOUSE $
(Map p182; r with fan 300-400B, with air-con 500-600B; ❄📶) The bright cement rooms, all with attached hot-water bathrooms and balcony, in this apartment block are a steal. Reception is at an unnamed restaurant on the main drag right opposite across the alley.

Akwa GUESTHOUSE $
(Map p182; ☎084 660 0551; www.akwaguesthouse.com; r from 750B; ❄@📶) Akwa's funky rooms come with bright colours, cartoon paintings and soft toys, but things are a little past their prime. There's no shortage of character and friendly service, however, and the branch a five-minute walk to the north of the original is fresher and newer.

Samui Hostel HOSTEL $
(Map p182; ☎089 874 3737; dm 200-300B, d 850B; ❄@) It doesn't look like much from the front, but this very neat, tidy and friendly place has

clean fan and air-con dorm rooms and spruce air-con doubles. Service is a cut above the rest and there's a popular room at the front with wooden tables for lounging and chatting.

★ Jungle Club BUNGALOW **$$**

(Map p178; ☎ 081 894 2327; www.jungleclubsamui.com; huts 800-1800B, houses 2700-4500B; ❄@📶🏊) The drive up the slithering road is worthwhile once you take in the views from the top. With a relaxed back-to-nature vibe, this isolated mountain getaway is a huge hit among locals and tourists alike. Guests chill around the stunning horizon pool or catnap under the canopied roofs of an open-air *săh·lah* (often spelt as *sala*).

Call ahead for a pick-up (from Chaweng only) – you don't want to spend your precious jungle vacation in a body cast.

Chaweng Garden Beach RESORT **$$**

(Map p182; ☎ 077 960394; www.chawenggarden.com; r 3600-33,000B; ❄@📶🏊) A huge variety of room types hide amid the abundant foliage, from fine if rather bland standards with balcony to an indulgent 33,000B private beachfront pool villa. The best value is found in those such as the modern Asian-inspired 'Shinto' rooms and polished wood bungalows. The whole place is well-tended with greenery and serviced by an extra-smiley and helpful staff.

Tango Beach Resort RESORT **$$**

(Map p182; ☎ 077 300451; www.tangobeachsamui.com; r 1600-7400B; ❄📶🏊) The colourful lobby suggests a youngish vibe, but Tango is really more a standard string of bungalows arranged along a teak boardwalk meandering away from an excellent but busy stretch of beach. The dark tinted windows make the place look a little tacky from the outside (and the dated pool doesn't help) but the 39 rooms are fresh enough.

Ark Bar Beach Resort RESORT **$$**

(Map p182; ☎ 077 422047; www.ark-bar.com; r 1700-5200B; ❄📶🏊) You'll find two of every party animal at clean and well-tended 328-room Ark Bar – frat boys, chilled-out hippies, teenagers, 40-somethings and so on. Contemporary, brightly painted rooms all come with balcony, within staggering distance from the bar that pumps out music all day and well into the night.

★ Library RESORT **$$$**

(Map p182; ☎ 077 422767; www.thelibrary.co.th; r from 9140B; ❄@📶🏊) This library is too cool for school. The entire resort is a sparkling white mirage accented with black trimming and slatted curtains. Besides the futuristic iMac computer in each page (rooms are 'pages' here), our favourite feature is the large monochromatic wall art – it glows brightly in the evening and you can adjust the colour to your mood.

Life-size statues are engaged in the act of reading, and if you too feel inclined to pick up a book, the on-site library houses an impressive assortment of colourful art and design books. The large rectangular pool is not to be missed – it's tiled in piercing shades of red, making the term 'bloodbath' suddenly seem appealing. It has an on-site restaurant (p188).

Buri Rasa Village RESORT **$$$**

(Map p182; ☎ 077 230222; www.burirasa.com; r 4850-8900B; ❄📶🏊) Thai-style wooden doors lead to private villa patios and simple yet elegant rooms. This Zen-feeling place is beautifully landscaped with palms and frangipani, central, well-priced and on a good stretch of busy beach, but the real reason to stay here is the bend-over-backwards friendly and helpful service.

Chaweng Regent Beach Resort RESORT **$$$**

(Map p182; ☎ 077 422390, 077 422389; www.chawengregent.com; r 6000-15,000B; ❄📶🏊) This delightful oasis of tree, vegetation, shady foliage and tropical seclusion is a welcome respite from frantic Chaweng Beach Rd. Enticingly secluded, the resort is navigated via wooden boardwalks leading to the beach, with two pools, goldfish ponds and a wide range of rooms.

Baan Haad Ngam RESORT **$$$**

(Map p182; ☎ 077 231500; www.baanhaadngam.com; bungalows 8700-33,500B; ❄@📶🏊) Very modern and stylish, with classy yet simple lime-green rooms, villas and pool villas tucked into a lush botanical garden cut with mini waterfalls and streams that lead to a small infinity pool that gazes over aqua sea. Its best asset, however, is its location, close to the action yet quiet and private.

Kirikayan Boutique Resort RESORT **$$$**

(Map p182; ☎ 077 332299; www.kirikayan.com; r from 4500B; ❄@📶🏊) Simple whites, lacquered teak and blazing red accents set the colour scheme at this small, hip address along Hat Chaweng's southern sands. It's a smooth and restful composition: wander past thick palm trunks and sky-scraping foliage to find the relaxing pool deck at the back.

Hat Chaweng

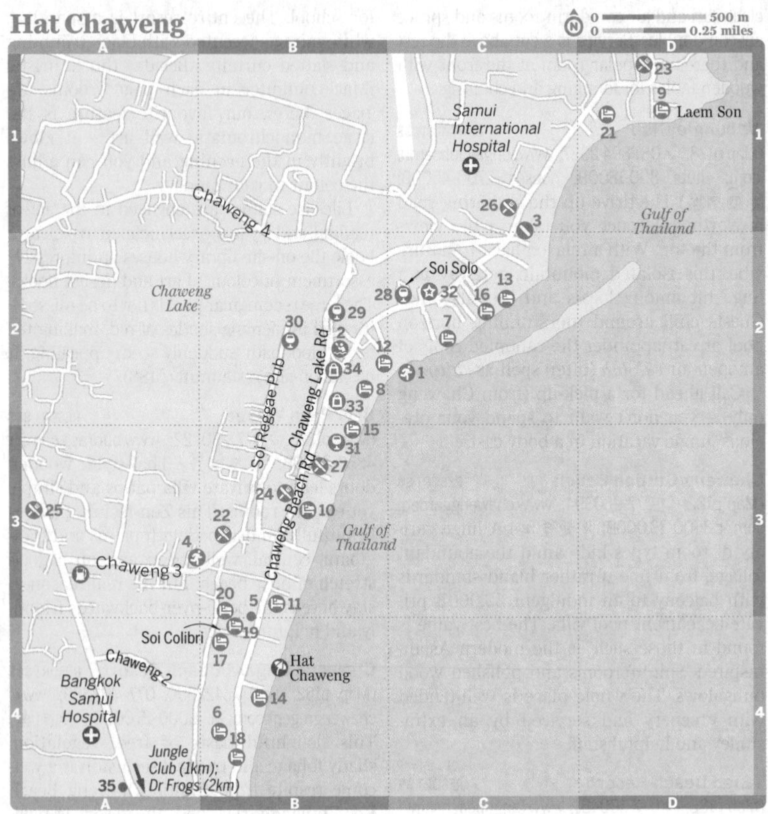

Centara Grand RESORT $$$
(Map p182; ☎077 230500; www.centralhotelsresorts.com; r 8900-21,500B;) Centara is a massive, manicured beachfront compound in the heart of Hat Chaweng, but the palm-filled property is so large you can safely escape the street-side bustle. Rooms are found in a hotel-like building, conspicuously Western in theme and decor. Babysitting and family-friendly services abound. Check online for big discounts out of high season.

Baan Chaweng Beach Resort RESORT $$$
(Map p182; ☎077 300564; www.baanchawengbeachresort.com; bungalows 4500-11,000B;) A bit of luxury without breaking the bank, Baan Chaweng draws in families and retired bargain-seekers who roast themselves on loungers along the lovely beach. The immaculate rooms are painted in various shades of peach and pear, with teak furnishings that feel both modern and traditional.

Hat Lamai

The central, powdery white area of Hat Lamai is packed with an amazing quantity of sunburned souls lounging on beach chairs, but head to the grainier northern or southern extremities and things get much quieter. Ban Lamai runs back from the main beach area. Unlike Hat Chaweng, the main party in Lamai takes place off the beach, so the sand here is generally free of a dance-beat soundtrack. However, the party scene that is here, mostly along the town's main drag and its smaller arteries, is of the seedier bar-girl-oriented variety.

Amarina Residence HOTEL $
(☎077 418073; www.amarinaresidence.com; r 1200-1800B;) A two-minute walk to the beach, this excellent-value small hotel has two storeys of big, tastefully furnished, tiled rooms encircling the lobby and an incongruous dipping pool.

Hat Chaweng

Activities, Courses & Tours
1 Aquapark C2
2 Blue Stars B2
3 Discovery Dive Centre C1
4 Samui Dog & Cat Rescue Centre A3
5 Samui Institute of Thai Culinary Arts B3

Sleeping
6 Akwa B4
7 Ark Bar Beach Resort C2
8 Baan Chaweng Beach Resort B2
9 Baan Haad Ngam D1
10 Buri Rasa Village B3
11 Centara Grand B3
12 Chaweng Garden Beach B2
13 Chaweng Regent Beach Resort C2
14 Kirikayan Boutique Resort B4
15 Library B3
16 Lucky Mother C2
17 P Chaweng B4
18 Pott Guesthouse B4
19 Queen Boutique Place B4
20 Samui Hostel B3
21 Tango Beach Resort D1

Eating
22 Laem Din Market B3
23 Larder D1
24 Ninja Crepes B3
Page .... (see 15)
25 Pepenero A3
26 Prego C1
27 Stacked B3

Drinking & Nightlife
Ark Bar .... (see 7)
28 Bar Solo C2
29 Green Mango B2
30 Reggae Pub B2
31 Tropical Murphy's Irish B3

Entertainment
32 Paris Follies Cabaret C2

Shopping
33 Bookazine B2
34 Central Festival B2

Transport
35 Bangkok Airways Office A4

New Hut BUNGALOW $
(☎077 230437; newhutlamai@yahoo.co.th; Lamai North; huts 300-800B; 📶) A-frame huts right on the beach all share a big, clean block of bathrooms. There's a lively restaurant, friendly enough staff and one of the most simple and happy backpacker vibes.

Spa Resort BUNGALOW $$
(☎077 230855; www.spasamui.com; Lamai North; bungalows 720-1200B; ❄📶🏊) Programs at this friendly spa include colonics, massage, aqua detox, hypnotherapy and yoga, just to name a few. With rattan furniture, traditional wall art and balconies, rooms are comfortable and excellent value, but book up quickly. Nonguests are welcome to partake in the spa programs and dine at the excellent (and healthy) open-air restaurant by the beach.

★ **Rocky Resort** RESORT $$$
(☎077 418367; www.rockyresort.com; Hua Thanon; r 8000-20,000B; ❄📶🏊) With a supremely calm reception area and two swimming pools, Rocky effortlessly finds the right balance between an upmarket ambience and an unpretentious, sociable vibe. During quieter months prices are a steal, since ocean views abound, and each room (some with pool) has been furnished with beautiful Thai-inspired furniture that seamlessly incorporates a modern twist.

Banyan Tree Koh Samui RESORT $$$
(☎077 915333; www.banyantree.com/en/samui/overview; villas from 23,300B; ❄@📶🏊) Occupying an entire bay, this sprawling over-the-top luxury delight encompasses dozens of pool villas hoisted above the foliage by spider-like stilts. Golf carts zip around the grounds carrying jet-setters between the myriad dining venues and the gargantuan spa (which sports a relaxing rainforest simulator). Service, however, could be improved.

Samui Jasmine Resort RESORT $$$
(☎077 232446; 131/8 Moo 3, Lamai; r & bungalows 4600-12,000B; ❄📶🏊) Smack dab in the middle of Hat Lamai, varnished-teak yet frilly Samui Jasmine is a great deal. Go for the lower-priced rooms – most have excellent views of the ocean and the crystal-coloured lap pool.

Choeng Mon

Choeng Mon is an area that holds several beaches that span the northeastern nub of the island. Samrong and Ton Son to the north are home to small communities and some of the most luxurious resorts in the world. Those with mortal budgets tend to stay on the beach at Choeng Mon proper whose perfect (although busy) half-moon of sand is considered by many to be the most beautiful beach on the island.

Bo Phut

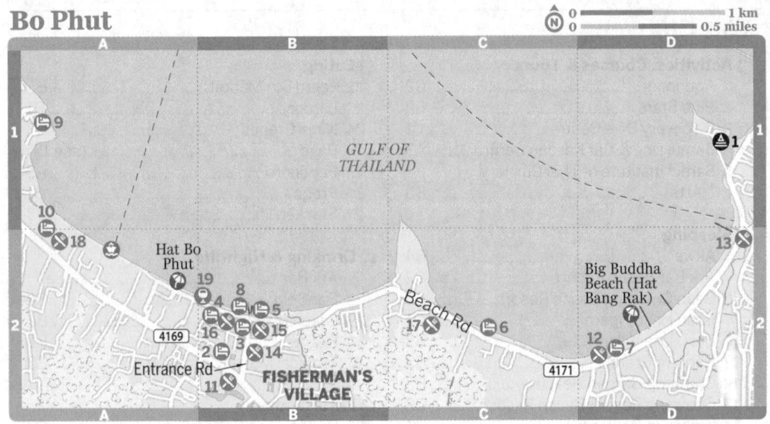

Samui Honey Cottages Resort RESORT **$$**
(Map p178; ☎077 427093; www.samuihoney.com; Choeng Mon; r incl breakfast 3500-6500B; ❄📶🏊) At the quieter southern part of the beach, this small resort (with an equally small pool) isn't anything that special but it's nicer than some of the other mediocre offerings in this price range on this beach. Expect attractive, classic Zen-style rooms.

★**Six Senses Samui** RESORT **$$$**
(Map p178; ☎077 245678; www.sixsenses.com/hideaway-samui/index.php; Samrong; bungalows from 13,000B; ❄@📶🏊) This hidden bamboo paradise is worth the once-in-a-lifetime splurge. Set in 9 hectares along a rugged promontory, Six Senses strikes the perfect balance between opulence and rustic charm, and defines the expression 'barefoot elegance'. Most of the 66 villas have stunning concrete plunge pools and offer magnificent views of the silent bay below.

The regal, semi-outdoor bathrooms give the phrase 'royal flush' a whole new meaning. Golf buggies move guests between their cottages and the stunning amenities strewn around the property – including a world-class spa and two excellent restaurants.

Tongsai Bay RESORT **$$$**
(Map p178; ☎077 245480; www.tongsaibay.co.th; Tong Son; ste 11,800-38,000B; ❄📶🏊) For serious pampering, head to this secluded luxury gem. Impeccably maintained, the 10-hectare hilly grounds make the cluster of bungalows look more like a small village. All the split-level suites have day-bed rest areas, romantic decor, stunning views, large terraces and creatively placed bathtubs (you'll see).

Facilities include two pools, a tennis court, a spa, a dessert shop, several restaurants and a private beach, of course.

Sala Samui RESORT **$$$**
(Map p178; ☎077 245888; www.salasamui.com; Choeng Mon; r 6700B, villas 9700-23,200B; ❄@📶🏊) Is the hefty price tag worth it? Definitely. The dreamy, deluxe design scheme is exquisite and modern – clean whites and lacquered teaks are lavish throughout, while subtle turquoise accents draw on the colour of each villa's private plunge pool. Heavenly.

Big Buddha Beach (Hat Bang Rak)

Named after the huge golden Buddha that presides over the small nearby quasi-island of Ko Fan, this beach's western half is by far the best, with its relatively empty stretch of white sand. The closer you get to the busy pier areas, the coarser and browner the sand becomes and the murkier the water. Big Buddha Beach's proximity to the airport means some overhead roaring (but quick and cheap taxi rides for flight arrivals).

Secret Garden Beach Resort BUNGALOW **$$**
(Map p184; ☎077 245255; www.secretgarden.co.th; bungalows 1700-3700B; ❄📶🏊) This refurbished and renewed Dutch-owned establishment has an excellent beach restaurant and bar and fresh, well-equipped bungalows in the eponymous garden and by the pool. There's live music on Sundays when locals, expats and tourists come to chill out and imbibe, but it's fairly subdued the rest of the time.

Bo Phut

Sights
1 Wat Phra Yai D1

Sleeping
2 Anantara B2
3 Castaway Guesthouse B2
4 Eden B2
5 Hacienda B2
6 Scent C2
7 Secret Garden Beach Resort D2
8 The Lodge B2
9 W Retreat Koh Samui A1
10 Zazen A1

Eating
11 69 .... B2
12 Antica Locanda D2
13 Catcantoo D2
14 Chez François B2
15 Karma Sutra B2
16 Shack Bar & Grill B2
17 The Hut C2
18 Zazen Restaurant A2

Drinking & Nightlife
Billabong Surf Club .... (see 8)
19 Coco Tam's B2
Woo Bar .... (see 9)

★ **Scent** RESORT $$$
(Map p184; ☎077 960123; www.thescenthotel.com; ste 8500-10,500B) Seek out the taste (and scent if you light your complimentary incense) of Indo-China at this tranquil gem that recreates the elegance of 1940s and '50s colonial Asia. The tall grey concrete structure is cut by elongated teak framed windows and surrounds a courtyard swimming pool and ornamental trees and plants.

Choose between European, Chinese or Thai-Chinese style rooms, each one spacious and decorated with tasteful opulence.

Bo Phut

Bo Phut's Fisherman's Village is a concentration of narrow Chinese shophouses, transformed into some of the island's trendiest (and often midrange) boutique hotels and eateries. The accompanying beach, particularly the eastern part, is slim and coarse but becomes whiter and lusher further west.

Hacienda GUESTHOUSE $$
(Map p184; ☎077 245943; www.samui-hacienda.com; r 1200-2800B, ste 2600-4450B; ❄📶🏊) Polished terracotta and rounded archways give the entrance a Spanish mission motif. Similar decor permeates the adorable rooms, which sport touches such as pebbled bathroom walls and translucent bamboo lamps. Hacienda Suites, the overflow property a few doors down, holds the cheaper 'eco' rooms which are minuscule and mostly window-less, but still clean and comfortable. The tiny rooftop pool has gorgeous ocean views.

The Lodge HOTEL $$
(Map p184; ☎077 425337; www.lodgesamui.com; r 2500-3000B; ❄📶) The Lodge feels like a colonial hunting chalet with pale walls, hardwood floors and dark wooden beams jutting across the ceiling, except it all looks out over blue-green sea. Each of the eight rooms has scores of wall hangings and a private balcony overlooking the beach; the 'pent-huts' on the top floor are particularly spacious.

You're really in the heart of the Fisherman's Village, making this a lively spot but somehow still intimate. It's extremely popular so reservations are a must.

Castaway Guesthouse GUESTHOUSE $$
(Map p184; ☎098 464 6562; r with fan/air-con 650-1500B; ❄📶) A block away from the beach, right in the Fisherman's Village, the newly renovated Castaway's 15 rooms are all clean, bright and cheery.

Eden BUNGALOW $$
(Map p184; ☎077 427645; www.edenbungalows.com; bungalows 1500-2300B; ❄📶🏊) The 10 bungalows and five rooms here are all tucked away in a garden with a small pool at its centre. Cheaper options are rather shabby but an upgrade gets you a more stylish suite with yellow walls and naturalistic wood furniture. It's about a two-minute walk to the beach.

★ **Anantara** RESORT $$$
(Map p184; ☎077 428300; samui.anantara.com; r 6400-22,775B; ❄@📶🏊) Anantara's stunning palanquin entrance satisfies fantasies of a far-flung oriental kingdom. Clay and copper statues of grimacing jungle creatures abound on the property's wild acreage, while guests savour wild teas in an open-air pagoda, swim in the lagoon-like infinity-edged swimming pool or indulge in relaxing treatments amid the lush tropical foliage of the beautiful spa.

Zazen RESORT $$$

(Map p184; ☎077 425085; www.samuizazen.com; r 6160-17,200B; ❄@☜🏊) Welcome to one of the boutique-iest boutique resorts on Samui – every inch of this charming getaway has been thoughtfully and creatively designed. It's 'Asian minimalism meets modern rococo' with a scarlet accent wall, terracotta goddesses, a dash of feng shui and a generous smattering of good taste. Guests relax poolside or on loungers gently shaded by canvas parasols on the very best stretch of this beach. Even better, the service is as luxe as the setting.

Mae Nam & Bang Po

Mae Nam's slim length of white sand slopes down to an aqua sea. One of the island's prettiest stretches of beach, it's popular with families and older couples, giving it an unhurried yet still vibrant ambience perfect for reading under the shade of a coconut tree, sleeping or having beach massages. Bang Po, just around the tiny peninsula, is even quieter.

Shangri-la BUNGALOW $

(☎077 425189; Mae Nam; bungalows with fan/air-con from 500/1300B; ❄☜) A backpacker's Shangri La indeed – these are some of the cheapest huts around and they're on a sublime part of the beach. Grounds are sparsely landscaped but the basic concrete bungalows, all with attached bathrooms (only air-con rooms have hot water), are well kept and the staff is pleasant.

Coco Palm Resort BUNGALOW $$

(Map p178; ☎077 425095; www.cocopalmbeachresort.com; Mae Nam; bungalows 3000-9450B; ❄☜🏊) The huge array of bungalows at this resort have been crafted with hard wood, bamboo and rattan touches. A rectangular pool is the centrepiece along the beach. The cheapest choices are the furthest from the beach, but even these are comfy; and if you want to make a real splash, aim for the beachfront pool villas.

Code HOTEL $$$

(Map p178; ☎077 602122; www.samuicode.com; Mae Nam; ste 3300-11,100B; ❄☜🏊) All sleek modern lines and dust-free white contrasts against the turquoise sea and the hotel's large infinity pool, making for a stunning piece of architecture. The all-ocean-view suites are spacious and efficient and the service is just as grand.

Of course, as with any fine piece of machinery, everything you need is at your fingertips including a gym, spa and restaurant.

W Retreat Koh Samui RESORT $$$

(Map p184; ☎077 915999; www.starwoodhotels.com/whotels; Mae Nam; r from 19,500B; ❄@☜🏊) A bejewelled 'W' welcomes guests on the curling road to the lobby, and upon arrival jaws immediately drop while staring out over the infinity pools and endless horizon. The trademark 'W glam' does its darnedest to fuse an urban vibe with tropical serenity throughout. Do note, though, that this hotel is on a hill and not on a beach.

Belmond Napasai RESORT $$$

(Map p178; ☎077 429200; www.napasai.com; Bang Po; r from 10,900B; ❄@☜🏊) Gorgeously manicured grounds welcome weary travellers as they glide past grazing water buffalo and groundsmen donning cream-coloured pith helmets. A generous smattering of villas dot the expansive landscape – all sport traditional Thai-style decorations, from the intricately carved wooden ornamentation to streamers of luscious local silks.

Na Thon

Chytalay Palace Hotel HOTEL $$

(☎077 421079; 152 Nathon Moo 3; d with fan 400B, d with air-con, 550-950B, tr 800-1000B; ❄☜) This quiet hotel on the beachfront road a short walk south from the pier has spacious rooms with balcony overlooking the sea. The perfectly good, cheaper, lower-floor rooms have electricity cables partially blocking the view but are 400B less than the newer rooms upstairs. All rooms have attached shower rooms. Service is pleasant, if rather reserved.

West Coast

With more Thai tourists, Samui's west coast has skinny beaches of grainy sand but the sunsets can be breathtaking, while the blue seas and views out to the Five Islands and the shadowy greens of the mainland are beguiling. It's a welcome escape from the often-draining east-side bustle.

Am Samui BUNGALOW $$

(Map p178; ☎077 235165; Taling Ngam; bungalows 1600-6000B; ❄☜🏊) Cast modesty aside, spread your curtains wide, and welcome sunshine and sea views in through your floor-to-ceiling windows. Getting out of the main tourist areas to this private beach with fantastic sunset views means your baht goes miles further in terms of room quality.

Sunset Beach Resort & Spa
RESORT $$$

(Map p178; ☎077 428200; www.thesunsetbeachresort.com; Ban Taling Nam; r 6000-14,300B, villa 11,000-35,800B;) While the views over the Five Islands at sunset, quiet (though slightly pebbly) beach and extra-clean, simple yet luxurious rooms are a draw, it's the smiling, attentive service that makes this place stand out among resorts in this area. Free mountain bikes get you around the sleepy surrounding village, but you'll want a vehicle to get further afield.

Four Seasons Koh Samui
HOTEL $$$

(Map p178; ☎077 243000; www.fourseasons.com/kohsamui; villas from 30,000B;) This hilly 17-hectare enclave of 60 villas, on a peninsula at the far western corner of Bang Po, feels more like a private village than a resort. Stunning views range out from the lobby, while each huge villa has a private plunge pool. A beautiful stretch of flaxen sand awaits, there's a Thai boxing ring and a gym with a view.

Mövenpick Resort Laem Yai Beach Samui
RESORT $$$

(Map p178; ☎077 421722; www.moevenpick-hotels.com; r incl breakfast 8100-21,900B;) Splendid and serene, this boutique spot on the west coast is a top choice for out-of-the-action beachcombing, coupled with fine sunsets and a sparklingly high degree of service. Facilities, including three pools, are top notch, as are the villas. Cabarets and fire shows kick off in the evening, but if it's nightlife you want, look elsewhere.

South Coast

The southern end of Ko Samui is spotted with rocky headlands and smaller coves of pebble sand that are used more as parking lots for Thai fishing boats than for lounge chairs. It's a great area to take a leisurely cycle through coconut palm groves and small Thai villages that aren't ruled by tourism.

Easy Time
BUNGALOW $$

(Map p178; ☎077 920111; www.easytimesamui.com; Phang Ka; villas 2300-4000B;) Safely tucked away from the throngs of tourists, this little haven – nestled a few minutes' walk to the beach around a serene swimming pool – doesn't have well-oiled service so be prepared to be master of your own off-the-beaten-path getaway. Duplex villa units and a chic dining space create an elegant mood that is refreshingly unpretentious.

Elements
RESORT $$$

(Map p178; ☎077 914678; www.elements-koh-samui.com; Phang Ka; r incl breakfast 7400-24,000B;) Peaceful Elements occupies a lonely strand of sand with views of the Five Islands, and is the perfect place for a meditative retreat or quiet couples romantic getaway. Chic rooms are arranged in condo-like blocks while hidden villas dot the path down to the oceanside lounge area. Free kayaks and bikes plus excellent service add to the calm.

Eating

If you thought it was hard to pick a place to sleep, the island has even more options when it comes to dining. From roasted crickets to beluga caviar, Samui's got it and is not afraid to flaunt it.

Influenced by the mainland, Samui is peppered with *kôw gaang* (rice and curry) shops, usually just a wooden shack displaying large metal pots of southern Thai-style curries. Folks pull up on their motorcycles, lift up the lids to survey the vibrantly coloured contents, and pick one for lunch. *Kôw gaang* shops are easily found along the Ring Rd (Rte 4169) and sell out of the good stuff by 1pm. Any build-up of local motorcycles is usually a sign of a good meal in progress.

The upmarket choices are even more numerous and although Samui's swank dining scene is laden with Italian options, visitors will have no problem finding flavours from around the globe. Lured by high salaries and spectacular weather, world-class chefs regularly make an appearance on the island.

Hat Chaweng

Dozens of the restaurants on the 'strip' serve a mixed bag of local bites, international cuisine and greasy fast food, but there's nothing worth making a trip for. For the best ambience head to the beach, where many bungalow operators set up tables on the sand and have glittery fairy lights at night.

Laem Din Market
MARKET $

(Map p182; dishes from 35B; ⏰4am-6pm, night market 6pm-2am) A busy day market, Laem Din is packed with stalls that sell fruits, vegetables and meats and stock local Thai kitchens. Pick up a kilo of sweet green oranges or wander the stalls trying to spot the ingredients in last night's curry. For dinner, come to the adjacent night market and sample the southern-style fried chicken and curries.

Ninja Crepes THAI $

(Map p182; dishes from 75B; ⊙11am-midnight) Rammed nightly, with flaming woks at the heart of things working double-time to keep the pace, this warehouse-sized restaurant serves up Thai seafood, curries, crepes, soups and desserts to throngs of eager patrons.

★ **Stacked** STEAK $$

(Map p182; www.stacked-samui.com; mains from 295B; ⊙noon-midnight;) All sharp lines, open grill, a team of busy staff plus a cracker of a menu, this burger restaurant is a visual and culinary feast. Burgers and steaks – bursting with flavour – are served up on slate slabs in generous portions. Go with a sizeable hunger as the inclination is to simply keep on ordering.

★ **Pepenero** ITALIAN $$

(Map p182; www.pepenerosamui.com; mains from 250B; ⊙5.30-10.30pm Mon & Wed-Sat, 6-10.30pm Sun) Pepenero has caused quite a stir on Ko Samui. What this excellent Italian restaurant lacks in views, is more than made up for by a terrific menu (including cutting boards with cheese and cold cuts) and the care and attention displayed to customers by the very sociable, hard-working hosts.

★ **Larder** EUROPEAN $$$

(Map p182; www.thelardersamui.com; mains 300-900B; ⊙noon-11pm;) This restaurant/bar/gastropub pulls out the stops in an invigorating menu of classic fare in a relaxing and tasteful setting, supported by a strong selection of wines and zesty cocktails. It's a winning formula, with dishes ranging from slow cooked lamb spare ribs to beer-battered snow fish and warm falafel with feta cucumber and chilli salad.

Page ASIAN FUSION $$$

(Map p182; www.thelibrary.co.th/the-page.html; dishes 300-1650B; ⊙7am-11.30pm;) If you can't afford to stay at the ultra-swanky Library (p181), have a meal at its beachside restaurant. It's not cheap, but lunch is a bit more casual and affordable.

Dr Frogs STEAK $$$

(Map p178; www.drfrogssamui.com; mains from 380B; ⊙noon-11pm) Perched atop a rocky overlook, Dr Frogs combines beautiful ocean vistas with international Italian grills, seafood, pasta, pizza and Thai favourites. Delectable steaks and crab cakes, and friendly owners, make it a winner. It's a romantic set-

SALT AND SPICE IN SOUTHERN THAI CUISINE

Don't say we didn't warn you: southern Thai cooking is undoubtedly the spiciest regional cooking style in a land of spicy regional cuisines. The food of Thailand's southern provinces also tends to be very salty, and seafood, not surprisingly, plays an important role, ranging from fresh fish that is grilled or added to soups, to pickled or fermented fish or served as sauces or condiments.

Two of the principal crops in the south are coconuts and cashews, both of which find their way into a variety of dishes. In addition to these, southern Thais love their greens, and nearly every meal is accompanied by a platter of fresh herbs and vegies, and a spicy 'dip' of shrimp paste, chillies, garlic and lime.

Dishes you are likely to come across in southern Thailand include the following:

Gaang đai Ƀlah An intensely spicy and salty curry that includes *đai Ƀlah* (salted fish stomach); much tastier than it sounds.

Gaang sôm Known as *gaang lĕu·ang* (yellow curry) in central Thailand, this sour/spicy soup gets its hue from the liberal use of turmeric, a root commonly used in southern Thai cooking.

Gài tôrt hàht yài The famous deep-fried chicken from the town of Hat Yai gets its rich flavour from a marinade containing dried spices.

Kà·nŏm jeen nám yah This dish of thin rice noodles served with a fiery curry-like sauce is always accompanied by a tray of fresh vegetables and herbs.

Kôo·a glîng Minced meat fried with a fiery curry paste is a southern staple.

Kôw yam A popular breakfast, this dish includes rice topped with sliced herbs, bean sprouts, dried prawns, toasted coconut and powdered red chilli, served with a sour/sweet fish-based sauce.

Pàt sà·đor This popular stir-fry of 'stink beans' with shrimp, garlic, chillies and shrimp paste is both pungent and spicy.

ting, and for harassed parents there's a kids playground in the front garden. Live guitar music from Tuesday to Thursday at 7.30pm.

Prego ITALIAN **$$$**
(Map p182; www.prego-samui.com; mains 280-860B; ⌚noon-11pm) Renovated and zestfully refreshed with a new bar/lounge zone, this cool restaurant serves up tantalising Italian cuisine, with a strong selection of vegetarian dishes, backed up by a tempting wine list.

Hat Lamai

As Samui's second-most populated beach, Hat Lamai has a surprisingly limited assortment of decent eateries when compared to Hat Chaweng next door. Most nights a few noodle and pancake stalls open up around the 'Lady Boxing' bars in the centre of town, and sell dishes from 50B that you can eat at outdoor plastic tables.

Hua Thanon Market MARKET **$**
(Map p178; dishes from 30B; ⌚6am-6pm) Slip into the rhythm of this village market slightly south of Lamai; it's a window into the food ways of southern Thailand. Vendors shoo away the flies from the freshly butchered meat and housewives load bundles of vegetables into their motorcycle baskets. Follow the market road to the row of food shops delivering edible Muslim culture: chicken *biryani*, fiery curries or toasted rice with coconut, bean sprouts, lemon grass and dried shrimp.

Lamai Day Market MARKET **$**
(dishes from 30B; ⌚6am-8pm) Lamai's market is a hive of activity, selling food necessities and takeaway food. Visit the covered area to pick up fruit or to see vendors shredding coconuts to make coconut milk. Or hunt down the ice-cream seller for homemade coconut ice cream. It's next door to a petrol station.

Pad Thai THAI **$**
(www.manathai.com/samui/phad-thai; mains from 70B; ⌚11am-11pm) On the corner of the huge Manathai hotel, this highly affordable, semi alfresco and smart restaurant is a fantastic choice for stir-fried and soup noodles, rounded off with a coconut ice cream.

Tandoori Nights INDIAN **$**
(mains from 150B; ⌚11am-11.30pm) The set meals at this welcoming Indian restaurant will only set you back 190B for a vegetable curry, soft drink and a papadum; otherwise select your spice level from the à la carte menu or take a deep breath and order up the eye-watering lamb vindaloo (290B).

★**La Fabrique** BAKERY **$$**
(set breakfasts from 120B; ⌚6.30am-10.30pm; 📶) Ceiling fans chop the air and service is snappy and helpful at this roomy French-styled boulangerie/patisserie away from the main drag, near Wat Lamai on Rte 4169. Choose from fresh bread, croissants, gratins, baguettes, meringues, yoghurts, pastries or unusually good set breakfasts that include fresh fruit and well-cooked eggs. Wash it down with a selection of coffees or teas. There's a smaller and noisier branch in Chaweng.

Baobab FRENCH **$$**
(☎084 838 3040; Hat Lamai; mains 150-380B; ⌚8.30am-6pm) Grab a free beach towel and crash out on a sun lounger after a full meal at breezy Baobab, or have a massage next door, but seize one of the beach tables (if you can). You'll need two hands to turn over the hefty menu, with its all-day breakfasts, French/Thai dishes, grills, pastas and popular specials, including red tuna steak (350B).

With the sound of the surf and lovely views, it's frequently a sell-out.

Radiance INTERNATIONAL **$$**
(meals 100-400B; ⌚7am-10pm; 📶🖉) Even if you're not staying at the Spa Resort, or not even a vegetarian for that matter, healthy food rarely tastes this good. It's not all brown rice: you'll find everything from an amazing raw *thom kha* (coconut green curry soup) to chocolate smoothies that can jive with anyone's dietary restrictions. Plus the semi-outdoor beach-side setting is tranquil, relaxing and unpretentious.

The Dining Room FRENCH **$$$**
(www.rockyresort.com/en/dining/dining-room; dishes 300-950B; ⌚lunch & dinner) The signature beef Rossini at this beachfront restaurant at Rocky's Resort is like sending your taste buds on a Parisian vacation as the views pop you into seventh heaven.

Choeng Mon & Big Buddha Beach (Hat Bang Rak)

Choeng Mon's lively main drag that runs parallel to this main northern beach has lots of eating options, although price tags are high even without the beach view. There are fewer eating options around Big Buddha Beach, west of Choeng Mon, and the setting is less glamorous, but prices are more reasonable.

Antica Locanda ITALIAN $$

(Map p184; ☎077 245163; www.anticasamui.com; Hat Bang Rak; mains from 240B; ⌚1-11pm; 📶) This friendly trattoria has pressed white tablecloths and caskets of Italian wine. Try the *vongole alla marinara* (clams in white wine; 240B), but also consider the succulent specials of the day.

Catcantoo INTERNATIONAL $$

(Map p184; www.catcantoo.com; Hat Bang Rak; mains 90-350B; ⌚9am-2am) Enjoy good-value breakfasts in the morning, succulent ribs at noon, or shooting pool later in the day.

★**Dining On The Rocks** ASIAN FUSION $$$

(Map p178; ☎077 245678; reservations-samui@sixsenses.com; Choeng Mon; menus from 2200B; ⌚5-10pm) Samui's ultimate dining experience takes place on nine cantilevered verandahs of weathered teak and bamboo that yawn over the gulf. After sunset (and wine), guests feel like they're dining on a barge set adrift on a starlit sea. Each dish on the six-course set menu is the brainchild of the cooks who regularly experiment with taste, texture and temperature.

If you're celebrating a special occasion, you'll have to book well in advance if you want to sit at 'table 99' (the honeymooners' table) positioned on a private terrace, complete with surprise menu. Dining On The Rocks is at the isolated Six Senses Samui. The bar and lounge opens an hour earlier, with dining starting at 6pm.

Bo Phut

The Fisherman's Village is the nicest setting for a meal but you'll find heaps of cheaper options on the road leading inland towards the main road.

The Hut THAI $

(Map p184; mains 60-550B; ⌚1-10pm) Basic, reasonably priced Thai specialities share space with more expensive fresh seafood and Western treats here, but the dozen or so tables fill fast so get here early or late if you don't want to wait. If you're a fisherman this is the place to get your own catch cooked up.

Karma Sutra INTERNATIONAL $$

(Map p184; mains 180-700B; ⌚8am-2am; 📶) A haze of purples and pillows, beanbags and low tables, this charming chow spot straddles the heart of Bo Phut's Fisherman's Village and serves up good international and Thai eats, with alfresco seating by the wayside.

69 THAI FUSION $$

(Map p184; mains from 149B; ⌚1-10pm; 📶) The simply roaring roadside setting puts it on the wrong side of the tracks and the dated, eclectic decor is looking rather limp and tired; that said, almost unanimous rave reviews for its creative twists on Thai favourites make this a really popular choice.

★**Chez François** FRENCH $$$

(Map p184; www.facebook.com/chezporte; 33/2 Moo 1 Fisherman's Village; set meal 1700B; ⌚6-11pm Tue-Sat) With no à la carte menu, but a reputation for outstanding cuisine that has sent waves across the culinary map of Ko Samui, Chez François serves a three-course surprise meal. Book ahead using the Facebook page and if you're only on Ko Samui for a few days, book early to get a table. It's tiny (and cash only).

Chez François is hidden away behind a wooden door near a pharmacy.

Shack Bar & Grill STEAK $$$

(Map p184; www.theshackgrillsamui.com; mains 450-800B; ⌚5.30-11pm) The Shack imports the finest cuts of meat from Australia and slathers them in a rainbow of tasty sauces from red wine to blue cheese. Booth seating and jazz over the speakers give the joint a distinctly Western vibe, though you'll find all types of diners coming here to splurge.

Zazen Restaurant ASIAN FUSION $$$

(Map p184; dishes 540-900B, set menu from 1300B; ⌚lunch & dinner) This superb romantic dining experience at the Zazen Resort comes complete with ocean views, dim candle lighting and soft music. Thai dancers animate things on Thursday and Sunday nights from 8pm. Reservations recommended.

Mae Nam & Bang Po

Mae Nam has tonnes of eating options from beachside huts serving a mix of Thai, Western and seafood dishes to classier places tucked along the inland, lily-pad pond-dotted tangle of roads. It's a lovely place to wander and find your own surprises.

Fish Restaurant INTERNATIONAL $

(mains from 50B; ⌚noon-10pm) With elegant Thai tablecloths and a well-priced, tasty menu of Thai seafood and pan-Asian dishes and international appetisers, this popular concrete-floor eatery pulls in a regular stream of diners, although portions are a bit on the teeny side and the relaxing music edges into muzak territory.

Bang Po Seafood SEAFOOD $$

(Bang Po; dishes from 100B; ⌚dinner) A meal at Bang Po Seafood is a test for the taste buds. It's one of the only restaurants that serves traditional Ko Samui fare: recipes call for ingredients such as raw sea urchin roe, baby octopus, sea water, coconut and local turmeric.

John's Garden Restaurant THAI $$

(Map p178; ☎077 247694; www.johnsgardensamui.com; mains from 160B; ⌚1-10pm) This delightful garden restaurant is a picture, with tables slung out beneath bamboo and palms and carefully cropped hedges. The signature dish on the Thai and European menu is the excellent massaman chicken. Mosquito repellent is generally provided, but pack some in case. It's particularly romantic when lantern-lit at night, so reserve ahead.

Farmer INTERNATIONAL $$$

(Map p178; ☎077 447222; Mae Nam; mains 350-1000B; ⌚lunch & dinner) Magically set in front of a photogenic rice field, fantastic Farmer is a choice selection, especially when the candlelight flickers on a starry night. The mostly European-inspired food is lovely and well-presented, there's a free pick-up for nearby beaches and service is attentive. At the time of writing, new resort villas were being constructed around the rice field.

West & South Coasts

The quiet west coast features some of the best seafood on Samui. Na Thon has a giant **day market** on Th Thawi Ratchaphakdi – it's worth stopping by to grab some snacks before your ferry ride.

Ging Pagarang SEAFOOD $

(Thong Tanote; meals from 50B; ⌚11.30am-8pm) Locals know this is one of the island's best beachside places to sample authentic Samui-style seafood. It's simple and family-run, but the food and views are extraordinary. Try the sea algae salad with crab, fried dried octopus with coconut or the spectacular fried fish or prawns with lemon grass.

Five Islands SEAFOOD $$$

(Map p178; ☎077 415359; www.thefiveislands-samui.com; dishes 250-790B; ⌚noon-11pm) Five Islands offers a unique (yet pricey) eating experience. First, a long-tail boat (tours for two including meal 7500B to 9250B) will take you out into the turquoise sea to visit the haunting Five Sister Islands where you'll learn about the ancient art of harvesting bird nests to make bird's-nest soup, a Chinese delicacy. When you return, a deluxe meal is waiting for you on the beach.

Lunch tours departs around 10am, and the dinner programs leave around 3pm. Customers are also welcome to dine without going on the tour and vice versa but if you want the tour, book two days in advance.

Drinking & Nightlife

Samui's biggest party spot is, without a doubt, noisy Hat Chaweng. Lamai and Bo Phut come in second and third respectively, while the rest of the island is generally quiet, as the drinking is usually focused around self-contained resort bars.

Hat Chaweng & Hat Lamai

Making merry in Chaweng is a piece of cake. Most places are open until 2am and there are a few places that go strong all night long.

Every Saturday night around dinner hours it's lady boxing time at Lamai's thus named 'Lady Boxing' bars, when two bar girls duke it out in the ring after weeks of training. The rest of the week the girls writhe and dance at these central open-air bars, which is particularly depressing when there are no clients.

Beach Republic BAR

(www.beachrepublic.com; 176/34 Mu 4, Hat Lamai; ⌚7am-11pm) Recognised by its thatch-patched awnings, Beach Republic could be the poster child of a made-for-TV, beachside, booze swilling holiday. There's a wading pool, lounge chairs, an endless cocktail list and even a hotel if you never, ever want to leave the party. The Sunday brunches here are legendary.

Ark Bar BAR

(Map p182; www.ark-bar.com; Hat Chaweng; ☎7am-2am;) Drinks are dispensed from the multicoloured bar to an effusive crowd, guests recline on loungers on the beach, and the party is on day and night.

Bar Solo BAR

(Map p182; Hat Chaweng) Bar Solo's bubbly party mood, decent DJs and evening drink specials lure in front-loaders preparing for a late, late night at the dance clubs on Soi Solo and Soi Green Mango.

Tropical Murphy's Irish BAR

(Map p182; Hat Chaweng; ⌚8am-2am; 📶) Come night-time, the live music kicks on and this place turns into the most popular Irish bar on Ko Samui (yes, there are a few). On the menu, there's steak-and-kidney pie, fish and chips, Ulster Fry (breakfast) and lamb chops and Irish stew (mains 60B to 300B).

Green Mango BAR
(Map p182; ww.thegreenmangoclub.com; Hat Chaweng) This place is so popular it has an entire soi named after it. Samui's favourite power drinking house is very big, very loud and very *fa·ràng*. Green Mango has blazing lights, expensive drinks and masses of sweaty bodies swaying to dance music.

Reggae Pub BAR
(Map p182; Hat Chaweng; 6pm-3am) This fortress of fun sports an open-air dance floor with music spun by foreign DJs. It's a towering two-storey affair with long bars, pool tables and a live-music stage. The whole place doubles as a shrine to Bob Marley; it's often empty early in the evening, getting going around midnight. The long road up to Reggae Pub is ladyboy central.

Northern & West Coast Beaches

Woo Bar BAR
(Map p184; Mae Nam; 11am-1am;) With serious wow factor, the W Retreat's signature lobby bar gives the word 'swish' a whole new meaning with cushion-clad pods of seating plunked in the middle of an expansive infinity pool that stretches out over the infinite horizon. This is, without a doubt, the best place on Samui for sunset cocktails. Mojitos are free-flow on Thursday nights (1300B).

Nikki Beach BAR
(Map p178; 077 914500; www.nikkibeach.com/kohsamui; Lipa Noi;) The acclaimed luxury brand brings international *savoir faire* to the secluded west coast of Ko Samui. Think: haute cuisine, chic decor and jet-setters. Themed brunch and dinner specials keep the masses coming throughout the week, and sleek villa accommodation is also on offer.

Coco Tam's BAR
(Map p184; Bo Phut; shisha pipes 500B; 5pm-1am) Plop yourself on a beanbag on the sand, order a cocktail served in a jar and take a toke on a shisha (water pipe). It's a bit pricey, but this boho, beach bum–chic spot oozes relaxation. There are fire dancers most nights.

Billabong Surf Club BAR
(Map p184; Bo Phut; 9am-1am;) Billabong's all about Aussie Rules football – it's playing on the TV and the walls are smothered with signed shirts and memorabilia from Down Undah. There are great views of Ko Pha-Ngan and hearty portions of ribs and chops to go with your draught beer.

Entertainment

Paris Follies Cabaret CABARET
(Map p182; Hat Chaweng; 8pm-midnight) This dazzling and fun cabaret offers one-hour *gà·teu·i* (ladyboys; also spelled *kàthoey*) cabaret every night at 8pm, 9pm, 10pm and 11pm and attracts a mixed clientele of both sexes. Admission is free, but you need to buy a drink (around 390B).

Shopping

Central Festival SHOPPING CENTRE
(Map p182; 11am-11pm) This new monster-mall is stuffed with shops and restaurants.

Island Books BOOKS
(9am-7pm) Tucked away on a lane off Rte 4169 and run by Liverpudlian Paul, Island Books in Lamai has the largest selection of used books on the island.

Bookazine BOOKS
(Map p182; 077 413616; Hat Chaweng; 11am-10pm) Chaweng Chain outlet selling new books, magazines and Lonely Planet guides.

Information

DANGERS & ANNOYANCES

The rate of road accident fatalities on Ko Samui is quite high. This is mainly due to the large number of tourists who rent motorcycles only to find out that the winding roads, sudden tropical rains and frenzied traffic can be lethal. If you decide to rent a motorcycle, protect yourself by wearing a helmet, and ask for one that has a plastic visor. Be warned that if you don't have an international driving licence, you may have problems in the event of an accident and your insurer might not cover you.

Beach vendors are registered with the government and should all be wearing a numbered jacket. No peddler should cause an incessant disturbance – seek assistance if this occurs.

A car bomb exploded in the Central Festival shopping centre in 2015, wounding six people.

EMERGENCY

Tourist Police (077 421281, emergency 1155) Based at the south of Na Thon.

IMMIGRATION

Located about 2km south of Na Thon is Ko Samui's **Immigration Office** (077 421069; 8.30am-noon & 1-4.30pm Mon-Fri). Officials here tend to issue the minimum rather than maximum visa extensions. During our visits here we've watched dozens of tourists wait through exhausting lines only to be curtly denied an extension for no particular reason. On a particularly bad day expect extensions to take the entire afternoon.

INTERNET ACCESS

Wi-fi is widespread at most accommodation choices, restaurants and bars. You may have to pay for wi-fi access at some high-end hotels, but it is provided free at most midrange and budget places.

MEDIA

Siam Map Company (www.siammap.com) Puts out quarterly booklets including a *Spa Guide*, *Dining Guide*, and an annual directory, which lists thousands of companies and hotels on the island. Its *Siam Map Company Samui Guide Map* is free and easily found throughout the island.

Samui Navigator (www.samuinavigator.com) This pamphlet is worth a look.

Samui Guide (www.samuiguide.com) This guide looks more like a magazine and features mostly restaurants and attractions.

MEDICAL SERVICES

Ko Samui has four private hospitals, all near Chaweng's Tesco Lotus supermarket on the east coast (where most of the tourists tend to gather). The government hospital (Samui Hospital) in Na Thon has seen significant improvements in the past couple of years but the service is still a bit grim because funding is based on the number of Samui's legal residents (which doesn't take into account the many illegal Myanmar workers).

Bandon International Hospital (☎077 245236, emergency 077 425748)

Bangkok Samui Hospital (Map p182; ☎077 429500, emergency 077 429555) Your best bet for just about any medical problem.

Hyperbaric Chamber (☎077 427427; Big Buddha Beach) The island's dive medicine specialists.

Samui International Hospital (Map p182; ☎077 230782; www.sih.co.th; Hat Chaweng) Emergency ambulance service is available 24 hours and credit cards are accepted. It's near the Amari Resort in Hat Chaweng.

MONEY

Changing money isn't a problem on the east and north coasts, and in Na Thon. Multiple banks and foreign-exchange booths offer daily services and there's an ATM every 200m. You should not have to pay credit card fees as you do on Ko Tao.

POST

In several parts of the island there are privately run post-office branches charging a small commission. You can almost always leave your stamped mail with your accommodation.

Main Post Office Near the TAT office; not always reliable.

TOURIST INFORMATION

Tourism Authority of Thailand (TAT; ☎077 420504; Na Thon; ⊙8.30am-4.30pm)

Getting There & Away

AIR

Ko Samui's **airport** (www.samuiairportonline.com) is in the northeast of the island near Big Buddha Beach. **Bangkok Airways** (www.bangkokair.com) operates flights roughly every 30 minutes between Samui and Bangkok's Suvarnabhumi International Airport (50 minutes). Bangkok Airways also flies direct from Samui to Phuket, Pattaya, Chiang Mai, Singapore, Kuala Lumpur, Hong Kong and other cities in Southeast Asia. **Firefly** (www.fireflyz.com.my) operates direct flights from Ko Samui to Kuala Lumpur's Subang airport and has three flights per week to Penang.

There is a **Bangkok Airways Office** (Map p182; ☎077 420519, 077 420512) in Hat Chaweng and another at the airport. The first (at 6am) and last (10pm) flights of the day are always the cheapest.

During the high season, make your flight reservations far in advance as seats often sell out. If the Samui flights are full, try flying into Surat Thani from Bangkok and taking the short ferry ride to Samui instead. Flights to Surat Thani are generally cheaper than a direct flight to the island, although they are much more of a hassle.

BOAT

To reach Samui, the main piers on the mainland are Ao Ban Don, Tha Thong, Don Sak and Chumphon – Tha Thong (in central Surat) and Don Sak being the most common. On Samui, the three oft-used ports are Na Thon, Mae Nam and Big Buddha Beach. Expect complimentary taxi transfers with high-speed ferry services.

To the Mainland

There are frequent boat departures between Samui and the mainland. Two options are the high-speed Lomprayah (p229; 450B), which departs from Na Thon, and the slower, stinkier Raja (☎022 768 2112; www.rajaferryport.com) car ferry (120B) to Don Sak, which departs from Thong Yang. Ferries take one to five hours, depending on the boat. A couple of these departures can connect with the train station in Phun Phin (for a nominal extra fee). The slow night boat to Samui (300B) leaves from central Surat Thani each night at 11pm, reaching Na Thon around 5am. It returns from Na Thon at 9pm, arriving at around 3am. Watch your bags on this boat.

To Ko Pha-Ngan & Ko Tao

There are almost a dozen daily departures between Ko Samui and Thong Sala on the west coast of Ko Pha-Ngan and many of these continue on to Ko Tao. These leave from the Na Thon, Mae Nam or Big Buddha Beach pier, take from 20 minutes to one hour and cost 200B to 300B to Ko Pha-Ngan, depending on the boat.

To go directly to Hat Rin, the *Haad Rin Queen* goes back and forth between Hat Rin and Big Buddha Beach four times a day, with double the number of sailings the day after the Full Moon Party and an extra trip laid on at 7.30am the same day. The voyage takes 50 minutes, costs 200B and the last boat leaves at 6.30pm.

Also for Hat Rin and the more remote east coast beaches of Ko Pha-Ngan, the small and rickety *Thong Nai Pan Express* runs once a day at noon from Mae Hat on Ko Samui to Hat Rin and then up the east coast, stopping at all the beaches as far as Thong Nai Pan Noi. Prices range from 200B to 400B, depending on the destination. The boat won't run in bad weather.

BUS & TRAIN

A bus–ferry combo is more convenient than a train–ferry package for getting to Ko Samui because you don't have to switch transportation in Phun Phin. However, the trains are much more comfortable and spacious – especially at night. If you prefer the train, you can get off at Chumphon and catch the Lomprayah catamaran service the rest of the way.

Several services offer these bus–boat combo tickets, the fastest and most comfortable being the Lomprayah which has two daily departures from Bangkok at 6am and 9pm and two from Samui to Bangkok at 8am and 12.30pm. The total voyage takes about 13½ hours and costs between 1400B and 1450B.

MOTORBIKE RENTAL SCAMS

Even if you escape unscathed from a motorbike riding experience, some shops will claim that you damaged your rental and will try to extort some serious cash. The best way to avoid this is to take copious photos of your vehicle (cars included) at the time of rental, making sure the person renting you the vehicle sees you do it (they will be less likely to make false claims against you if they know you have photos). If they still make a claim against you, keep your cool. Losing your temper won't help you win the argument and could significantly escalate the problem. The situation is just as bad on Ko Pha-Ngan, a bit less so on Ko Tao.

If things get really bad call the **tourist police** (p192), not the regular police.

Getting Around

You can rent motorcycles (and bicycles) from almost every resort on the island. The going rate is 150B to 200B per day, but for longer periods try to negotiate a better rate.

Drivers of *sŏrng·tăa·ou* (pick-up trucks) love to try to overcharge you, so it's always best to ask a third party for current rates, as they can change with the season. These vehicles run regularly during daylight hours. It's about 50B to travel between beaches, and no more than 100B to travel halfway across the island. Figure about 20B for a five-minute ride on a motorcycle taxi.

Taxi service is quite chaotic due to the plethora of cabs. In the past taxi fares were unwieldy; these days prices are more standardised across the islands (though fares are still ridiculously inflated compared to Bangkok). Taxis typically charge around 500B for an airport transfer. Some Hat Chaweng travel agencies can arrange minibus taxis for less.

Ko Pha-Ngan เกาะพงัน

POP 12,500

Hippie-at-heart Ko Pha-Ngan has become so synonymous with the massive Full Moon Party on Hat Rin that the rest of the island gets eclipsed, and forgotten. This is a massive shame, as there's so much else to enjoy and explore. For one week a month, the island sees some 30,000 people cramming one beach partying their minds out and then, off they all go on the next boat, and the beaches and accommodations are left half empty. It's at this time, however, that budget-conscious serenity seekers can retreat into a fog of the backpacker days of old and nab a fan-cooled beach shack from 400B (on the northern beaches at least). This may change overnight with the future opening of the island's airport, but for now this exceptionally gorgeous island is in a sleepy sweet spot where you can even find a solid bungalow on Hat Rin for around 1000B outside of full moon mania.

Ko Pha-Ngan has plenty to offer the more clean-cut, comfort-seeking traveller as well; its peace and quiet make it a great choice for families. Remote Hat Thong Nai Pan Noi in particular feels like a miniature version of Ko Samui with its elegant resorts fronted by rows of cushion-clad beach loungers, while the easier-to-access west coast has attracted a handful of new upscale resorts and a few older places have been revamped to attract a more ritzy market.

Ko Pha-Ngan

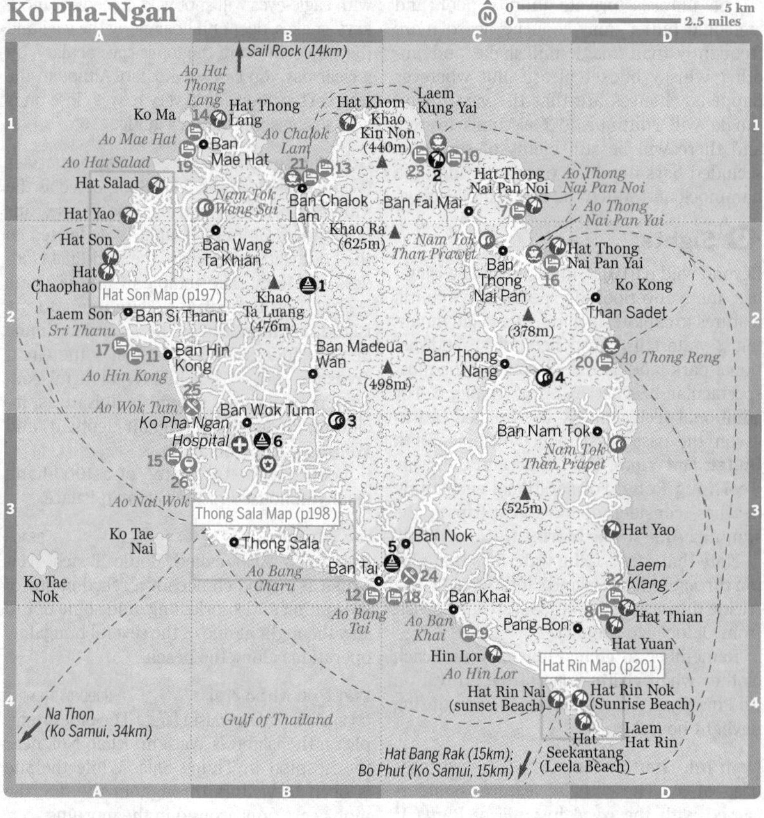

Ko Pha-Ngan

Sights

1 Guanyin Temple ... B2
2 Hat Khuat ... C1
Ko Pha-Ngan's tallest Yang Na Yai Tree ... (see 5)
3 Nam Tok Phaeng ... B3
4 Nam Tok Than Sadet ... C2
5 Wat Pho ... C3
6 Wat Phu Khao Noi ... B3

Sleeping

7 Anantara Rasananda ... C1
8 Bamboo Hut ... D4
Barcelona ... (see 8)
9 Bay Lounge & Resort ... C4
Boom's Cafe Bungalows ... (see 9)
10 Bottle Beach II ... C1
11 Chills Resort ... A2
12 Divine Comedie ... B3
13 Fantasea ... B1
14 Island View Cabana ... B1
15 Kupu Kupu Phangan Beach Villa ... A3
16 Longtail Beach Resort ... C2
17 Loyfa Natural Resort ... A2
18 Mac Bay ... C3
19 Mae Hat Beach View Resort ... A1
20 Mai Pen Rai ... D2
21 Mandalai ... B1
Pariya Resort & Villas ... (see 8)
22 Sanctuary ... D3
23 Smile Bungalows ... C1

Eating

Bamboo Hut ... (see 8)
Cucina Italiana ... (see 21)
24 Fabio's ... C3
Fisherman's Restaurant ... (see 12)
25 JJ's Restaurant ... A2
Sanctuary ... (see 22)

Drinking & Nightlife

26 Amsterdam ... A3
Flip Flop Pharmacy ... (see 16)
Jam ... (see 25)

The phrases 'private infinity pool' and 'personal butler' may soon be heard more frequently than 'magic milkshake' and 'another whisky bucket please'. But whatever happens, chances are that the vast inland jungle will continue to feel undiscovered, and there will be still plenty of stunning, secluded bays in which you can string up a hammock and watch the tide roll in. Enjoy!

Sights

Beyond wild partying, this large jungle island has many overlooked, spectacular natural features to explore, including tree-clad mountains, waterfalls, unspoiled forest and national park land as well as some of the most spectacular beaches in all of Thailand. For additional seclusion, try the isolated beaches on the east coast, which include **Than Sadet**, **Hat Yuan**, **Hat Thian** and the teeny **Ao Thong Reng**. For additional enchanting beaches, consider doing a day trip to the stunning **Ang Thong Marine National Park**.

Note that most of the waterfalls that glisten throughout the island's interior slow to a trickle during the dry season, so aim to visit from October to January.

Remember to change out of your beach clothes when visiting one of the 20 wát on Ko Pha-Ngan. Most temples are open during daylight hours.

Nam Tok Than Sadet WATERFALL
(Map p195) These falls feature boulders carved with the royal insignia of Rama V, Rama VII and Rama IX. King Rama V enjoyed this hidden spot so much that he returned over a dozen times between 1888 and 1909. The river waters of Khlong Than Sadet are now considered sacred and used in royal ceremonies. Also near the eastern coast, **Than Prawet** is a series of chutes that snake inland for approximately 2km.

Nam Tok Phaeng WATERFALL
(Map p195) Nam Tok Phaeng is protected by a national park; this waterfall is a pleasant reward after a short, but rough, hike. After the waterfall (dry out of season), it's a further exhilarating 15-minute climb up a root-choked path (along the Phaeng-Domsila Nature Trail) to the fantastic Domsila Viewpoint, with ranging views. The two- to three-hour trail then continues on through the jungle in a loop, past other waterfalls before bringing you back. Take water and good shoes.

It's possible to continue up to Khao Ra, the highest mountain on the island at 625m. Those with eagle-eyes will spot wild crocodiles, monkeys, snakes, deer and boar along the way, and the viewpoint from the top is spectacular – on a clear day you can see Ko Tao. Although the trek isn't arduous, it is very easy to lose one's way, so consider finding a guide.

Guanyin Temple BUDDHIST TEMPLE
(Map p195; 40B; ⏲7am-6pm) Signposted as the 'Goddess of Mercy Shrine Joss House', this fascinating Chinese temple is dedicated to the bodhisattva Guanyin, the Buddhist Goddess of Mercy. The temple's Chinese name (普岳山) on the entrance gate refers to the island in China that is the legendary home of the goddess. The main hall – the Great Treasure Hall – is a highly colourful confection, containing several bodhisattvas, including Puxian (seated on an elephant) and Wenshu (sitting on a lion).

Look out for the statue of a 1000-hand Guanyin, housed in the Guanyin Palace.

Hat Khuat BEACH
(Map p195) Also called Bottle Beach, Hat Khuat is a good choice for a relaxing day of swimming and snorkelling, and some opt to stay the night at one of the several bungalow operations along the beach.

Wat Phu Khao Noi BUDDHIST TEMPLE
(Map p195; ⏲dawn-dusk) FREE The oldest temple on the island is Wat Phu Khao Noi, near the hospital in Thong Sala. While the site is open to visitors throughout the day, the monks are only around in the morning.

Ko Pha-Ngan's Tallest Yang Na Yai Tree TREE
(Map p195) Near Wat Pho, Ko Pha-Ngan's tallest Yang Na Yai (dipterocarpus alatus; ยางนา) is an astonishing sight as you veer round the bend for the diminutive Wat Nok temple, a small shrine tucked away in the greenery. These colossal giants grow to over 50m in height and, for tree lovers, are real beauties. This imposing specimen is often garlanded with colourful ribbons.

Wat Pho BUDDHIST TEMPLE
(Map p195; ⏲herbal sauna 1-7pm) FREE With a dazzling gateway and extensive temple grounds, Wat Pho, near Ban Tai, has a **herbal sauna** (admission 50B) accented with natural lemon grass. When we last visited, a new temple hall was under construction.

Wat Khao Tham BUDDHIST TEMPLE
(Map p198; www.kowtahm.com; ⏲dawn-dusk) FREE With resident female monks, Wat

Khao Tham, near Ban Tai, sits among the trees high on a hill. A bulletin board details a meditation retreat at the temple; see the website for details. Don't miss the temple hall at the top of the steps with the colourful glass, housing a sleeping Buddha.

Activities

With Ko Tao, the high-energy diving behemoth, just a few kilometres away, Ko Pha-Ngan enjoys a much quieter, more laid-back diving scene focused on fun diving rather than certifications. A recent drop in Open Water certification prices has made local prices competitive with Ko Tao. Group sizes tend to be smaller on Ko Pha-Ngan since the island has fewer divers in general.

Like the other islands in the Samui Archipelago, Pha-Ngan has several small reefs dispersed around the island. The clear favourite snorkelling spot is **Ko Ma**, a small island in the northwest connected to Ko Pha-Ngan by a charming sandbar. There are also some rock reefs of interest on the eastern side of the island.

A major perk of diving from Ko Pha-Ngan is the proximity to **Sail Rock** (Hin Bai), the best dive site in the Gulf of Thailand and a veritable beacon for whale sharks. This large pinnacle lies about 14km north of the island. An abundance of corals and large tropical fish can be seen at depths of 10m to 30m, and there's a rocky vertical swim-through called 'The Chimney'.

Dive shops on Ko Tao sometimes visit Sail Rock; however, the focus tends to be more on shallow reefs (for newbie divers) and the deep-dive waters at Chumphon Pinnacle. The most popular trips departing from Ko Pha-Ngan are three-site day trips which stop at **Chumphon Pinnacle**, Sail Rock and one of the other premier sites in the area. These three-stop trips cost from around 3650B to 4000B and include a full lunch. Two-dive trips to Sail Rock will set you back around 2500B to 2800B.

Lotus Diving and Haad Yao Divers are the main operators on the island with a solid reputation.

Hiking and snorkelling day trips to **Ang Thong Marine National Park** generally depart from Ko Samui, but recently tour operators are starting to shuttle tourists from Ko Pha-Ngan as well. Ask at your accommodation for details about boat trips as companies often come and go due to unstable petrol prices.

Hat Son

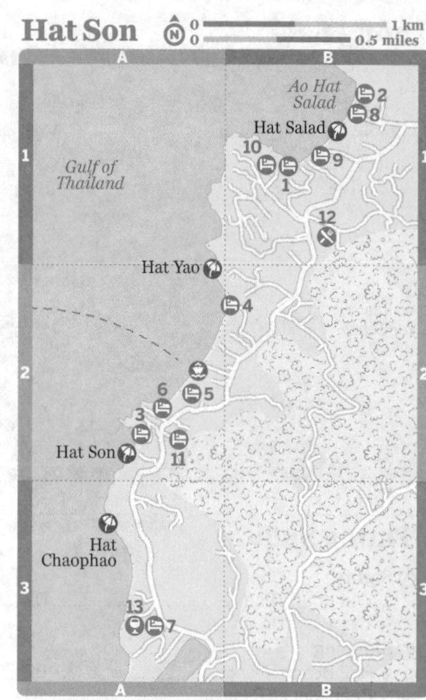

Hat Son

Sleeping

1 Cookies Salad B1
2 Green Papaya B1
3 Haad Son Resort & Restaurant A2
4 Haad Yao Bay View Resort B2
5 Haad Yao See Through Boutique Resort A2
6 High Life A2
7 Pha-Ngan Paragon A3
8 Salad Beach Resort B1
9 Salad Hut B1
10 Shiralea B1
11 Tantawan Bungalows A2

Eating

12 Peppercorn B1

Drinking & Nightlife

13 Belgian Beer Bar A3

Many of the larger accommodation options can hook you up with a variety of aquatic equipment such as jet skis and kayaks, and the friendly staff at Backpackers Information Centre (p210) can attend to any of your other water-sports needs.

Chaloklum Diving DIVING

(☎077374025; www.chaloklum-diving.com; ⏰6am-8pm) One of the more established dive shops on the island (based on the main drag in

Thong Sala

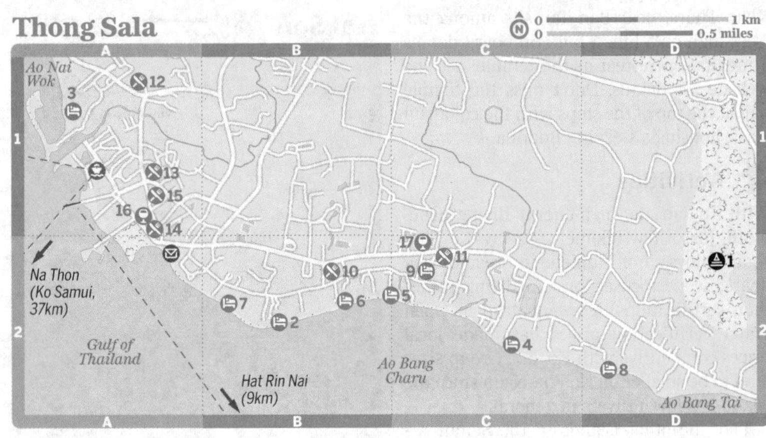

Thong Sala

Sights

1 Wat Khao Tham D2

Sleeping

2 B52 Beach Resort B2
3 Baan Manali Resort A1
4 Charu Bay Villas C2
5 Coco Garden B2
6 Hacienda Resort B2
7 Lime n Soda B2
8 Milky Bay Resort D2
9 V-View Beach Resort C2

Eating

10 Ando Loco B2
11 Food Factory C2
12 Mason's Arms A1
13 Night Market A1
14 Nira's A1
15 Vintage Burgers A1

Drinking & Nightlife

16 Harp A1
17 Outlaws Saloon C2

Ban Chalok Lam) has quality equipment and high standards.

Lotus Diving DIVING
(☎077 374142; www.lotusdiving.com) This dive centre gets the thumbs up from divers. Trips can be booked at its Ban Chalok Lam office, or at the Backpackers Information Centre.

Haad Yao Divers DIVING
(☎086 279 3085; www.haadyaodivers.com; Hat Yao) Established in 1997, this dive operator has garnered a strong reputation by maintaining European standards of safety and customer service.

Wake Up WAKEBOARDING
(☎087 283 6755; www.wakeupwakeboarding.com; ⏲Jan-Oct) Jamie passes along his infinite wakeboarding wisdom to eager wannabes at his water sports school in Chalok Lam. Fifteen minutes of 'air time' will set you back 1200B, which is excellent value considering you get one-on-one instruction. Kiteboarding, wakeskating and waterskiing sessions also available.

Jungle Gym GYM
(Map p201; Hat Rin) One of several Thai boxing places on Ko Pha-Ngan, this very conveniently located gym was one of the island's first and also offers yoga and well-maintained fitness equipment.

Tours

Eco Nature Tour TOUR
(☎084 850 6273) This popular outfit offers a selection of island day trips. We suggest the one-day 'safari' including snorkelling, a visit to a Chinese temple, a stunning viewpoint and Nam Tok Phaeng waterfall (1500B). Elephant trekking is also available, but it's worth reading up on the animal welfare issues involved before considering that option. Bookings can be made at its office in Thong Sala or at the Backpackers Information Centre.

Sleeping

Ko Pha-Ngan's legendary history of laid-back revelry has solidified its reputation as *the* stomping ground for the gritty backpacker lifestyle. Even so, many local mainstays have recently collapsed their bamboo huts and constructed newer, sleeker accommodation aimed at the ever-growing legion of 'flashpackers'.

On other parts of the island, new tracts of land are being cleared for Samui-esque five-star resorts. But backpackers fear not – it will still be a while before the castaway lifestyle goes the way of the dodo. For now, Ko Pha-Ngan can revel in having excellent choices to suit every budget. Pha-Ngan also caters to a subculture of seclusion seekers who crave a deserted slice of sand. The northern and eastern coasts offer just that – a place to escape.

Sleeping options start in Hat Rin, move along the southern coast, head up the west side, across the northern beaches and down the quiet eastern shore. The accommodation along the southern coast is the best bang for your baht on Ko Pha-Ngan, while the west coast is seeing a lot of development. The atmosphere here is a pleasant mix of quiet seclusion and a sociable vibe, although some of the beaches, particularly towards the south, aren't as picturesque as other parts of the island. Price tags are also higher than north or south of here.

Stretching from Chalok Lam to Thong Nai Pan, the dramatic northern coast is a wild jungle with several secluded beaches – it's the most scenic coast on the island.

The east coast is the ultimate hermit hang-out. For many of these refuges, you'll have to hire a boat from Thong Sala, Chalok Lam and Hat Rin, and 4WD taxis from Thong Sala are an option for those that have dirt roads. The *Thong Nai Pan Express* boat runs daily at noon from Hat Mae Nam on Ko Samui, stopping at Hat Rin and the east coast beaches as far as Thong Nai Pan Noi. The boat is a casual, rickety fishing-style vessel and won't run in rough weather.

Hat Rin

The thin peninsula of Hat Rin features three separate beaches. Beautiful blonde Hat Rin Nok (Sunrise Beach) is the epicentre of Full Moon tomfoolery, Hat Rin Nai (Sunset Beach) is the much less impressive stretch of sand on the far side of the tiny promontory, and Hat Seekantang (also known as Hat Leela), just south of Hat Rin Nai, is a smaller, lovely white and more private beach. The three beaches are linked by Ban Hat Rin (Hat Rin Town) – a small inland collection of restaurants and bars. It takes only a few minutes to walk from one beach to another.

Hat Rin sees Thailand's greatest accommodation crunch during the Full Moon festivities. At this time, bungalow operations expect you to stay for a minimum number of days (usually five). If you plan to arrive the day of the party (or even the day before), we strongly suggest booking a room in advance, or else you'll probably have to sleep on the beach (which you might end up doing anyway). A new breed of cattle car–style dorms stack and cram a seemingly impossible number of beds into dark small rooms and shared toilets are few. These start at around 200B outside of the Full Moon chaos then escalate to 650B and up for party times. Even though these grim options have added a significant number of beds to the town, everything still manages to fill up. Check hostel booking websites for dorm bed availability. Catering to the deluge, new operations constantly set up.

Full Mooners can also stay on Ko Samui or other beaches on Ko Pha-Ngan and take speedboat shuttles to access the festivities – prices will depend on how far away you're staying but the money you'll save on staying anywhere besides Hat Rin itself will probably make it worth it. With gory and often fatal accidents monthly, driving on Ko Pha-Ngan during the festivities is an absolutely terrible idea.

Expect room rates to increase by 20% to 300% during Full Moon.

Lighthouse Bungalows BUNGALOW $
(Map p201; ☎077 375075; www.lighthousebungalows.com; Hat Seekantang; bungalows 400-1000B; ❄📶) This outpost perched on the rocks has simple fan options and newer spacious air-con bungalows, all great value and with sweeping views of the sea; plus there's a cushion-clad restaurant/common area and high-season yoga classes. To get there, follow the wooden boardwalk southeast from Hat Leela or take the high road (motorbike). Beware the monthly techno parties (check), unless that's in your wishlist.

Seaview Sunrise BUNGALOW $
(Map p201; www.seaviewsunrise.com; Hat Rin Nok; r 500-1400B; ❄📶) Budget Full Moon revellers who want to sleep inches from the tide: apply here. Some of the options back in the jungle are sombre and musty, but the solid, beachfront models have bright, polished wooden interiors facing onto a line of coconut trees and the sea.

Paradise Bungalows BUNGALOW $
(Map p201; ☎077 375244; Hat Rin Nok; bungalows 1200-4500B;) The world-famous Full Moon Party was first hatched here way back, and the place has been milking it ever since, but the original plot has been divided up and what's left is a rather charmless series of hillside and poolside units and two-storey blocks, with more going up at the time of writing.

Same Same GUESTHOUSE $
(Map p201; ☎077 375200; www.same-same.com; Ban Hat Rin; dm 400B, r 650B;) A sociable spot for Scandinavians during the Full Moon madness, Same Same offers simple but bright rooms and plenty of party fun.

Blue Marine BUNGALOW $$
(Map p201; ☎077 375079; www.bluemarinephangan.com; Hat Rin Nai; bungalows 1000-1200B;) This cluster of identical concrete bungalows with blue tiled roofs surrounds a manicured green lawn; the best have dreamy views over the whitest and cleanest part of quiet Sunset Beach. Every unit is spacious, clean and has air-con, fridge, hot water and TV.

Cocohut Village RESORT $$
(Map p201; ☎077 375368; www.cocohut.com; Hat Seekantang; bungalows incl breakfast 2600-9500B;) This super-social place on a stunning stretch of sand is very popular with Israelis, but prices are high. The most expensive options, including the cliff villas and beachfront bungalows, are some of the best bets in Hat Rin but budget choices are far less appealing. A fantastic buffet breakfast is included in the room rate.

Pha-Ngan Bayshore Resort RESORT $$
(Map p201; ☎077 375224; www.phanganbayshore.com; Hat Rin Nok; r 2300-6000B;) This neat and well-maintained hotel-style operation soaks up an ever-increasing influx of Hat Rin flashpackers. Staff are on the ball and welcoming, while sweeping beach views and a giant swimming pool nudge it into one of the top addresses on Sunrise Beach, especially if you are able to nab a special promotion.

Delight GUESTHOUSE $$
(Map p201; ☎077 375527; www.delightresort.com; Ban Hat Rin; r 800-6400B;) In the centre of Hat Rin, friendly Delight offers some of the best lodging around. Spic-and-span rooms in a Thai-style building come with subtle designer details (such as peacock murals) and are sandwiched between an inviting swimming pool and a lazy lagoon peppered with lily pads.

Tommy Resort RESORT $$
(Map p201; ☎077 375215; www.tommyresort.com; Hat Rin Nok; r incl breakfast 1850-7500B;) Tommy is a trendy address in the heart of Hat Rin, striking a balance between chic boutique and carefree flashpacker hang-out. Wander down to a lovely strip of white sand, past flowering trees, an azure slab of a pool at the heart of things and helpful, obliging staff. Rooms come with air-con, fridge and safe.

Palita Lodge BUNGALOW $$
(Map p201; ☎077 375172, 077 375170; www.palitalodge.com; Hat Rin Nok; bungalows 1800-6400B;) Smack in the heart of the action, family-run Palita is notable for its welcoming service. Spacious concrete bungalows look a bit ramshackle from the outside but the wooden accents and modern design elements make the interiors very comfy. It's on a beachy wedge of sand and the restaurant serves good Thai food. Nonguests can use the pool for 200B.

Sea Breeze Bungalow BUNGALOW $$
(Map p201; ☎077 375162; Ban Hat Rin; bungalows 500-6000B;) Sea Breeze gets a good report card from our readers, and we agree; the labyrinth of secluded hillside cottages is a pleasant retreat for any type of traveller. Several bungalows, poised high on stilts, deliver stunning views of Hat Rin and the sea. There's a big range of options here from fan rooms up and a lovely forested setting.

Sarikantang RESORT $$$
(Map p201; ☎077 375055; www.sarikantang.com; Hat Seekantang; bungalows 2500-5600B;) Cream-coloured cabins, framed with teak posts and lintels, are sprinkled among swaying palms and crumbling winged statuettes on one of Hat Rin's best stretches of beach. Inside, the rooms are an Ikea chic that's not ageing well but still offers a comfy stay.

The Coast RESORT $$$
(Map p201; ☎077 951567; www.thecoastphangan.com; Hat Rin Nai; 3700-10,800B;) This dark-grey, sharp-angled and stylish resort leads to a slim but OK stretch of beach away from the party hub. Swanky room interiors are polished cement and beds topped with white duvets, while an infinity pool overlooks the sea and service pulls out the stops. Hip, cool and minimalist, but comfy.

Hat Rin

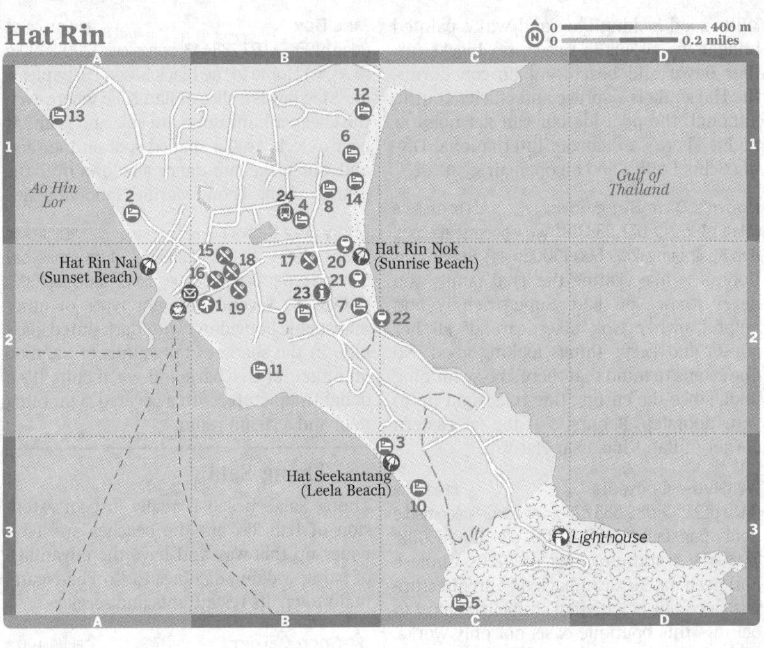

Hat Rin

Activities, Courses & Tours

1 Jungle Gym B2

Sleeping

2 Blue Marine A1
3 Cocohut Village C3
4 Delight B1
5 Lighthouse Bungalows C3
6 Palita Lodge B1
7 Paradise Bungalows B2
8 Pha-Ngan Bayshore Resort B1
9 Same Same B2
10 Sarikantang C3
11 Sea Breeze Bungalow B2
12 Seaview Sunrise B1
13 The Coast A1
14 Tommy Resort B1

Eating

15 Lazy House B2
16 Lucky Crab B2
17 Matt's Joint B2
18 Monna Lisa B2
19 Om Ganesh B2

Drinking & Nightlife

20 Cactus Bar B2
21 Drop-In Bar B2
22 Rock C2
Sunrise (see 8)
Tommy (see 14)

Information

23 Backpackers Information Centre B2

Transport

24 Sǒrng•tǎa•ou to Thong Sala B1

Ban Khai to Ban Tai

The waters at Ban Tai tend to be shallow and opaque, especially during low season, but lodging options are well-priced compared to other parts of the island, and you're close to Thong Sala and not too far from Hat Rin. Like Ban Tai, Ban Khai's beaches aren't the most stunning, but the accommodation is cheap and there are beautiful views of Ang Thong Marine National Park in the distance.

These beaches are where many of the moon-but-not-full-moon parties happen so even if your resort seems quiet, there's probably some boozed-up action nearby.

Hacienda Resort BUNGALOW $
(Map p198; ☎077 238825; www.beachresorthacienda.com; dm 300B, r 500-1500B; ❄📶🏊)

With good-looking blue and white painted bungalows, rooms in two-storey blocks further down and beachfront air-con dorms, the Hacienda is a spruce and efficient outfit, although the poolside bar can get noisy at night. There's a Phangan International Diving School office and an open air gym.

Boom's Cafe Bungalows BUNGALOW **$**
(Map p195; 077 238318; www.boomscafe.com; Ban Khai; bungalows 600-1000B;) Staying at Boom's is like visiting the Thai family you never knew you had. Super-friendly and helpful owner Nok takes care of all her guests and keeps things looking good. No one seems to mind that there's no swimming pool, since the curling tide rolls right up to your doorstep. Boom's is at the far eastern corner of Ban Khai, near Hat Rin.

★ **Divine Comedie** RESORT **$$**
(Map p195; 080 885 8789; www.ledivinecomedie.com; Ban Tai; r 1900-3600B, ste 3100-6900B;) A stunning mix of 1920s Chinese and perhaps Mexican hacienda architecture with a colour palette that shifts from mint to ochre – this boutique oasis not only works, it's beguiling. Junior suites have rooftop terraces, the elongated pool runs to the slim beach and there's an on-site restaurant serving Myanmar specialities.

V-View Beach Resort BUNGALOW **$$**
(Map p198; 077 377436; r 600-2100B;) An air of seclusion settles over this beach resort and although the sea can be a bit swampy, there are hammocks galore and a fine pool, decent bungalows and a helpful owner.

B52 Beach Resort BUNGALOW **$$**
(Map p198; www.b52-beach-resort-phangan.info; bungalows 1500-4200B;) It doesn't cost a bomb at B52's campus of Thai-styled bungalows sporting plenty of thatch, polished concrete floors and rustic tropical tree trunks leading down to the sea.

Bay Lounge & Resort RESORT **$$**
(Map p195; 077 377892; www.bayloungeresort.com; Ban Khai; bungalows incl breakfast 3200-3700B;) On a private white nugget of beach sandwiched by jungle-topped boulders, this is an intimate, chic choice. Bungalows mingle with the natural surroundings yet inside look quite urban with distressed concrete and modern art. It's midway between Hat Rin's Full Moon Party and the Half Moon Party in Ban Khai – the resort offers transport to each. Check-out time is late at 1pm.

Mac Bay BUNGALOW **$$**
(Map p195; 077 238443; bungalows 1200-8500B;) Home to the Black Moon Party, pleasant Mac Bay is a slice of Ban Khai where even the cheaper bungalows are spic and span. At beer o'clock, grab a shaded spot on the sand and watch the sun dance shadows over the islands of Ang Thong Marine National Park.

Milky Bay Resort RESORT **$$$**
(Map p198; 077 238566; http://milkybaythailand.com; Ban Tai; bungalows 1800-13,200B; @) Several different types of minimalist chic bungalows with dark tinted glass hide in the shade of tall stands of bamboo on a floor of tree bark and wood chip. It's a delightful picture, with a covered swimming pool and a steam room.

Thong Sala

Thong Sala's beach is really just an extension of Ban Tai but the beaches are a bit wider up this way and have the advantage of being walking distance to Ko Pha-Ngan's main town, its restaurants and services.

★ **Coco Garden** BUNGALOW **$**
(Map p198; 086 073 1147, 077 377721; www.cocogardens.com; Thong Sala; bungalows 550-1100B;) The best budget hang-out along the southern coast, fantastic Coco Garden one-ups the nearby resorts with well-manicured grounds and 25 neat bungalows and an excellent beach bar.

Baan Manali Resort BUNGALOW **$$**
(Map p198; 077 377918; bungalows 2200-3150B;) Quiet, clean and attractively laid out among the coconut trees, 14-bungalow Baan Manali is a convenient, relaxing and well-run choice with an infinity pool and excellent restaurant, close to the action at Thong Sala.

Lime n Soda RESORT **$$**
(Map p198; www.limesodathailand.com; bungalows 700-2300B;) Clean and simple tiled bungalows hide in the shade of bamboo and coconut palms along a breakwater above the beach. Ignoring the 'Ko Pha-Ngan's first Eco-Friendly beachfront resort' waffle, it's all in all a solid, decent choice.

Charu Bay Villas VILLA **$$$**
(Map p198; 084 191 1266; www.backpackersthailand.com; villas 8640-11,520B;) These fully equipped villas on the bay of Ao Bang Charu, just southeast of Thong Sala, are great value if you're a group. The Beachfront Villa is a three-bed with large Jacuzzi and

is big enough to sleep up to 10; the two-bed Seaview Villa sleeps up to four.

Ao Nai Wok to Ao Sri Thanu

Close to Thong Sala, the resorts peppered along this breezy west-coast strip mingle with small beaches between patches of mangroves. Despite the lack of sand, the prices are cheap and the sunsets are memorable.

Chills Resort RESORT $$
(Map p195; ☎089 875 2100; Ao Sri Thanu; r 1000-2300B;) Under new management and set along a stunning and secluded stretch of stony outcrops, Chills' cluster of delightfully simple-but-modern rooms all have peaceful ocean views letting in plenty of sunlight, sea breezes and gorgeous sunset views. Book through www.agoda.com.

Loyfa Natural Resort BUNGALOW $$
(Map p195; ☎077 349022; www.loyfanaturalresort.com; Ao Sri Thanu; r 750B, bungalows 1300-3100B, villas from 3825B;) Loyfa scores high marks for its friendly, French-speaking Thai staff, charming gardens and sturdy huts guarding sweeping ocean views. Modern bungalows tumble down the promontory onto an exclusively private sliver of ash-coloured sand. Cheapest rooms are in a hotel block.

Kupu Kupu Phangan Beach Villa RESORT $$$
(Map p195; ☎077 377384; www.kupuphangan.com; Ao Nai Wok; villas from 8500B;) This supreme Balinese-style resort is one of the island's most swoon-worthy, with lily ponds, tall palms, a swimming pool straight from a luxury magazine centrefold and rocky boulders that meet the sea. The gorgeous wooden villas have pools and elegant interiors.

Hat Chaophao

Like Hat Yao up the coast, this rounded beach on the west coast is lined with a variety of bungalow operations.

Pha-Ngan Paragon BUNGALOW $$$
(Map p197; ☎084 728 6064; bungalows 1750-12,000B; @) A tiny hideaway with just seven rooms, the Paragon has decor that incorporates stylistic elements from ancient Khmer, India and Thailand, without forfeiting any modern amenities. The 'royal bedroom' deserves a special mention – apparently the canopied bed was imported from Kashmir.

Hat Yao & Hat Son

One of the busier beaches along the west coast, Hat Yao sports a swimmable beach, numerous resorts and a few extra services such as ATMs and convenience stores. With a delightful sense of seclusion, Hat Son is a quiet, smaller beach that feels like a big secret.

Tantawan Bungalows BUNGALOW $
(Map p197; ☎077 349108; www.tantawanbungalow.com; Hat Son; bungalows 900-3300B;) This relaxed and recently renovated 11-bungalow (fan and air-con) teak nest, tucked among jungle, has fantastic views and a fine pool but it's a bit of a steep climb with luggage.

High Life BUNGALOW $
(Map p197; ☎077 349114; www.haadyaohighlife.com; Hat Yao; air-con bungalows 1200-3500B;) We can't decide what's more conspicuous: the dramatic ocean views from the infinity-edged swimming pool, or the blatant double entendre in the resort's name. True to its moniker, the 25 bungalows, of various shapes and sizes, sit on a palmed outcropping of granite soaring high above the sea.

Shiralea BUNGALOW $
(Map p197; ☎080 719 9256; www.shiralea.com; Hat Yao; dm 250B, bungalows 600-1300B;) The fresh-faced poolside bungalows are simple but the new air-con dorms are great and the ambience, with an on-site bar with draught beer, is convivial. It's about 100m away from the beach and it fills up every few weeks with Contiki student tour groups.

Haad Son Resort & Restaurant RESORT $$
(Map p197; ☎077 349104; http://haadsonresort.net; Hat Son; bungalows 1000-8000B; @) There's a mixed bag of rooms here from big, older wooden bungalows with terraces on the hillside to brand-new polished cement suites and rooms along the beachfront. The secluded beach setting is spectacular and is highlighted by one of the most beachy-chic restaurants on the island on a jungle- and boulder-clad peninsula overlooking the sea.

Haad Yao See Through Boutique Resort HOTEL $$
(Map p197; ☎077 349315; www.haadyao.net; Hat Yao; r 2350-2550B;) This towering polished cement double-storey complex with elongated Chinese-style wooden doors has a long but uninviting pool that's hard to access. The building looks bizarrely placed,

but room interiors are comfortable and the resort has a central beachfront location.

Haad Yao Bay View Resort RESORT $$$

(Map p197; ☎077 349193; www.haadyao-bayviewresort.com; Hat Yao; r & bungalows incl breakfast 1500-7000B;) This arrangement of bungalows and hotel-style accommodation looks like a tropical mirage on Hat Yao's northern headland. There's a huge array of options but our pick are the tiny but good-value rooms that hover right over the sea. For more luxe head up to the hillside sea-view bungalows. It's a busy, businesslike place.

Hat Salad

This slim, pretty beach on the northwest coast is fronted by shallow blue water – a clutch of photogenic long-tail boats tend to park at the southern end. It's slightly rustic, with local Thai fishermen coming out to throw their nets out at sunset, yet with plenty of amenities and comfortable accommodation.

Cookies Salad RESORT $$

(Map p197; ☎083 181 7125, 077 349125; www.cookies-phangan.com; bungalows 1800-3300B;) Sling out on a hammock at this resort with private Balinese-styled bungalows on a steep hill, orbiting a two-tiered lap pool tiled in various shades of blue. Shaggy thatching and dense tropical foliage give the realm a certain rustic quality, although you won't want for creature comforts. It's super friendly and books up fast.

Salad Hut BUNGALOW $$

(Map p197; ☎077 349246; www.saladhut.com; bungalows 2200-5000B;) Totally unpretentious despite sharing a beach with some distinctly upscale options, this small clutch of Thai-style bungalows sits but a stone's throw from the rolling tide, but the pool is rather small. Watch the sun gently set below the waves from your lacquered teak porch or the beach bar.

Salad Beach Resort BUNGALOW $$

(Map p197; ☎077 349149; www.phangan-saladbeachresort.com; bungalows 2000-3920B;) A full-service retreat along the sands of Hat Salad. Room decor employs an unusual palette of colours, but the grounds are tasteful and understated – especially around the pool.

Green Papaya BUNGALOW $$$

(Map p197; ☎077 374230; www.greenpapayaresort.com; bungalows 3600-10,200B;) In a tranquil and elegant setting, the polished wooden bungalows at Green Papaya are a clear stand-out along the lovely beach at Hat Salad; however, they come at quite a hefty price.

Ao Mae Hat

The relatively undeveloped northwest tip of the island has excellent ocean vistas, plenty of white sand and little Ko Ma is connected to Pha-Ngan by a stunning sandbar.

Island View Cabana BUNGALOW $

(Map p195; ☎077 374173; islandviewcabana@gmail.com; Ao Mae Hat; bungalows 400-1500B;) Well positioned for sunsets, the bungalows here are really big, though not that new, but this is a lovely spot at the end of the beach right at the isthmus to Ko Ma. Cheaper fan bungalows are at the rear.

Mae Hat Beach View Resort BUNGALOW $

(Map p195; ☎089 823 9756; bungalows 400-1500B;) At the listless southern end of the beach, this quiet but rather neglected spot sees little action. It's an option if you just want peace and quiet, with fan-cooled bamboo bungalows with solid tiled floors and a solitary air-con model.

Ban Chalok Lam (Chaloklum) & Hat Khom

In the north of the island, the cramped and quiet fishing village at Ban Chalok Lam is like no other place on Ko Pha-Ngan. The conglomeration of teak shanties and huts is being slowly infiltrated with the occasional European-style bakery and authentic Italian restaurant. For much of the time, locals still outnumber tourists and that's refreshing, but the new road is pumping up visitor numbers and there's not much of a beach.

Sŏrng·tăa·ou ply the route from here to Thong Sala for around 150B per person. There's a dirt road leading from Chalok Lam to Hat Khom, and water taxis are available to a number of beaches.

Fantasea BUNGALOW $

(Map p195; ☎089 443 0785; www.fantasea.asia; Chalok Lam; bungalows with fan/air-con 500/800B;) This friendly place is one of the better of a string of family-run bungalow operations along the quiet, eastern part of Chalok Lam. There's a thin beach out front with OK swimming and an elevated Thai-style restaurant area to chill out in.

Mandalai HOTEL $$$
(Map p195; 077 374316; www.mandalaihotel.com/web2014; Chalok Lam; r 1800-5600B;) With a couple of surreal-looking Louis XIV armchairs in reception, this lovely small boutique hotel quietly towers over the surrounding shantytown of fishermen's huts. Floor-to-ceiling windows command views of tangerine-coloured fishing boats in the bay, and there's a small but inviting pool in the main courtyard, mere steps from the sand.

Hat Khuat (Bottle Beach)

This isolated dune in the north of the island has a reputation as a low-key getaway, so it's pretty popular. During high season, places can fill up fast so it's best to arrive early. Grab a long-tail taxi boat from Chalok Lam for 100B to 150B (depending on the boat's occupancy).

Smile Bungalows BUNGALOW $
(Map p195; 085 429 4995; www.smilebungalows.com; Bottle Beach/Hat Khuat; bungalows 520-920B; closed Nov) At the far western corner of the beach, family-run Smile features an assortment of all-fan wooden huts climbing up a forested hill. The two-storey bungalows (920B) are our favourite.

Bottle Beach II BUNGALOW $
(Map p195; 077 445156; Bottle Beach/Hat Khuat; bungalows 600-1100B; closed Nov;) At the far eastern corner of the beach, this string of basic bungalows is the ideal place to chill out – if you don't need many creature comforts.

Thong Nai Pan

The pair of rounded bays at Thong Nai Pan, in the northeast of the island, are some of the most remote yet busy beaches on the island; Ao Thong Nai Pan Yai (*yai* means 'big') is the southern half that has some excellent budget and midrange options, and Ao Thong Nai Pan Noi (*noi* means 'little') is Pha-Ngan's most upscale beach that curves just above. Both bays are equally beautiful and great for swimming and hiking. A taxi between the two is around 100B. The road from Thong Sala to Thong Nai Pan is now excellent, so visitor numbers are increasing.

Longtail Beach Resort BUNGALOW $
(Map p195; 077 445018; www.longtailbeachresort.com; Thong Nai Pan; bungalows with fan/air-con from 550/2590B;) Tucked away at the southern end of the beach by the forest, Longtail offers backpackers charming abodes that wind up a lush garden path.

Anantara Rasananda RESORT $$$
(Map p195; 077 239555; http://phangan-rasananda.anantara.com; villas from 7500B;) Blink and you'll think you've been transported to Ko Samui. This five-star luxury resort is a sweeping sand-side property with a smattering of semi-detached villas – many bedecked with private plunge pools. A savvy mix of modern and traditional *săh·lah* styling prevails, and superb Anantara management assures service is polished.

Than Sadet

A new road runs all the way to Than Sadet, so the lovely bay here is totally accessible. Otherwise catch the *Thong Nai Pan Express* boat from Ko Samui.

Mai Pen Rai BUNGALOW $
(Map p195; 081 894 5076, 077 445090; www.thansadet.com; Than Sadet; bungalows 550-1200B;) This quiet, beachy bay elicits nothing but sedate smiles. Trek up to Nam Tok Than Sadet falls, hike an hour to Thong Nai Pan or explore by sea with a rented kayak. Bungalows mingle with Plaa's next door on the hilly headland, and sport panels of straw weaving with gabled roofs. Family bungalows are available for 900B and there's a friendly on-site restaurant.

Hat Thian & Hat Yuan

Both Hat Thian and Hat Yuan, near the southeastern tip of the island, have a few bungalow operations, and are quite secluded. You can walk between the two in under 10 minutes via the rocky outcrop that seperates them. Hat Yuan is the more developed beach and has the whiter, wider stretches of sand, while Hat Thian is relatively empty and is back-to-nature pretty.

To get here hire a long-tail from Hat Rin (300B to 400B for the whole boat) or organise a boat pick-up from your resort. A dirt road to Hat Yuan has been cleared for 4WDs, but is only passable in the dry season; even then the voyage by sea is much easier.

Bamboo Hut BUNGALOW $
(Map p195; 087 888 8592; Hat Yuan; bungalows 400-1000B;) Beautifully lodged up on the bouldery outcrops that overlook Hat Yuan and back into the jungle, groovy, hippie village, Bamboo Hut is a favourite for yoga retreats and meditative relaxation. Dark wood bungalows are small and have terraces.

Barcelona BUNGALOW $

(Map p195; 077 375113; Hat Yuan; bungalows 400-700B) Old, rickety wood bungalows with balconies – some with hammocks – climb up the hill on stilts behind a palm garden and have good vistas. Price depends on the view, but there's not a huge amount of variation, so grab a cheap one.

★ **Sanctuary** BUNGALOW $$

(Map p195; 081 271 3614; www.thesanctuarythailand.com; Hat Thian; dm 220B, bungalows 770-6000B) A friendly forested enclave of relaxed smiles, the Sanctuary is a haven of splendid lodgings, yoga classes and detox sessions. Accommodation, in various manifestations of twigs, is scattered along a tangle of hillside jungle paths while Hat Thian is wonderfully quiet and is great for swimming. Note that payment is cash only.

Pariya Resort & Villas RESORT $$$

(Map p195; 087 623 6678; www.pariyahaadyuan.com; Hat Yuan; villas 8000-17,000B;) The swankiest option on these beaches is found right in front of the softest sands of Hat Yuan in majestic burnt-yellow painted concrete, but it's not cheap. the octagonal, pagoda-topped bungalows are spacious yet sparsely furnished.

Eating

Most visitors quickly adopt the lazy lifestyle and wind up eating at their accommodation, which is a shame as Ko Pha-Ngan has some excellent restaurants scattered around the island; at the very least, it's another reason to get exploring.

Hat Rin

Hat Rin has the largest conglomeration of restaurants and bars on the island, yet most of them are pretty lousy so don't come here for the food. The infamous Chicken Corner is a popular intersection stocked with several faves and a decent new arrival or two.

Matt's Joint BARBECUE $$

(Map p201; mains from 189B; 10.30am-midnight) With Marvel posters, tonnes of elbow room and choice positioning at the Chicken Corner intersection, this brash-looking US-styled newcomer is an obvious, if rather unsubtle, choice among very middling competition. The all-you-can-eat BBQ buffet (299B) at 6.30pm is a winner, and breakfasts and burgers pull in hungry punters throughout the day.

Lazy House INTERNATIONAL $$

(Map p201; Hat Rin Nai; dishes 90-270B; lunch & dinner) Back in the day, this joint was the owner's apartment – everyone liked his cooking so much that he decided to turn the place into a restaurant and hang-out spot. Today, Lazy House is easily one of Hat Rin's best places to veg out in front of a movie with a scrumptious shepherd's pie.

Lucky Crab SEAFOOD $$

(Map p201; Hat Rin Nai; dishes 100-450B; 9am-11pm) Rows of freshly caught creatures are presented nightly atop miniature long-tail boats loaded with ice. Once you've picked your prey, grab a table inside amid dangling plants and charming stone furnishings.

Om Ganesh INDIAN $$

(Map p201; Hat Rin Nai; mains from 100B; 9am-11pm) Seasoned old-timer Om Ganesh sees a regular flow of customers for its north Indian curries, *biryani* rice, roti and lassis, with a token spread of Chinese dishes for good measure. Set meals start at 300B.

Monna Lisa ITALIAN $$

(Map p201; Hat Rin Nai; pizza & pasta from 200B; 1-11pm) Travellers rave about the pizza here, and the pasta gets a thumbs-up as well. It's run by a team of friendly Italians and has a basic, open-air atmosphere.

Southern Beaches

On Saturday evenings from 4pm to 10pm, a side street in the eastern part of Thong Sala becomes **Walking Street** – a bustling pedestrian zone mostly filled with locals hawking their wares to other islanders. There's plenty on offer, from clothing to food.

Night Market MARKET $

(Map p198; Thong Sala; dishes 25-180B; 2-11pm) A heady mix of steam and snacking locals, Thong Sala's night market is a must for those looking for doses of culture while nibbling on low-priced snacks. Wander the stalls for a galaxy of Thai street food, from vegetable curry puffs to corn on the cob, spicy sausages, kebabs, spring rolls and coconut cake.

Nira's BAKERY $

(Map p198; snacks from 80B; 7am-7pm) With outstanding service, a bright interconnected two-room interior, scrummy baked goodies, tip-top coffee (and rarities such as Marmite) and trendy furniture, Nira's is second to none in Thong Sala, and perhaps the entire island. This is *the* place for breakfast. Music is of the Grover Washington school.

Ando Loco MEXICAN $

(Map p198; www.andoloco.com; Ban Tai; mains from 50B; ⊙2-10.30pm Wed-Mon) This super-popular outdoor Mexican hang-out gets the universal thumbs up. Grab a jumbo margarita, down a drunken fajita, line up a quesadilla or two and sink a round of balls on the pool table.

★ Fisherman's Restaurant SEAFOOD $$

(Map p195; ☎084 454 7240; Ban Tai; dishes 50-600B; ⊙1-10pm) Sit in a long-tail boat looking out over the sunset and a rocky pier. Lit up at night it's one of the island's nicest settings and the food, from the addictive yellow curry crab to the massive seafood platter to share, is as wonderful as the ambience. Reserve ahead, especially during party time.

★ Fabio's ITALIAN $$

(Map p195; ☎083 389 5732; Ban Khai; dishes 150-400B; ⊙5-10pm Mon-Sat) An intimate, and delicious Italian place with golden walls, cream linens and bamboo furniture. There are only seven tables, so reserve in advance. House-made delicacies like seafood risotto, pizzas and iced limoncello are as artfully presented as they are fresh and delicious.

Vintage Burgers BURGERS $$

(Map p198; mains from 220B; ⊙5-10pm; 📶) This fantastic Portuguese-run gourmet burger spot in Thong Sala really hits the nail on the head with six types of superb patties, including a vegie, tuna and kids burger option, backed up by scrummy salt and oregano French fries and a sociable vibe.

Mason's Arms BRITISH $$

(Map p198; Thong Sala; mains 160-350B; ⊙10am-10.30pm, till midnight high season) Surreally emerging from the swaying palms, this Tudor-style black-and-white affair is seemingly plucked straight from Stratford-upon-Avon and deposited in the steamy jungle. It's one blood pudding away from being an official British colony, with a classic British menu – the fish 'n' chips (290B) is a winner every time and Marmite on toast (80B) awaits salt-deficient diners.

Food Factory INTERNATIONAL $$

(Map p198; mains from 180B; ⊙24hr; 📶) Serving up pizza and burgers around the clock on the busy road to Ban Tai and divided into restaurant and bar, this hard-working spot is all signed football shirts, sports TV check table cloths, '80s sounds, really terrific milkshakes and winning breakfasts (150B).

Other Beaches

★ Cucina Italiana ITALIAN $$

(Jenny's; Map p195; Chalok Lam; pizzas 180-200B; ⊙5-10pm) If it weren't for the sand between your toes and the long-tail boats whizzing by, you might think you had been transported to the Italian countryside. The friendly Italian chef is passionate about his food, and creates everything from his pasta to his tiramisu daily, from scratch.

Sanctuary HEALTH FOOD $$

(Map p195; www.thesanctuarythailand.com; Hat Thian; mains from 130B; 📶) The Sanctuary's restaurant proves that wholesome food (vegetarian and seafood) can also be delicious. Enjoy a tasty parade of plates – from massaman curry to crunchy Vietnamese spring rolls. Don't forget to wash it all down with a blackberry, soya milk and honey immune booster. No credit cards.

Peppercorn STEAK $$

(Map p197; www.peppercornphangan.com; Hat Salad; mains 160-400B; ⊙4-10pm Mon-Sat; 🖉) Escargot and succulent steaks in a rickety jungle cottage? You bet. Peppercorn may be tucked in the brush away from the sea, but that shouldn't detract foodies from seeking out some of Pha-Ngan's best international cuisine, with a fine selection of good vegetarian dishes to boot. No MSG or artificial ingredients.

Bamboo Hut WESTERN, THAI $$

(Map p195; Hat Yuan; dishes 100-300B; ⊙breakfast, lunch & dinner; 📶🖉) Lounge on a Thai-style cushion or sit at a teak table that catches sea breezes and looks over infinite blue. There are plenty of options from vegetarian specialities and fresh juices for those coming off a fast or cleanse, to classic, very well-prepared Thai dishes with all assortments of beef, chicken and prawns.

Two Brothers SEAFOOD $$

(Chalok Lam; barbecue sets from 250B; ⊙breakfast, lunch & dinner) One of the best of a string of Chalok Lam's seafood restaurants where fisher families serve you their bounty straight off the boats.

JJ's Restaurant THAI $$

(Map p195; ⊙9am-9pm) Drop off at JJ's come sunset to swoon before stirring visuals over the young mangroves at Ao Wok Tum while devouring tasty treats from the kitchen and toasting it all with a chilled beer.

Drinking & Nightlife

Every month, on the night of the full moon, pilgrims pay lunar tribute to the party gods with trancelike dancing, wild screaming and glow-in-the-dark body paint. The throngs of bucket-sippers and fire twirlers gather on the infamous Sunrise Beach (Hat Rin Nok) and party until the sun replaces the moon in the sky.

A few other noteworthy spots can be found around the island for those seeking something a bit mellower.

Hat Rin

Hat Rin is the beating heart of the legendary Full Moon fun. When the moon isn't lighting up the night sky, partygoers flock to other spots on the island's south side. Most party venues flank Hat Rin's Sunrise Beach from south to north.

Rock BAR, CLUB
(Map p201) The superb views of the party from the elevated terrace on the far south side of the beach are matched by the best cocktails in town.

Drop-In Bar BAR, CLUB
(Map p201) This dance shack blasts the chart toppers that we all secretly love. This is one of the liveliest places but things go quiet on non–Full Moon nights.

Cactus Bar BAR, CLUB
(Map p201) Smack in the centre of Hat Rin Nok, Cactus pumps out a healthy mix of old-school tunes, hip-hop and R&B. It's popular and lively, although a DJ was shot dead here a few years back.

Sunrise BAR, CLUB
(Map p201) A spot on the sand where trance beats shake the graffiti-ed walls, with drum 'n bass coming into its own at Full Moon.

Tommy BAR, CLUB
(Map p201) One of Hat Rin's largest venues lures the masses with loungers, low tables, black lights and blaring Full Moon trance music.

Thong Sala

Harp PUB
(Map p198; ⏲8am-midnight) With chatty staff and a prime location on the corner straight down from the pier, cavernous wood-floored Harp is the sports bar of choice for those crucial Premier League fixtures, draught beer and outstanding Sunday roasts (250B) plus other solid pub fare.

Other Beaches

Belgian Beer Bar BAR
(Map p197; www.seetanu.com; Surat Thani; ⏲8am-10pm) Run by the affable Quentin, this enjoyable bar defies Surat Thani's appropriation by yogis and the chakra-balancing crowd with a heady range of Belgian beer, the most potent of which (Amber Bush) delivers a dizzying 12.5% punch. If the yogic flying doesn't give you wings, this might.

Jam BAR
(Map p195; Hin Kong; ⏲8pm-2am Tue & Sat) It's DIY live music at this friendly nightspot on the west coast. Saturday nights are open mic, and the rest of the week you'll usually catch a few locals jamming on their guitars. By appointment, musicians can practise their songs from 6pm.

Outlaws Saloon BAR
(Map p198; ⏲4pm-2am) With its buffalo skulls, US flags, sounds from Elvis and other American icons, this fun ranch-style saloon is quite a sight on a lively night. There's a meaty menu, excellent Sunday roast dinners and imported beers and ciders.

It's on the north side of the road between Thong Sala and Ban Tai.

Flip Flop Pharmacy BAR
(Map p195; Thong Nai Pan; ⏲noon-1am; 📶) With flip flops on the wall, this open-air bar on the sands of Thong Nai Pan has a fine beach perspective (and a pool table).

Amsterdam BAR
(Map p195; Ao Plaay Laem) Near Ao Wok Tum on the west coast, Amsterdam attracts tourists and locals from all over the island, who are looking for a chill spot to watch the sunset.

Information

DANGERS & ANNOYANCES

Some of your fondest holiday memories can hatch on Ko Pha-Ngan; just be mindful of the following situations where things can go pear-shaped.

Drugs You're sunning on the beach when a local walks up and offers you some local herb at a ridiculously low price. 'No thanks,' you say, knowing that the penalties for drug use in

Thailand are fierce. But the vendor drops his price even more and practically offers you the weed for free. Too good to be true? Obviously. As soon as you take a toke, the seller rats you out to the police and you're whisked away to the local prison to pay a wallet-busting fine. This is a regular scenario on Ko Pha-Ngan so it's best to avoid the call of the ganja.

Another important thing to remember: your travel insurance does not cover drug-related injuries or treatment. Drug-related freak-outs *do* happen – we've heard firsthand accounts of partiers slipping into extended periods of delirium. Suan Saranrom (Garden of Joys) Psychiatric Hospital in Surat Thani has to take on extra staff during Full Moon and other party periods to handle the number of *fa·ràng* who freak out on magic mushrooms, acid or other abundantly available hallucinogens.

Women Travellers Female travellers should be particularly careful when partying on the island. We've received numerous reports about drug- and alcohol-related rape (and these situations are not limited to Full Moon Parties). Another disturbing problem is the unscrupulous behaviour of some of the local motorcycle taxi drivers. Several complaints have been filed about drivers groping female passengers; there are even reports of severe sexual assaults.

Motorcycles Ko Pha-Ngan has more motorcycle accidents than injuries incurred from Full Moon tomfoolery, although bad motorcycle driving coincides with the Full Moon revelries. Nowadays there's a decent system of paved roads (recently extended to Than Sadet), but some tracks remain rutted dirt-and-mud paths and the island is also hilly, with some steep inclines.The island now has a special ambulance that trawls the island helping injured bikers. If you don't have an international driving licence, you will also be driving illegally and your insurance may not cover you in the event of an accident, so costs could pile up fast.

Drowning Rip currents and alcohol don't mix well. Drownings are frequent; if swimming, it's advisable to be clear-headed rather than plunging into the sea on a Full Moon bender.

Fake Alcohol This is a common scam during the Full Moon mania at the bucket stalls on the beach and along the road. Buckets may be filled with low-grade moonshine rice whisky, or old bottles filled with homemade alcohol. Apart from obvious health risks, dodgy alcohol is also a prime mover in many of the accidents at the time of the Full Moon, from motorcycle accidents to drownings, fights and burns from jumping fire ropes.

Glass on the Beach Beware nasty cuts from broken glass in the sand at Full Moon Party time – don good footwear.

EMERGENCY

Main Police Station (Map p195; ☎077 377114, 191) Located about 2km north of Thong Sala. Come here to file a report. You might be charged between 110B and 200B to file the report, which is for insurance and refusing to pay may lead to complications. If you are arrested you have the right to an embassy phone call; you don't have to accept the 'interpreter' you are offered.

If you have committed a serious offence, do not sign anything written only in Thai, or write on the document that you do not understand the language and are signing under duress.

LAUNDRY

If you got fluorescent body paint on your clothes during your Full Moon romp, don't bother sending them to the cleaners – it will never come out. Trust us, we've tried. For your other washing needs, there are heaps of places that will gladly wash your clothes. Prices hover around 40B per kilo, and express cleanings shouldn't be more than 60B per kilo.

MEDICAL SERVICES

Medical services can be a little crooked in Ko Pha-Ngan – expect unstable prices and under-qualified, mercenary doctors. Many clinics charge a 3000B entrance fee before treatment. Serious medical issues should be dealt with on nearby Ko Samui.

Ko Pha-Ngan Hospital (Map p195; ☎077 377034; Thong Sala; ⏲24hr) About 2.5km north of Thong Sala; has 24-hour emergency.

MONEY

Thong Sala, Ko Pha-Ngan's financial 'capital', has plenty of banks, currency converters and several Western Union offices. Hat Rin has numerous ATMs and a couple of banks at the pier. There are also ATMs in Hat Yao, Chalok Lum and Thong Nai Pan.

POST

Main Post Office (Map p198; ⏲8.30am-4.30pm Mon-Fri, 9am-noon Sat) In Thong Sala; there's a smaller office (Map p201) right near the pier in Hat Rin.

TOURIST INFORMATION

There are no government-run Tourist Authority of Thailand (TAT) offices on Ko Pha-Ngan; instead tourists get their information from local travel agencies and brochures. Most agencies are clumped around Hat Rin and Thong Sala. Agents take a small commission on each sale, but collusion keeps prices relatively stable and standardised. Choose an agent you trust if you are spending a lot of money – faulty bookings do happen on Ko Pha-Ngan, especially since the island does not have tourist police.

Several mini-magazines also offer comprehensive information about the island's accommodation, restaurants, activities and Full Moon Parties. Our favourite option is the pocket-sized quarterly Phangan Info (www.phangan.info), also available as a handy app.

Backpackers Information Centre (Map p201; ☎077 375535; www.backpackersthailand.com; Hat Rin; ⊙11am-8pm) A must for travellers looking to book high-quality tours (diving, live-aboards, jungle safaris etc) and transport. Not just for backpackers, it's an expat-run travel agency that offers peace of mind with every purchase – travellers are provided with the mobile phone number of the owners should any problems arise. Service is first rate and staff are forever helpful. It also runs the Crystal Dive shop next door.

WEBSITES

www.backpackersthailand.com Everything you need to know about Ko Pha-Ngan, from booking accommodation to finding out the Full Moon Party schedule. Doubles as a vast resource for the whole country as well.

www.phangan.info Handy and informative resource for Ko Pha-Ngan, with detailed maps and reviews.

Getting There & Away

As always, the cost and departure times are subject to change. Rough waves are known to cancel ferries between the months of October and December.

AIR

Ko Pha-Ngan's new airport was due to open in 2014, but when we stopped by in 2015 it was still not operational and no date was set for an official opening. At the time of writing, there were issues relating to the airport encroaching on land belonging to Than Sadet-Koh Phangan National Park, so everything was in the air, so to speak. If and when operational, it is expected that Kan Air flights will connect Ko Pha-Ngan with Bangkok, with flights taking 80 minutes. It's also expected that services will increase over the next few years to include more Bangkok flights and other destinations as well.

BOAT

To Bangkok, Hua Hin & Chumphon

The Lomprayah and Seatran Discovery services have bus–boat combination packages (from around 1300B) that depart from the Th Khao San area in Bangkok and pass through Hua Hin and Chumphon. The whole voyage takes about 17 hours.

It is also quite hassle-free (unless your train breaks down, which happens a lot) to take the train from Bangkok or Hua Hin to Chumphon and switch to a ferry service. In this case expect to pay 300B for a 2nd class seat on a train from Bangkok to Chumphon (about 8½ hours); the boat from Chumphon to Ko Pha-Ngan takes around 2½ hours and costs 800B to 1000B depending on the boat.

To Ko Samui

There are around a dozen daily departures between Thong Sala on Ko Pha-Ngan and Ko Samui. These boats leave throughout the day from 7am to 6pm, take from 20 minutes to an hour and cost 200B to 300B depending on the boat.

The **Haad Rin Queen** (☎077 484668) goes back and forth between Hat Rin and Big Buddha Beach on Ko Samui four times a day. The voyage takes 50 minutes and costs 200B.

The *Thong Nai Pan Express* is a wobbly old fishing boat (not for the faint-hearted) that runs once a day from Mae Hat on Ko Samui to Hat Rin on Ko Pha-Ngan and then up the east coast, stopping at all the beaches as far as Thong Nai Pan Noi. Prices range from 200B to 400B depending on the destination. The boat won't run in bad weather.

To Ko Tao

Ko Tao-bound **Lomprayah** ferries (500B to 600B) depart from Thong Sala on Ko Pha-Ngan at 8.30am, 1pm and 5.45pm and arrive at 9.45am, 2.15pm and 6.45pm. The **Seatran** service (430B, 90 minutes) departs from Thong Sala at 8.30am, 1.30pm and 5pm daily. Taxis depart Hat Rin for Thong Sala one hour before the boat departure. The cheaper-but-slower **Songserm** (350B) leaves Ko Pha-Ngan at 12.30pm and alights at 2.30pm, before continuing to Chumphon.

To Surat Thani & the Andaman Coast

There are approximately eight daily departures between Ko Pha-Ngan and Surat Thani on the **Songserm Express** (350B, 4½ hours) or **Lomprayah** (550B, 2¾ hours) services, both travelling via Ko Samui. These boats leave from Thong Sala throughout the day from 7am to 8pm. Every night, depending on the weather, a night boat runs from Surat (400B, seven hours), departing at 11pm. Boats in the opposite direction leave Ko Pha-Ngan at 10pm.

Combination boat–bus tickets are available at any travel agency. Simply tell them your desired destination and they will sell you the necessary links in the transport chain. Most travellers will pass through Surat Thani as they swap coasts.

Getting Around

You can rent motorcycles all over the island for 150B to 250B per day. Always wear a helmet – it's the law on Ko Pha-Ngan, and local policemen are starting to enforce it. But whatever the law, if you come off even at quite a low speed and hit your head, you can sustain serious injuries. Check that the motorcycle has enough space in the underseat compartment to store your helmet. If you plan on riding over dirt tracks it is imperative that you rent a bike comparable to a Honda MTX125 – gearless scooters cannot make the journey. Bicycle rentals are discouraged unless you're fit enough to take on the Tour de France.

Pick-up trucks and *sŏrng·tăa·ou* chug along the island's major roads and the rates double after sunset. Ask your accommodation about free or discount transfers when you leave the island. The trip from Thong Sala to Hat Rin is 100B; further beaches will set you back around 150B to 200B.

Long-tail boats depart from Thong Sala, Chalok Lam and Hat Rin, heading to far-flung destinations such as Hat Khuat (Bottle Beach). Expect to pay anywhere from 50B for a short trip, and up to 300B for a lengthier journey. You can charter a private boat ride from beach to beach for about 150B per 15 minutes of travel.

Ko Tao

เกาะเต่า

POP 2032

Once the baby of the Samui–Pha-Ngan–Tao trio, Ko Tao may still be the smallest in size but in many other ways it's grown up. The island is consistently gaining popularity and going more upscale, but for now this jungle-topped cutie has the busy vibe of Samui mixed with the laid-back nature of Pha-Ngan. But Tao also has its wild card, something the others don't: easy-to-get-to, diverse diving right off its shores. Cavort with sharks and rays in a playground of tangled neon coral, toast the day with sunset cocktails on a white beach then get up and do it all over again the next day. But even while the island may be synonymous with diving, there is much more to the place. Hikers and hermits can re-enact an episode from *Lost* in the dripping coastal jungles. And when you're Robinson Crusoe-ed out, hit the pumpin' bar scene that rages on until dawn.

Activities

Diving

If you've never been diving before, Ko Tao is *the* place in Thailand to lose your scuba virginity. The shallow bays scalloping the island are perfect for newbie divers to take their first stab at scuba; the waters are crystal clear, there are loads of neon reefs and the temperatures feel like bathwater. With many sheltered dive sites, waters around Ko Tao can be dived all year round, and it's only during the monsoon months that diving may stop for a day or two if the waters are too choppy, but this is actually quite rare. The best dive sites are found at offshore pinnacles within a 20km radius of the island, but seasoned scubaholics almost always prefer the top-notch sites along the Andaman coast. The local marine wildlife includes groupers, moray eels, batfish, bannerfish, barracudas, titan triggerfish, angelfish, clownfish (Nemos), stingrays, reef sharks and frequent visits by mighty whale sharks.

Onshore, over 40 dive centres are ready to saddle you up with gear and teach you the ropes in a 3½-day Open Water certification course. The intense competition among scuba schools means that certification prices are unbeatably low and the standards of service top-notch; dozens of dive shops vie for your baht, so be sure to shop around. The island issues more scuba certifications than anywhere else in the world.

ACE Marine Expeditions DIVING

(Map p218; ☎077 456547; www.divephotothai.com) The luxe choice. Go out on this James Bond–worthy speedboat and get to sites in a fraction of the time. The ingenious 'whaleshark watch' program keeps up-to-the-moment tabs on where sightings are taking place – they'll whisk you out to where the creatures are so your chances of seeing them are greatly increased.

Ban's Diving School DIVING

(Map p218; ☎077 456466; www.bansdivingresort.com; Sairee Beach) A well-oiled diving machine that's relentlessly expanding, Ban's is one of the world's most prolific diver certification schools yet it retains a five-star feel. Classroom sessions tend to be conducted in large groups, but there's a reasonable amount of individual attention in the water. A breadth of international instructors means that students can learn to dive in their native tongue.

Big Blue Diving DIVING

(Map p218; ☎077 456050; www.bigbluediving.com; Sairee Beach) If Goldilocks were picking a dive school, she'd probably pick Big Blue – this mid-size operation (not too big, not too small) gets props for fostering a sociable vibe while maintaining a high standard of service. Divers of every ilk can score dirt-cheap accommodation at their resort.

Buddha View DIVING

(☎077 456074; www.buddhaview-diving.com; Chalok Ban Kao) One of several big dive operations on Ko Tao, Buddha View offers the standard fare of certification and special programs for technical diving (venturing

Ko Tao

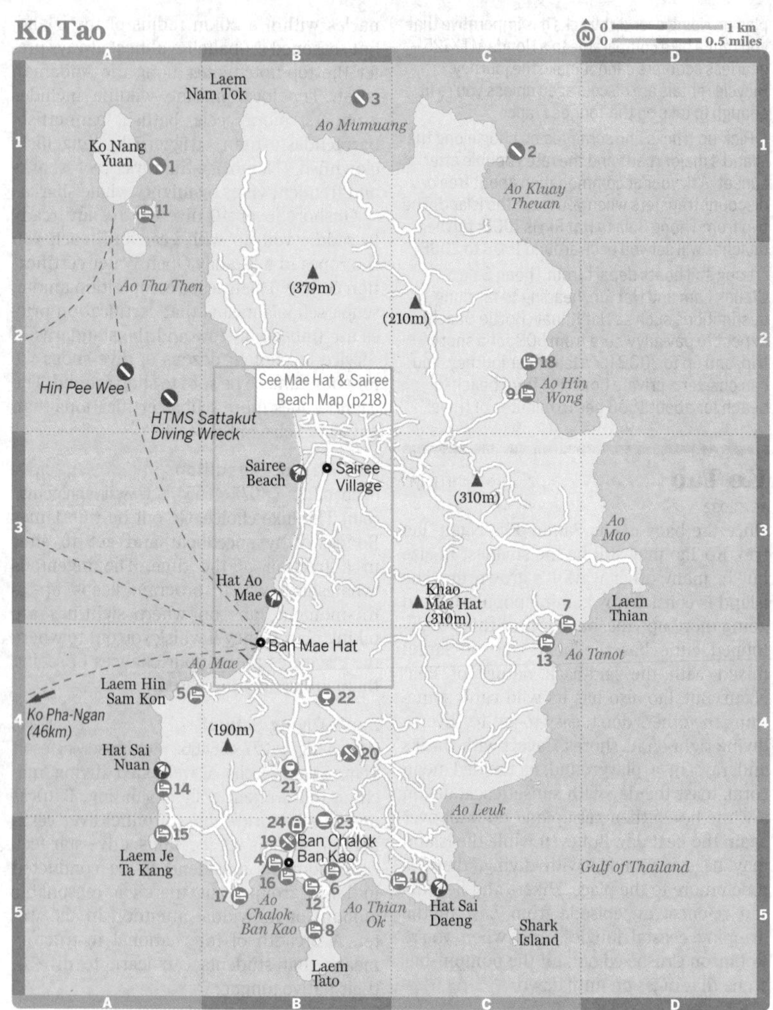

beyond the usual parameters of recreational underwater exploration). Discounted accommodation is available at its friendly resort.

Crystal Dive DIVING
(Map p218; ☎077 456106; www.crystaldive.com; Mae Hat) Crystal is the Meryl Streep of diving operators, winning all the awards for best performance year after year. It's one of the largest schools on the island (and around the world), although high-quality instructors and intimate classes keep the school feeling quite personal. Multilingual staff members, air-conditioned classes and two on-site swimming pools sweeten the deal. Highly recommended.

New Heaven DIVING
(☎077 457045; www.newheavendiveschool.com; Chalok Ban Kao) The owners of this small diving operation dedicate a lot of their time to preserving the natural beauty of Ko Tao's underwater sites by conducting regular reef checks and contributing to reef restoration efforts. A special CPAD research diver certification program is available in addition to the regular order of programs and fun dives.

Ko Tao

Activities, Courses & Tours
1 Japanese Gardens Dive Site A1
2 Light House Point C1
3 Mango Bay B1

Sleeping
4 Buddha View Dive Resort B5
5 Charm Churee Villa A4
6 Chintakiri Resort B5
7 Family Tanote C3
8 Freedom Beach B5
9 Hin Wong Bungalows C2
10 Jamahkiri Resort & Spa C5
JP Resort ..... (see 16)
11 Ko Nangyuan Dive Resort A1
12 Ko Tao Resort B5
13 Poseidon C4
14 Sai Thong Resort A4
15 Tao Thong Villa A5
16 Tropicana B5
17 View Point Resort B5
18 View Rock C2

Eating
19 I (Heart) Salad B5
20 Long Pae B4
Viewpoint Restaurant ..... (see 17)

Drinking & Nightlife
21 Castle B4
22 Earth House B4
23 Natural High Cafe B5

Shopping
24 Hammock Cafe Plaeyuan B5

Scuba Junction DIVING
(Scuba J; Map p218; ☎077 456164; www.scuba-junction.com; Sairee Beach) These instructors lure travellers that are looking for an intimate dive experience.The outift guarantees a maximum of four people per group.

Snorkelling

Snorkelling is a popular alternative to diving, and organising your own snorkelling trip here is simple, since the bays on the east coast have bungalow operations offering equipment rental for between 100B and 200B per day.

Most snorkel enthusiasts opt for the do-it-yourself approach on Ko Tao, which involves swimming out into the offshore bays or hiring a long-tail boat to putter around further out. Guided tours are also available and can be booked at any local travel agency. Tours range from 500B to 800B (usually including gear, lunch and a guide/boat captain) and stop at various snorkelling hotspots around the island. **Laem Thian** is popular for its small sharks, **Shark Island** has loads of fish (and ironically no sharks), **Ao Hin Wong** is known for its crystalline waters, and **Light House Point** (Map p212), in the north, offers a dazzling array of colourful sea anemones. Dive schools will usually allow snorkellers on their vessels for a comparable price – but it's only worth snorkelling at the shallower sites such as Japanese Gardens. Note that dive boats visit the shallower sites in the afternoons.

Freediving

Over the last couple of years freediving (exploring the sea using breath-holding techniques rather than scuba gear) has grown rapidly in popularity. Several small schools have opened across the island. We recommend the capable staff at **Apnea Total** (Map p218; ☎081 956 5720, 081 956 5430; www.apneatotal.com; Sairee Beach) who have earned awards in the freediving world and have a knack for easing newbies into this sport. The student-teacher ratio of three to one also ensures plenty of attention to safety. Also worth a special mention is **Blue Immersion** (Map p218; ☎081 188 8488; www.blue-immersion.com; Sairee Beach) run by friendly Akim, a martial arts expert and a freediving pro – he was one of the first people in the world to freedive below 100m – where a one-day introduction to freediving costs 3000B. Freediving prices are standardised across the island as well – a 2½-day SSI beginner course will set you back 5500B.

Technical Diving & Cave Diving

Well-seasoned divers and hardcore Jacques Cousteaus should contact **Tech Thailand** (www.techthailand.com) or one of a handful of other tech diving schools if they want to take their underwater exploration to the next level and try a technical dive. According to PADI, tec diving, as it's often known, is 'diving other than conventional commercial or recreational diving that takes divers beyond recreational diving limits'. Technical diving exceeds depths of 40m and requires stage decompressions, and a variety of gas mixtures are often used in a single dive. You must be a certified tech diver to undertake tech dives; training courses are available at many schools on the island, offering various tech diving certifications.

TAKING THE PLUNGE: CHOOSING A DIVE SCHOOL ON KO TAO

It's no surprise that this underwater playground has become exceptionally popular with beginners. But before you dive in (so to speak) it's important to look around at the various dive schools available.

When you alight at the pier in Mae Hat, touts will try to coax you into staying at their dive resort with promises of a 'special price for you'. But there are dozens of dive centres on Ko Tao, so it's best to arrive armed with the names of a few reputable schools. If you're not rushed for time, consider relaxing on the island for a couple of days before making any decisions – you will undoubtedly bump into swarms of scubaphiles and instructors who will offer their advice and opinions.

Remember: the success of your diving experience will largely depend on how much you like your instructor. Other factors to consider are the size of your diving group, the condition of your equipment and the condition of the dive sites, to name a few.

For the most part, diving prices are somewhat standardised across the island, so there's no need to spend your time hunting around for the best deal. A **PADI** (www.padi.com) Open Water Diver (OWD) certification course costs 9800B; an **SSI** (www.ssithailand.com) OWD certificate is slightly less (9000B) because you do not have to pay for instruction materials. An Advanced Open Water Diver (AOWD) certification course will set you back 8500B, a rescue course is 9500B and the Divemaster program costs a cool 25,000B. Fun divers should expect to pay roughly 1000B per dive, or around 7000B for a 10-dive package. These rates include all dive gear, boat, instructors/guides and snacks. Discounts are usually given if you bring your own equipment. Be wary of dive centres that offer too many price cuts – safety is paramount, and a shop giving out unusually good deals is probably cutting too many corners.

Most dive schools will hook you up with cheap or even free accommodation. Almost all scuba centres offer gratis fan rooms for anyone doing beginner coursework. Expect large crowds and booked-out beds throughout December, January, June, July and August, and a monthly glut of wannabe divers after every Full Moon Party on Ko Pha-Ngan.

Several years ago, Tech Thailand's old boat, MV *Trident,* made a name for itself in the diving community after successfully locating dozens of previously undiscovered wrecks in the Gulf of Thailand. Its most famous discovery was the USS *Lagarto,* an American naval vessel that sank during WWII. The gulf has long been an important trading route and new wrecks are being discovered all the time, from old Chinese pottery wrecks to Japanese *marus* (merchant ships). In 2010 the *Trident* was purposefully sunk off the coast of Ko Tao to create an artificial reef. A miscalculation with the explosives has left the wreck a bit too deep for beginners. The HTMS *Sattakut* wreck and deeper pinnacle dive sites are also good for tech diving.

Cave diving has taken Ko Tao by storm, and the most intrepid scuba buffs are lining up to make the half-day trek over to Khao Sok National Park. Beneath the park's main lake lurks an astonishing submarine world filled with hidden grottos, limestone crags and skulking catfish. In certain areas divers can swim near submerged villages that were flooded in order to create a reservoir and dam. Most cave-diving trips depart from Ko Tao on the afternoon boat service and return to the island on the afternoon boat service of the following day. Overnight stays are arranged in or near the park.

Underwater Photography & Videography

If your wallet is already full of diving certification cards, consider renting an underwater camera or enrolling in a marine videography course. Many scuba schools hire professional videographers to film Open Water Diver certifications, and if this piques your interest, you could potentially earn some money after completing a video internship. Your dive operator can put you in touch with any of the half-dozen videography crews on the island. We recommend **ACE Marine Images** (Map p218; ☎077 457054; www.acemarineimages.com; Sairee Beach), one of Thailand's leading underwater videography studios. An introductory course including camera, diving and instruction is 4500B and can also be used towards an Advanced PADI certification. **Crystal Images** (☎092 476 4110; www.crystalimageskohtao.com) and **Oceans Below** (www.oceansbelow.net) offer videography courses and internships and each have their own special options.

Other Activities

★Flying Trapeze Adventures ACROBATICS
(FTA; Map p218; ☎080 696 9269; www.gtadventures.com; Sairee Beach; ⏰4-8pm, lessons 3.30-5.30pm) Find out if you're a great catch during a 90-minute small group beginner trapeze lesson (1200B). Afternoon courses are taught by super-friendly Gemma and her posse of limber sidekicks, who take you from circus neophyte to soaring savant in four jumps or less. There are occasional nightly shows, involving audience participation. Class times vary depending on sundown; reserve ahead.

Participants must be at least six years old.

The Gallery Spa MASSAGE
(Map p218; ☎077 456547; www.thegallerykohtao.com; 400B) The traditional Thai massage will make you feel brand-new. Book in advance.

Goodtime Adventures HIKING, ADVENTURE SPORTS
(Map p218; ☎087 275 3604; www.gtadventures.com; Sairee Beach; ⏰noon-late) Dive, hike through the island's jungle interior, swing from rock to rock during a climbing and abseiling session, or unleash your inner daredevil during an afternoon of cliff jumping (at your own risk). Alternatively, take a shot at all of them on the full-day Koh Tao Adventure (3500B). The Goodtime office, along the Sairee sands, doubles as a friendly cafe.

Dorms and doubles are also available.

Monsoon Gym & Fight Club MARTIAL ARTS
(Map p218; www.monsoongym.com) This Sairee Beach club combines Thai boxing programs

DIVE SITES AT A GLANCE

In general, divers don't have much of a choice as to which sites they explore. Each dive school chooses a smattering of sites for the day depending on weather and ocean conditions. Deeper dive sites such as Chumphon Pinnacle are usually visited in the morning. Afternoon boats tour the shallower sites such as Japanese Gardens. Recently, two large vessels have been sunk off the coast, providing scubaphiles with two new wreck dives. Divers hoping to spend some quality time searching for whale sharks at Sail Rock should join one of the dive trips departing daily from Ko Pha-Ngan.

Chumphon Pinnacle (36m maximum depth), 13km west of Ko Tao, has a colourful assortment of sea anemones along the four interconnected pinnacles. The site plays host to schools of giant trevally, tuna and large grey reef sharks. Whale sharks are known to pop up once in a while.

Green Rock (25m maximum depth) is an underwater jungle gym featuring caverns, caves and small swim-throughs. Rays, grouper and triggerfish are known to hang around. It's a great place for a night dive.

Japanese Gardens (Map p212; 12m maximum depth), between Ko Tao and Ko Nang Yuan, is a low-stress dive site perfect for beginners. There's plenty of colourful coral, and turtles, stingray and pufferfish often pass by.

Mango Bay (Map p212; 16m maximum depth) might be your first dive site if you are putting on a tank for the first time. Lazy reef fish swim around as newbies practise their skills on the sandy bottom.

Sail Rock (40m maximum depth), best accessed by Ko Pha-Ngan, features a massive rock chimney with a vertical swim-through, and large pelagics like barracuda and kingfish. This is one of the top spots in Southeast Asia to see whale sharks; in the past few years they have been seen year round, so there's no clear season.

Southwest Pinnacle (33m maximum depth) offers divers a collection of pinnacles that are home to giant groupers and barracudas, and whale sharks are sometimes spotted.

White Rock (29m maximum depth) is home to colourful corals, angelfish, clownfish and territorial triggerfish. Another popular spot for night divers.

HTMS Sattakut was sunk in 2011 southeast of Hin Pee Wee at a depth of 30m and has become one of the most popular wreck diving sites.

and air-con dorm accommodation (300B) for students signed up to get to grips with the fighting art. It's an excellent and exhilarating way to spend time in Ko Tao, if diving isn't your scene. The well-equipped concrete gym is right alongside the Muay Thai ring. Drop-in fight training costs 300B, monthly unlimited use is 7000B.

Shambhala YOGA
(Map p218; ☎084 440 6755; www.shambhalayogakohtao.com; Sairee Beach) Ko Tao's full-time yoga centre is housed in beautiful wooden *săh·lah* on the forested grounds of Blue Wind in Sairee Beach. The two-hour classes, led by Kester, the energetic yogi, cost 300B.

Ko Tao Bowling & Mini Golf BOWLING, GOLF
(☎077 456316; ⊙noon-midnight) On the main road between Mae Hat and Chalok Ban Kao, Ko Tao Bowling & Mini Golf has several homemade bowling lanes where the employees reset the pins after every frame (300B per hour). The 18-hole mini-golf course has a landmark theme – putt your ball through Stonehenge or across the Golden Gate Bridge.

Sleeping

If you are planning to dive while visiting Ko Tao, your scuba operator will probably offer you free or discounted accommodation to sweeten the deal. Some schools have on-site lodging, while others have deals with bungalows. It's important to note that you only receive your discount on the days you dive. So, for example, if you buy a 10-dive package, and decide to take a day off in the middle, your room rate will not be discounted on that evening. Also, a restful sleep is important before diving, so scope out these 'great room deals' before saying yes – some of them are one cockroach away from being condemned.

There are also many sleeping options that have absolutely nothing to do with the island's diving culture. Ko Tao's secluded eastern coves are dotted with stunning retreats that still offer a true getaway experience, but these can be difficult to reach due to the island's dismal network of roads. You can often call ahead of time and arrange to be picked up from the pier in Mae Hat.

Note that many budget rooms are only available on a first come, first served basis and often aren't even advertised on hotel websites. Many midrange resorts offer budget rooms so take a look at all our listings to see each resort's (usually very big) price range. These rooms book fast so it can be prudent to call ahead and find out what may be available before you arrive.

Sairee Beach

Giant Sairee is the longest and most developed strip on the island, with a string of dive operations, bungalows, travel agencies, minimarkets and internet cafes. The northern end is the prettiest and quietest while there's more of a party scene and noise from the bars to the south. For most people, this is the choice beach to stay since it has a great blend of scenery and action.

Blue Wind BUNGALOW $
(Map p218; ☎077 456116; bluewind_wa@yahoo.com; bungalows 350-1400B; ❄📶) Blue Wind is a great rustic but relaxing alternative to the high-intensity dive resorts strung along Sairee Beach. Sturdy bamboo huts are peppered along a dirt trail behind the beachside bakery. Large, tiled air-conditioned cabins and attractive rooms in blocks with balcony boast hot showers and TVs. Reception is shut in the evenings and wi-fi is limited to the beach area.

Spicytao Backpackers HOSTEL $
(Map p218; ☎082 278 7115; www.spicyhostels.com/Home.html; dm 200-250B; ❄📶) Like your own super-social country hang-out, Spicytao is hidden off the main drag in a rustic garden setting. Backpackers rave about the ambience and staff who are always organising activities. Book in advance!

Ban's Diving Resort RESORT $$
(Map p218; ☎077 456466; www.bansdivingresort.com; r 600-10,000B; ❄@📶🏊) This dive-centric party palace offers a wide range of quality accommodation from basic backpacker digs to sleek hillside villas, and it's growing all the time. Post-scuba chill sessions take place on Ban's prime slice of beach or at one of the two swimming pools tucked within the strip of jungle between the two-storey, pillared and terraced white hotel blocks.

Sairee Cottage BUNGALOW $$
(Map p218; ☎077 456374; www.saireecottagediving.com; bungalows 500-3000B; ❄📶🏊) Bungalows are connected by a sand path through a sun-splotched garden of palms and hibiscus. Even the smallest, most budget options here are of a higher standard than most and very good value. The beach out front is slim and under the shade of a giant ironwood tree.

Big Blue Resort BUNGALOW $$

(Map p218; ☎077 456050; www.bigbluediving.com; dm 400B, r 1000-7000B; ❄@) This scuba-centric resort has a summer camp vibe – diving classes dominate the daytime, while evenings are spent en masse, grabbing dinner or watching fire twirling. Both the basic fan bungalows and motel-style air-con rooms offer little when it comes to views, but you can grade up if you want ocean panoramas.

Palm Leaf Resort BUNGALOW $$

(Map p218; ☎077 456731; www.kohtaopalmleaf.com; bungalows 2000-3500B; ❄🛜🏊) Palm Leaf rooms are good though nothing spectacular, but the location, at the quieter northern section of silky Sairee Beach, can't be beat.

Seashell Resort BUNGALOW $$

(Map p218; ☎077 456271; www.seashell-kohtao.com; bungalows 1000-4000B; ❄🛜🏊) Another huge mix of lodging from simple wood fan bungalows to hotel-style rooms in a block, this is a busy resort with nicely tended grounds but prices are out of whack with what you can find elsewhere. It's a good backup, however, that welcomes divers and non-divers.

★**Place** RESORT $$$

(Map p218; www.theplacekohtao.com; villas 8000-9000B; ❄🛜) About a 15-minute walk or five-minute taxi ride from its hilltop location to Sairee Beach, this romantic boutique choice has nine private luxury villas nestled in leaf-clad hills with sweeping ocean views. Honeymooners will rejoice: a private plunge pool is standard and private chef services satisfy those who choose to remain in their nuptial nest instead of venturing out for calories.

Ko Tao Cabana BUNGALOW $$$

(Map p218; ☎077 456505; www.kohtaocabana.com; bungalows 6100-16,700B; ❄@🛜🏊) This prime piece of quiet beachside property offers timber-framed villas and white adobe huts with woven roofs dotted along the beach and up the hill, as paths wind through the fern-laden, manicured jungle. The private villas are one of the more upscale options on the island, although service can be lacking and a bit of TLC wouldn't go amiss.

Mae Hat

All ferry arrivals pull into the pier at the busy village of Mae Hat and nearly all the resorts on this beach will have a view and be in earshot of the constant ebb and flow of boat arrivals and departures. As such this isn't the best beach for a tranquil getaway although it's a good hub if your main goal is diving. Accommodation is spread throughout, but the more charming options extend in both directions along the sandy beach, both north and south of the pier.

Sai Thong Resort BUNGALOW $

(Map p212; www.saithongresort.info; Hat Sai Nuan; bungalows 500-2500B; ❄🛜) As the rush of Mae Hat dwindles away along the island's southwest shore, Sai Thong emerges along quiet, sandy Hat Sai Nuan. Bungalows, in various, rustic incarnations of weaving and wood, have colourful porch hammocks and palm-filled vistas. It's secluded and serene: guests frequent the restaurant's relaxing sun deck. Wi-fi only in the restaurant.

The resort is accessed by a quick ride from the Mae Hat pier by long-tail boat, or a 25-minute walk.

Ko Tao Central Hostel HOSTEL $

(Map p218; ☎077 456925, 093 761 2398; www.kohtaohostel.com; dm 310B; ❄🛜) Identified by its London Underground–style logo, this clean, central and friendly Mae Hat hostel has good 12-bed dorms, if all you need is a handy dorm near to the pier. Check-out is at 11am. Reception is in Island Travel next door; no towel service, so bring your own.

Tao Thong Villa BUNGALOW $

(Map p212; ☎077 456078; Ao Sai Nuan; bungalows 400-1800B; ❄@🛜) Popular with long-termers seeking peace and quiet, these no-frills bungalows have killer views. Tao Thong actually straddles two tiny beaches on a craggy cape about halfway between Mae Hat and Chalok Ban Kao. To reach it, grab a boat taxi for a short ride from the Mae Hat pier.

Crystal Dive Resort BUNGALOW $$

(Map p218; ☎077 456106; www.crystaldive.com; bungalows 800-1500B; ❄🛜🏊) The bungalow and motel-style accommodation at Crystal is reserved for its divers, and prices drop significantly for those taking courses. Guests can take a dip in the refreshing pool when it isn't overflowing with newbie divers.

Ananda Villa HOTEL $$

(Map p218; ☎077 456478; www.anandavilla.com; r 500-1800B; ❄🛜) This friendly, two-storey hotel with verandahs and lined with decorative palms and plumeria has a colonial feel, not far from the jetty. The cheapest rooms are fan only and are in another older room block a bit further from the beach.

Mae Hat & Sairee Beach

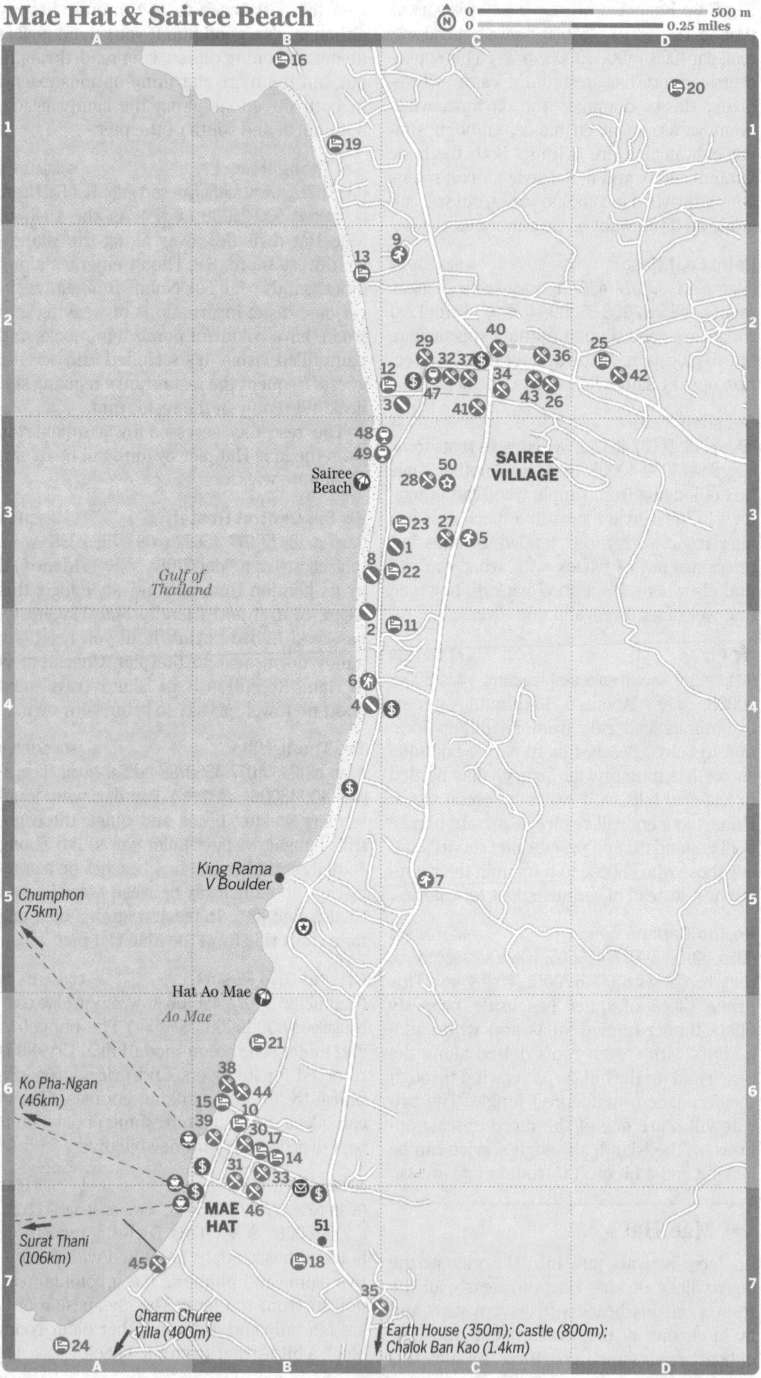

0 — 500 m
0 — 0.25 miles

A B C D
1 2 3 4 5 6 7

16
20
19
9
13
40
29
32
37
36
25
12
47
34
43
26
42
3
41
48
49
SAIREE VILLAGE
Sairee Beach
50
28
23
27
5
1
8
22
Gulf of Thailand
2
11
6
4
King Rama V Boulder
7
Chumphon (75km)
Hat Ao Mae
Ao Mae
21
38
44
Ko Pha-Ngan (46km)
15
10
39
30
17
14
31
33
MAE HAT
46
Surat Thani (106km)
51
45
18
35
Charm Churee Villa (400m)
Earth House (350m); Castle (800m); Chalok Ban Kao (1.4km)
24

Mae Hat & Sairee Beach

Activities, Courses & Tours

- ACE Marine Expeditions ....(see 43)
- ACE Marine Images ....(see 43)
- 1 Apnea Total C3
- 2 Ban's Diving School B4
- 3 Big Blue Diving C2
- 4 Blue Immersion B4
- Crystal Dive .... (see 15)
- 5 Flying Trapeze Adventures C3
- 6 Goodtime Adventures B4
- 7 Monsoon Gym & Fight Club C5
- 8 Scuba Junction B3
- 9 Shambhala C2
- The Gallery Spa ....(see 43)

Sleeping

- 10 Ananda Villa B6
- 11 Ban's Diving Resort C4
- 12 Big Blue Resort C2
- 13 Blue Wind B2
- 14 Captain Nemo Guesthouse B6
- 15 Crystal Dive Resort B6
- 16 Ko Tao Cabana B1
- 17 Ko Tao Central Hostel B6
- 18 Nadapa Resort B7
- 19 Palm Leaf Resort B1
- 20 Place D1
- 21 Regal Resort B6
- 22 Sairee Cottage C3
- 23 Seashell Resort C3
- 24 Sensi Paradise Resort A7
- 25 Spicytao Backpackers D2

Eating

- 26 995 Roasted Duck C2
- 27 Bang Burgers C3
- 28 Barracuda Restaurant & Bar C3
- 29 Café Corner C2
- 30 Café del Sol B6
- 31 Cappuccino B6
- 32 Chopper's Bar & Grill C2
- 33 Dolce Vita B6
- 34 Farango's C2
- 35 Greasy Spoon B7
- 36 Los Pollos Hermanos C2
- 37 Oishi Kaiso C2
- 38 Pranee's Kitchen B6
- 39 Safety Stop Pub B6
- 40 Simple Life C2
- 41 Su Chili C2
- 42 Taste of Home D2
- 43 The Gallery C2
- 44 This is a Book Cafe B6
- 45 Whitening A7
- 46 Zest Coffee Lounge B7

Drinking & Nightlife

- 47 Diza C2
- 48 Fizz C3
- 49 Lotus Bar C3

Entertainment

- 50 Queen's Cabaret C3

Transport

- 51 Lederhosenbikes B7

Captain Nemo Guesthouse GUESTHOUSE $$
(Map p218; www.captainnemo-kohtao.com; d 1000-3000B;) With only five rooms, this popular, small choice a short walk from the pier is nearly always full, so book upfront. The owners are responsive, friendly and helpful and everything is kept clean.

Regal Resort RESORT $$
(Map p218; 077 456007; www.kohtaoregal.com; r 2000-4500B;) Just north of the pier, this resort gives you all the commotion along with your pretty stretch of white sand – the main pool (of three) is filled with divers most of the day. Rooms are large and some have beautiful sea views but things tend to break down. Decent value for the price though.

Nadapa Resort RESORT $$
(Map p218; 077 456495; www.nadaparesort.com; tw & d 1500B;) It's not really a resort and not the choice if what you want is a pool and a beach front, but reliable Nadapa is bright, clean and comfortable, with colour-coded rooms in a block with balcony and bungalows. Away from, but not far from, the action and close to the pier.

Charm Churee Villa RESORT $$$
(Map p212; 077 456393; www.charmchureevilla.com; bungalows 3600-39,100B;) Tucked under sky-scraping palms on a 48-hectare jungle plot away from the bustle of the pier, the luxuriant villas of Charm Churee are dedicated to the flamboyant spoils of the Far East. Staircases, chiselled into the rock face, dribble down a palmed slope revealing teak huts strewn across smoky boulders. The villas' unobstructed views of the swishing waters are beguiling.

Sensi Paradise Resort RESORT $$$
(Map p218; 077 456244; www.sensiparadise.com; bungalows 2100-7000B;) 'Natural chic' on the prettiest stretch of Mae Hat proper, right up against some boulder outcrops. You won't escape the noise of the pier, however. Rooms on the hillside are worn and not worth the price while newer models closer to the beach are quite lovely. Friendly

caretakers and several airy teak *săh·lah* add an extra element of charm.

Chalok Ban Kao

Ao Chalok Ban Ko, about 1.7km south of Mae Hat by road, has one of the largest concentrations of accommodation on Ko Tao. This is a slim stretch of sand in a scenic half-circle bay framed by boulders at either end. The milky blue water here is quite shallow and at low tide a sandbar is exposed that's fun to wade out to for prime sunbathing. This is the quietest of the main beaches but there's still a good selection of restaurants, diving and a more mellow but fun nightlife scene.

Tropicana GUESTHOUSE **$**
(Map p212; 077 456167; www.koh-tao-tropicana-resort.com; r 450-2500B) This friendly place has 56 basic, low-rise units peppered across a sandy, shady garden campus with fleeting glimpses of the ocean between fanned fronds and spiky palms.

JP Resort GUESTHOUSE **$**
(Map p212; 077 456099; r from 700-1300B;) A colourful but rather old menagerie of motel-style rooms stacked on a small scrap of jungle across the street from the sea.

★ **View Point Resort** RESORT **$$**
(Map p212; 077 456444; www.kohtaoviewpoint.com; bungalows 2500-14,000B;) Lush grounds of ferns and palms meander across a boulder-studded hillside offering stunning views over the sea and the bay. All options, from the exquisite private suites that feel like Tarzan and Jane's love nest gone luxury to the huge, view-filled bungalows, use boulders, wood and concrete to create comfortable, naturalistic abodes. It's under new management and fantastic value.

Freedom Beach BUNGALOW **$$**
(Map p212; 077 456596; www.freedombeachresort.info; bungalows 700-3500B;) On its own secluded beach shaded by tall bushes and connected to Ao Chalok Ban Kao by a boardwalk, Freedom feels like a classic backpacker haunt. Steep paths link the seaside bar to the accommodation (from wooden shacks to sturdier huts with air-con) that runs from the beach to high on the cliff. Reception is next door at Taahtoh Resort.

New Heaven Resort BUNGALOW **$$**
(077 456422; www.newheavenkohtao.com; r & bungalows 700-3800B;) Just beyond the clutter of Chalok Ban Kao, New Heaven delivers colourful huts perched on a hill over impossibly clear waters. A steep path of chiselled stone tumbles down the shrubby rock face revealing views ripped straight from the pages of *National Geographic*.

Buddha View Dive Resort BUNGALOW **$$**
(Map p212; 077 456074; www.buddhaview-diving.com; r 800-1300B;) Like other large diving operations on the island, Buddha View offers its divers discounted on-site digs in a super-social atmosphere. Wi-fi costs 100B.

Ko Tao Resort RESORT **$$$**
(Map p212; 077 456133; www.kotaoresort.com; r & bungalows 1900-6500B;) Rooms at this resort are split between 'pool side' and 'paradise zone' – all are well stocked, water sports equipment is on offer, and there are several bars primed to serve an assortment of fruity cocktails.

Chintakiri Resort RESORT **$$$**
(Map p212; 077 456133; www.chintakiri.com; r & bungalows 3200-6200B;) Perched high over the gulf waters overlooking Chalok Ban Kao, Chintakiri is one of Ko Tao's more luxurious properties, helping the island furtively creep upmarket. Rooms are spread around the inland jungle, and sport crisp white walls with lacquered finishing.

Hin Wong

A sandy beach has been swapped out for a boulder-strewn coast on the serene east side of the island, but the water is crystal clear. The road to Hin Wong is paved in parts, but sudden sand pits and steep hills can toss you off your motorbike. A taxi to Sairee Beach will cost you around 200B.

Hin Wong Bungalows BUNGALOW **$**
(Map p212; 077 456006; Hin Wong; bungalows 500-700B;) Above boulders strewn to the sea, these 11 pleasant corrugated roof huts are scattered across a lot of untamed tropical terrain – it all feels a bit like *Gilligan's Island*. A rickety dock, jutting out just beyond the breezy restaurant, is the perfect place to dangle your legs and watch schools of black sardines slide through the cerulean water.

View Rock BUNGALOW **$**
(Map p212; 077 456549, 077 456548; viewrock@hotmail.com; Hin Wong; bungalows 500-2000B;) When coming down the dirt road into Hin Wong, follow the signs as they lead you north of Hin Wong Bungalows. View Rock is

precisely that: views and rocks; the hodgepodge of wooden huts, which resembles a secluded fishing village, is built into the steep crags, offering stunning views of the bay.

Ao Tanot (Tanote Bay)

Boulder-strewn Ao Tanot is more populated than some of the other eastern coves, but it's still rather quiet and picturesque. Note that the road is paved quite a fair bit, but then dissolves into a deeply pitted dirt track, so go slow. Discounted taxis (around 100B) bounce back and forth between Tanote Bay and Mae Hat; ask at your resort for a timetable.

Poseidon BUNGALOW $
(Map p212; 077 456735; poseidonkohtao@hotmail.com; Ao Tanot; bungalows 800-1500B;) Poseidon keeps the tradition of the budget bamboo bungalow alive with 150 or so basic-but-sleepable fan huts scattered near the sand. Wi-fi in restaurant.

Family Tanote BUNGALOW $$
(Map p212; 077 456757; Ao Tanot; bungalows 800-3500B;) This family-run scatter of hillside bungalows is a good choice for solitude seekers. Strap on a snorkel mask and swim around with the fish at your doorstep, or climb up to the restaurant for a tasty meal and beautiful views of the bay.

Ao Leuk & Ao Thian Ok

Jamahkiri Resort & Spa RESORT $$$
(Map p212; 077 456400; www.jamahkiri.com; bungalows incl breakfast 8400-30,000B;) Wooden masks and stone fertility goddesses abound amid mosaics and multi-armed statues at this whitewashed estate. Hoots from monkeys confirm the jungle theme, as do the thatched roofs and tiki-torched soirees. There are lots of steps, but views are gorgeous, the spa is top-of-the-range and the dive centre is excellent.

Ko Nang Yuan

Photogenic Ko Nang Yuan, just off the northwest coast of Ko Tao, is easily accessible by the Lomprayah catamaran, and by water taxis that depart from Mae Hat and Sairee (100B each way). There's a 100B tax for all visitors to the island.

Ko Nangyuan Dive Resort BUNGALOW $$$
(Map p212; 077 456088; www.nangyuan.com; bungalows incl breakfast 1500-14,000B;) The rugged collection of wood and aluminium bungalows winds its way across three coolie-hat-like conical islands connected by an idyllic beige sandbar. Yes, this is a private island paradise but note it gets busy with day trippers. Prices include round-trip to Ko Tao.

Eating

With super-sized Ko Samui lurking on the horizon, it's hard to believe that quaint little Ko Tao holds its own in the gastronomy category. Most resorts and dive operators offer on-site dining, and stand-alone establishments are multiplying at in Sairee Beach and Mae Hat. The diverse population of divers has spawned a broad range of international cuisine dining options, including Mexican, French, Italian, Indian and Japanese. On our quest to find the tastiest Thai fare on the island, we discovered, not surprisingly, that our favourite local meals were being dished out at small, unnamed roadside restaurants.

Sairee Beach

★**995 Roasted Duck** CHINESE $
(Map p218; mains from 70B; 9am-9pm) You may have to queue a while to get a seat at this shack and wonder what all the fuss is about. The fuss is excellent roast duck, from 70B for a steaming bowl of roasted waterfowl with noodles to 700B for a whole bird.

Bang Burgers BURGERS $
(Map p218; mains from 100B; 10am-10pm) You may have to dig your heels in and wait in line at this terrific burger bar that does a roaring trade in Sairee. There's around a half dozen burgers on the menu, including a vegie choice for meat-free diners.

Su Chili THAI $
(Map p218; dishes 85-225B; 10am-10.30pm) Inviting and bustling, Su Chili serves fresh and tasty Thai dishes, with friendly staff always asking how spicy you want your food. Try the delicious northern Thai specialities or Penang curries. There's a smattering of Western comfort food for homesick diners.

Oishi Kaiso JAPANESE $
(Map p218; mains from 90B; 11.30am-10.30pm) This neat *gyoza* (dumpling) sized establishment is often full, doing a brisk trade in *nigiri*, *sashimi* and *maki*. A couple of Thai dishes are thrown in for good measure, but you can find them elsewhere. The *gyoza* are very tempting indeed.

Los Pollos Hermanos BARBECUE $
(Map p218; www.lospolloshermanos-kohtao.com; mains from 140B; ⏲8am-midnight) No, there's no Nandos on Ko Tao. But there's *Los Pollos Hermanos*, which does a mighty fine job of grilling up peri-peri chicken with sauces arriving in three different grades of spiciness. We hope they lose the wooden plates though. It's tucked away along an alley off the main drag.

Simple Life INTERNATIONAL $
(Map p218; mains from 80B; ⏲7.30am-10.30pm) The menu is kind of average but excellent deals are noteworthy here: the all-you-can-eat pizza buffet (199B) brings in crowds four nights a week (Sunday, Monday, Wednesday and Friday) and the all-you-can-eat breakfasts (170B) and free-flow coffees do a roaring trade each morning.

★**Barracuda Restaurant & Bar** ASIAN FUSION $$
(Map p218; ☎080 146 3267; mains 240-590B; ⏲6-10.30pm) Chef Ed Jones caters for the Thai princess when she's in town but you can sample his exquisite cuisine for mere pennies in comparison to her budget. Locally sourced ingredients are sourced for creative, fresh, fusion masterpieces. Try the seafood platter, sesame-seared tuna fillet or braised lamb shank – then wash it down with a lemon grass, ginger mojito.

There's another branch a five-minute walk away.

The Gallery THAI $$
(Map p218; ☎077 456547; www.thegallerykohtao.com; mains 120-420B; ⏲noon-10pm) One of the most pleasant settings in town, next to owner Chris Clark's gallery of beautiful island photography, the food here is equally special. The signature dish is *mok maprao* (chicken, shrimp and fish curry served in a young coconut) but the white snapper fillet in creamy red curry sauce is also excellent.

Taste of Home INTERNATIONAL $$
(Map p218; mains 120-250B; ⏲11am-1pm & 6-11pm; 📶) German-run and serving a bit of everything (Swedish meatballs, Turkish kofta, Hungarian goulash and Wiener schnitzel to name a few), but everything is delicious and prepared with heart. It's a small, simple setting popular with expats.

Chopper's Bar & Grill INTERNATIONAL $$
(Map p218; www.choppers-kohtao.com; mains 160-300B; ⏲9am-midnight) Frequently rammed and a fixture on the Ko Tao pub crawl, Chopper's is a riotously popular two-storey hangout with live music, sports on the TVs, billiards, a cinema room and decent pub grub. Happy hour is 5pm to 8pm.

Café Corner CAFE $$
(Map p218; snacks & mains 30-180B; ⏲breakfast & lunch) Prime real estate, mod furnishings and tasty iced coffees have made Café Corner a Sairee staple over the last few years. Swing by at 5pm to stock up for tomorrow morning's breakfast; the scrumptious baked breads are buy-one-get-one-free before being tossed at sunset.

Farango's PIZZA $$
(Map p218; dishes 80-230B; ⏲lunch & dinner) Things are cookin' at his busy pizzeria doing a fine trade in Sairee Village with decent pizzas and other signature Italian fare. Payment is cash only.

Mae Hat

Zest Coffee Lounge CAFE $
(Map p218; dishes 70-200B; ⏲6am-6pm; 📶) All brick and wood with a scuffed red floor, Zest pulls out the stops to brew up some excellent coffee. Eggs Benedict gets the morning off on the right foot, while idlers and snackers can nibble on ciabatta sandwiches or sticky confections while nursing their creamy caffe latte. There's a second branch in Sairee, although we prefer this location.

Cappuccino CAFE $
(Map p218; Mae Hat; dishes from 30B; ⏲7am-6pm) With marble table tops, wall mirrors and good grooves, Cappuccino's decor falls somewhere between the New York deli on *Seinfeld* and a French brasserie – it's a great place to grab a coffee and croissant.

Safety Stop Pub INTERNATIONAL $
(Map p218; mains 60-250B; ⏲7am-11pm; 📶) A haven for homesick Brits, this pier-side restaurant and bar feels like a tropical beer garden. Stop by on Sundays to stuff your face with an endless supply of barbecued goodness; and the Thai dishes also aren't half bad.

Pranee's Kitchen THAI $
(Map p218; dishes 50-150B; ⏲7am-10pm; 📶) An old Mae Hat fave, Pranee's serves scrumptious curries and other Thai treats in an open-air pavilion sprinkled with lounging pillows, wooden tables and TVs. English-language movies are shown nightly at 6pm.

Greasy Spoon BREAKFAST $
(Map p218; English breakfast 140B; ⏲6.30am-3pm; 📶) Although completely devoid of character, Greasy Spoon stays true to its name by offering a variety of heart-clogging breakfast treats: black pudding, eggs, sausage, hash browns, chips (and vegie options) that'll bring a tear to any Brit's eye.

★ **Whitening** INTERNATIONAL $$
(Map p218; dishes 150-400B; ⏲1pm-1am; 📶) This starched, white, beachy spot falls somewhere between being a restaurant and a chic seaside bar – foodies will appreciate the tasty twists on indigenous and international dishes. Dine amid dangling white Christmas lights while keeping your bare feet tucked into the sand. And the best part? It's comparatively easy on the wallet.

Café del Sol INTERNATIONAL $$
(Map p218; mains from 100B; ⏲8am-10.30pm; 📶) This corner cafe steps away from the pier is an excellent choice to down a French (120B), Full English (190B) or Divers (140B) breakfast and watch the morning Ko Tao world go by. Lunch and dinner dishes range from hearty pepper hamburgers to homemade pasta, though prices tend to be quite inflated.

This is a Book Cafe CAFE $$
(Map p218; ⏲7am-9pm; 📶) With lovely white walls, books on shelves, a small scattering of trendy furniture (and a dissonant 1970s fat-screen TV in the corner) and floral sofa, this charming and very quiet choice is perfect for a coffee, ice cream, baked goodies and doses of tranquillity.

Dolce Vita ITALIAN $$
(Map p218; pizzas 170-270B; ⏲noon-10pm) For the best Italian on Ko Tao, come and taste Dolce Vita's homemade pastas and fine pizzas.

Chalok Ban Kao

I ♥ Salad CAFE $$
(Map p212; mains from 120B; ⏲8am-9pm; 📶) This rustic choice offers a healthy array of salads using fresh ingredients, with a good supply of vegetarian and vegan dishes and sticky desserts to follow. There are also real fruit juices and healthy egg white–only breakfasts.

Viewpoint Restaurant INTERNATIONAL $$$
(Map p212; ☎077 456444; 250-1100B; ⏲7.30am-10pm) On a deck overlooking Ao Chalok Ban Kao, this is one of the most romantic settings on the island. The food is also the most upscale and holds its own against Samui's best – try the braised pork belly or the whole tuna from the oven. Apart from the Australian beef dishes, prices are reasonable.

Long Pae STEAK $$$
(Map p212; mains from 160B; ⏲10am-midnight) Ensconced off the radar from most of the island's tourist traffic, 'Uncle Pae' sits on a terrace in hilly jungle with distant views of the sea down below. The speciality here is steak, which goes well with a generous smattering of pan-Asian appetisers. If the weather's clear, try to tie in sunset, but if the winds blow, hold on to your napkins.

Drinking & Nightlife

After diving, Ko Tao's favourite pastime is drinking, and there's no shortage of places to get tanked. In fact, the island's three biggest dive centres each have bars – **Fishbowl Beach Bar**, **Crystal Bar** and **Buddha On The Beach** in Chalok Bak Kao – that attract swarms of travellers and expats alike. It's well worth stopping by even if you aren't a diver.

Flyers detailing upcoming parties are posted on various trees and walls along the island's west coast (check the two 7-Elevens in Sairee). Also keep an eye out for posters touting 'jungle parties' held on nondescript patches of scrubby jungle in the centre of the island. There's also a **Koh Tao Pub Crawl** (www.kohtaopubcrawl.com) that starts at Chopper's Bar & Grill (p222) on Hat Sairee every Monday, Wednesday and Friday at 6pm before departing at 7.30pm to four other watering holes, taking in cabaret, live music and fire shows. The 400B cover includes a bucket, two shots and a T-shirt, so it's not a bad deal. If you go again, it's 300B and then 200B.

Several places, such as Chopper's and Safety Stop Pub (p222), double as great hang-out joints for a well-deserved post-dive beer.

Just remember: don't drink and dive.

Clumped at the southern end of Sairee Beach, **AC Party Pub**, **In Touch** and **Maya Bar** take turns reeling in the partiers throughout the week.

★ **Earth House** BEER GARDEN
(Map p212; www.theearthhousekohtao.com; ⏲noon-midnight Mon-Sat) Run by Kelly from Worcester, this relaxing, secluded and rustic spot serves up a global selection of 40 beers, craft labels and ciders in a dreamy garden setting. With its own relaxing treehouse, there's also a restaurant for bites (9am to noon and 1pm to 6pm Monday to Saturday) and bungalows

for going prone if you overdo it on the Green Goblin (cider).

Earth House is on the road to Ao Tanot, just before the turn-off for Ao Leuk.

★Fizz BAR
(Map p218; Sairee Beach) Sink into a bean bag, order up a designer cocktail and let the hypnotic surf roll in amid a symphony of ambient sounds. Fantastic.

Castle CLUB
(Map p212; www.thecastlekohtao.com; Mae Hat) Located along the main road between Mae Hat and Chalok Ban Kao, the three-floor Castle is the top hip-hop, garage, electro and funk party venue on the island, luring an array of local and international DJs to its triad of parties each month.

Lotus Bar BAR
(Map p218; Sairee Beach) Lotus is the de facto late-night hang-out spot along the northern end of Sairee. Muscular fire twirlers toss around flaming batons, and the drinks are so large there should be a lifeguard on duty.

Diza BAR
(Map p218; Sairee Beach) Diza is a packed hang-out at the crossroads of Sairee Village, flogging cheap beer and drowning and cranking the volume up as loud as it can go.

Natural High Cafe CAFE
(Map p212; ⏲10.30am-midnight) With a fine elevated open-air terrace and ranging views in all directions over the profuse island greenery, hammocks for lying around in, ambient chill-out sounds and coffee served up in enamel cups, this cafe is ideal for zoning out, but there's pool for fidgets. It's on a hill on the road to Hat Sai Daeng; look out for the signs.

☆ Entertainment

★Queen's Cabaret CABARET
(Map p218; ⏲10.15pm nightly) Every night is different at this intimate bar where acts range from your standard sparkling Abba and leg kicks extravaganza to steamy topless croons. If you're male, note you may get 'dragged' into the performance if you're sitting near the front. The show is free but it's expected that you will purchase a (pricey) drink – which is totally worth it.

Raw Art Moovment LIVE MUSIC
(⏲10am-late) A place for art, music, socialising, drinking and, most importantly, the Sunday Art Jam when the island's talented musicians perform and the vibe is like a big, fun (free!) party at someone's house (in fact the venue is part of owner's Denny and Lisa's house). The first chords are strummed at 7.30pm, but come by any time.

Shopping

Although most items are cheap when compared to prices back home, diving equipment is a big exception to the rule. On Ko Tao you'll be paying Western prices plus shipping plus commission on each item (even with 'discounts') so it's better to do your scuba shopping at home or on your computer. The main 7-Eleven at the intersection in Sairee Village is often rammed with punters waiting in line, especially at night; if you're after beer, soft drinks or anything else you might find at a smaller, local shop, it's quicker to hunt around. There are a few family-run shops up the road past the Gallery, for example. Ubiquitous pharmacists charge very high prices for imported sunscreen, shampoos, mosquito repellent and other items; check in smaller shops and branches of 7-Eleven to see if you can find better-priced equivalents.

Hammock Cafe Plaeyuan HOMEWARES
(Map p212; ⏲9am-6pm) This small cafe on the road to Chalok Ban Kao doubles as a hammock shop, selling a fantastic selection of vivid and brightly coloured Mlabri handwoven hammocks, some with up to 3km worth of fabric. Prices start at around 1700B for a sitting hammock, and up to 5000B for the most elaborate.

Information

The ubiquitous *Koh Tao Info* booklet lists loads of businesses on the island and goes into some detail about the island's history, culture and social issues.

DANGERS & ANNOYANCES

There's nothing more annoying than enrolling in a diving course with your friends and then having to drop out because you scraped your knee in a motorcycle accident. The roads on Ko Tao are slowly being paved but some remain dangerous. While hiring a scooter is extremely convenient, this is not the place to learn how to drive. The island is rife with abrupt hills and sudden sand pits along gravel trails; if driving a scooter, stick to good roads and if you are unsure, turn back. Even if you escape unscathed, scamming bike shops may claim that you damaged your rental and will try to extort some serious cash from you (ensure you check the bike carefully prior to hire and identify scratches and dents).

Also be aware that mosquito-borne dengue fever is a real and serious threat. The virus can spread quickly due to tightly packed tourist areas and the small size of the island.

EMERGENCY

Police Station (Map p218; ☎077 456631) Between Mae Hat and Sairee Beach along the rutted portion of the beachside road.

INTERNET ACCESS

Wi-fi is widely available at resorts, bars and restaurants.

MEDICAL SERVICES

All divers are required to sign a medical waiver before exploring the sea. If you have any medical condition that might hinder your ability to dive (including mild asthma), you will be asked to get medical clearance from a doctor on Ko Tao. If you're unsure about whether or not you are fit to dive, consider seeing a doctor before your trip as there are no official hospitals on the island, and the number of qualified medical professionals is limited. Also, make sure your traveller's insurance covers scuba diving. On-island medical 'consultations' (and we use that term very lightly) cost 300B. There are several walk-in clinics and mini hospitals scattered around Mae Hat and Sairee, but all serious medical needs should be dealt with on Ko Samui. If you are diving, ask your outfitter to point you in the proper direction of medical advice. The nearest hyperbaric chamber is on Big Buddha Beach (Hat Bang Rak) on Ko Samui; in emergencies, a speedboat makes the journey.

MONEY

There are 24-hour ATMs at the island's 7-Elevens. There's also a cluster of ATMs orbiting the ferry docks at Mae Hat. There is a money exchange window at Mae Hat's pier and a second location near Chopper's in Sairee Beach. There are several banks near the post office in Mae Hat, at the far end of town along the island's main inland road. They are usually open 9am to 4pm on weekdays. Almost all dive schools accept credit cards, however there is usually a 3% or 4% handling fee.

POST

Post Office (Map p218; ☎077 456170; ⏰9am-5pm Mon-Fri, 9am-noon Sat) A 10- to 15-minute walk from the pier; at the corner of Ko Tao's main inner-island road and Mae Hat's 'down road'.

TOURIST INFORMATION

There's no government-run TAT office on Ko Tao. Transportation and accommodation bookings can be made at most dive shops or at any of the numerous travel agencies, all of which take a small commission on services rendered.

WEBSITES

www.kohtaocompleteguide.com Handy website and an excellent quarterly free hard copy guide in book form.

www.kohtaoonline.com An online version of the *Koh Tao Info* booklet.

Getting There & Away

As always, costs and departure times are subject to change. Rough waves are known to cancel ferries between the months of October and December. When the waters are choppy we recommend taking the Seatran rather than the Lomprayah catamaran if you are prone to seasickness. The catamarans ride the swell, whereas the Seatran cuts through the currents as it crosses the sea. Note that we highly advise purchasing your boat tickets *several* days in advance if you are accessing Ko Tao from Ko Pha-Ngan after the Full Moon Party.

AIR

Nok Air (www.nokair.com) jets passengers from Bangkok's Don Mueang airport to Chumphon once or twice daily in each direction while **Happy Air** (www.happyair.co.th) has several flights per day from Bangkok's Suvarnabhumi International Airport and a flight five days a week to Ranong. Flights to/from Bangkok are usually around 3300B. Upon arriving in Chumphon, travellers can make a seamless transfer to the catamaran service bound for Ko Tao.

BOAT

To Ko Pha-Ngan

The Lomprayah catamaran offers a thrice-daily service (500B to 600B), leaving Ko Tao at 6am, 9.30am and 3pm and arriving on Ko Pha-Ngan around 7am, 10.30am and 4pm. The Seatran Discovery Ferry (430B) offers a similar service, but its earliest boat departs at 6.30am. The Songserm express boat (350B) departs daily at 9.30am and arrives on Ko Pha-Ngan at 11.30am. Hotel pick-ups are included in the price.

To Ko Samui

The **Lomprayah** catamaran offers a twice-daily service (600B), leaving Ko Tao at 9.30am and 3pm and arriving at Mae Nam on Ko Samui via Ko Pha-Ngan, around 11.20am and 4.40pm. An earlier boat at 6am goes to Na Thon on Ko Samui, arriving at 7.45am. The **Seatran Discovery Ferry** (600B) offers a similar service, with departures at 6.30am, 9am and 3pm. The **Songserm** express boat (450B) departs daily at 9.30am and arrives on Samui (again via Ko Pha-Ngan) at 1.15pm. Hotel pick-ups are included in the price.

To Surat Thani & the Andaman Coast

The easiest option is to stop over on either Ko Pha-Ngan or Ko Samui to shorten the trip and lessen the number of connections. Otherwise, a combination bus–boat ticket from travel agents around the island shouldn't cost more than going it alone. But if you don't feel like being herded like a sheep onto a tourist bus, there are two routes you can take. The first, and more common, approach is to board a Surat-bound boat (you may have to transfer boats on Ko Pha-Ngan or Ko Samui), then transfer to a bus upon arrival.

The second option is to take a ferry to Chumphon on the mainland and then switch to a bus or train bound for the provinces further south.

BUS

Bus-boat package tickets to/from Bangkok are available from travel agencies all over Bangkok and the south; tickets cost around 1000B and the whole voyage takes around 12 hours. Buses switch to boats in Chumphon, and Bangkok-bound passengers can choose to disembark in Hua Hin (for the same price as the Ko Tao–Bangkok ticket).

TRAIN

Travellers can plan their own journey by taking a boat to Chumphon, then making their way to Chumphon's town centre to catch a train up to Bangkok (or any town along the upper southern gulf); likewise in the opposite direction. A 2nd-class ticket to Bangkok will cost around 300B and the trip takes around 8½ hours.

From Ko Tao, the high-speed Lomprayah catamaran departs for Chumphon at 10.15am and 2.45pm (600B, 1½ hours), and a Songserm express boat makes the same journey at 2.30pm (500B), arriving at 5pm. There may be fewer departures if the swells are high.

Getting Around

MOTORCYCLE

Renting a motorcycle is a dangerous endeavour if you're not sticking to the main, well-paved roads. Daily rental rates begin at 150B for a scooter. Larger bikes start at 350B. Discounts are available for weekly and monthly rentals. Try **Lederhosenbikes** (Map p218; ☎0817 528994; www.kohtaomotorbikes.com; Mae Hat; ⊙8.30am-6pm Mon-Sat). Reconsider renting all-terrain-vehicles (ATVs) or jet skis – accidents are not uncommon.

SŎRNG·TĂA·OU

In Mae Hat *sŏrng·tăa·ou*, pick-up trucks and motorbikes crowd around the pier as passengers alight. If you're a solo traveller, you will pay 200B to get to Sairee Beach or Chalok Ban Kao. Groups of two or more will pay 100B each. Rides from Sairee to Chalok Ban Kao cost 150B per person, or 300B for solo tourists. These prices are rarely negotiable, and passengers will be expected to wait until their taxi is full unless they want to pay an additional 200B to 300B. Prices double for trips to the east coast, and drivers will raise the prices when rain makes the roads harder to negotiate. If you know where you intend to stay, we highly recommend calling ahead to arrange a pick-up. Many dive schools offer free pick-ups and transfers as well.

WATER TAXI

Boat taxis depart from Mae Hat, Chalok Ban Kao and the northern part of Sairee Beach (near Vibe Bar). Boat rides to Ko Nang Yuan will set you back at least 100B. Long-tail boats can be chartered for around 1500B per day, depending on the number of passengers carried.

Ang Thong Marine National Park

อุทยานแห่งชาติหมู่เกาะอ่างทอง

The 40-some jagged jungle islands of Ang Thong Marine National Park stretch across the cerulean sea like a shattered emerald necklace – each piece a virgin realm featuring sheer limestone cliffs, hidden lagoons and perfect peach-coloured sands. These dream-inducing islets inspired Alex Garland's cult classic novel, *The Beach*.

February, March and April are the best months to visit this ethereal preserve of greens and blues; crashing monsoon waves mean that the park is almost always closed during November and December.

Sights

Every tour stops at the park's head office on **Ko Wua Talap**, the largest island in the archipelago.

The naturally occurring stone arches on **Ko Samsao** and **Ko Tai Plao** are visible during seasonal tides and weather conditions. Because the sea is quite shallow around the island chain, reaching a maximum depth of 10m, extensive coral reefs have not developed, except in a few protected pockets on the southwest and northeast sides. There's a shallow coral reef near Ko Tai Plao and Ko Samsao that has decent but not excellent snorkelling. There are also several novice dives for exploring shallow caves and colourful coral gardens and spotting banded sea snakes and turtles. Soft powder beaches line **Ko Tai Plao**, **Ko Wuakantang** and **Ko Hintap**.

Viewpoint VIEWPOINT

The island's viewpoint might just be the most stunning vista in all of Thailand. From the top, visitors will have sweeping views of the jagged islands nearby as they burst through the placid turquoise water in easily anthropomorphised formations. The trek to the lookout is an arduous 450m trail that takes roughly an hour to complete. Hikers should wear sturdy shoes and walk slowly on the sharp outcrops of limestone. A second trail leads to **Tham Bua Bok**, a cavern with lotus-shaped stalagmites and stalactites.

Emerald Sea LAKE

The Emerald Sea (also called the Inner Sea) on **Ko Mae Ko** is a popular destination. This large lake in the middle of the island spans an impressive 250m by 350m and has an ethereal minty tint. You can look but you can't touch; the lagoon is strictly off limits to the unclean human body. A dramatic **viewpoint** can be found at the top of a series of staircases nearby.

Tours

The best way to experience Ang Thong is by taking one of the many guided tours departing Ko Samui and Ko Pha-Ngan. The tours usually include lunch, snorkelling equipment, hotel transfers and (with fingers crossed) a knowledgeable guide. If you're staying in luxury accommodation, there's a good chance that your resort has a private boat for providing group tours. Some midrange and budget places also have their own boats, and if not, they can easily set you up with a general tour operator. Dive centres on Ko Samui and Ko Pha-Ngan offer **scuba trips** to the park, although Ang Thong doesn't offer the world-class diving that can be found around Ko Tao and Ko Pha-Ngan.

Tour companies tend to come and go like the wind. Ask at your accommodation for a list of current operators.

Sleeping

Ang Thong does not have any resorts; however, on Ko Wua Talap the national park has set up five bungalows, each housing between two and eight guests. Campers are also allowed to pitch a tent in certain designated zones. Online bookings are possible, although customers must forward a bank deposit within two days of making the reservation. For advance reservations contact the **National Parks Services** (☎077 286025; www.dnp.go.th; bungalows 500-1400B).

Getting There & Around

The best way to reach the park is to take a private day tour from Ko Samui or Ko Pha-Ngan (28km and 32km away, respectively). The islands sit between Samui and the main pier at Don Sak; however, there are no ferries that stop off along the way.

The park officially has an admission fee (adult/child 400/200B), although it should be included in the price of every tour (ask your operator if you are unsure). Private boat charters are also another possibility, although high petrol prices will make the trip quite expensive.

SURAT THANI PROVINCE

Surat Thani อำเภอเมืองสุราษฎร์ธานี

POP 128,990

Known in Thai as 'City of Good People', Surat Thani was once the seat of the ancient Srivijaya empire. Today, this unglamorously typical Thai town is a busy transport hub moving cargo and people around the country. Travellers rarely linger here as they make their way to the popular islands of Ko Samui, Ko Pha-Ngan and Ko Tao, but it's a great stop if you enjoy real Thai working cities, good southern-style street food and nosing around colourful Chinese temples.

Sleeping

Staying in central Surat puts you in a bustling Thai city that can be refreshing, and indeed fascinating, after sojourns in the primped-for-tourists gulf islands. Prices are low and you get a lot for relatively few baht.

For more modern amenities, hop on a *sŏrng·tăa·ou* heading towards the Phang-Nga district. When you climb aboard, tell the driver 'Tesco Lotus', and you'll be taken about 2km to 3km out of town to a large, boxlike shopping centre. A handful of more upscale hotel options orbit the mall.

If you're on a very tight budget, consider zipping straight through town and taking the night ferry to reach your island destination.

My Place @ Surat Hotel HOTEL $

(☎077 272288; 247/5 Th Na Meuang; d 490-590B, f 620B; ❄📶) All smiles and nary a speck of dust at this excellent, central Chinese hotel,

Surat Thani

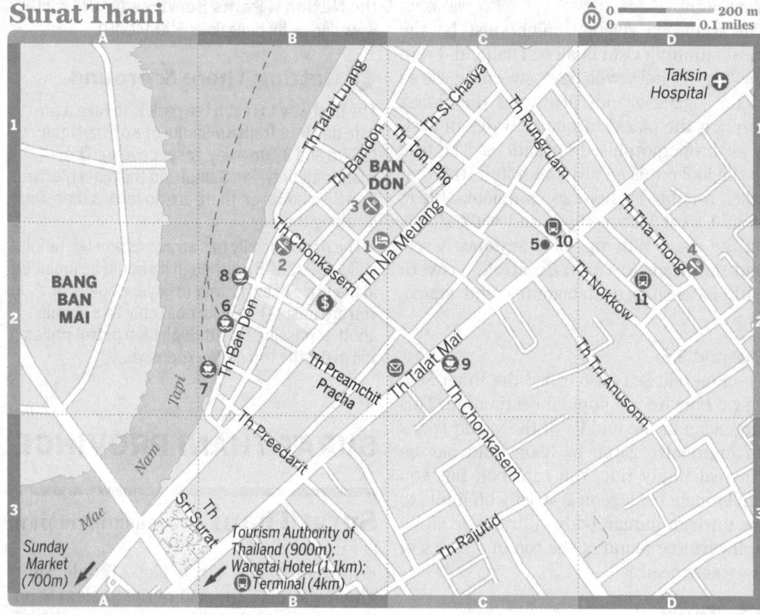

Surat Thani

Sleeping

1 My Place @ Surat Hotel B2

Eating

2 Milano B2
3 Night Market B1
4 Vegetarian Restaurant D2

Information

5 Pranthip Co C2

Transport

6 Ko Tao Night Ferry Pier B2
Lomprayah .... (see 8)
7 Night Boat to Ko Pha-Ngan B2
8 Seatran Discovery B2
9 Seatran Office C2
Songserm .... (see 8)
10 Talat Kaset 1 Bus Terminal C2
11 Talat Kaset 2 Bus Terminal D2

which offers spacious, very clean rooms, colourful throw cushions, modern art on the walls, power showers and value for money. It may be budget, but it will suit almost anyone. Breakfast is served in the cafe next door.

Wangtai Hotel HOTEL $$
(☎077 283020; 1 Th Talad Mai; r 790-2000B; ❄@☎≋) Across the river from the TAT office, the 230-room Wangtai is a smart, marbled choice in the centre of town, offering pleasant and comfortable, if rather generic, rooms with good views of the city.

Eating

Surat Thani is packed with delicious street food for lunch and dinner. Aside from the central night market, stalls near the departure docks open for the daily night boats to the islands, and there's an afternoon **Sunday market** (⊙4-9pm) near the TAT office. During the day, many food stalls near the downtown bus terminal sell *kôw gài òp* (marinated baked chicken on rice).

Night Market MARKET $
(Sarn Chao Ma; Th Ton Pho; dishes from 35B; ⊙6-11pm) A fantastic smorgasbord of food including masses of melt-in-your-mouth marinated meats on sticks, fresh fruit juices, noodle dishes and desserts. It's not that big so it's easy to browse the stalls before making a selection.

Milano PIZZA $
(Th Bandon; mains from 110B; ⊙noon-10pm) This Italian restaurant near the pier bakes up

a tasty selection of pizza, while pasta and a choice of other international dishes and comfort food round out a surprisingly good menu.

Vegetarian Restaurant VEGETARIAN $
(47/7 Th Tha Thong; mains from 30B; ⏲7am-3pm; 🖉) This simple but friendly vegie restaurant can serve you a bowl of rice and curried vegies, washed down with an enamelled cup of water for 30B. Look for the yellow banners with the Chinese character 斋 (meaning 'vegetarian').

Information

Th Na Meuang has a bank on virtually every corner in the heart of downtown.

Post Office (☎077 281966, 077 272013; ⏲8.30am-4.30pm Mon-Fri, 9am-noon Sat & Sun) West of Wat Thammabucha.

Taksin Hospital (☎077 273239; Th Talat Mai) The most professional of Surat's three hospitals. Just beyond the Talat Mai Market in the northeast part of downtown.

Tourism Authority of Thailand (TAT; ☎077 288818; 5 Th Talat Mai; ⏲8.30am-4.30pm) This friendly office southwest of town has useful brochures and maps, and staff speak good English.

Getting There & Away

In general, if you are departing Bangkok or Hua Hin for Ko Pha-Ngan or Ko Tao, consider taking the train or a bus–boat package that goes through Chumphon rather than Surat. You'll save time, and the journey will be more comfortable. Travellers heading to/from Ko Samui will most likely pass through town. If you require any travel services, try reliable **Pranthip Co** (Th Talat Mai; ⏲7.30am-5.30pm).

AIR

Although flights from Bangkok to Surat Thani are cheaper than the flights to Samui, it takes quite a bit of time to reach the gulf islands from the airport. Air Asia offers a convenient bus and boat shuttle with its flights that can alleviate some of the stress. There are daily shuttles to Bangkok on **Thai Airways** (☎077 272610; 3/27-28 Th Karunarat), **Air Asia** (www.airasia.com) and **Nok Air** (www.nokair.com).

BOAT

Various ferry companies offer services to the islands. Try **Lomprayah** (☎077 4277 656; www.lomprayah.com), **Seatran Discovery** (☎077 275063; www.seatrandiscovery.com) or **Songserm** (☎077 377704; www.songserm-expressboat.com).

Bus–Boat Combination Tickets

In the high season travellers can usually find bus–boat services to Ko Samui and Ko Pha-Ngan directly from the Phun Phin train station (which is 14km west of Surat). These services don't cost any more than those booked in Surat Thani and can save you some serious waiting time.

There are also several ferry and speedboat operators that connect Surat Thani to Ko Tao, Ko Pha-Ngan and Ko Samui. Most boats – such as the Raja and Seatran services – leave from Don Sak (about one hour from Surat; bus transfers are included in the ferry ticket) although the Songserm leaves from the heart of Surat town. Be warned that the Raja service can be a very frustrating experience, especially for travellers who are tight on time. The boat trip usually takes around 1½ hours to Ko Samui and 2½ hours to Ko Pha-Ngan, although often the captain will cut the engines to half propulsion, which means the journey can take up to five hours.

Night Ferry

From the centre of Surat there are nightly ferries to Ko Tao (600B, eight hours, departs at 11pm), Ko Pha-Ngan (400B, seven hours, departs at 11pm) and Ko Samui (300B, six hours, departs at 11pm). These are cargo ships, not luxury boats, so bring food and water and watch your bags.

BUS & MINIVAN

The most convenient way to travel around the south, frequent buses and minivans depart from two main locations in town known as Talat Kaset 1 and Talat Kaset 2. Talat Kaset 1, on the north side of Th Talat Mai (the city's main drag), offers speedy service to Nakhon (120B, 1½ hours). This is also the location of Pranthip Co, one of the more trustworthy agencies in town. Buses to Phun Phin also leave from Talat Kaset 1.

At Talat Kaset 2, on the south side of Th Talat Mai, you'll find frequent transportation.

The 'new' bus terminal (actually a few years old now, but still referred to as new by the locals) is 7km south of town on the way to Phun Phin. This hub services traffic to and from Bangkok (380B to 800B, 11 to 14 hours).

BUSES & MINIVANS FROM SURAT THANI

DESTINATION	FARE (B)	DURATION (HR)
Bangkok	421-856	10
Hat Yai	160-290	5
Khanom	100	1
Krabi	150	2½
Phuket	250	6
Trang	160	2

TRAIN

When arriving by train you'll actually pull into Phun Phin, a nondescript town 14km west of Surat. From Phun Phin, there are buses to Phuket, Phang-Nga and Krabi – some via Takua Pa, a junction for Khao Sok National Park. Transport from Surat moves with greater frequency, but it's worth checking the schedule in Phun Phin first – you might be lucky and save yourself a slow ride between towns.

If you plan on travelling during the day, go for the express train. Night travellers should opt for the air-con couchettes. Trains passing through Surat stop in Chumphon and Hua Hin on their way up to the capital, and in the other direction you'll call at Trang, Hat Yai and Sungai Kolok before hopping across the border. The train station at Phun Phin has a 24-hour left-luggage room that charges around 20B a day. The advance ticket office is open from 6am to 6pm daily (with a nebulous one-hour lunch break somewhere between 11am and 1.30pm). The trip to Bangkok takes over 8½ hours and costs 297B to 1379B depending on class.

Getting Around

Air-conditioned vans to/from Surat Thani airport cost around 100B per person and they'll drop you off at your hotel.

To travel around town, *sŏrng·tăa·ou* cost 10B to 30B (it's around 30B to reach Tesco Lotus from the city centre).

Fan-cooled Orange buses run from Phun Phin train station to Surat Thani every 10 minutes (15B, 25 minutes). For this ride, taxis charge a cool 200B for a maximum of four people, while share taxis charge 100B per person. Other taxi rates are posted just north of the train station (at the metal pedestrian bridge). If you have to overnight in Phun Phin, the Queen Hotel is very basic and unfriendly, but is cheap and can put a roof over your head for a similar price as a taxi to Surat Thani.

NAKHON SI THAMMARAT PROVINCE

Ao Khanom อ่าวขนอม

Lovely Ao Khanom, halfway between Surat Thani and Nakhon Si Thammarat, quietly sits along the blue gulf waters. Overlooked by tourists who flock to the jungle islands nearby, this pristine region, simply called Khanom, is a worthy choice for those seeking a serene beach setting unmarred by enterprising corporations.

The beach area is actually quite long and is comprised of two beaches: the main, long Hat Nadan and the smaller and more out of the way Hat Nai Plao.

Sights

This area is home to a variety of pristine geological features including **waterfalls** and **caves** but the highlight for many are the pink dolphins.

Caves CAVE

Two beautiful caves are along the main road (Hwy 4014) between Khanom and Don Sak. Khao Wang Thong has a string of lights guiding visitors through the network of caverns and narrow passages. A metal gate covers the entrance; stop at the house at the base of the hill to retrieve the key (and leave a small donation). Turn right off the main highway at Rd 4142 to find Khao Krot, with two large caverns (but bring a torch).

Samet Chun Waterfall WATERFALL

This is the largest waterfall in the area with tepid pools for cooling off, and great views of the coast. To reach the falls, head south from Ban Khanom and turn left at the blue Samet Chun sign. Follow the road for about 2km and, after crossing a small stream, take the next right and hike up into the mountain following the dirt road. After about a 15-minute walk, listen for the waterfall and look for a small trail on the right.

Hin Lat Falls WATERFALL

The scenic Hin Lat Falls is the smallest of the cascades in the area, but also the easiest to reach. There are pools for swimming and several huts providing shade. It's south of Hat Nai Plao.

Dat Fa Mountain MOUNTAIN

For a postcard-worthy vista of the undulating coastline, head to Dat Fa Mountain, about 5km west of the coast along Hwy 4014. The hillside is usually deserted, making it easy to stop along the way to snap photos.

Tours

Pink Dolphin Viewing Tours WILDLIFE WATCHING

(day tours 1700B) The most special feature of Khanom are the pink dolphins – a rare albino breed with a stunning pink hue. They are regularly seen from the old ferry pier and the electric plant pier around dawn and dusk but resorts are now offering full-day tours that include viewing the dolphins by boat and a car tour to the area's caves and waterfalls.

If you just want to see the dolphins you can hire a boat for a few hours (for up to six people) for 1000B. Enquire at your hotel.

Sleeping & Eating

Despite talk of further developing Khanom's beaches into a more laid-back alternative to the nearby islands, it remains a very low-key and quiet retreat. Many of the resorts see very few customers and constant disuse (not regularly flushing the toilets etc) means that some rooms are dank. In general, it's advisable to stay away from the large hotels and stick to beachside bungalow operations. Note that all options are spaced very far apart so unless you have your own wheels don't expect to just show up and wander around looking for a place to stay.

For some cheap eats, head to **Hat Kho Khao** at the end of Rd 4232 where you'll find a steamy jumble of barbecue stands offering some tasty favourites such as *mŏo nám đòk* (spicy pork salad) and *sôm·đam*. On Wednesday and Sunday there are markets further inland near the police station.

Suchada Villa BUNGALOW $
(075 528459; www.suchadavilla.com; Hat Naiplau; bungalows weekday/weekend incl breakfast 800/1000B;) Right off the main road and a five-minute walk to the beach, Suchada offers a cache of brightly coloured, quite cute bungalows. Friendly, English-speaking staff.

Khanom Hill Resort BUNGALOW $$
(075 529403, 081 956 3101; www.khanom.info; Hat Naiplau; bungalows 2900-3900B;) Travellers rave about this lovely spot on a very small hill, that leads to a half-circle of dreamy white beach. Choose from modern, concrete villas with thatched roofs, cheaper models with Thai-style architecture or big family-sized apartments; all are clean and comfy.

Talkoo Beach Resort BUNGALOW $$
(075 528397; yok_hana@yahoo.com; Hat Nadan; bungalows 1000-1500B;) An efficiently run place on Hat Nadan, Talkoo has a range of bungalows in a garden on the beach and cheaper ones across the main road in a more dry, sparse area. All are in good shape, spacious, comfortable and include charming touches like naturalistic bathrooms.

CC Beach Bar & Bungalows BUNGALOW $$
(www.ccbeachbarthai.wordpress.com; bungalows from 1500B;) A social spot that's sprung from a friendly, fun beach bar on a stunning stretch of Hat Nadan. The clean and modern concrete bungalows are priced higher for what you can find elsewhere, with a foreigner-specific, chummy ambience.

Racha Kiri RESORT $$$
(075 300245; www.rachakiri.com; bungalows 3550-7150B;) With spa and pool, Khanom's upscale retreat is a beautiful campus of rambling villas. The big price tag means no crowds, which can be nice, although the resort feels like a white elephant when the property isn't being used as a corporate retreat.

WORTH A TRIP

WÁT SUAN MOKKHAPHALARAM

Wát Suan Mokkhaphalaram (www.suanmokkh-idh.org; Wat Suanmokkh) Surrounded by lush forest, Wat Suan Mokkhaphalaram ('the Garden of Liberation'), charges 2000B for a 10-day program including food, lodging and instruction (although technically the 'teaching' is free). Retreats, run by the International Dharma Hermitage, begin on the first day of every month and registration takes place the afternoon before. Founded by Ajan Buddhadasa Bhikkhu, arguably Thailand's most famous monk, the temple's philosophical teachings are ecumenical in nature, comprising Zen, Taoist and Christian elements, as well as the traditional Theravada schemata.

For details on reaching the temple, located 7km outside of Chaiya, check out the website.

Information

The police station and hospital are just south of Ban Khanom at the junction leading to Hat Kho Khao. There's a 7-Eleven (with an ATM) in the heart of Khanom town.

Getting There & Away

Minivans from both Surat Thani and Nakhon leave every hour on the hour from 5am to 5pm daily and drop passengers off in Khanom town, which is several kilometres from the beach. From Khanom town you can hire motorcycle taxis out to the beaches for about 20B to 80B depending on the distance you're going. If you've booked in advance your hosts may offer to pick you up in Khanom town for free.

A taxi to/from Don Sak pier for the gulf islands is 1000B and a motorcyle taxi is 300B.

Once at your lodging you'll be stranded unless you hire your own transport or take a tour with your hotel.

Nakhon Si Thammarat

อำเภอเมืองนครศรีธรรมราช

POP 120,836

With one of the most significant temples in the kingdom, the historic city of Nakhon Si Thammarat (usually shortened to 'Nakhon') is a natural and rewarding stop between Hat Yai and Surat Thani.

Hundreds of years ago, an overland route between the western port of Trang and the eastern port of Nakhon Si Thammarat functioned as a major trade link between Thailand and the rest of the world. This ancient influx of cosmopolitan conceits is still evident today in the local cuisine, and housed in the city's temples and museums.

Sights

Most of Nakhon's commercial activity (hotels, banks and restaurants) takes place in the northern part of the downtown. South of the clock tower, visitors will find the city's awe-inspiring Wat Mahathat, while tantalising remains of the historic **red brick city walls** can be seen near the park and public square of **Sanam Na Muang** off the long, long main thoroughfare of Th Ratchadamnoen, itself teeming with cheap *sŏrng·tăa·ou* zipping north and south. Sanam Na Muang is a delightful sight in the late afternoon, when locals come out to play football and hacky sack and jog or walk in the cooler air. Note also the gold-coloured statues of the 12 animals of the Thai zodiac atop lampposts along Th Ratchadamnoen, each of which also represents one of the 12 city states that were tributary to the Nakhon Si Thammarat kingdom.

★Wat Phra Mahathat Woramahawihaan TEMPLE

(Th Si Thamasok; 8.30am-4.30pm) The most important wát in southern Thailand, stunning Wat Phra Mahathat Woramahawihaan (simply known as Mahathat) boasts an imposing 77m white *chedi* (stupa) crowned by a gold spire piercing the sky. According to legend, Queen Hem Chala and Prince Thanakuman brought relics to Nakhon over 1000 years ago, and built a small pagoda to house the precious icons. The temple has since grown into a huge site, and today crowds gather daily to purchase the popular Jatukham amulets.

Within the courtyard beneath the towering *chedi* rise up scores of further grey *chedi*. Don't miss the hall enclosing a splendid stairway and the **museums** featuring antique statues from all eras and corners of Thailand including an 18th-century reclining Buddha. Frequently stuffed with visiting school kids who apply gold leaf to the temple statuary, the wát is a 10B *sŏrng·tăa·ou* ride from the Thai Hotel area.

Shadow Puppet Museum MUSEUM

(Th Si Thamasok Soi 3; 9am-4.30pm) There are two styles of local shadow puppets: *năng đà·lung* and *năng yài*. At just under 1m tall, the former feature movable appendages and parts; the latter are nearly life-sized, and lack moving parts. Both are intricately carved from cow hide. Suchart Subsin's puppet house has a small museum where staff can demonstrate the cutting process and performances for visitors (50B).

Look out for the shadow puppets from the 18th century upstairs and others from the WWII era which were smaller than the traditional size and include a bi-plane.

National Museum MUSEUM

(Th Ratchadamnoen; admission 150B; 9am-4pm Wed-Sun) When the Tampaling (also known as Tambralinga) kingdom traded with merchants from Indian, Arabic, Dvaravati and Champa states, the region around Nakhon became a melting pot of crafts and art. Today, many of these relics are on display in this absorbing national museum.

Sleeping & Eating

Nakhon is a great place to sample cuisine with a distinctive southern twist. In the evening, Muslim food stands sell delicious *kôw mòk gài* (chicken *biryani*), *má·đà·bà* (*murdabag;* Indian pancake stuffed with chicken or vegetables) and roti. A good hunting ground is along Th Neramit, which turns into Th Pak Nakhon – the street bustles with food stalls every night.

Thai Hotel HOTEL $

(075 341509; fax 075 344858; 1375 Th Ratchadamnoen; r with fan 350B, with air-con 430-550B;) The most central sleeping spot in town, and not far from the train station, the

DON'T MISS

KHAO LUANG NATIONAL PARK

Khao Luang National Park (อุทยานแห่งชาติเขาหลวง; ☎075 300494; www.dnp.go.th; adult/child 400/200B) Known for its beautiful mountain and forest walks, cool streams, waterfalls and orchards, Khao Luang National Park surrounds the 1835m peak of Khao Luang. A soaring mountain range covered in virgin forest and a habitat for a plethora of bird species, it's a good spot for any budding ornithologist. There are over 300 species of orchid in the park, some of which are found nowhere else on earth.

It's possible to rent **park bungalows** (per night 600-2000B), sleeping six to 12 people. There's a **restaurant** at park headquarters. **Camping** is permitted along the trail to the summit.

To reach the park, take a *sŏrng·tăa·ou* (around 35B) from Nakhon Si Thammarat to Lan Saka; drivers will usually take you the extra way to park headquarters. The entrance to the park and the offices of the Royal Forest Department are 33km from the centre of Nakhon on Rte 4015, an asphalt road that climbs almost 400m in 2.5km to the office and a further 450m to the car park. Plenty of up-to-date details are available on the park's website.

Thai Hotel is a semi-smart bargain. Walls may be a bit thin and the wi-fi twitchy, but rooms are clean and a good deal for the price. Each room has a TV and the higher floors have good views of the urban bustle, while staff are lovely.

Nakorn Garden Inn HOTEL $
(☎075 323777; 1/4 Th Pak Nakhon; r 445B; ❄📶) There's a lovely forested setting more like a shady jungle than the centre of town, but most of the bare brick rooms are gloomy, although they come with air-con, TV, hot water and fridge. It's a nice rustic change from a cement block, though, and prices are a steal, although staff speak zero English.

Twin Lotus Hotel HOTEL $$
(☎075 33777; www.twinlotushotel.net; 97/8 Th Phattanakan Khukhwang; r 1500-2500B; ❄📶🏊) It's looking a bit tired, but the 401-room Twin Lotus is still the place to go a little more upscale when in Nakhon. This 16-storey behemoth sits 2km southeast of the city centre.

★Krua Talay THAI $
(1204/29-30 Th Pak Nakhon; dishes 40-300B; ⏰4-10pm) Opposite the Nakorn Garden Inn, this fantastic restaurant serves awesome seafood dishes. Take a seat in the rear garden area and order up fried prawn cake, crispy cat fish with hot and spicy salad, or stir-fried vegetables in oyster sauce, and make a meal of it. There's no English sign, but look for the red, yellow and blue sign and potted plants outside.

Hao Coffee CAFE $
(☎075 346563; Bovorn Bazaar; dishes 30-60B; ⏰breakfast & lunch) This charming, shuttered and well-staffed cafe is always stuffed with talkative locals and decorated with an eclectic array of collectibles and knick-knacks from pith helmets to rifles and assorted ceramics. It's a great place for a scrambled eggs breakfast, a larger meal or a caffeine fix, either inside or at one of the tables out front.

Rock 99 INTERNATIONAL $
(1180/807 Bovorn Bazaar; mains from 65B; ⏰4pm-midnight) In Bovorn Bazaar, Rock 99 may be rather rough and ready, but has a good enough selection of international fare, from taco salads to pizzas (avoid the Thai fare though) and live music several nights a week. A glass of wine is 70B.

ℹ Information

Several banks and ATMs hug Th Ratchadamnoen in the northern end of downtown. There is an English-language bookstore on the 3rd floor of Robinson Ocean shopping mall.

Most hotels have free maps to give to guests, but not all are that useful.

Police Station (☎1155; Th Ratchadamnoen)

Post Office (Th Ratchadamnoen; ⏰8.30am-4.30pm Mon-Fri, 9am-noon Sat & Sun)

Tourism Authority of Thailand (TAR; ☎075 346515; ⏰8.30am-4.30pm) Housed in a fine 1926-vintage building in the northern end of the Sanam Na Muang (City Park), this office has some useful brochures, but spoken English is limited.

ℹ Getting There & Away

AIR

Several carriers such as Nok Air, Air Asia and Orient Thai Airlines (plus Thai Airways) fly from Bangkok to Nakhon everyday. There are about six daily one-hour flights. One-way fares are around 1500B.

BUS

Ordinary buses to Bangkok leave from the bus terminal (mostly in the afternoon or evening), but a couple of private buses leave from booking offices on Th Jamroenwithi, where you can also buy tickets. The journey takes 12 hours and costs 454B to 1142B depending on the class of bus.

When looking for minivan stops to leave Nakhon, keep an eye out for small desks along the side of the downtown roads (minivans and waiting passengers may or may not be present nearby). It's best to ask around as each destination has a different departure point. Krabi and Don Sak minivans are grouped together – just make sure you don't get on the wrong one. Stops are scattered around Th Jamroenwithi, Th Wakhit and Th Yommarat.

TRAIN

There are two daily train departures to/from Bangkok to Nakhon (133B to 652B; stopping through Hua Hin, Chumphon and Surat Thani along the way). All are 12-hour night trains. These trains continue on to Hat Yai and Sungai Kolok.

Getting Around

Sŏrng·tăa·ou run north–south along Th Ratchadamnoen and Th Si Thammasok for 10B (a bit more at night). Motorcycle-taxi rides start at 30B and cost up to 50B for longer distances.

SONGKHLA PROVINCE

Songkhla Province's two main commercial centres, Hat Yai and Songkhla, are less affected by the political turmoil plaguing the cities further south, although some state travel advisories warn against travel here. You won't be tripping over foreign backpackers, but you'll see a fair number of tourists drawn to wandering through local markets, savouring Muslim-Thai fusion cuisine, relaxing on breezy beaches and tapping into Hat Yai's fun and eclectic urban vibe.

Songkhla & Around สงขลา

POP 90,780

'The great city on two seas' is photogenic in parts; however, slow-paced Songkhla doesn't see much in the way of foreign tourist traffic. Although the town hasn't experienced any of the Muslim separatist violence plaguing the provinces further south, it's still catching the same bad press.

The population is a mix of Thais, Chinese and Malays, and the local architecture and cuisine reflect this fusion at every turn.

Sights

The **aquarium** (สงขลาอะควาเรี่ยม; www.songkhlaaquarium.com; admission adult/child 300/200B; ⌚9.30am-3.45pm Tue-Fri, 9.30am-4.45pm Sat & Sun) is a good outing if you have kids in tow.

★National Museum MUSEUM

(พิพิธภัณฑสถานแห่งชาติสงขลา; Th Wichianchom; admission 150B; ⌚9am-4pm Wed-Sun, closed public holidays) This 1878 building was originally built in a Chinese architectural style as the residence of a luminary. The museum is easily the most picturesque national museum in Thailand and contains exhibits from all Thai art-style periods, particularly the Srivijaya. Walk barefoot on the wood floors to view elaborate wood carvings, historical photos and pottery salvaged from a shipwreck.

Hat Samila BEACH

(หาดสมิหลา) Stroll this beautiful strip of white sand with the giggling local couples and enjoy the kite flying (a local obsession). A bronze **Mermaid sculpture**, in tribute to Mae Thorani (the Hindu-Buddhist earth goddess), sits atop some rocks at the northern end of the beach. Locals treat the figure like a shrine, tying the waist with coloured cloth and rubbing the breasts for good luck.

Don't expect to sunbathe here – the local dress code is too modest – but it's a wholesome spot to meet locals and enjoy a distinctly Thai beach scene, and it's a gorgeous spot for a wander at sundown.

Ko Yo ISLAND

(เกาะยอ) A popular day trip from Songkhla is this island in the middle of Thale Sap. It is actually connected to the mainland by bridges and is famous for its cotton-weaving industry. There's a roadside market selling cloth and ready-made clothes at excellent prices.

If you visit Ko Yo, don't miss **Wat Phrahorn Laemphor**, with its giant reclining Buddha, and check out the **Thaksin Folklore Museum** (☎074 591618; admission 100B; ⌚8.30am-4.30pm), which actively aims to promote and preserve the culture of the region.

The pavilions here are reproductions of southern Thai-style houses and contain folk art and traditional household implements.

Tours

Singora Tram Tour TRAM TOUR
(9am-3pm) FREE These free 40-minute tours (six daily) in an open-air tram leave from next to the National Museum. You'll be lucky if you get any English narration but you will get a drive through the old part of town past the Songkhla mosque, a Thai temple, Chinese shrine and then out to Hat Samila.

Sleeping & Eating

Songkhla's hotels tend to be lower priced than other areas in the gulf, which makes going up a budget level a relatively cheap splurge.

For quality seafood, head to the street in front of the BP Samila Beach Hotel – the best spot is the restaurant directly in the roundabout. If market munching is your game, you'll find a place to sample street food most days of the week. On Sundays try the bustling market that encircles the Pavilion Hotel. Monday, Tuesday and Wednesday feature a night market (which closes around 9pm) near the local fish plant and bus station, and the Friday morning market sits diagonally opposite the City Hall.

Sook Soom Boon 2 HOTEL $
(074 323809; 14 Th Saiburi; d 550B;) The owner speaks good English and rooms are excellent value at this centrally located choice.

BP Samila Beach Hotel HOTEL $$
(074 440222; 8 Th Ratchadamnoen; r 1600-2500B;) This landmark hotel is a great deal – you'd pay nearly double for the same amenities on the islands. The beachfront establishment offers large rooms with fridges, satellite TVs and a choice of sea or mountain views (both are pretty darn good), although it's rather set in its ways and checking on wi-fi reception in your room first is prudent.

★ **Blue Smile Cafe** CAFE $
(254 Th Nakhonnai; mains from 100B; 10am-10pm Tue-Fri & Sun, 10am-midnight Sat) A fine place for a snack, some alcohol or cool beats; we're not sure what we like best at this Canadian-owned place: the roof garden, *The Blues Brothers* poster, the B52s and Bob Dylan pics, the live jazz (from 7.15pm Friday and Saturday) or the homemade waffles. There's even a double room if you need to crash out.

Ong Heap Huad CAFE $
(Th Nakhonnai; 8am-6pm) This astonishing family-run curiosity shop-slash-cafe has a mesmerising museum-like collection of ancient Chinese and Thai shop signs, antiques, statuette, lamps, stuffed animal heads and more. It's an enchanting place for a glass of tea. Look for the shop with the urns and bric-a-brac outside and the Chinese shop sign saying 黄協發, opposite No 239.

Information

Banks can be found all over town.

Indonesian Consulate (074 311544; www.kemlu.go.id/songkhla; 19 Th Sadao)

Malaysian Consulate (074 311062; 4 Th Sukhum, Songkhla; 8.15am-noon & 1-4pm Mon-Thu, 8.15am-noon & 2-4pm Fri)

Police Station (074 321868; Th Laeng Phra Ram) North of the town centre.

Post Office (Th Wichianchom) Opposite the market; international calls can be made upstairs.

Getting There & Around

BUS

The bus and minibus station is a few hundred metres south of the Viva Hotel. Three 2nd-class buses go daily to Bangkok (693B to 1070B), stopping in Nakhon Si Thammarat and Surat Thani, among other places. For Hat Yai, buses (21B) and minivans (30B to 40B) take around 40 minutes, and leave from Th Ramwithi. *Sŏrng·tăa·ou* also leave from here for Ko Yo.

TRAIN

From Songkhla you'll have to go to Hat Yai to reach most long-distance destinations in the south (trains no longer pass through town).

Hat Yai หาดใหญ่

POP 191,696

Welcome to the urban hub of southern Thailand, where Western-style shopping malls mingle with wafts of Cantonese street eats and curry from the eclectic range of busy street food stalls as Old Chinese men sit and watch the world go by on rickety chairs outside junk shops. It's a mix of busy city and laid-back tropics and Hat Yai has long been a favourite stop for Malaysian men on their weekend hooker tour. You'll notice that the town's tourism scene is still predominantly Malaysian mixed with a few Western expats. Come evenings, Hat Yai's cosy pubs and bouncing clubs come into their own.

The town is often said to be safe from the violent hullabaloo of the far south; however, it hasn't been ignored. The Lee Gardens Plaza Hotel was bombed in 2012, killing four people in a subsequent fire and injuring 400. Three bombs exploded in Hat Yai in 2014, injuring eight. In earlier years pubs, malls, department stores and hotels have been targeted in other bombings.

It's up to you if you want to stop here, but changing transport shouldn't be too risky. Those who get out and explore will be rewarded with some of the best food in the region and the dynamic flavour of the big smoke of southern Thailand.

Sleeping

Hat Yai has dozens of business-style hotels in the town centre, within walking distance of the train station.

Cathay Guest House HOSTEL $
(074 243815; 93/1 Th Niphat Uthit 2; s 200B, d & tw 240B, tr 290B;) There are very helpful staff and plentiful information about onward travel at this central cheapie; although rooms are simple (with squat loos), prices are rock bottom. Wi-fi is 30B for one hour.

Hat Yai Backpackers HOSTEL $
(www.hatyaibackpackershostel.com; 226 Th Niphat Uthit 1; dm 240B, d 350B;) With four-bed female dorms, eight-bed mixed dorms and double rooms (all fan), this new central choice is a decent bet, and there's helpful staff at hand for Hat Yai pointers.

Red Planet HOTEL $
(074 261011; www.redplanethotels.com; 152-156 Th Niphat Uthit 2; r from 900B;) In a great, central location, this hotel offers cleanliness, affordability and good service, with uncluttered, functional rooms. The atmosphere and theme is generically charmless and prices depend a lot on how far in advance you book. The 200B upgrade for the room with the kettle is not worth it.

Centara HOTEL $$$
(074 352222; www.centarahotelsresorts.com; 3 Th Sanehanusorn; r 4000-4700B, apt 5300-7000B, ste 8500B;) The centrally located, 244-room Centara is a particularly smart choice with pool, excellent rooms, terrific service and some fine views from the upper floors. Evening live jazz in the foyer bar brings some style.

Eating

The city is the unofficial capital of southern Thailand's cuisine, offering Muslim roti and curries, Chinese noodles, duck rice and dim sum, and fresh Thai-style seafood from both the gulf and Andaman coasts. You'll find hawker stalls everywhere but a particularly good hunting ground is along Th Supasarnrangsan. Meals here cost between 25B to 80B.

Night Market MARKET $
(Th Montri 1) The night market boasts heaps of local eats including several stalls selling the famous Hat Yai–style deep-fried chicken and *kà·nŏm jeen* (fresh rice noodles served with curry), as well as a couple of stalls peddling grilled seafood.

Daothiam CAFE $
(79/3 Thammanoonvithi Rd; mains from 60B; 7am-7pm;) Serving Hat Yai patrons since 1959, this traditional Chinese cafe has framed bank notes on its walls, friendly staff, a reliable menu of Thai/Chinese dishes and fine breakfasts. Curiously, its name means 'Satellite'. It's opposite the Odean Shopping Mall.

Gedi Chadian CHINESE $
(134-136 Th Niphat Uthit 3; mains from 50B) This big, open, spacious and very busy restaurant serves steaming bowls of scrumptious *wonton* noodles, chicken rice, *chā shāo* pork and other filling Chinese staples.

Drinking

Hive Bar BAR
(127 Th Niphat Uthit 2; 3pm-midnight) A cut above the rest, Hive bar is a decent downtown hang-out in Hat Yai with a traveller, expat and local fan base, serving up a solid menu of pub food. Pool enthusiasts won't be disappointed.

Information

Immigration Office (Th Phetkasem) Near the railway bridge, it handles visa extensions.

Tourism Authority of Thailand (TAT; www.tourismthailand.org/hatyai; 1/1 Soi 2, Th Niphat Uthit 3; 8.30am-4.30pm) The very helpful staff here speak excellent English and have loads of info on the entire region.

Tourist Police (Th Niphat Uthit 3; 24hr) Near the TAT office.

Getting There & Away

AIR

Air Asia (www.airasia.com) and **Nok Air** (www.nokair.com) have daily flights to and from Bangkok.

Thai Airways International (THAI; www.thaiairways.com; 182 Th Niphat Uthit 1) Runs several flights daily between Hat Yai and Bangkok.

BUS

Most interprovincial buses and southbound minivans leave from the bus terminal 2km southeast of the town centre, while most northbound minivans now leave from a minivan terminal 5km west of town at Talat Kaset, a 60B túk-túk ride from the centre of town. Buses link Hat Yai to almost any location in southern Thailand.

Prasert Tour (Th Niphat Uthit 1) runs quicker minibuses to Surat Thani (4½ hours, 8am to 5pm), and **Cathay Tour** (93/1 Th Niphat Uthit 2) can also arrange minivans to many places in the south.

BUSES FROM HAT YAI

DESTINATION	FARE (B)	DURATION (HR)
Bangkok	688-1126	15
Krabi	182-535	5
Nakhon Si Thammarat	140	4
Pak Bara	130	2
Phuket	360	7
Songkhla	40	1½
Sungai Kolok	200	4
Surat Thani	235	5
Trang	100	2

TRAIN

There are four overnight trains to/from Bangkok each day (259B to 945B), and the trip takes at least 16 hours; trains go via Surat Thani (105B). There are also seven trains daily that run along the east coast to Sungai Kolok (92B) and two daily trains running west to Butterworth (332B) and Padang Besar (57B), both in Malaysia.

There is an advance booking office and left-luggage office at the train station; both are open 7am to 5pm daily.

Getting Around

An **Airport Taxi Service** (182 Th Niphat Uthit 1; 100B per person; ⏲6.30am-6.45pm) makes the run to the airport six times daily (6.45am, 10am, 12.15pm, 1.45pm, 3pm and 6.15pm). A private taxi for this run costs 320B.

Sŏrng·tăa·ou run along Th Phetkasem (10B per person). Túk-túk and motorcycle taxis around town cost 20B to 40B per person.

DEEP SOUTH

Yala ยะลา

POP 61,250

Landlocked Yala wiggles its way south to the Malaysian border, making it Thailand's southernmost province. Its eponymous capital appears very different from other Thai metropolises. The city's big boulevards and well-organised street grid are set around a huge circular park and feel distinctly Western. Around three-quarters of the population are Muslim and it is a university town; the educational centre of the Deep South.

Sights

Yala's biggest attraction is **Wat Kuha Pi Muk** (also called Wat Na Tham or Cave-front Temple), one of the most important pilgrimage points in southern Thailand. Located 8km west of town on the road connecting Yala to Hat Yai (Rte 409), the Srivijaya-period cave temple features a reclining Buddha that dates back to AD 757. A statue of a giant guards the temple's entrance and, inside, small natural openings in the cave's roof let in the sun's rays to illuminate a variety of ancient Buddhist cave drawings.

Further south, Betong is home to the largest **mail box** in Thailand, first built in 1924. Betong also functions as a legal, but inconvenient, border crossing to Malaysia; contact Yala's **immigration office** (☎073 231292; ⏲8.30am-4.30pm).

Sleeping & Eating

Many of Yala's cheapest lodgings double as unofficial brothels. There are excellent restaurants that are scattered around the park's perimeter.

Yala Rama HOTEL $

(☎073 212815; 21 Th Sri Bumrung; r 600B; ❄📶) Like most hotels in the region, this central and reputable place would be more expensive if it weren't in the tourist-free Deep South. Clean, comfortable rooms and an OK attached restaurant.

TRAVEL IN THE DEEP SOUTH: SHOULD YOU GO?

Despite the conflict, almost everyone in the Deep South – whether ethnic Malay Muslim or a Thai soldier – is happy to see a *fa·ràng*. So few foreigners make it here that you're guaranteed a lot of attention from the locals.

Nor have tourists, or any Westerners, ever been targeted by the insurgents; this is a very insular war.

Yet, by nature insurgencies are unpredictable, and bombs kill indiscriminately. Explosive devices planted on parked motorbikes outside shops, or in markets, are a common tactic of the separatists and are frequently used in the city centres of Yala, Pattani, Narathiwat and Sungai Kolok.

It's best not to linger on the streets for too long; you could be in the wrong place at the wrong time. Nor is travel in the countryside in the early morning or after dark advisable. This isn't an area to be driving a motorbike in if you can't be identified as a foreigner.

But perhaps the biggest drawback to travel in the region is that the insurgency has stifled tourism to such an extent that there is very little infrastructure for visitors. Travel between the major centres apart, you'll need private transport to get around. There are few hotels and restaurants, and almost no nightlife, while those beautiful beaches have absolutely no facilities.

If you do want to travel here, research the current situation carefully and take advice from your embassy.

Getting There & Around

Yala's bus station is south of the city centre. There are three daily buses to and from Bangkok's southern bus terminal (711B to 1422B, 14 hours). The 4pm bus from Bangkok carries onto Betong.

Four trains a day run between Bangkok and Yala (22 hours). Two trains travel daily between Yala and Sungai Kolok (three to four hours). The train station is just north of the city centre.

Buses to Hat Yai (160B, 2½ hours) stop several times a day on Th Sirirot, outside the Prudential TS Life office.

Minivans to Betong and Sungai Kolok (100B, two hours) depart hourly from opposite the train station.

Pattani ปัตตานี

POP 44,234

Once the heart of a large Muslim principality that included the neighbouring provinces of Yala and Narathiwat, Pattani Province has never adjusted to Thai rule. Although today's political situation has stunted the area's development, Pattani Town has a 500-year history of trading with the world's most notorious imperial powerhouses. The Portuguese established a trading post here in 1516, the Japanese passed through in 1605, the Dutch in 1609 and the British flexed their colonial muscle in 1612.

Yet despite the city's fascinating past, there's little of interest in Pattani. There are some decent beaches nearby, but the ongoing insurgency has made most of these sandy destinations unsafe for the independent traveller.

Sights

The Mae Nam Pattani (Pattani River) divides the older town to the east and the newer town to the west. Along Th Ruedi you can see what is left of old Pattani **architecture** – the Sino-Portuguese style that was once so prevalent in this part of southern Thailand. On Th Arnoaru there are several ancient but still quite intact, Chinese-style homes.

Pattani could be one of the better beach destinations in the region. The coastline between Pattani Town and Narathiwat Province is stunning: untouched and deserted apart from fishing villages. But exploring much of this area independently is not a safe option at this time.

Locals frequent **Laem Tachi**, a sandy cape that juts out over the northern end of Ao Pattani. It can be reached by boat taxi from Pattani pier. **Thepha district**, 35km northwest of Pattani, is the most developed beach destination in the area, although it is technically in Songkhla Province. There you'll find a few resorts and beachfront restaurants that cater mostly to middle-class Thais. To reach Thepha, hop on any Songkhla-bound bus from Pattani (or vice versa); mention the name of your resort and you'll be deposited at the side of the road for the brief walk to the beach.

Matsayit Klang MOSQUE
(Th Naklua Yarang) Thailand's second-largest mosque is the Matsayit Klang, a traditional structure with a green hue that is probably still the south's most important mosque. It was built in the 1960s. Non-Muslims can enter outside of prayer times.

Sleeping & Eating

Palace Hotel HOTEL $
(☎073 349171; 10-12 Pipit Soi Talattewiwat 2; r 200-350B; ❄) There's nothing palatial about this place. But it is the only budget option in town for foreigners and close to the night market. Go for the air-con rooms with hot water.

CS Pattani Hotel HOTEL $$
(☎073 335093; www.cspattanihotel.com; 299 Moo 4, Th Nong Jik; r from 1400B; ❄@🛜≋) The safest and best hotel, with soldiers outside and a metal detector in the lobby, this is where Thai politicians stay on their rare visits to the Deep South. The paucity of tourists mean you get great rooms and facilities for a bargain price. It's 2km north of the centre of town.

Night Market SOUTHERN THAI $
(Soi Talattewiwat; ⌚4-9pm) Pattani shuts down far earlier than most Thai towns, but the night market offers solid seafood, as well as southern Thai-style curries and the usual noodle and fried-rice options.

Information

There are several banks along the southeastern end of Th Pipit, near the Th Naklua Yarang intersection.

Pattani Hospital (☎073 323411, 073 323414; Th Nong Jik)

Police Station (☎073 349018; Th Pattani Phirom)

Getting There & Around

Minivans and buses depart from Pattani's bus station on the western fringes of town. There are frequent daytime departures to Hat Yai (100B, 1½ hours), Narathiwat (100B, 1½ hours) and Sungai Kolok (140B, 2½ hours).

There are two daily buses to and from Bangkok's southern bus terminal (920B to 1220B, 15 hours).

Motorbike taxis charge 30B for hops around town, but they become very scarce after dark.

Narathiwat นราธิวาส

POP 41,342

Sitting on the banks of the Bang Nara River, Narathiwat is probably the most Muslim city in Thailand, with many mosques scattered around town. There are still a few old Sino-Portuguese buildings lining the riverfront (although blink and you'll miss them), and there are some excellent beaches just outside town. But few tourists pass through, due to the security situation.

Sights

Matsayit Klang MOSQUE
Towards the southern end of Th Pichitbumrung stands Matsayit Klang, a wooden mosque built in the Sumatran style and known locally as the 'central mosque'. It was reputedly built by a prince of the former kingdom of Pattani over a hundred years ago. Non-Muslims can enter outside of prayer times.

Ao Manao BEACH
Five kilometres south of town, Ao Manao is a superb strip of palm tree-fringed sand. You'll likely have it all to yourself, unless it's a public or Muslim holiday.

Hat Narathat BEACH
Just north of town is Hat Narathat, a 5km-long sandy beach fronted by towering pines, which serves as a public park for locals. The beach is only 2km from the town centre – you can easily walk there or take a săhm·lór.

Wat Khao Kong BUDDHIST TEMPLE
(⌚9am-5pm) FREE The tallest seated-Buddha image in southern Thailand is at Wat Khao

MOBILE PHONES

At the time of writing, Thailand was unveiling a nationwide mobile (cell) phone registration program. It's a scheme that started in the Deep South, where mobile phones are frequently used by insurgents to set off bombs. If you buy a Thai SIM card, your number should be registered automatically. But if you reach the Deep South and your phone stops working, then you'll need to visit any local phone shop to reactivate it. Hand over your passport and your details will be noted and, an hour later, your phone will work again.

THAILAND'S FORGOTTEN WAR

It may seem fantastic as you laze on the beach, or meditate at a peaceful hilltop temple, but the Deep South is home to one of Southeast Asia's longest-running and bloodiest conflicts.

Just 300km or so south of the party islands of Ko Samui and Ko Pha-Ngan, a guerrilla war between ethnic Malay Muslims and the overwhelmingly Buddhist Thai state has claimed almost 6000 lives since 2004.

The Deep South, which borders Malaysia, is a different world from the rest of the country. Foreign visitors are nonexistent and the pristine beaches deserted. Military convoys rumble through the villages and towns, checkpoints dominate the roads and residents are subject to compulsory DNA tests designed to make identifying suspected insurgents easier.

Around 80% of the 1.8 million people who live in Thailand's three southernmost provinces of Pattani, Narathiwat and Yala are ethnic Malay Muslims. They speak a Malay dialect and many want their own independent state, as the region once was hundreds of years ago.

For the estimated 12,500 to 15,000 separatist fighters here, the Deep South is 'Patani': the name given to the Qatar-sized sultanate during its glory days in the 14th and 15th centuries. The insurgents view the Thai government as a colonial power and Thai Buddhists as interlopers in their land.

Ranged against the separatists are around 150,000 soldiers, police and militias. Targeted in ambushes along the coconut tree–lined roads of the region, or by increasingly sophisticated IEDs (improvised explosive devices), barely a week goes by without a member of the Thai security forces being killed or wounded.

At the same time, the insurgency has set neighbours against each other. Gruesome tit-for-tat killings occur, with both Buddhist and Muslim civilians being gunned down as they ride home on their motorbikes or beheaded in the rubber plantations that are the mainstay of the local economy. Bombs are planted outside shops and in the markets of the towns, claiming random victims. The few remaining Buddhist monks in the region have to be escorted by the army when they collect alms every morning for fear they will be assassinated, while mosques are riddled with bullet holes.

Yet despite the appalling violence, the insurgency remains little known both at home and overseas. With almost 25 million visitors a year, Thailand is fiercely proud and protective of its reputation as the 'Land of Smiles'. The media downplay the security situation, while Thai politicians act as if they are in denial about the sheer scale of the conflict.

The insurgents. too, have resisted attacking targets outside the Deep South, a tactic that would do huge damage to the Thai psyche and would garner them far more attention

Kong, 6km southwest on the way to the train station in Tanyongmat. Located in a park, the image is 17m long and 24m high, and made of reinforced concrete covered with tiny gold-coloured mosaic tiles that glint magically in the sun.

Sleeping & Eating

Most of the town's accommodation is located on and around Th Puphapugdee along the Bang Nara river.

Ocean Blue Mansion HOTEL $

(☎073 511109; 297 Th Puphapugdee; r 400-500B; ❄📶) The decent-sized rooms are a little beaten up, but some have fine river views and this is still the best budget choice.

Tanyong Hotel HOTEL $$

(☎073 511477; www.tanyonghotel.com; 16/1 Th Sophaphisai; r 690-890B; ❄📶) Respectable, welcoming hotel with big, comfortable rooms and an OK attached restaurant. Some English spoken.

Ang Mo CHINESE $

(cnr Th Puphapugdee & Th Chamroonnara; dishes 50-150B; ⏱10am-10pm) This popular Chinese restaurant is both cheap and tasty, and has even fed members of the Thai royal family.

Mangkorntong THAI $

(433 Th Puphapugdee; dishes 55-200B; ⏱11am-9pm) Perched over the river, there are two terraces to dine on here. There's a wide selection of seafood dishes plus a number of vegie options, and it serves alcohol.

around the world. Nor do they appear to be connected to the more extreme Islamic militants of Indonesia and the Philippines.

Instead, they stay in the shadows, rarely issuing statements or talking to the press. Operating in independent cells, they belong to a number of different organisations all likely linked to each other. But there seems to be no common leader of the groups. That renders the sporadic peace talks that take place between the separatists and the Thai government meaningless, as no one is really sure if the representatives of the insurgents have any true control over them.

While the insurgency kicked into life in earnest in 2004, after 32 suspected Muslim rebels were cornered in an ancient mosque in Pattani Town and brutally killed by the Thai army, its roots go back hundreds of years. From the 16th century on, the sultanate of Patani was unwillingly under Thai rule for brief periods. But it wasn't until the Anglo-Siamese Treaty of 1909 that the Deep South was absorbed into Thailand proper. Britain recognised Thai sovereignty over the region, in return for Bangkok abandoning its claims to other parts of what were then the British-ruled Malay States.

Since then, Thailand, the most populous Buddhist country in the world, has set about attempting to remake the Deep South in its own image. Muslim schools have been shut down and all children made to study in Thai, even though most of them speak it only as a second language. They are also forced to learn about Buddhism, a part of the Thai national curriculum, despite following Islam. Officials from other parts of the country are imported to run the region.

By turns heavy-handed and paternalistic, the Thai government's policies began to fuel a separatist movement. Having their children subject to the Thai school system remains a huge source of resentment for many Muslims. Regarded as symbols of the hated Thai state by the insurgents, over 300 schools have been burned down in recent years, while more than 150 Buddhist teachers have been assassinated.

But with the insurgency entirely confined to just three provinces, and a small part of neighbouring Songkhla Province, few Thais are even aware of why the fighting is taking place. Nor are they willing to contemplate giving into the separatists' demands. Imbued with the nationalism taught in their schools, the idea that the Deep South should want to secede from Thailand is unthinkable, both to ordinary Thais and the authorities.

Yet, some form of autonomy for the region is likely the only way to end the violence. Until that happens, Thailand's forgotten war will carry on and the grim list of casualties will continue to grow.

Information

The **Tourism Authority of Thailand** (TAT; ☎ Narathiwat 073 522411, nationwide call centre 1672) is inconveniently located a few kilometres south of town, just across the bridge on the road to Tak Bai.

Getting There & Around

Air Asia (☎ nationwide call centre 02 515 9999; www.airasia.com) flies daily to and from Bangkok (from 1783B, 1½ hours).

Minivans and buses leave from Narathiwat's **bus terminal** (☎ 073 511552), 2km south of town on Th Rangae Munka. There are two daily buses to and from Bangkok's southern bus terminal (860B to 1338B, 15 to 17 hours).

There are frequent minivans heading to Hat Yai (170B, three hours), Pattani (100B, two hours), Sungai Kolok (70B, one hour) and Yala (100B, 1½ hours).

Narathiwat is small enough to navigate by foot. Motorcycle taxis charge 30B to get around.

Sungai Kolok สุไหงโกลก

POP 41,590

It's not the most prepossessing place to enter or exit the 'Land of Smiles', but Sungai Kolok is the main gateway between Thailand and Malaysia. As such, it's a scuzzy border town best known for smuggling and prostitution. Less of a target than the other major towns in the region, the unstable situation in the Deep South has nevertheless severely diminished its 'sin city' reputation in recent years, with the Malaysian men who once came here for wild weekends now

GETTING TO MALAYSIA: SUNGAI KOLOK TO RANTAU PANJANG

Getting to the Border The Thai border (open 5am to 9pm) is about 1.5km from the centre of Sungai Kolok or the train station. Motorbike taxis charge 30B.

At the Border This is a hassle-free border crossing. After completing formalities, walk across the Harmony Bridge to the Malaysian border post.

Moving On Shared taxis and buses to Kota Bharu, the capital of Malaysia's Kelantan State, can be caught 200m beyond the Malaysian border post. Shared taxis cost RM$10 per person (90B) or RM$50 (450B) to charter the whole car yourself. The ride takes around 40 minutes. Buses make the hour-long journey for RM$5.10 (45B).

It's possible to continue south by the so-called 'jungle train', but the closest station is at Pasir Mas, located along taxi/bus routes to Kota Bharu.

Tak Bai, also in Narathiwat Province, and Betong, further south in Yala, are also legal crossing points for foreigners, but Sungai Kolok is by far the most convenient place to cross the border.

favouring safer Hat Yai. Fewer travellers, too, leave Thailand here now; more come in the opposite direction and immediately hop on a train heading north.

Sleeping & Eating

Most hotels here are uniform in quality and price. Many of the real cheapies won't accept foreigners.

Stand-out restaurants are in short supply, although there is some tasty Malaysian and Chinese food around.

Merlin Hotel HOTEL **$$**
(☎ 073 611003; 68 Th Charoenkhet; r 600B; ❄ ☎) Fixtures and furniture from a different age, but clean and handy for the train station.

Genting Hotel HOTEL **$$**
(☎ 073 613231; 250 Th Asia 18; r 700B; ❄ @ ☎ ≈) More respectable than most hotels in town and, if you're the nervous type, the security is efficient. But the midrange rooms are rather scuffed for the price. It's a few hundred metres west of the train station on the other side of the road.

Kakyah Restaurant MALAYSIAN **$**
(43/11 Th Charoenkhet; dishes from 30B; ⏲ 10am-10pm) Decent Malaysian food is on offer at this reliable, alcohol-free, Muslim-run place.

Information

There is an **immigration office** (☎ 073 614114; Th Charoenkhet; ⏲ 8am-5pm Mon-Fri) opposite the Merlin Hotel with helpful, English-speaking staff. A tourist police office sits at the border. There are ATMs and foreign-exchange booths close to the train station.

Getting There & Away

The long-distance **bus station** (Th Asia 18) is 3km east of the train station. There are four buses daily to and from Bangkok's southern bus terminal (707B to 1414B, 17 to 20 hours). Minvans to Hat Yai (200B, four hours) leave from here too.

Minivans heading north to Narathiwat (70B, one hour), Pattani (130B, 2½ hours) and Yala (120B, two hours) depart from opposite the train station.

Two daily trains (11.30am and 2.20pm, 24 hours) connect Sungai Kolok with Bangkok. Trains in the Deep South are often delayed and subject to army and police searches.

Getting Around

Motorcycle taxis zoom around town for a flat rate of 30B.

Phuket & the Andaman Coast

Includes ➜

Best Places to Eat

- Suay (p277)
- Aziamendi (p264)
- Krua Thara (p310)
- Pad Thai Shop (p290)
- Trang Night Market (p337)

Best Places to Stay

- Point Yamu by Como (p303)
- Iniala Beach House (p264)
- Pak-Up Hostel (p305)
- Six Senses Hideaway (p268)
- Castaway Resort (p356)

Why Go?

The Andaman is Thailand's turquoise coast; one of those places you see on a postcard that makes you want to quit your job and live in flip-flops…forever. For once, the beauty exceeds the hype. Pure-white beaches, some of the world's softest sand, cathedral-esque limestone cliffs and hundreds of jungle-covered isles extend down the Andaman Sea from the border of Myanmar to Malaysia. Phuket is the glitzy show-stealer, but head north and you'll uncover world-class dive sites, little-visited isles and Ranong's Thai-Myanmar flavour. To the south, you can lazily island-hop past karst towers down to the Malaysian border.

The catch? The Andaman Coast is no secret and its beaches are becoming increasingly crowded with backpackers, package tourists, high-end jet-setters and everyone in between. Flashy resorts are pushing out the bamboo shacks, and authenticity largely now hides in the backwaters. But your postcard dream is still here – if you're willing to look.

When to Go

- May to October is the rainy season. At this time, swells pick up, some islands become inaccessible, many resorts close and others slash their prices. In Phuket, Trang and other southern towns, the Vegetarian Festival is held in late September or October and involves parades of pierced-faced worshippers, endless firecrackers and fantastic meat-free food.
- December to January is the peak season for tourism and conditions are ideal for diving and snorkelling. Prices soar, transport links increase, and accommodation and transport must be booked well in advance.

Phuket & the Andaman Coast Highlights

1. Buzzing glassy waters between white-sand beaches in the **Trang Islands** (p340).
2. Exploring a heady mix of luxury lodgings and street-food treats on **Phuket** (p269).
3. Traipsing through the real-life Jurassic Park of **Khao Sok National Park** (p256).
4. Snorkelling over colourful corals off **Ko Lipe** (p353).
5. Scaling limestone cliffs above blissful jade waters in **Railay** (p311).
6. Blending into the laid-back beach scene on **Ko Lanta** (p326).
7. Floating in a cerulean sea, then

dancing into the night on **Ko Phi-Phi** (p316).

8 Looking for elusive whale sharks in the **Surin** (p254) and **Similan Islands** (p262).

9 Kayaking into the spectacular *hôrng* (island caves) of jaw-dropping **Ao Phang-Nga** (p265).

10 Falling into the mellow beach-bar vibe of **Ko Phayam** (p250).

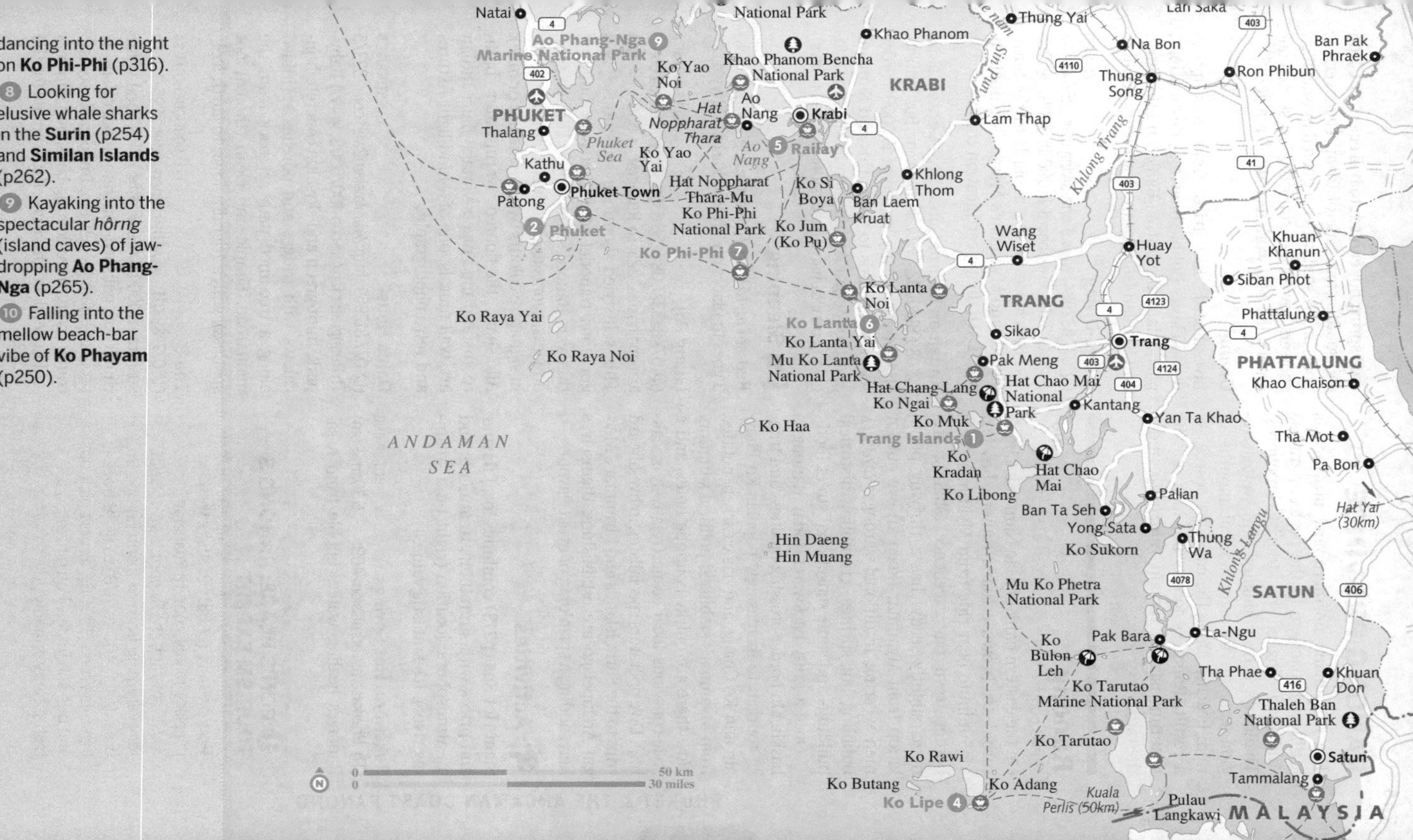

RANONG PROVINCE

The Andaman's northernmost province is a different package to the perfect-paradise Andaman flogged on tourist brochures. Thailand's least populated and wettest region gets up to eight annual months of rain; beaches along the coast are scarce. As a result, Ranong's forests are lush and its beautiful islands remain *relatively* under the radar.

Ranong ระนอง

POP 53,000

On the eastern bank of Mae Nam Pak Chan's turbid, tea-brown estuary, Ranong lies just a 45-minute boat ride from Myanmar. This border town par excellence (shabby, frenetic, slightly seedy) has a thriving population from Myanmar (keep an eye out for men wearing traditional sarongs, *longyi*), bubbling hot springs, crumbling historical buildings and some sensational street food.

Once a gritty backwater, today Ranong is basking in border-crossing business and transit tourism to increasingly popular Ko Phayam and Ko Chang, and has clearly benefitted from Myanmar's stabilised political situation. Now there are quirky boutique hotels and a style-conscious local scene (relatively speaking). Dive operators specialising in live-aboard trips to the Surin Islands and Myanmar's Mergui Archipelago are establishing themselves here, adding a sprinkling of expat flavour.

Activities

Siam Hot Spa (p278) combines local flavour and prices with sumptuous treatments and an atmospheric location (right on a steaming river). It's fantastic value.

Rakswarin Hot Springs HOT SPRING
(Th Phetkasem; admission 40B; ⏲6.30am-9pm) Ranong's healing waters bubble from a sacred spring hot enough to boil eggs (65°C), on the southeastern side of town. The riverside pools are blessed with chequered mosaic tiles, showers, towels and sunbeds. Just stretch out and let the heat work its natural magic.

Diving

Live-aboard dive trips from Ranong to world-class bubble-blowing destinations, particularly the Burma Banks and the Surin and Similan Islands, are deservedly popular.

A-One-Diving DIVING
(☎077 832984; www.a-one-diving.com; 256 Th Ruangrat; 3-day live-aboard 17,900-18,900B; ⏲Oct-Apr) Specialises in live-aboards to the Surin Islands and Myanmar's Mergui Archipelago, plus PADI diving certification courses.

Andaman International Dive Center DIVING
(☎089 814 1092; www.aidcdive.com; Bus Terminal, Th Phetkasem; 4-day live-aboard 19,000B; ⏲Oct-Apr) Live-aboards to the Surins and Similans and the Mergui Archipelago in Myanmar, focusing on extensive excursions (six to 14 days).

Sleeping

Red *sŏrng·tăa·ou* (passenger pick-up truck) 3 goes to places on Th Phetkasem (Hwy 4).

Luang Poj GUESTHOUSE $
(☎077 833377, 087 266 6333; www.facebook.com/luangpojhostel; 225 Th Ruangrat; r 500B; ❄📶) This self-styled 'boutique guesthouse' is a gorgeous remodel of a 1920s-era building that was Ranong's first hotel. Though windowless, rooms are spotless, comfy and cosy, in signature colours (we like the hot orange). All share tile-floored warm-water bathrooms and mod-meets-vintage flair: Indian art, wall murals, one-of-a-kind light fixtures and retro photography.

Dahla House GUESTHOUSE $
(☎077 812959; http://dahla.siam2web.com; 323/5 Th Ruangrat; r fan/air-con 400/500B; ❄📶) Baby-pink, mint-green and sky-blue concrete bungalows with fridges and porches sprinkled along a tree-lined path set back from the main road. Simple and clean (though not spotless), with a friendly down-to-earth feel.

The B BOUTIQUE HOTEL $$
(☎077 823111; www.thebranong.com; 295/1-2 Th Ruangrat; r 1100-1600B; ❄📶🏊) This good-value chunk of polished-concrete modernism is proof of Ranong's new era. Impeccably stylish, comfy rooms have floating beds, rain showers and tasteful, bright decor. Extra points for the

> **PON'S PLACE: RANONG'S TOURISM EXPERT**
>
> **Pon's Place** (☎081 597 4549; www.ponplace-ranong.com; Th Ruangrat; ⏲7.30am-7pm; 📶) Ranong's go-to spot for everything from wi-fi and European breakfasts (40B to 70B) to flight bookings, visa runs (1300B), airport pick-ups and bus schedules. Pon himself is a high-energy, friendly guy.

Ranong

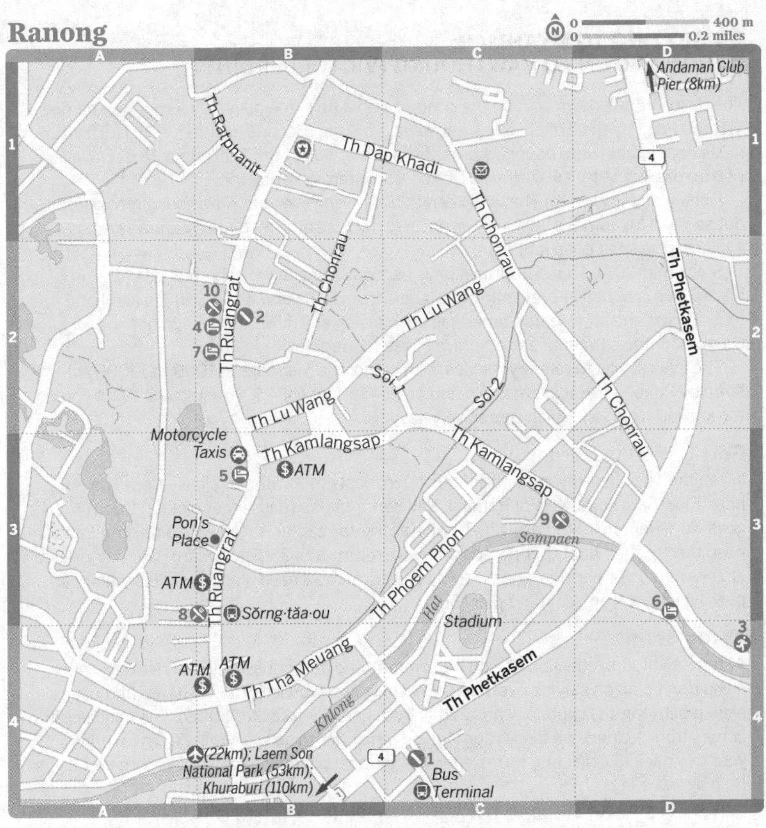

snooker bar, the open-air **bar-restaurant** (mains 100-250B; ⏲7am-1am; 📶), and, particularly, the rooftop infinity pool overlooking Ranong and the surrounding green hills.

Thansila HOTEL **$$**
(☎081 797 4674, 077 823405; www.facebook.com/thansilahotspringresort; 129/2 Th Phetkasem; r fan/air-con 1000/1600B; ❄📶) A homely spot with artsy flair, 800m west of the hot springs on the southeast edge of town. The best digs are exposed-stone, lodge-style rooms overlooking the river, with grotto-like hot-water bathrooms and wooden mirrors. It's owned by a Thai architect who renovated over two years.

Eating & Drinking

Ranong has a lively, young, very local drinking scene involving lots of karaoke.

★Day Market MARKET **$**
(Th Ruangrat; dishes 40-50B; ⏲5am-midnight) Ranong's bubbly day market offers delicious, inexpensive Thai and Burmese meals. It's a wonderfully local scene.

Ranong

Activities, Courses & Tours
1 Andaman International Dive Center C4
2 A-One-Diving B2
3 Rakswarin Hot Springs D4

Sleeping
4 Dahla House B2
5 Luang Poj B3
6 Thansila D3
7 The B B2

Eating
8 Day Market B3
9 Night Market C3
10 Ranong Hideaway B2
The B Restaurant .... (see 7)

GETTING TO MYANMAR: RANONG TOWN TO KAWTHOUNG (VICTORIA POINT)

The dusty, tumbledown port on the southernmost tip of mainland Myanmar was named Victoria Point by the British, but is known as Ko Song (Second Island) by Thais. The Burmese appellation, Kawthoung, is probably a corruption of the Thai name. Most travellers pop across just to renew their visas, but it's an interesting day trip.

Fishing and trade with Thailand keep things ticking over, but Kawthoung also churns out some of Myanmar's best kickboxers. Nearby isles are inhabited by *chow lair* (sea gypsies; also spelt *chao leh*).

Since mid-2014, Thai authorities have been cracking down on in-out visa runs. In theory, this is aimed at preventing foreigners from living and working in Thailand on tourist visas and, at research time, was not causing any difficulty for regular travellers. Do monitor the situation; ask other travellers for updates.

The easiest way to renew your visa is on one of the 'visa trips' (1100B to 1300B) offered by Ranong travel agencies, including Pon's Place (p246). You'll save 200B if you do the legwork yourself, which is relatively easy.

Getting to the Border

When the Thailand–Myanmar border is open, boats to Kawthoung leave from Tha Saphan Plaa, 5km southwest of Ranong. Red *sŏrng·tăa·ou* (passenger pick-up truck) 4 goes from Ranong to the pier (20B), where long-tail captains lead you to the immigration post, then to their boat (per person one-way/return 125/250B). Confirm whether prices are per person or per ride, and one-way or return. You'll need a photocopy of your passport, which you can get at the pier (5B).

At the Border

At the Kawthoung checkpoint, you must inform the authorities that you're a day visitor if you don't plan on staying overnight – in which case you'll pay a US$10 fee (it must be a crisp bill; long-tail captains can get this from harbour touts for 500B). The only hassle comes from 'helpers' on the Myanmar side, who offer to do everything from carrying your day pack to collecting forms, then ask for tips, but they're generally more friendly than aggravating.

If you're just renewing your Thai visa, the whole process takes two hours. When returning to Thailand, bear in mind that Myanmar's time is 30 minutes behind Thailand's. This has previously caused problems for returning travellers who got through **Myanmar Immigration** (⏲7am-5pm) before its closing time only to find the Thai Immigration post (p249) closed. It's worth checking Thai immigration closing hours when leaving the country; if you don't get stamped in you'll have to return to Myanmar the next day.

A quicker, easier and much more polished alternative (albeit sterilised and less interesting) is via the **Andaman Club Pier** (☎077 871081; www.andamanclub.com; off Rte 4004; ⏲8.30am-4pm), 8km northwest of town, off Rte 4004. At the terminal, you'll get your passport stamped immediately, and a Myanmar-bound speedboat (950B return, 15 minutes each way) leaves hourly from 8.30am to 3.30pm, docking at a flash casino. The whole trip takes one hour. For an additional 550B you can add a two-hour tour along Myanmar's coast from the casino.

Moving On

It's possible to stay overnight in one of Kawthoung's dingy, overpriced hotels, but you'd probably rather not. If you have a valid Myanmar visa, which you'll have to apply for in advance at the Myanmar Embassy in Bangkok (or a third country), you'll be permitted to stay for up to 28 days and exit anywhere you like.

Night Market MARKET $

(Th Kamlangsap, off Hwy 4; dishes 30-50B; ⏲2-7pm) The night market, which is located just northwest off the highway, sizzles up some brilliant Thai dishes offered at killer prices.

BUSES FROM RANONG

DESTINATION	FARE (B)	DURATION (HR)	FREQUENCY
Bangkok	445-692	9-10	hourly 7am-1pm, 3pm, 5pm, 7pm & 8pm (VIP)
Chumphon	120	2	hourly 7am-5pm
Hat Yai	420	7	6am, 10am & 8pm
Khao Lak	180	3½	hourly 6.30am-5.45pm
Krabi	197	6	7.30am, 10.15am & 2pm
Phang-Nga	190	5	7.30am, 10.15am & 2pm
Phuket	250	5-6	hourly 6.30am-5.45pm
Surat Thani	190	4-5	6am & 2pm

Ranong Hideaway THAI, INTERNATIONAL **$$**
(☎077 832730; www.ranonghideaway.com; 323/7 Th Ruangrat; mains 90-300B; ⏰10am-11pm; 📶) A long-time favourite of expats and border businessmen, this attractive (if weathered) international eatery unfurls beneath a stilted bamboo roof, offering decent pastas, meaty mains, Thai curries and international breakfasts along with a pizza oven, a pool table and a well-stocked bar.

ℹ Information

Most guesthouses and restaurants have wi-fi. ATMs are clustered around the intersection of Th Ruangrat and Th Tha Meuang.

Ranong Immigration Office (Th Chalermprakiat; ⏰8.30am-5pm) Main immigration office, 4km southwest of town; handles visa extensions.

Ranong Immigration Post (Tha Saphan Plaa; ⏰8am-5pm) If you're just popping in and out of Myanmar's Kawthoung, visiting this small immigration post, 5km southwest of town, is sufficient.

ℹ Getting There & Away

AIR

Ranong Airport is 22km south of town. **Nok Air** (☎02 900 9955; www.nokair.com) flies twice daily to Bangkok (Don Muang).

BUS

The **bus terminal** (Th Phetkasem) is 1km southeast of the centre. *Sŏrng·tăa·ou* 2 (blue) passes the terminal. From here, minivans head to Surat Thani (190B, 3½ hours, 6am and 2pm) and Chumphon (150B, two hours, hourly 7am to 5pm).

ℹ Getting Around

Motorcycle taxis (50B) take you almost anywhere in town, including **Tha Saphan Plaa**, 5km southwest of the centre, for boats to Myanmar, and **Tha Ko Phayam**, 6km southwest of the centre, for Ko Chang and Ko Phayam. *Sŏrng·tăa·ou* 4 (red) stops near the piers (20B).

Pon's Place (p246) helps with motorcycle and car rentals and offers shuttle vans from its office/the airport to the piers (70/200B).

Ko Chang เกาะช้าง

This little-visited rustic isle is a long way (in every respect) from its much more popular Trat Province namesake. The speciality here is no-frills living, and, yes, electricity and wi-fi are frills here, but their absence from most places gives as much as it denies. An all-pervading quiet saturates 'Little Ko Chang'. The buzz of modern life is replaced by the slosh of the sea, the murmur of cicadas or the far-off rumbling of a long-tail. In the fringe and low-season months, it's beyond mellow.

Wide west-coast **Ao Yai** (Long Beach) has gorgeous marbled white-black sand in the south, which obscures the otherwise clear sea. White-sand snobs will be happiest on Ao Yai's north end. A short trail leads south over the bluff to **Ao Tadaeng**, a boulder-strewn beach and the island's best sunset spot.

Stroll the beaches, explore the tiny village capital (halfway between east and west coasts) or wind around the island's dirt trails. If you're lucky, you'll spot sea eagles, Andaman kites and hornbills floating above the mangroves and the jungled east coast. Trails lead south from the village and Ao Yai to west-coast **Ao Kai To** and the park ranger station, where you'll find the island's best stretch of intact jungle; elsewhere it's been tamed into cashew orchards and rubber plantations.

Activities

Aladdin Dive Safari DIVING
(☎087 274 7601; www.aladdindivesafari.com; Cashew Resort, Ao Yai; 2/3 dives 4900/6500B,

3-day live-aboard 15,800-19,800B; ⌚10am-6pm Nov-Apr) A relatively flash live-aboard operation that runs day trips to the Surin and Similan Islands, Open Water Diver (OWD) courses (18,700B to 19,800B) and live-aboards to Myanmar's Mergui Archipelago, the Surins, the Similans, Ko Phi-Phi, Hin Daeng and Hin Muang.

Om Tao YOGA
(☎085 470 9312; www.omtao.net; Ao Yai; class 300B) German-run studio with daily yoga (8.30am) November to April. Classes are by request at other times; tai chi and qi-gong also offered.

Sleeping & Eating

Basic bamboo huts reign supreme on Ko Chang. They're mostly only open from November to mid-April. Electricity is limited; a few places have solar and wind power.

Ao Yai is where you'll find most lodgings. A few more places are tucked away on Ao Tadaeng, immediately south, and linked to Ao Yai via a short walking track. More isolated options lie on the beaches to the north and far south of the island.

★ **Crocodile Rock** GUESTHOUSE $
(☎080 533 4138; tonn1970@yahoo.com; Ao Yai; bungalows 400-700B) Outstanding bamboo bungalows perched on Ao Yai's serene southern headland with superb bay views. The classy kitchen turns out homemade yoghurt, breads, cookies, good espresso, and a variety of vegie and seafood dishes. It's popular, so book ahead.

Little Italy BUNGALOW $
(☎084 851 2760; daniel060863@yahoo.it; Ao Yai; r 400-650B) Just three immaculate bungalows attached to an Italian restaurant amid the trees towards the southern end of Ao Yai. Two are stilted split-level concrete-and-wood jobs encircled by wraparound verandas. The third concrete bungalow is back on earth, with a tiled bathroom. At research time, the friendly Italian owner was planning upgrades, so prices may rise. Book well ahead.

Sunset Bungalows BUNGALOW $
(☎084 339 5224; Ao Yai; bungalows 300-500B; ⌚Oct–mid-Apr) Sweet wooden bungalows with bamboo decks and attached Thai-style bathrooms sit back in the trees along Ao Yai's finest (northern) patch of beach. Staff are as friendly as they come.

Sawasdee BUNGALOW $
(☎086 906 0900; www.sawadeekohchang.com; Ao Yai; bungalows 350-950B; ⌚Nov–mid-Apr) A-frame wooden bungalows have vented walls to keep things cool, sunken bathrooms painted bright colours and hammocks on terraces, at the southern end of Ao Yai.

Eden BUNGALOW $
(☎080 628 7590; Ao Yai; r 200-300B) These rickety, barebones-basic bungalows (forget bathrooms doors) and no-frills shared-shower rooms at the north end of Ao Yai are kept clean by a friendly family who'll whip you up a sensational massaman curry. It's popular with returnees, electricity runs 6pm to 11pm and there's a social beachside bar-restaurant.

Information

There are no banks or cars, but wi-fi has arrived at a few shops and resorts, including Koh Chang Resort (southern Ao Yai).

Getting There & Around

From Ranong, *sŏrng·tăa·ou* (20B) or motorcycle taxis (50B) go from Th Ruangrat to Tha Ko Phayam (p249) near Saphan Plaa.

Two daily long-tail taxi boats (150B, two hours) leave for Ko Chang at 9.30am and 1pm. In high season, they stop at the west-coast beaches, returning at approximately 8.30am and 1.30pm. During the monsoon, only morning long-tails make the crossing (weather permitting), docking at the main pier on the northeast coast.

During the November-to-April high season, several daily speedboats (350B, 30 minutes, 8am to 4.30pm) run between Ranong's Tha Ko Phayam and Ko Chang's northeast-coast pier.

High-season Ko Phayam–Ranong speedboats often drop off and pick up passengers in Ko Chang (350B) on request, though they're unreliable; get your resort to make (and confirm!) the booking. You can charter long-tails to Ko Phayam (2000B) through Koh Chang Resort.

Motorcycle taxis meet boats, charging 100B between the northeast-coast pier and Ao Yai.

Ko Phayam เกาะพยาม

Technically part of Laem Son National Park (p252), increasingly popular Ko Phayam is fringed with beautiful soft-white beaches and, for now, is continuing to go mainstream while still holding onto its soul. If you're coming from Phuket or Ko Phi-Phi, it'll feel refreshingly wild and dozy. The spectacular northwest and southwest coasts are dotted with rustic bungalows, small-scale resorts, breezy sand-side restaurants and barefoot beach bars. Fauna includes wild pigs, monkeys, snakes and tremendous bird life (sea eagles, herons, hornbills).

The island's one 'village' (on the east coast, beside the main pier) caters mostly to tourists. But hit it during a festival (say the February Cashew Festival) and you'll see that islanders still have a firm grip on their homeland.

Narrow motorcycle pathways, concrete roadways and dirt trails run across the island's wooded interior; some are rutted to the point of hazardous – drive slowly.

Sights & Activities

Ko Phayam's main drawback is that the snorkelling isn't great; high sea temperatures have killed off all the coral. But the Surin Islands are close, and you can hop on live-aboard dive expeditions or speedboat transfers.

Wat Phayam BUDDHIST TEMPLE
(วัดเกาะพยาม; dawn-dusk) FREE Shrouded in jungle just north of the main pier, on Ko Phayam's east coast, you'll find a majestic golden Buddha flanked by a three-headed *naga* (mythical serpent).

Phayam Divers DIVING
(086 995 2598; www.phayamlodge.com; Ao Yai; 2 dives 6400B, 3-day live-aboard 16,000-17,000B; Nov-Apr) At the north end of Ao Yai. Offers one-day snorkelling (4000B) and dive trips to the Surins, plus multi-day live-aboards to the Surins and Ko Bon.

Aladdin Dive Safari DIVING
(087 274 7601; www.aladdindivesafari.com; Ao Yai; 2/3 dives 4900/6500B, 3-day live-aboard 15,800-19,800B; 8am-8pm Nov-Apr) A relatively flash live-aboard operation, 500m inland from central Ao Yai. It runs day trips to the Surin and Similan Islands, Open Water Diver courses (18,700B to 19,800B) and live-aboards to Myanmar's Mergui Archipelago, the Surins, the Similans, Ko Phi-Phi, Hin Daeng and Hin Muang.

Sleeping & Eating

Room capacity has sky-rocketed in recent years. Many resorts now stay open year-round, with attached eateries serving middling Thai fare. The best, cheapest Thai eats are in town near the pier. Plenty of resorts have 24-hour power, though some still have limited electricity.

The most popular beaches to use as a base are Ao Yai, to the southwest, and Ao Khao Kwai to the northwest. Other quieter, less known options are the east-coast beaches of Ao Hin Khow and Ao Mea Mai, north and south of the pier respectively

Ao Yai อ่าวใหญ่

Aow Yai Bungalows BUNGALOW $
(083 389 8688; www.aowyai.com; bungalows 400-800B;) This French-Thai operation, southeast end of Ao Yai, is the thatched bamboo bungalow pioneer that kicked it all off two decades ago. Choose between decent, rustic small wooden-and-bamboo bungalows amid towering palms and pines, and larger beachfront wood models or concrete bungalows. Electricity 10am to 3am.

Frog Beach House HOTEL $
(083 542 7559; www.frogbeachhouse.com; bungalows 500-1400B;) Well-kept, traditional Thai-style hardwood chalets with wooden floors, outdoor bathrooms, glass sinks and mosquito nets line up behind a nice slab of sand beside a small stream at the north end of Ao Yai.

Cede BOUTIQUE HOTEL $$
(081 622 6464; cedekohphayam@gmail.com; r 2000-2400B;) A 2015 baby, Italian-run Cede brings a dash of low-key sophistication to northwest end of Ao Yai. Interiors are gleaming, boutique-y and inviting; two front rooms soak in sea panoramas. Star of the show is the sprawling wide-open beachfront bar-restaurant deck. There's 24-hour electricity, along with evenings-only air-con, a coffee shop and motorbike rental (200B).

Ban Nam Cha INTERNATIONAL $
(dishes 100-180B; 9am-6.30pm, hours vary;) Twinkling lights, prayer flags and driftwood signs adorn this artsy, easygoing food shack. Tuck into fantastic homemade panini (garlic mushroom, cashew-nut pesto), sandwiches, cakes and a range of Burmese, European and vegetarian treats, and peruse a paperback from the lending library. It's 500m inland from central Ao Yai.

Ao Khao Kwai อ่าวเขาควาย

Heaven Beach BUNGALOW $$
(082 806 0413; www.ppland-heavenbeach.com; r 1500-2000B;) A sweet four-year-old resort on an idyllic slice of central beachfront real estate. Tiled bungalows in shades of pastel are cutesy, characterful and super-spacious without losing comfort, and feature flower motifs, open-air bathrooms, hot showers,

all-day electricity and wide decks with rattan lounges.

Mr Gao BUNGALOW $$
(077 870222; www.mr-gao-phayam.com; bungalow 1200-1600B; Nov-Apr;) These sturdy, varnished wood-and-brick or bamboo bungalows in the centre of Ao Khao Kwai are popular with activity-oriented couples and families and have character, mosquito nets, tiled bathrooms and front decks. The owner arranges kayak rental, snorkelling and multiday trips to the Surin Islands. A makeover (including 24-hour electricity) was underway at research time in 2015.

Baan Klong Kleng BUNGALOW $$
(089 772 5090; www.baanklongkleng.com; r 1200-1700B; mid-Oct–Apr;) Simple, clean wooden bungalows cascade through trees to a luscious chunk of beach. They're comfy, if not overly exciting, with stylish ceramic-bowl sinks and semi-open bathrooms. The fabulous open-walled beachside **restaurant** (mains 140-180B; 8am-10pm mid-Oct-Apr;) has a fun vibe, dishing up fragrant Thai curries (veg versions available), delicious breakfasts and fusion specials like green-curry pasta. It's in the centre of Ao Khao Kwai.

Ao Hin Khow & Ao Mea Mai อ่าวหินขาว/อ่าวแม่หม้าย

★ **PP Land** BUNGALOW $
(081 678 4310; www.ppland-heavenbeach.com; Ao Hin Khow; bungalows 700-1400B;) A stunning Thai-Belgian–owned ecolodge, just north of the pier on the little-visited east coast. Beautifully designed concrete bungalows are powered by wind and sun, with 24-hour electricity and hammocks on terraces overlooking the sea. The knowledgeable owners bake cakes, run an organic garden, treat sewage and make their own all-natural laundry detergent. Excellent value.

Sabai Sabai BUNGALOW $
(087 895 4653; www.sabai-bungalows.com; Ao Mea Mai; bungalows 250-1400B;) Five minutes' walk south of the east-coast pier, this fab, social travellers' hideaway has heaps of clean, (mostly) fan-cooled, budget-friendly options. Cheap and cheerful bamboo huts share bathrooms. Simple doubles come with sea views, sunken bathrooms and plenty of style. Best is the two-floor, loft-style room with balcony. There's a chilled-out bar, plus hammocks, movie nights and electricity 8am to 1am.

Information

Many resorts now have wi-fi. There are no ATMs; get cash out in Ranong before heading over to Ko Phayam.

Getting There & Away

A daily 10am ferry runs from Ranong's Tha Ko Phayam (p249), 6km southwest of town, to Ko Phayam itself (200B, two hours), returning at 3pm. During the November-to-April high season, speedboats (350B, 35 minutes) make the run at least hourly from 7.45am to 4.30pm, returning to the mainland at 8am, 9am, 9.30am, 11.30am, noon, 3.30pm, 4pm and 4.30pm. High-season speedboats go from Ko Phayam to Ko Chang (350B, 20 minutes) en route to Ranong at 8.30am, 9am, noon, 12.30pm, 3pm and 3.30pm, though they aren't 100% reliable.

Getting Around

Ko Phayam has no cars. Motorcycle taxis from the pier to Ao Khao Kwai/Ao Yai cost 50/80B. Walking distances are long; it's about 45 minutes from the pier to Ao Khao Kwai, the nearest bay. You can rent motorbikes (200B) in the village (best) and from larger resorts; you'll need one to explore properly.

Laem Son National Park อุทยานแห่งชาติแหลมสน

This serene 315-sq-km **national park** (077 861431; www.dnp.go.th; adult/child 200/100B; 8am-4.30pm) covers 60km of Andaman coastline (Thailand's longest protected shore) and over 20 islands, including much-loved Ko Phayam (p250). It's 85% open sea. Much of the coast is fringed by mangroves and laced with tidal channels, home to fish, deer, macaques, civets, giant squirrels and over 100 bird species, including white-bellied sea eagles.

The most accessible beach is gorgeous, casuarina-backed 3km **Hat Bang Ben**, home to the park headquarters and accommodation. To the south, peninsulas jut out into the ocean concealing isolated coves accessible only by long-tail. All these beaches are allegedly safe for swimming year-round. From Hat Bang Ben, spot Ko Kam Yai, Ko Kam Noi, Mu Ko Yipun, Ko Khang Khao and, to the north, Ko Phayam. If there's a prettier sunset picnic spot in the northern Andaman, we missed it.

Hat Praphat, 56km south of Hat Bang Ben, is a turtle nesting ground.

Activities

Nature trails wind off from the park headquarters, where you can arrange one-day boat trips (2500B, maximum 10 people) to nearby islands. Turn left (south) towards the pier just before park headquarters to access the beach without paying park fees.

Sleeping & Eating

Most accommodation is at Hat Bang Ben.

Wasana Resort BUNGALOW $
(077 861434; www.wasanaresort.org; Hat Bang Ben; bungalow fan 450B, air-con 650-750B;) A family-run ring of cosy concrete bungalows with bamboo beds wraps around the colourful on-site **restaurant** (mains 80-200B; 7.30am-9pm). The welcoming Dutch-Thai owners make a gloriously authentic gado-gado, organise Laem Son day trips, lend bicycles and are full of fantastic ideas for exploring the park (ask about the stunning 10km trek around the headland). If you've booked, they'll collect you from the highway.

There are larger four-person bungalows for families.

Laem Son National Park Accommodation BUNGALOW, CAMPGROUND $$
(077 861431, in Bangkok 02 562 0760; www.dnp.go.th; Hat Bang Ben; d/q 1000/1800B, camp site per person 30B, with tent hire 270B;) Simple air-conditioned concrete bungalows under a shady beachside casuarina canopy, or camping in the grounds or on the sand.

Getting There & Away

The Laem Son National Park turn-off is 44km south of Ranong on the west side of Hwy 4, between the Km 657 and Km 658 markers. Buses heading south from Ranong will drop you here (ask for Hat Bang Ben; 65B, one hour). You'll have to flag down a vehicle going towards the park or grab a taxi (200B) at the roadside agency. It's 10km from Hwy 4 to the park entrance.

PHANG-NGA PROVINCE

Phang-Nga's jungle mountains are carved up by muddy rivers leading to aqua bays sprinkled with limestone karsts and, below, some of Thailand's finest underwater treasures.

More than a decade after the 2004 Boxing Day tsunami, Phang-Nga's touristy areas feel pretty much back to normal. There's a tangible sense of progress, especially around Khao Lak, which has surpassed all prior expectations of development. Many fishing communities, however, have had their way of life changed forever, either by the loss of key family members, the destruction of fishing equipment or being forced to relocate inland.

Phang-Nga remains very seasonal. From mid-October to mid-April, visitors descend en masse for its clear waters, white beaches and colourful reefs. Many establishments close during the May-to-October monsoon, when the region feels slightly haunted.

Khuraburi คุระบุรี

Blink and you'll miss it. But, if you keep your eyes wide open, you'll enjoy this soulful, roadside gateway to the Surin Islands and some of southern Thailand's best community-based tourism opportunities. For local inhabitants, Khuraburi is a market town relied on by hundreds of squid fishermen.

For tourist information, contact **Tom & Am Tour** (086 272 0588; 298/1 Mu 1, Hwy 4; 24hr), opposite the bus station road.

Tours

Andaman Discoveries TOUR
(087 917 7165; www.andamandiscoveries.com; 120/1 Mu 1, Khuraburi; 3-day trip per person 6000B; 8.30am-5.30pm Mon-Fri) Highly recommended community-based one- and multi-day tours, featuring cycling, cultural and handicraft activities, snorkelling trips, village homestays on Ko Phra Thong and ecotours to Khao Sok National Park. They also manage community projects that take volunteers.

Sleeping & Eating

★ **Boon Piya Resort** GUESTHOUSE $
(081 752 5457; 175/1 Th Phetkasem; bungalows 650B;) In a garden compound just off the main road at Khuraburi's north end, these spacious, modern concrete bungalows with tiled floors, hot-water bathrooms and little balconies are a wonderful surprise. The helpful owner books transport to/from the Surin Islands and Ko Phra Thong.

Morning Market MARKET $
(Hwy 4; dishes 20-40B; 6-10am) Don't miss the morning market at the north end of town. Stalls fry chicken, grill coconut waffles, and bubble kettles with Thai doughnuts to be dipped in thick, sugary green curry. Tea (10B) arrives caramel coloured and floating on a layer of condensed milk. You'll be among very few *fa·ràng* (Westerners) here.

Getting There & Around

Most buses running between Ranong (105B, two hours) and Phuket (150B, four hours) stop in Khuraburi. Take a Phuket-bound bus to Takua Pa (70B, 1½ hours), 55km south, to transfer to further destinations including Khao Sok National Park.

The pier for the Surin Islands and Ko Phra Thong is 9km northwest of town. Whoever books your boat to the islands will arrange free pier transfer.

Surin Islands Marine National Park

อุทยานแห่งชาติหมู่เกาะสุรินทร์

The five gorgeous isles of the **Surin Islands Marine National Park** (076 472145; www.dnp.go.th; adult/child 500/300B; mid-Oct–mid-May) sit 60km offshore, 5km from the Thailand–Myanmar marine border. Healthy rainforest, pockets of white-sand beach in sheltered bays and rocky headlands that jut into the ocean characterise these granite-outcrop islands. Perfectly clear water makes for easy marine-life spotting, with underwater visibility of up to 30m outside monsoon. These shielded waters attract *chow lair* (sea gypsies; also spelt *chao leh*), an ethnic group of Malay origin who live on Ko Surin Tai during the May-to-November monsoon. Here they're known as Moken, from the local word *oken* ('salt water').

The spectacular flaxen sand, the purpling depths, the sparkling bays in never-ending shades of jade and turquoise, and the sheer granite peninsulas that tumble down in a permanent geological avalanche, forming arrow-like points and natural breakwaters, are what you'll remember.

Ko Surin Tai (south) and Ko Surin Neua (north) are the two largest islands. Park headquarters, an **information office** (7.30am-8.30pm mid-Oct–mid-May) and all visitor facilities are at Ao Chong Khad on southwest Ko Surin Neua.

Khuraburi is the park's jumping-off point. The pier is 9km northwest of town, alongside the helpful mainland **national park office** (076 472145; www.dnp.go.th; Tha Khuraburi; 8.30am-4.30pm mid-Oct–mid-May).

Sights & Activities

Ban Moken VILLAGE

(Ao Bon, Ko Surin Tai) Ban Moken on east Ko Surin Tai welcomes visitors. Post-tsunami, the Moken (from the Sea Gypsy ethnic group) have re-settled in this sheltered bay, where a major ancestral worship ceremony, **Loi Reua** takes place each April. The colourfully carved *labong* poles dotted around embody Moken ancestors. This population experienced no casualties during the 2004 Boxing Day tsunami that wiped out the village, because they understood nature's signs and evacuated to the hilltop.

The Surin Islands Marine National Park runs two-hour trips from Ko Surin Neua to Ban Moken (per person 150B, minimum five people). You'll stroll through the stilted village, where you can ask permission/guidance for hiking the 800m **Chok Madah trail** over the jungled hills to an empty beach. Handicrafts for sale help support the local economy and clothing donations are accepted. Please refrain from bringing along alcohol and sweets; alcoholism is a growing problem among Moken.

Diving & Snorkelling

The park's dive sites include **Ko Surin Tai**, **Ko Torinla** (south) and **HQ Channel** between the two main islands. **Richelieu Rock**, a seamount 14km southeast, is also technically in the park and happens to be one of the Andaman's best dive sites (if not *the* best). Manta rays pay visits and whale sharks are sometimes spotted here during March and April.

There's no dive facility inside the park, so dive trips (four-day live-aboards from 20,000B) must be booked through centres in Khao Lak (p258), Phuket (p269) and Ranong (p246). Transfers are usually included. There's a 200B park diving fee per day, plus the national park fee (adult/child 500/300B), which is valid for five days.

Though recent bleaching of hard corals means snorkelling isn't quite as fantastic as it once was, you'll still see plenty of colourful fish and soft corals. The most vibrant soft corals we saw were at **Ao Mai Yai**, off southwest Ko Surin Neua. There's good snorkelling at **Ao Sabparod** and **Ao Pak Kaad**, where you might spot turtles, off east and south Ko Surin Tai. More fish swim off tiny **Ko Pajumba**, but the coral isn't great. **Ao Suthep**, off north Ko Surin Tai, has hundreds of colourful fish.

The nearest decompression chamber is in Phuket. In the case of an accident, dive operators will contact the chamber's Khao Lak-based SSS Ambulance (p262), which meets boats and rushes injured divers south to Phuket.

Half-day snorkelling trips (per person 150B, snorkel hire 160B) leave the island headquarters at 9am and 2pm. You'll be mostly in the company of Thais, who generally splash around fully clothed in life jackets. For more serene snorkelling, charter a long-tail from the national park (per day 3000B) or, better yet, directly from the Moken in Ban Moken (p254).

Tour operators in Khuraburi (p253) and Khao Lak (p258) organise snorkelling day trips to the park (adult/child 3500/2100B).

Greenview SNORKELLING
(☎076 472070; greenviewtour99@gmail.com; Tha Khuraburi; adult/child one-day tour 3500/2100B; ⊙7.30am-9pm) Impressive in safety, service and value, Greenview runs excellent Surin Islands snorkelling day trips with knowledgeable guides. Rates include transfers, snacks, equipment and a delicious lunch. Also organises multi-night stays in the Surins.

Wildlife & Hiking

Around park headquarters, you can explore the forest fringes and spot crab-eating macaques and some of the 57 resident bird species, including the beautiful Nicobar pigeon, endemic to the Andaman islands, and the elusive beach thick-knee. Along the coast you're likely to see Brahminy kites and reef herons. Twelve species of bat live here, most noticeably the tree-dwelling fruit bat (flying fox).

Nature Trail WALKING
(Ko Surin Neua) FREE Behind Ao Chong Khad's campground, a rough-and-ready nature trail winds 2km along the coast and through forest to the campsite at Ao Mai Ngam. At low tide, it's easy to stroll along the coast between the two campsites.

Sleeping & Eating

Park accommodation is decent, though it can feel seriously crowded when full (around 300 people). The clientele is mostly Thai, giving the place a lively holiday-camp vibe.

Surin Islands Marine National Park Accommodation BUNGALOW, CAMPGROUND $$
(☎076 472145; www.dnp.go.th; Ko Surin Neua; d/q 2000/3000B, camping site per person 80B, with tent hire 300B; ⊙mid-Oct–mid-May; ❄) Bungalows, at Ao Chong Khad, have wooden floors, private bathrooms, front terraces and fans from 9.30pm to 7am or air-con from 6pm to 9.30pm. Electricity runs 6pm to 7am. You can camp on Ao Chong Khad and Ao Mai Ngam. The former has the more spectacular beach; the latter fills up last, is more secluded and, with its narrow shallow white-sand bay, feels wilder.

Book ahead online or through the mainland national park office.

Ao Chong Khad Restaurant THAI $$
(Ko Surin Neua; mains 80-180B, set menu 120-280B; ⊙7.30-9am, noon-2pm & 6.30-8pm) The park restaurant on Ko Surin Neua serves authentically good Thai food. This is where day trips stop for lunch.

Ao Mai Ngam Restaurant THAI $$
(Ko Surin Neua; mains 80-180B, set menu 120-280B; ⊙7.30-9am, noon-2pm & 6.30-8pm) The national park's restaurant at Ao Mai Ngam does decent Thai food.

Getting There & Away

Tour operator speedboats (return 1700B, 1¼ hours one-way) leave around 9am, return between 1pm and 4pm and honour open tickets. Return whenever you please, but confirm your ticket with Ko Surin Neua's park office the night before.

Ko Phra Thong & Ko Ra เกาะพระทอง/เกาะระ

According to legend, many centuries ago, pirates buried a golden Buddha beneath the sands at Ko Phra Thong (Golden Buddha Island). The statue was never found, but the island's modern-day treasures are its endless sandy beaches, mangroves, vast bird life and rare orchids.

This long, slender, wooded island is as quiet as a night on the open ocean. Fishing (squid, prawns, jellyfish) remains its key industry; the local delicacy is pungent *gà·Ъì* (fermented prawn paste). On the southern west coast lies 10km of virgin golden-sand beach kissed by blue sea.

Immediately north is even quieter Ko Ra, encircled by golden beaches and mangroves. This small isle is a mountainous jungled slab with impressive wildlife (including over 100 bird species, leopard cats, flying lemurs, wild pigs, monitor lizards, scaly anteaters and slow lorises) and a welcoming population of fisherfolk.

Sleeping & Eating

Mr Chuoi's BUNGALOW $
(☎084 855 9886, 087 898 4636; www.mrchuoibarandhut.com; Ko Phra Thong; bungalows 500-1200B) Simple, wood-and-bamboo bungalows,

on the island's northwest coast, with evening electricity. You'll also find a fun bar and excellent restaurant, enlivened by Mr Chuoi himself. Call ahead and he'll arrange transport to Ko Phra Thong.

Horizon BUNGALOW **$$**
(☎081 894 7195; www.horizonecoresort.com; Ko Phra Thong; d 1300-1900B) This northwest beach ecolodge has seven roomy, shaggy-haired, wood-and-bamboo bungalows made from natural local products from renewable sources (wherever possible); they only use fansa and sleep two or four. Horizon organises hiking tours to neighbouring Ko Ra (1600B, minimum three people) and has the island's only dive school, **Blue Guru** (☎080 144 0551; www.blue-guru.org; 2 dives 4500-6500B), ideally positioned for underwater explorations of the nearby Surin Islands.

★**Golden Buddha Beach Resort** BUNGALOW **$$$**
(☎081 895 2242, 081 892 2208; www.goldenbuddharesort.com; Ko Phra Thong; bungalows 2700-14,000B;) The area's poshest resort attracts yogis, couples and families keen for a secluded getaway. Accommodation is in uniquely designed, naturalistic-chic, privately owned wooden houses, short- or long-term; there are big family-sized house options too. Rooms have open-air bathrooms, wood-carved interiors and glimpses of the fabulous 10km beach through surrounding forest and gardens. Everyone congregates at the mosaic-floored club house **restaurant-bar** (mains 220-300B; ⏲7.30am-9.30pm;).

Getting There & Away

You could theoretically charter a long-tail from the Khuraburi pier to Ko Phra Thong (one-way around 1500B); but boatmen are hard to find. It's worth enquiring in Khuraburi about the 'daily local ferry' to the island, though timings and reliability vary. It's easiest to contact your resort in advance to arrange transport.

Khao Sok National Park อุทยานแห่งชาติเขาสก

If your leg muscles have atrophied after too much beach-bumming, venture inland to the wondrous 738-sq-km **Khao Sok National Park** (☎077 395154; www.khaosok.com; adult/child 300/150B; ⏲8am-5pm), halfway between the Andaman and Gulf coasts. Many believe this lowland jungle (Thailand's rainiest spot) is over 160 million years old, one of the world's oldest rainforests. Dramatic limestone formations and waterfalls cascade through juicy thickets drenched with rain and morning dew. A network of dirt trails snakes through, allowing visitors to spy on an exciting array of indigenous creatures.

Khao Sok's vast terrain makes it one of the last viable habitats for large mammals. During rainy months you may spot bears, boars, gaurs, tapirs, gibbons, deer, marbled cats, wild elephants and perhaps even a tiger. And you'll find more than 300 bird species, 38 bat varieties and one of the world's largest (and smelliest) flowers, the increasingly rare *Rafflesia kerrii*, which, in Thailand, lives only in Khao Sok. These giant flowers can reach 80cm in diameter.

The best time to visit is during the December-to-April dry season. During the June-to-October monsoon, trails get slippery, flash flooding is common and leeches come out in force, though European summer holidays keep the park busy. Animals leave their hidden reservoirs throughout the wet months, so you're more likely to stumble across big fauna.

Sights & Activities

Kayaking (700B), rafting (1100B; high season) and tubing (400B; rainy season) are popular activities. Elephant rides are available, but it's worth reading up on the animal welfare issues involved (p327) if you're considering these.

The road leading 1.8km northeast from Rte 401 to park headquarters is lined with simple, sweet guesthouses offering park tours and guide services. We recommend a two-day, one-night canoeing and hiking trip (per person 2500B) to Chiaw Lan, where you sleep on the lake in floating huts. Book through the park headquarters (p258) or any tour agency.

Chiaw Lan Lake LAKE
(เขื่อนเชี่ยวหลาน; day/overnight trip 1500/2500B) This stunning 165-sq-km lake sits 65km (an hour's drive) east of park headquarters. It was created in 1982 by an enormous shale-clay dam called Ratchaprapha (Kheuan Ratchaprapha or Chiaw Lan). Limestone outcrops protruding from the lake reach up to 960m, over three times higher than Phang-Nga's formations. Most lake visits involve a day or overnight tour (including transfers, boats and guides). Charter boats (per day 2000B) from local fishermen at the

dam's entrance to explore the coves, canals, caves and cul-de-sacs along the lakeshore.

Two caves can be accessed by foot from the southwestern shore. **Tham Nam Thalu** FREE, contains striking limestone formations and subterranean streams. Visiting during the rainy season isn't recommended; there have been fatalities. **Tham Si Ru** FREE features four converging passageways used as a hideout by communist insurgents between 1975 and 1982.

Hiking

Khao Sok hiking is excellent. Most guesthouses and agencies arrange hiking tours (full day 1500B to 2000B); just ensure you find a certified guide (they wear official badges).

The park headquarters (p258) hands out hiking maps. You can hike independently from the headquarters to waterfalls at **Wing Hin** (2.8km) and **Bang Hua Rad** (3km). Hikes to the waterfalls at **Than Sawan** (6km) and **Than Kloy** (7km) require guides. At research time, the 4km trail to the 11-tiered waterfall at **Sip-Et Chan** was off-limits.

Sleeping & Eating

Jungle Huts BUNGALOW $

(077 395160; www.khaosokjunglehuts.com; 242 Mu 6; r fan 300-700B, air-con 1000B;) This popular budget hang-out, 1km northeast off Rte 401, contains an ever-growing collection of decent, individually styled bungalows, all with bathrooms and porches. Choose from plain stilted bamboo huts, bigger wooden editions, pink-washed concrete bungalows, or air-con rooms along vertiginous walkways.

Art's Riverview Jungle Lodge GUESTHOUSE $$

(098 826 6967, 090 167 6818; www.facebook.com/Arts-Riverview-Lodge-Travel-1562090180732965; 54/3 Mu 6; bungalows fan 650-1000B, air-con 1200-1500B;) In a monkey-filled jungle bordering a rushing river with a limestone cliff-framed swimming hole, Art's enjoys Khao Sok's prettiest setting. Stilted brick, shingled and all-wood bungalows are spacious and comfy, many with river views, though they could use a refresh. There's a variety of rooms, including family-sized options, and a host of family-friendly activities. It's signposted 1.5km northeast off Rte 401.

Tree Tops River Huts BUNGALOW $$

(077 395129, 087 862 9656; www.treetopsriverhuts.com; d fan/air-con 1000/1300B;) Clean and sturdy, if ageing, fan-cooled bungalows with porches sit high on stilts in the trees at this busy riverside spot overlooking park headquarters. Stone-walled air-con rooms are perfectly comfy, though less exciting. All have hot showers.

> **KHAO SOK TOURS**
>
> Tours in and around Khao Sok can be up to 50% cheaper when booked through guesthouses or travel agents around the park itself. Tours booked from further-afield destinations (Phuket or Khao Lak) include higher-priced transport and tour agent commissions.

★ **Elephant Hills** RESORT $$$

(076 381703; www.elephanthills.com; 170 Mu 7, Tambon Klong Sok; d all-inclusive from 13,585B;) Whether you're a five-strong family, honeymooning backpacker couple or a soloist, this resort makes everyone smile. Above Mae Nam Sok, at the foot of stunning limestone mountains draped in misty jungle, Khao Sok's only top-end tented camp offers rootsy Serengeti-style luxury. Airy tents have wood furnishings, full bathrooms, skylights and hammocks on porches.

All-inclusive prices cover meals, guided hikes and canoe trips downriver to its elephant camp, where 12 lovely ladies (rescues from other camps where they were forced to carry tourists around) are treated kindly. You can't ride them, but you get to feed, bathe, and spend quality time with them. It's a special experience. Consider adding a night at their floating **Rainforest Camp** (076 381703; www.elephanthills.com; Chiaw Lan Lake; d all-inclusive from 19,355B). Reservations only.

Jasmine Garden RESORT $$$

(082 282 3209; www.khaosokjasmine.com; 35/6 Mu 6; d/q 2200/3000B;) A 2015 arrival, family-run Jasmine hosts some of Khao Sok's classiest non-luxury lodgings, plus cooking classes (800B). Orange-toned concrete bungalows open onto roomy terraces overlooking a warm-blue pool with sensational cliff vistas. Delicate interiors involve wood-carved beds, Buddha paintings, tiled floors and plenty of teak. It's 1km northeast off Rte 401.

Pawn's Restaurant THAI $

(park access road; mains 100-150B; 9am-9pm;) A friendly all-female team heads up this humble eatery: your go-to spot for deliciously spiced curries, from searing red pumpkin-and-veg to beautifully creamy tofu or chicken massaman, and huge hearty breakfasts. It's 500m southwest of park headquarters.

Information

There are many ATMS. Most guesthouses have wi-fi.

Khao Sok National Park Headquarters (☎077 395154; www.khaosok.com; ⊙8am-5pm) About 1.8km northeast off Rte 401, exiting near the Km 109 marker; helpful maps and information.

Getting There & Around

From Surat catch a bus going towards Takua Pa; from the Andaman coast, take a Surat Thani–bound bus. Buses stop on Rte 401, 1.8km southwest of the visitors centre. If touts don't meet you, you'll have to walk to your chosen guesthouse (50m to 2km).

Daily minivan departures include the following:

DESTINATION	FARE (B)	DURATION (HR)
Bangkok	850	11
Khao Lak	150	1¼
Ko Lanta	750	5
Ko Tao	1100	8
Krabi	350	3
Surat Thani	250	1

Khao Lak & Around เขาหลัก

When people refer to Khao Lak, they're usually talking about a series of white-sand beaches hugging Phang-Nga's west coastline, backed by forested hills, about 70km north of Phuket. With easy day trips to the Similan and Surin Islands, Khao Sok and Khao Lak/Lam Ru National Parks, or even Phuket, the area is a central, kick-back base for exploring the northern Andaman.

Southernmost **Hat Khao Lak** gives way to **Hat Nang Thong**, making up a beach for those who shun the glitz and cheesiness of Phuket's bigger resort towns, but still crave comfort, shops and plenty of facilities. Khao Lak proper (Khao Lak Town), a jumble of restaurants, tourist markets and low-rise hotels along grey Hwy 4, is bland but convenient; you'll probably spend your days further afield.

About 2.5km north, **Hat Bang Niang** is a quieter version of sandy bliss with skinnier beaches. **Hat Pakarang** and **Hat Bang Sak**, 12km to 13km north of Hat Khao Lak, are a sleepy, unbroken sandy stretch surrounded by thick mangroves, rolling pasture and plantations of rubber trees forming a wide buffer between the coast and highway. You'll feel like you've really escaped it all here.

Sights

Khao Lak/Lam Ru National Park NATIONAL PARK
(อุทยานแห่งชาติเขาหลัก-ลำรู่; ☎076 485243; www.dnp.go.th; adult/child 200/100B; ⊙8am-4.30pm) Immediately south of Hat Khao Lak, this vast 125-sq-km park is a collage of sea cliffs, 1000m-high hills, beaches, estuaries, waterfalls, forested valleys and mangroves. Wildlife includes hornbills, drongos, tapirs, serows, monkeys, Bengal monitor lizards and Asiatic black bears. The park office and visitors centre, 3km south of Khao Lak proper off Hwy 4, has little printed information, but there's a scenic open-air **restaurant** (mains 100-200B; ⊙8.30am-8.30pm) perched on a shady slope overlooking the sea. From here, there's an easy 3km (one-hour) round-trip nature trail south along the cape to often-deserted **Hat Lek**.

Boat 813 MEMORIAL
(Bang Niang) This police boat was hurled into an open field 1km inland from Hat Bang Niang (2.5km north of central Khao Lak) by the powerful 2004 Boxing Day tsunami. A decade later, it remains the region's most prominent reminder of the disaster. There's a regal monument-worthy entryway and an information booth with a tsunami timeline in Thai and English.

International Tsunami Museum MUSEUM
(พิพิธภัณฑ์สึนามิระหว่างประเทศ; Hwy 4, Bang Niang; adult/child 100/50B; ⊙9am-7pm) On Hwy 4, 2.5km north of Khao Lak proper and just north of Boat 813, is the International Tsunami Museum, with English-language displays, photos and videos that spare no detail about the effects of the disaster in one of Thailand's worst hit regions.

Activities

Diving and snorkelling day excursions to the Similan and Surin Islands are immensely popular but, if you can, go for a live-aboard. The islands are around 70km from the mainland (1½ hours by speedboat), so live-aboards allow you a more relaxing trip sans masses of day trippers. Dive shops offer live-aboard trips from around 19,000/35,000B for three-/six-day packages and day trips for 5000B to 6000B.

On these three- to seven-day trips, you'll slink below the ocean's surface up to four

Khao Lak

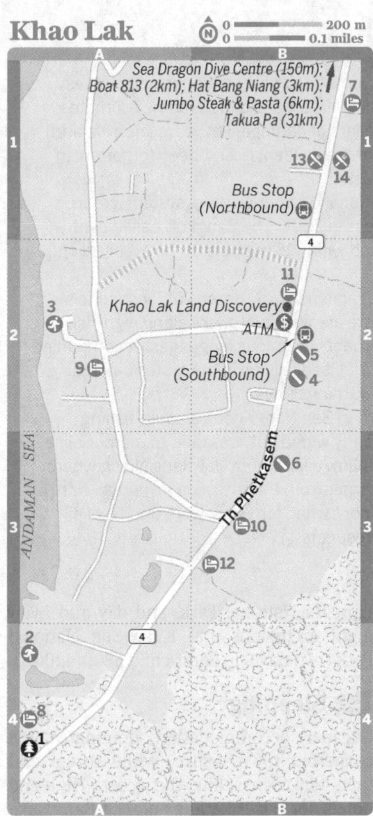

Khao Lak

Sights
1 Khao Lak/Lam Ru National Park........A4

Activities, Courses & Tours
2 Hat Khao Lak........A4
3 Hat Nang Thong........A2
4 IQ Dive........B2
5 Sea Bees........B2
6 Wicked Diving........B3

Sleeping
7 Fasai House........B1
8 Khao Lak/Lam Ru National Park Accommodation........A4
9 Nangthong Bay Resort........A2
10 PhuKhaoLak........B3
11 To Zleep........B2
12 Walker's Inn........B3

Eating
13 Go Pong........B1
14 Jai........B1
Khao Lak/Lam Ru National Park Restaurant........(see 8)
PhuKhaoLak........(see 10)

times daily in what's commonly considered one of the world's top 10 diving realms. While both the Similan and Surin Islands have experienced vast coral bleaching recently, Richelieu Rock (p254) in the Surin Islands is still the crème de la crème of the region's dive sites, frequented by whale sharks from March to April. Ko Bon (p262) is a rewarding Similan site due to the traffic of giant manta rays.

Most dive shops welcome snorkellers on selected day dives and live-aboards, with around 30% discount. Otherwise, tour agencies offer cheaper snorkelling trips to the Similans (1900B). Open Water certification costs between 10,500B and 18,000B, depending on where you dive. Beginners can join one-day Similans Discover Scuba trips for around 6500B. Rates exclude the 700B national park diving fee.

The Similans' dive season runs from mid-October to mid-May, when the national park is open. April and May trips are weather dependent.

★Wicked Diving DIVING
(☎076 485868; www.wickeddiving.com; Th Phetkasem, Khao Lak; 2 dives 5700B, snorkelling day/overnight trip 2900/8100B; ⊙Oct-May) An exceptionally well-run, environmentally conscious outfit that offers diving and snorkelling day and overnight trips, a range of live-aboards (three-day Similans trip from 20,700B) and conservation trips, and a range of dive courses (PADI Open Water certification costs 17,000B).

★Fantastic SNORKELLING
(☎076 485998; www.fantasticsimilan.com; adult/child 2300/1700B; ⊙mid-Oct–mid-May) Fantastic is an over-the-top frolic of a Similans snorkelling tour featuring players from the local cross-dressing cabaret as guides. It's a trip duplicated nowhere else on earth; they get you to the prime snorkel sites too. Prices include hotel pick-ups from Phuket or Khao Lak. Bookings essential online or by phone.

Sea Dragon Dive Centre DIVING
(☎076 485420; www.seadragondivecenter.com; Th Phetkasem, Khao Lak; 2 dives 5100B, snorkelling day trip 2700B; ⊙Oct-May) One of Khao Lak's older dive centres, super-efficient Sea Dragon maintains high standards, running

TSUNAMI EARLY WARNING SYSTEM

On 26 December 2004, an earthquake off the Sumatran coast sent enormous waves crashing into Thailand's Andaman coast, claiming almost 5400 lives (some estimates have it much higher) and causing millions of dollars of damage. Ten years later, life and business on this stretch have bounced back, but the incident hasn't been forgotten. In fact, it's inspired action to prevent a repeat disaster.

In 2005, Thailand officially inaugurated a national disaster warning system, created in response to the country's lack of preparedness in 2004. The Bangkok-based centre anticipates that a tsunami warning can be issued within 15 minutes of the event being detected by existing international systems.

The public will be warned via the nationwide radio network, dozens of TV channels and SMS messages. For non-Thai speakers, there are warning towers along high-risk beachfront areas that will broadcast announcements in various languages, accompanied by flashing lights. Recent reports (2014) have criticised failings in the system, including insufficient alert towers and two out-of-action warning buoys.

The wave-shaped **Tsunami Memorial Park** in Ban Nam Khem, a squid-fishing village 26km north of Hat Khao Lak that was nearly wiped out, was built to memorialise those who lost their lives. **Boat 813** (p258) lies 1km inland from Hat Bang Niang where it was deposited by the wave, just around the corner from the **International Tsunami Museum** (p258). The moving memorials augment what, for years, were unofficial pilgrimage sites for those who came to pay their respects.

diving and snorkelling day trips, wreck dives (2600B), Open Water Diver certification (10,500B to 17,500B) and an array of Similan and Surin Islands live-aboards (three-day trip from 12,600B).

Sea Bees DIVING
(076 485434; www.seabees.com; Th Phetkasem, Khao Lak; 2 dives 5600B; mid-Oct–May) This well-organised German-run dive operation offers two-dive Similan day trips, one-day tasters (9600B), Open Water courses (18,050B) and advanced diver courses, plus Similans live-aboards (three-day trip from 18,900B). Snorkellers can join day trips (2800B).

IQ Dive DIVING
(076 485614; www.iq-dive.com; Th Phetkasem, Khao Lak; 2/3 dives 5000/6000B) A quality dive school focused on diving and snorkelling (2700B) day trips. Also offers Open Water certification (15,000B to 17,000B), one-day Discover Scuba (6500B), and low-season dives off Phuket and Ko Phi-Phi.

Tours

Khao Lak Land Discovery ADVENTURE TOUR
(076 485411; www.khaolaklanddicovery.com; 21/5 Mu 7, Th Phetkasem, Khao Lak; 9am-8pm) This multilingual agency, one of Khao Lak's most reliable, runs adventure-activity day trips (adult/child 2500/1800B) to Khao Lak/Lam Ru National Park, and day and overnight excursions into Khao Sok National Park (two-day trip adult/child 5800/4200B).

Sleeping

Cheaper accommodation dominates the congested town centre, while three- and four-star resorts line the coast. High-end hotels dot Hat Pakarang and Hat Bang Sak.

Fasai House GUESTHOUSE $
(076 485867; www.fasaihouse.com; 5/54 Mu 7, Khao Lak; r 650-900B;) Arguably Khao Lak's top budget choice, Fasai wins us over with its delightful staff and immaculate, motel-style air-con rooms set in a warm yellow-washed block framing a little pool. It's signposted west off Hwy 4 towards the northern end of Khao Lak.

To Zleep GUESTHOUSE $
(076 485899; www.tozleep.com; Th Phetkasem, Khao Lak; r 700-1200B;) If you can forgive the name, this chequered roadside block is a tasteful, hostel-feel guesthouse full of colourful wall murals and small, spotlessly smart rooms. Some have bunks, others doubles. All come coolly kitted out with minimalist Ikea-style furnishings, concrete floors and colour-on-white themes. Biggest and brightest are corner mountain-view doubles.

Walker's Inn GUESTHOUSE $
(084 840 2689; www.walkersinn.com; 26/61 Mu 7, Th Phetkasem, Khao Lak; dm/r 200/600B;) A long-running backpacker fave and classic old-school guesthouse that features bright, spacious air-con rooms, decent single-sex dorms, and a popular downstairs pub dishing up full English breakfasts. It also does laundry and hire motorbikes (per day 200B).

Khao Lak/Lam Ru National Park Accommodation BUNGALOW $
(076 485243, in Bangkok 02 562 0760; www.dnp.go.th; Hat Khao Lak; bungalows fan/air-con 800/2000B;) Just beyond the southern end of Khao Lak Town, the national park headquarters has a handful of no-frills two-, four- and 10-person bungalows. Nothing fancy, but the shady hillside setting and low-key vibe will suit anyone after an eco-experience.

Nangthong Bay Resort RESORT $$
(076 485088; www.nangthong.com; 13/5 Mu 7, Hat Nang Thong; r 1800-3000B;) The massive turquoise pool dominates lush grounds that ramble to the beach and service is good. Free-standing bungalows follow a minimalist black-and-white chic design, with open-air showers. Cheaper rooms are set back from the beach, but are still fantastic value. It's popular with holidaying Thai families for the lovely big pool and four-person rooms, and an absolute steal in low season.

PhuKhaoLak BUNGALOW $$
(089 874 1018, 076 485141; www.phukhaolak.com; Mu 7, Th Phetkasem, Khao Lak; r fan/air-con 800/1800B; Oct-May;) Air-con rooms are stylish stand-alone casitas with high ceilings, dark-wood furnishings, ceramic-tiled floors, huge bathrooms, and beanbags loaded on verandahs. Fan rooms, fronted by porches, are basic but spotless. All curve around an aqua-tiled pool and a palm grove sprawling back against jungled hills. The open-walled Thai restaurant (p262) is good.

★ **Sarojin** HOTEL $$$
(076 427900; www.sarojin.com; Hat Pakarang; r 13,100-24,100B;) A gloriously peaceful and romantic retreat with stellar service and an elegant, intimate setting amid lotus ponds, 12km north of Khao Lak proper. The very private spa (p278), which takes in views of coconut groves and mangroves, is one of the Andaman's best. Glossy-chic rooms are impeccably styled in warm woods, with huge swish bathrooms sporting free-standing circular tubs. No kids allowed.

Both the beachside **Thai seafood kitchen** and the gorgeous candle-lit **Mediterranean restaurant** tucked into the trees are exceptional, and there are weekly guests-only cocktail parties. **Cooking classes** happen on the banks of Mae Nam Takua Pa, where you can watch water buffalo amble by. The resort contributes to local community projects, including animal welfare and landscape replanting.

Casa de La Flora DESIGN HOTEL $$$
(076 428999; www.casadelaflora.com; 67/213 Mu 5, Hat Bang Niang; r incl breakfast 12,420-24,050B;) Folded into trim seaside grounds dotted with contemporary art, this sleekly modern belle is composed of smart cube-like glass-and-concrete villas and suites adorned with warm-wood-panelled walls, double-sided mirrors, chunky concrete bathtubs and private plunge pools. Thoughtful touches include iPod docks, in-room espresso machines, hairdryers and, of course, pillow menus. Pod-style lounge beds fringe the sea-view infinity pool.

The service strikes that perfect friendly-but-efficient balance.

Eating & Drinking

This is no culinary capital, but tourists congregate at a few local haunts to rehash the day's diving. Early-morning divers will struggle to find breakfast before 8.30am.

Go Pong THAI $
(Th Phetkasem, Khao Lak; dishes 40-120B; 10am-11pm) Get a real taste of local flavours at this terrific streetside diner where they stir-fry noodles and sensational spicy rice dishes and simmer aromatic noodle soups that attract a loyal lunch following. Dishes are packed full of flavour.

Jai THAI $
(5/1 Mu 7 Th Phetkasem, Khao Lak; mains 80-250B; 8am-9pm;) Under a soaring peaked roof at the northern end of central Khao Lak, this semi-open-air, family-run eatery has a gigantic menu of fresh grilled seafood, spiced stir fries and all the curries, rices and noodles. Satisfying, friendly and convenient.

Takieng THAI $$
(26/43 Mu 5, Bang Niang; mains 120-350B; noon-10pm;) Of two open-air Thai restaurants beneath stilted tin roofs on Hwy 4, 2.5km north of Khao Lak Town,

Takieng is the most popular and attractive. It steams fresh fish in sweet green curry, does a scintillating chicken or pork *lâhp*, bubbles up beautifully spiced curries, and fries squid in a delicious chilli paste. Service is impeccable.

Jumbo Steak & Pasta ITALIAN **$$**
(☎098 059 8293; Th Phetkasem, Ban Khukkhuk; mains 70-280B; ⊙noon-10.30pm Thu-Tue) A hole-in-the-wall joint on the west side of Hwy 4, 6km north of Khao Lak proper, launched by a former Le Meridien line chef who does beautiful pasta dishes in all kinds of flavours: penne arrabiata, hot-and-spicy seafood spaghetti, creamy spinach tagliatelle, a host of pizzas and terrific steaks. Dishes are great value in terms of quality, though portions aren't huge.

PhuKhaoLak INTERNATIONAL, THAI **$$**
(☎076 485141; www.phukhaolak.com; Mu 7, Th Phetkasem, Khao Lak; mains 100-350B; ⊙7am-10pm Oct-May;) With cloth-covered tables spilling to the lawn edge at the south end of Khao Lak's highway strip, it's hard to miss. And you shouldn't, because there's a never-ending, well-prepared Thai-European menu of fried/grilled/steamed fish, sirloin steaks, pastas and sandwiches, and a dedicated veg section featuring such delights as spicy tofu with peanut sauce.

Information

SSS Ambulance (☎076 209 347, emergency 081 081 9000) For diving-related emergencies, the SSS Ambulance rushes injured persons to Phuket International Hospital (p273), and can also be used for car or motorcycle accidents.

Getting There & Around

Any bus following Hwy 4 between Takua Pa (55B, 45 minutes) and Phuket (100B, two hours) will stop at Hat Khao Lak if you ask.

Khao Lak Land Discovery (p260) runs shared minibuses to Phuket International Airport (600B, 1¼ hours). Alternatively, you can take **Cheaper Than Hotel** (☎085 786 1378, 086 276 6479; cheaperkhaolak1@gmail.com) taxis to Phuket airport (1000B) and points south. Otherwise, taxis cost 1500B from Khao Lak to the airport. Or tell a Phuket-bound bus driver to drop you at the 'airport'; you'll be let off at an intersection from which motorcycle taxis usually take you to the airport (10 minutes, 100B).

Numerous travel agencies and guesthouses rent motorbikes (per day 250B), including Khao Lak Land Discovery.

Similan Islands Marine National Park

อุทยานแห่งชาติหมู่เกาะสิมิลัน

Known to divers the world over, the beautiful 70-sq-km **Similan Islands Marine National Park** (☎076 453272; www.dnp.go.th; adult/child 500/300B ; ⊙mid-Oct–mid-May) lies 70km offshore from Phang-Nga Province. Its smooth granite islands are as impressive above the bright-aqua water as below, topped with rainforest, edged with blindingly white beaches and fringed by coral reefs. Unfortunately, coral bleaching has killed off many hard corals, but soft corals are still intact, the fauna is there and it remains a lovely (popular) place to dive.

In 1998, the nine-island park was expanded to include **Ko Bon** and Ko Tachai. Two of the 11 islands, Ko Miang (Island 4) and **Ko Similan** (Island 8), have accommodation. The park visitors centre and most facilities are on Ko Miang. 'Similan' comes from the Malay *sembilan*, meaning 'nine'; while each island is named, they're more commonly known by numbers.

Hat Khao Lak, home to most dive schools, is the park's jumping-off point. The pier and mainland **national park headquarters** (☎076 453272; www.dnp.go.th; 93 Mu 5, Thap Lamu; ⊙8am-5pm mid-Oct–mid-May) are at Thap Lamu, 12km south (Hwy 4, then Rte 4147). There's a **visitors centre** (Ko Miang; ⊙7.30am-8pm mid-Oct–mid-May) on Ko Miang's north-coast beach.

Sadly, the onslaught of mass tourism means that many Similan beaches and dive/snorkel sites get completely packed with day trippers. It's clear that nobody is monitoring these numbers, to the park's detriment. There are huge queues to climb viewpoints and some snorkelling outfits even feed the fish, a big ecological no-no. That would never happen if this were a national park! Oh, wait...

Sights & Activities

Diving & Snorkelling

The Similans offer diving for all levels, at depths from 2m to 30m. There are rock reefs at **Ko Hin Pousar** (Island 7) and dive-throughs at **Hin Pousar** (Elephant Head Rock), with marine life ranging from tiny plume worms and soft corals to schooling fish, manta rays and rare whale sharks. **Ko Bon**, largely unscathed by coral bleaching,

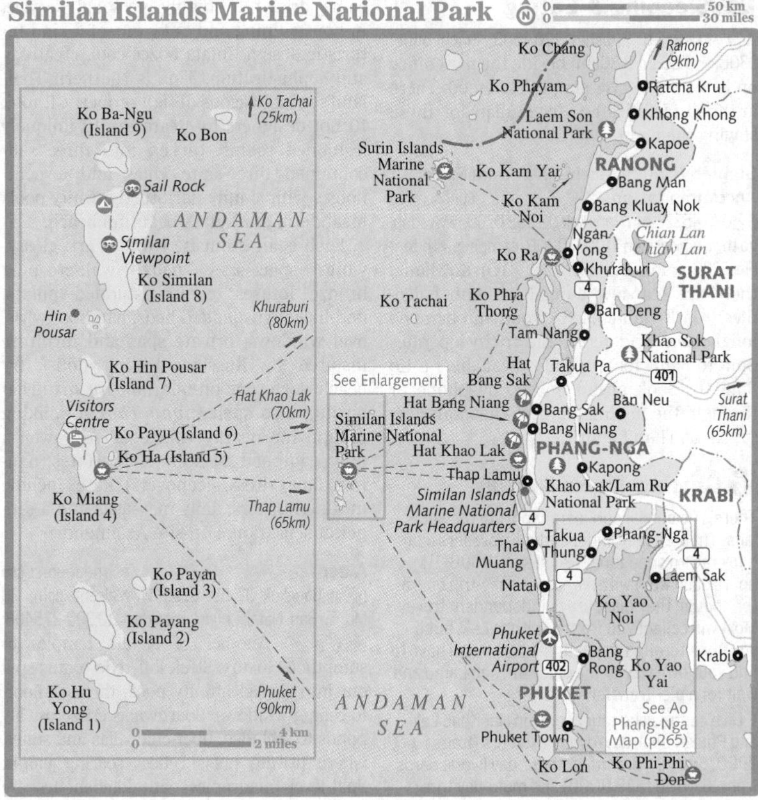

has some of the better diving and snorkelling areas. There are dive sites at each of the islands north of **Ko Miang**. The park's southern section (Islands 1, 2 and 3) is an off-limits turtle nesting ground.

No facilities for divers exist in the national park, so you'll be taking a dive tour. Dive schools in Hat Khao Lak (p258) book day trips (two dives 5000B to 6000B) and live-aboards (three-/six-day trip from around 19,000/35,000B), as do Phuket dive centres (two-dive day trip from 5600B, three-day live-aboard from 19,000B).

Agencies situated in Khao Lak offer snorkelling-only day/overnight trips from 1900/4700B. Day-trip operators usually visit three or four snorkelling sites.

Wildlife & Hiking

The forest around Ko Miang's visitors centre has some walking trails and great wildlife. The fabulous Nicobar pigeon, with its wild mane of grey-green feathers, is common here. Endemic to the islands of the Andaman Sea, it's one of the park's 39 bird species. Hairy-legged land crabs and fruit bats (flying foxes) are relatively easy to spot in the forest, as are flying squirrels.

A small beach track, with information panels, leads 400m east from the visitors centre to a tiny snorkelling bay. Detouring from the track, the **Viewpoint Trail**, about 500m or 30 minutes of steep scrambling, has panoramic vistas from the top. A 500m (20-minute) walk west from the visitors centre leads through forest to smooth west-facing granite platform **Sunset Point**.

On Ko Similan, there's a 2.5km forest hike to a **viewpoint**, and a shorter, steep scramble off the north-coast beach to **Sail Rock** (Balance Rock), during daylight it's clogged with visitors.

Sleeping & Eating

A **restaurant** (dishes 120-150B, lunch buffet 230B; 7.30am-8.30pm) beside the park office on Ko Miang serves simple Thai food. There are food facilities on Ko Similan for those staying the night.

Similan Islands Marine National Park Accommodation BUNGALOW $$
(076 453272, in Bangkok 02 562 0760; www.dnp.go.th; r fan/air-con 1100/2000B, camping with tent hire 570B; mid-Oct–mid-May;) On Ko Miang, there are sea-view bungalows with balconies, dark fan-cooled wood-and-bamboo longhouses, and tents. Electricity operates 6pm to 6am. Tents are also available on Ko Similan. Book ahead online, by phone or through the mainland park headquarters (p262) at Thap Lamu.

Getting There & Away

There's no official public transport to the Similans. Theoretically, independent travellers can book return speedboat transfers (1900B, 1½ hours each way) with a Khao Lak day-trip operator, though they discourage independent travel. Most will collect you from Hat Khao Lak, but if you book through the national park you'll have to find your own way to the office in Thap Lamu and wait for a pier transfer.

Dive centres and tour agents in Hat Khao Lak and Phuket book day/overnight tours (from 2900/5000B), dive trips (three-day live-aboards from 16,000B to 19,000B) and multi-day trips including park transport, food and lodging, which cost little more than what you'd pay getting to the islands independently, which is not encouraged.

Natai นาใต้

Officially in Phang-Nga Province, Natai is like a misleadingly laid-back outpost of high-life Phuket – but, in reality, even more fabulous. Just 26km north of Phuket International Airport, this budding luxury bolthole lies within easier reach of Phuket than parts of Phuket itself. There's little else out here yet, apart from a delicious broad blonde beach that disappears into turquoise waters. And, of course, some of southern Thailand's finest dining and lodgings.

Sleeping & Eating

★ **Iniala Beach House** DESIGN HOTEL $$$
(076 451456; www.iniala.com; 40/14 Mu 6, Ban Natai; d all-inclusive $1290-2820;) From expertly concocted passion-fruit welcome drinks to highly personal service, in-house dining and bold, one-of-a-kind futuristic design, Iniala oozes cool, creativity and sophistication. This is southern Thailand's most luscious design property. It took 10 hot designers to create the 10 uniquely fashioned rooms, tucked into three self-contained three-suite villas and a penthouse, with skinny dark-tiled infinity pools meandering to Natai's beautiful beach.

Each is an exquisite work of art: glossy-white space-agey pads, wall-creeping bronze lotuses, ceramic-studded pillars, pod-like or suspended beds, bamboo twirls, oval windows, private spas and furniture inspired by Russian nesting dolls. Try beach yoga, one-on-one *moo·ay tai* (Thai boxing; also spelt *muay Thai*) or biking around the nearby village. There's even a fully equipped 24-hour Kids' Hotel (nannies, fancy dress, sleepovers). Rates include meals, transfers, daily massages and a dinner at sensational on-site Aziamendi.

Aleenta BOUTIQUE HOTEL $$$
(in Bangkok 02 514 8112; www.aleenta.com; 33 Mu 5, Ban Natai; r incl breakfast 10,300-21,540B;) Another of Natai's temples to sumptuous luxury. Sleek loft-style rooms spill out into shared infinity pools through floor-to-ceiling windows. Boardwalks crisscross lily ponds to secluded, uber-chic villas and suites, where private pools reflect soaring palms. Split-level quadruples with kitchenettes are ideal for families. Swish cabanas dot the black-tiled seafront infinity pool and there's an elegant spa, plus brand-new villas on the way.

★ **Aziamendi** FUSION $$$
(083 006 5277; www.aziamendi.com; Iniala Beach House, 40/14 Mu 6, Ban Natai; 10-course tasting menu from 5300B; 6.30-9pm Tue-Sat Dec-Apr) Topping many fine-dining dream lists, the south's hottest new restaurant comes courtesy of three-Michelin-star Basque chef Eneko Atxa (of Azurmendi, Spain, fame) and an internationally acclaimed culinary team. Dining at avant-garde Aziamendi takes the shape of ambitious, inventive 10-course tasting menus that fuse Basque techniques with Thai flavours, unearthing such wonderful complex creations as truffled eggs, deconstructed picnics and sea bass with tsuyu tartare.

It all unfolds alongside a prize-winning wine list, in a stunning space loaded with gold Andaman-inspired ceilings, fluffy black carpets and elaborate Southeast Asian art.

Getting There & Away

Taxis to/from Phuket airport cost 700B.

Ao Phang-Nga อ่าวพังงา

Between turquoise bays peppered with craggy limestone towers, brilliant-white beaches and tumbledown fishing villages, Ao Phang-Nga is one of the Andaman's most spectacular landscapes. Little wonder then that it was here, among looming cliffs and swifts' nests, that James Bond's nemesis, Scaramanga *(The Man with the Golden Gun)*, chose to build his lair. Modern-day wanted assassins with world-domination goals would doubtless skip the place, as it's swarming with tourists, motorboats and sea kayaks year-round. Much of the bay, and some of the coastline, makes up Ao Phang-Nga National Park (p266).

Phang-Nga พังงา

POP 12,000

Phang-Nga is a scruffy, unremarkable town set against sublime limestone cliffs. There isn't much to see or do unless you're here during the annual **Vegetarian Festival** (late September or October). Hotels and amenities are mostly on Th Phetkasem.

Tours

Although it's nice to create your own Ao Phang-Nga itinerary by chartering a boat (p266), it's easier (and cheaper) to join a tour with one of Phang Nga's agencies, most of which are at the bus station. Quality varies, but all offer near-identical itineraries and prices.

Sayan Tours BOAT TOUR

(☎090 708 3211, 076 430348; www.sayantour.com; bus station, off Th Phetkasem; half/full day 800/1100B) A long-standing Ao Phang-Nga tour company offering day trips to Ko Panyi, Ko Phing Kan and Tham Lod (covered in stalactites), and overnight stays on Ko Panyi (1350B).

Mr Kean Tour BOAT TOUR

(☎076 430619, 089 871 6092; bus station, off Th Phetkasem; half/full day 800/1100B) Mr Kean has been running tours of Ao Phang-Nga for over 20 years. Half- and full-day tours include Tham Lod, Ko Phing Kan and Ko Panyi. You can add kayaking and trekking, or spend the night on Ko Panyi (1450B to 1750B).

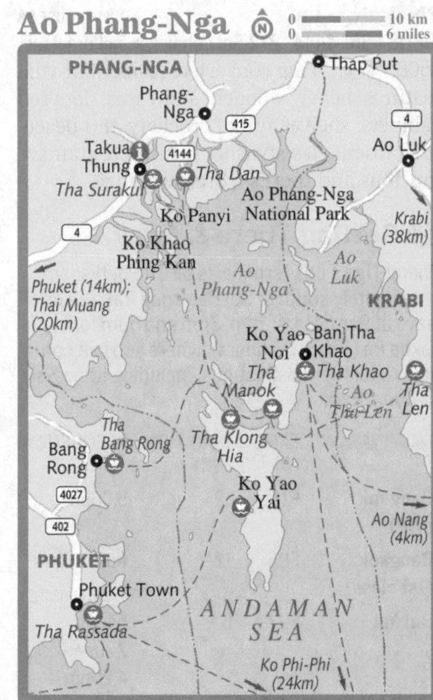

Sleeping & Eating

Several food stalls along Th Phetkasem sell delicious *kà·nŏm jeen* (thin wheat noodles) with chicken curry, *náam yah* (spicy ground-fish curry) or *náam prík* (spicy sauce). There's a small night market on Th Phetkasem just north of the bus station, beside 7-Eleven.

Thaweesuk Hotel GUESTHOUSE $

(☎076 412100; www.thaweesukhotel.com; 76 Th Phetkasem; r incl breakfast with fan 450B, air-con 700-800B; ❄📶) A welcoming, family-run guesthouse tucked behind a colourful mosaic-floor lobby, on north Th Phetkasem. Ground-floor cold-water fan/air-con rooms are simple and clean. Hot-water air-con pads on the 1st floor are significantly more stylish, with varnished-wood floors and lots of tiles.

Baan Phang Nga GUESTHOUSE $$

(☎076 413276; baanphangngabandb@gmail.com; 100/2 Th Phetkasem; r 650-850B; ❄📶) This is a homey, retro-style place with spacious, bright, spotless rooms in an old relic towards the north end of Th Phetkasem. Ceilings are high, varnished-concrete floors are colourful and hot-water bathrooms have rain showers. Good coffee, European breakfasts and Thai fare are served in the delightful downstairs **bakery** (dishes 65-160B; ⏰8am-9pm; 📶).

Phang-Nga Inn GUESTHOUSE $$

(☎084 851 4444; 2/2 Soi Lohakit; r incl breakfast 850B; ❄📶) This converted residential villa features heavy wooden staircases, louvred cabinets, shelves full of crockery and peaceful gardens. It's stylishly furnished, staff are gracious and there's a breezy lounge.

Getting There & Away

Phang-Nga's bus terminal is off Th Phetkasem, immediately south of Soi Bamrung Rat. Buses leave at 9am, 11am, 1pm, 3pm and 5pm for Takua Pa (150B, 1½ hours), where you can connect to further destinations, including Khao Sok National Park.

DESTINATION	FARE (B)	DURATION (HR)	FREQUENCY
Bangkok (VIP)	916	12	5.30pm
Bangkok (1st class)	585	12	6pm & 7pm
Hat Yai	292	6	hourly 7.30am-4.20pm
Krabi	80	1½	hourly 7.30am-6pm
Phuket	90	1½	hourly 9am-4pm
Ranong	170	5	10.30am & 1.30pm
Surat Thani	150	4	9.30am, 11.30am, 1.30pm & 3.30pm
Trang	185	3½	hourly 7.30am-4.20pm

Ao Phang-Nga National Park อุทยานแห่งชาติอ่าวพังงา

Established in 1981, 400-sq-km **Ao Phang-Nga National Park** (☎076 481188; www.dnp.go.th; adult/child 300/100B; ⏲8am-4pm) is famous for its classic karst scenery. Huge vertical cliffs frame 42 islands, some with caves accessible only at low tide and leading into hidden *hôrng* (semi-submerged island caves). The bay is composed of large and small tidal channels (Khlong Ko Phanyi, Khlong Phang-Nga, Khlong Bang Toi and Khlong Bo Saen), which run north to south through vast mangroves functioning as aquatic highways for fisherfolk and island inhabitants. These are Thailand's largest remaining primary mangrove forests.

Ao Phang-Nga's marine limestone environment conceals reptiles like Bengal monitor lizards, two-banded monitors (reminiscent of crocodiles when swimming), flying lizards, banded sea snakes, shore pit vipers and Malayan pit vipers. Mammals include serows, crab-eating macaques, white-handed gibbons and dusky langurs.

In high season (November to April) the bay becomes a clogged package-tourist superhighway. But if you explore in the early morning (ideally from the Ko Yao Islands) or stay out later, you might just find a slice of beach, sea and limestone karst of your own. The best way to explore is by kayak.

Sights & Activities

You can charter boats to explore Ao Phang-Nga's half-submerged caves and oddly shaped islands from Tha Dan, 9km south of central Phang-Nga.

Two- to three-hour tours (per person 1000B) head to well-trodden Ko Phing Kan, Ko Panyi and elsewhere in the park. Tha Surakul, 13km southwest of Phang-Nga in Takua Thung, has private boats for hire at similar prices to tours. From the national park headquarters, you can hire boats (1400B, maximum four passengers) for three-hour islands tours. From Phuket, John Gray's Seacanoe (p276) is the top choice for Ao Phang-Nga kayakers.

Ko Khao Phing Kan ISLAND

(เกาะเขาพิงกัน, James Bond Island) Ao Phang-Nga's top tourist drawcard is known to Thais as Ko Phing Kan ('Leaning on Itself Island'). Once used as a location setting for *The Man with the Golden Gun*, today the island is packed with photo-snapping visitors and vendors hawking coral and shells that should have stayed in the sea.

Ko Panyi ISLAND

(เกาะปันหยี) A stilted Muslim village clings to this small karst island, where most tours dock for lunch. It's busy, but several Phang-Nga town tours (p265) enable you to stay overnight and soak up the scenery without crowds.

Sleeping & Eating

Ao Phang-Nga National Park Accommodation BUNGALOW $

(☎076 481188, in Bangkok 02 562 0760; www.dnp.go.th; Rte 4144; bungalows 700-1000B) Simple air-con bungalows sleep two to three, in quiet shady grounds 8.5km south of central Phang-Nga. There's a basic waterside Thai restaurant.

Getting There & Around

From central Phang-Nga, drive 7km south on Hwy 4, turn left onto Rte 4144 (the road to Tha Dan) and travel 2.6km to the park headquarters. Otherwise take a *sǒrng·tǎa·ou* to Tha Dan (30B).

Ko Yao เกาะยาว

With mountainous backbones, unspoilt shorelines, hugely varied birdlife and a population of friendly Muslim fisherfolk, Ko Yao Yai and Ko Yao Noi are laid-back vantage points for soaking up Ao Phang-Nga's beautiful karst scenery. The islands are part of Ao Phang-Nga National Park (p266), but most easily accessed from Phuket (30km away).

Despite being the relative pipsqueak of the Ko Yao Islands, Ko Yao Noi is the main population centre, with fishing, coconut farming and tourism sustaining its small, year-round population. Bays on the east coast, where most resorts are, recede to mud flats at low tides. That said, **Hat Pasai**, on the southeast coast, and **Hat Paradise**, on the northeast coast, are both gorgeous, and **Hat Tha Khao**, on the east coast, has its own dishevelled charm. **Hat Khlong Jark** is a beautiful sweep of sand with good sleeping options.

Ko Yao Yai is more remote and less developed; it's twice the size of Yao Noi with a fraction of the infrastructure. The most accessible beaches are slightly developed **Hat Lo Pared**, on the southwest coast, and powder-white **Hat Chonglard** on the northeast coast.

Please respect local beliefs and dress modestly away from the beaches.

Sights & Activities

Cycling

Amazing Bike Tours (p286) runs popular small-group day trips to Ko Yao Noi from Phuket. If you're keen to explore the numerous dirt trails on Ko Yao Noi or Ko Yao Yai independently, most guesthouses rent mountain bikes (per day 200B), though they're more readily available on Ko Yao Noi.

Diving & Snorkelling

Half-day three-island snorkelling tours (1800B) of Ao Phang-Nga are easily arranged through guesthouses or at the piers.

Elixir Divers DIVING
(☎087 897 0076; www.elixirdivers.com; Glow Elixir, 99 Mu 3, Ko Yao Yai; 2 dives 3500-5500B, 4-day live-aboard 17,900-22,900B; ⏰Oct-Apr) Ko Yao Yai's only dive school is an on-the-ball operator covering a range of PADI courses, two-dive day trips locally and to Ko Phi-Phi, and live-aboards to Hin Daeng, Hin Muang and the Similans, plus snorkelling excursions to Ao Phang-Nga, Krabi and Ko Phi-Phi. If you're staying on Ko Yao Noi, they'll help with transfers.

Yoga

Island Yoga YOGA
(☎089 290 0233; www.thailandyogaretreats.com; 4/10 Mu 4, Hat Tha Khao, Ko Yao Noi; class 600B; ⏰classes 7.30am & 4.30pm) A popular yoga school hosting daily drop-in classes, and multi-day yoga and tai chi retreats. Enquire ahead for schedules.

Kayaking

Kayaks (per day 500B) are widely available on Ko Yao Noi, including at Sabai Corner (p268).

Rock Climbing

Mountain Shop Adventures ROCK CLIMBING
(☎083 969 2023; www.themountainshop.org; Tha Khao; half-day 3200B) There are over 150 climbs on Ko Yao Noi; Mountain Shop owner Mark has routed most of them himself. Trips range from beginner to advanced and many involve boat travel to remote limestone cliffs.

Sleeping & Eating

Ko Yao Noi

Suntisook BUNGALOW $$
(☎089 781 6456, 075 582750; www.facebook.com/suntisookresort; 11/1 Mu 4, Hat Tha Khao; r 2200B; ❄📶) Suntisook's comfy, stylish varnished-wood bungalows are sprinkled across gorgeous butterfly-filled gardens just metres from a quiet beach. All have spacious hammock-laden verandahs, clear-glass sinks, mugs, drinking water, fridges and pot plants. It's efficiently run by a helpful English-speaking Thai family, who offer a good authentic **restaurant** (mains 70-140B; ⏰7.30am-9pm; 📶) and kayak hire. Rates include motorbike use.

Hill House BUNGALOW $$
(☎089 593 9523; www.hillhouse-kohyaonoi.com; Hat Tha Khao; r 1000-1200B; 📶) A friendly, simple hillside spot where dark-wood, hot-water, fan-cooled bungalows are swathed in mosquito nets and have beautiful views

through trees to Ao Phang-Nga's limestone karsts from hammock-loaded terraces.

Sabai Corner Bungalows GUESTHOUSE $$
(☎076 597497; www.sabaicornerbungalows.com; Hat Khlong Jark; bungalows 1800B) Pocketed into a rocky headland, these super-clean no-fuss bungalows with whizzing fans, mosquito nets and hammocks on terraces are blessed with gorgeous sea views. The good, chilled-out waterside **restaurant** (mains 85-260B; ⊙8am-10pm) is a bubbly place to hang out, and it rents kayaks.

★**Six Senses Hideaway** RESORT $$$
(☎076 418500; www.sixsenses.com; 56 Mu 5, btwn Hat Khlong Jark & Hat Tha Khao; villa incl breakfast 27,485-61,500B;) This elegant five-star property, with 56 hillside pool villas and an exquisite spa (p278) built into an existing rubber plantation, exceeds every expectation. Views of Ao Phang-Nga are as jaw-dropping at pink tinged-sunset as at fresh-blue morning; its clifftop infinity pool is a dream; its lounge bar and white-sand beach are well worthy of the frequenting fashionistas; and its commitment to sustainability is unparalleled among global high-end hotels.

Ko Yao Island Resort RESORT $$$
(☎076 597474; www.koyao.com; 24/2 Mu 5, Hat Khlong Jark; villa 6500-21,600B; @) Open-concept thatched bungalows offer serene views across a palm-shaded garden and beach-facing infinity pool to a white strip of sand. We love the graceful, airy, near safari-esque feel of the villas, with their fan-cooled patios and indoor-outdoor bathrooms. There's a snazzy bar-restaurant area and service is stellar.

Chaba Café INTERNATIONAL $
(www.facebook.com/Chaba-Café-and-Gallery-481886365211171; Hat Khlong Jark; mains 90-120B; ⊙9am-5pm Mon-Sat;) Rustic-cute Chaba is a haven of pastel-painted prettiness, with driftwood walls, mellow music and a small gallery. Organic-oriented offerings include honey-sweetened juices, coconut-milk-and-avocado shakes, chrysanthemum tea and home-baked paninis, cookies and cakes, plus soups, pastas and Thai dishes. It's just beyond northern Hat Khlong Jark.

★**Rice Paddy** INTERNATIONAL, THAI $$
(☎082 331 6581, 076 454255; Hat Pasai; mains 180-280B; ⊙noon-10.30pm Tue-Sun Oct-Apr, 6-10.30pm Tue-Sun May-Sep;) On the roadside corner at the southwest end of Hat Pasai, this sweet, all-wood, German-owned Thai-international kitchen is very special. Chunky wooden menus reveal flash-fried *sôm đam*, fantastic falafel and hummus, spicy whole-fish coconut curry and fresh salads. There are excellent vegie dishes with meat substitutes like shiitake 'lamb'. The massaman curry is divine. So are the mojitos.

Ko Yao Yai

Thiwson Beach Resort BUNGALOW $$$
(☎081 956 7582; www.thiwsonbeach.com; 58/2 Mu 4, Hat Chonglard; bungalows with fan & breakfast 1800B, air-con & breakfast 2300-3600B;) Easily the sweetest of the island's humbler bungalow properties. Here are proper wooden thatch- or tin-topped huts with polished floors, outdoor bathrooms and wide patios overlooking the island's prettiest, northeast-coast beach, fronted by an aqua pool. Beachfront bungalows are biggest, but fan rooms are excellent low-season value.

Glow Elixir RESORT $$$
(☎087 808 3838; www.glowbyzinc.com; 99 Mu 3, Prunai; bungalows incl breakfast 4000-14,900B; @) Beside its own silky beach in the southwest corner of the island, the oldest of Yao Yai's four-star resorts offers tasteful beachfront and hillside peaked-roof villas steeped in classic Thai style: dark-wood floors, outdoor showers and fish-patterned ceramic-bowl sinks. Some have private pools. You'll also enjoy a high-season dive centre (p267), massage pagodas and spectacular sunsets over Phuket.

ℹ Information

There are a few ATMs in Ta Khao, Ko Yao Noi's largest settlement, and there's an east-coast ATM opposite the Six Senses Hideaway entrance.

On Ko Yao Yai, three ATMs were operating at research time. It's still wise to carry plenty of cash in low season; resupplying can be an issue.

ℹ Getting There & Away

TO/FROM AO NANG

From November to April, there's an 11am speedboat from the pier at Hat Noppharat Thara to Ko Yao Noi and Ko Yao Yai (both 650B, 45 minutes). It continues to Phuket's Tha Bang Rong, returning at 3pm.

TO/FROM PHUKET

From Phuket's Tha Bang Rong, there are daily speedboats (200B, 30 minutes) to Ko Yao Noi at 7.50am, 8.40am, 9.50am,11.30am, 1pm, 1.30pm, 2.30pm, 3pm and 5.40pm, plus long-tails (120B, one hour) at 9.15am, 12.30pm and 5pm. They stop en route at Tha Klong Hia on Ko Yao Yai (200B, 25 minutes). Boats return to Phuket between 6.30am and 4.40pm.

Returning to Phuket from Ko Yao, taxis run from Tha Bang Rong to Phuket's resort areas for 600B to 800B, and *sŏrng·tăa·ou* (50B) leave for Phuket Town at 7am, 8.30am, 11am and 2.30pm daily.

TO/FROM KO PHI-PHI

Three weekly speedboats run to/from Ko Phi-Phi (1500B), October to April.

TO/FROM KRABI

From 9am to 5.30pm daily, there are frequent long-tails (150B) between Ko Yao Noi's Tha Khao and Krabi's Tha Len (33km northwest of Krabi Town). *Sŏrng·tăa·ou* (100B) run between Tha Len and Krabi's Th Maharat via Krabi's bus terminal.

TO/FROM PHANG-NGA

From Tha Dan in Phang-Nga there's a 1pm ferry to Ko Yao Noi (200B, 1½ hours), returning at 7.30am.

Getting Around

Frequent shuttle boats run from Ko Yao Noi's Tha Manok to Ko Yao Yai's Tha Klong Hia (per person 50B). On the islands, túk-túk (pronounced *đúk đúk*) rides cost about 150B, and most guesthouses rent motorbikes (per day 250B to 300B). It's 100B for *sŏrng·tăa·ou* transport to the resorts.

PHUKET PROVINCE

The island of Phuket has long been misunderstood. Firstly, the 'h' is silent. And secondly, Phuket doesn't feel like an island at all. It's so huge (49km long, the biggest in Thailand) that you rarely feel surrounded by water, which is probably why Ko ('island') was dropped from its name. Branded the 'pearl of the Andaman', this is Thailand's original flavour of tailor-made fun in the sun.

Phuket's sin city of Patong is the biggest town and busiest beach. It's the ultimate gong show where beachaholics sizzle off their hangovers and go-go girls play ping pong… without paddles. But there's space for all kinds here. Phuket Town has morphed into an artsy, culturally rich capital, while Rawai on the island's southern tip remains blissfully laid-back, despite development. The twin west-coast beaches of Kata and Karon reel in holidaymakers who like their trips easy. An upmarket twist awaits along Hat Surin and Ao Bang Thao, while, further north, things quieten down as you thread through Sirinat National Park and Khao Phra Thaew reserve.

Ultimately, the island's affinity for luxury far outshines its other stereotypes. Jet-setters swing through in droves, getting pummelled during swanky spa sessions and sipping sundowners at fashion-forward nightspots or on rented yachts. And you don't have to be an heiress to tap into Phuket's style-packed to-do list. With deep-sea diving, high-end dining, luxury shopping, fabulous white beaches and some of Thailand's swankiest hotels at your fingertips, you might forget to leave.

Activities

Diving & Snorkelling

Phuket enjoys an enviable central location relative to the Andaman's top diving destinations. The much-talked-about Similan Islands lie 100km northwest, while dozens of dive sites orbit Ko Phi-Phi and Ko Lanta, 40km and 72km southeast. Trips from Phuket to these awesome destinations cost slightly more than from places closer to the sites, as you'll be forking out extra baht for boat petrol. Most Phuket operators take divers to the nine decent sites orbiting the island, like **Ko Raya Noi** and **Ko Raya Yai** (Ko Racha Noi and Ko Racha Yai), but these spots rank lower on the wow-o-meter. The reef off the southern tip of Raya Noi is the best spot, with soft corals and pelagic fish species aplenty, though it's usually reserved for experienced divers. Manta and marble rays are frequently glimpsed here and, if you're lucky, you might spot a whale shark.

One-day two-dive trips to nearby sites typically cost 3000B to 4000B. Nondivers (and snorkellers) can tag along for a significant discount. Open Water certification costs 12,000B to 18,000B for three days' instruction. Some schools charge 500B extra for equipment.

From Phuket, you can join a huge range of live-aboard diving expeditions to the Similan Islands (p262) and Myanmar's Mergui Archipelago.

Snorkelling isn't wonderful off Phuket proper, though mask, snorkel and fins (per day 200B) are available in most resort areas. As with diving, you'll find better snorkelling (with greater visibility and variety of marine life) along the shores of small outlying islands, such as Ko Raya Yai and Ko Raya Noi.

As elsewhere in the Andaman Sea, the best diving months are November to April when weather is good and seas smooth and clear, though most dive shops power on

Phuket Province

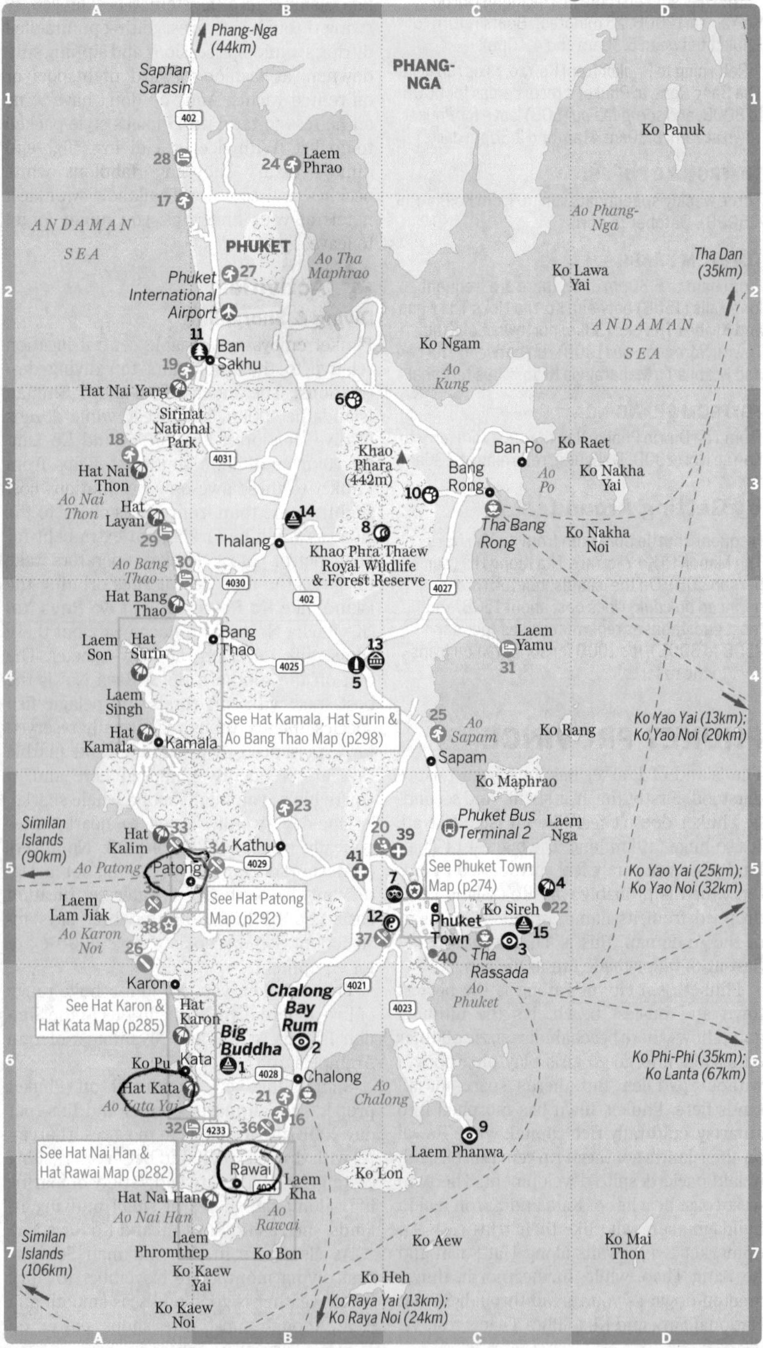

Phuket Province

(weather permitting) through the low season, with good discounts.

Highly recommended dive schools have branches across Phuket, including in Patong (p291), Kata (p285) and Karon (p289).

Sea Kayaking

Several Phuket-based companies offer canoe tours of scenic Ao Phang-Nga. Kayaks can enter semi-submerged caves inaccessible to long-tail boats. A day paddle (per person around 4000B) includes meals, equipment and boat transfer. Some outfits run all-inclusive, three-day (from 13,500B) or six-day (from 23,500B) kayaking and camping trips, covering Ao Phang-Nga and Khao Sok National Park. John Gray's Seacanoe (p276) is the island's star operator.

Surfing

Phuket is an undercover surf destination. With the monsoon's midyear swell, glassy seas fold into barrels. The best waves arrive between June and September, when annual competitions are held on Hat Kata Yai (p284), Phuket's most popular surf spot, and Hat Kalim, just north of Patong. Phuket Surf (p285) is based at the south end of Kata Yai near the best break, which tops out at 2m. Hat Nai Han (p283) gets bigger waves (up to 3m), in front of the yacht club. Both Kata and Nai Han have vicious undertows that can claim lives.

Hat Kalim is sheltered and has a consistent break that gets up to 3m. This is a hollow wave, and is considered the best break on the island. The northernmost stretch of Hat Kamala (p295) has a nice 3m beach break. Laem Singh (p295), 1km north, gets very big and fast, plus it's sheltered from wind by a massive headland. Hat Surin (p296) gets some of Phuket's most challenging waves.

Hat Nai Yang (p300) has a consistent (if soft) wave that breaks more than 200m offshore. Hat Nai Thon gets better shape. Swells get up to 3m high a few times per year.

In the low season, you can rent surfboards (per hour 250B to 300B) on most of these beaches.

Kitesurfing

One of the world's fastest-growing sports is also one of Phuket's latest addictions. The best kitesurfing spots are Hat Nai Yang (p300) from April to October and Rawai (p283) from mid-October to March. All listed kitesurfing outfitters are affiliated with the International Kiteboarding Organization (www.ikointl.com).

Adventure Sports

There's no shortage of adrenaline-fuelled activities on Phuket (bungee jumps, zip lines). Equipment quality and safety levels vary, and there have been serious, even fatal, accidents. Ask for recommendations and, if you have any doubts, don't proceed.

Yachting

Phuket is one of Southeast Asia's main yachting destinations. You'll find all manner of craft anchored along its shores, from 80-year-old wooden sloops to the latest in high-tech motor cruisers.

Marina-style facilities with year-round anchorage are available at several locations. Marinas can advise in advance on the latest port-clearance procedures. Expect to pay from 14,500B per day for a high-season, bareboat charter.

Royal Phuket Marina BOATING
(Map p270; ☎076 360811; www.royalphuketmarina.com; off Hwy 402) The US$25 million east-coast Royal Phuket Marina is 13km north of Phuket Town. It's luxurious, with high-end condos and upscale restaurants overlooking 350 berths, and does repairs.

Phuket Yacht Haven Marina BOATING
(Map p270; ☎076 206704; www.pyhmarina.com; 141/2 Mu 2, Laem Phrao) This recently revamped marina, on Phuket's northeastern tip, boasts 320 high-tech berths with deep-water access. Popular with superyachts.

Asia Marine BOATING
(Map p270; ☎076 206653; www.asia-marine.net; Phuket Yacht Haven Marina, 141/2 Mu 2, Laem Phrao) One of Phuket's first yacht charters and with a diverse Andaman fleet, Asia Marine has a boat for everyone, from sleek fibreglass catamarans to wooden junks. High-season bareboat charters start at 14,3000B.

 Courses

Popular Thai cooking classes are held in Kata (p286), Phuket Town (p276), Ko Sireh (p281) and Patong (p291).

 Tours

We recommend opting for a bike tour (p286) instead of supporting the questionable animal welfare and environmental standards of Phuket's elephant ride and 4WD tour operators. For more on the elephant debate see p327 and p759.

 Information

DANGERS & ANNOYANCES

Assaults We've had reports of late-night motorbike muggings and stabbings on the road leading from Patong to Karon and from Kata to the Rawai–Hat Nai Han area. Random sexual assaults on women can also happen. Think twice before sunbathing topless (a big no-no in Thailand anyway) or alone, especially on isolated beaches. It can also be dangerous to run alone at night or early in the morning.

Jet skis Keep an eye out for jet skis when you're swimming. Although the Phuket governor declared jet skis illegal in 1997 and they've been re-banned as part of the recent island clean-up, enforcement of the rule is another issue. Long-tails can be hazardous; do not expect the boatman to see you!

Motorcycles Renting a motorbike can also be hazardous. Thousands of people are injured or killed every year on Phuket's highways. If you must, make sure you at least know the basics and wear a helmet. Rental rarely includes insurance.

Undertows During the May-to-October monsoon, large waves and fierce undertows sometimes make swimming dangerous. Dozens of drownings occur every year on Phuket's beaches, especially Laem Singh, Kamala, Karon and Patong. Heed the red flags signalling serious rips.

MEDIA

The weekly English-language *Phuket Gazette* (www.phuketgazette.net) publishes information on island-wide activities, dining and entertainment, plus the latest scandals. *Phuket Wan*

PHUKET TAXIS

Since taking over in 2014, the Thai military has cracked down on Phuket's infamous 'taxi mafia', an organisation of overpriced chartered cars which, until recently, had a monopoly on the island's transport industry. Numerous drivers suspected of extortion and intimidation have been arrested, and taxi salas, where drivers gathered, have been torn down. Some drivers deny involvement, saying they are simply earning a living.

Price boards around the island outline *maximum* journey rates; you're free to negotiate down. Meters have been introduced but, at research time, metered taxis remained tricky to find.

To avoid being overcharged, jot down the phone number of a metered taxi and use the same driver throughout your stay. The best way to do this is to take a metered taxi from the airport (the easiest place to find them) when you arrive. Metered taxis are 50m to the right as you exit airport arrivals. Set rates are 50B for the first 2km, 12B per kilometre for the next 15km and 10B per kilometre thereafter, plus a 100B 'airport tax'. That's no more than 700B to anywhere on the island from the airport.

Driver-booking apps Uber and GrabTaxi have landed on Phuket, opening up more transport options, though not necessarily at lower prices.

(www.phuketwan.com) is frequently juicier and more newsworthy. *Phuket News* (www.thephuketnews.com) is another excellent source on up-to-date island life.

MEDICAL SERVICES

Local hospitals are equipped with modern facilities, emergency rooms and outpatient-care clinics. Both hospitals listed below have hyperbaric chambers.

Bangkok Hospital Phuket (Map p270; ☎076 254425; www.phukethospital.com; Th Hongyok Uthit) Reputedly the favourite among locals, 3km north of Phuket Town.

Phuket International Hospital (Map p270; ☎076 361818, 076 249400; www.phuketinternationalhospital.com; 44 Th Chalermprakiat) International doctors rate this hospital as the island's best.

USEFUL WEBSITES

Jamie's Phuket (www.jamie-monk.blogspot.com) A fun, intelligent insider's blog written by a long-time Phuket expat, with excellent photos and travel tips.

Phuket Dot Com (www.phuket.com) A compendium of island-wide information and recommendations, including accommodation.

Getting There & Away

AIR

Phuket International Airport (Map p270; ☎076 327230; www.phuketairportthai.com) is 30km northwest of Phuket Town. It takes 45 minutes to an hour to reach the southern beaches from here. A number of carriers serve domestic destinations:

Air Asia (Map p292; ☎02 515 9999; www.airasia.com; 39 Th Thawiwong, Hat Patong; ⏰11am-9.30pm)

Bangkok Airways (Map p274; ☎076 225033; www.bangkokair.com; 158/2-3 Th Yaowarat, Phuket Town; ⏰8am-5.30pm Mon-Sat)

THAI (Map p274; ☎076 360444; www.thaiairways.com; 78/1 Th Ranong, Phuket Town; ⏰8am-4.30pm)

BUS

Interstate buses depart from **Phuket Bus Terminal 2** (Map p270; Th Thepkrasattri), 4km north of Phuket Town.

FERRY & SPEEDBOAT

Phuket's **Tha Rassada** (Map p270), 3km southeast of Phuket Town, is the main pier for boats to Ko Phi-Phi, Krabi, Ao Nang, Ko Lanta, the Trang Islands, Ko Lipe and even as far as Pulau Langkawi in Malaysia (which has ferry connections to Penang). Additional services to Krabi and Ao Nang via Ko Yao leave from **Tha Bang Rong** (Map p270), 26km north of Tha Rassada.

MINIVAN

Phuket travel agencies sell tickets (including ferry fare) for air-con minivans to destinations across southern Thailand, including Krabi, Ranong, Trang, Surat Thani, Ko Samui and Ko Pha-Ngan. Prices are usually slightly higher than for buses.

Getting Around

Local Phuket transport is terrible. The systems in place make tourists either stay on their chosen beach, rent a car or motorbike or take overpriced taxis or túk-túk. *Sŏrng·tăa·ou* run from Phuket Town to the beaches, but often you'll have to go via Phuket Town to get from one beach to another (say Hat Surin to Hat Patong), which takes hours.

That said, thanks to the recent crackdown on Phuket's 'taxi mafia' (p273), the stranglehold local drivers have enjoyed may be coming to an end, particularly when it comes to transport to and from the airport.

Phuket Town เมืองภูเก็ต

POP 77,600

Long before flip-flops and selfie sticks, Phuket was an island of rubber trees, tin mines and cash-hungry merchants. Attracting entrepreneurs from the Arabian Peninsula, China, India and Portugal, Phuket Town was a colourful blend of cultural influences, cobbled together by tentative compromise and cooperation. Today the city is testament to the island's historical soul. Wander down streets clogged with Sino-Portuguese architecture housing arty coffee shops, eccentric galleries, bright textiles stores, fantastic cheap restaurants and inexpensive boutique-chic guesthouses, and peek down alleyways to serene incense-cloaked Chinese Taoist shrines.

But it's not just some lost-in-time cultural archive. Bubbling up throughout the emerging Old Town is an infusion of current art, music and food attracting a very style-conscious, mostly Thai crowd. Investors have finally caught on that culture, not just beaches and girly bars, is a commodity. Century-old shophouses and homes, once left to rot, have been restored, resulting in flash-forward gentrification. It *can* feel like every other building is now a trendy polished-concrete cafe or a quirky guesthouse, but the city is still a wonderfully refreshing cultural break from Phuket's beaches.

Despite inflated real estate prices, Phuket Town has the island's best lodging bargains, and regular *sŏrng·tăa·ou* run to most beaches. Stay a few days to soak it all up, if you can.

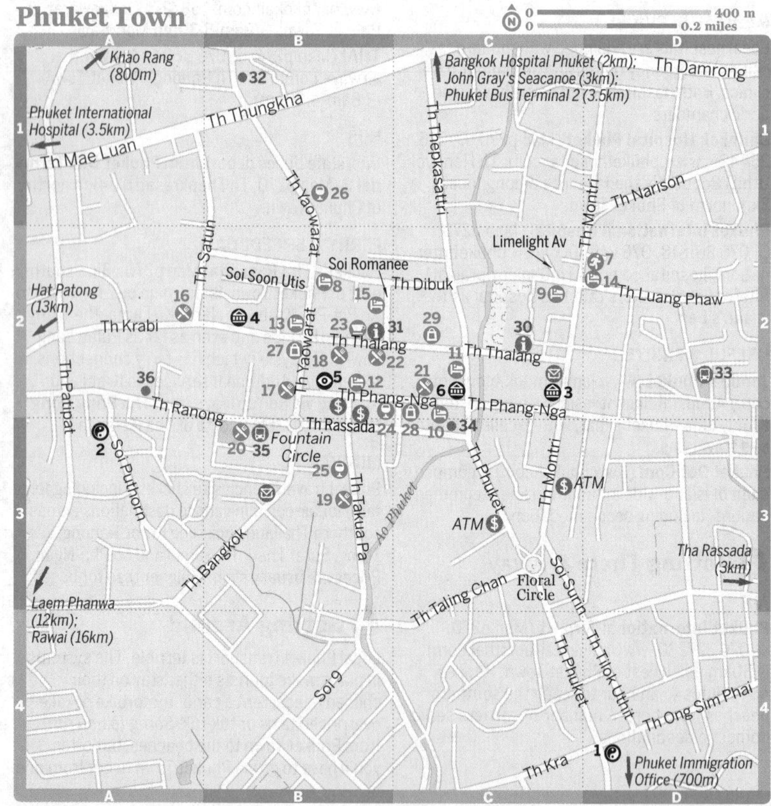

Sights

Phuket Thaihua Museum MUSEUM

(พิพิธภัณฑ์ภูเก็ตไทยหัว; Map p274; ☎076 211224; 28 Th Krabi; admission 200B; ⊙9am-5pm) Formerly a Chinese language school, this flashy museum is filled with photos and English-language exhibits on Phuket's history, from the Chinese migration (many influential Phuketian families are of Chinese origin) and the tin-mining era to local cuisine, fashion and literature. There's an overview of the building's history, which is a stunning combination of Chinese and European architectural styles, including art deco, Palladianism and a Chinese gable roof and stucco.

Shrine of the Serene Light CHINESE SHRINE

(ศาลเจ้าแสงธรรม, Saan Jao Sang Tham; Map p274; Th Phang-Nga; ⊙8.30am-noon & 1.30-5.30pm) FREE A handful of Chinese temples pump colour into Phuket Town, but this restored shrine, tucked away up a 50m alley, is particularly atmospheric, with its Taoist etchings on the walls and the vaulted ceiling stained from incense plumes. The altar is always fresh with flowers and burning candles. The shrine is said to have been built by a local family in the 1890s.

Khao Rang VIEWPOINT

(เขารัง, Phuket Hill; Map p270; P) For a bird's-eye view of the city, climb (or drive) up Khao Rang, 3km northwest of the town centre. A new viewing platform has opened up the commanding panoramas across Phuket Town and all the way to Chalong Bay, Laem Phanwa and Big Buddha. It's at its best during the week, when the summit is relatively peaceful. There are a few restaurants up here. It's about an hour's walk, but don't try it at night. A taxi up costs 700B.

Sino-Portuguese Architecture

Stroll along Ths Thalang, Dibuk, Yaowarat, Ranong, Phang-Nga, Rassada and Krabi for a glimpse of Phuket Town's Sino-Portuguese architectural treasures. The most magnificent examples are the **Standard Chartered Bank** (Map p274; Th Phang-Nga), Thailand's oldest foreign bank; the THAI office (p273); and the **old post office building**, which now houses the **Phuket Philatelic Museum** (Map p274; Th Montri; ⊙10am-5pm Mon-Sat) FREE. Some of the most colourfully revamped buildings line Soi Romanee, off Th Thalang, once home to brothels, gamblers and opium dens.

Phuket Town

Sights
1 Bang Niew Shrine ... D4
2 Jui Tui Shrine ... A3
3 Phuket Philatelic Museum ... C2
4 Phuket Thaihua Museum ... B2
5 Shrine of the Serene Light ... B2
6 Standard Chartered Bank ... C2

Activities, Courses & Tours
Blue Elephant Cooking School ... (see 16)
7 Raintree Spa ... D2
Suay Cooking School ... (see 19)

Sleeping
8 Ai Phuket Hostel ... B2
9 Baan Suwantawe ... C2
10 Best Stay Hostel ... C2
11 Casa Blanca ... C2
12 Memory at On On Hotel ... B2
13 RomManee Classic ... B2
14 Sino House ... D2
15 The RomManee ... B2

Eating
16 Blue Elephant ... A2
17 Gallery Cafe ... B2
18 Kopitiam by Wilai ... B2
19 Suay ... B3
20 Thanon Ranong Day Market ... B3
21 The Cook ... C2
22 Walking St ... B2

Drinking & Nightlife
23 Bo(ok)hemian ... B2
24 Comics ... B2
25 Ka Jok See ... B3
26 Timber Hut ... B1

Shopping
27 Ban Boran Textiles ... B2
28 Drawing Room ... C2
29 Ranida ... C2

Information
30 Tourism Authority of Thailand ... C2
31 Tourist Information Centre ... B2

Transport
32 Bangkok Airways ... B1
33 Phuket Bus Terminal 1 ... D2
34 Pure Car Rent ... C3
35 Sŏrng·tăa·ou to Beaches ... B3
36 THAI ... A2

PHUKET FOR CHILDREN

While the seedier side of Thailand's sex industry is on show in Patong (we'd be reluctant to bring our kids here, though many people do), the rest of Phuket is fairly G-rated.

Visits to **Phuket Aquarium** (p281), **Soi Dog** (p301) and the **Phuket Gibbon Rehabilitation Project** (p302) are terrific animal-themed activities for kids. Adrenaline-addled older kids can tackle kitesurfing in **Rawai** (p281) and **Hat Nai Yang** (p300).

Phuket's main family-flogged feature is **Phuket Fantasea** (p296) which, while popular, does not set an ecologically sound (let alone responsible) example to kids big or small. Elephant rides are particularly plentiful on Phuket, but carry complex yet significant animal welfare concerns (p409). For those with children who insist, ask around about more responsible outfits.

Phuket Wake Park (Map p270; ☎089 873 0187; www.phuketwakepark.com; 86/3 Mu 6, Th Vichitsongkram, Kathu; adult/child 2hr 650/350B, day pass 1150/550B; ⏲7.30am-11pm; 👪) Buzz Kathu's marvellous hill-backed lake on a wakeboard. This outfit, mostly aimed at teenagers and older kids, offers rides in two-hour blocks, by the day or as lessons (per hour 1000B). Gear rental is available (from 350B), as are hotel transfers.

Surf House (Map p285; ☎081 979 7737; www.surfhousephuket.com; 4 Mu 2, Th Pak Bang, Hat Kata; ⏲9.30am-11.30pm; 👪) Across the street from Hat Kata Yai, this bar-entertainment spot serves both beer and artificial waves. Kids will love the sloped surf slide on which riders show off wakeboarding skills for as long as they can stay upright. The bar pours icy Chang and serves pub grub.

The best-restored residential properties lie along Ths Thalang, Dibuk and Krabi. The fabulous 1903 **Phra Phitak Chyn Pracha Mansion** has been refurbished into the upscale Blue Elephant restaurant (p278) and culinary school.

Activities

★John Gray's Seacanoe KAYAKING
(Map p270; ☎076 254505; www.johngray-seacanoe.com; 86 Soi 2/3, Th Yaowarat; adult/child from 3950/1975B) The original, the most reputable and by far the most ecologically sensitive kayaking company on Phuket. The Hong by Starlight trip dodges the crowds, involves sunset paddling and will introduce you to Ao Phang-Nga's famed after-dark bioluminescence. Like any good brand in Thailand, John Gray's 'Seacanoe' name and itineraries have been frequently copied. He's 3.5km north of Phuket Town.

Courses

★Suay Cooking School COOKING COURSE
(Map p274; ☎081 797 4135; www.suayrestaurant.com; 50/2 Th Takua Pa; per person 1800B) Learn from one of Phuket's top chefs at the most laid-back, soulful and fun cooking school around. Noy Tammasak will lead you through the local market and teach you how to make three dishes, before cracking open a bottle of wine to enjoy with your culinary creations. Highly recommended; minimum three people.

Blue Elephant Cooking School COOKING COURSE
(Map p274; ☎076 354355; www.blueelephant.com; 96 Th Krabi; half-day class 3270B) Master the intricate art of royal Thai cooking in a stunningly restored Sino-Portuguese mansion. Options range from half-day group lessons to private eight-dish vegetarian classes (7000B). Morning sessions visit the market. Book ahead.

Sleeping

Phuket Town is a treasure trove of affordable lodging. Head to the beaches for midrange and top-end options.

Ai Phuket Hostel HOSTEL $
(Map p274; ☎076 212881; www.aiphukethostel.com; 88 Th Yaowarat; dm 259B, d 650-850B; ❄@📶) Doubles are tight but characterful with wood floors, black-and-white photos, muralled ceilings and, for some, private bathrooms. Dorms are bright, colourful and clean, sleeping six (girls only) to eight. All share polished-concrete hot-water bathrooms and a cramped downstairs hangout lounge.

Best Stay Hostel HOSTEL $
(Map p274; ☎099 301 9499; www.beststayhostel.com; 88 Th Phang-Nga; dm/r 250/600B; ❄📶) Another fresh Phuket Town hostel, featuring

shiny-white eight- to 10-person dorms with gleaming green floors and chunky-framed bunks with individual lamps and white duvets, plus boxy doubles. It's friendly and has a cute tile-floored cafe downstairs.

★The RomManee BOUTIQUE HOTEL $$
(Map p274; ☎089 728 9871; www.therommanee.com; Th Romanee; r 1200B; ❄📶) On Phuket Town's prettiest street, this 'boutique guesthouse' definitely packs in plenty of style with its turquoise-toned exterior, varnished-concrete floors and wood-block reception bar. The four spacious rooms have an arty modern feel with wood floors, flat screens, colour feature walls, neon-washed chairs and tasteful lighting. Stairs are steep and there's no lift. There's another comfy, less-friendly **branch** (Map p274; ☎076 355488; 4-6 Th Krabi; r 1000-1200B; ❄📶) a block away.

Casa Blanca BOUTIQUE HOTEL $$
(Map p274; ☎076 219019; www.casablancaphuket.com; 26 Th Phuket; r 2300-2800B; ❄📶🏊) All whites and pastels, this elegantly revamped Sino-Portuguese beauty gets extra boutique spark from Spanish-themed touches like patterned tiles and a plant-lined patio. Modern art adorns smart rooms, in soft greens and pale blues. Deluxes have balconies with city panoramas; superiors overlook the little pool. A teensy cafe doles out fresh-from-the-oven pastries in the bubbly bright lobby.

Memory at On On Hotel HOTEL $$
(Map p274; ☎076 216161; www.thememoryhotel.com; 19 Th Phang-Nga; dm 300B, r incl breakfast 1700-3400B; ❄📶) This longtime bare-bones classic played a dingy backpacker dive in *The Beach* (2000). But a smart revamp put the antiquated shine on Phuket's first hotel, transforming it into a contemporary budget-to-midrange guesthouse. Four- to six-bed dorms are fantastic, thanks to wooden flooring, ceramic sinks, old-school office desks, draped bunks and excellent shared facilities.

Stylish private rooms have concrete floors, rain showers, flat screens and vibrant shutters (though some seem stuffy).

Baan Suwantawe HOTEL, APARTMENT $$
(Map p274; ☎076 212879; www.baansuwantawe.com; 1/10 Th Dibuk; r 1800-3200B; P❄@📶🏊) With Zen art, hardwood floors, good-sized bathrooms, colourful bedspreads and comfy lounge areas, these spacious studio-style rooms are a steal. Higher-priced rooms have terraces overlooking the pool and lily pond, and the whole place basks in a lemongrassy scent that seems to be synonmous of many upmarket Asian hotels.

Sino House HOTEL $$
(Map p274; ☎076 232494; www.sinohousephuket.com; 1 Th Montri; r incl breakfast 1600-2500B; P❄@📶) Shanghai style meet 1960s chic at this impressive Phuket Town offering. Massive airy rooms are more like small apartments, with modern furnishings, handmade ceramic basins, tea/coffee sets, unique wall murals and quarter-moon showers in the bathrooms. The on-site Raintree Spa (p278) is excellent. Long-term discounts available.

Eating

There's great food in Phuket Town; meals here cost a lot less than at the beach.

Kopitiam by Wilai THAI $
(Map p274; ☎083 606 9776; www.facebook.com/kopitiambywilai; 18 Th Thalang; mains 80-120B; ⊙11am-10pm Mon-Sat; 📶) Kopitiam serves Phuket soul food. It does Phuketian *pàt tai* (thin rice noodles with egg, tofu and/or shrimp) with a kick, and a fantastic *mee sua*: noodles sautéed with egg, greens, prawns, chunks of sea bass, and squid. Wash it all down with fresh chrysanthemum or passionfruit juice.

The Cook THAI, FUSION $
(Map p274; ☎076 258375; 101 Th Phang-Nga; mains 65-240B; ⊙8am-9.30pm Tue-Sun) The Thai owner-chef used to cook Italian at a mega-resort, so when he opened this ludicrously inexpensive Old Town restaurant he successfully fused the two cultures. Try one of the sensational green chicken curry or *đôm yam* (spicy Thai soup) pizzas, or a classic pasta plate, and you'll see what the fuss is about.

★Suay INTERNATIONAL, THAI $$
(Map p274; ☎081 797 4135; www.suayrestaurant.com; 50/2 Th Takua Pa; mains 15-400B; ⊙5pm-midnight) Fabulous fusion at this converted house, just south of old town proper, means mouth-melting glass noodle salad, bright pomelo salad with salmon carpaccio and roasted chilli dressing, lamb-chop massaman curry, turmeric-infused sea bass wrapped in banana leaf, smoked eggplant with chilli-coconut dressing and crab meat, and an innovative *sôm·đam* (spicy green papaya salad) featuring flavour-popping mangosteen.

Tables are sprinkled across the romantically lit house, garden and wraparound porch. Don't miss the flamed mango with sticky rice and black sesame ice cream.

DON'T MISS

FIVE SPARKLING SPAS OF THE NORTHERN ANDAMAN

There's a massage shop on every Andaman corner, especially on Phuket. Most are low-key family affairs where traditional one-hour 300B Thai massages are a real steal. Service quality varies and staff turnover is high. Go with your gut instinct or ask locally for recommendations.

If you fancy a more Europen-style spa experience, book into one of Phuket's resort spas. Though often affiliated with a glitzy hotel, most of these high-class affairs with sumptuous Zen designs and extensive treatment menus accept nonguests. Of course there are gorgeous spas to be found across the northern Andaman.

Siam Hot Spa (☎077 813551; www.siamhotsparanong.com; 73/3 Th Phetkasem, Ranong Town; treatment 300-750B; ⏲11am-8pm) This is a highly recommended, classier mineral bath experience than the public hot springs opposite in Ranong Town. Soak in a private hot tub, then add a salt scrub or a classic Thai massage.

Cool Spa (Map p270; ☎076 371000; www.coolspaphuket.com; Sri Panwa, 88 Mu 8, Th Sakdidej, Laem Phanwa, Phuket; massages 2400-4000B; ⏲10am-8.30pm) An elegant wonderland of fruit-infused wraps, facials and scrubs, and hilltop ocean-view pools. Oh, and then there's the dreamy setting, on the southernmost tip of Phuket's Laem Phanwa.

Six Senses Spa (☎076 418500; www.sixsenses.com; 56 Mu 5, btwn Hat Khlong Jark & Hat Tha Khao, Ko Yao Noi; massage 3900-6500B; ⏲8am-9pm) No luxury brand presents back-to-nature elegance like the Six Senses stilted 'spa village'. Therapists are trained in massage traditions and organic-fuelled treatments from China, India and Thailand. The 'Signature Yao Noi Ritual' is a blissful 3½-hour scrub, massage and facial blend.

Pathways Spa (☎076 427900; www.sarojin.com; Sarojin, Hat Bang Sak, Khao Lak; massage 2100-2600B; ⏲10am-9pm) One of the finest massage settings of your life awaits. Sala-style treatment rooms wander to the edge of mangroves and coconut groves, open to the ocean breeze. Relax and let the talented therapists take you through signature Sarojin flower scrubs and herbal wraps, and royal oriental massages.

Raintree Spa (Map p274; ☎081 892 1001; www.theraintreespa.com; Sino House, 1 Th Montri, Phuket Town; massages 600-1000B; ⏲10am-9.30pm) Tucked into tranquil tropical grounds, Raintree is a step up in price, quality and atmosphere from Phuket Town's storefront spas. Skilled therapists don't just go through the motions here. Get silky-smooth with an aloe-cucumber body wrap or indulge in a two-hour 'fruit salad' scrub (pineapple, papaya, mango).

The wine list is short but proper, and affable chef/owner Noy Tammasak offers good cooking classes (p276).

Gallery Cafe CAFE $$

(Map p274; www.gallerycafe-phuket.com; 19 Th Yaowarat; mains 160-270B; ⏲8am-8pm; 📶) Settle in on comfy cushions at this popular brunch cafe, surrounded by varnished-wood booths and yellow walls hung with art. The menu is full of hearty international and Thai goodies: all-day egg breakfasts, pizzas, pastas, salads, sandwiches, smoothies, homemade veggie burgers. We're still dreaming about the brilliant breakfast bagels and zingy passionfruit, lemongrass and ginger juices.

Blue Elephant THAI $$$

(Map p274; ☎076 354355; www.blueelephant.com; 96 Th Krabi; mains 670-1000B, set menus 1350-2400B; ⏲11.30am-2.30pm & 6.30-10.30pm; 📶🍷) Royal Thai cuisine in royal Thai surrounds. Set in the beautifully restored, mustard-yellow Phra Phitak Chyn Pracha Mansion overlooking manicured lawns, Blue Elephant is elegant in every way, from the brass cutlery and ornately carved doors to the chequered tiled floors, stellar service and superbly prepped and presented dishes.

Choose a tasting menu, a three-main set or go à la carte: it's all exquisite. The Blue Elephant Cooking School (p276) is also here.

Drinking & Nightlife

Phuket Town is where you can party like a local. Bars buzz until late, patronised almost exclusively by Thais and local expats.

Timber Hut CLUB

(Map p274; ☎076 211839; 118/1 Th Yaowarat; ⏲6pm-2am) Thai and expat locals have been packing out this two-floor pub-club nightly for 25 years, swilling whiskey and swaying to live bands that swing from hard rock to pure pop to hip-hop. No cover charge.

Comics BAR

(Map p274; www.facebook.com/Comics-Cafe-Bar-358086567609208; 44 Th Phang-Nga; 6pm-midnight) A youthful all-Thai clientele crams into this bubbly, blue-lit, comic-covered space for mellow live music enjoyed with Thai and international beers, ciders, wines and cocktails.

Bo(ok)hemian CAFE

(Map p274; 098 090 0657; www.bookhemian.com; 61 Th Thalang; 9am-7pm Mon-Fri, to 8.30pm Sat & Sun;) Every town should have a coffee house this cool, with a split-level design that feels simultaneously warm and cutting-edge. Used books (for sale) line the front room, bicycles hang from the wall, and it does gourmet coffee and tea, and damn good chocolate cake.

Ka Jok See CLUB

(Map p274; 076 217903; kajoksee@hotmail.com; 26 Th Takua Pa; buffet per person 2500B; 8pm-1am Nov-Apr, reduced hours May-Oct) Dripping with Old Phuket charm and the owner's fabulous trinket collection, this intimate century-old house has two identities: half glamorous eatery, half crazy party venue. There's good Thai food, but once the tables are cleared it becomes a bohemian madhouse party with top-notch music and – if you're lucky – some sensationally extravagant cabaret. Book a month or two ahead. There's no sign.

Shopping

There are some gorgeous bohemian-chic boutiques scattered throughout Old Town selling jewellery, women's fashions, fabrics and souvenirs, plus an ever-growing number of whimsical art galleries.

★Ranida ANTIQUES, FASHION

(Map p274; 119 Th Thalang; 10.30am-7.30pm Mon-Sat) An elegant antique gallery and boutique featuring antiquated Buddha statues and sculpture, organic textiles, and ambitious, exquisite high-fashion clothing inspired by vintage Thai garments and fabrics.

Drawing Room ARTS

(Map p274; isara380@hotmail.com; 56 Th Phang-Nga; 10am-9pm) With a street-art vibe reminiscent of pre-boom Brooklyn or East London, this wide-open cooperative is by far the stand-out gallery in a town full of them. Canvases might be vibrant abstract squiggles or comical pen-and-ink cartoons. Metallic furniture and bicycles line concrete floors. House music thumps at low levels.

Ban Boran Textiles TEXTILES

(Map p274; 076 211563; 51 Th Yaowarat; 11am-6.30pm) Shelves at this hole-in-the-wall are stocked high with quality silk scarves, Burmese lacquerware, sarongs, linen shirts, cute colourful bags and cotton textiles from Chiang Mai.

Information

There are numerous ATMs on Ths Phuket, Ranong, Montri and Phang-Nga.

FLIGHTS TO/FROM PHUKET

DESTINATION	AIRLINE	FREQUENCY	FARE (B)
Bangkok (Don Muang)	Air Asia	14 daily	1400
Bangkok (Don Muang)	Nok Air	8 daily	1600
Bangkok (Suvarnabhumi)	Bangkok Airways	7-9 daily	1790
Bangkok (Suvarnabhumi)	THAI	9-10 daily	1800
Chiang Mai	Air Asia	3 daily	1900
Dubai	Emirates	1-2 daily	15,000
Hat Yai	Bangkok Airways	daily	1400
Hong Kong	Air Asia	daily	3700-6000
Ko Samui	Bangkok Airways	4-5 daily	3200
Kuala Lumpur	Air Asia	5 daily	2000-3000
Seoul	Korean Air	daily	13,000
Shanghai	China Eastern	2 daily	9800
Singapore	Air Asia	daily	1500-2500

BUSES FROM PHUKET BUS TERMINAL 2

DESTINATION	BUS TYPE	FARE (B)	DURATION (HR)	FREQUENCY
Bangkok	VIP	1011	13	5pm, 5.20pm, 6.20pm, 6.30pm & 7pm
	air-con	650	13-14	hourly 3.30pm-7pm
Chiang Mai	VIP	1826	22	3pm
Hat Yai	VIP	560	7	9.45pm
	air-con	360	7	hourly 7.30am-12.30pm, 7.30pm & 9.30pm
Ko Samui	air-con	450	8 (bus/boat)	9am
Ko Pha-Ngan	air-con	550	9½ (bus/boat)	9am
Krabi	air-con	155	3½	hourly 6.20am-7pm
Phang-Nga	air-con	85	2½	8.15am, 10.15am, 12.15pm & 8.15pm
Ranong	air-con	250	6	hourly 5.30am-6.10pm
Satun	air-con	364	7	8.15am, 10.15am, 12.15pm & 8.15pm
Surat Thani	air-con	195	5	8am, 10am, noon & 2pm
Trang	air-con	252	5	hourly 7.30am-12.30pm, 7.30pm & 9.30pm

Phuket Immigration Office (Map p270; ☎076 221905; www.phuketimmigration.go.th; 482 Th Phuket; ⊙8.30am-4.30pm Mon-Fri) Handles visa extensions.

Police (Map p270; ☎076 212046, 191; Th Chumphon)

Post Office (Map p274; Th Montri; ⊙8.30am-4.30pm Mon-Fri, 9am-noon Sat & Sun)

Tourism Authority of Thailand (TAT; Map p274; ☎076 211036; www.tourismthailand.org/Phuket; 191 Th Thalang; ⊙8.30am-4.30pm) Has maps, brochures, transport advice and info on boat trips to nearby islands.

Tourist Information Centre (Map p274; Th Thalang; ⊙9am-4.30pm) Maps, brochures, historical displays.

Getting There & Around

TO/FROM THE AIRPORT

Despite what airport touts say, an hourly bright-orange government airport bus (www.airportbusphuket.com) runs between the airport and Phuket Town (100B, one hour) via the Heroines Monument from 6.30am to 8.30pm. Taxis from the airport to Phuket Town cost 550B.

BUS

Phuket Bus Terminal 1 is mostly used by minivans. From here, a 'local bus' (actually a minivan) to Patong (50B) operates from 7am to 5pm.

Interstate buses depart from **Phuket Bus Terminal 2** (p273), 4km north of Phuket Town. Taxis or túk-túk do the run from Phuket Town for 300B.

CAR & MOTORCYCLE

Th Rassada has cheap car-rental agencies near **Pure Car Rent** (Map p274; ☎076 211002; www.purecarrent.com; 75 Th Rassada; ⊙8am-7pm), a good central choice. Cars cost around 1200B per day (including insurance), though rates drop in low season and for rentals of over three days.

Rates are usually better at local places than at the better-known internationals (which have desks at the airport), though you might find deals with familiar companies if you book ahead.

You can rent motorcycles on Th Rassada, including at Pure Car Rent, or from countless places at the beaches, for 250B to 300B per day. Bigger bikes (over 125cc) can be rented at shops in Patong, Kata, Rawai and Karon.

MINIVAN

From **Phuket Bus Terminal 1** (Map p274; Th Phang-Nga), 500m east of Phuket Town centre, minivans run to destinations across southern Thailand. Departures include the following:

DESTINATION	FARE (B)	DURATION (HR)
Hat Yai	360	7
Ko Lanta	280	5
Krabi	140	3
Surat Thani	200	4

SŎRNG·TĂA·OU & TÚK-TÚK

Large bus-sized *sŏrng·tăa·ou* run regularly from Th Ranong near the day market to Phuket's beaches (per person 25B to 40B, 30 minutes to 1½ hours), from 7am to 6pm; otherwise you'll have to charter a túk-túk to the beaches, which costs 400B (Rawai, Kata and Ao Bang Thao), 500B (Patong, Karon and Surin) or 600B (Kamala). Beware of tales about the tourist office being 5km away, or that the only way to reach beaches is by taxi.

For a ride around town, túk-túk drivers charge 100B to 200B and motorcycle taxis 30B.

Ko Sireh เกาะสิเหร่

This tiny island, 4km east of Phuket Town and connected to Phuket by a bridge, is known for its hilltop reclining Buddha at **Wat Sireh** (Map p270; Th Sireh; dawn-dusk) FREE and its **chow lair village** (Map p270).

Thailand's largest settlement of *chow lair* (sea gypsies) is little more than a poverty-stricken cluster of stilted tin shacks. The Urak Lawoi, the most sedentary of the three *chow lair* groups, live only between here and the Tarutao-Langkawi archipelago, and speak a mixture of Malay and Mon-Khmer.

A single road loops the island, passing a few villas, prawn farms, rubber plantations, a bit of untouched forest and east-coast **Hat Teum Suk** (Map p270).

Courses

Phuket Thai Cookery School COOKING COURSE
(Map p270; 076 252355; www.phuketthaicookery.com; 1-day course 2900B; 8am-3pm) Get intimate with aromatic Thai spices at this terrific cooking school on a quiet seafront plot on Ko Sireh's east coast, 7km east of Phuket Town. Courses take in a market tour and a cookbook and last up to six hours. Hotel pick-up is provided.

Laem Phanwa แหลมพันวา

An elongated jungle-covered cape jutting into the sea just south of Phuket Town, Laem Phanwa is an all-natural throwback. Some say this is the last vestige of Phuket as it once was. The biggest bloom of development is near the harbour at the cape's tip, 12km south of Phuket Town. On either side of the harbour, the beaches and coves remain rustic, protected by rocky headlands and mangroves and reached by a dreamy, sinuous coastal road. If you're seeking peace and quiet on Phuket, head here by taking Rte 4021 south, then heading southeast down Rte 4023 just south of Phuket Town.

Sights

Phuket Aquarium AQUARIUM
(สถานแสดงพันธุ์สัตว์น้ำภูเก็ต; Map p270; 076 391126; www.phuketaquarium.org; 51 Th Sakdidej; adult/child 180/100B; 8.30am-4.30pm; P) Get a glimpse of Thailand's wondrous underwater world at Phuket's popular aquarium, by the harbour on the tip of Laem Phanwa. There's a varied collection of tropical fish, sharks and other marine life, with helpful English-language displays. Check out the blacktip reef shark, the tiger-striped catfish resembling a marine-like zebra and the electric eel with up to 600V.

Sleeping & Eating

The seafood restaurants (mains 100B to 300B) along the harbour waterfront are a great place to relax and watch painted fishing boats bobbing by.

★ **Sri Panwa** RESORT $$$
(Map p270; 076 371000; www.sripanwa.com; 88 Mu 8, Th Sakdidej; d incl breakfast 18,090-38,000B; P) From the mosaic-filled lobby and classy orange-grey colour scheme to the sensational pool-lined Cool Spa (p278), Sri Panwa is as decadent as the cape gets, poised idyllically on its jungle-cloaked southernmost tip. Multi-room villas feature hot tubs, outdoor showers, private pools and personal sound systems. More affordable rooms are still wonderfully comfy.

There is a games room, several pools, tennis courts and two-bedroom villas designed for families. The rooftop **Baba Nest** (5-9pm) lounge-bar, flooded with unimaginably beautiful ocean-and-island views, is magical. On-site food offerings range from all-day international staples to Mexican tapas and Japanese specialities.

Panwa Beach Resort RESORT $$$
(Map p270; 076 393300; www.thepanwabeachresort.com; 5/3 Mu 8, Ao Yon; r incl breakfast 4500-5500B; P) With its own stretch of beachfront and views of Chalong, Rawai and Big Buddha, this slightly dated resort on the cape's west coast offers seclusion, sizeable rooms and four-star service at good-value rates.

Rawai ราไวย์

Now this is a place to live, which is exactly why Phuket's rapidly developing south coast is teeming with retirees, artists, Thai and

Hat Nai Han & Hat Rawai

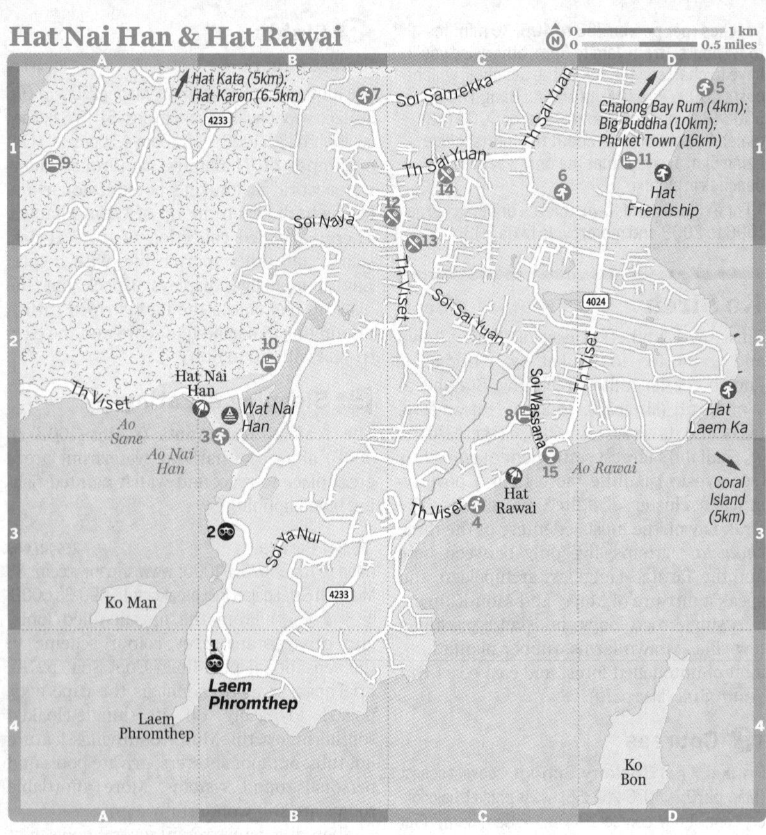

Hat Nai Han & Hat Rawai

Top Sights

1 Laem Phromthep ... B4

Sights

2 Secret Viewpoint ... B3

Activities, Courses & Tours

Boat Charters ... (see 4)
3 Hat Nai Han ... B2
4 Hat Rawai ... C3
5 Kite Zone ... D1
6 Rawai Supa Muay Thai ... C1
7 Sinbi Muay Thai ... B1

Sleeping

8 Good 9 at Home ... C2
9 Sabai Corner ... A1
10 Sunsuri ... B2
11 Vijitt ... D1

Eating

12 Da Vinci ... C1
13 German Bakery ... C1
14 Rum Jungle ... C1
Sabai Corner ... (see 9)

Drinking & Nightlife

15 Nikita's ... C3

expat entrepreneurs, and a service sector that, for the most part, moved here from somewhere else.

The region is defined not just by its beaches but also by its lush coastal hills that rise steeply and tumble into the Andaman Sea, forming **Laem Phromthep** (Map p282; Rte 4233) Phuket's beautiful southernmost point; for a more secluded sunset spot, seek out the **secret viewpoint** (Map p282; Rte 4233) 1.5km north. These hills are home to pocket neighbourhoods and cul-de-sacs knitted together by just a few roads – although more are being carved into the hills each year and you can almost envision real-estate money chasing away all the seafood grills and tiki bars. Let's hope that's several decades off. Or at least one. Even with the growth you can still feel nature, especially when you hit the beach.

Activities

Rawai is the centre of Phuket's growing *moo·ay tai* mania, home to half a dozen schools where students (of both sexes) live and train traditional-style in camps with professional *moo·ay tai* fighters.

Hat Rawai is an excellent place to arrange **boat charters** (Map p282) to neighbouring islands. Destinations include quiet Ko Bon (long tail/speedboat 1200/2400B) and Coral island (1800/3500B, maximum eight people) for snorkelling.

Hat Nai Han BEACH
(Map p282) Ask a Phuket local or expat which their favourite beach is and they should say Hat Nai Han, though they'll probably send you off somewhere else and keep this one to themselves. One of Rawai's great swimming spots (be careful of rips in low season), this is a beautifully curved white crescent on the west side of the cape, with minimal development and backed by casuarinas and a seafront wát.

Hat Rawai BEACH
(Map p282) Not really good for lounging, Hat Rawai is a rocky long-tail and speedboat harbour with a string of seafood grills on the east side of the cape. This is where most of the luxury condo development seems to be proliferating.

Rawai Supa Muay Thai THAI BOXING
(Map p282; ☎076 226495; www.supamuaythaiphuket.com; 43/42 Mu 7, Th Viset; per session/week 300/3000B; ⊙7am-7pm Mon-Sat, 9am-6pm Sun) Strap up those wrists and get fired up at this Thai boxing gym opened by a former *moo·ay tai* champion (he doesn't teach here). People come from around the world to learn how to fight alongside seasoned Thai professionals. It's a mix of Thais and foreigners who live in on-site dorms, but tourists can join drop-in classes and yoga (400B).

Sinbi Muay Thai THAI BOXING
(Map p282; ☎083 391 5535; www.sinbi-muaythai.com; 100/15 Mu 7, Th Sai Yuan; per session/week 400/4800B; ⊙7.30am-7pm Mon-Sat) A well-respected boxing training camp for both men and women.

Kite Zone KITESURFING
(Map p282; ☎083 395 2005; www.kitesurfthailand.com; Hat Friendship; 1hr lesson 1100B, 3-day course 10,000-15,000B) Rawai is a fine place to tackle kitesurfing and this cool young school has a tremendous perch on Hat Friendship. Courses range from one-hour tasters to three-day, 10-hour courses. From April to October, classes happen at Hat Nai Yang (p300) on the northwest side of the island. Also rents kit (per hour/day 1200/3500B) and runs stand-up paddle trips (from 700B).

Bob's Kite School KITESURFING
(Map p270; ☎092 459 4191; www.kiteschoolphuket.com; Rte 4024; 1hr lesson 1500B, 3hr course 3500B; ⊙Nov-Apr) Phuket's very first, German-run kite school is still going strong with keen, friendly staff. From May to mid-October they operate on the northwest of the island at Hat Nai Yang (p300). Equipment hire costs 1000B per hour.

Phuket Riding Club HORSE RIDING
(Map p270; ☎076 288213; www.phuketridingclub.com; 95 Th Viset; 1/2hr 1000B/2000B; ⊙7.30am-6.30pm) The perfect opportunity to live out that horse-riding through the tropics dream. Phuket Riding Club offers fun one- to two-hour rides in the jungle around Rawai. Book a day ahead.

Sleeping

Good 9 at Home GUESTHOUSE $
(Map p282; ☎088 457 6969; www.facebook.com/good9athome; 62 Mu 6, Soi Wassana; r incl breakfast 900B; ❄📶) Beside a cute patio, these seven small but wonderfully fresh, gleaming contemporary-style rooms spiced up with colour feature walls, tiled bathrooms and the odd bit of artwork make for good-value digs, 300m up the street from Hat Rawai. The lime-green-and-grey house is kept clean, cosy and friendly, with a thoughtful little coffee corner thrown into the mix.

Vijitt RESORT $$$
(Map p282; ☎076 363600; www.vijittresort.com; 16 Mu 2, Th Viset; villa incl breakfast 6800-27,500B; P❄📶🏊) Arguably the area's most elegant property, peaceful Vijitt is sprinkled with frangipani trees and deluxe villas that boast limestone floors, large bathtubs, outdoor showers and gorgeous sea views from private terraces (some with their own pools). The stunning, multilevel, black-bottom infinity pool overlooks Hat Friendship.

Sunsuri RESORT $$$

(Map p282; ☎076 336400; www.sunsuri-phuket.com; 11/5 Mu 1, Hat Nai Han; r 4600-5000B; P❄@📶🏊) Sprawling over a ridge behind Hat Nai Han, this luxe 132-room compound is made up of vaguely modernist cubes swathed in earthy tones that make it feel a bit like Jurassic Park. Almost all of the smart, straight-lined rooms enjoy ocean views, along with free-standing baths, plush linens and hardwood-on-limestone decor. Three huge swimming pools round off the package.

Eating

Hat Rawai is lined with a dozen locally owned seafood grills sizzling fresh catch along the roadside (mains 90B to 300B), with seating on plastic chairs or blankets on the floor.

Som Tum Lanna THAI $

(Map p270; ☎081 597 0569; 3/7 Th Sai Yuan; mains 80-150B; ⊙9am-5pm Tue-Sun) When it comes to *sôm·đam*, order it mild – it'll still bring some serious heat. And while the fish at this Isan soul food shack is good, its equal exists elsewhere. The chicken on the other hand is outstanding.

German Bakery EUROPEAN $

(Map p282; Th Viset; mains 80-140B; ⊙7.30am-4.30pm) This fun, friendly restaurant run by a German-Thai couple does the best pastries in the area. It makes fine brown bread, serves excellent breakfasts (try the pineapple pancakes) and has amazing bratwurst and sauerkraut. Surfers come here to fuel up before an early session.

Da Vinci ITALIAN $$

(Map p282; ☎076 289574; www.davinciphuket.com; 28/46 Mu 1, Th Viset; mains 320-900B; ⊙5.30-10.30pm; 👪) Alfresco wining and dining on crisp white-linen tables at this modern, authentic Italian kitchen is perfect on a balmy night. Staff are lovely and warm, the pizza is wood-fired, breads are fresh and pastas arrive full of flavour. The world-roaming wine list is excellent and there's complimentary after-dinner limoncello up for grabs. Popular with families for the kids' play area.

★**Rum Jungle** INTERNATIONAL $$$

(Map p282; ☎076 388153; www.facebook.com/Rum-Jungle-Cafe-Rawai-Phuket-173738946050909; 69/8 Mu 1, Th Sai Yuan; mains 240-620B; ⊙11.30am-2pm & 6-10.30pm; 🍷) One of Rawai's finest, this semi-open thatched-roof restaurant with an exceptional world-beat soundtrack is family-run and spearheaded by a terrific Aussie chef. The New Zealand lamb shank is divine, as are the steamed clams, and the pasta sauces are all made from scratch. Tempting veggie choices include eggplant parmigiana and pasta Gorgonzola.

Drinking & Nightlife

Nikita's BAR

(Map p282; ☎076 288703; www.nikitas-phuket.com; Hat Rawai; mains 150-350B; ⊙10am-midnight; 📶) This beautifully chilled-out open-air hang-out gazes over the sea just west of Rawai's pier, with coffee, green tea and a good selection of shakes and cocktails. A mango margarita, perhaps? If you're hungry, it also does decent watering-hole food such as omelettes, pastas, burgers and wood-fired pizzas.

Getting There & Away

Rawai is 18km southwest of Phuket Town. *Sŏrng·tăa·ou* (40B) run to Rawai from Phuket Town's Th Ranong between 7am and 5.30pm. Some continue to Hat Nai Han (40B), but not all, so ask first. Taxis from Rawai to Nai Han cost 200B.

Taxis go from Rawai and Hat Nai Han to Phuket airport (750B), Patong (700B) and Phuket Town (500B).

Hat Kata หาดกะตะ

Classier than Karon and without Patong's seedy hustle, Kata attracts travellers of all ages and walks of life for its shopping, surfing and lively beach. While you won't bag a secluded strip of sand, you'll still find lots to do.

Enjoy surfing in the shoulder and wet seasons, terrific day spas, fantastic (if pricey) food, and a top-notch yoga studio. The gold-sand beach is carved in two by a rocky headland. **Hat Kata Yai** lies on the north side; more secluded **Hat Kata Noi** unfurls to the south. The road between them is home to Phuket's original millionaire's row.

The main commercial street, Th Kata, runs parallel to the beach. There are cheaper restaurants, bars and guesthouses on Th Thai Na, which branches inland just south of where Th Kata heads up over the hill into Karon.

Sights & Activities

The small island of **Ko Pu** is just offshore, but be careful of rip tides, heed the red flags and don't go past the breakers in the rainy

Hat Karon & Hat Kata

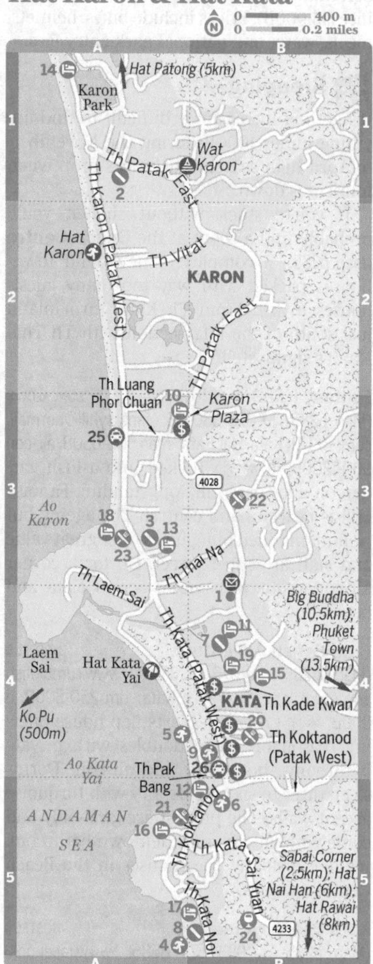

Hat Karon & Hat Kata

season unless you're a strong, experienced ocean swimmer.

Both Kata's beaches offer decent surfing from April to November. Hiring stand-up paddle kit or kayaks costs 300/900B per hour/day.

There's a branch of highly rated **Sea Fun Divers** (Map p285; ☎076 330124; www.seafundivers.com; Katathani, 14 Th Kata Noi; ⏲9am-6pm) on Kata Noi.

Phuket Surf SURFING
(Map p285; ☎087 889 7308; www.phuketsurfing.com; Hat Kata Yai; lesson 1500B, board rental per hr/day 150/500B; ⏲8am-7pm Apr-late Oct) Offers private 1½-hour surf lessons plus board rentals. Check the website for info on local surf breaks.

Rumblefish Adventure DIVING
(Map p285; ☎095 441 8665; www.rumblefishadventure.com; 98/79 Beach Centre, Th Kata; 2/3 dives 2900/3700B; ⏲10am-7pm) A terrific boutique dive shop offering all the standard courses, day trips and live-aboards from its Beach Centre location in Kata. The PADI

Open Water course costs 11,900B. There's a hostel attached.

Dive Asia DIVING

(Map p285; ☎076 330 598; www.diveasia.com; 24 Th Karon; 2/3 dives 3400/3900B; ⊙10am-9pm) Runs an extensive range of PADI certification courses (Open Water 11,600B to 16,020B) plus day-trip dives to Ko Phi-Phi and live-aboards to the Similan and Surin Islands (from 21,000B). There's another branch (p289) in Karon.

Kata Hot Yoga YOGA

(Map p285; ☎076 605950; www.katahotyoga.com; 217 Th Koktanod, Hat Kata; per class 550B; ⊙classes 9am, 5.15pm & 7.15pm Mon-Fri, 9am & 5.15pm Sat & Sun) Craving more heat? At Kata Hot Yoga, Bikram's famous asana series is taught over 90 minutes in a sweltering room by the expert owner and an international roster of visiting instructors. All levels welcome; no bookings needed. Multi-class packages offer good deals.

Re Ká Ta Beach Club BEACH CLUB

(Map p285; ☎076 330421; www.rekataphuket.com; 184 Th Koktanod, Hat Kata; day pass 1500B) Of Phuket's (controversially) popular beach clubs, gleaming-white Re Ká Ta is one of the chicest. It's part of the Boathouse family. Entry bags you a day of glamour, lounging on faux-leather beds or sipping passionfruit mojitos in the beachfront infinity pool surrounded by colour-changing lamps – and goes towards drinks and food (mains 300B to 1000B). Wednesdays mean free admission and manicures for girls.

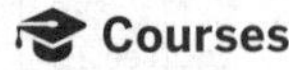

Courses

Boathouse Cooking Class COOKING COURSE

(Map p285; ☎076 330015; www.boathousephuket.com; 182 Th Koktanod; 1-/2-day class 2570/4095B; ⊙class 10am Wed, Sat & Sun) Kata's top fine-dining restaurant offers fantastic Thai cooking classes with its renowned chef.

Tours

Amazing Bike Tours CYCLING

(Map p285; ☎087 263 2031; www.amazingbiketoursthailand.asia; 191 Th Patak East; day trip adult/child 2900/2500B) This highly popular Kata-based adventure outfitter leads small groups on half-day bicycle tours through Khao Phra Thaew Royal Wildlife & Forest Reserve. It also runs terrific day trips around Ko Yao Noi and more challenging three-day adventures rides around Khao Sok National Park (14,900B) and Krabi Province (15,900B). Prices include bikes, helmets, meals, water and national park entry fees.

Sleeping

It's getting increasingly difficult to find anything under 1000B during the November-to-April high season, but prices drop when tourism is down.

If you're stuck without shelter, you'll probably find a room at the **Beach Centre** (Map p285), a complex of new-build townhouses packed with way too many guesthouses to list. From Th Kata, turn inland just south of the intersection with Th Thai Na; it's signposted.

Fantasy Hill Bungalow BUNGALOW $

(Map p285; ☎076 330106; fantasyhill@hotmail.com; 8/1 Th Kata, Hat Kata; r fan 500-650B, air-con 900-1200B; P❄📶) Tucked into a lush garden on a low-rise hill, longstanding Fantasy Hill is peaceful and central. The ageing but well-maintained bungalows offer great value and staff are super sweet. Go for a corner air-con room with views across Kata and beyond.

Rumblefish Adventure HOSTEL $

(Map p285; ☎076 330315; www.rumblefishadventure.com; 98/79 Th Kata; dm 250-300B, d 800B; ❄📶) A water-sports flop house offering reasonably clean doubles with private bathrooms, hot water and air-con. Dorms sleep three to six and are airy with turquoise accent walls. The priciest are girls-only and come with air-con and their own bathroom. It's one of many guesthouses in the Beach Centre complex.

Kata Beach Homestay HOSTEL $

(Map p285; ☎093 574 8586; www.facebook.com/Kata-Beach-Homestay-490941801079830; 9 Th Kade Kwan; dm 250B, d 650-950B; 📶) This modern-feel hostel-guesthouse offers cheap sleeps in a spotless, chequered-floor, eight-bed dorm with two bathrooms. Tile-floored super-clean doubles, in shared- or private-bathroom editions, have fridges, colourful cushions and purple walls, and there's a large communal lounge. Enter through the ground-floor herb shop/travel agency.

Sabai Corner BUNGALOW $$

(Map p282; ☎089 875 5525; www.facebook.com/Sabai-Corner-150517525037992; Hat Kata, off Rte 4233; r 2000B; P📶) No room on this island offers the fabulous 270-degree ocean view available from these three isolated hillside

DON'T MISS

CHALONG BAY RUM: THE SPIRIT OF PHUKET

When Marine Lucchini and Thibault Spithakis, each born into a prestigious French wine family, met and fell in love, they bonded over booze – fine rum, in particular. Which is why they became master distillers and launched their own distillery, **Chalong Bay Rum** (Map p270; ☎093 575 1119; www.chalongbayrum.com; 14/2 Mu 2, Soi Palai 2; tour 300B; ⏰tours hourly 2-6pm; P).

They knew they wanted to make natural rum in the French style, the kind they make in Martinique, which meant distilling sugarcane juice, rather than molasses (as is used for most rum). Thailand is the world's fourth-largest sugarcane producer with over 200 varieties currently in cultivation and, in 2012, nobody was distilling anything at all on Phuket, so they imported 40-year-old copper Armagnac stills and incorporated one of the world's great islands into their brand.

For now, their rum is white, though there's dark rum on the horizon. It has great flavour, took a gold medal at the 2015 San Francisco World Spirits Competition, and makes a mean mojito – which you'll be sipping as you tour the facility, learning way more about rum than you could ever imagine.

Book ahead, because you'll need directions. About 3km north of Chalong Circle, turn east at the signs to the zoo; it's signposted shortly after.

chalets. Each is a spacious independent concrete studio with pebbled bathroom, canopied four-poster bed, wall-mounted TV, fridge, sofa and safe, as well as a large outdoor terrace with lounge chairs. There's a fourth, wooden bungalow on the way.

From Kata, head 2.5km south on Rte 4233 (towards Rawai/Hat Nai Han). Though it isn't signposted, turn right (downhill) immediately beyond Karon Viewpoint and after 1.5km you're here.

★ **Sawasdee Village** BOUTIQUE HOTEL $$$
(Map p285; ☎076 330979; www.phuketsawasdee.com; 38 Th Kade Kwan, Hat Kata; r 4400-7400B, villa 9800-16,500B; ❄@📶🏊) This opulent boutique resort mixes classic Thai style with Moroccan-esque flourishes and is immersed in a lush tropical landscape laced with canals, waterfalls, Buddhist art installations and a stunning **spa** (massage 1300-2600B; ⏰10am-10pm). Ornate, peaked-roof bungalows have wooden floors, beamed ceilings and lots of character.

Villas are exquisite two-floor homes with free-standing baths, super-comfy beds, elaborate domed ceilings and direct access to one of two romantic pools.

Kata Rocks DESIGN HOTEL $$$
(Map p285; ☎076 370777; www.katarocks.com; 186/22 Th Koktanod, Hat Kata; d 24,900-33,300B; P❄📶🏊) Kata's newest luxury offering is a coolly contemporary all-white beauty, poised on cliffs between the two beaches. Villas are insanely modern, minimalist-chic apartments with iPad-controlled sound systems, full kitchens, Nespresso machines, private pools and electric blinds. Semi-submerged sunbeds dot the pale-turquoise sea-view infinity pool. The innovative **Infinite Luxury Spa** (massages 4200B; ⏰10am-10pm) blends traditional therapies with bang-up-to-date technology like anti-jetlag pods.

Katathani Resort & Spa RESORT $$$
(Map p285; ☎076 330124; www.katathani.com; 14 Th Kata Noi, Hat Kata Noi; r incl breakfast 6400-12,300B, ste 8600-18,000B; P❄📶🏊👪) Taking over a huge portion of (relatively) quiet Hat Kata Noi, this glitzy resort offers all the usual trimmings in stylish surrounds. It features six pools and heaps of space and activities, though rooms could be smarter. **The Shore** (Map p270; ☎076 330124; www.theshore.katathani.com; Hat Kata Noi; villa incl breakfast 19,000-24,200B; ❄📶🏊) complex is an ultra-luxurious and peaceful, private world of pastel-painted villas fronted by a luscious infinity pool practically on the beach.

Excellent low-season deals are often available. There are several child-friendly pools, a kids' club, kids' menus, a host of activities and babysitting service.

Boathouse BOUTIQUE HOTEL $$$
(Map p285; ☎076 330015; www.boathousephuket.com; 182 Th Koktanod; r incl breakfast 7650-9775B, ste 14,300-17,600B; P❄📶🏊) For Thai politicos, pop stars, artists and celebrity authors, the intimate, elegant boutique Boathouse is still the only place to stay on Phuket. Dark-wood rooms are grand, spacious and gorgeous, some sporting large

BIG BUDDHA

Big Buddha (พระใหญ่; Map p270; www.mingmongkolphuket.com; off Rte 4021; 6am-7pm; P) High atop the Nakkerd Hills, northwest of Chalong circle, and visible from half of the island, the 45m-high Big Buddha sits grandly on Phuket's finest viewpoint. Though it's a tad touristy, tinkling bells and flapping flags give this space an energetic pulse. Pay your respects at the tented golden shrine, then step up to Big Buddha's glorious plateau, where you can peer into Kata's perfect bay, glimpse the shimmering Karon strand and, to the southeast, survey the pebble-sized channel islands of Chalong Bay.

Construction began on Big Buddha in 2007. He's dressed in Burmese alabaster, which isn't cheap. All in all, the price tag is around 100 million baht (not that anybody minds). Phuketians refer to the Big Buddha as Phuket's most important project in the last 100 years, which means a lot considering that construction on Phuket hasn't stopped for the last 20 years.

From Rte 4021, follow signs 1km north of Chalong circle to wind 6km west up a steep country road, passing terraces of banana groves and tangles of jungle.

breezy verandahs. The on-site Boathouse Wine & Grill is one of the island's top restaurants and the attached Re Ká Ta Beach Club (p286) oozes glamour.

Eating

There's some surprisingly classy cuisine in Kata, though you'll be paying for it. For cheaper eats, head to Th Thai Na or the cluster of casual seafood restaurants at the southern end of Hat Kata Yai.

Kata Mama THAI $
(Map p285; Hat Kata Yai; mains 50-400B; 8am-9pm) Our pick of several cheapie seafood huts hidden at the southern end of Hat Kata Yai, Kata Mama keeps busy thanks to its charming management, reliably tasty Thai standards and the low-key beachside setting.

★**Sabai Corner** INTERNATIONAL, THAI $$
(Map p282; 089 875 5525; www.facebook.com/Sabai-Corner-150517525037992; Hat Kata, off Rte 4233; mains 100-400B; 10am-10pm;) There's no better Phuket view than the one you'll glimpse from this wide deck: all the way to Karon in one direction and an endless horizon of blue ocean wrapping around the island in the other. It's rare that a location like this gets the restaurant it deserves, but this popular Thai-Swiss-American-owned indoor-outdoor eatery is a stellar nature-fringed find frequented by local expats.

Here are a soaring thatched roof, a pool table, an island bar and a flatscreen for sports. The menu isn't innovative – wandering from fried rice, grilled fish and searing Thai curries to salads, pastas and pizza – but it satisfies. From Kata, head 2.5km south towards Rawai/Hat Nai Han on Rte 4233, turn downhill right behind Karon Viewpoint and drive 1.5km.

Capannina ITALIAN $$
(Map p285; 076 284318; www.capannina-phuket.com; 30/9 Mu 2, Th Kata, Hat Kata; mains 160-800B; 11am-11pm Nov-Apr, 5.30-11pm May-Oct) Everything at this modern semi-open-air eatery – from pastas to sauces – is made fresh. Service can be inconsistent, but the four-cheese ravioli is memorable, the risotto comes highly recommended, and there are excellent pizzas, calzones and bruschettas, plus weekly specials on the board. It gets crowded during the high season, so you may want to book ahead.

★**Boathouse Wine & Grill** INTERNATIONAL $$$
(Map p285; 076 330015; www.boathousephuket.com; 182 Th Koktanod, Hat Kata; mains 470-1750B, tasting menu 1800-2200B; 11am-10.30pm) The perfect place to wow a special date, this is the pick of the bunch for many a local foodie. The atmosphere can feel a little old-school stuffy, but it's all very glam – plus the Thai and Mediterranean food (think: tiger prawn risotto and lobster soufflé) is fabulous, the wine list famously expansive and the sea views sublime. Special sharing platters are prepared at your table.

Drinking & Nightlife

Kata's nightlife is pretty mellow.

★**Ska Bar** BAR
(Map p285; www.skabar-phuket.com; 186/12 Th Koktanod; noon-late) Tucked into rocks on the southernmost curl of Hat Kata Yai and seemingly intertwined with the trunk of a

grand old banyan tree, Ska is our choice for seaside sundowners. The Thai bartenders add to the laid-back Rasta vibe, and buoys, paper lanterns and flags dangle from the canopy. Hang around if there's a fire show.

After Beach Bar BAR

(Map p285; ☎081 894 3750; Rte 4233; ⏲9am-10.30pm) It's impossible to overstate how glorious the 180-degree views are from this stilted, thatched reggae bar clinging to a cliff above Kata: rippling sea, rocky peninsulas and palm-dappled hills. Now wack on the Bob Marley and you've got the perfect sunset-watching spot. When the fireball finally drops, lights from fishing boats blanket the horizon. It also does some flavour-bursting *pàt tai*.

Information

There are plenty of ATMs and wi-fi along Kata's main drag.

Post Office (Map p285; Rte 4028; ⏲8.30am-4.30pm Mon-Fri, 9-11am Sat)

Getting There & Around

Sŏrng·tăa·ou run from Th Ranong in Phuket Town to Kata (per person 35B) from 7.30am to 6pm, stopping on Th Pak Bang (opposite Kata Beach Resort).

Taxis from Kata go to Phuket airport (1200B), Phuket Town (600B), Patong (500B) and Karon (300B). There's a minibus service from the airport to Kata (per person 200B, minimum 10 people).

Motorbike rentals (per day 300B) are widely available.

Hat Karon

หาดกะรน

Hat Karon is like Hat Patong and Hat Kata's baby: chilled-out, reaching for glamour and a tad sleazy. Despite the megaresorts, there's still more sand space per capita here than at Patong or Kata. The further north you go the more beautiful the broad golden beach gets, culminating at the northernmost edge (accessible from a rutted road past the roundabout) where the water is like turquoise glass.

Within the inland network of streets and plazas you'll find a harmless mess of good local food, more Russian signage than seems reasonable, low-key girly bars, T-shirt vendors and pretty Karon Park, with its artificial lake and mountain backdrop. The northern end of town, near the roundabout, feels tatty, while southern Karon filters into more sophisticated Kata.

Activities

During the April-to-October low season, you can take surf lessons (one hour 1200B) and rent surfboards/bodyboards (per hour 250/100B) at the south end of Hat Karon.

Kata-based Dive Asia has an **office** (Map p285; ☎076 396 199; Th Patak East) in north Karon.

Sunrise Divers DIVING

(Map p285; ☎084 626 4646, 076 398040; www.sunrise-divers.com; 269/24 Th Patak East, Hat Karon; 2/3 dives 3200/3800B, live-aboards from 12,900B; ⏲9am-5pm) Managed by a long-time Phuket blogger, Phuket's biggest live-aboard agent organises a range of budget to luxury multi-day dives to the Similan and Surin Islands, Myanmar's Mergui Archipelago and Ko Phi-Phi. Also arranges day-trip dives, including to Ko Phi-Phi and the Similans.

Sleeping

Pineapple Guesthouse GUESTHOUSE $

(Map p285; ☎076 396223; www.pineapplephuket.com; 291/4 Karon Plaza; dm 280B, r fan/air-con 500/1100B; ❄📶) Pocketed away 400m inland from Hat Karon, Pineapple is an excellent budget choice under warm Thai-English management. It's full of brilliantly kept, bright hot-water rooms adorned with colourful feature walls, fridges and, in some cases, small balconies, and there's a simple, clean 10-bed dorm.

★**Bazoom Haus** GUESTHOUSE $$

(Map p285; ☎076 396414; www.bazoomhostel.com; 269/5 Mu 3, Karon Plaza; dm 400B, r 2300-3500B; ❄📶) The bold modern exterior suggests something special. Fabulous doubles have wood floors and furnishings, concrete walls, recessed lighting, mosaic showers and, for some, private terraces. There are DJ decks and colourful art in the polished-concrete, in-house Korean restaurant (the helpful young owners are Korean), plus a dive shop. Dorms sleep six. Up to 60% off in low season.

Marina Phuket RESORT $$$

(Map p285; ☎076 330625; www.marinaphuket.com; 47 Th Karon; r incl breakfast & dinner 8100-11,800B; P❄📶🏊) Stilted boardwalks lead through lush, hushed gardens to comfy, secluded sea-

and jungle-facing rooms and villas decked out in classic Thai style. All enjoy breezy terraces, warm-wood decor, teak furniture and silk throws. Villas have hot tubs. Garden rooms were getting an upgrade at research time. The modern-Asian Red Chopsticks restaurant is excellent. Up to 50% discount in low season.

In On The Beach HOTEL $$$
(Map p285; ☎076 398220; www.karon-inonthebeach.com; 695-697 Mu 1, Th Patak West, Hat Karon; r incl breakfast 3500B; P❄📶🏊) Though nothing fancy, this is a sweet, tasteful inn on Karon Park. The slightly dated, cream-walled rooms line a deep-blue pool and come with marble floors, air-con, ceiling fans and sea views. The wonderful location is the thing. With substantial low-season discounts, it's an ideal surf lair.

Eating

There are cheap Thai and seafood places at the north end of Hat Karon and on the main road near south Hat Karon.

★Pad Thai Shop THAI $
(Map p285; Th Patak East, Hat Karon; dishes 50B; ⏲9am-6pm) This glorified roadside food shack does rich, savoury chicken stew and absurdly good *kôw pàt Ƀoo* (crab fried rice), *pàt see·éw* (fried noodles) and noodle soup. It also serves up some of the best *pàt tai* we've ever tasted: spicy and sweet, packed with tofu, egg and peanuts, and plated with a side of spring onions, beansprouts and lime. Don't miss the house-made chilli sauces.

Mama Noi's THAI, ITALIAN $
(Map p285; Karon Plaza; mains 90-185B; ⏲9am-10pm; 📶) This simple tile-floored cafe with faded Italy photos, a good local vibe and dangling pot-plants has been feeding the expat masses for a generation. They do fantastic versions of all the Thai dishes plus a huge list of popular pastas – anyone for red-curry spaghetti? Cheap, tasty and friendly.

Red Chopsticks THAI $$
(Map p285; ☎076 330625; 47 Th Karon; mains 80-250B; ⏲noon-midnight; 📶) This great contemporary-Thai eatery, just beyond south Hat Karon, is a welcome breath of sophistication. Dine in a smart, fashionable food lounge full of cosy striped chairs, thick wood pillars and dangling low-light lamps, where busy waiters deliver clay-pot seafood grills, light bubbling curries and herb-infused stir-fries from the open-plan kitchen. The cocktail list is suitably long.

Getting There & Around

Sŏrng·tăa·ou run frequently from Th Ranong in Phuket Town to Hat Karon (per person 30B) from 7.30am to 6pm. Taxis from Karon go to Phuket airport (1000B), Phuket Town (550B), Patong (400B) and Kata (200B). A minibus runs from the airport to Karon (per person 200B, minimum 10 people). Motorbike rental costs 250B per day.

THE BIG PHUKET BEACH CLEAN-UP

As of Thailand's 2014 military takeover, the governing Thai junta has been tackling Phuket's notoriously widespread corruption. Most noticeably, this has involved a firm crackdown on illegal construction and consumer activity on the island's overcrowded beaches, and on its 'taxi mafia' (p273).

Initially, all rental sunbeds, deckchairs and umbrellas were banned, with thousands removed under the watch of armed soldiers. Vendors, masseuses and restaurants on the sand were ordered off the beach. Illegally encroaching buildings were bulldozed, including well established beach clubs and restaurants, and others dramatically reduced in size.

How does all this affect travellers? At the time of writing, beach mats and umbrellas are still available to rent, in limited numbers and in '10%' allocated areas; sunbeds remain banned. Tourists may pitch their own umbrellas and chairs within the '10%' zone. Of course, people aren't necessarily following these new regulations. Jet skis, which were suspended to begin with, are still very much operating on Patong and Kamala. Some businesses have defied close-down orders and popped back up elsewhere.

For now, you'll be enjoying Phuket's beautiful beaches in refreshingly tidier, less-hassle versions, albeit with more limited amenities. This is a trial run that may be extended to other parts of Thailand, and the situation is complex and open to change.

Hat Patong หาดป่าตอง

Sun-scorched Russians in bad knock-off T-shirts, an overwhelming disregard for managed development and a knack for turning the midlife crisis into a full-scale industry make Patong rampant with unintentional comedy. But for all the concrete, silicon and moral bending, there's something honest about this place.

Patong is a free-for-all. Anything, from a Starbucks venti latte to, ahem, companions for the evening, is available for the right price. And while that's true of dozens of other destinations, Patong doesn't try to hide it.

Of course, that doesn't mean you're going to like it. But when you arrive you'll take one look at the wide white-sand beach and its magnificent crescent bay, and you'll at least understand how the whole thing started.

Diving and spa options abound, along with upscale dining, streetside fish grills, extravagant cabaret, Thai boxing, dusty antique shops, one of Thailand's coolest shopping malls and, obviously, dusk-'til-dawn parties.

Activities

★Sea Fun Divers DIVING
(Map p270; 076 340480; www.seafundivers.com; 29 Soi Karon Nui; 2/3 dives 4100/4500B, Open Water certification 18,400B; 9am-6pm) An outstanding, very professional diving operation, with high standards, impeccable service and keen, knowledgeable instructors. It's based at Le Meridien resort at the southern end of Patong; there's a second location (p285) in Kata Noi.

Sea Bees DIVING
(Map p270; 076 292969; www.sea-bees.com; Amari Coral Beach Resort; 2 dives 3750B; 9am-6pm) An excellent German-managed diving school offering fun dives to Ko Phi-Phi and King Cruiser Wreck, Open Water certification (15,000B) and Similan Islands liveaboards (from 18,900B). Branches across Phuket and Khao Lak.

Courses

Pum Thai Cooking School COOKING COURSE
(Map p292; 076 346269; www.pumthaifoodchain.com; 204/32 Th Rat Uthit; class 500-7500B) This restaurant and cookery school (with branches in Thailand, France and the UK) holds several daily one-dish (30 minutes) to six-hour classes. Popular, four-hour 'Little Wok' classes include a market tour and a take-home cookbook.

Sleeping

It's getting tricky to find anything in Patong under 1000B between November and April. Outside this time rates drop by 40% to 60%.

★Lupta Hostel HOSTEL $
(Map p292; 076 602462, 092 934 6453; www.luptahostel.com; 138 Th Tawiwong; dm 490-590B, d 1200B; @) Just 100m from Th Bangla, this wonderful, warm, modern newcomer feels more European posh-tel than Patong crashpad. Small, comfy four- to eight-person dorms in light woods and whites share smartish bathrooms. Each bed gets its own locker, plug socket and tiny shelf. Enjoy light breakfast in the social lobby loaded with cushions, high stools and rattan lamps. There's a girls-only dorm.

Patong Backpacker Hostel HOSTEL $
(Map p292; 076 341196; 140 Th Thawiwong; dm 250-450B;) This busy budget spot has a great location across the road from the beach and a welcoming communal lounge. Colour-walled dorms sleep three to 10. The top floor is brightest, but dorms on the lower floors each have their own attached bathrooms.

Baipho GUESTHOUSE $$
(Map p292; 076 292074; www.baipho.com; 205/12-15 Th Rat Uthit ; r incl breakfast 2000-4500B;) Tucked into a quiet soi, this artsy, characterful boutique guesthouse overflows with Buddha imagery, paintings of dancers, floral motifs and Zen-like trimmings that mingle with modern art and urban touches. The dimly lit but stylish nest-like rooms are all unique, so ask the friendly management if you can see a few.

Merrison Inn HOTEL $$
(Map p292; 076 340383; www.merrisoninn.com; 5/35 Th Hat Patong; r incl breakfast 1500-2000B;) Polished-concrete floors, colourful-tiled bathrooms, wall-mounted flat-screen TVs, queen-sized beds, friendly staff and more than a little Asian kitsch make this place an excellent deal.

Red Planet HOTEL $$
(Map p292; 076 341936; www.redplanethotels.com; 56 Th Rat Uthit; r 1200-2500B; P) Part of a budding Southeast Asian brand, this red-and-white block offers no-frills, tidy, three-star living. And it works. Rooms

Hat Patong

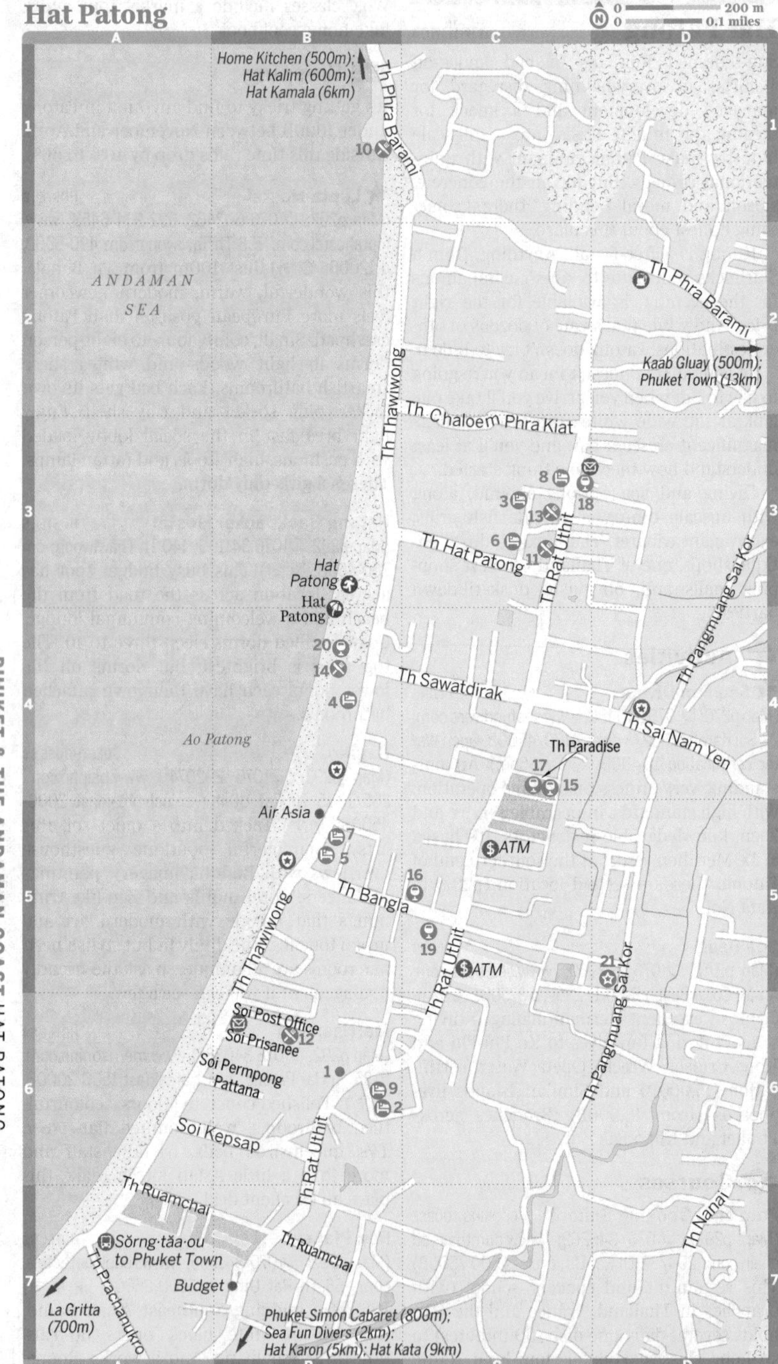

Home Kitchen (500m); Hat Kalim (600m); Hat Kamala (6km)
Th Phra Barami
ANDAMAN SEA
Th Phra Barami
Kaab Gluay (500m); Phuket Town (13km)
Th Thawiwong
Th Chaloem Phra Kiat
Th Hat Patong
Th Rat Uthit
Th Pangmuang Sai Kor
Hat Patong
Hat Patong
Th Sawatdirak
Th Sai Nam Yen
Ao Patong
Th Paradise
Air Asia
ATM
Th Bangla
ATM
Th Thawiwong
Th Rat Uthit
Soi Post Office
Soi Prisanee
Soi Permpong Pattana
Soi Kepsap
Th Rat Uthit
Th Pangmuang Sai Kor
Th Ruamchai
Th Ruamchai
Th Nanai
Sŏrng·tăa·ou to Phuket Town
Budget
Th Prachanukro
La Gritta (700m)
Phuket Simon Cabaret (800m); Sea Fun Divers (2km); Hat Karon (5km); Hat Kata (9km)

Hat Patong

Activities, Courses & Tours

are a tight fight, but smart, cushy and well-equipped with wood floors, hairdryers and plush linens.

Sino House GUESTHOUSE $$
(Map p292; ☎076 293272; 205/10-11 Th Rat Uthit; r 1400-1800B; ❄📶) A sweet guesthouse with Chinese art hanging on the flagstone hallway walls, an elaborately tiled lobby, and clean and large, if basic, rooms with wood furnishings, burgundy drapes, safety boxes and floor-to-ceiling headboards.

★**BYD Lofts** APARTMENT $$$
(Map p292; ☎076 343024; www.bydlofts.com; 5/28 Th Hat Patong; apt 6500-17,400B; ❄📶🏊) Three-block BYD feels like it's been torn straight out of an upmarket interior design magazine. If style and comfort win over beachfront location (it's only a minute's walk), look no further. Urban-chic apartments coated in white (floors, walls, blinds), sharp lines and colourful art feel angelic compared to the seedy world outside. Some rooms have private pools. For everyone else there's a turquoise rooftop pool.

Impiana Phuket Cabana HOTEL $$$
(Map p292; ☎076 340138; www.impiana.com; 41 Th Thawiwong; r 5300-10,600B, ste 12,750-29,700B; P❄📶🏊) Cabana-style and bang on the best (north) part of the beach, Impiana's rooms are laden with sophisticated creature comforts and still close to all the action. There's good Asian-Mediterranean fusion food at poolside **Sala Bua** (mains 300-1900B; ⏰11am-11pm), while indulgent treatments at the on-site **Swasana Spa** (massage 1100-1900B; ⏰10am-9pm) see you nestled in a cool glass cube with ocean views.

Eating

Patong has loads of restaurants, for all budgets. The trick is to steer around the abundant watered-down Thai and poorly executed Western kitchens. The swishest restaurants are huddled together above the cliffs on the north edge of town.

Bargain seafood and noodle stalls pop up across town at night. Try the sois around Th Bangla, and **Patong Food Park** (Map p292; Th Rat Uthit; dishes 50-200B; ⏰4.30pm-midnight) once the sun drops.

Kaab Gluay THAI $
(Map p270; ☎076 346832; 58/3 Th Phra Barami; dishes 60-165B; ⏰11am-2am; 📶) It's hardly Patong's most peaceful spot, but this easy-going roadside eatery is a hit for its authentic, affordable Thai food, with switched-on staff and well-spelt (!) menus to match. Unpretentious dining happens under a huge tin roof. Expect red-curry prawns, chicken satay, sweet-and-sour fish, deep-fried honeyed chicken, classic noodles and stir-fries, and 30-plus takes on spicy Thai salads.

Chicken Rice Briley THAI $
(Map p292; ☎081 597 8380; Patong Food Park, Th Rat Uthit; meals 50-60B; ⏰6am-9pm) One of few diners in Patong Food Park to offer sustenance while the sun shines. Steamed chicken breast is served on a bed of rice with a bowl of chicken broth with crumbled bits of meat; dip it in the fantastic chilli sauce. It does a popular stewed pork on rice, plus

mango with sticky rice. There's a reason it's perennially packed.

Ella INTERNATIONAL $$
(Map p292; ☎076 344253; www.facebook.com/EllaBistro; 100/19-20 Soi Post Office; mains 200-400B; ⏲9am-11pm; 📶) A moulded-concrete, industrial-feel bistro-cafe that's a lovely surprise. Inventive all-day breakfasts feature spicy Rajasthani scrambled eggs, massaman chicken tacos, omelettes stuffed with chicken and veg, and baguette French toast with caramelised banana. It has similarly styled **rooms** (r 3200-5400B; ❄📶) upstairs.

The Beach THAI, SEAFOOD $$
(Map p292; ☎076 345944; 49 Th Thawiwong; mains 180-350B; ⏲8am-11.30pm) If you fancy decent Thai food and a string of predictable, reliable seafood choices by the beach, wander over to this long-running shack. It's slightly overpriced, but the setting is fantastic.

★ **Home Kitchen** INTERNATIONAL $$$
(Map p270; ☎093 764 6753; www.facebook.com/HOME.kitchen.bar.bed; 314 Th Phra Barami, Hat Kalim; mains 300-800B; ⏲5am-1am; 📶) White leather, faded tables, floaty fabrics, burning lanterns and neon lighting crash together with Mediterranean flair. This crazily beautiful, quirky-chic dining room/cocktail bar shaped like a ship's hull is a stunning work of art. And the creative Thai-Mediterranean food is fab too. Try avocado and crabmeat salad, squid-ink pasta with salmon, massaman Wagyu beef, deep-fried *pá·aang*-curry sea bass and perfectly crispy Parmesan-coated chips.

Baan Rim Pa THAI $$$
(Map p292; ☎076 340789; www.baanrimpa.com; 223 Th Phra Barami; mains 290-750B; ⏲noon-10pm) Refined Thai fare is served with a side order of spectacular views at this institution. Standards are high, with prices to match, but romance is in the air, with candlelight and piano music aplenty. Book ahead, button up and tuck in.

La Gritta ITALIAN $$$
(Map p270; ☎076 292697; www.lagritta.com; Amari Coral Beach Resort; mains 400-800B; ⏲10am-midnight; 📶) A spectacularly positioned, modern Italian restaurant serving up huge portions of deliciously creamy pastas and gourmet pizzas. With comfy booths, gorgeous beach views and a deck just centimetres above the boulder-strewn shore at the south end of Hat Patong, there are few better settings for a sunset Chalong Bay Rum mojito (p287).

Drinking & Nightlife

Some visitors may find that Patong's bar scene puts them off their *pàt tai*, but, if you're in the mood for plenty of winking neon and short skirts, it's certainly a once-in-a-lifetime experience.

Th Bangla is beer and bar-girl central, featuring spectacular go-go extravaganzas with the usual mix of gyrating Thai girls and often red-faced Western men. The techno is loud, the clothes are all but nonexistent and the decor is typically slapstick with plenty of phallic imagery. The atmosphere is more carnival than carnage and you'll find plenty of peers fighting through the throng to the bar.

TIGER KINGDOM

At some point during your stay, you'll inevitably be handed a brochure flaunting Phuket's controversial Tiger Kingdom. Launched in 2013, Tiger Kingdom Phuket (like its original in Chiang Mai) offers hundreds of daily visitors the chance to stroke, feed and pose over-enthusiastically with its 'domesticated' tigers, both tiny cubs and full-grown adults.

As with Thailand's other tiger-centric attractions, worries of animal welfare and human safety abound, and there are constant concerns about animals being maltreated, confined to small cages and sedated to keep them docile. Like the infamous Tiger Temple in Kanchanaburi, Tiger Kingdom denies all allegations that its tigers are mistreated.

In 2014, an Australian tourist was seriously mauled while visiting Tiger Kingdom. The tiger in question was 'retired'.

Given the significant animal welfare issues involved, Lonely Planet does not recommend visiting Tiger Kingdom. For more on the thorny issues surrounding Thailand's animal attractions, see p148.

★ Seduction CLUB

(Map p292; www.facebook.com/seductiondisco; 70/3 Th Bangla; ⏱10pm-5am) International DJs, professional-grade sound system and forever the best dance party on Phuket, without question.

Illuzion CLUB

(Map p292; www.illuzionphuket.com; 31 Th Bangla; ⏱10pm-6am) Patong's hottest new mega-club is a sparkly multi-level mishmash of dance and gymnastics shows, international DJs, regular ladies' nights, all-night electronic beats, and more bars than you could ever count.

Sole Mio BAR

(Map p292; ☎081 5378116; Th Thawiwong; ⏱10am-midnight; 📶) A whimsically decorated Caribbean-feel bar, crafted from reused corrugated tin, strings of shells and reclaimed pastel-washed wood. It's right by the beach, pulses with pop songs and is fuelled by middling cocktails and Chang draught. There are worse ways to spend an afternoon.

Nicky's Handlebar BAR

(Map p292; ☎076 343211; www.nickyhandlebars.com; 41 Th Rat Uthit ; ⏱7.30am-1am; 📶) This fun biker bar welcomes all, wheels or no wheels. Once a bit of a dive, Nicky's has never looked better. Ashtrays crafted from bike parts rest on the metal bar and weighty menus are made from hubcaps and heavy disk brakes. You can get your own wheels here by asking about Harley tours and hire (from 4800B).

☆ Entertainment

Cabaret shows and Thai boxing are Patong's specialities.

Phuket Simon Cabaret CABARET

(Map p270; ☎076 342114; www.phuket-simoncabaret.com; 8 Th Sirirach; adult 700-800B, child 500-600B; ⏱shows 6pm, 7.45pm & 9.30pm) About 500m south of town, Simon puts on fun colourful trans cabarets. The 600-seat theatre is grand, the costumes are glittery, feathery extravaganzas and the ladyboys are convincing. It's noticeably geared towards an Asian audience and the house is usually full – book ahead.

Bangla Boxing Stadium SPECTATOR SPORT

(Map p292; ☎076 273416; www.banglaboxingstadiumpatong.com; Th Pangmuang Sai Kor; admission 1700-2500B; ⏱9pm Wed, Fri & Sun) Old name, same game: a packed line-up of competitive *moo·ay tai* bouts featuring Thai and foreign fighters.

ℹ Information

There are ATMs, currency-exchange facilities and wi-fi across town.

Post Office (Map p292; Th Rat Uthit; ⏱8.30am-4.30pm Mon-Fri, 9am-noon Sat & Sun)

Tourist Police (Map p292; ☎1669, 076 342719; cnr Th Thawiwong & Th Bangla)

ℹ Getting There & Around

Túk-túks circle Patong for around 200B per ride. Numerous places rent motorbikes (250B); Nicky's Handlebar (p295) rents Harleys (from 4800B). The mandatory helmet law is strictly enforced in Patong, where roadblocks/checkpoints can spring up suddenly. **Budget** (Map p292; ☎089 873 0234; www.budget.co.th; Patong Merlin Hotel, 44 Th Thawiwong; ⏱8am-6pm) hires cars at the south end of town.

Sŏrng·tăa·ou from Th Ranong in Phuket Town go to the south end of Hat Patong (30B) from 7am to 6pm. From here you can walk or hop on motorbike taxis (30B per ride) or túk-túk. After-hours túk-túk charters from Phuket Town cost 500B. A 'local bus' runs between Phuket Town's Bus Terminal 1 (p280) and Patong (50B) from 7am to 5pm.

Taxis to/from the airport cost 800B. There's a shared minibus from the airport to Patong (per person 180B, minimum 10 people).

Hat Kamala หาดกมลา

A chilled-out hybrid of Hat Karon and Hat Surin, Kamala lures in a mix of longer-term, low-key visitors, families and young couples. The bay is magnificent and serene. Palms and pines mingle on the leafy, rocky northern end, where the water is a rich emerald green and the snorkelling around the rock reef is halfway decent. The entire beach is backed by a paved path and lush rolling hills, which one can only hope are left alone...forever. Flashy new resorts are carved into the southern bluffs and jet skis make an appearance, but Kamala is quietish and laid-back, by Phuket standards.

Activities

During the May-to-October monsoon, you can hire surfboards (per hour 300B) and take surf classes (1500B) on south Hat Kamala.

Laem Singh BEACH

(Map p298) Local beach addicts will tell you that cliff-framed Laem Singh, 1km north of Kamala, conceals one of the island's most beautiful beaches. Park on the headland and clamber down a steep jungle-frilled path, or

> **PHUKET FANTASEA**
>
> It's impossible to ignore the brochures, billboards and touts flogging **Phuket Fantasea** (Map p298), the US$60 million 'cultural theme park' located just east of Hat Kamala and relentlessly promoted as one of the island's top 'family-friendly' attractions. We recommend reading up on the numerous animal welfare issues associated with this Vegas-style spectacle, at which animals are forced to 'perform' here daily, before choosing to support it.

you could charter a long-tail (1000B) from Hat Kamala. It gets crowded.

Sleeping

Papa Crab BOUTIQUE HOTEL **$$**
(Map p298; ☎076 385315; www.phuketpapacrab.com; 93/5 Mu 3; r 1900B; ❄📶) This elegant boutique guesthouse combines homey lodgings, peaceful location and discreet, friendly service. A wooden bridge trails over the lobby's lily pond to tastefully styled terracotta-floor rooms with darkwood beds, Lemongrass toiletries and soothing lime-green-and-white colour schemes, topped up by fresh frangipani flowers.

Cape Sienna HOTEL **$$$**
(Map p298; ☎076 337300; www.capesienna.com; 18/40 Mu 6, Th Nakalay; r 4950-16,900B; ❄📶🏊) This flashy, romantic hotel sprawls up the southern headland offering magnificent azure bay views from the lobby, the pool, the sunken in-pool cabanas and every room. Rooms are bright, smart and modern, with all amenities and splashes of orange and turquoise. Deluxes have balcony hot tubs. Up above is Kamala's breeziest cocktail bar, **Vanilla Sky** (⏲5pm-midnight), and there's polished Mediterranean-Thai cuisine at on-site **Plum** (mains 400-1000B; ⏲6-11pm, closed Mon May-Oct; 🍷).

Layalina Hotel BOUTIQUE HOTEL **$$$**
(Map p298; ☎076 385944; www.layalinahotel.com; 75-75/1 Mu 3, Hat Kamala; r incl breakfast 6050-8500B; ❄📶🏊) Bag one of the split-level suites with private rooftop terraces at this beachfront boutique spot for sunset views. The decor is simple, Thai and chic, full of fluffy white duvets and honey-toned wooden furniture. The pool is ridiculously tiny, but that aqua ocean *is* only steps away. Good low-season discounts.

Eating

Meena Restaurant THAI **$**
(Map p298; mains 80-150B; ⏲9am-5pm) This family-run beachside shack with rainbow-striped and leopard-print sarongs for tablecloths is a real find. The owners couldn't be more welcoming. The tasty authentic Thai food is exceptional and so are the fresh fruit shakes. The rustic setting is exactly what you (most likely) came to Kamala for. It's at the north end of the beach.

Mam's Restaurant THAI, INTERNATIONAL **$$**
(Map p298; ☎089 032 2009; 32/32 Soi 8; mains 90-280B; ⏲noon-10pm) There's no beach view, but local expats swear by this quiet, simple place with just a handful of tables sprinkled across the patio of a family home. Mam's plates up all the usual Thai suspects in meat, shrimp or vegie versions packed full of flavour, along with burgers, pastas, kebabs, sandwiches and, yes, even fish 'n' chips. It's about 400m east (inland) from the main highway.

Getting There & Away

Sŏrng·tăa·ou run between Phuket Town's Th Ranong and Kamala (35B) from 7am to 5pm. *Sŏrng·tăa·ou* also go from Kamala to Hat Surin (20B). Taxis to/from the airport cost 700B.

Hat Surin หาดสุรินทร์

With a wide, blonde beach, water that blends from pale turquoise in the shallows to a deep blue on the horizon, and lush, boulder-strewn headlands, Surin could easily attract visitors on looks alone. Ah, but there are stunning galleries, fabulous boutiques, five-star spa resorts, wonderful beachfront dining and a fun party vibe too.

Phuket's beach clean-up operation (p290) has hit Surin particularly hard. At research time, all establishments on the sand had been cleared away (leaving behind a scruffy mess), and there were mixed messages about the fate of remaining businesses. *In theory*, this means you'll now enjoy Hat Surin's full untarnished beauty.

Sleeping

Hat Surin hosts some of Phuket's classiest resorts, but little for those on a budget.

Benyada Lodge HOTEL $$

(Map p298; ☎076 271261; www.benyadalodge-phuket.com; 106/52 Mu 3, Hat Surin; r incl breakfast 2800-5500B; ❄📶🏊) Stellar service and stylish, modern rooms – with black louvred closets, tiled bathrooms, lounging corners and vibrant silk pillows on tight white sheets – make Benyada one of Surin's better deals. Admire the sunset from the rooftop bar. It's just a couple of minutes' walk from the beach.

Surin Bay Inn HOTEL $$

(Map p298; ☎076 271601; 106/11 Mu 3; r incl breakfast 1800-3000B; ❄📶) A welcoming no-frills midranger 300m back from the beachfront. Tiled floors, white sheets and colourful cushions smarten up spacious, simple kettle-equipped rooms. Larger rooms at the front, with terraces and sea glimpses, are best.

★ **Twin Palms** RESORT $$$

(Map p298; ☎076 316500; www.twinpalms-phuket.com; 106/46 Mu 3; r incl breakfast 8100-18,400B, ste 14,100-29,100B; ❄@📶🏊) Classic yet completely contemporary, Twin Palms is what Surin is all about. Delicate white frangipani trees fringe a maze of artsy minimalist pools. Even the simplest rooms are modern and extra spacious, with oversized bathrooms, free-standing baths, sublimely comfortable beds and a supreme sense of calm. Staff are professional, the **Sun Spa** (treatment 1500-2400B; ⏲11am-9pm) is fantastic, and the beach lies just minutes away.

There's a popular Sunday brunch (1970B).

★ **Surin Phuket** RESORT $$$

(Map p298; ☎076 316400; www.thesurinphuket.com; 118 Mu 3, Hat Pansea; r incl breakfast 10,500-41,200B; P❄📶🏊) Almost any establishment on a secluded beach this quiet and stunning would be a top pick. But bungalows at the Surin, hidden beneath hillside foliage, offer homey, earthy, luxurious interiors that make the site that much better, and the six-sided sea-view pool is gorgeously abstract. It's quite a walk up hills and over wooden walkways to many of the 'cottages'.

Amanpuri Resort RESORT $$$

(Map p298; ☎076 324333; www.amanresorts.com; Hat Pansea; villa US$990-3450; P❄📶🏊) Understated, luxurious and unbelievably peaceful, celebrity magnet Amanpuri is one of Phuket's most exclusive hotels. Graceful traditional-design bungalows are all about the location, with sea-facing cabanas, warm-wood decor and enormous bathrooms. There's a huge array of activities on offer (yoga, kayaking, surfing), plus a jet-black pool, first-rate service and a well-stocked library.

Eating & Drinking

Surin has some excellent upmarket restaurants. For cheap seafood, head to the numerous delicious seafront dining rooms. The most affordable eats are at the food stalls in the beachside parking lot and the couple of roadside shacks heading inland on Rte 4025.

Twin Brothers THAI $$

(Map p298; Hat Surin; mains 120-350B; ⏲11am-10pm) By day, one brother mans the wok, stirring up decent seafood-focused Thai food at (almost) local prices. At night, the other fires up a fresh seafood grill. It's more down to earth than Surin's other options.

Taste FUSION $$

(Map p298; ☎076 270090; www.tastesurinbeach.com; dishes 200-420B; ⏲noon-11pm Tue-Sun; 📶) Minimalist modern lines, top-notch service, a sophisticated but chilled-out vibe and delicious Thai-Mediterranean fusion food make this urban-meets-surf eatery an outstanding choice. Dine indoors or alfresco on meal-sized salads (try the goats' cheese with smoked almonds), weekly specials or a variety of creative starters and mains. Ceramic fish swim above the bathroom door.

Sugo ITALIAN $$

(Map p298; ☎076 386599; www.sugo-phuket.com; 117 Mu 3, Th Srisoonthorn; mains 250-570B; ⏲5-10.30pm Tue-Sun) A Sicilian chef leads this popular new 'rustic Italian' spot, 700m east of Hat Surin on Rte 4025. It's smart and full of style, with specials chalked up on the walls. Slip into a bright-red booth or sneak into the back courtyard to feast on carefully crafted wood-fired pizza, pasta, bruschetta, meaty mains or antipasti platters.

★ **Catch** INTERNATIONAL $$$

(Map p298; ☎076 316567; www.catchbeachclub.com; mains 400-600B; ⏲noon-2am; 📶) Throw on your breeziest island-chic outfit to dine overlooking the sea at Surin's glitziest beach club. It's classy at every turn, from ambience to cocktails and international cuisine (pastas, salads, burgers, pizzas). Club admission (low/high season 1000/2000B) buys you a beach mat and pillow for the day, and goes towards food

Hat Kamala, Hat Surin & Ao Bang Thao

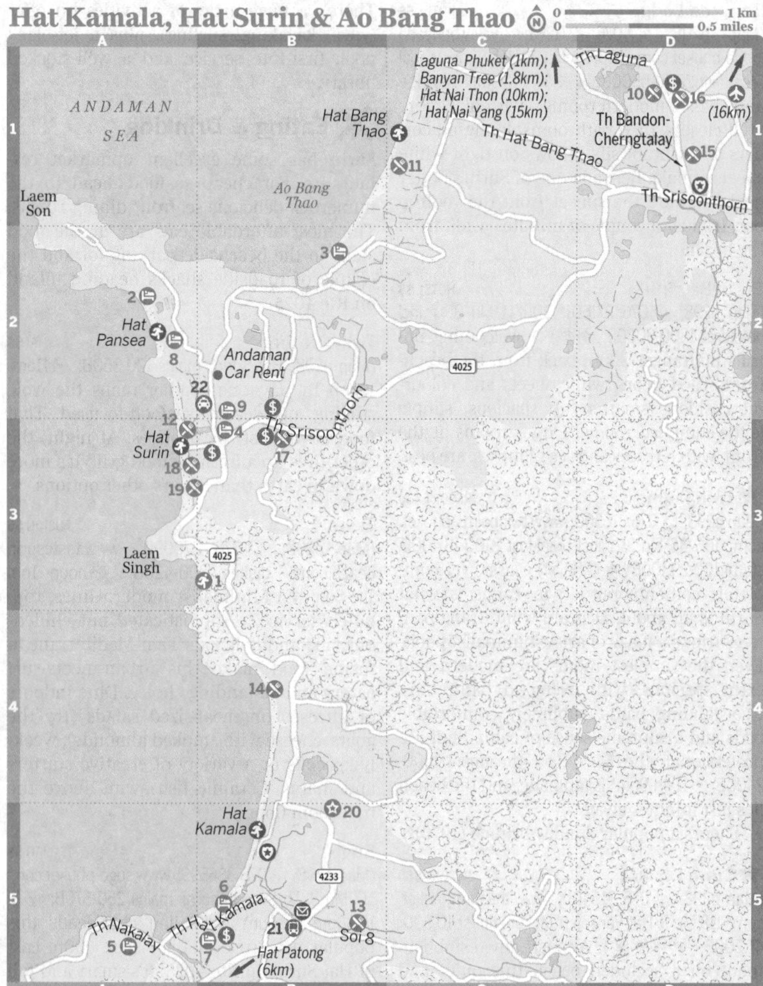

and drinks. Or just grab a table and order off the menu.

Getting There & Away

Sŏrng·tăa·ou go from Phuket Town's Th Ranong to Hat Surin (30B) from 7am to 5pm, continuing to Hat Kamala; túk-túk charters cost 500B. Taxis to/from the airport cost 700B.

Andaman Car Rent (Map p298; ☎076 621600; www.andamancarrent.com; 112/12 Mu 3, Hat Surin; ⏰9am-7pm) This agency, 300m north of Twin Palms, rents vehicles (per day 800B).

Ao Bang Thao อ่าวบางเทา

Even more beautiful than Hat Patong, stunning 8km-long white-sand Hat Bang Thao is the glue that binds this area's disparate elements. The southern half of the region is dotted with three-star bungalow resorts, plus the swanky Bliss Beach Club. Further inland you'll find an old fishing village laced with canals, a number of upstart villa subdivisions and some stellar restaurants. If you see a herd of water buffalo grazing beside a gigantic construction site...well, that's how fast Bang Thao has developed.

Hat Kamala, Hat Surin & Ao Bang Thao

Activities, Courses & Tours
1 Laem Singh ... B3
Sun Spa ... (see 9)

Sleeping
2 Amanpuri Resort ... A2
3 Andaman Bangtao Bay Resort ... B2
4 Benyada Lodge ... B3
5 Cape Sienna ... A5
6 Layalina Hotel ... B5
7 Papa Crab ... B5
Surin Bay Inn ... (see 4)
8 Surin Phuket ... A2
9 Twin Palms ... B2

Eating
Andaman Restaurant ... (see 3)
10 Bampot ... D1
11 Bliss Beach Club ... C1
12 Catch ... A3
13 Mam's Restaurant ... B5
14 Meena Restaurant ... B4
15 Pesto ... D1
Plum ... (see 5)
16 Siam Supper Club ... D1
17 Sugo ... B3
18 Taste ... A3
Tatonka ... (see 16)
19 Twin Brothers ... A3

Drinking & Nightlife
Vanilla Sky ... (see 5)

Entertainment
20 Phuket Fantasea ... B5

Transport
21 Sŏrng·tăa·ou to Hat Surin & Phuket Town ... B5
22 Taxi Stop ... B2

Smack in the centre of it all is the somewhat bizarre Laguna Phuket complex, a network of five four- and five-star resorts tied together by an artificial lake (patrolled by tourist shuttle boats) and a paved nature trail. At the northern end, nature reasserts itsself, and a lonely stretch of powder-white sand and tropical blue sea extends past the bustle into the peaceful bliss you originally had in mind.

Sleeping

Laguna Phuket has seven luxury resorts, an 18-hole golf course and over 30 restaurants. Guests can use the dining and recreation facilities at all of them. Frequent shuttle buses make the rounds of the hotels, as do pontoon boats (via the linked lagoons).

★ Anantara Phuket Layan RESORT $$$
(Map p270; 076 317200; www.anantara.com; 168 Mu 6, Soi 4, Hat Layan; P ❄ 📶 🏊 👪) On its own secluded, wild-feel bay just north of Hat Bang Thao, this is an exquisite top-end addition. Chic, contemporary-Thai rooms come decked out with dark woods, marble floors, ceramic-bowl sinks and Apple gadgets. Villas have dark-tiled pools and 24-hour butlers. A laid-back lounge-bar overlooks the bubbling beachside pool. Dine at two excellent on-site restaurants (Thai, international/Italian) or in a private beach cabana.

An arts and crafts kids' club keeps the little ones happy.

Banyan Tree RESORT $$$
(Map p270; 076 372400; www.banyantree.com; 33 Mu 4, Th Srisoonthorn, Laguna Phuket; d incl breakfast 18,600-28,250B; P ❄ @ 📶 🏊) One of Phuket's finest hotels, and the first to introduce bungalows with their own personal pools, the sprawling Banyan Tree is a lushly shaded oasis of sedate, understated luxury. Accommodation is situated in sophisticated villas, with free-standing, open-air baths and private pools, and there's also an adults-only pool. Don't miss the on-site **spa** (treatment 2900-7000B; 8am-9pm).

Andaman Bangtao Bay Resort HOTEL $$$
(Map p298; 076 270246; www.andamanbangtaobayresort.com; 82/9 Mu 3, Hat Bang Thao; r incl breakfast 2000-8450B; P ❄ 📶 🏊) Most bungalows have sea views and there's a summer-camp vibe at this pleasant little resort at the southern end of Hat Bang Thao. The design is very Thai, with woodcarvings on the walls and coconuts hanging from the roofs, but we'd expect a little more luxury at these prices. Tuck into BBQ seafood and Thai curries at the simple sand-side **restaurant** (mains 195-295B; 8am-10pm; 📶).

Eating & Drinking

Some of Phuket's finest restaurants are just outside Laguna's main gate.

Pesto THAI, INTERNATIONAL **$$**
(Map p298; ☎082 423 0184; Th Bandon-Cherngtalay; mains 69-479B; ⏲11.30am-11pm Sun-Fri, 5-11pm Sat; ✎) Mix a Paris-trained Thai chef with a tiny roadside shack and you've got a fantastic find for delicious, wallet-friendly Thai and international food. Light pesto pasta, lobster lasagne and roast-pumpkin salad whizz you across the Mediterranean. Otherwise, stay local with *đôm yam gûng* (spicy-sour prawn soup), deep-fried turmeric fish of the day, and all your favourite curries.

★ **Bampot** INTERNATIONAL **$$$**
(Map p298; ☎093 586 9828; www.bampot.co; 19/1 Mu 1, Th Laguna; mains 500-600B; ⏲6pm-midnight Tue-Fri, noon-3pm & 6pm-midnight Sat & Sun) The latest fabulous arrival on Bang Thao's food scene is suitably classy with a modern, urban edge. Cool-blue booths, dangling pans, black-topped tables and white brick walls hung with art set the scene for ambitious European-inspired meals (lobster mac and cheese, sea bass ceviche with pomelo) straight from the open-plan kitchen. Creatively concocted cocktails and international wines round things off.

Bliss Beach Club INTERNATIONAL **$$$**
(Map p298; ☎076 510150; www.blissbeachclub.com; 202/88 Mu 2; mains 400-720B; ⏲11am-late; 📶) Even if you don't commit to the Sunday party or a day indulging in these plush turquoise-and-orange-on-white surrounds (per person 300B), swing by Bliss for a tasty lunch or dinner. The Thai-international menu of 13in wood-fired pizzas, roast pumpkin and quinoa salad, chicken satay, burgers and quesadillas is served on a breezy beachside deck with gorgeous sea views.

Siam Supper Club INTERNATIONAL **$$$**
(Map p298; ☎076 270936; www.siamsupperclub.com; 36-40 Th Laguna; mains 290-1250B; ⏲6pm-1am; ✎) One of the swishest spots on Phuket, where the glamorous come to sip cocktails, listen to jazz and eat an excellent meal. The menu is predominantly international with gourmet pizzas, grilled goats' cheese and hearty mains such as barbecued Tasmanian salmon, plenty of pastas and truffle-honey roast chicken.

Tatonka INTERNATIONAL **$$$**
(Map p298; ☎076 324349; 382/19 Mu 1, Th Laguna; dishes 180-790B; ⏲6-10pm Mon-Sat; ✎) Tatonka bills itself as the home of 'globetrotter cuisine', which owner-chef Harold Schwarz has developed by combining local products with cooking techniques learned in Europe, Colorado and Hawaii. The eclectic, tapas-style selection includes inventive vegetarian and seafood dishes and such delights as Peking duck pizza, green-curry pasta and eggplant 'cookies' with goats' cheese. Book ahead in high season.

ℹ Getting There & Away

Sŏrng·tăa·ou run between Phuket Town's Th Ranong and Ao Bang Thao (25B) from 7am to 5pm. Túk-túk charters are 400B. Taxis to/from the airport cost 700B.

Sirinat National Park อุทยานแห่งชาติสิรินาถ

Comprising the exceptional beaches of Nai Thon, Nai Yang and Mai Khao, along with the former Nai Yang National Park and Mai Khao wildlife reserve, **Sirinat National Park** (Map p270; ☎076 327152, 076 328226; www.dnp.go.th; adult/child 200/100B; ⏲8.30am-4pm) encompasses 22 sq km of coastline and 68 sq km of sea, stretching from the north end of Ao Bang Thao to Phuket's northernmost tip. This is one of the sweetest slices of the island.

The whole area is 15 minutes or under from Phuket International Airport.

Activities

During the April-to-October monsoon, Hat Nai Yang is great for kitesurfing. Three fine schools include **Kiteboarding Asia** (Map p270; ☎081 591 4594; www.kiteboardingasia.com; Hat Nai Yang; 1hr lesson 1300B, 3-day course 11,000B; ⏲Apr-Oct), **Kite Zone** (Map p270; ☎083 395 2005; www.kitesurfthailand.com; Hat Nai Yang; 1hr lesson 1100B, 3-day course 10,000-15,000B; ⏲May–late-Oct) and Rawai-based Bob's Kite School (p283).

Hat Nai Thon BEACH
(Map p270) If you're after a lovely arc of fine golden sand, away from Phuket's busy buzz, come to west-coast Hat Nai Thon, 7km south of the airport. Swimming is good (except at the height of the monsoon), and there's coral near the headlands at either end of the bay. Many beach restaurants here have been demolished by the island clean-up.

Hat Nai Yang BEACH
(Map p270) Hat Nai Yang's bay, 3km south of the airport, is sheltered by a reef that slopes 20m below the surface – which means good snorkelling in high season and fantastic

surfing/kitesurfing during the monsoon. Behind is a seemingly endless strip of seafood restaurants, hotels and mellow bars.

Hat Mai Khao BEACH
(Map p270) Phuket's longest beach is a beautiful, secluded 10km stretch of sand extending from just south of the airport to the island's northernmost point. Except on weekends and holidays, you'll mostly have it to yourself. Sea turtles lay eggs here between November and February. Take care with the strong year-round undertow.

Soi Dog VOLUNTEERING
(Map p270; ☎081 788 4222; www.soidog.org; 167/9 Mu 4, Soi Mai Khao 10; admission by donation; ⊙9am-noon & 1-3.30pm Mon-Fri, tours 9.30am, 11am & 1.30pm) This nonprofit foundation, 2km inland from Hat Mai Khao, protects 50 cats and 450 dogs (many rescued from the illegal dog-meat trade), focusing on sterilisation, castration, re-homing and animal welfare awareness. Visits are by in-depth tour. The 'old dogs' enclosure can be upsetting, but they're in a happy home. Visitors can play with the animals, or become a dog-walking or long-term volunteer.

Sleeping & Eating

Hat Nai Thon หาดในทอน

Pullman RESORT $$$
(Map p270; ☎076 303299; www.pullmanphuketarcadia.com; 22/2 Mu 4; r 6500-32,350B; P ❄ @ 📶 🏊) Set high on cliffs above northern Hat Nai Thon, this 227-room resort is a belle. The lobby alone will send you into relax mode, with its arched bridge, soothing grey-and-lavender colour scheme, treasure-chest desks and exposed rough-cut limestone walls. A dreamy network of reflection pools extends out above the sea. Service is divine. Cool two- and three-storey chalets are spacious and modern, with terraces.

Enjoy upmarket Thai cuisine and Friday seafood BBQs at the on-site **Elements** (mains 320-1100B; ⊙6.30-11pm) restaurant.

Hat Nai Yang หาดในยาง

Sirinat National Park Accommodation CAMPGROUND, BUNGALOW $
(Map p270; ☎076 327152, in Bangkok 02 562 0760; www.dnp.go.th; camping per person 30B, bungalow 700-1000B) At the park headquarters at the north end of Hat Nai Yang you'll find campsites (bring your own tent) and large, concrete, air-con bungalows just back from the beach on a gorgeous, shady, white-sand bluff. Book ahead online or by phone.

Discovery Beach Resort GUESTHOUSE $
(Map p270; ☎082 497 7500; discovery-phuket@hotmail.com; 90/34 Mu 5; r fan/air-con 800/1500B; ❄ 📶) With wooden Thai accents featured on the facade, lacquered timber handrails and furnishings, and fridges in the rooms, this spotless budget place is a perfectly decent choice. It's nothing fancy, but the location – right on the beach – makes it great value.

★ **Dewa** BOUTIQUE HOTEL $$$
(Map p270; ☎076 372300; www.dewaphuketresort.com; 65 Mu 1; r from 7000B; P ❄ 📶 🏊) An independently owned boutique property that offers one- and two-bedroom apartments and luscious pool villas, just steps from the national park. Full-kitchen apartments are more spacious, but villas are secluded pods with reclaimed wood accents, vintage wrought-iron motifs and huge outdoor bathrooms with soaker tubs that spill into gorgeous gardens dominated by sizeable plunge pools.

The **Terrace Grill** (mains 250-440B; ⊙6.30am-10.30pm; 📶) is sensational and borders the sultry common pool/bar area. Service could not be better.

Indigo Pearl RESORT $$$
(Map p270; ☎076 327006; www.indigo-pearl.com; 116 Mu 1; r 8250-16,500B; P ❄ 📶 🏊) One of Phuket's most unique megaresorts takes its design cues from the island's tin-mining history. Hardware (vices, scales and other mining tools) feature in the delicate decor – even the toilet-paper rolls are big bolts – and common lounge areas are infused with indigo light. Perks include a sports bar, a pool oasis, cooking classes (3000B) and the fantastic **Coqoon Spa** (treatment 2200-7000B; ⊙9am-8pm).

Mr Kobi THAI $$
(Map p270; mains 150-200B; ⊙10am-10pm) The sign says, 'Broken English spoken here perfect', but the ever-popular Mr Kobi speaks English very well. Tuck into inexpensive Thai faves in refreshingly scruffy surrounds. One wall is dedicated to telling the story of the 2004 tsunami.

Hat Mai Khao หาดไม้ขาว

Anantara Phuket HOTEL $$$
(Map p270; ☎076 336100; www.phuket.anantara.com; 888 Mu 3; villa from 13,125B;) This romantic all-villa property opens onto a serene lotus-filled lagoon crisscrossed by timber boardwalks beneath swaying palms. Luxurious, classic Thai pool villas are impeccably elegant, some with private lagoon salas. It also offers a handsome **spa** (treatment 3500-5900B; ⏲10am-10pm) and every activity under the sun (yoga, pilates, cycling, tennis, *moo·ay tai*).

Getting There & Away

Taxis to/from the airport cost 200B. A túk-túk charter from Phuket Town costs 550B.

Khao Phra Thaew Royal Wildlife & Forest Reserve

อุทยานสัตว์ป่าเขาพระแทว

This **reserve** (Map p270; off Rte 4027 & Hwy 402; adult/child 200/100B) protects 23 sq km of virgin island rainforest on north Phuket. Because of its royal status, it's better protected than the average Thai national park. The highest point is Khao Phara (442m).

Tigers, Malayan sun bears, rhinos and elephants once roamed here, but nowadays residents are limited to humans, wild boar, monkeys, slow loris, langurs, gibbons, deer, civets, flying foxes, cobras, pythons, squirrels and other smaller creatures.

A German botanist discovered the rare 3m to 5m white-backed palm (*langkow* palm) in Khao Phra Thaew about 50 years ago. This fan-shaped plant is found only here and in Khao Sok National Park.

To get to Khao Phra Thaew from Phuket Town, take Th Thepkasattri 13km north to Thalang District. At the Heroines Monument, drive 9km northeast on Rte 4027, turn left (west) towards Nam Tok Bang Pae and after 1km you're at the Phuket Gibbon Rehabilitation Project (p302). The reserve is also accessible off Hwy 402, 6km northwest of the Heroines Monument.

Sights & Activities

There are pleasant hill hikes and some photogenic waterfalls, including **Nam Tok Ton Sai** (Map p270; ☎076311998; off Hwy 402; adult/child 200/100B) and **Nam Tok Bang Pae** (Map p270; off Rte 4027; adult/child 200/100B) (300m along a jungle-fringed path from the Gibbon Project). The falls are most impressive during the June-to-November monsoon. Park rangers may guide hikers in the park on request; payment is negotiable.

Phuket Gibbon Rehabilitation Project WILDLIFE SANCTUARY
(โครงการคืนชะนีสู่ป่า; Map p270; ☎076 260492; www.gibbonproject.org; off Rte 4027; admission by donation; ⏲9am-4.30pm, to 3pm Thu; P) Financed by donations (1800B cares for a gibbon for a year), this tiny sanctuary adopts gibbons that have been kept in captivity in the hope that they can be reintroduced to the wild. The centre has volunteer opportunities that include providing educational information to visitors, cleaning cages, feeding and tracking released gibbons. Swing by around 9am to hear the gibbons' morning song. Note that you can't get too close to them, which may disappoint kids, but the volunteer work done here is outstanding.

Gibbon poaching is a big problem on Phuket, fuelled in no small part by tourism: captive gibbons are paraded around tourist bars. Phuket's last wild white-handed gibbon was poached in the early 1980s. You can help by choosing not to have your photo taken with Phuket's captive gibbons.

Thalang District อำเภอถลาง

Unfolding around the **Heroines Monument** (Map p270; Hwy 402), 13km north of Phuket Town, untouristed Thalang has some worthwhile cultural attractions.

Sights & Activities

Thalang National Museum MUSEUM
(พิพิธภัณฑสถานแหงชาติ ถลาง; Map p270; ☎076 379895; Th Srisoonthorn (Rte 4027); admission 100B; ⏲9am-4pm Wed-Sun; P) This excellent museum chronicles Phuket's history, from prehistoric Andaman inhabitants to the tin-mining era, with Thai and English displays. It traces southern Thailand's varied ethnicities and dialects, and recounts the legend of the 'two heroines' (immortalised on the nearby Heroines Monument), who supposedly drove off an 18th-century Burmese invasion by convincing the island's women to dress like men. The prize entrance-hall artefact is a 2.3m-tall 9th-

century stone statue of Vishnu, found in Takua Pa in the early 20th century.

It's 200m northeast of the Heroines Monument, on Rte 4027.

Wat Phra Thong BUDDHIST TEMPLE

(วัดพระทอง; Map p270; off Hwy 402; ⌚ dawn-dusk; P) FREE About 7km north of the Heroines Monument, Phuket's 'Temple of the Golden Buddha' is half buried, so only the head and shoulders are visible. According to legend, those who have tried to excavate the image have become very ill or encountered serious accidents. The temple is particularly revered by Thai-Chinese, who believe the image hails from China. During Chinese New Year, pilgrims descend from Phang-Nga, Takua Pa and Krabi. Also here are a **crematorium** and a **historical museum**.

Sleeping & Eating

★ **Point Yamu by Como** RESORT $$$

(Map p270; ☎076 360100; www.comohotels.com/pointyamu; 225 Mu 7, Pa Klok, Laem Yamu; d incl breakfast 7060-47,480B; P ❄ 📶 🏊 👪) Breeze into the soaring lobby, where chunky white-mosaic pillars frame ponds reflecting encircling palms, and fall in love. This five-star stunner blends Thai influences (monk-robe orange, lobster traps as lamps) into a coolly contemporary, Italian-designed creation. A huge array of rooms, some with private pools, comes in royal-blue or turquoise, intensifying the endless sea and Ao Phang-Nga panoramas from the entire property.

Laze in the soft-blue pool, the aqua-tiled spa and the private beach club, or join complimentary yoga, pilates, tai chi and bike tours. Two- and three-bedroom villas accommodate families, and there's a babysitting service. Two fantastic restaurants provide southern Italian and refined southern Thai fare. It's 20km northeast of Phuket Town, but you'll never want to leave.

★ **Breeze Restaurant** INTERNATIONAL $$$

(Map p270; ☎081 271 2320; www.breezecapeyamu.com; Laem Yamu; mains 275-750B; ⌚ noon-10pm Wed-Sat, to 4pm Sun ; 📶 🌿) Classy yet understated, one of Phuket's finest restaurants sits in glorious hilltop, sea-surrounded seclusion, 20km northeast of Phuket Town. Blue beanbags overlook pool and sea from the pillared open-walled dining hall. Mini upside-down graffitied cars patrol the log ceiling. Weekly-changing menus triumph with divine, inventive European-style dishes infused with local produce. Pair with classic cocktails given a Thai twist. Book for Sunday brunch (1930B).

KRABI PROVINCE

When travellers talk dreamily about the amazing Andaman, they usually mean Krabi, with its trademark karst formations curving along the coast like a giant limestone fortress of adventure. Rock climbers will find their nirvana in Railay, while castaway wannabes should head to Ko Lanta, Ko Phi-Phi or any of the other 150-plus islands swimming off this 120km-long bleach-blonde shoreline.

Krabi Town กระบี่

POP 30,500

Bustling Krabi Town is majestically situated among impossibly angular limestone karsts jutting from the mangroves, but mid-city you're more likely to be awe-struck by the sheer volume of guesthouses, travel agencies and building work packed into this quirky, compact town. It's a key transport hub, around which a busy traveller scene continues to evolve. Western restaurants and free wi-fi are ubiquitous, as are gift shops selling the usual trinkets.

And yet, if you hang around a while, you'll see that there's also a very real provincial scene going on between the cracks.

Sights & Activities

★ **Wat Tham Seua** BUDDHIST TEMPLE

(วัดถ้ำเสือ, Tiger Cave Temple) This sprawling hill and cave temple complex 9km northwest of Krabi Town is an easy, worthwhile day trip. At the park entrance you'll come to a gruellingly steep 1260-step staircase leading to a 600m karst peak. After a 30- to 40-minute climb, the fit and fearless are rewarded with golden Buddha statues, a gilded stupa and spectacular views out to sea beyond Ao Nang. Start early and bring water; there are drinking taps at the top.

The best of the rest of the grounds can be found by following a loop trail through a little forest valley behind the ridge where the *bòht* (central sanctuary) is located. Here you'll find several limestone caves that are hiding Buddha images, statues and altars.

Krabi Town

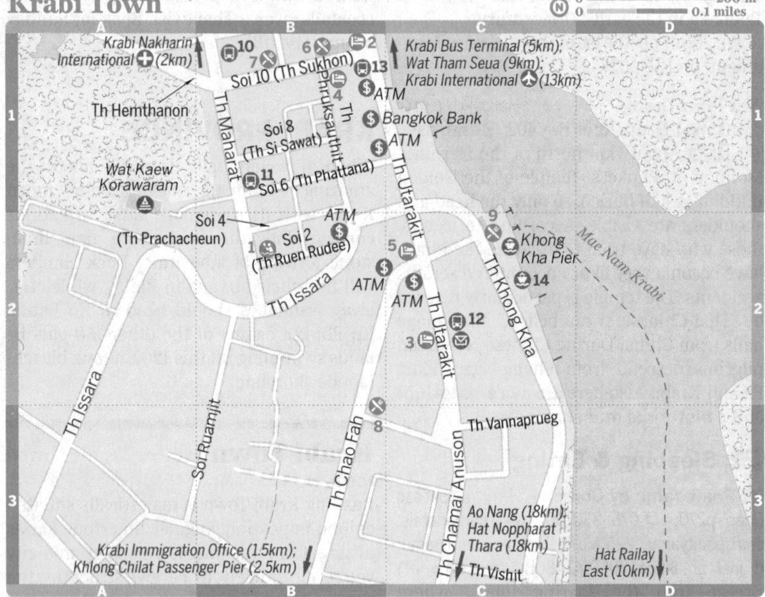

Krabi Town

Activities, Courses & Tours

1 Sea Kayak Krabi B2

Sleeping

2 Apo B1
3 Chan Cha Lay C2
4 Hometel B1
5 Pak-Up Hostel C2

Eating

6 Day Market B1
7 May & Mark's B1
8 Mr Krab-i B3
9 Night Market C2

Drinking & Nightlife

Playground .... (see 5)

Transport

10 Sŏrng·tăa·ou to Ao Luk B1
11 Sŏrng·tăa·ou to Ao Nang & Hat Noppharat Thara B1
12 Sŏrng·tăa·ou to Ao Nang & Hat Noppharat Thara C2
13 Sŏrng·tăa·ou to Krabi Bus Terminal B1
14 Tha Khong Kha C2

This is a sacred area of worship: please dress appropriately by covering shoulders to knees and avoiding tight outfits.

Motorcycle taxis or túk-túk from Krabi cost 100B. A *sŏrng·tăa·ou* from Krabi's Th Utarakit is 50B.

Sea Kayak Krabi KAYAKING
(☎089 724 8579, 075 630270; www.seakayak-krabi.com; 40 Th Ruen Rudee) A wide variety of sea-kayaking tours, including to Ao Tha Len (half/full day 1050/1500B), which has looming sea cliffs; Ko Hong (full day 2200B), famed for its emerald lagoon; and Ban Bho Tho (full day 1700B), which has karsts and sea caves with 2000- to 3000-year-old cave paintings. Rates include guides, transfers, lunch and water.

Tours

Many companies offer day trips to Khlong Thom, 45km southeast of Krabi on Hwy 4, taking in hot springs and freshwater pools, for 1200B to 2000B (including transport, guides, lunch and beverages). Bring decent shoes. Various other 'jungle tours' and mangrove and island trips are available.

Sleeping

Exceptional cheap sleeps abound in Krabi. Head to Ao Nang if you crave luxury.

★Pak-Up Hostel HOSTEL $
(☎075 611955; www.pakuphostel.com; 87 Th Utarakit; dm 280-390B, d 400-500B; ❄@📶) This snazzy hostel features contemporary, polished-cement four- to 10-bed air-con dorms with big wooden bunks built into the wall, each with its own locker. Massive, modern shared bathrooms have cold-water stalls and hot-water rain showers. The two doubles share bathrooms and women-only dorms are available. There are two on-site bars and a young, fun-loving, club-like vibe; you'll never want to leave.

Chan Cha Lay GUESTHOUSE $
(☎075 620952; www.lovechanchalay.com; 55 Th Utarakit; r fan 350-600B, air-con 450-800B; ❄@📶) The en-suite, air-con rooms at ever-busy Chan Cha Lay, done up in Mediterranean blues and whites with white-pebble and polished-concrete open-air bathrooms, are among Krabi's most comfortable and characterful. Shared-bathroom, fan-only rooms are plainer but spotless, with firm beds. Service ranges from rude to delightful.

Hometel GUESTHOUSE $
(☎075 622301; hometel_2012@hotmail.com; 7 Soi 10, Th Maharat ; r 750B; ❄📶) A modern, friendly boutique sleep with 10 rooms on three floors crafted entirely from polished concrete. Abstract art brings colour, some rooms have two terraces and all have rain showers and high ceilings. The lack of windows might not suit everyone. There's a tour/transport desk plus a sunny cafe serving international breakfasts.

Apo HOTEL $$
(☎075 631189; www.apohotel.com; 189 Th Utarakit; r 1500-2000B; ❄📶) The best-value of several fresh, modern guesthouses in this otherwise unremarkable block, Apo has gleaming, minimalist-smart rooms decorated with a single colourful swirl and wall-mounted TVs, spread across two buildings. Some have river views from little balconies.

Eating & Drinking

★Night Market MARKET, THAI $
(Th Khong Kha; meals 30-60B; ⏲4-10pm) Beside Tha Khong Kha, this market is the most popular, pleasant spot in town for an evening meal. Try authentic *sôm·đam*, wok-fried noodles, *đôm yam gûng* (prawn and lemon grass soup), grilled snapper, all things satay, plus creamy Thai desserts and freshly pressed juices. English menus are a bonus.

Day Market MARKET, THAI $
(Th Sukhon; meals 20-60B; ⏲noon-8pm) Among bouquets of flowers and weighty tropical-fruit stands are simmering curry pots and banquet trays of steaming noodles with fried squid, sautéed beef, fried fish and boiled corn. Eat daringly.

May & Mark's INTERNATIONAL, THAI $
(34 Th Sukhon; mains 85-150B; ⏲7am-10.30pm; 📶) A classic travellers' spot with a bold varnished concrete coffee bar, May and Mark's is always busy. We love it for the delicious espresso and excellent breakfast omelettes, pancakes and home-baked bread. It also does popular Thai meals, plus international salads, sandwiches and mains.

Mr Krab-i INTERNATIONAL $$
(www.facebook.com/MrKRAB-i-Thailand-518357558204883; 27-29 Th Chao Fah; mains 150-280B; ⏲11am-1am Mon-Sat, 5pm-1am Sun; 📶✎) A sociable, open-brick lounge bar and chilled-out eatery that hits all the right traveller notes: oven-baked pizzas, pastas, salads, and burgers, plus cool cocktails, friendly management and a pool table. Good vegie options.

Playground BAR
(www.facebook.com/krabiplaygroundbar; 87 Th Utarakit; ⏲5.30pm-2am; 📶) The rollicking downstairs courtyard bar at Pak-Up Hostel is where Krabi fun happens. From beer pong and open-mic nights to live music and giant Jenga, there's always something going on.

Information

There are numerous banks and ATMs. Most guesthouses and restaurants offer free wi-fi.

Krabi Immigration Office (☎075 611097; 382 Mu 7, Saithai; ⏲8.30am-4.30pm Mon-Fri) Handles visa extensions; 4km southwest of Krabi.

Krabi Nakharin International Hospital (☎075 626555; www.krabinakharin.co.th; 1 Th Pisanpob) Located 2km northwest of town.

Post Office (Th Utarakit; ⏲8.30am-4.30pm Mon-Fri, 9am-noon Sat & Sun)

Getting There & Away

AIR

The airport is 14km northeast of Krabi on Hwy 4. Most domestic carriers fly between Bangkok and Krabi. Bangkok Air (www.bangkokair.com) flies daily to Ko Samui and Air Asia (www.airasia.com) to Chiang Mai.

BUS

Krabi Bus Terminal (☎075 663503; cnr Th Utarakit & Hwy 4) is 5km north of central Krabi at Talat Kao, near the Th Utarakit and Hwy 4 junction.

BOAT

Ferries to Ko Phi-Phi and Ko Lanta leave from the Khlong Chilat Passenger Pier (Tha Khlong Chilat), 4km southwest of Krabi. Travel agencies selling boat tickets include free transfers.

Hat Railay East Long-tail boats (150B, 45 minutes) leave from Krabi's Tha Khong Kha between 7.45am and 6pm. Boatmen wait until eight people arrive before leaving; otherwise, you can charter the whole boat (1200B). Boats to Hat Railay West leave from Ao Nang.

Ko Jum From November to late April, Ko Lanta boats stop at Ko Jum (400B, one hour), where long-tails shuttle you to shore.

Ko Lanta From November to late April, one daily boat (400B, two hours) leaves at 11.30am. During the rainy season, you can only get to Ko Lanta by frequent air-con minivans (250B to 300B, 2½ hours), which also run in high season.

Ko Phi-Phi Year-round boats (250B to 300B, 1½ to two hours) leave at 9am, 10.30am, 1.30pm and 3pm, returning at 9am, 10.30am, 1.30pm and 3.30pm. Ferries may be cancelled in low season.

Phuket & Ko Yao Islands The quickest route is with direct boats from the pier at Hat Noppharat Thara (p310), 19km southwest of Krabi. *Sŏrng·tăa·ou* (50B) run between Krabi's Tha Khong Kha and the pier at Hat Noppharat Thara; taxis cost 600B. Boats also run several times daily to Ko Yao Noi from Tha Len, 33km northwest of Krabi Town.

MINIVAN

Travel agencies run air-con minivans and VIP buses to popular southern tourist centres, but you'll end up crammed cheek-to-jowl with other backpackers. Most offer combined minivan-boat tickets to Ko Samui (500B, five hours) and Ko Pha-Ngan (650B, seven hours). More (usually cheaper) minivans depart from the bus terminal. Departures from Krabi include the following:

DESTINATION	FARE (B)	DURATION (HR)
Hat Yai	230	4
Ko Lanta	250-300	2½
Phuket	140-450	2-3
Satun	200	4
Surat Thani	180	2½
Trang	150	2

SŎRNG·TĂA·OU

Sŏrng·tăa·ou run from the bus station to Krabi (20B) and on to Hat Noppharat Thara (50B), Ao Nang (50B) and the Shell Cemetery at Ao Nam Mao (50B) between 6am and 7pm. In high season there are less frequent services until 10pm for a small surcharge. For Ao Luk (80B, one hour) there are frequent *sŏrng·tăa·ou* from Th Maharat, just north of Th Sukhon; the last service leaves around 3pm.

ℹ Getting Around

You can explore central Krabi on foot. *Sŏrng·tăa·ou* between the bus terminal and Krabi (20B) stop on Th Utarakit, outside the River View Hotel.

TO/FROM THE AIRPORT

Taxis between the airport and Krabi Town cost 350B; motorcycle taxis cost 200B. Agencies and Pak-Up Hostel (p305) can arrange seats on the airport bus (130B).

CAR & MOTORCYCLE

Most travel agencies and guesthouses, including Pak-Up Hostel (p305), rent motorbikes (per day 200B). Several international car-rental companies have offices at the airport (vehicle hire per day 1000B to 1200B).

BUSES FROM KRABI

DESTINATION	FARE (B)	DURATION (HR)	FREQUENCY
Bangkok (VIP)	955	12	5pm
Bangkok (air-con)	640-650	12	8am, 8.20am, 4pm, 5.30pm & 6pm
Hat Yai	230	4½	hourly 9am-3.20pm
Phuket	150	3	every 30min 7.30am-5.30pm
Ranong	210	5	8.30am & noon
Satun	234	5	11am, 1pm & 3pm
Surat Thani	150	2½	hourly 4.30am-4.30pm
Trang	120	2	hourly 9am-3.20pm

Ao Nang อ่าวนาง

POP 12,200

First, the hard truths. Thanks to its unchecked and unsightly development huddled in the shadows of stunning karst scenery, Ao Nang is ugly pretty, but it's an easy, if blandly touristy, destination to visit. There's a slightly seedy undercurrent too, with booze crawls and naughty bar-girl sois.

So, yes, it's a little trashy, but if you forgive all that and focus on the beaches, framed by limestone headlands tied together by narrow strips of golden sand, there's an awful lot to like. In the dry season the sea glows a turquoise hue; during the monsoon, currents stir up the mocha shallows. If you're hankering for a swim in clearer waters, you can easily book a trip to the little local islands that dot the horizon, which generally enjoy less-murky water, at any time of the year.

Ao Nang is compact and straightforward to navigate. The surge of attractive, mid-range development means accommodation standards are high (and substantial discounts possible). It's nowhere near as cheap or authentic as Krabi Town, but it's cleaner, sunnier and, obviously, beach-ier. With plenty to do (dive trips, mangrove tours, snorkelling, kitesurfing) and only 40 minutes away from Krabi airport and a smooth 15-minute long-tail boat ride from dramatic Railay, it's easy to see why visitors flock here year-round.

Sights

Shell Cemetery NATURE RESERVE

(สุสานหอย, Gastropod Fossil, Su-San Hoi; adult/child 200/100B; 8am-6pm) About 8km east of Ao Nang at the eastern end of Ao Nam Mao is the Shell Cemetery: giant slabs formed from millions of tiny 75-million-year-old fossil shells. There's a dusty **visitors centre** (8am-4.30pm), with mildly interesting geological displays, plus stalls selling snacks. *Sŏrng·tăa·ou* from Krabi/Ao Nang cost 60/40B.

Activities

Loads of activities are possible at Ao Nang. Kids under 12 typically get a 50% discount.

Diving & Snorkelling

Ao Nang has numerous dive schools offering trips to 15 local islands, including Ko Si, Ko Ha, Ko Poda, Yava Bon and Yava Son. Two local dives cost 2700B to 3400B. Ko Mae Urai is one of the more unique local dives, with two submarine tunnels lined with soft and hard corals. As of 2013, the area has three new wreck dives created by the deliberate sinking of three decommissioned Thai navy ships, though these are only suitable for advanced-level divers and trips are very limited.

Other trips run further afield to King Cruiser Wreck (p318) for 3600B to 4700B, to Ko Phi-Phi (p318) for 3600B to 4500B, and Hin Daeng, Hin Muang and Ko Haa (p327) south of Ko Lanta for 5700B to 6600B. An Open Water course costs 14,900B. Most dive companies also arrange snorkelling trips (from 1800B).

Aqua Vision DIVING

(086 944 4068; www.diving-krabi.com; 76/12 Mu 2, Ao Nang; 2/3 dives 2700/3600B; 9am-7pm) A reliable, well-informed dive school offering local dives, two-dive trips to Ko Phi-Phi (3600B to 4400B), a realm of diving courses courses (OWD 14,900B) and 'safaris' to Hin Daeng, Hin Muang and Ko Haa (5700B to 6600B), plus local snorkelling trips (1800B).

The Dive DIVING

(082 282 2537; www.thediveaonang.com; 249/2 Mu 2; 2/3 dives 2700/3600B; 11am-8pm) This relatively new, keen Ao Nang diving team with an excellent reputation runs trips to Ko Phi-Phi (3500B), which snorkellers can join (2500B), and Ko Haa (6200B). Open Water certification costs 14,900B.

Kon-Tiki DIVING

(075 637826; www.kontiki-krabi.com; 161/1 Mu 2; 2/3 dives 3400/4000B; 9am-9pm) A well regarded, large-scale operation, Kon-Tiki does fun dives to Ko Phi-Phi (3900B) and Ko Haa (6300B), local after-dark dives (3800B), snorkelling 'safaris' (2700B) and Open Water courses (14,900B).

Cycling

Krabi Eco Cycle CYCLING

(081 607 4162, 075 637250; www.krabiecocycle.com; 309/5 Mu 5; half-/full-day tour 800/2000B) The recommended full-day 20km pedal leads you through rubber and oil plantations, small villages, hot springs and, finally, to the 'Emerald Pool'. Lunch is included on all tours except the half-day bike-only tour. It also rents bikes (per day 250B).

Kayaking

Several companies offer kayaking tours to surrounding mangroves and islands. Popular destinations include the hidden lagoon at Ko Hong (1800B to 2500B) to view collection points for sea swallow nests (spurred by the ecologically dubious demand for bird's-nest soup). There are also trips to the lofty sea cliffs at Ao Tha Len (half/full day 700/1100B) and to the sea caves and 2000- to 3000-year-old paintings at Ban Bho Tho (half/full day 1000/1500B). Rates vary (some companies use speedboats), but always include lunch, water, kayaks and guides.

Last Café (p309), at the southeastern end of Hat Ao Nang, rents kayaks (250B).

Kitesurfing

Kiteboarding Asia (p310) offers lessons and courses from nearby Hat Noppharat Thara.

Tours

All agencies can book you on popular four- or five-island tours for 900B to 1200B, depending on whether you choose long-tail or speedboat. Ao Nang Long-Tail Boat Service and Ao Nang Long-Tail Boat Service Club (p309) offer private charters to Hong Island (2500B) and Bamboo Island (3800B), the standard five-island tour (2200B) and half-day trips to Ko Kai (Chicken Island) and Ko Poda (1700B); maximum six people.

Tour agencies offer half-day tours to Khlong Thom (adult/child 800/1200B), including visits to freshwater pools and hot springs.

You can arrange speedboat day tours to Ko Phi-Phi (adult/child 1800/1200B) with Green Planet (p310), departing at 9am and visiting Ao Maya, Ao Pileh and Bamboo Island.

Sleeping

Prices drop by 50% during low season.

★Glur HOSTEL $

(075 695297, 089 001 3343; www.krabiglurhostel.com; 22/2 Mu 2, Soi Ao Nang; dm/d 600/1500B; P ❄ @ ☏ ≋) A sneaky, fabulous Krabi-area hostel that's much better value than many nearby 'hotels'. Designed, built, owned and operated by a talented Thai architect and his wife, this gleaming white lodge complex incorporates shipping containers, glass, and moulded and polished concrete to create sumptuous dorms, with curtained-off turquoise beds, bright-orange pillows, and airy doubles. The pale-blue pool is fringed by tropical gardens.

It's a walkable 1.5km northeast of Ao Nang proper.

Slumber Party Hostel HOSTEL $

(075 637089; www.slumberpartyhostel.com; Th Ao Nang; dm 400-500B; ❄ ☏) You're here for the social scene not the z's. Catering to a lively young crowd, Slumber Party's pod-like, purple-washed, 12-bed air-con dorms with private bathrooms are straightforward but comfy and contemporary. Booze cruises, beer pong, pub crawls, island trips, cultural tours – it does it all. Reception is the downstairs bar.

It's 2km northeast of central Ao Nang, where there's another **branch** (075 656850; Th Ao Nang; ❄ ☏) just back from the beach.

Mini House BOUTIQUE HOTEL $$

(075 810678; www.minihouseaonang.com; 675 Mu 2; r incl breakfast 1850-2100B; ❄ ☏) Local-life murals, warm-wood furnishings, an airy reception lounge and a trickling river feature bring a boutique-y edge to this fresh grey-washed block. Slickly minimalist modern rooms are delicately kitted out with chunky wooden beds, feature walls, tiled bathrooms and balconies; some suites are loft-style abodes reached by smart ladders. It's 900m up the main road leading northeast out of Ao Nang.

Anawin BUNGALOW $$

(081 677 9632, 075 637664; www.anawinbungalows.com; 263/1 Mu 2; bungalow 1400B; ❄ ☏) This zingy-yellow collection of clean, compact concrete cabins with TVs and fronted by little verandahs is tucked into a quiet flowery corner 400m northeast of Ao Nang beach.

Ban Sainai RESORT $$$

(075 819333; www.bansainairesort.com; 11/1 Mu 2, Soi Ao Nang; bungalow incl breakfast 4950-7200B; P ❄ ☏ ≋) A relatively new property 1.5km northeast of the main strip, Ban Sainai sports cushy, thatched faux-adobe bungalows in burnt orange, sprinkled amid the palms and crushed up so close to the cliffs you can almost kiss them. Expect high-end tiled floors, coloured-concrete bathrooms, timber wash basins and pebbled showers. Low-season deals (2625B) are wonderful.

Phra Nang Inn HOTEL $$$

(075 637130; www.vacationvillage.co.th; Th Ao Nang; r incl breakfast 2800-5500B; ❄ ☏ ≋) A thatched explosion of rustic coconut wood,

shell curtains, bright orange and purple paint and elaborate Thai tiles with Mexico-inspired flair. There are two pools, and a similarly styled branch across the road from the original. Some rooms could use a refresh, but it's a sweet perch with plenty of life and a beachfront bar.

Red Ginger Chic HOTEL $$$
(☎075 637999; www.redgingerkrabi.com; 168 Mu 3; r 3200-8000B; ❄📶🏊) On a hotel-filled boulevard at the far western end of Ao Nang, Red Ginger is fashionable and colourful with detailed tiles, red paper lanterns, draped fabrics and a frosted glass bar in the lobby. Spacious rooms feature elegant wallpaper, modern furnishings and big balconies overlooking an expansive pool.

Eating

Ao Nang is full of mediocre roadside restaurants serving overpriced Italian, Scandinavian, Indian, Thai and fast food. For budget meals, stalls pop up in the evening on the road to Krabi (near McDonald's). You'll find *roti* (pancakes), *gài tôrt* (fried chicken), hamburgers and the like, and around lunchtime street stalls set up just north of Krabi Resort. The best meal in the area (and beyond) is at Krua Thara (p310), in nearby Hat Noppharat Thara.

Soi Sunset SEAFOOD $$
(Soi Sunset; dishes 200-450B; ⏲noon-10pm) At the northwest end of the beach is this packed pedestrian-only alley where several samey seafood restaurants with gorgeous sea views show off the day's catch. One of the best (and most popular) is **Krua Ao Nang Cuisine** (☎075 695260; mains 200-450B; ⏲7.30am-10pm), at the far end.

Wang Sai Seafood SEAFOOD, THAI $$
(☎075 638128; Hat Noppharat Thara; mains 80-300B; ⏲10.30am-10pm) Come to this huge open-walled dining hall (just beyond the northwestern end of Ao Nang) for the breezy seaside setting. Fresh seafood and no-fuss Thai fare keep the masses happy: red-curry snapper, cashew-nut fried prawns, lemon-steamed squid and garlic-infused fish cooked every which way. Cutesy cafe attached.

Drinking & Nightlife

Last Café BAR
(Hat Ao Nang; ⏲11am-late) For a welcome blast of natural Ao Nang, hit this barefoot beach bar with cold beer, cool breezes and plastic tables in the far southern corner of Hat Ao Nang. 'Open until sunrise'.

Information

All information offices on the strip are private tour agencies. Cafes and hotels have wi-fi. Several banks on the main drag have ATMs and foreign-exchange windows (open approximately 10am to 8pm).

Getting There & Around

TO/FROM THE AIRPORT

White airport buses (150B) run hourly from 9am to 5pm, stopping outside McDonald's on the Krabi road. Private taxis (600B) and minivans (150B) go to/from the airport.

BOAT

Boats to Railay's Hat Railay West (15 minutes) are run by **Ao Nang Long-Tail Boat Service** (northwestern end of Hat Ao Nang; ⏲8am-4pm, to 2pm May-Oct) and **Ao Nang Long-Tail Boat Service Club** (southeastern end of Hat Ao Nang; ⏲8am-midnight, to 8pm May-Oct). Fixed rates are 100B per person from 8am to 6pm or 150B per person from 6pm to midnight. Boats leave with eight passengers; you can charter the whole boat for the eight-person price.

Boats leave for Ko Phi-Phi, Ko Lanta, Phuket and the Ko Yao Islands from the pier at Hat Noppharat Thara (p310).

CAR

Dozens of agencies along the main strip rent out motorcycles (200B). Budget Car Hire (www.budget.co.th) has desks at bigger resorts and the airport (vehicle rental per day 1200B to 1500B).

MINIVAN

Minivans (often combined boat-minivan tickets) go to destinations across southern Thailand.

DESTINATION	FARE (B)	DURATION (HR)
Khao Sok	350	3
Ko Lanta	350	3
Ko Lipe	1000	6
Ko Samui	500	4
Ko Tao	800	7
Ko Pha-Ngan	600	5
Phuket	300-350	3

SŎRNG·TĂA·OU

Sŏrng·tăa·ou run to/from Krabi (50B, 20 minutes). The route goes from Krabi's bus terminal via Th Maharat to Krabi's Tha Khong Kha and on to Hat Noppharat Thara, Ao Nang and the Shell Cemetery. From Ao Nang to Hat Noppharat Thara or the Shell Cemetery it's 30B.

Hat Noppharat Thara หาดนพรัตน์ธารา

North of Ao Nang, the golden beach turns more au naturel as it curves 4km around a less developed headland, until the sea eventually spills into a busy natural lagoon at **Hat Noppharat Thara-Mu Ko Phi-Phi National Park** (อุทยานแหงชาติหาดนพรัตนธารา-หมูเกาะพีพี; ☎075 661145; www.dnp.go.th; adult/child Ko Phi-Phi 400/200B, other islands 200/100B) headquarters. The **visitors centre** (⏰8.40am-4pm) has displays on coral reefs and mangrove ecology in Thai and English.

Several resorts here deceptively advertise a 'central Ao Nang' location though you may well prefer it if you end up a little out of town here anyway.

Activities

Kiteboarding Asia KITESURFING
(☎084 628 5786; www.kiteboardingasia.com; 1-day course 4000B; ⏰May-Sep & Nov–mid-Mar) Thailand's kitesurfing craze has hit Krabi. Here you can test the waters with one-hour private lessons (2000B) or jump straight in with one-/three-day courses (4000/11,000B).

Sleeping & Eating

Several restaurants serving typical Thai snacks (fried chicken, papaya salad) cluster near the national park headquarters. There are seafood restaurants along the seafront road.

Hat Noppharat Thara-Mu Ko Phi-Phi National Park Accommodation BUNGALOW, CAMPGROUND $$
(☎075 661145; www.dnp.go.th; bungalow 1000B, camping per person 30B, incl tent hire 250B) Rustic but well maintained concrete, air-con, 24-hour-electricity bungalows, located just over the road from the beach. Camping is just behind the park headquarters, near the harbour. Prices stay the same year-round. Book ahead online or at the visitors centre.

Sabai Resort HOTEL $$
(☎075 637791; www.sabairesort.com; 79/2 Mu 3; bungalow fan 1300-1600B, air-con 1600-2200B;) This is the most professionally run of the area's bungalow properties. Tiled-roof, mint-green bungalows come in fan-cooled or air-coniditioned editions, with pebbled concrete patios thatt are overlooking a palm-shaded pool and flower-filled gardens. There are four-person family-sized rooms.

★ **Krua Thara** SEAFOOD $$
(☎075 637361; 82 Mu 5; mains 100-400B; ⏰11am-10pm) This cavernous, tin-roof delight is one of the best restaurants in the South Andaman and one of the finest seafood kitchens in southern Thailand (which places it high in the running for best worldwide). There's no style or pretension, just the freshest fish, crab, clams, oysters, lobster, squid and prawns done dozens of ways, some of them very special.

The crab stir-fried in yellow curry and topped with curry scramble is spectacular. The fried rice is fluffy and light. The snapper fried in red curry is one of the best fish dishes we've ever eaten in Thailand (and we've had hundreds). If seafood isn't your thing, there are lip-smacking versions of all your other Thai faves too. Service is super-efficient and the place is packed.

Getting There & Away

Sŏrng·tăa·ou between Krabi (50B) and Ao Nang (30B) stop in Hat Noppharat Thara. In April 2015, an *Ao Nang Princess* ferry sank en route from Krabi to Phuket; one passenger died. At research time, these ferries were still operating despite the incident.

Ko Phi-Phi The *Ao Nang Princess* runs between Hat Noppharat Thara's pier, beside the national park headquarters, and Ko Phi-Phi (450B, two hours) daily from around November to April, and on Wednesday, Friday and Sunday from May to October. Boats leave at 9.30am, returning from Ko Phi-Phi at 3.30pm, via Railay.

Ko Lanta In high-season only, a 10.30am *Ao Nang Princess* boat runs to Ko Lanta (550B, 2¾ hours).

Phuket From November to April, the fastest option to Phuket is the **Green Planet** (☎075 637488; www.krabigreenplanet.com) speedboat from Hat Noppharat Thara to Tha Bang Rong (1200B, 1¼ hours), via Ko Yao Noi and Ko Yao Yai (both 650B, 45 minutes). The boat leaves Hat Noppharat Thara's pier at 11am, returning from Phuket at 3pm; transport to your Phuket accommodation is included. There's also a 3pm *Ao Nang Princess* boat to Phuket (700B, three hours; reduced services May to October).

Railay ไร่เล

Krabi's fairy-tale limestone crags come to a dramatic climax at Railay (also spelt Rai Leh), the ultimate jungle gym for rock-climbing fanatics. Accessible only by boat, this slice of paradise fills in the sandy gaps between each craggy flourish. It's just around the bend from Ao Nang, so the tourist hustle sometimes spills over, but the atmosphere here remains one of laid-back, Thai-Rasta bliss.

Sights

Tham Phra Nang CAVE

(ถ้ำพระนาง, Princess Cave; Hat Tham Phra Nang) At the eastern end of the beach, Tham Phra Nang is an important shrine for local fishermen (Muslim and Buddhist), who make offerings of carved wooden phalluses in the hope that the inhabiting spirit of a drowned Indian princess will provide a good catch. According to legend, a royal barge carrying the princess foundered here in a storm during the 3rd century BC. Her spirit took over the cave, granting favours to all who paid their respects.

Sa Phra Nang LAGOON

(Holy Princess Pool) Halfway along the trail linking Hat Railay East to Hat Tham Phra Nang, a sharp 'path' leads up the jungle-cloaked cliff wall to this hidden lagoon. The first section is a steep 10-minute uphill climb (with ropes for assistance). Fork right for the lagoon, reached by sheer downhill climbing. If you fork left, you'll quickly reach a dramatic cliffside **viewpoint**; this is a strenuous but generally manageable, brief hike.

Tham Phra Nang Nai CAVE

(Inner Princess Cave, Diamond Cave; adult/child 200B/free; ⌚9am-4.30pm) A wooden boardwalk leads through this series of illuminated caverns full of beautiful limestone formations (and squeaking bats) but, with shifting rain patterns, the water is gone and with it the luminescent effects that won it the diamond moniker. It's pricey for what you see. Follow signs north off Walking St (five minutes' walk).

Activities

Overnight trips to deserted islands can be arranged with local boat owners, but you'll need your own camping gear and food.

Rock Climbing

With over 700 bolted routes, ranging from beginner to challenging advanced climbs, all with unparalleled cliff-top vistas, it's no surprise that Railay is among the world's top climbing spots. You could spend months climbing and exploring – many people do. Deep-water soloing, where free-climbers scramble up ledges over deep water, is incredibly popular. If you fall you'll probably just get wet, so even daring beginners can try.

Most climbers start at **Muay Thai Wall** and **One, Two, Three Wall**, at the southern end of Hat Railay East, which have at least 40 routes graded from 4b to 8b on the French system. The **Thaiwand Wall** sits at the southern end of Hat Railay West, offering a sheer limestone cliff with some of the most challenging climbing routes, graded from 6a to 7c+.

Other top climbs include **Hidden World**, with its classic intermediate routes, **Wee's Present Wall**, an overlooked 7c+ winner, **Diamond Cave**, a busy beginner-to-intermediate favourite, and **Ao Nang Tower**, a three-pitch climbing wall reached only by boat. There's excellent climbing information online at www.railay.com.

Climbing courses cost 800B to 1000B for a half-day and 1500B to 2000B for a full day. Private instruction runs 3000B for a half-day and 4500B to 5000B for a full-day. Three-day courses (6000B) involve lead climbing, where you clip into bolts on the rock face as you ascend. Experienced climbers can rent gear sets for two people from the climbing schools for around 1000B per day (quality can vary); the standard set consists of a 60m rope, two climbing harnesses and climbing shoes. If you're planning to climb independently, you're best off bringing your own gear, including plenty of slings and quickdraws, chalk (sweaty palms are inevitable in the tropics) and a small selection of nuts and cams as backup for thinly protected routes. If you forget anything, some climbing schools sell a limited range of imported climbing gear.

Several locally published books detail climbs in the area. *Rock Climbing in Thailand and Laos* (2014; Elke Schmitz) is one of the more complete and up-to-date guides.

★ **Basecamp Tonsai** ROCK CLIMBING

(☎081 149 9745; www.tonsaibasecamp.com; Hat Ton Sai; half/full day 800/1500B, 3-day course 6000B; ⌚8am-5pm & 7-9pm) Arguably Railay's most professional outfit and big on deep-water soloing (700B).

Highland Rock Climbing ROCK CLIMBING

(☎084 443 9539; www.highlandrockclimbingthailand.weebly.com; Railay Highlands; half/full day

Railay

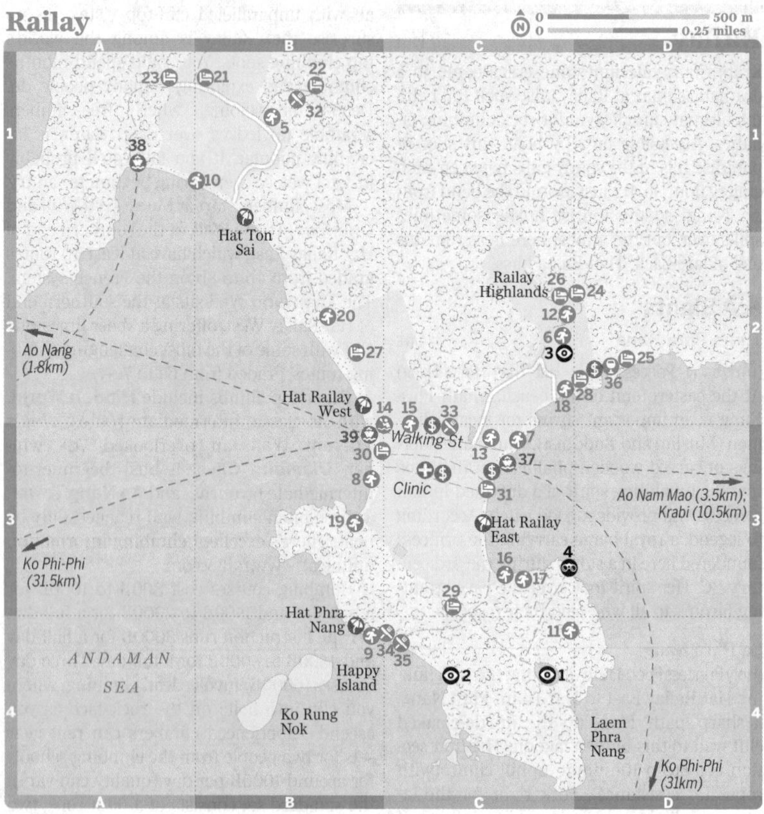

1000/1800B, 3-day course 6000B; ⊙8am-10pm) If you're sleeping on the mountain, Mr Chao is the man to climb with.

Hot Rock ROCK CLIMBING
(☎085 641 9842; www.railayadventure.com; Hat Railay East; half/full day 1000/2000B, 3-day course 6000B; ⊙9am-8pm) Owned by one of the granddaddies of Railay climbing, Hot Rock has a good reputation.

King Climbers ROCK CLIMBING
(☎081 797 8923; www.railay.com; Walking St; half/full day 1000/1800B, 3-day course 6000B; ⊙8.30am-9pm Mon-Fri, to 6pm Sat & Sun) One of the biggest, oldest, most reputable and commercial schools.

Real Rocks ROCK CLIMBING
(Hat Railay East; half/full day 1000/1800B, 3-day course 6000B; ⊙8am-10pm) A newer, Thai-American–run operation that's efficiently managed and gets good reports.

Diving & Snorkelling

Dive operations in Railay run trips out to local dive sites, including Ko Poda. Two dives cost 2500B; an Open Water dive course is 13,500B. There are also dive trips to Ko Phi-Phi (4000B) and King Cruiser Wreck (p318) for 4500B. Most dive operators in Ao Nang, where there's more choice, will pick up from Railay.

Full-day, multi-island snorkelling trips to Ko Poda, Ko Hong, Ko Kai and beyond can be arranged through resorts and agencies for 450B to 1400B, or you can charter a long-tail (half/full-day 1800/2800B) from Hat Railay West. One-day snorkelling tours to Ko Phi-Phi cost 1400B to 2000B. If you're just snorkelling off Railay, most resorts rent mask sets and fins for around 150B each.

Kayaking

Rent kayaks on Hat Railay West or Hat Ton Sai (per hour/day 200/800B).

Railay

Sights
1 Sa Phra Nang C4
2 Tham Phra Nang C4
3 Tham Phra Nang Nai C2
4 Viewpoint C3

Activities, Courses & Tours
5 Basecamp Tonsai B1
6 Diamond Cave C2
7 Hat Railay East C3
8 Hat Railay West B3
9 Hat Tham Phra Nang B4
10 Hat Ton Sai B1
11 Hidden World C4
12 Highland Rock Climbing C2
13 Hot Rock C3
Kayak Rental .... (see 38)
14 Kayak Rental C3
15 King Climbers C3
16 Muay Thai Wall C3
17 One, Two, Three Wall C3
18 Real Rocks C2
19 Thaiwand Wall B3
20 Wee's Present Wall B2

Sleeping
21 Chill Out B1
22 Forest Resort B1
23 Paasook A1
24 Railay Cabana D2
25 Railay Garden View D2
26 Railay Phutawan Resort C2
27 Railei Beach Club B2
28 Rapala Rockwood Resort D2
29 Rayavadee C3
30 Sand Sea Resort B3
31 Sunrise Tropical Resort C3

Eating
32 Mama's Chicken B1
33 Mangrove Restaurant C3
Sunset Restaurant .... (see 30)
34 The Grotto B4
35 The Terrace C4

Drinking & Nightlife
Chill Out .... (see 21)
Highland Rock Climbing .... (see 12)
36 Last Bar D2

Transport
37 Ferry Jetty C3
Long-Tail Boats to Ao Nam Mao .... (see 37)
38 Long-Tail Boats to Ao Nang A1
39 Long-Tail Boats to Ao Nang B3
Long-Tail Boats to Krabi .... (see 37)

Sleeping & Eating

Hat Railay East
หาดไร่เลย์ทิศตะวันออก

Rapala Rockwood Resort BUNGALOW $

(☎075 622586; bungalow 800-900B; 📶) These ramshackle wooden bungalows have been spruced up with gleaming paint and hammocks on verandahs. Within lie colourful linens, cold-water bathrooms, mosquito nets and fans. There's a teensy paddling pool beside a couple of sun loungers. The hilltop location means breezes, sea panoramas and some steep steps. Walk-ins only.

Railay Garden View BUNGALOW $$

(☎085 888 5143; www.railaygardenview.com; bungalow incl breakfast 1450-1950B; 📶) A collection of tin-roof, woven-bamboo and shiny-wood bungalows, stilted between tropical gardens high above the mangroves at the northeastern end of the beach. Some look weather-beaten from outside, but all are spacious and decently clean, graced with Thai fabrics, creative concrete bathrooms and floor cushions. Bring mosquito repellent and a torch for after-dark walks.

Sunrise Tropical Resort RESORT $$$

(☎075 819418; www.sunrisetropical.com; bungalow incl breakfast 3200-6950B; ❄@📶🏊) Swish 'chalets' and 'villas' here rival some of the finest on Hat Railay West but are priced for Hat Railay East – so we reckon this is one of the best deals in Railay. Expect soothing smart decor, hardwood floors, four-poster beds or wooden mattress-platforms, lush bathrooms with aqua-tiled floors and private balconies or patios.

Mangrove Restaurant THAI $

(Walking St; dishes 80-150B; ⏲9am-10pm; 📶) This humble, heaving, local-style place, set beneath a stilted thatched roof between east and west beaches, turns out all the spicy Thai favourites cheaply, from glass-noodle salad and cashew-nut stir-fry to curries, *sôm đam* and the wonderful creation that is egg-grilled sticky rice. Praise goes to the kitchen's matriarch.

Hat Railay West หาดไร่เลย์ทิศตะวันตก

You can't go wrong with any of the beach-front resort restaurants.

WHERE TO STAY IN RAILAY

There are four beaches around Railay, or you can sleep up on the headland. It's a five-minute walk between Hat Railay East, Hat Railay West, Hat Tham Phra Nang and the highlands.

Hat Railay East (Hat Sunrise) Railay's most developed beach, this shallow, muddy, mangrove-lined bay recedes to mud flats during low tide, gets steamy hot if the breezes aren't blowing and isn't appealing for swimming. That said, it's lined with affordable hotels, guesthouses and restaurants and is only a five-minute walk to better beaches. Rates drop by 50% for low season.

Hat Railay West A near flawless white wonder and the best place to swim, join an afternoon pick-up football game or watch a fiery sunset. It's all tasteful midrange and top-end resorts here, but rates can drop by up to 50% in low season. Long-tail boats to/from Ao Nang pick up and drop off here.

Hat Tham Phra Nang Quite possibly one of the world's most beautiful beaches, on the southwest side of the headland and with a crescent of pale, golden sand, framed by cave-carved karst cliffs and Ko Kai (Chicken Island) and Ko Poda peeking out of the cerulean sea. There's only one place to stay here – the peninsula's most exclusive resort, Rayavadee. Anyone can drop a beach towel.

Hat Ton Sai The grittier climbers' and budgeteers' retreat. The beach itself isn't spectacular, but with so many good climbs all around, most people don't mind. Bars and bungalows are nestled further back in the jungle and it's a lively, fun scene.

At research time, a private development had walled off and ripped up a vast section of the jungle fringing the beach, unearthing mountains of rubbish; Ton Sai lovers have retaliated with witty wall graffiti. It's a pretty ugly mess.

To get to the other beaches you'll need to take a long-tail (50B) or hike – it takes about 20 minutes to scramble over the rocks from Hat Railay West at low tide or 30 minutes through the jungle with lots of up and downs.

Railay Highlands About 500m inland from Hat Railay West or East, this is Railay's most recently developed area. Sea breezes cool the jungle canopy and lodgings are good value. From Hat Railay West, follow Walking St and veer left (north) onto the path to Tham Phra Nang Nai (Diamond Cave). From Hat Railay East head right (north) on the cement road accessible via Diamond Cave Resort.

Sand Sea Resort RESORT $$$
(075 819463; www.krabisandsea.com; Hat Railay West; bungalow incl breakfast 3990-6800B;) The lowest-priced resort on this sublime beach offers everything from ageing 'superior' bungalows to newly remodelled cottages and smart, sparkly, contemporary rooms with every amenity. The grounds aren't as swanky as the neighbours', but rooms are comfy and there are two peaceful foliage-enclosed pools, one with karst views.

At the recommended beachfront **Sunset Restaurant** (mains 180-400B; 11am-9pm;), red-shirted waiters take seafood-grill and Thai-curry orders on iPads.

★**Railei Beach Club** VILLA $$$
(086 685 9359; www.raileibeachclub.com; house 3000-20,000B;) At the northern end of the beach, hidden in forested grounds that stretch back to luscious limestone cliffs, is this collection of individually designed Thai-style homes for six to eight people, rented out on behalf of absent owners. They come with patios, kitchens and amenities, and there are also a few smaller but impeccably stylish dark-wood doubles. Only a few homes have air-con.

It's a superb, unique deal and a romantic location; book well ahead. In-house chefs prepare fresh Thai meals on request.

Hat Tham Phra Nang
หาดถ้ำพระนาง

★**Rayavadee** HOTEL $$$
(075 620740; www.rayavadee.com; pavilion incl breakfast 16,900-50,300B, villa 106,500-162,600B;) Arguably one of Thailand's finest chunks of beachfront property, this exclusive resort sprawls across grounds filled with banyan trees, flowers and meandering

ponds. The two-storey, mushroom-domed pavilions are packed with antique furniture, locally sourced spa products and every mod con (including butler service). Some have private pools.

There are yoga classes, tours in luxury speedboats and a first-rate spa, plus a range of kids-only activities, and family-sized villas. Nonguests are welcome for pricey but divine cuisine courtesy of the four onsite eateries. **The Grotto** (mains 460-820B; ⏲noon-10pm) plates up Mediterranean treats half-inside an illuminated cave fronting Hat Tham Phra Nang, where you might alternatively dine on upscale Thai fare at **the Terrace** (mains 400-1100B; ⏲6-11pm; ✍).

Railay Highlands

Railay Cabana BUNGALOW $

(☎075 621733, 084 534 1928; Railay Highlands; bungalow 500B) Superbly located in a bowl of karst cliffs, this is your tropical hippie mountain hideaway. Creaky yet clean thatched-bamboo bungalows with 24-hour electricity are surrounded by mango, mangosteen, banana and guava groves. It's just north of Tham Phra Nang Nai, inland from Hat Railay East.

Railay Phutawan Resort HOTEL $$

(☎084 060 0550, 075 819479; www.railayphutawan.com; Railay Highlands; r fan 800B, air-con 2500-3500B; ❄@📶🏊) The spacious cottages highlighted with creamy yellow walls and big rain-shower bathrooms offer all the trimmings of a high-end resort, though the surly service doesn't. Tiled rooms in an apartment-style block are a step down in luxury, but comfortable. Musty but decent-value fan bungalows are for walk-ins only. Watch rock-climbers in action from the sea-and-cliff-view infinity pool.

Hat Ton Sai หาดต้นไทร

For the best cheap eats, follow the path leading inland beyond bungalows.

Chill Out BUNGALOW $

(☎087 699 4527, 084 186 8138; www.chilloutbarkrabi.com; Hat Ton Sai; dm/d 400/600B; 📶) While no more luxurious than Ton Sai's other offerings, Chill Out's bungalows bring a sociable, laid-back atmosphere and a pinch more style. Vibrantly painted international flags are plastered across the doors of basic tin-topped, wood-floored huts, which have terraces, cold-water bathrooms and mosquito nets. The bar gets busy. Electricity and wifi in evenings only.

Paasook BUNGALOW $

(☎081 893 9220; juaaup@gmail.com; bungalow 600-900B) Cheaper, concrete-floored bungalows are clean and just about do-able, but the wooden cottages are huge, with floor-to-ceiling windows and tiled bathrooms. The gardens are lush and management is friendly.

Forest Resort BUNGALOW $$

(☎084 440 4335; www.basecamptonsai.com; r 600-900B, bungalow 600-1200B) The bamboo bungalows are slightly less scruffy than the sparse three-person, concrete-floor cells. The best bet are the wood-and-brick bungalows with tiled floors, red-brick bathrooms, private porches and tin roofs. All are fan cooled when the electricity is running (6pm to 1am). If there's no one around, ask at Basecamp Tonsai (p311), which manages the place.

Mama's Chicken THAI $

(70-100B; ⏲7am-10pm; ✍) Relocated to the jungle path leading inland to Hat Railay East and West, Mama's remains one of Ton Sai's favourite food stops for its international breakfasts, fruit smoothies and extensive range of cheap Thai dishes, including a rare massaman tofu and other vegetarian-friendly adaptations.

Drinking & Nightlife

There's a bunch of beachside places where you can unwind.

★**Last Bar** BAR

(Hat Railay East; ⏲11am-late) A reliably packed-out multi-level tiki bar that rambles to the edge of the mangroves, with bunting, balloons and cushioned seats on one deck, candlelit dining tables on another, live music at the back and waterside fire shows.

Highland Rock Climbing CAFE

(☎084 443 9539; Railay Highlands; ⏲8am-8pm) Part climbing school, part cafe, this driftwood-clad place sources beans from sustainable farms in Chiang Rai and serves some of the peninsula's best coffee.

Chill Out BAR

(Hat Ton Sai; ⏲11am-late, hours vary; 📶) Kick back over some cold beers, live music, DJ beats and frenzied fire shows at Ton Sai's top jungle reggae bar.

Information

There's lots of local information on www.railay.com. There are ATMs on Hat Railay East and on the paths leading to Hat Railay West. Bigger resorts change cash. Wi-fi is widely available.

Clinic (084 378 3057; Railay Bay Resort, Hat Railay West; 8am-10pm) For minor injuries.

Getting There & Around

Long-tails run to Railay from Krabi's Tha Khong Kha and from the seafront at Ao Nang and Ao Nam Mao. Boats between Krabi and Hat Railay East leave between 7.45am and 6pm when they have eight people (150B, 45 minutes). Chartering the boat costs 1200B.

Boats to Hat Railay West or Hat Ton Sai from the southeastern end of Ao Nang (15 minutes) cost 100B from 8am to 6pm or 150B from 6pm to midnight. Boats don't leave until eight people show up. Private charters cost 800B. Services stop as early as 5pm May to October.

During exceptionally high seas, boats from Ao Nang and Krabi stop running; you may still be able to get from Hat Railay East to Ao Nam Mao (100B, 15 minutes), where you can pick up a *sŏrng·tăa·ou* to Krabi or Ao Nang.

A year-round ferry runs to Ko Phi-Phi (400B, 1¼ hours) from Hat Railay East at 9.45am; long-tails motor over to meet it. Boats to Ko Lanta (500B, two hours, 10.45am daily) operate only during the October-to-April high season. For Phuket (700B, 2¼ hours), there's a year-round ferry at 3.15pm. Some ferries pick up off Hat Railay West.

Ko Phi-Phi Don เกาะพีพีดอน

Oh, how beauty can be a burden. About 38km southwest of Krabi, the insanely pretty islands of Ko Phi-Phi Don and Ko Phi-Phi Leh are Thailand's Shangri-La: a hedonistic paradise where tourists cavort in azure seas, party all night long on packed-out sands and snap pictures of long-tails puttering between craggy cliffs. With its flashy, curvy, bleach-blonde beaches and bodacious jungles, it's no wonder Phi-Phi has become the darling of the Andaman coast.

Unfortunately, nothing can withstand this pace forever. Phi-Phi's stunning looks have become its own demise and, unless limits are set, these beloved islands will continue speeding towards ecological disaster.

Ko Phi-Phi Don is practically two islands joined together by a narrow isthmus, flanked on either side by Ao Ton Sai and Ao Lo Dalam. Boats dock at Ao Ton Sai and a narrow path, crammed full of tour operators, restaurants and souvenir shops, stretches east along the beach to **Hat Hin Khom** (Map p317). This central sandbar is a cramped, chaotic mess of relentless construction and overpriced accommodation. **Hat Yao** (Long Beach; Map p317), facing south, is more attractive.

On the island's more isolated eastern coast it's a slightly different story: here you'll still find sensational snow-white coves and a beachy scene unpolluted by pounding bass. The beautifully languid, long eastern bays of **Hat Laem Thong** (Map p317) and **Ao Lo Bakao** (Map p317) are reserved for top-end resorts, while the smaller bays of **Hat Phak Nam** (Map p317) and **Hat Rantee** (Map p317) host low-key bungalows.

Choose carefully, tread lightly, manage your expectations, and Phi-Phi may well seduce you as it has thousands of other travellers. You might, equally, find you can't wait to leave.

Sights

★Phi-Phi Viewpoint VIEWPOINT
(จุดชมวิวเกาะพีพีดอน; Map p317; admission 30B) The strenuous Phi-Phi viewpoint climb is a steep, rewarding 20- to 30-minute hike up hundreds of steps and narrow twisting paths. Follow the signs on the road heading northeast from Ton Sai Village; most people will need to stop for a break (don't forget your water bottle). The views from the top are exquisite: Phi-Phi's lush mountain butterfly brilliance in full bloom.

From here, head over the hill through the jungle to the peaceful eastern beaches.

Activities

Watersports Experience WATER SPORTS
(www.watersportsexperience.com; per person without/with sports 1500/2500B; tour 10am) Zip around in a speedboat and stand-up paddle (SUP), wakeboard, water ski, cliff-jump and snorkel the waters around Phi-Phi Don and Phi-Phi Leh. Anyone who doesn't fancy getting sporty is welcome at a discount. Book at any Ton Sai Village agency.

Diving

Crystalline water and abundant marine life make the perfect recipe for top-notch scuba (p318).

Phi-Phi has fixed island-wide dive prices. Open Water certification costs 13,800B, while standard two-dive trips cost 2500B to

Ko Phi-Phi Don

Top Sights
1 Phi-Phi Viewpoint C3

Activities, Courses & Tours
2 Ao Lo Bakao C2
3 Blue View Divers C3
4 Hat Hin Khom C4
5 Hat Laem Thong B1
6 Hat Phak Nam C2
7 Hat Rantee C3
8 Hat Yao C4
9 Hin Taak Climbing Area B4
10 Ton Sai Tower Climbing Area B3

Sleeping
11 P.P. Erawan Palms Resort B1
12 Paradise Pearl Bungalow C4
13 Paradise Resort Phi Phi C4
14 Phi Phi Island Village B2
15 PP Rantee C3
16 Rantee Cliff Beach Resort C3
17 Relax Beach Resort C2
18 Sunflower Boathouse C3
19 Viking Natures Resort C4
20 Zeavola B1

Eating
Paradise Pearl Bungalow .... (see 12)
Relax Beach Resort .... (see 17)

Drinking & Nightlife
Sunflower Bar .... (see 18)

3500B and Discover Scuba costs 3400B. Hin Daeng and Hin Muang, 60km south, are expensive ventures from Ko Phi-Phi (5500B); it's slightly cheaper to link up with a dive crew in Ko Lanta.

★ **Adventure Club** DIVING
(Map p320; ☎ 081 895 1334; www.diving-in-thailand.net; Ton Sai Village; 2 dives 2500B, Open Water certification 13,800B; ⏲ 8am-10pm) Our favourite

KO PHI-PHI DIVE SITES

Leopard sharks and hawksbill turtles are common on Ko Phi-Phi's dive sites. Whale sharks sometimes make cameo appearances around Hin Daeng, Hin Muang, Hin Bida and Ko Bida Nok in February and March. November to February boasts the best visibility. Top dives around Ko Phi-Phi include the following:

DIVE SITE	DEPTH (M)	FEATURES
Anemone Reef	17-26	Hard coral reef with plentiful anemones and clownfish
Hin Bida Phi-Phi	5-30	Submerged pinnacle with hard coral, turtles, leopard sharks and occasional mantas and whale sharks
Hin Muang	19-24	Submerged pinnacle with a few leopard sharks, groupers, barracudas, moray eels and occasional whale sharks
King Cruiser Wreck	12-30	Sunken passenger ferry (1997) with snappers, leopard sharks, barracudas, scorpionfish, lionfish and turtles
Kledkaeo Wreck	14-26	Deliberately sunk decommissioned Thai navy ship (2014) with lionfish, snappers, groupers and barracudas
Ko Bida Nok	18-22	Karst massif with gorgonians, leopard sharks, barracudas and occasional whale sharks and mantas
Phi-Phi Leh	5-18	Island rim covered in coral and oysters, with moray eels, octopuses, seahorses and swim-throughs

Phi-Phi diving operation runs an excellent assortment of educational, responsible diving and snorkelling tours. You won't mind getting up at 6am for the popular shark-watching snorkel trips (800B) on which you're guaranteed to cavort with at least one reef shark.

Blue View Divers DIVING
(Map p317; ☎075 819 395; www.blueviewdivers.com; Phi Phi Viewpoint Resort, Ao Lo Dalam; 2 dives 2500B; ⏲10am-8pm) A professional, well-organised outfit that focuses on community involvement, beach clean-ups and environmental conservation, with two-dive trips, night dives (1900B), Open Water courses (13,800B) and Discover Scuba (3400B).

Sea Frog Diving DIVING
(Map p320; ☎087 920 0680, 075 601073; www.ppseafrog.com; Ton Sai Village; 2 dives 2500B; ⏲7am-10pm) A long-running dive shop with a solid reputation. Offers Open Water certification (13,800B) and Discover Scuba (3400B), plus the standard two-dive trips.

Snorkelling

Ko Mai Phai (Bamboo Island), 6km north of Phi-Phi Don, is a popular shallow snorkelling spot where you may see small sharks. There's good snorkelling along the eastern coast of **Ko Nok** (near Ao Ton Sai), along the eastern coast of **Ko Nai**, and off **Hat Yao**. Most resorts rent out snorkel, mask and fins sets (per day 200B).

Snorkelling trips cost 700B to 2500B, depending on whether you travel by long-tail or motorboat. You can tag along with dive trips, and many dive operators also offer specialised snorkelling tours. Those with the Adventure Club (p317) come highly recommended.

Rock Climbing

Yes, there are good limestone cliffs to climb on Phi-Phi, and the views are spectacular. The main climbing areas are **Ton Sai Tower** (Map p317), at the western edge of Ao Ton Sai, and **Hin Taak** (Map p317), a short long-tail boat ride around the bay.

Ibex Climbing & Tours ROCK CLIMBING
(Map p320; ☎075 601370, 084 309 0445; www.ibexclimbingandtours.com; Ton Sai Village; half/full day 1100/1950B) One of Phi-Phi's newest and best rock-climbing operators. Rates include instruction and gear.

Courses

Pum Restaurant & Cooking School COOKING COURSE
(Map p320; ☎081 521 8904; www.pumthaifoodchain.com; 125/40 Mu 7, Ton Sai Village; per person 500-4000B; ⏲classes 11am, 4pm & 6pm) Thai-food fans can take highly recommended cooking courses ranging from half-hour, one-dish sessions to five-hour 'healthy lifestyle' extravaganzas. You'll learn the secrets behind some of the excellent dishes served in their Ton Sai Village restaurant and go home with a cookbook.

Tours

Ever since Leo (DiCaprio) smoked a spliff in the film rendition of Alex Garland's *The Beach*, Phi-Phi Leh has been something of a pilgrimage site. Aside from long-tail boat trips to Phi-Phi Leh and Ko Mai Phai, tour agencies organise sunset tours around Phi-Phi Leh that include Monkey Bay and the beach at Wang Long.

PP Original Sunset Tour BOAT TOUR
(Map p320; Ton Sai Village; per person 900B; ⏲tour 1pm) A sensational sunset cruise that sees you bobbing around Phi-Phi Leh aboard a double-decker boat to mellow beats, snorkelling and kayaking between Ao Pi Leh's sheer-sided cliffs and dining on fried rice off Maya Beach, led by an enthusiastic, organised team. Bliss.

Maya Bay Sleepaboard BOAT TOUR
(www.mayabaytours.com; per person 3000B) You can no longer camp on Phi-Phi Leh's Maya Beach, but you can spend the night just offshore. Prices include food, sleeping bags and national park entry fees; tours depart at 3pm, returning at 10am the following morning. The same team runs the popular **Plankton Sunset Cruise** (www.mayabaytours.com; per person 1200B; ⏲3-8pm) to Phi-Phi Leh. Book at any Ton Sai travel agent.

Captain Bob's Booze Cruise BOAT TOUR
(Map p320; ☎084 848 6970; www.phiphiboozecruise.com; women/men 2500/3000B; ⏲tour 1pm) Phi-Phi's latest buzz-worthy excursion: you're cruising the waters around Phi-Phi Don and Phi-Phi Leh, on a sail boat, adult beverage in hand.

Sleeping

Finding accommodation on this popular island has never been easy. Expect serious room shortages and extortionate rates, especially at peak holiday times. Masses of touts meet incoming boats and, while often annoying, can make your life easier.

Break-ins are a problem: lock the door while you sleep and close all windows when you go out.

Ton Sai Village & Ao Lo Dalam บ้านต้นไทร/อ่าวโละดาลัม

The flat, packed-out, hourglass-shaped land between Ao Ton Sai and Ao Lo Dalam is crammed with lodging options. Central Ton Sai is called the 'Tourist Village'.

Framed by stunning karst cliffs, the beach at Ao Lo Dalam is arguably Phi-Phi's prettiest. But it's clogged with people and long-tail boats, and polluted by beach bars and day visitors.

There's an insane amount of (loud) construction going on in this area. More and more identical, basic-job dorm rooms are popping up, particularly behind popular clubs on Ao Lo Dalam.

Blanco HOSTEL $
(Map p320; ☎093 638 3781; Ao Lo Dalam; dm 470-625B; ❄📶) This bare-bones (bring your own top sheet!) but modern party hostel offers four- to eight-bed dorms in concrete-floor bamboo chalets. Digs are cramped, there's usually sand on the floor and mattresses are gym-mat hard, but this is where the hardcore revellers stay, thanks to the fun-loving vibe and super-sociable beach bar with cushioned lounges and a pool table.

Prepare to keep vampire hours.

Ibiza House HOSTEL, HOTEL $
(Map p320; ☎075 601274, 080 537 1868; ibizahouseppth@gmail.com; Ao Lo Dalam; dm 450-700B, r incl breakfast 2000-5500B; ❄📶🏊) Ibiza House stacks up points for its popular, well-kept (slightly sandy) 10-bed air-con dorms with hot showers, safes and wi-fi, and lively party atmosphere, and also has a collection of shiny white doubles and 'villas'. All guests can use the pool – which hosts regular Sunday parties.

Rock Backpacker HOSTEL $
(Map p320; ☎081 607 3897; Ton Sai Village; dm 300B, r fan/air-con 800/1600B; ❄📶) A proper hostel on the village hill, with clean dorms lined with bunk beds, tiny private rooms, an inviting restaurant-bar and a rugged, graffiti-scrawled exterior. It's still one of Ton Sai's cheaper pads and there's a buzzing backpacker scene – just don't expect a friendly welcome. Walk-ins only.

Ton Sai Village

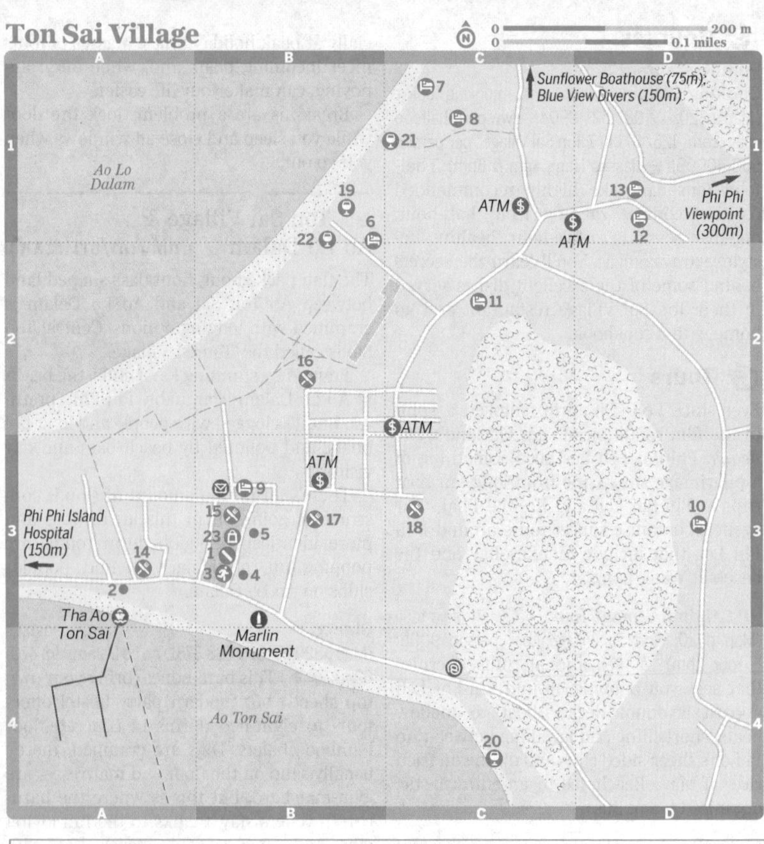

Ton Sai Village

Activities, Courses & Tours
1 Adventure Club ... B3
2 Captain Bob's Booze Cruise ... A3
3 Ibex Climbing & Tours ... B3
4 PP Original Sunset Tour ... B3
5 Pum Restaurant & Cooking School ... B3
Sea Frog Diving ... (see 15)

Sleeping
6 Anita Resort ... B1
7 Blanco ... C1
8 Ibiza House ... C1
9 JJ Residence ... B3
10 Oasis Guesthouse ... D3
11 Rock Backpacker ... C2
12 Tropical Garden Bungalows ... D1
13 Up Hill Cottage ... D1

Eating
14 Le Grand Bleu ... A3
15 Local Food Market ... B3
16 Only Noodles ... B2
17 Papaya 2 ... B3
18 Papaya Restaurant ... C3
Unni's ... (see 15)

Drinking & Nightlife
19 4Play ... B1
20 Carlito's ... C4
21 Ibiza ... C1
22 Slinky ... B1

Shopping
23 D's Bookshop ... B3

Oasis Guesthouse GUESTHOUSE $
(Map p320; ☎075 601207; 115 Mu 7, Ton Sai Village; r 700-800B; ❄📶) Up the side road east of central Ton Sai you'll find this cute, simple guesthouse with wooden shutters, surrounded by trees. Freshly painted rooms have

gleaming bathrooms. Staff can be surly. No reservations: it's first-come, first-served.

JJ Residence HOTEL $$
(Map p320; ☎075 601098; www.jjresidence.com; 95 Mu 7, Ton Sai Village; r 2500B; ❄📶🏊) Spacious tiled rooms with smart wood panelling, beamed ceilings, duvets, mini fridges, built-in desks and wardrobes and private terraces make this one of Ton Sai's better choices. Rooms on the 1st floor spill out onto the pool with its feature waterfall. A new, similar-style block directly opposite should be ready by the time you read this.

Up Hill Cottage BUNGALOW $$
(Map p320; ☎075 601124; www.phiphiuphillcottage.com; 140 Mu 7, Ton Sai Village; r fan 1200B, air-con 2000-2500B; ❄📶) These newly renovated, cream-painted wood-panelled bungalows come in cute pastels offset by colourful bed runners and snazzily tiled bathrooms. Most enjoy island views from private balconies. Cheaper fan rooms are simple but still clean. It's *slightly* beyond the madness, at the eastern end of the main street heading north from Ton Sai Village. Beware the hundreds of stairs.

Tropical Garden Bungalows BUNGALOW $$
(Map p320; ☎089 729 1436; www.thailandphiphitravel.com; Ton Sai Village; r fan 1100-1300B, air-con 1400-2300B; ❄📶🏊) If you don't mind walking 10 minutes to eat, drink or sunbathe, you'll love Tropical Garden, near the viewpoint path. Rooms are offered in a million shapes, sizes and budgets: frontier-style log cabins, modern concrete air-con rooms, and even the smallest options have a bit of character. There's a flower-fringed pool with a swim-up bar.

Anita Resort RESORT $$
(Map p320; ☎075 601282; www.phiphianitaresort.com; Ao Lo Dalam ; r 2700-4500B; ❄📶🏊) Just back from Ao Lo Dalam, this three-star resort has shiny-floored bungalows tastefully done up with pink-tiled bathrooms, wood-carved-elephant lamps, those rare floor-to-ceiling headboards and sliding glass doors that open onto private decks overlooking the pool. Opposite, newer 'deluxe' rooms with flat-screen TVs are more contemporary.

Sunflower Boathouse GUESTHOUSE $$
(Map p317; ☎080 038 3374; www.facebook.com/pages/Sunflower-Boathouse-Phi-Phi/101127755691; Ao Lo Dalam; r fan/air-con 1200/1500B; ❄📶) Lovingly built, varnished dark-wood rooms with a bit of space and character sporting colourful bed-throws are spread across a thatch-roofed, ship-like structure, cosied up to the wonderfully chilled-out Sunflower Bar (p323) at the northern end of Ao Lo Dalam. Simple and welcoming.

Hat Hin Khom หาดหินคม

A 15-minute beach or jungle walk east of Ao Ton Sai, this area has a few small white-sand beaches in rocky coves.

Viking Natures Resort BUNGALOW $$
(Map p317; ☎083 649 9492, 075 819399; www.vikingnaturesresort.com; Hat Hin Khom; bungalow 1200-6000B; ❄📶) OK, it's wacky in every way (and definitely not the place to stay if you're afraid of jungle critters), but if it's character you're after, Viking's wood, thatch and bamboo bungalows (decorated with driftwood, shell curtains, stone-cut sinks and hammock-decked lounging spaces that enjoy fabulous views of Phi-Phi Leh) are just the ticket.

We say splurge on the large wooden lodge rooms that open onto inviting verandas.

Hat Yao หาดยาว

This lively stretch of pure-white south-coast beach is perfect for swimming, but don't expect it to yourself. You can walk here in 30 minutes from Ton Sai via Hat Hin Khom or take long-tails (100B to 150B) from Ton Sai pier.

Paradise Pearl Bungalow RESORT $$
(Map p317; ☎075 601248; www.phiphiparadisepearl.com; Hat Yao; r incl breakfast 3000-6000B; ❄📶) A sprawling complex of dark-wood Thai chalets, decked out with art and updated electronics, tucked into the rocky headland on the northern curl of Hat Yao. Delightfully old-fashioned beach-facing wooden 'houses' have four-poster beds, lace curtains and tea/coffee stands. The loungey **restaurant** (mains 120-400B; ⏰7.30am-10pm; 📶), typically packed with young couples, rambles to the edge of the sand.

★**Paradise Resort Phi Phi** HOTEL $$$
(Map p317; ☎081 968 3982; www.paradiseresort.co.th; Hat Yao; bungalow 2900-6500B; ❄📶) Freshly built, impeccably kept seafront villas at this sparkly white resort are plush with floor-to-ceiling windows, massive semi-open-air bathrooms, indoor-outdoor showers, colour feature walls, kettles, fridges, hairdryers and wooden sun loungers on the front deck. Older villas at the back are per-

fectly comfy, bright and clean, and they also have smart wood-panelled 'Thai-modern' rooms. Superb low-season deals. Online bookings only.

Hat Rantee หาดรันตี

Still low-key, this small, remote, grey-gold eastern bay has modest family bungalows and good snorkelling. Arrive by long-tail from Ton Sai's pier (600B; return per person 200B, minimum four people; resorts provide free pick up if you've booked) or via the strenuous 45-minute hike over the viewpoint.

Rantee Cliff Beach Resort BUNGALOWS $$
(Map p317; 087 474 7770; www.phiphirantee-cliff.com; bungalow incl breakfast 2500-5000B;) Fronted by swaying orange and purple hammocks, Rantee's newest offering surprises with character-packed, pointy-roofed chunky bamboo bungalows overlooking a gorgeous patch of sand. All have bright-blue throws, in-room sinks, soaring thatched ceilings, sunken bathrooms, gauzy mosquito netting, tea/coffee kits and fridges. It's tucked into the headland at the southern end of Hat Rantee.

PP Rantee BUNGALOW $$
(Map p317; 092 124 0599; bungalow fan 1500B, air-con 2500-4500;) Basic, acceptable woven bamboo bungalows and newer, clean, tiled concrete bungalows with air-con and wide porches overlooking a trim garden path that leads to the sand. It also has an excellent restaurant and a wooden tree-swing out front.

Hat Phak Nam หาดผักน้ำ

This gorgeous white-sand beach shares its bay with a small fishing hamlet. Charter a long-tail from Ao Ton Sai (1000B; 200B by shared taxi boat to return) or make the sweaty one-hour hike over the viewpoint.

★**Relax Beach Resort** BUNGALOW $$
(Map p317; 089 475 6536; www.phiphirelaxresort.com; bungalow 2100-5200B;) These 47 lacquered Thai-style bungalows, with wood floors, thatched roofs, two-tiered terraces with lounging cushions and mosaic bathrooms (in the best rooms), are rimmed by lush jungle. There's a good seafood-focused Thai/international **restaurant** (Map p317; Hat Phak Nam; dishes 100-350B; 7.30am-9pm;) and breezy bar, and it's run by charming staff who treat guests like family.

Ao Lo Bakao อ่าวโละบาเกา

Ao Lo Bakao's fine stretch of northeastern palm-backed sand, ringed by dramatic hills, is one of Phi-Phi's loveliest, with offshore views over aqua bliss to Bamboo and Mosquito Islands. A long-tail charter from Ao Ton Sai costs 1000B.

Phi Phi Island Village BUNGALOW $$$
(Map p317; 075 628900; www.phiphiislandvillage.com; r incl breakfast 8400-22,000B;) The 156 wood-and-concrete bungalows take up most of the beachfront, with palms swaying between them. Amenities vary from the family-friendly and casual to romantic dining experiences, pampering spa treatments and dozens of activities. If you have the means, it's good living with a hint of old-school luxury. The resort arranges long-tail transfers to/from Ton Sai.

SLEEPING (OR TRYING TO) ON KO PHI-PHI

Noise pollution on Phi-Phi is terrible and focused on central Ao Ton Sai and Ao Lo Dalam. Don't expect an early night on Hat Hin Khom either. At research time, bars in Dalam and Ton Sai had a 2am curfew (which is more or less observed) though that doesn't stop inebriated revellers from making plenty of other noise (door slamming, dry heaving) or builders bashing away at all hours.

For a shot at peaceful Phi-Phi accommodation, try one of the following:

- Phi-Phi's east coast
- the back road connecting southeast Ao Ton Sai with Ao Lo Dalam
- the hill near the road up to Phi-Phi Viewpoint (p316)
- Hat Yao (p316)

Of course, the best option is probably to grab a bucket and join the fun.

Hat Laem Thong หาดแหลมทอง

Despite the upmarket offerings, this north-eastern white-sand beach is busy and has a small, rubbish-strewn *chow lair* (sea gypsy) settlement at its northern end. Long-tail charters from Ao Ton Sai cost 1200B; hotels arrange transfers.

★Zeavola HOTEL $$$
(Map p317; 075 627000; www.zeavola.com; bungalow incl breakfast 10,600-21,800B;) Hibiscus-lined pathways lead to shady teak bungalows with sleek, distinctly Asian indoor-outdoor floorplans. Each comes with floor-to-ceiling windows on three sides, beautiful 1940s fixtures and antique furniture, huge ceramic sinks, indoor/outdoor showers, tea and coffee pods on a private terrace and impeccable service. The finest villas enjoy their own infinity pools and there's a fabulous couples-oriented spa.

P.P. Erawan Palms Resort HOTEL $$$
(Map p317; 075 627500; www.pperawanpalms.com; r incl breakfast 4200-9000B;) Step onto the grounds and let the stress fall away as you follow a meandering path through gardens to bright, spacious, modern yet traditional-feel 'cottages' and smaller rooms decorated with Thai art and handicrafts. There's an inviting pool bar plus excellent service.

Eating

Most resorts and bungalows have restaurants. Ao Ton Sai is home to some reasonably priced restaurants, but don't expect haute cuisine.

Local Food Market MARKET, THAI $
(Map p320; Ton Sai Village; meals 60-80B; 7am-10pm) Phi-Phi's cheapest, most authentic eats are at the market (which was being renovated at research time), on the narrowest sliver of the isthmus. A handful of enthusiastic local stalls serve up scrumptious *pàt tai*, fried rice, *sôm·đam* and smoked catfish.

Only Noodles THAI $
(Map p320; Ton Sai Village; dishes 60-120B; 11am-10pm) The name tells no lies. You're at this popular tucked-away spot for straightforward, flavour-packed *pàt tai*, served up with your choice of noodles in meat, seafood or veg format at just two simple streetside tables.

Papaya Restaurant THAI $
(Map p320; 087 280 1719; Ton Sai Village; dishes 100-350B; 10am-10.30pm) Cheap, tasty and spicy. Here's some real-deal Thai food served in heaping portions. It has your basil and chilli, all the curries, *sôm·đam* and *đôm yam*, too. There's a second branch, **Papaya 2** (dishes 100-350B; 10am-10pm), a block away.

★Unni's INTERNATIONAL $$
(Map p320; 081 979 2865; Ton Sai Village; mains 200-350B; 8am-midnight;) Swing by this local expat fave for homemade breakfast bagels topped with everything from smoked salmon to meatballs or specials like avocado-and-feta toast. Other excellent global treats include massive Greek salads, pastas, burritos, nachos, burgers, tapas, cocktails and more. It's a chic cafe-lounge–style place with contemporary mood music.

Le Grand Bleu THAI, FRENCH $$
(Map p320; 081 979 9739; 137 Mu 7, Ton Sai Village; mains 160-360B; 6.30-11pm) Thai–French fusion in a charming wooden house with a trickling fountain, wall art and a colourful concrete bar, just off the main pier. Here you can get duck oven-roasted with honey, shrimp as ravioli, king prawns cooked in pesto and creamy mushroom tagliatelle, plus a selection of southern Thai specialities, accompanied by international wines.

Drinking & Nightlife

A rowdy party scene saturates Phi-Phi. Buckets of cheap whiskey and Red Bull and sickly-sweet cocktails make this the domain for gap-year craziness and really bad hangovers. If you're crashing within earshot of the party, you might as well enjoy it.

★Sunflower Bar BAR
(Map p317; Ao Lo Dalam; 11am-2am;) Poetically ramshackle, this driftwood gem is still Phi-Phi's most chilled-out bar. Destroyed in the 2004 tsunami, it was rebuilt with reclaimed wood. The long-tail booths are named for the four loved ones the owner lost in the deluge.

Slinky CLUB
(Map p320; Ao Lo Dalam; 9pm-2am) Forever the beach dancefloor of the moment. One of several Dalam nightspots with standard over-the-top fire shows, buckets of candy-juice cocktails and throngs of Thais, expats and tourists mingling, flirting and flailing to throbbing bass on the sand.

BOATS TO/FROM KO PHI-PHI DON

DESTINATION	FARE (B)	DURATION (HR)	TO KO PHI-PHI	FROM KO PHI-PHI
Ao Nang	350	1¾	9.30am	3.30pm
Ko Lanta	250-700	1½	8am, 12.30pm, 1pm & 4pm	11.30am & 3pm
Krabi	250-300	1½-2	9am, 10.30am, 1.30pm & 3	9am, 10.30am, 1.30pm & 3.30pm
Phuket	250-300	1¼-2	9am, 11am & 3pm	9am, 2pm, 2.30pm & 3.30pm
Railay	350-400	1¼	9.45am	3.30pm

Ibiza CLUB
(Map p320; Ao Lo Dalam; ⊙9pm-2am) Another of Dalam's beach dens of inebriation and iniquity (but, you know, in a good way). Relax on beachside cushions and marvel at expert fire twirlers and drunken daredevils as they jump through fiery hoops and limbo beneath a fiery cane, while everyone else dances and fist-pumps to bone-rattling bass.

4Play CLUB
(Map p320; Ao Lo Dalam; ⊙9pm-2am) If Dalam's frenzied clubs start to feel the same after a few (buckets), that's because they're pretty much identical: 4Play has the usual mix of electrifying fire throwing, tight-rope walking and throbbing bass.

Carlito's BAR
(Map p320; www.carlitosbar.net; Ao Ton Sai; ⊙11am-1am) For a (slightly) toned-down take on Dalam's fire-twirling madness, pull up a plastic chair on the sand at this fairy-light-lit beachside bar, which puts on fun fire shows and attracts beer- and cocktail-seeking *fa·ràng* (Westerners). It can get a bit rowdy on party nights.

Shopping

D's Bookshop BOOKS
(Map p320; Ton Sai Village; ⊙10am-10pm) Swaps and sells new and used fiction and travel guides (English, German, French, Italian).

ℹ Information

ATMs are spread thickly throughout the Tourist Village but aren't available on the eastern beaches. Wi-fi is everywhere.

Phi Phi Island Hospital (Map p317; ☎075 622 151; Ao Ton Sai) Emergency care, at the west end of Ao Ton Sai. For anything truly serious, you're on the first boat to Krabi or Phuket.

Post Office (Map p320; Ton Sai Village; ⊙9am-5pm Mon-Fri & 9am-1pm Sat)

ℹ Getting There & Away

Ko Phi-Phi can be reached from Ao Nang, Krabi, Phuket, Railay and Ko Lanta. Most boats moor at Ao Ton Sai, though a few from Phuket use isolated, northern Tha Laem Thong (Map p317). Phuket, Krabi and Ao Nang ferries operate year-round, while Ko Lanta boats only run from October to April.

There are also combined boat-minivan tickets to destinations across Thailand, including Bangkok (550B to 600B, 11 hours, 5pm and 5.30pm), Ko Samui (400B to 500B, 6½ hours, 11am and 4pm) and Ko Pha-Ngan (500B to 600B, seven hours, 11am and 4pm).

ℹ Getting Around

There are no roads on Ko Phi-Phi Don. Transport is mostly by foot, though long-tails can be chartered at Ao Ton Sai for short hops around both islands.

Long-tails leave Ao Ton Sai pier for Hat Yao (100B to 150B), Hat Rantee (600B), Hat Phak Nam and Ao Lo Bakao (1000B), Laem Thong (1200B) and Viking Cave (on Ko Phi-Phi Leh; 600B). Chartering a long-tail for three/six hours costs 1500/3000B; a half-day speedboat charter costs 5000B.

Ko Phi-Phi Leh เกาะพีพีเล

Rugged Phi-Phi Leh is the smaller of the two Phi-Phi Islands, protected on all sides by soaring, jagged cliffs. Coral reefs crawling with marine life lie beneath the crystal-clear waters and are hugely popular with day-tripping snorkellers (so there's some coral damage and a huge amount of rubbish).

There are no places to stay on Phi-Phi Leh. Most people visit on a day trip or sunset cruise with one of the ludicrously popular tours (p319) out of Phi-Phi Don. Tours last half a day, including various snorkelling stops around the island and detours to Viking Cave and Ao Maya. Long-tail trips cost 700B to 800B; by motorboat you'll pay 2500B. The national park day-use fee (adult/child 400/200B) is payable upon landing.

You can no longer camp on Phi-Phi Leh, but you can still swing by Maya Beach at dusk and sleep on a boat bobbing offshore with Maya Bay Sleepaboard (p319).

Sights & Activities

Viking Cave CAVE

(Tham Phaya Naak) On the northeastern tip of the island, Viking Cave is a major collection point for outrageously valuable swifts' nests, the key components of Chinese speciality bird's-nest soup. Nimble collectors scamper up fragile bamboo scaffolding to the roof of the cave to gather the nests. Before ascending, they pray and make offerings of tobacco, incense and liquor. The cave gets its misleading moniker from the 400-year-old boat graffiti created by crews of passing Chinese fishing junks.

At research time, visitors were not allowed inside the cave, but most tour boats slow down for a good glimpse.

Ao Pileh LAKE

Of the two gorgeous emerald lagoons that await in Phi-Phi Leh's interior, Pileh lies on the eastern coast. It's predictably busy, but the thrill of kayaking between these towering limestone walls never gets old.

Ao Maya BAY

(Maya Bay; adult/child 400/200B) Dramatically flanked by green-clad cliffs, majestic Ao Maya sits on Phi-Phi Leh's western shoreline. In 1999, its beautiful sands were controversially used as a set for *The Beach*, based on Alex Garland's cult novel. Natural sand dunes were flattened and extra palm trees planted to increase the paradisaical backdrop and, although the production's team restored things, many claim the damage to the ecosystem has been permanent.

The level of boat traffic here nowadays somewhat detracts from the serenity, but the setting is still spectacular.

Ko Jum & Ko Si Boya เกาะจำ/เกาะศรีบอยา

Just north of Ko Lanta, Ko Jum and its low-lying neighbour Ko Si Boya have surprisingly little development; what's there is tucked away in the trees. There's little more to do than wander the long, broad beaches and soak up the islands' refreshingly rustic beauty.

Ko Jum was once the exclusive domain of Lanta's *chow lair* people, but ethnic Chinese began arriving after Chairman Mao came to power in the 1950s. At the time there were no Thai people living here at all, but eventually the three cultures merged into one, a mix best sampled early in the morning amid the ramshackle poetry of Ban Ko Jum, the fishing village on the southeast side of the island.

Although technically one island, local people consider only the flatter southern part of Ko Jum to be Ko Jum. The northern hilly bit is Ko Pu.

Activities

Koh Jum Divers DIVING

(082 273 7603; www.kohjum-divers.com; Koh Jum Beach Villas, Ko Jum; 2 dives 4600-5500B, Open Water certification 15,800B; 10am-7pm) Ko Jum's only, west-coast dive operation hits all the Lanta and Phi-Phi sites. Snorkellers can tag along for about half price.

Sleeping & Eating

Accommodation is strung out along Ko Jum's west coast. Most resorts have on-site restaurants; some close for the May-to-October low season.

Bodaeng BUNGALOW $

(081 494 8760; Hat Yao, Ko Jum; bungalow 250-300B) A good old-fashioned hippie vortex with dirt-cheap bamboo bungalows and a couple of slightly newer wood huts, sprinkled in the trees. Expect squat toilets in the corrugated-tin bathrooms and very limited electricity. Nonetheless, it's a hit with returning travellers, who bring along a sociable high-season scene, and the owner is a charmer.

Siboya Bungalows BUNGALOW $

(081 979 3344; www.siboyabungalows.com; Ko Si Boya; bungalow 350B, house 500-1200B; @) OK, Ko Si Boya's beach isn't spectacular. But the mangrove setting is wild and full of life, the bungalows and private homes are large, stylish and affordable, and the excellent restaurant is wired with high-speed internet. No wonder ever-smiling, secretive 50-somethings flock here like it's a retiree's version of Alex Garland's *The Beach*. There are family-friendly homes that sleep four people.

★Woodland Lodge BUNGALOW $$

(☎081 893 5330; www.woodland-koh-jum.com; Hat Yao, Ko Jum; standard/family bungalow 1100/1500B;) Tasteful, clean, fan-cooled bamboo huts with proper thatched roofs, polished wood floors and verandahs, spaciously laid out across shady grounds, make this our favourite spot on Ko Jum. Concrete-and-wood family bungalows sleep three. The friendly British-Thai owners organise boat trips and run the excellent on-site **Fighting Fish Restaurant** (mains 100-200B; ⏲8am-4pm & 6-10pm;).

Koh Jum Beach Villas VILLA $$$

(☎086 184 0505; www.kohjumbeachvillas.com; Hat Yao, Ko Jum; villa incl breakfast 12,800-26,900B;) Spacious, elegant privately owned wooden homes with four-poster beds, cosy decks and sea views sprawl back among frangipani- and bougainvillea-filled gardens from a luscious golden beach. Some have romantic private infinity pools. The team keeps things as environmentally and socially responsible as possible. Staff are delightful, the **restaurant** (mains 190-350B; ⏲8am-10pm;) and bar scrumptious.

There's no air-con, but villas are built to catch ocean breezes. Some have up to five bedrooms, making them ideal for families.

Koh Jum Lodge RESORT $$$

(☎089 921 1621; www.kohjumlodge.com; Hat Yao, Ko Jum; bungalow incl breakfast 4500-7000B; ⏲Nov-Apr;) An ecolodge with style: lots of hardwoods and bamboo, gauzy mosquito netting, coconut palms, Thai carvings, silk throws, manicured grounds, massage pavilions and a hammock-strewn curve of white sand out front. It strikes that hard-to-get balance of authenticity and comfort.

Hong Yong Restaurant THAI $

(Ban Ting Rai, Ko Jum; mains 80-100B; ⏲8am-10pm) Local food talk sends you inland to this pastel-pink makeshift village restaurant, where bubbly Rosa sizzles up huge portions of delicious Thai curries, stir fries and international breakfasts. Try the fragrant massaman curry or the seasonal seafood specials. Also known as Rosa's.

ℹ Getting There & Away

From November to May, the boat from Krabi to Ko Lanta will drop you at Ko Jum, for the full fare (400B, one hour, 11.30am); boats return from Lanta at 8.30am. In high season, daily boats run from Ko Jum to Ko Phi-Phi (600B, 1½ hours) at 8.30am, collecting guests from the Hat Yao resorts; boats return from Phi-Phi at 2.30pm.

There are year-round long-tails to Ko Jum from Ban Laem Kruat, 38km southeast of Krabi at the end of Rte 4036, off Hwy 4. Boats (100B, 30 minutes) leave at 9am, 10am, 11.30am, 1pm, 2.30pm, 4pm, 5.30pm and 6.15pm, and return at 6.30am, 7.15am, 7.35am, 7.55am, 8.10am, 1.30pm, 2.30pm and 4pm.

If you're arriving on Ko Jum via Laem Kruat, note that boats run to three different piers; Ban Ko Jum and Mu Tu piers are most convenient. Guesthouses will arrange transfers from the piers if you call in advance. Otherwise, you're relying on the kindness of strangers.

Daily boats to Ko Si Boya (50B, 15 minutes) run from Laem Kruat every hour between 8am and 5.30pm, returning hourly from 6.15am to 5pm. Call Siboya Resort (p325) to arrange transfer from the pier.

Sŏrng·tăa·ou meet boats at Laem Kruat and go to Krabi (100B), via Krabi airport and Nua Khlong (where you can connect for Ko Lanta).

ℹ Getting Around

Several places in Ban Ko Jum and some Ko Jum guesthouses rent bicycles (100B) and motorbikes (250B).

Ko Lanta เกาะลันตา

POP 26,800

Once the domain of backpackers and sea gypsies, Lanta has morphed from a luscious southern Thai backwater into a mid-range-to-luxury getaway for mostly-European tourists, who come for the divine miles-long beaches unpolluted by jet skis (though the northern coast is alarmingly eroded) and nearby dive spots of Hin Daeng, Hin Muang and Ko Haa.

Within eyeshot of Phi-Phi, charming Lanta remains far more calm, real and culturally rich, and effortlessly caters to all tastes and budgets. It's also relatively flat compared to its karst-formation neighbours, and laced with good roads that run 22km from north to south, so is easily explored by motorbike. A quick loop reveals a colourful crucible of cultures – fried-chicken stalls sit below slender minarets, stilted *chow lair* villages cling to the island's east side, and small Thai wát hide within green-brown tangles of curling mangroves.

Ko Lanta is technically called Ko Lanta Yai. Boats pull into dusty two-street Ban Sala Dan, on the northern tip of the island.

Sights

★ Ban Si Raya — VILLAGE

(บ้านศรีรายา, Lanta Old Town; Map p330) Halfway down Lanta's eastern coast, Ban Si Raya was the island's original port and commercial centre, providing a safe harbour for Arabic and Chinese trading vessels sailing between Phuket, Penang and Singapore. It was Lanta's administrative capital from 1901 to 1998. Some of the gracious, well-kept wooden century-old stilt houses and shopfronts have been transformed into beautifully dated guesthouses. Pier restaurants offer fresh catch overlooking the sea, and there are some cute bohemian shops dotted around.

Tham Khao Maikaeo — CAVE

(ถ้ำเขาไม้แก้ว; Map p330; ☎089 288 8954; tour 300B) Monsoon rains pounding away at limestone crevices for millions of years have created this complex of caverns and tunnels. There are cathedral-size chambers, dripping with stalactites and stalagmites, tiny passages you have to squeeze through on hands and knees, and even a subterranean pool. A local family runs hourly treks to the caves (with headlamps). The full trip takes two hours; sensible shoes essential. It's signposted off the main road from Hat Khlong Tob to the east coast. Phone ahead for timings.

Tham Seua — CAVE

(ถ้ำเสือ, Tiger Cave; Map p330; tour 200B; ⏲Oct-Apr) Reached via a signposted track heading east off the national park headquarters road, 2km south of Hat Khlong Nin, Tham Seua has interesting tunnels to explore via guided one-to-two-hour tours (with individual headlamps).

Activities

Diving & Snorkelling

Some of Thailand's top diving spots are within arm's reach of Lanta. The best diving can be found at the undersea pinnacles of Hin Muang (p318) and **Hin Daeng**, 45 minutes away by speedboat. These lone mid-sea coral outcrops act as important feeding stations for large pelagic fish such as sharks, tuna, barracudas and occasionally whale sharks and manta rays. Hin Daeng is commonly considered to be Thailand's second-best dive site after Richelieu Rock (p254), near the Myanmar border.

The sites around **Ko Haa** have consistently good visibility, with depths of 18m to

Ko Lanta

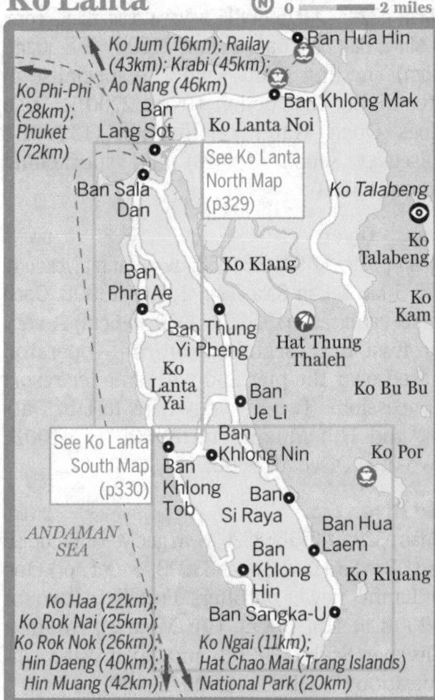

34m, plenty of marine life (including turtles) and a three-chamber cave known as 'the Cathedral'. Lanta dive outfitters run trips up to King Cruiser Wreck (p318), Anemone Reef (p318) and Ko Phi-Phi (p318).

Lanta's dive season is November to April, though some operators run weather-dependent dives during low season. Trips to Hin Daeng and Hin Muang cost 3400B to 4500B; Ko Haa dives are 3100B to 4000B. PADI Open Water courses cost 13,900B to 17,900B. Rates usually exclude national park fees.

From mid-October to April, agencies across Lanta offer four-island snorkelling and kayaking tours (1200B to 1800B) to Ko Rok Nok (p334), the Trang Islands and other nearby isles.

Scubafish — DIVING

(Map p330; ☎075 665095; www.scubafish.com; Ao Kantiang; 2 dives 3500B; ⏲8am-8pm) A long-running southern-based operator with a stellar reputation, Scubafish offers personable, personal programs, including the Liquid Lense underwater photography courses. The three-day dive packages (9975B) are popular. One-day Discover Scuba is 3200B; Open Water certification costs 15,900B to 17,900B; for Hin Daeng/Hin Muang you'll pay 4500B for two dives.

Blue Planet Divers DIVING
(Map p329; ☎075 668165; www.divinglanta.com; 3 Mu 1, Ban Sala Dan; 2 dives 3100B; ⊙8.30am-9pm) The first Lanta school to specialise in free-diving instruction (from 2700B). Also does Open Water certification (13,700B), Discover Scuba (4300B) and snorkelling tours (1500B).

Lanta Diver DIVING
(Map p329; ☎075 668058; www.lantadiver.com; 197/3 Mu 1, Ban Sala Dan; 2 dives 2900B, Open Water certification 13,900B; ⊙10am-6pm) A very professional Scandinavian-run operator, based near the pier and with smaller resort concessions. Two-dive day trips to Hin Daeng and Hin Muang run 3900B to 4700B; two-dive Discover Scuba is 4500B.

Go Dive DIVING
(Map p329; ☎075 668320; www.godive-lanta.com; 6 Mu 1, Ban Sala Dan; 2 dives 3300B; ⊙Oct-Apr) One of Lanta's newer outfitters. Fun dives (two for 4200B at Hin Daeng/Hin Muang), two-dive Discover Scuba (3900B) and Open Water certification (PADI/SSI 13,900/12,900B).

Yoga

Relax Bay (p329) offers high-season drop-in classes (400B), as does Sri Lanta (p331) for 500B.

Oasis Yoga YOGA
(Map p329; ☎085 115 4067; www.oasisyoga-lanta.com; Hat Khlong Dao; class 400B) A dedicated studio halfway down Hat Khlong Dao, with up to four daily high-season drop-in Hatha, Ashtanga or flow yoga, plus detox retreats and teacher training. Reduced schedule May to October; check its website.

Volunteering

Lanta Animal Welfare VOLUNTEERING
(Map p329; ☎084 304 4331; www.lantaanimalwelfare.com; 629 Mu 2, Ban Phra Ae; tour by donation; ⊙9am-5pm) This long-standing animal rescue centre cares for 30 dogs and 60 cats through feeding, sterilising and re-homing, and vaccination and local awareness campaigns. Visitors can join hourly 40-minute facilities tours (low season noon and 3pm only) and play with kittens. The centre also welcomes casual dog-walking visitors and volunteers for longer placements.

Courses

Time for Lime COOKING COURSE
(Map p329; ☎075 684590; www.timeforlime.net; Hat Khlong Dao; class 1800B; ⊙class 4pm) On south Hat Khlong Dao, this popular school-restaurant offers excellent cooking courses with a slightly more exciting recipe selection than most Thai cookery schools, in a professional moulded-concrete kitchen. Five-hour courses can be adapted for vegetarians and there are multiple-class discounts. Profits finance Lanta Animal Welfare. Book ahead.

Sleeping

Ban Sala Dan ท่าศาลาด่าน

Lanta House GUESTHOUSE $
(Map p329; ☎095 547 3873, 075 656277; lantahouse@gmail.com; r fan/air-con 350/450B; ❄📶) A fine budget choice run by an exceptionally friendly family, Lanta House has windowless but sparkling-clean, fan-cooled rooms with dark walls, bamboo beds and lots of style for this price. An extra 100B gets you air-con, a window and a balcony. All share bathrooms.

Hat Khlong Dao หาดคลองดาว

★**Costa Lanta** HOTEL $$$
(Map p329; ☎075 668186; www.costalanta.com; r incl breakfast 6800-9900B; ❄📶🏊) These Zen-like standalone abodes are nestled in a coconut-palm garden laced with tidal canals at the north end of Hat Khlong Dao. Everything from the floors to the walls to the washbasins is polished concrete, and the barn doors of each minimalist-chic cabana open on two sides to maximise space and breezes.

The restaurant is stunning, as is the service and the black sand-edge spill-over pool. Discounts are available if booked online; low-season rates are excellent.

Hat Phra Ae หาดพระแอ

Andaman Sunflower BUNGALOW $
(Map p329; ☎089 969 2610, 075 684668; bungalow 750-1350B; ⊙Oct-Mar; 📶) Hidden amid bougainvillea- and palm-filled gardens, this is a terrific set of wood and bamboo bungalows with built-in platform beds, high palm-leaf ceilings, polished-wood floors, glass-bowl bathroom sinks and hammock-laden verandas. Set back from the beach, these are some of the best upper-budget bungalows around Hat Phra Ae.

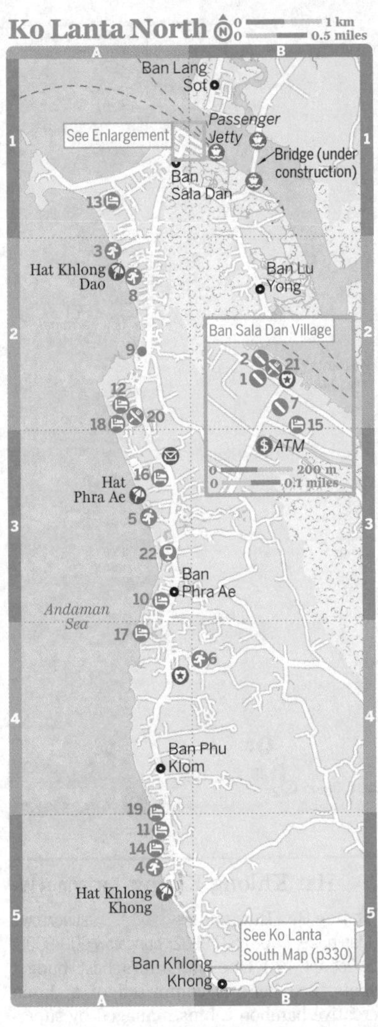

Ko Lanta North

Activities, Courses & Tours
1 Blue Planet Divers....B2
2 Go Dive....B2
3 Hat Khlong Dao....A2
4 Hat Khlong Khong....A5
5 Hat Phra Ae....A3
6 Lanta Animal Welfare....B4
7 Lanta Diver....B2
8 Oasis Yoga....A2
9 Time for Lime....A2

Sleeping
10 Andaman Sunflower....A3
11 Bee Bee Bungalows....A5
12 Chill Out House....A2
13 Costa Lanta....A1
Hutyee Boat....(see 10)
14 Isara Lanta....A5
15 Lanta House....B3
16 Layana Resort....A3
17 Relax Bay....A4
18 Somewhere Else....A2
19 Where Else!....A4

Eating
20 Cook Kai....A2
21 Lanta Seafood....B2
Manao....(see 17)
Red Snapper....(see 10)

Drinking & Nightlife
Feeling Bar....(see 19)
22 Irish Embassy....A3

Chill Out House HOSTEL $
(Map p329; ☎082 183 2258; www.facebook.com/ChillOutHouse; dm 150B, d 220-275B; 📶) This buzzing backpacker 'treehouse community' has simple four-bed dorms, shared bathrooms, chalkboard doors and rickety en-suite doubles. It's basic, but you can't beat the laid-back vibe (or the price): swings at the bar, a communal iPod dock, and a wonderful (yes) chill-out lounge heavy on hammocks.

Hutyee Boat BUNGALOW $
(Map p329; ☎083 633 9723; bungalow 500-700B) A hidden, hippie paradise of big, solid bungalows on stilts with tiled bathrooms, mini fridges and swinging hammocks in a forest of palms and bamboo. It's just back from the beach (behind Nautilus Resort) and run by a friendly Muslim family.

Relax Bay HOTEL $$
(Map p329; ☎075 684194; www.relaxbay.com; Ao Phra Ae; bungalow incl breakfast with fan 1600-2450B, air-con 2450-5100B, luxury tent 2750-3250B; ❄📶🏊) This gorgeous French-run place sprawls over a tree-covered headland by a small beach. Yellow- and red-toned, wood-and-bamboo bungalows sit on stilts with large decks overlooking the bay. There's a lovely tropical-feel pool, plus the good, stylish semi-open-air **Manao restaurant** (mains 140-400B; ⏰7am-9.30pm; 📶) and bar and high-season yoga (400B). It's sightly overpriced, but an absolute steal in low season.

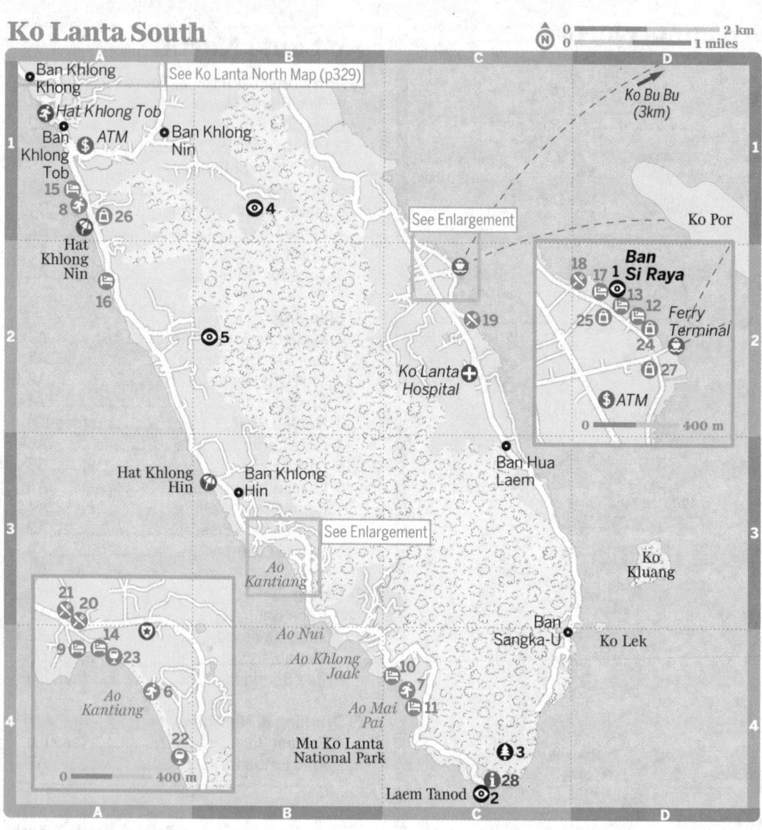

Somewhere Else BUNGALOW **$$**
(Map p329; ☎081 536 0858; bungalow 800-1700B;) Choose between basic thatched bamboo huts with terracotta-tiled bathrooms and bigger octagonal polished-concrete bungalows, all of which dot a shady lawn right on a very popular, social and lounge-worthy stretch of beach.

Layana Resort RESORT **$$$**
(Map p329; ☎075 607100; www.layanaresort.com; r incl breakfast 16,900-28,100B;) The beachfront location, fabulous palm-lined pool and impeccable service make anyone lucky to stay at the slickly contemporary adults-only Layana. Comfy, spacious hardwood rooms with soothing neutral decor, complimentary fruit bowls and a pillow menu mean it's all the more attractive. Rack rates are steep but internet deals can make it a bargain; expect 50% discounts in low season.

Hat Khlong Khong หาดคลองโขง

★ **Bee Bee Bungalows** BUNGALOW **$**
(Map p329; ☎081 537 9932; bungalow 600-900B; Oct-Apr;) One of Lanta's best budget spots, Bee Bee's is comprised of a dozen creative bamboo cabins managed by superfriendly staff. Each bungalow is unique; a few are stilted in the trees. The on-site restaurant has a library of tattered paperbacks to keep you occupied while you wait for your delicious Thai staples.

Where Else! BUNGALOW **$**
(Map p329; ☎075 667173, 081 536 4870; where else_lanta@yahoo.com; bungalow 800-2000B) One of Lanta's little slices of bohemia, thatched bungalows with semi-outdoor cold-water bathrooms are pretty shaky; if you're trying to avoid late-night parties and tropical critters look elsewhere. Still, the place buzzes with backpackers

Ko Lanta South

Top Sights
1 Ban Si Raya ... D2

Sights
2 Laem Tanod ... C4
3 Mu Ko Lanta National Park ... C4
4 Tham Khao Maikaeo ... B1
5 Tham Seua ... B2

Activities, Courses & Tours
6 Ao Kantiang ... A4
7 Ao Mai Pai ... C4
8 Hat Khlong Nin ... A1
Scubafish ... (see 9)

Sleeping
9 Baan Laanta Resort & Spa ... A4
10 Baan Phu Lae ... C4
11 La Laanta ... C4
12 Mango House ... D2
Mu Ko Lanta National Park Accommodation ... (see 28)
13 Old Times ... D2
14 Phra Nang Lanta ... A4
15 Round House ... A1
16 Sri Lanta ... A2
17 Sriraya ... D2

Eating
18 Beautiful Restaurant ... D2
19 Caoutchouc ... C2
20 Drunken Sailors ... A3
La Laanta ... (see 11)
21 Phad Thai Rock'n'Roll ... A3

Drinking & Nightlife
22 Same Same But Different ... A4
23 Why Not Bar ... A4

Shopping
24 Hammock House ... D2
25 Malee Malee ... D2
26 Monkey Biziness ... A1
27 Sunday Market ... D2

Information
28 Mu Ko Lanta National Park Headquarters ... C4
Mu Ko Lanta National Park Visitors Centre ... (see 28)

and there's a fun barefoot-beach vibe that culminates in the popular Feeling Bar (p335). Pricier bungalows are multilevel abodes sleeping up to four.

Low season rates drop by 50% to 70%.

Isara Lanta BUNGALOW **$$**
(Map p329; 088 823 2184; www.isaralanta.com; bungalow fan 500-1300B, air-con 1200-2500B;) A popular little set of neat, pastel-painted, tin-roofed concrete bungalows with woven bamboo flourishes lining a simple flowery path that spreads back behind a rustic blue-and-white-washed restaurant-bar.

Hat Khlong Nin หาดคลองนิน

Round House GUESTHOUSE **$$**
(Map p330; 086 950 9424; www.lantaroundhouse.com; r 1600B, bungalow without/with bathroom 600/1500B, house 3000B;) A cute multi-option find on the north end of the beach. Stilted bamboo and wood fan bungalows are simply styled with (mostly) shared hot-water bathrooms, and are just behind the breezy beachfront restaurant. Also available is a cool two-person adobe round house, concrete rooms fronted by porches and an air-con beach house perfect for families. Good low-season and solo-traveller discounts.

Sri Lanta BOUTIQUE HOTEL **$$$**
(Map p330; 075 662688; www.srilanta.com; r 3400-6900B; Sep-May;) At the southern end of the beach, this decadent ecospot consists of minimalist wooden villas in wild gardens stretching from the beach to a landscaped hillside. There's a chic flower-fringed beachside area with an infinity pool, restaurant and private massage pavilions. The resort strives for low environmental impact by using biodegradable products and minimising energy use and waste.

It also hosts yoga classes (500B) and some retreats.

Ao Kantiang อ่าวกันเตียง

★ **Baan Laanta Resort & Spa** HOTEL **$$**
(Map p330; 075 665091; www.baanlaanta.com; bungalow incl breakfast 2500-4500B;) Landscaped grounds wind around stylish wooden bungalows with terraces and a sultry dark infinity pool refreshed by elephant fountains and surrounded by frangipani trees, all overlooking an idyllic white sandy beach. The bungalows' centrepiece is a futon-style bed on a raised wooden platform under a delicate veil of mosquito netting, beside which lie lounge sofas on varnished terracotta tiles. The Scubafish (p327) dive school is on-site.

WHERE TO STAY ON KO LANTA

Ko Lanta has masses of long good-looking golden beaches, most on the western coast. You'll experience the island in different incarnations depending on where you bed down. Some resorts close for the May-to-October low season; others drop rates by 50%. Resorts usually have their own restaurants and tour-booking facilities.

The building boom means that there are now dozens of good-value roadside spots available, though views are lacking. Reservations are essential in high season.

Ban Sala Dan Decent budget accommodation has sprung up in characterful Ban Sala Dan. It's handy for local-flavoured seafood restaurants and boat arrivals/departures, but not on the beach.

Hat Khlong Dao Once an outstanding 2km white-sand stretch perfect for swimming, this beach has become so eroded that at high tide there's no sand at all. That's a big issue throughout northern Lanta.

Hat Phra Ae (Long Beach) A large travellers' village (*fa·ràng*-oriented restaurants, beach bars, tour offices) has grown up along sandy Hat Phra Ae, 3km south of Ban Sala Dan. The beach has suffered erosion recently, but there's a nice stretch on its northern flank.

Hat Khlong Khong This is thatched-roof, Rasta-bar bliss with beach volleyball, moon parties and the occasional well-advertised mushroom shake, 9km south of Ban Sala Dan. It's all pretty low-key. The thinning yet ample stretch of beach goes on forever in either direction lapped by turquoise shallows.

Hat Khlong Nin The main road heading south forks 13km south of Ban Sala Dan (after Hat Khlong Tob). The left road leads to the east coast; the right road hugs the coastline for 14km to Ko Lanta's southernmost tip. On the right fork the first beach is lovely white-sand Hat Khlong Nin, which has lots of small, flashpacker-type guesthouses at its north end. Shop around.

Ao Kantiang This superb southwestern sweep of sand backed by mountains is also its own self-contained village with mini-marts, motorbike rental and restaurants. It's upmarket-ish and far from everything. Don't expect to move much.

Ao Mai Pai A lush nearly forgotten cove at the southwestern curve just before the cape, Ao Mai Pai is one of Lanta's finest beaches. Backed by elegant palm groves, with a rock reef jutting north, a jungle-swathed headland to the south and jade waters between.

Laem Tanod The wild, jungled, mountainous southern tip of the island has sheer drops and massive views.

Ban Si Raya There are a handful of guesthouses in Lanta's oft-ignored, wonderfully dated and incredibly rich east-coast Old Town, which has its own bohemian groove.

Phra Nang Lanta HOTEL $$$

(Map p330; ☎075 665025; www.vacationvillage.co.th/phrananglanta; r 5900-9500B; ❄@🛜🏊) These 15 gorgeous, Mexican-style, adobe-looking concrete studios are straight off the pages of an interiors magazine. Think: clean lines, hardwoods and whites accented with vibrant colours, lounge cushions and ceramic sinks. Outside, flowers and foliage climb over bamboo lattice sunshades, and the pool and restaurant-bar look over the beautiful beach. Excellent low-season deals.

Ao Mai Pai อ่าวไม้ไผ่

Baan Phu Lae BUNGALOW $$

(Map p330; ☎075 665100, 085 474 0265; www.baanphulaeresort.com; Ao Mai Pai; bungalow fan 1800B, air-con 2000-2400B; ❄🛜) Set on secluded rocks at the northern end of the final beach before Lanta's southern cape, this collection of cute, canary-yellow concrete fan and air-con bungalows have thatched roofs, colourful art, bamboo beds and private porches. Just behind stand stilted, wooden, air-con bungalows. They also arrange diving and snorkelling trips, cooking classes, massages and transport.

★**La Laanta** BOUTIQUE HOTEL $$$
(Map p330; ☎087 883 9977, 087 883 9966; www.lalaanta.com; bungalow incl breakfast 2800-6200B;) Operated by a young English-speaking Thai-Vietnamese couple, this is the grooviest spot on Lanta. Thatched bungalows have polished-concrete floors, platform beds, floral-design murals and decks overlooking a sandy volleyball pitch, which blends into a rocky beach. The laid-back **restaurant** (mains 120-350B; ⏱8am-9pm;) does a tasty Thai menu with lots of veggie-friendly choices. It's the last turn before the national park, far from everything else.

They provide extra beds for children and there's a kids' swimming pool. Steep low-season discounts.

Laem Tanod แหลมโตนด

Mu Ko Lanta National Park Accommodation BUNGALOW, CAMPGROUND $
(Map p330; ☎075 660711, in Bangkok 02 561 4292; www.dnp.go.th; bungalow 1500-3000B, camp site per person 40B, with tent hire 300B) Engulfed by craggy outcrops and the sound of crashing waves, the secluded national park headquarters grounds are a gloriously serene place to stay, in simple four- to eight-person bungalows or tents. There are toilets, running water and a shop, but bring your own food. You can also get permission for camping on Ko Rok here.

The road to the marine national park headquarters fords the *klorng* (canal; also spelt *khlong*), which can get deep during the monsoon.

Ban Si Raya บ้านศรีรายา

Sriraya GUESTHOUSE $
(Map p330; ☎075 697045; punpun_3377@hotmail.com; r with shared bathroom 500B) Sleep in a simple but beautifully restored, thick-beamed Chinese shophouse with plenty of style and a friendly welcome. Walls are brushed in earth tones and sheets are bright. Go for the street-front balcony room overlooking the Old Town's characterful centre.

Old Times GUESTHOUSE $$
(Map p330; ☎075 697255, 098 567 2855; www.theoldtimeslanta.com; Ban Si Raya; r fan 900B, air-con 1200-2000B;) A fabulous new Old Town addition, tucked into two stylishly revamped 100-year-old teak houses facing each other across the street. Impeccably styled rooms grace various sizes and budgets, under music-inspired names like 'Yellow Submarine'. The best – bright and decked with black-and-white photos – jut out over the sea on the jetty, where there's a cushioned communal chill-out area. Fun, fresh and friendly.

★**Mango House** GUESTHOUSE $$$
(Map p330; ☎095 014 0658; www.mangohouses.com; ste 2500-3000B, 2-person villa 4000B;) These century-old Chinese teak pole houses and former opium dens are stilted over the harbour. The original time-worn wood floors are intact, ceilings soar and the three, house-sized suites are kitted out with kitchenettes, satellite TVs, DVD players and ceiling fans. There are also newly built Old Town–style seafront villas sleeping two to six people. Rates drop by 50% in low season.

Eating

The best-value places for a feed are the seafood restaurants along the northern edge of Ban Sala Dan, which offer fresh seafood sold by weight (including cooking costs) on verandahs over the water.

Phad Thai Rock'n'Roll THAI $
(Map p330; www.facebook.com/phadthairock77; Ao Kantiang; mains 90-150B; ⏱11am-9pm) It's not every day you get your spiced-to-taste *pàt tai* whipped up streetside by a guitarist. Choose from just six options ('jazz' fried rice, 'blues' fried noodles; veg, meat or seafood), swiftly and artfully prepared in simple contemporary surrounds. With about as many tables as dishes, it's deservedly popular, so you may have to wait.

Cook Kai THAI $
(Map p329; www.cook-kai.com; Hat Phra Ae; mains 75-350B; ⏱8am-10pm;) A huge family-run eatery where shells dangle from a thatched roofed. Cook Kai is best for its wide selection of straightforward local staples, which takes in everything from spicy Thai salads, noodle soups and fried rice to sizzling seafood hotpans and deep-fried or steamed fish.

★**Drunken Sailors** INTERNATIONAL, THAI $$
(Map p330; ☎075 665076; www.facebook.com/DrunkenSailors; Ao Kantiang; mains 90-150B; ⏱9am-3pm & 6-10pm;) This relaxed octagonal pod is smothered in beanbags, hammocks and low-lying tables spilling out onto a terrace. The global, want-to-eat-it-all

WORTH A TRIP

MU KO LANTA NATIONAL PARK

Mu Ko Lanta National Park (อุทยานแห่งชาติหมู่เกาะลันตา; Map p330; ☎075 660711, in Bangkok 02 561 4292; www.dnp.go.th; adult/child/motorbike 200/100/20B; ⊙8am-6pm) Established in 1990, this marine national park protects 16 islands in the Ko Lanta group, including the southern tip of Ko Lanta Yai. The park is increasingly threatened by the runaway development on west-coast Ko Lanta Yai, though other islands in the group have fared slightly better.

Ko Rok Nai is still very beautiful, with a crescent-shaped bay backed by cliffs, fine coral reefs and a sparkling white-sand beach. Camping is permitted on adjacent **Ko Rok Nok** with permission from the park headquarters. On the eastern side of Ko Lanta Yai, **Ko Talabeng** (Map p327) has some dramatic limestone caves that you can visit on sea-kayaking tours (1300B). National park fees apply if you visit any of the islands. Ko Rok Nai, Ko Rok Nok and **Ko Haa** (p327) are off limits to visitors from 16 May to 31 October.

The **national park headquarters** (Map p330; ☎075 660711, in Bangkok 02 561 4292; ⊙8am-4pm) and **visitors centre** (Map p330; ⊙8am-6pm) are at Laem Tanod, on the southern tip of Ko Lanta Yai, reached by a steep paved road. There are some basic hiking trails, two twin beaches and a gorgeously scenic lighthouse, plus camping facilities and bungalows amid wild, natural surroundings.

menu roams from pastas, baguettes and burgers to top-notch Thai, starring perfectly spiced ginger stir fries and red curries cooked to personal taste. Coffees, cakes and juices are another forte.

Lanta Seafood SEAFOOD $$
(Map p329; Ban Sala Dan; mains 80-250B; ⊙11am-9pm) The best of Ban Sala Dan's seafood-by-weight options, with all your other Thai favourites too. Try the *Ƀlah tôrt kà·mîn:* deep-fried white snapper rubbed with fresh, hand-ground turmeric and garlic.

Beautiful Restaurant SEAFOOD $$
(Map p330; ☎086 282 1777; Ban Si Raya; mains 100-350B; ⊙10am-9pm; 📶) Tables are scattered on four piers that extend into the sea at the northwest end of the Old Town. Fish is fresh and exquisitely prepared.

Caoutchouc INTERNATIONAL, THAI $$
(Map p330; ☎075 697060; www.facebook.com/Caoutchouc-125216317555399; Ban Si Raya; dishes 150-300B; ⊙10am-9pm) For Thai-international flavours blended into delectable creative concoctions, hunt down this rustic-chic, French-run restaurant with a short but special changing menu served on a panoramic stilted deck, 800m south of the Old Town pier. You might just uncover a deliciously fresh feta-and-rice or shrimp curry salad, served alongside mango or pineapple lassi.

Red Snapper INTERNATIONAL $$$
(Map p329; ☎087 885 6965; www.redsnapper-lanta.com; Hat Phra Ae; tapas 60-295B, mains 315-625B; ⊙5-11pm Thu-Tue; 🌱) When local expats fancy a splurge, they head to this Dutch-run roadside tapas restaurant, serving everything from Indian lentil-and-pumpkin curry and house marinated olives to a popular beef tenderloin steak and a huge variety of cheese platters, in a romantic garden setting. Decent vegetarian choices too. When we stopped by, there were plans to relocate nearby in mid-2016.

Drinking & Nightlife

If you're after heaving clubs, pick another island. If you fancy a more low-key bar scene with music wafting well into the night, Lanta has options on most beaches, and particularly around Hat Phra Ae. Things move around depending on the day, so check out posters island-wide for upcoming events. Low season is beyond mellow.

Why Not Bar BAR
(Map p330; www.facebook.com/WhyNotBarKohLanta; Ao Kantiang; ⊙11am-midnight) A buzzing, driftwood-clad hang-out that keeps things simple with a killer mix of fire twirlers, sturdy cocktails, bubbly bar-staff and fantastic nightly live music jams, best enjoyed at low-slung wooden tables on a raised deck.

Feeling Bar BAR

(Map p329; Hat Khlong Khong; ⏲11am-late) Joined to the rickety but much-loved Where Else! (p330) bungalows, Feeling keeps that original Lanta hippie-backpacker vibe alive with its 'Friday Feeling' beach parties.

Same Same But Different BAR

(Map p330; ☎081 787 8670; www.facebook.com/samesamebutdifferentlanta; Ao Kantiang; ⏲10am-10pm) In an island-chic seaside setting, you can sample middling Thai cuisine (mains 120B to 300B) and sip cocktails beneath massive trees, thatched pagodas or in a bamboo chair sunk into the sand. The location is the thing.

Irish Embassy PUB

(Map p329; www.irishembassylanta.com; Ban Phra Ae; ⏲4pm-midnight) Few may come to Lanta looking for a pub, but this warm, friendly expat favourite has all the quiz nights, sports screens, pool competitions and darts fun you could ask for if you do.

Shopping

★Malee Malee FASHION

(Map p330; ☎075 697235; 55/3 Mu 2, Ban Si Raya; ⏲9am-9pm) A bohemian wonderland of quirky homemade goods, from silk-screened and hand-painted T-shirts and silk scarves to journals, toys, baby clothes, paintings, jewellery and handbags. Prices are low, it's super fun to browse and a sweet cafe (coffees around 80B) sits on the doorstep.

Hammock House HOMEWARES

(Map p330; www.jumbohammock.com; Ban Si Raya; ⏲10am-5pm) For unique, quality, colour-bursting hammocks, crafted by rural villagers and threatened Mlabri tribespeople in northern Thailand, don't miss Hammock House. It sometimes closes for low season (May to October).

Monkey Biziness FASHION

(Map p330; Hat Khlong Nin; ⏲10am-7pm Sep-May; 📶) Floaty, soft-toned Thai-made women's clothing and accessories, plus home decor pieces and a relaxed cafe (drinks 60B).

Sunday Market MARKET

(Map p330; Ban Si Raya; ⏲8-11am) There's a small Sunday market in Ban Si Raya.

Information

Ban Sala Dan has plenty of ATMs, restaurants, mini-marts, travel agencies, dive shops and motorcycle rentals. There are 7-Elevens spread along the island's west coast, most with ATMs. Lanta Pocket Guide (www.lantapocketguide.com) is helpful.

Ko Lanta Hospital (Map p330; ☎075 697017; Ban Si Raya) About 1km south of the Ban Si Raya Old Town.

Police Station (Map p329; ☎075 668192; Ban Sala Dan)

Getting There & Away

Transport to Ko Lanta is by boat or air-con minivan. If arriving independently, you'll need to use the frequent **vehicle ferries** (motorcycle/pedestrian/car 20/20/200B; ⏲6am-10pm) between Ban Hua Hin and Ban Khlong Mak (Ko Lanta Noi) and on to Ko Lanta Yai.

BOAT

Ban Sala Dan has two piers. The passenger jetty is 300m from the main strip of shops; vehicle ferries leave from a **jetty** (Map p329) 2km east.

From mid-October to mid-April, the high-speed **Tigerline** (☎075 668428; www.tigerlinetravel.com) ferry runs between Phuket (1500B, two hours) and Ban Sala Dan (Ko Lanta) and on to Ko Lipe (1700B, five hours), via Ko Ngai (750B, one hour), Ko Kradan (850B, 1½ hours) and Ko Muk (850B, two hours). The service heads south at 10am, returning from Lipe at 10am the following day and stopping on Ko Lanta around 3pm before continuing north.

Ko Phi-Phi Ferries between Ko Lanta and Ko Phi-Phi run only during the October-to-April high season. Boats leave Ko Lanta at 8am and 1pm (250B, 1½ hours), returning from Ko Phi-Phi at 11.30am and 3pm. There are also high-season speedboats between Lanta and Phi-Phi (700B to 800B, one hour).

Krabi From November to late April, boats leave Ko Lanta for Krabi's Khlong Chilat (p306) pier at 8.30am and 1.30pm (400B, two hours) and return from Krabi at 11.30am. During high season, they stop at Ko Jum (400B, one hour).

Phuket From Ko Phi-Phi you can transfer to ferries to Phuket; you can book tickets all the way through to Phuket from Lanta. Ko Lanta to Ko Phi-Phi is 250B to 350B. From Ko Lanta to Phuket it's 700B.

Trang Islands From November to early April, speedboats buzz from Ko Lanta to the Trang Islands, including the **Satun Pak Bara Speedboat Club** (☎099 404 0409; www.tarutaolipeisland.com) and **Bundhaya Speedboat** (☎075 668043; www.bundhayaspeedboat.com). Stops include Ko Ngai (650B, 30 minutes), Ko Muk (900B, one hour), Ko Kradan (1150B, 1¼ hours), Ko Bulon Leh (1600B, two hours) and Ko Lipe (1900B, three hours).

MINIVAN

Minivans, your easiest option from the mainland, run year-round, but they're particularly packed in this region and traffic jams for vehicle ferries can cause delays. Most minivans offer pick ups from resorts. Frequency is reduced in low season.

Minivans to Krabi airport (300B, 2½ hours) and Krabi Town (300B, three hours) run hourly between 7am and 4pm in both directions. You can connect in Krabi for further destinations, including Khao Lak and Bangkok. Departures from Lanta include the following:

DESTINATION	FARE (B)	DURATION (HR)	FREQUENCY
Ko Pha-Ngan	1000-1200	8½	8am & 10.30am
Ko Samui	900-1100	6½	8am & 10.30am
Phuket	400	6	9am, 10am & 1.30pm
Trang	380	3	8am, 9.20am, 10.40am, noon & 1.30pm

Getting Around

Most resorts send vehicles to meet the ferries – a free ride to your resort. In the opposite direction expect to pay 100B to 400B. Alternatively, take a motorcycle taxi from outside 7-Eleven in Ban Sala Dan; fares run from 50B to 400B, depending on distance.

Motorbikes (per day 250B) can be rented everywhere (without insurance). Agencies in Ban Sala Dan rent out small 4WDs (per day 1300B).

TRANG PROVINCE

South of Krabi, Trang Province has an impressive limestone-covered Andaman coast with several sublime islands. For the adventurous, there's plenty of big nature to explore in the lush interior, including dozens of scenic waterfalls and limestone caves. And it's nowhere near as popular as Krabi, which means you're more likely to see working rubber plantations here than rows of T-shirt vendors. Transport links continue improving every year, and during the high season you can easily island-hop all the way to Malaysia.

Trang ตรัง

POP 60,590

Most visitors to Trang are in transit to nearby islands, but if you're an aficionado of culture, Thai food or markets, stay a day or more. Here is an easy-to-manage, old-school Thai town where you can get lost in wet markets, hawker markets and late-night Chinese coffee shops. At nearly any time of year, there'll be some minor festival that oozes local colour.

Most tourist facilities lie along Th Praram VI, between the **clock tower** and the train station.

Sights

Trang is more a business centre than a tourist town. The lively, colourful wet and dry markets on **Th Ratchadamnoen** and **Th Sathani** are worth exploring.

Wat Tantayaphirom BUDDHIST TEMPLE
(วัดตันตยาภิรม; Th Tha Klang) FREE Wat Tantayaphirom has a huge white-and-gold *chedi* (stupa) enshrining a footprint of the Buddha that's mildly interesting.

Meunram Shrine CHINESE TEMPLE
(ศาลเจ้าพ่อหมื่นราม; btwn Th Visetkul & Th Ratsada) FREE Hazy with incense smoke, the Chinese Meunram Shrine conceals a surprisingly elaborate interior behind a blander facade and sometimes sponsors southern Thai shadow theatre.

Activities

Tour agencies around the train station and Th Praram VI offer boat trips to Hat Chao Mai National Park and the Trang Islands (750B, plus park fees), snorkelling trips to Ko Rok (per person 1300B) and private car trips to local caves and waterfalls (1500B, maximum three people).

Festivals & Events

Vegetarian Festival CULTURAL
(late Sep-Oct) Trang's Chinese population celebrates this wonderful festival to coincide with Phuket's Vegetarian Festival.

Sleeping & Eating

Trang is famous for its *mŏo yâhng* (crispy barbecued pork), spongy cakes, early-morning dim sum breakfasts and *ráhn go·Ъíi* (coffee shops) that serve real filtered coffee. You can find *mŏo yâhng* in the mornings at some

Trang Province

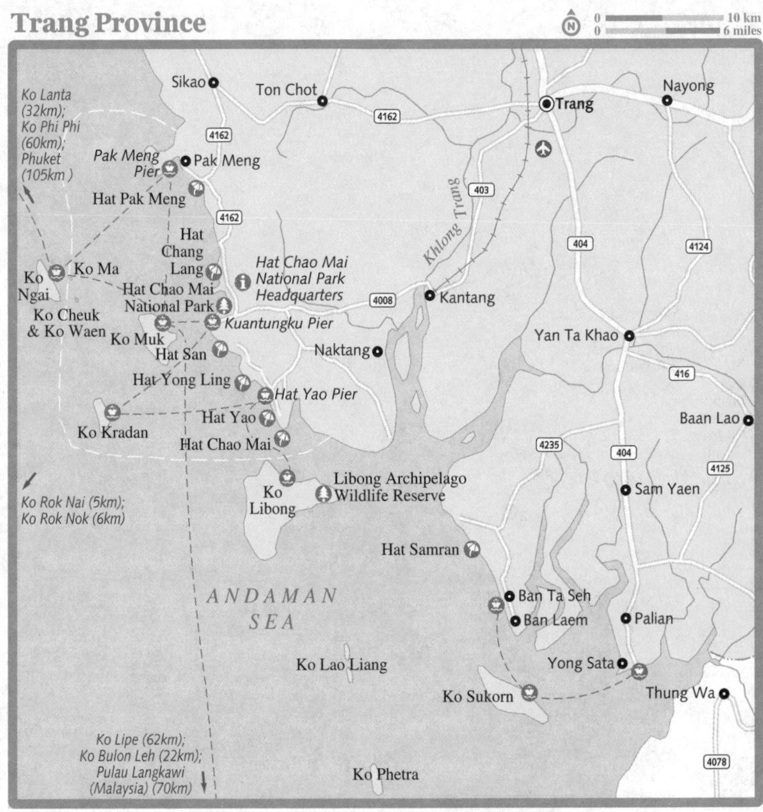

coffee shops or by weight at the wet market on Th Ratchadamnoen. To really get into the local scene, stay out late at the coffee shops along Th Ratsada.

Yamawa Guesthouse GUESTHOUSE $

(☎099 402 0349, 075 216617; www.yamawaguesthouse.blog.com; 94 Th Visetkul; r fan/air-con 350/450B; ❄📶) With simple, spotless fan or air-con rooms equipped with fridges, and sweet local owners who hand out detailed Trang maps, this popular budget spot is often full.

Sri Trang Hotel HOTEL $$

(☎075 218122; www.sritranghotel.com; 22-26 Th Sathani; r 600-800B; ❄📶) This renovated old building (which has been open for business since 1952) hosts a range of fan-cooled and air-con rooms, playing up its dated design with retro travel trunks, high ceilings, a winding wooden staircase and colourful paint jobs. Downstairs is the cosy contemporary-style **1952 Café** (dishes 65-250B; ⏱8am-8pm; 📶), perfect for coffee and mushroom omelettes while studying the Trang map wall mural.

Rua Rasada Hotel HOTEL $$$

(☎075 214230; www.ruarasadahotel.com; 188 Th Phattalung; r incl breakfast 2900-7100B; ❄📶🏊) Trang's slickest choice is handily located opposite the bus station, a 10-minute 3.5km (40B) túk-túk ride northeast from the train station. Modern, corporate-smart rooms come in dusky blue, dark mauve and grey, with huge windows, rectangular sinks and comfy beds.

★ **Night Market** MARKET $

(btwn Th Praram VI & Th Ratchadamnoen; dishes around 30B; ⏱4-9pm) The finest night market on the Andaman coast will have you salivating over bubbling curries, fried chicken and fish, deep-fried tofu, *pàt tai* and an array of Thai desserts. Go with an empty stomach

Trang

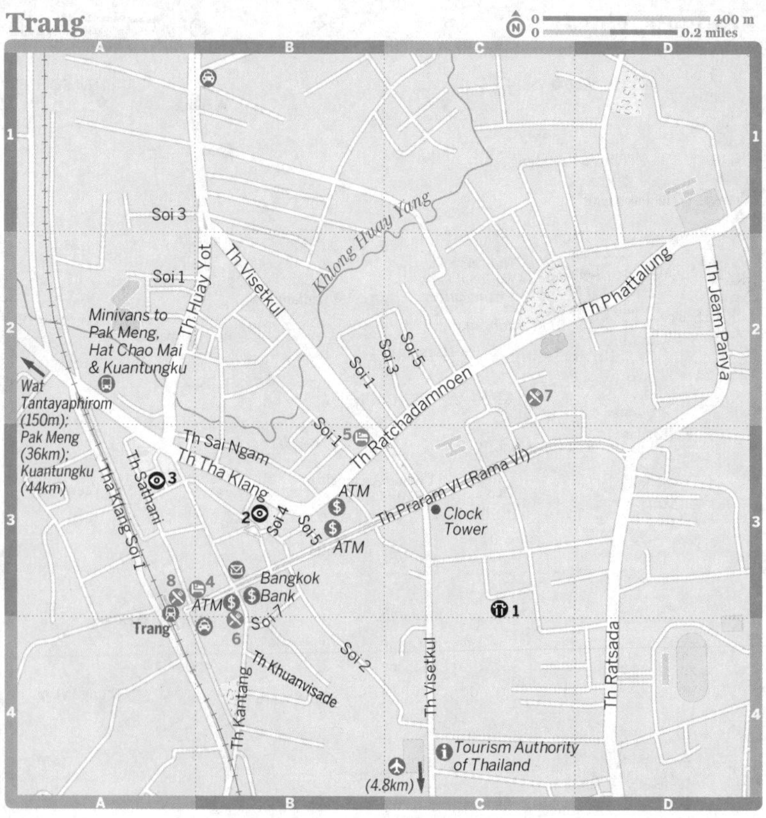

Trang

Sights

1 Meunram Shrine ... C3
2 Wet & Dry Market ... B3
3 Wet & Dry Market ... A3

Sleeping

4 Sri Trang Hotel ... B3
5 Yamawa Guesthouse ... B3

Eating

1952 Café ... (see 4)
6 Asia Ocha ... B4
7 Night Market ... C2
8 Night Market ... A3

and a sense of adventure. There's a second, equally glorious weekend **night market** (Train Station; dishes around 30B; ⏲6-10pm Thu-Sun) opposite the train station.

Asia Ocha THAI $
(Th Kantang; dishes 35-50B; ⏲6.30am-5pm) In business for 60 years, this antiquated spot serves filtered coffee (20B) to an all-Thai clientele who sit at vintage marble tables. Come here for delicious roast duck, crispy pork and noodle soups.

Information

ATMs and foreign-exchange booths line Th Praram VI. Hotels have wi-fi.

Post Office (cnr Th Praram VI & Th Kantang; ⏲8.30am-4.30pm Mon-Fri, 9am-noon Sat)

Tourism Authority of Thailand (TAT; ☎075 211580, 075 215867; www.tourismthailand.org; 199/2 Th Visetkul; ⏲8.30am-4.30pm)

Getting There & Away

AIR

Nok Air (☎02 900 9955; www.nokair.com) and **Air Asia** (☎02 900 9999; www.airasia.com) fly

BUSES TO/FROM TRANG

DESTINATION	FARE (B)	DURATION (HR)	FREQUENCY
Hat Yai	100	3	every 30min 5.30am-5.30pm
Krabi	120	2	hourly 5.30am-6.30pm
Phang-Nga	185	4	hourly 5.30am-6.30pm
Phuket	252	5	hourly 5.30am-6.30pm

daily from Bangkok (Don Muang) to Trang. The airport is 5km south of Trang.

Minivans to town (90B) meet flights. In the reverse direction, taxis, motorbike taxis or túk-túk cost 100B to 120B. Agencies at airport arrivals sell combined taxi-boat tickets to Trang's islands, including Ko Ngai (1000B).

BUS

Buses leave from Trang's **New Bus Terminal** (Th Phattalung), 3.5km northeast of the train station. There are 1st-class air-con buses to Bangkok (646B, 12 hours) at 8.30am, 9.30am, 4.30pm and 5pm, and more comfortable VIP 24-seat buses at 5pm and 5.30pm (1050B). From Bangkok, VIP/air-con buses leave between 6.30pm and 7.30pm. There are plenty of services to other destinations.

MINIVAN

Minivans depart from Trang's New Bus Terminal. Agencies sell minivan tickets including in-town pick-up.

Local transport is by air-con minivan rather than *sŏrng·tăa·ou*. From the bus station, minivans leave regularly from 7.30am to 4pm for Pak Meng (80B, one hour), Hat Chao Mai (100B, one hour) and Kuantungku (100B, one hour), stopping in town just east of where Th Tha Klang crosses the railway tracks.

Other departures include the following:

Hat Yai (120B, two hours, hourly 6am to 6pm)
Ko Lanta (250B, 2½ hours, five daily 9.50am to 4.30pm)
Krabi (100B, two hours, hourly 7am to 5pm)
Satun (120B, two hours, every 40 minutes 6am to 6pm)
Surat Thani (160B, three hours, hourly 7am to 5pm)

TRAIN

Only two trains run between Bangkok and Trang: the express 83 and the rapid 167, which leave from Bangkok's Hualamphong station at 5.05pm and 6.30pm and arrive in Trang the next morning at 8.05am and 10.30am respectively.

From Trang, trains leave at 1.30pm and 5.25pm, arriving in Bangkok at 5.35am and 8.35am the following morning. Fares are around 1480/761B for a 1st-/2nd-class air-con sleeper and 285B for 3rd class.

Getting Around

Túk-túk and motorbike taxis congregate near the train station, charging 40B for local trips. Travel agencies rent motorbikes (per day 250B). Most agencies arrange car rental (per day 1200B). You can rent cars at the airport.

An orange 'local bus' runs from the train station to the New Bus Terminal (12B).

Trang Beaches

Trang's beaches are mostly just jumping-off points to the Trang Islands, but, if you have time, stop and enjoy the scenery: limestone karsts rising from steamy palm-studded valleys and swirling seas.

Sights & Activities

Thirty-nine kilometres west of Trang in Amphoe Sikao (Sikao District) you'll hit Hat Pak Meng; immediately south is **Hat Chang Lang**.

Pak Meng's tour agencies organise one-day boat tours to Ko Muk, Ko Cheuk, Ko Ma and Ko Kradan, and snorkelling day tours, all including lunch (per person 750B, plus Hat Chao Mai National Park fees). Mask and snorkel sets and fins can be rented by the pier (50B each).

Hat Chao Mai National Park NATIONAL PARK
(อุทยานแห่งชาติหาดเจ้าไหม; ☎075 203308; www.dnp.go.th; adult/child 200/100B; ⊗9am-4pm) This 231-sq-km park covers the shoreline from Hat Pak Meng to Laem Chao Mai, and encompasses the islands of Ko Muk, Ko Kadran and Ko Cheuk (plus a host of small islets). While touring the coast and islands, you may spot endangered dugongs and rare black-necked storks, as well as more common species like barking deer, sea otters, macaques, langurs, wild pigs, pangolins, little herons, Pacific reef egrets, white-bellied sea eagles and monitor lizards.

Park headquarters are at the southern end of Hat Chang Lang, where the beachfront road turns inland.

Hat Pak Meng BEACH

There's a wild-looking stretch of coastline at Hat Pak Meng, 39km west of Trang. Though the beach is scruffy, the spectacular jutting limestone karsts here rival the best of Railay and Phi-Phi. Pak Meng's pier, the jumping-off point for Ko Ngai, is at the north end of the beach. Several seafood restaurants, popular with Thai day trippers and weekenders, stand where Rte 4162 meets the coast.

Sleeping & Eating

Hat Chao Mai National Park Accommodation CAMPGROUND, BUNGALOW $

(075 203308; www.dnp.go.th; Hat Chang Lang; bungalow 800B, camp site per person 30B, with tent hire 225B) Simple fan-cooled cabins sleep two to six people or you can camp under the casuarinas. There's also a restaurant.

Anantara Si Kao HOTEL $$$

(075 205888; www.sikao.anantara.com; Hat Chang Lang; r incl breakfast 6500-11,200B, ste 13,300-18,250B; P ❄ ᯤ ≋) Deluxe oceanfront rooms with rich wood floors, floating desks and delicious views of Pak Meng's signature karsts bring Anantara's trendy glamour to northern Hat Chang Lang. Impressive timber columns and Balinese furnishings line the lobby, there's a host of activities on offer, and the sea-views from Italian restaurant **Acqua** (mains 300-700B; 6.30-10.30pm) are jaw-dropping.

Shuttle over to the guests-only beach club on seductive Ko Kradan.

Getting There & Away

Air-con minivans run regularly from Trang's New Bus Terminal to Hat Pak Meng (80B, one hour) and Hat Chao Mai (100B, one hour) between 7.30am and 4pm, via Trang's Th Tha Klang. Taxis from Trang cost 1000B.

Boats leave Ko Ngai for Pak Meng at 9.30am daily, returning to Ko Ngai at noon (350B, one hour). Long-tail charters cost 1500B.

The Hat Chao Mai National Park headquarters is 1km off the main road, down a clearly signposted track.

Trang Islands

The mythical Trang Islands feel like lost fragments of the Andaman's iconic limestone that have tumbled into the sea. Most have tangles of verdant jungle and pure white-sand beaches home to roving sea gypsies.

Ko Ngai เกาะไหง (ไห)

Encircled by coral and clear waters, densely forested Ko Ngai (Ko Hai) is the most developed of the Trang Islands. The long blonde wind-swept beach on the eastern coast spills into turquoise water with a sandy bottom (perfect for children) that ends at a reef drop-off with good snorkelling. It's a stunning place. With no indigenous population, a bunch of snazzy resorts have the whole island to themselves.

Although technically part of Krabi Province, Ko Ngai's mainland link is with Pak Meng, 16km northeast. Pricier resorts have wi-fi.

Activities

Ko Ngai has a couple of dive centres (dives from 1300B). Resorts rent snorkel sets and fins (50B each) and sea kayaks (per hour 150B), or you can join half-day snorkelling tours of nearby islands (from 600B).

Sleeping & Eating

Most places are decidedly upper-midrange, with restaurants and 24-hour electricity. The pier is at Koh Ngai Resort, but long-tails usually drop you at your resort. Most resorts arrange transfers.

Ko Ngai Seafood Bungalows BUNGALOW $$

(081 367 8497, 095 014 1853; kob_1829@hotmail.com; bungalow 1000-1500B; year-round) Boosted by its friendly family-style set-up in the middle of main beach, this collection of simple, well-kept, fan-cooled bungalows with sea-view porches is essentially a few rooms tacked onto a popular seafood-focused **restaurant** (081 367 8497; mains 80-280B; 7am-9pm Sep-Apr). Its coconut-milk crab curry with chunks of de-shelled fresh crab is a dream come true.

★ **Coco Cottage** BUNGALOW $$$

(089 724 9225; www.coco-cottage.com; bungalow 3400-5000B; Oct-May; ❄ @ ᯤ) Cottages at the north end of main beach are coconut thatched-roof extravaganzas with coconut-wood walls and coconut-shell lanterns. Wake up to twinkling Andaman vistas through floor-to-ceiling windows in sea-view bungalows. It's impeccably styled, with decks and interiors catching plenty of breezes. Other perks include bamboo

BOATS TO/FROM KO NGAI

DESTINATION	BOAT COMPANY	FARE (B)	DURATION
Ko Lanta	Tigerline	750	1hr
	Speedboat	650	30min
Ko Lipe	Tigerline	1300	4hr
	Speedboat	1600	2½hr
Ko Kradan	Tigerline	450	30min
	Satun Pakbara Speedboat Club	400	25min
Ko Muk	Tigerline	350	1hr
	Speedboat	350	30min
Ko Phi-Phi	Tigerline	1200	2½hr
	Satun Pakbara Speedboat Club	1350	2hr
Phuket	Tigerline	1800	3½hr
	Satun Pakbara Speedboat Club	2350	3hr

loungers, massage pavilions and a fantastic Thai/fusion beachfront **restaurant-bar** (mains 160-280B; ⌚7-10am, 11am-4pm & 6-9.30pm).

Thanya Resort BUNGALOW **$$$**
(☎086 950 7355, 075 206967; www.kohngaithanyaresort.com; south end of main beach; r incl breakfast 3500-5200B; ⌚Oct-Apr; ❄@📶🏊) Ko Ngai's Bali-chic choice has dark but stylish, spacious teak bungalows that have indoor hot showers and outdoor country-style bucket showers (don't knock it until you've tried it). Laze in the gorgeous beachside pool and gaze across the frangipani-filled lawn rolling out towards the sand from your terrace. There's an on-site **dive centre** (☎085 056 3455; 1 dive 1300-1500B) plus a breezy Thai **restaurant** (mains 170-310B; ⌚7am-10pm Oct-Apr; 📶).

Thapwarin Resort RESORT **$$$**
(☎081 894 3585; www.thapwarin.com; north end of main beach; garden/sea view bungalow incl breakfast 2700/4700B; ⌚mid-Jun–mid-May; ❄📶) Thapwarin's airy, attractive bamboo cottages sprawl back into trees. With private decks, tumbling mosquito netting, paper lanterns and semi-outdoor showers, they're comfy and cosy, if a tad overpriced. Catch evening fire shows at the beach-facing **bar-restaurant** (mains 200-500B; ⌚7am-10pm mid-Jun–mid-May; 📶), which tackles everything from grilled snapper to pizza and pasta.

ℹ Getting There & Away

Ko Ngai Villa runs daily boats from Ko Ngai to Pak Meng (350B, one hour) at 9.30am, returning to Ko Ngai at noon. You can also charter long-tails to/from Pak Meng (1500B), Ko Muk (1500B), Ko Kradan (1800B) and Ko Lanta (2000B); enquire at Ko Ngai Seafood (p340) or Ko Ngai Villa.

From mid-October to mid-April, **Tigerline** (☎075 590490, 081 358 8989; www.tigerlinetravel.com) ferries stops just off Ko Ngai en route between Phuket and Ko Lipe. From November to early April, **Satun Pakbara Speedboat Club** (☎099 414 4994, 099 404 0409; www.tarutaolipeisland.com) and **Bundhaya Speedboat** (☎083 653 0323, 075 668043; www.bundhayaspeedboat.com) offer faster/comfier island-hopping transport.

Ko Muk เกาะมุก

Motoring toward jungle-clad Ko Muk is unforgettable, whether you land on sugary white eastern sand bar **Hat Sivalai**, on humble, local-flavoured **Hat Lodung** or on southwest **Hat Farang** (Hat Sai Yao, Charlie's Beach), where jade water kisses a perfect beach.

Unfortunately, the lodging options aren't amazing, and there's a steady stream of Speedo-clad package tourists tramping the beach and day-tripping over to Tham Morakot (p342) from Ko Lanta. Still, the west-coast sunsets are glorious, it's an easy hop from here to every island in the province, and you'll be mixing in with a blend of travellers more likely to relish the calm than party all night.

Sights & Activities

Between Ko Muk and Ko Ngai are two small karst islets, **Ko Cheuk** and **Ko Waen**, both with small sandy beaches and good snorkelling (though there's some coral damage).

Koh Mook Garden Resort rents out bikes (per day 100B) with self-guided maps, several resorts rent kayaks (per hour 100B to 300B) and motorbikes (per day 250B), and you can spend hours walking through rubber plantations and the island's devout Muslim sea shanty villages (remember to cover up).

Tham Morakot CAVE

(ถ้ำมรกต, Emerald Cave) This beautiful limestone tunnel leads 80m into a *hôrng* on Ko Muk's west coast. No wonder long-gone pirates buried treasure here. You have to swim or paddle through the tunnel, part of the way in pitch blackness, to a small white-sand beach surrounded by lofty limestone walls. A piercing shaft of light illuminates it around midday. National park fees (adult/child 200/100B) apply.

The cave features prominently on most tour itineraries, so it can get ridiculously crowded in high season. It's best to charter a long-tail boat (800B to 1000B) or rent a kayak and zip over at daybreak or late afternoon when you'll have it to yourself, but note that you can't get inside at high tide.

Sleeping & Eating

Most places on Hat Sivalai and Hat Lodung are a short walk from the main pier, on Ko Muk's eastern side. Hat Lodung is west of the pier beyond a stilt village and mangroves; Hat Sivalai wraps around the peninsula to the east. Though beautiful, these shores get lapped by murky backwash from the mainland mangrove villages.

The sea is cleaner on Hat Farang, where budget-friendly resorts lie inland from the beach. Most boats will pick up and drop off here; otherwise it's a 10-minute motorbike taxi to/from the pier (50B).

Koh Mook Garden Resort GUESTHOUSE $

(081 748 3849; kohmookgardenresort@hotmail.com; Hat Lodung; r 400-800B;) In shady grounds, the tile-floored, concrete, semi-sea-view rooms and new bungalows here are clean and airy, while older bamboo bungalows are small and basic. You'll be looked after by an enthusiastic local family who take guests snorkelling, lend bikes, rent kayaks (per hour 200B), organise transport and give out detailed maps of the island's secret spots.

Pawapi Resort BUNGALOW $$

(089 662 3169; www.pawapi.com; Hat Sivalai; bungalow 2800-5000B;) These upscale bamboo bungalows with balconies are perched on stilts 1.5m off the ground so that breezes ventilate the room, but it's the insane 180-degree view of islands, white sand and sparkling sea that steals the show. At research time, new rooms were under construction, so expect a hike in rates.

Sivalai HOTEL $$$

(089 723 3355; www.komooksivalai.com; Hat Sivalai; bungalow incl breakfast 5000-7000B;) Straddling an arrow-shaped white-sand peninsula framed by views of karst islands and the mainland, Sivalai wins the award for Ko Muk's most fabulous location. Elegant, exotic thatched-roof cottages splashed with colour are almost encircled by glass doors and many have wraparound verandas. The pool lacks style, but the beach is exquisite and there's a handy spa (massages from 700B).

Kayak rental is 300B per hour.

Hilltop Restaurant THAI $

(mains 50-300B; 9am-10pm) About 800m inland from Hat Farang, this welcoming, family-run operation serves up all your Thai favourites with an extra kick (on request) at wooden picnic-style benches in an open-air jungle-cloaked setting.

Getting There & Away

Boats to Ko Muk (100B to 300B, 30 minutes) leave daily from the pier at Kuantungku at noon, 1pm and 5pm November to April, returning to

THE 50B SURCHARGE

Tigerline (p343) ferries and speedboats often stop in the sea off the Trang and Satun islands. There's a 50B surcharge for long-tail transfers on/off islands, which you'll be asked for once you're aboard the long-tail; boatmen usually refuse to continue until you pay up. Yes, it's frustrating, but it'll hardly ruin your trip, so it's worth keeping change handy.

the mainland at 8am, 9am and 2pm. Services peter out in November and April, but the cheapest, 1pm 'local' ferry runs year-round. Minibus-boat combo tickets take you to/from Trang (250B to 450B, 1½ hours) and Trang airport (500B, 1½ hours). You can also charter long-tails to/from Kuantungku (600B to 800B, 30 minutes).

From November to early April, Ko Muk is a stop on the speedboats connecting Ko Lanta (900B, one hour), Ko Ngai (350B to 400B, 30 minutes) and Ko Lipe (1400B, two hours). The Phuket–Ko Lipe **Tigerline** (☎075 590490, 081 358 8989; www.tigerlinetravel.com) stops off Hat Farang mid-October to mid-April.

Long-tail charters from Ko Muk to Ko Kradan (600B, 30 minutes), Ko Ngai (1000B, one hour) and Pak Meng (1500B, 45 minutes to one hour) are easily arranged on the pier or on Hat Farang at Rubber Tree Bungalow or Ko Yao Viewpoint.

Ko Kradan เกาะกระดาน

Beautiful Ko Kradan is dotted with slender, silky, white-sand beaches, bathtub-warm shallows and dreamy views across the twinkling turquoise sea to Ko Muk, Ko Libong and limestone karsts from its main, east-coast beach. The water is clean, clear and inviting, and there's a small but lush tangle of remnant jungle inland.

Activities

Hat Sunset BEACH

A short signposted track at the south end of the main beach leads past Paradise Lost guesthouse and over the ridge to Sunset Beach, a mostly wet and rocky patch of sand facing open seas – and a fun place to get a little beachside privacy over a flaming pink sunset.

Hat South SNORKELLING

Although some of Kradan's coral structure has been decimated, there's good snorkelling off the island's South Beach, which you can reach in a 10-minute walk along a jungly path from Paradise Lost, signposted at the south end of the main beach.

Sleeping & Eating

Kradan's lodgings and restaurants are overpriced; blame the idyllic location.

Paradise Lost GUESTHOUSE $$

(☎089 587 2409; www.kokradan.wordpress.com; dm 300B, bungalow with/without bathroom 1200/700B) One of Kradan's first lodgings, this inland, Thai-American–founded property has easy access to more secluded beaches. Despite a little wear, it's still your best lower-range choice, with 24-hour electricity, a friendly vibe, and an airy new five-bed, fan-cooled dorm. Small bamboo huts have wood floors, mosquito nets and shared bathrooms; bigger wooden bungalows come with private facilities.

The open-plan **kitchen** (mains 120-300B; ⏰8am-9pm) dishes up Kradan's tastiest homemade food in giant portions.

Seven Seas Resort HOTEL $$$

(☎082 490 2552, 082 490 2442; www.sevenseasresorts.com; r incl breakfast 7000-7980B, villa 11,300-15,100B; ❄📶🏊) This boutique resort's super-sleek rooms have terrazzo floors, indoor-outdoor bathrooms blending into tropical gardens, enormous low-slung beds and, for some, private cabanas. Hugging the jet-black infinity pool, the breezy **restaurant** (mains 330-520B; ⏰7am-10pm; 📶) serves pricey Thai-international dishes. Beach

BOATS TO/FROM KO KRADAN

DESTINATION	BOAT COMPANY	FARE (B)	DURATION
Hat Yao	Tigerline	550	1hr
Ko Lanta	Tigerline	850	1½hr
	Satun Pakbara Speedboat Club	1150	1¼hr
Ko Lipe	Tigerline	1450	3½hr
	Satun Pakbara Speedboat Club	1400	2hr
Ko Muk	Satun Pakbara Speedboat Club	300	15min
Ko Ngai	Tigerline	450	30min
	Satun Pakbara Speedboat Club	400	45min

bums will love this sandy stretch, halfway up Kradan's main beach.

Reef Resort HOTEL $$$

(☎086 948 8559; www.reefresortkradan.com; r incl breakfast 3500-4000B; ❄📶🏊) Bright, minimalist, modern-design rooms frame a palm-lined pool at this fresh Italian-run arrival, steps from aqua waters at the northern, wooded end of Kradan's main beach. The thatched-roof beach bar is perfect sundowner land; the Thai-Italian **restaurant** (mains 170-300B; ⏰8-10am, noon-3pm & 6-9pm; 📶) is decent.

Getting There & Away

For boat tickets (and wi-fi), visit Kradan Beach Resort. From November to April, daily boats to Kuantungku leave at 9am and noon; tickets include connecting minibuses to Trang (450B) or Trang airport (550B). From Trang, minibus-boat services depart for Ko Kradan at 11am and 4pm. You can charter long-tails to/from Kuantungku (1500B, 45 minutes to one hour), Ko Muk (800B, 30 minutes) and Ko Ngai (1800B, one hour).

The Phuket–Ko Lipe **Tigerline** (☎075 590490, 081 358 8989; www.tigerlinetravel.com) stops off Ko Kradan from mid-October to mid-May. November to early April, **Satun Pakbara Speedboat Club** (☎099 404 0409, 099 414 4994; www.tarutaolipeisland.com) offers faster links (p343).

Ko Libong เกาะลิบง

Trang's largest island is just 30 minutes by long-tail from mainland Hat Yao. Less visited than neighbouring islands, it's a gorgeous, lush mountainous pearl, wrapped in rubber trees, thick with mangroves and known for its captivating flora and fauna (especially the resident dugongs and migrating birds) more than its thin gold-brown beaches. The island is home to a small Muslim fishing community and has a few west-coast resorts. With its scruffy sweetness and untouristy backwater charm, Libong has a way of drawing you in, if you let it.

Sights

Libong Archipelago Wildlife Reserve NATURE RESERVE

This large mangrove area on Ko Libong's east coast at Laem Ju Hoi is protected by the Botanical Department. The sea channels are one of the last habitats of the endangered dugong: over 100 graze on the sea grass that flourishes in the bay. Most of Ko Libong's resorts offer dugong-spotting boat tours, led by trained naturalists, for 1000B to 1500B.

Sleeping & Eating

Libong Sunset Resort BUNGALOW $

(☎089 766 3341, 087 276 5484; www.libongsunsetresort.com; r 500B, bungalow fan/air-con 1000/2000B; ⏰Oct–mid-Apr; ❄📶) Tucked up against a headland on its own rocky, sandy beach, the simple spotless air-con and fan-cooled bungalows at this sweet family-owned resort make good-value (though potentially isolated) crash pads. All have private sea-view porches. The biggest air-con options come with sofas and TVs, while basic shared-bathroom doubles do a straightforward budget job.

Libong Beach Resort BUNGALOW $$

(☎084 849 0899, 081 747 4600; bungalow fan 800-1000B, air-con 1000-2000B; ❄📶) This cute spot has everything from bland slap-up shacks behind a murky stream to comfy varnished wood-and-thatch beachfront chalets with semi-outdoor bathrooms. It also offers wildlife-spotting trips, transport info and motorbike rental (per day 300B). We love the restaurant; try the *pàt see·éw* (fried noodles) or the *đôm yam kà·mîn* (turmeric fish soup).

Libong Relax Beach Resort BUNGALOW $$

(☎091 825 4886, 094 582 5113; www.libongrelax.com; r incl breakfast fan 1200-2300B, air-con 2500-3000B; ❄📶) Top choice at this friendly, laid-back resort are rustic-stylish wood-and-bamboo bungalows with terracotta sinks, shiny floors and shuttered doors that open up to the sea. Fan-cooled cottages come simply but smartly designed, and there's a selection of bird- and dugong-spotting and snorkelling trips, plus kayak rental (per hour 200B). The low-key, thatch-roofed beachside **restaurant** (mains 80-350B; ⏰7.30am-3pm & 5-9pm; 📶) does a good line in Thai staples.

Getting There & Around

During daylight hours, long-tail boats to Ban Ma Phrao on Ko Libong's east coast leave hourly from Hat Yao (per person 50B, 30 minutes). On Ko Libong, motorcycle taxis run across to the west-coast resorts (per person 100B). Chartered long-tails from Hat Yao to the resorts cost 900B. You can charter boats to Ko Kradan (1800B), Ko Muk (1500B) and Ko Ngai (2300B).

Ko Sukorn เกาะสุกร

Little-visited Ko Sukorn is a cultural paradise of tawny beaches, light-green sea, jungle-shrouded black-rock headlands, and stilted shack neighbourhoods home to 2600 Muslim inhabitants whose rice fields, watermelon plots and rubber plantations unfurl along narrow concrete roads. Spin past fields occupied only by water buffalo, through pastel villages where people are genuinely happy to see you and sleep soundly through deep, silent nights. Sukorn's stillness is breathtaking, its authenticity a tonic to the jaded, road-weary soul.

With few hills, expansive panoramas, plenty of shade and lots of opportunities to meet islanders, Sukorn is best explored by rented bike (200B). The main beach, dotted with a few low-key resorts, extends along the island's southwestern coast. Please cover up away from the beach.

Sleeping & Eating

★Yataa Island Resort RESORT $$
(081 444 9989, 089 647 5550; www.yataaresort.com; bungalow incl breakfast 1350-3000B;) Rebranded under new management, these pastel-painted, green-roofed concrete air-con bungalows frame a cool blue pool and have tasteful varnished-wood verandahs. Older concrete-and-wood, air-con bungalows amid boungainvillea-filled gardens are comfy too. Staff offer Sukorn maps, guided island tours (per person 500B) and bicycle/motorbike rental (150/200B). Enjoy fiery pink sunsets over outlying islands from the gorgeous long beach out front. The **restaurant** (mains 100-150B; 7.30am-9pm;) is excellent.

Sukorn Cabana BUNGALOW $$
(089 724 2326; www.sukorncabana.com; bungalow incl breakfast 900-1500B;) Sloping landscaped grounds dotted with papaya, frangipani and bougainvillea hold large, clean, well-managed bungalows sporting thatched roofs, fridges, polished-wood interiors and plush verandahs. On the hill up above are spacious modern-style rooms overlooking the pretty beach and Ko Phetra through floor-to-ceiling windows.

Getting There & Around

The easiest way to get to Sukorn is by private transfers from Trang, arranged through your resort (per person 1900B). The cheapest way is to take a *sŏrng·tăa·ou* from Trang to Yan Ta Khao (80B, 40 minutes), then transfer to Ban Ta Seh (50B, 45 minutes), from where long-tails to Ban Saimai (50B), Sukorn's main village, leave when full. Trang guesthouses and travel agents arrange *sŏrng·tăa·ou*-and-boat transfers (250B to 350B) to Ban Saimai via Ban Ta Seh, departing Trang at 11am daily.

Otherwise, book a taxi from Trang to Ban Ta Seh (1200B). The resorts are a 3km walk or 100B moto-taxi ride from Ban Saimai. You can charter long-tails directly to the beach resorts (1000B).

SATUN PROVINCE

The Andaman's southernmost region, Satun was until recently mostly overlooked, but that's all changed thanks to the dynamic white sands of Ko Lipe – a one-time backpacker secret turned mainstream beach getaway. Beyond Ko Lipe, the rest of the province passes by in the blink of an eye, as visitors rush north to Ko Lanta or south to Pulau Langkawi (Malaysia). Which means, of course, that they miss the untrammelled beaches and sea caves of Ko Tarutao, the rugged trails and ribbon waterfalls of Ko Adang, the rustic beauty of Ko Bulon Leh and the scruffy urban buzz of Satun itself.

Largely Muslim in make-up, Satun has seen little of the political turmoil (p584) that plagues neighbouring Yala, Pattani and Narathiwat. Around 60% of inhabitants speak Yawi or Malay as a first language, and the few humble wát in the region are vastly outnumbered by mosques.

Satun สตูล

POP 23,610

Lying in a steamy jungle valley surrounded by limestone cliffs and a murky river, isolated Satun is a surprisingly bustling little city: the focal point of a province home to over 300,000 people. Most visitors whizz through en route to Malaysia; Malaysia-based yachties, dropping in for cheap repairs in Satun's acclaimed boat yard, are the only travellers who hang around. But if you explore before you leave, you'll uncover intriguing religious architecture, deliciously authentic food, lots of friendly smiles and plenty of gritty charm.

Sights & Activities

Satun National Museum MUSEUM
(พิพิธภัณฑสถานแห่งชาติสตูล, Kuden Mansion; Soi 5, Th Satun Thanee; admission 50B; 9am-

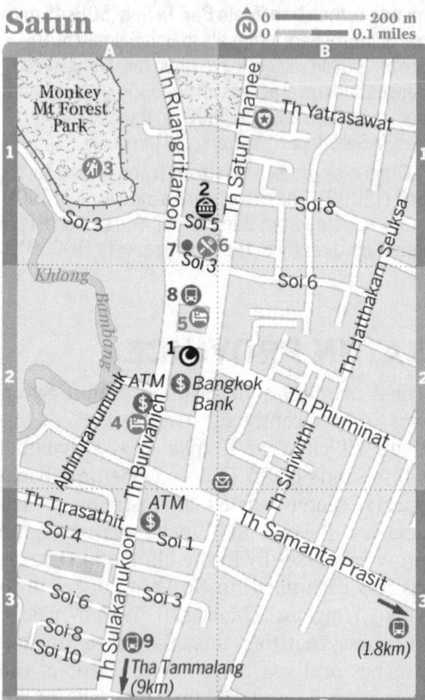

Satun

Sights

1 Masjid Mambang ... A2
2 Satun National Museum ... A1

Activities, Courses & Tours

3 Monkey Mountain ... A1

Sleeping

4 On's Guesthouse ... A2
5 Satun Tanee Hotel ... A2

Eating

@On's the Kitchen ... (see 4)
6 Night Market ... A1

Information

7 Immigration Office ... A1

Transport

8 Buses to Trang and Hat Yai ... A2
9 Sŏrng•tăa•ou to Tha Tammalang ... A3

4pm Wed-Sun) Housed in a restored bright white, mint-green-windowed 1902 Sino-Portuguese mansion, Satun's excellent museum was originally constructed as a home for King Rama V during a royal visit, but the governor snagged the pad when the king failed to show up. The building exhibits feature dioramas with soundtracks covering every aspect of Muslim life in southern Thailand.

Monkey Mountain WALKING

Soak up Satun's refreshing shabby beauty by hiking this jungled mound of limestone teeming with macaques. You can also walk over a bridge here to a stilted fishing village 1km west of town.

Sleeping

On's Guesthouse GUESTHOUSE $

(074 724133; onmarch13@hotmail.com; 36 Th Burivanich; dm/r 250/650B;) Satun's dynamic tourism matriarch, On, has transformed an old downtown shophouse into a sparkling, affordable guesthouse of spacious air-con rooms featuring wood furnishings, cute end tables and desks, plus other homey touches. Now she's added a massive, spotless six-bed dorm decked out in pastel wallpaper, with lockers.

Satun Tanee Hotel GUESTHOUSE $

(074 711010, 074 712309; www.satuntaneehotel.com; 90 Th Satun Thanee; r fan 300B, air-con 350-570B) Behind this jazzed-up, lime-green-and-orange exterior lie newly revamped, fresh-painted rooms modernised by tight white sheets and wood-panelled floors, plus dingier, cheaper, unrenovated air-con and fan rooms. It's a bit institutional, but the updated rooms are good value and you get a warm welcome.

Eating

Quick, cheap Chinese and Muslim restaurants are on Th Burivanich and Th Samanta Prasit. Chinese food stalls specialise in *kôw mŏo daang* (red pork with rice); Muslim restaurants offer roti with southern-style chicken curry.

★**Night Market** MARKET $

(off Th Satun Thanee; dishes around 35B; 5-9pm) Satun's popular, bubbly night market springs to life with flavour-packed *pàt tai*, fried fish, chicken satay and spicy, southern-style curries. There's a larger Saturday night market on Th Burivanich.

@On's the Kitchen THAI, INTERNATIONAL $$

(074 724133; 36 Th Burivanich; mains 60-250B; 8am-10pm;) Frequented by visiting yachties, young expat English teachers and a few locals, the lively ground-floor cafe at On's Guesthouse dishes out tasty baguettes, pastas, pizzas, salads and Thai mains, along

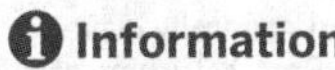

with popular steak dinners and European breakfasts.

Information

Most hotels have wi-fi. ATMs line Th Burivanich.

Immigration Office (074 711080; Soi 3, Th Burivanich; 8.30am-4.30pm Mon-Fri) Handles visa issues and extensions. It's easier for tourists to exit and re-enter Thailand via the border checkpoint at Tha Tammalang (p347).

Post Office (cnr Th Satun Thanee & Th Samanta Prasit; 8.30am-4.30pm Mon-Fri, 9am-noon Sat)

Getting There & Away

BUS

Buses leave from Satun Bus Terminal, 2km south of town. Buses to Hat Yai (70B, two hours, hourly 5am to 5pm) and local (non air-con) buses to Trang (100B, two hours, hourly 5am to 4.30pm) pick up passengers on Th Satun Thanee.

Departures include the following:

Bangkok – VIP (1150B, 14 hours, 4.30pm)

Bangkok – air-con (731B to 742B, 14 hours, 6am and 4pm)

Krabi (234B, five hours, 8.15am, 10.15am, 12.15pm and 8pm)

Phuket (364B, eight hours, 8.15am, 10.15am, 12.15pm and 8pm)

MINIVAN

Minivans run from Satun Bus Terminal to Hat Yai (100B, two hours, 6am to 5pm), Krabi (200B, five hours, 7am and 2pm) and Trang (120B, two hours, hourly 5am to 5pm). Direct minivans run between Tha Tammalang and Hat Yai (86B, two hours, 6.30am to 7pm).

Getting Around

Orange *sŏrng·tăa·ou* to Tha Tammalang (30B, 15 minutes; for boats to Malaysia) leave from the 7-Eleven on Th Sulakanukoon every 30 to 40 minutes. Motorcycle taxis from here cost 80B. *Sŏrng·tăa·ou* to the bus station cost 40B per person.

GETTING TO MALAYSIA

Since mid-2014, Thai authorities have been clamping down on in-out visa runs. This is particularly aimed at foreigners living/working in Thailand on tourist visas and, at research time, was not causing any problems for regular travellers. Do monitor the situation carefully and research latest updates.

Keep in mind that Malaysia is one hour ahead of Thai time.

Ko Lipe to Pulau Langkawi

From mid-October to mid-April, **Tigerline** (p357), **Bundhaya Speedboat** (p357) and **Satun Pakbara Speedboat Club** (099 414 4994, 099 404 0409; www.tarutaolipeisland.com) run daily from Ko Lipe to Pulau Langkawi in Malaysia (1000B to 1400B, 1½ hours). Departures are at 10am, 10.30am, 11am and 4pm. Head to the **immigration office** (Map p354; 8am-6pm) at Bundhaya Resort (east end of Hat Pattaya) 1½ hours ahead to get stamped out. In reverse, boats leave Pulau Langkawi for Ko Lipe at 9am, 9.30am, 2pm and 2.30pm Malaysian time.

Satun to Kuala Perlis or Pulau Langkawi

Daily boats to Malaysia's Pulau Langkawi leave from Tha Tammalang (10km south of Satun) at 9.30am, 1.30pm and 4pm (300B, 1½ hours). In the reverse direction, boats (M$30) return from Pulau Langkawi at 9am, 1pm and 5pm Malaysian time. Get stamped out in advance at Satun's immigration office or, much easier, exit Thailand via the Tammalang border checkpost. If you're just doing a visa run, the whole process is doable in a day.

Public long-tails no longer run from Tha Tammalang to Kuala Perlis in Malaysia. It's possible to take a 9am minivan from Satun to Kuala Perlis (400B) via the Wang Prajan/Wang Kelian border crossing; On's Guesthouse sells tickets.

At the Border

Citizens of the US, EU, Australia, Canada and several other countries may enter Malaysia for up to 90 days without prior visa arrangements. If you have questions about your eligibility, check with the nearest Malaysian embassy or consulate and apply for a visa in advance.

Pak Bara ปากบารา

Pak Bara, 60km northwest of Satun, is the main jumping-off point for the dazzling southern islands in the Mu Ko Phetra and Ko Tarutao Marine National Parks. Facilities are slowly improving as Pak Bara becomes increasingly packed with tourists. The peaceful fishing town has forgettable sleeping options, and, aside from great seafood, there's no pressing reason to stick around.

The main road from La-Ngu (Rte 4052) terminates at the pier, which is basically a massive passenger waiting terminal for Lipe- and Tarutao-bound speedboats, with travel agencies, cheap restaurants, ATMs and stalls flogging beach gear. The Ko Tarutao Marine National Park **visitors centre** (Map p350; ☎074 783485; ⊙8am-5pm) is by the pier; here you can book Ko Tarutao and Ko Adang accommodation, buy speedboat tickets and obtain camping permission. Local travel agents arrange one-day tours (2000B) to the parks' islands.

Getting There & Away

BUS

From Satun, take an ordinary Trang bus and get off at La-Ngu (50B, 30 minutes), continuing by *sŏrng·tăa·ou* to Pak Bara (20B, 15 minutes).

MINIVANS

Air-con minivans run every 45 minutes between 7.30am and 6.30pm from Hat Yai to Pak Bara pier (130B, two hours). Minivan services may be reduced mid-May to mid-October. Departures from Pak Bara include the following:

Hat Yai (150B, two hours, 11.30am and 3.30pm)
Hat Yai Airport (250B, two hours, 11.30am and 3.30pm)
Ko Lanta (450B, three hours, 11.30am)
Krabi (450B, four hours, 11.30am)
Phuket (650B, six hours, 11.30am)
Trang (200B, two hours, 11.30am)

BOAT

From mid-October to mid-May speedboats run from Pak Bara to Ao Pante Malacca on Ko Tarutao (450B, 30 minutes), and on to Ko Lipe (650B, 1½ hours) at 10.30am and 11.30am. There are further speedboats to Ko Lipe at 9.30am, 12.30pm, 2pm and 3pm. Boats return from Ko Lipe at 9am, 9.30am, 12.15pm, 1pm, 1.30pm and 4pm.

For Ko Bulon Leh (400B, 30 minutes), boats depart at 12.30pm and buzz on to Ko Lipe. If you miss the Bulon boat, you can charter long-tails from local fishermen (2000B, 1½ hours). D uring low season, services to Ko Lipe are weather dependent, but generally leave daily from Pak Bara at 11.30am, returning at 9.30am.

Ko Bulon Leh เกาะบุโหลนเล

Gracious Ko Bulon Leh, 23km west of Pak Bara, is surrounded by the Andaman's signature clear waters and has its share of faultless alabaster beaches with swaying casuarinas. This gorgeous island is in that perfect phase of being developed enough to offer comfortable facilities, yet it's not so popular that you have to book beach-time days in advance (though bungalow numbers are on the rise).

The exceptional, main white-sand beach extends along the east coast from Bulone Resort (p349), on the northeast cape, to Pansand Resort. In places it narrows, especially where buffered by gnarled mangroves and strewn with thick sun-bleached logs, making it easy to find a secret shady spot with dreamy views.

Sights & Activities

Bulon's lush interior is interlaced with tracks and trails that are fun to explore, though the dense, jungled rock that makes up the western half remains inaccessible on foot. The island's wild beauty is accessible on the northern coast at blue, coral-gravel-laden **Ao Panka Yai**, which has decent snorkelling. This bay is linked by a small paved path to **Ao Panka Noi**, a fishing village with beautiful karst views, long-tails docking on a gravel beach and a clutch of good, simple restaurants, on the eastern half of the northern coast. Follow a signposted trail nearby west through remnant jungle and rubber plantations – with eyes open wide lest you miss one of Bulon's enormous monitor lizards – to wind your way south to **Ao Muang** (Mango Bay), where there's an authentic *chow lair* squid-fishing camp.

There's good coral off **Laem Son** on the northeastern edge of the island and down the eastern coast. You can rent masks, snorkels and fin sets (200B) and kayaks (per hour 200B) at Bulone Resort and Pansand Resort. Snorkelling is best at low tide.

Resorts can arrange guided snorkelling trips (1700B, four hours, maximum six people) to other islands in the Ko Bulon group.

Tours usually take in the glassy emerald waters of **Ko Gai** (Map p350) and **Ko Ma** (Map p350), whose gnarled rocks have been ravaged by wind and time. But the most stunning sight is **White Rock** (Map p350): bird-blessed spires shooting out of the open sea. Beneath the surface is a mussel-crusted rock reef teeming with colourful fish.

Sleeping & Eating

Most places close from mid-April to November. For food, it's worth wandering over to Ao Panka Noi. There are a few local restaurants and shops in the Muslim village between Ao Panka Noi and Ao Panka Yai.

Chaolae Homestay BUNGALOW $
(Map p350; ☎086 967 0716, 086 290 2519; Ao Panka Yai; bungalow 500-600B; ⏲Dec-Apr) These classy, good-value, bamboo-and-wood bungalows have varnished wood interiors, thatched roofs and polished-cement bathrooms (with squat toilets). It's a blissfully quiet, shady spot, run by a welcoming *chow lair* family, and steps away from decent snorkelling at Ao Panka Yai.

Bulon Hill Resort BUNGALOW $$
(Map p350; ☎086 960 3890, 086 296 5809; www.bulonhill.com; bungalow 1300-1800B; ⏲Oct–mid-Apr) A collection of spacious, Thai-German-owned, concrete-and-wood bungalows and smaller bamboo ones, all with fans, stilted on the flower-strewn hill just inland from the northeast end of Bulon's main beach (it's signposted behind Bulone Resort). Electricity runs from 6pm to 6am. The recommended restaurant was being renovated at research time.

Bulone Resort HOTEL $$
(Map p350; ☎081 897 9084; www.bulone-resort.com; Main Beach; bungalow incl breakfast with fan 3500B, air-con 3000-4000B; ⏲Nov-Apr; ❄📶) Perched on Bulon's northeast cape with access to two exquisite white-sand stretches, Bulone Resort steals the island's top location. Cute whitewashed-wood bungalows (some fan, some air-con) come with queen-sized beds, iron frames and ocean breezes. Huge new alpine-chalet-style air-con rooms tower behind on stilts, with glorious views. Enjoy 24-hour electricity, a Thai-international **restaurant** (Map p350; mains 180-250B; ⏲7.30-10am & 6-10pm; 📶) and a coffee corner.

Su's Corner THAI, BREAKFAST $
(Map p350; ☎081 189 7183; Ao Panka Noi; dishes 80-100B; ⏲7am-8pm) Anyone who can transform vegie fried rice into something magical deserves high praise. This simple open-air cafe, with only a few tables scattered under palms just inland from Ao Panka Noi, is deservedly popular for its baguettes, shakes, cakes and Thai staples done with flair.

Information

Bulone Resort and Pansand Resort have wi-fi (nonguests per minute 3B). Bulone Resort also offers battery-charging services (free for restaurant clients).

Getting There & Away

From November to April, speedboats to Ko Bulon Leh (400B, 30 minutes) leave from Pak Bara at 12.30pm daily. Long-tail ship-to-shore transfers cost 50B; ask to be dropped off on the beach closest to your resort. In the reverse direction, the boat moors in the bay in front of Pansand Resort at 9am. You can charter long-tails to/from Pak Bara (2000B, 1½ hours).

From November to April, daily speedboats (600B, one hour) run from Ko Bulon Leh to Ko Lipe at 1pm, stopping in front of Pansand Resort. Boats originate in Ko Lanta (1600B, two hours) and make stops at Ko Ngai (1050B, 1½ hours), Ko Muk (900B, one hour) and Ko Kradan (900B, one hour), returning from Lipe at 9am.

Ko Tarutao Marine National Park

อุทยานแห่งชาติหมู่เกาะตะรุเตา

One of Thailand's most exquisite, unspoilt regions, **Ko Tarutao Marine National Park** (☎074 783485; www.dnp.go.th; adult/child 200/100B; ⏲mid-Oct–mid-May) encompasses 51 islands blanketed by well-preserved rainforest teeming with fauna, surrounded by healthy coral reefs and radiant white beaches. Born in 1974, it's the country's second marine national park. Within, you might spot dusky langurs, crab-eating macaques, mouse deer, wild pigs, sea otters, fishing cats, tree pythons, water monitors, Brahminy kites, sea eagles, hornbills, reef egrets and kingfishers.

The park's main accommodation consists of small, ecofriendly, government-run cabins. Pressure from big developers to build resorts on the islands has so far (mostly) been ignored, though concessions were made for the filming of American reality-TV series

Ko Tarutao Marine National Park & Around

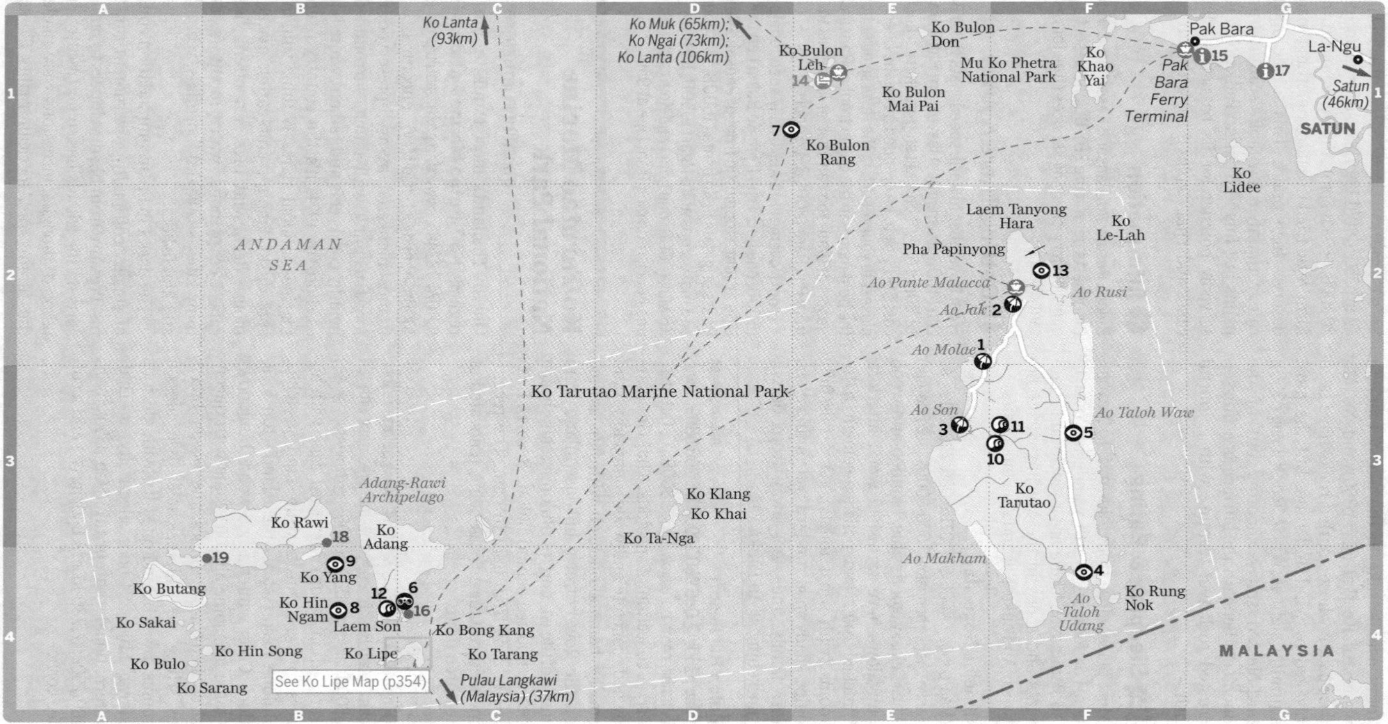

0 10 km
0 5 miles

Ko Lanta (93km)
Ko Muk (65km); Ko Ngai (73km); Ko Lanta (106km)
Ko Bulon Leh
14
Ko Bulon Don
Mu Ko Phetra National Park
Ko Khao Yai
Pak Bara
15
17
La-Ngu
Satun (46km)
Pak Bara Ferry Terminal
SATUN
Ko Bulon Mai Pai
7
Ko Bulon Rang
Ko Lidee
ANDAMAN SEA
Laem Tanyong Hara
Ko Le-Lah
Pha Papinyong
13
Ao Pante Malacca
Ao Rusi
Ao Jak
2
Ao Molae
1
Ko Tarutao Marine National Park
Ao Son
3
11
10
5
Ao Taloh Waw
Ko Tarutao
Adang-Rawi Archipelago
Ko Klang
Ko Khai
Ko Ta-Nga
Ko Rawi
18
Ko Adang
19
9
Ko Yang
Ao Makham
4
Ko Butang
12
6
16
Ko Hin Ngam
8
Laem Son
Ao Taloh Udang
Ko Rung Nok
Ko Sakai
Ko Bong Kang
Ko Hin Song
Ko Lipe
Ko Tarang
MALAYSIA
Ko Bulo
Ko Sarang
See Ko Lipe Map (p354)
Pulau Langkawi (Malaysia) (37km)

Ko Tarutao Marine National Park & Around

Sights
1 Ao Molae E2
2 Ao Pante Malacca F2
3 Ao Son E3
4 Ao Taloh Udang F4
5 Ao Taloh Waw F3
6 Chado Cliff C4
7 Ko Gai D1
8 Ko Hin Ngam B4
Ko Ma .... (see 7)
9 Ko Yang B4
10 Nam Tok Lo Po F3
11 Nam Tok Lu Du F3
12 Pirate's Falls B4
13 Tham Jara-Khe F2
Toe-Boo Cliff .... (see 2)

Activities, Courses & Tours
White Rock .... (see 7)

Sleeping
Ao Molae National Park Accommodation .... (see 1)
Ao Pante Malacca National Park Accommodation .... (see 2)
Ao Son National Park Accommodation .... (see 3)
Bulon Hill Resort .... (see 14)
14 Bulone Resort E1
Chaolae Homestay .... (see 14)
Ko Tarutao Marine National Park Accommodation .... (see 16)

Eating
Ao Pante Malacca Canteen .... (see 2)
Ao Son Canteen .... (see 3)
Bulone Resort .... (see 14)
Su's Corner .... (see 14)

Information
Ao Molae Ranger Station .... (see 1)
Ao Son Ranger Station .... (see 3)
Ao Taloh Udang Ranger Station .... (see 4)
Ao Taloh Waw Ranger Station .... (see 5)
Ko Tarutao Marine National Park Headquarters .... (see 2)
15 Ko Tarutao Marine National Park Visitors Centre G1
Ko Tarutao Visitors Centre .... (see 2)
16 Laem Son Ranger Station C4
17 Mu Ko Phetra National Park Headquarters G1
18 Ranger Station B3
19 Ranger Station B4

Survivor (2002). And there is the minor issue of a private resort on Ko Adang, which is supposedly off-limits to developers. It was originally scheduled to open in 2010, but local environmentalists have managed to keep it shut, so far.

Rubbish on the islands is a problem. Removal of beach and visitor refuse only happens sporadically, though successful Trash Hero (p355) clean-ups are improving things. Do your part and tread lightly.

Ko Tarutao is the biggest and second-most visited island in the group (after Ko Lipe). It's home to the park headquarters (p352) and most government-run accommodation. There are no foreign-exchange facilities on Ko Tarutao; you can change cash at travel agencies in Pak Bara and there are ATMs in Pak Bara and La-Ngu.

Most travellers choose to stay on Ko Lipe (p353) which, despite being inside the park, has rapidly morphed into a popular, increasingly paved resort island overflowing with tourist facilities and hotels. Curiously, the island has managed to evade the park's protection because it is home to communities of *chow lair*, making it exempt from zero development laws.

Long-tail tours to outlying islands can be arranged through travel agencies in Satun or Pak Bara, through the national park headquarters on Ko Tarutao, or through Ko Lipe's resorts and long-tail boat operators.

Ko Tarutao เกาะตะรุเตา

Most of Ko Tarutao's whopping 152 sq km is covered in old-growth jungle, rising sharply to the park's 713m peak. Just 22km southwest of Pak Bara, this is one of Thailand's wildest islands. Mangrove swamps and impressive limestone cliffs circle much of Tarutao. The western coast is dotted with caves and peaceful white-sand beaches.

Tarutao's sordid history partly explains its preservation. Between 1938 and 1948, more than 3000 Thai criminals, including 70 political rebels, were incarcerated here. Among them were interesting inmates such as So Setabutra, who compiled the first Thai–English dictionary while imprisoned on Tarutao, and Sittiporn Gridagon, son of Rama VII. During WWII, food and medical supplies from the mainland were severely depleted and hundreds of prisoners died from malaria, starvation and maltreatment. Prisoners and guards allied and mutinied, taking to piracy in the nearby Strait of Malacca until they were suppressed by British troops in 1946.

The park entrance fee (adult/child 200/100B) is payable on arrival at **park headquarters** (Map p350; Ao Pante Malacca; ⊙8am-5pm) on Tarutao's northwest side. The **visitors centre** (Map p350; ⊙8am-5pm) here hands out maps and has detailed displays on local history, geography, fauna and flora, plus a fascinating dusty library.

Sights & Activities

With a navigable river and long paved roads, Tarutao is perfect for independent exploration. Hire kayaks (per hour/day 200/500B) or mountain bikes (50/250B) from park headquarters.

Ao Pante Malacca BEACH

(อาวพันเตมะละกา; Map p350) Ao Pante Malacca, on the northwest Ko Tarutao, is the island's main arrival and departure point, with a lovely creamy beach shaded by pandanus and casuarinas. It is also home to the park headquarters and most park accommodation.

Toe-Boo Cliff VIEWPOINT

(จุดชมวิวผาโต๊ะบู; Map p350) Behind park headquarters at Ao Pante Malacca, on the northwest side of the island, a steep 500m (20-minute) trail winds through the jungle below a limestone karst dripping with precipitation, then climbs a series of stone-cut steps to this dramatic rocky outcrop with fabulous views across Ko Tarutao towards Ko Adang and other surrounding isles.

Tham Jara-Khe CAVE

(ถ้ำจระเข้, Crocodile Cave; Map p350) The large stream flowing inland from Ao Pante Malacca, on northwest Ko Tarutao, leads to Tham Jara-Khe, once home to deadly saltwater crocodiles. The cave is navigable for 1km at low tide and can be visited on long-tail tours (500B) from Ao Pante Malacca's jetty.

Ao Molae BEACH

(อาวเมาะและ; Map p350) Quiet, wonderfully secluded and unbelievably beautiful, Ao Molae has an exquisite white-sand beach backed by a ranger station, bungalows and a campsite, all a (very) hilly 4km walk/cycle south of Ao Pante Malacca.

Ao Son BEACH

(อาวสน; Map p350) On the western coast, a 30-minute boat ride (1500B) or 8km walk/cycle south of Ao Pante Malacca, is this isolated bay. A signposted track 300m inland from the beach leads to **Nam Tok Lu Du** (Lu Du Waterfall; Map p350) (3km, 1½ hours each way). You can also hike inland to **Nam Tok Lo Po** (Lo Po Waterfall; Map p350) (5km, 2½ hours each way) via a trail that starts 500m south down Ao Son's beach.

Ao Taloh Waw BAY

(อาวตะโละวาว; Map p350) The prison camp for civilian prisoners was on Ko Tarutao's isolated eastern coast, 12km southeast of Ao Pante Malacca. A historical trail leads through Ao Taloh Waw's old **prison site**, though the original buildings are long gone. Long-tails from Ao Pante Malacca charge 2500B return.

Ao Taloh Udang BAY

(อาวตะโละอุดัง; Map p350) The overgrown ruins of Tarutao's **political prisoners' camp** can be seen at Ao Taloh Udang, 24km southeast of the park headquarters. Return long-tail charters from the jetty at Ao Pante Malacca cost 3500B (about three hours).

Sleeping & Eating

There's government-run accommodation at Ao Pante Malacca, Ao Molae and Ao Son. Water is rationed, rubbish is (sporadically) transported back to the mainland and electricity runs from 6.30pm to 6am.

Camping (site per person 30B, with tent hire 225B) is permitted under casuarinas at Ao Molae and Ao Son, where there are toilets and showers, and on the wild beaches of Ao Makham, Ao Taloh Waw and Ao Taloh Udang, where you'll need to be self-sufficient. Monkeys often wander into tents, destroying or eating everything they find inside, so shut it all tight.

Accommodation can be booked online or, more easily, at the park's visitors centre (p348) in Pak Bara.

Ao Pante Malacca National Park Accommodation BUNGALOW $

(Map p350; Ao Pante Malacca; r 500-1000B; ⊙Nov–mid-May) The biggest spread of government-run sleeping options, conveniently near the facilities and park offices. Newer, fan-cooled bungalows with balconies sleep two. Simpler longhouse rooms with shared bathroom fit up to four people. The semi-open-air **canteen** (mains 80-180B; ⊙7.45am-2.30pm & 5.30-8.30pm) does good, straightforward Thai cooking. There's beer at the small convenience shop.

Ao Molae National Park Accommodation BUNGALOW $

(Map p350; www.dnp.go.th; Ao Molae; r 600B; ⌚Nov–mid-May) Simple and reasonably clean (not spotless) one- and two-room duplexes with classic mint-green national-park bedding stand right on the edge of the beach amid palms and casuarinas. Thai meals are available at the small **canteen** (mains 70-140B; ⌚7am-2pm & 5-9pm).

Ao Son National Park Accommodation BUNGALOW $

(Map p350; www.dnp.go.th; Ao Son; r 300-500B; ⌚Nov–mid-May) Basic, clean-enough, concrete rooms with shared showers and toilets, just back from isolated Ao Son's beautiful beach. Also here is a **canteen** (mains 60-140B; ⌚7am-8pm) offering simple Thai fare, drinks and snacks.

Getting There & Around

From 21 October to mid-May, the 10.30am and 11.30am speedboats from Pak Bara to Ko Lipe stop at Ko Tarutao (450B, 30 minutes). Only the 9am boat from Lipe to Pak Bara drops passengers at Tarutao. The island officially closes from mid-May to mid-October. During high season, you can visit on speedboat day tours from Pak Bara (around 2000B; includes park fees, lunch, drinks and snorkelling).

If you're staying at Ao Molae, take a shared van from Ao Pante Malacca at 11am or 1pm daily (per person 50B; demand-dependent).

Ko Lipe เกาะหลีเป๊ะ

Ko Lipe is this decade's poster child for untamed development in Thailand's islands. Blessed with two wide white-sand beaches separated by jungled hills and within spitting distance of protected coral reefs, seven or eight years ago the island was only spoken about in secretive 'rising star' whispers. Then the whispers became small talk, which quickly turned into a roar – you know, the kind generally associated with bulldozers. The biggest losers have been the 700-strong community of *chow lair* (sea gypsy) villagers, whose ancestors were gifted Lipe as a home by King Rama V in 1909, but eventually sold to a Thai developer with suspected mafia ties in the 1970s.

The big fear continues to be whether or not Lipe will become another Phi-Phi: a victim of its own beauty. Those fears were stoked back in 2009 when a bass-heavy nightclub arrived on Hat Pattaya. Although the club was shut down, development hasn't stopped. Walking St arrived in 2010 and, in between the glorious beaches, there's an ever-expanding concrete maze of cafes, travel agencies, shops and salons. Even 7-Eleven has landed.

But there's still plenty to love, and love deeply, about Lipe: gorgeous salt-white sand crescents, perfectly chilled-out reggae bars, some sensational dive sites, a jungle-clad interior, a contagiously friendly vibe and a good few inhabitants keen to minimise their environmental impact. You'll just have to look a little harder to find it all.

There are ATMS on Walking St. Most hotels offer free (often slow) wi-fi.

Activities

There are few experiences as relaxing as put-putting between the jungled gems of Ko Rawi, Ko Adang and surrounding islets. The best way to see the archipelago is to hire a *chow lair* captain from the **Taxi Boat** (Map p354) stand on Hat Sunrise. You can rent kayaks (per hour 250B) across the island, including at Sabye Divers (p355) and Daya's (p357).

Beaches

Be careful while swimming, especially in low season. A swimmer was killed in 2013 when a long-tail ran him down. Don't expect boats to see you!

Do not try to swim the narrow strait between Lipe and Adang at any time of year; currents are swift and can be deadly.

Hat Pattaya BEACH

(Map p354) Busy Hat Pattaya on Lipe's southern coast has some terrific beach bars, seafood and a party vibe during the high season, though long-tails often crowd out swimmers.

Hat Sunrise BEACH

(Map p354) Windswept Hat Sunrise, a sublime long stretch of powder-fine sand, runs along the island's east coast. From its northernmost point you'll have spectacular Ko Adang views.

Hat Sunset BEACH

(Map p354) With its golden sand, gentle jungled hills and serene bay that spills into the Adang Strait on the western side of the island, Hat Sunset has an altogether different feel to Lipe's other beaches and, blissfully, retains the island's wild soul.

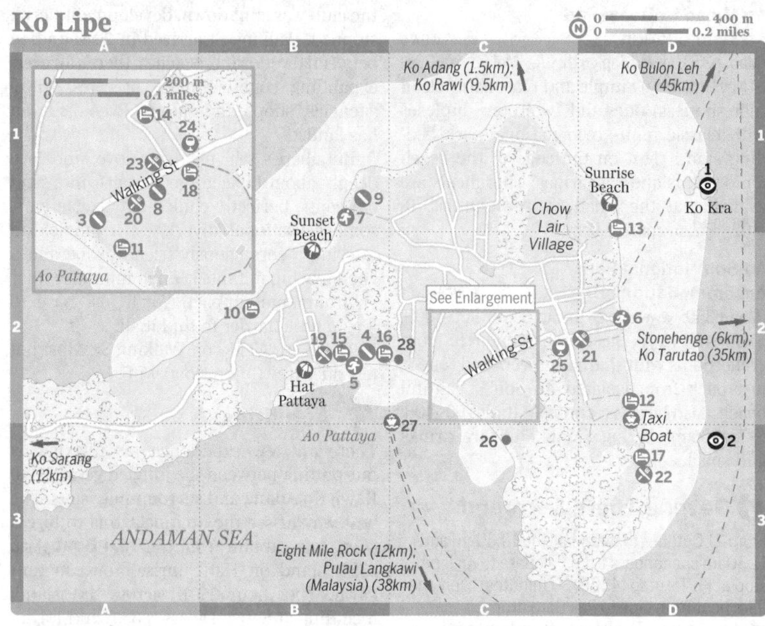

Ko Lipe

Sights

1	Ko Kra	D1
2	Ko Usen	D3

Activities, Courses & Tours

	Castaway Divers	(see 12)
	Davy Jones' Locker	(see 15)
	Forra Dive	(see 13)
3	Forra Dive	A1
4	Forra Dive	B2
5	Hat Pattaya	B2
6	Hat Sunrise	D2
7	Hat Sunset	B1
8	Ko Lipe Diving	A1
9	Sabye Divers	B1

Sleeping

10	Bila Beach	B2
11	Blue Tribes	A2
12	Castaway Resort	D2
13	Forra Dive	D1
	Forra Dive 2	(see 4)
14	Gecko Lipe	A1
15	Koh Lipe Backpackers Hostel	B2
16	Mali Resort	B2
17	Serendipity	D3
18	The Box	A1

Eating

19	Daya's	B2
20	Elephant Coffee House	A1
21	Nee Papaya	D2
22	On The Rocks	D3
23	Papaya Mom	A1
	The Box	(see 18)

Drinking & Nightlife

24	Maya Bar	A1
25	Pooh's Bar	C2

Information

26	Immigration Office	C3

Transport

27	Ferry Jetty	C2
28	Satun Pak Bara Speedboat Club	C2

Diving

While it would be a stretch to call the diving here world-class most of the year, it's outstanding when the visibility clarifies, somewhat counter-intuitively, in the early part of the wet season (15 April to 15 June). There are some fun drift dives and two rock-star dive sites.

Eight Mile Rock is a deep pinnacle that attracts devil rays and (very) rare whale sharks. It's the only site in the area to see pelagics. **Stonehenge** is popular because of its beautiful soft corals, resident seahorses, rare leopard sharks and the reef-top boulders behind its inspired name. **Ko Sarang** is another stunner with gorgeous soft corals, a ripping current and solar flares of fish that make it many people's favourite Lipe dive spot.

Forra Dive DIVING

(Map p354; ☎084 407 5691; www.forradiving.com; Hat Sunrise; 1/2 dives 1500/2800B; ⊙Nov-mid-May) French-owned Forra is one of Lipe's longest running outfitters. It offers snorkelling trips (from 650B), Discover Scuba (2500B), Open Water Diver courses (13,500B) and Lipe's only live-aboard operation (three-day trip 10,000B). These 'marine safaris' visit Hin Daeng and Hin Muang, one of Thailand's top dive sites, en route north to Ko Phi-Phi. Branches on **Walking St** and **Hat Pattaya**.

Castaway Divers DIVING

(Map p354; ☎087 478 1516; www.kohlipedivers.com; Castaway Resort, Hat Sunrise; 1/2 dives 1600/3000B; ⊙10am-8pm) Offers a range of specialised courses (night diving, underwater photography) along with the usual, and more intimate dives off long-tail boats. Maximum four people per group.

Ko Lipe Diving DIVING

(Map p354; ☎088 397 7749, 087 622 6204; www.kolipediving.com; Walking St; 1/2 dives 1700/2800B; ⊙8am-10pm) Well-organised, professional dive operator with consistently glowing reviews for its selection of specialist courses and fun dives focused on diving education. Two-dive Discover Scuba costs 3000B; SSI/PADI OWD certification is 14,000/14,500B.

Sabye Divers DIVING

(Map p354; ☎089 464 5884; www.sabyesports.com; Hat Sunset; 2/3 dives 2700/3500B; ⊙8.30am-8pm) Longstanding Sabye Divers is a small Greenfins-certified shop owned by a long-time expat. They're experienced and do a selection of PADI certification courses (from 10,500B) plus fun dives and Discover Scuba (2400B).

Snorkelling

There's good coral located along the southern coast and around **Ko Kra** (Map p354) and **Ko Usen** (Map p354), the islets that are opposite Hat Sunrise (be careful with oncoming long-tailed boats). Most resorts rent out mask and snorkel sets and fins (200B), and arrange various four-point snorkelling trips to Ko Adang, Ko Rawi and other coral-fringed islands (a group trip per person 550B; private 1700B, a maximum of five people).

Volunteering

Trash Hero VOLUNTEERING

(www.trashhero.org) The pioneering, increasingly successful brainchild of a Thai-Swiss duo, Trash Hero organises regular Monday volunteer clean-ups to preserve Lipe's beloved white-sand beaches and others in Ko Tarutao Marine National Park. The program launched in December 2013 with the straightforward aim of protecting the islands' beaches using only materials and people-power to hand. Local businesses quickly pledged support, supplying long-tailed boats, food, drinks and rubbish bags.

Over 1000 volunteers (locals and tourists) have since removed 21,000kg of rubbish from local beaches. Trash Hero now runs weekly clean-ups at 11 official points across Thailand and Indonesia.

Yoga

Swing by Castaway Resort (p356) for high-season yoga (450B; 7am and 4.30pm).

Sleeping

More and more Ko Lipe resorts are staying open year-round. A few humble bamboo bungalows still stand strong, but charmless package-tour type resorts are colonising, particularly on Hat Pattaya. Book well ahead during high season and holidays, when prices skyrocket.

Koh Lipe Backpackers Hostel HOSTEL $

(Map p354; ☎085 361 7923; www.kohlipebackpackers.com; Hat Pattaya; dm 400-500B, r 2500-3000B; ❄📶) The first of its kind on Lipe, this classic 21st-century backpacker pad houses spotless, spacious, air-conditioned eight-bed dorms in a contemporary-style concrete block on west Hat Pattaya. Showers are shared, but you get private lockers, wi-fi, an on-site **Davy Jones' Locker dive school** (dives from 2500B) and a fun young vibe. Upstairs are comfy air-con doubles brushed in pastels.

The Box BOUTIQUE HOTEL $$

(Map p354; ☎086 957 2480; www.theboxliperesort.com; Walking St; r incl breakfast with fan 1200-1900B, air-con 1600-2900B; ❄📶) Bang in the middle of Walking St is this alluring boutique hotel crafted from shipping containers, dressed up in natural wood panelling and connected by wooden paths through gardens. Interiors are stylishly minimalist with bamboo beds, colour feature walls and square wash basins. Linger over tasty tapas in the superb Spanish-Mediterranean restaurant (p357) out front.

Forra Dive BUNGALOW $$

(Map p354; ☎084 407 5691; www.forradiving.com; Hat Sunrise; bungalow 1000-1400B; 📶) Forra captures the look of Lipe's pirate spirit with a range of those beloved bamboo bungalows and lofts, the best of which sport indoor-outdoor bathrooms and hammock-strung terraces. Divers get same-day 25% off lodging and there's a second location with similar-style bungalows on Hat Pattaya. Sometimes it's divers-only.

Bila Beach BUNGALOW $$

(Map p354; ☎087 570 3684; www.bilabeachresort.com; Hat Sunset; bungalow 1500B) A killer bamboo reggae bar and beachfront restaurant lurk below stylish shaggy-haired cliffside bungalows set above a tiny, secluded white-sand cove, which is strewn with boulders and adjacent to Hat Sunset. It's the perfect setting for your hippie honeymoon and a short sweaty walk over the hill from Hat Pattaya.

Gecko Lipe BUNGALOW $$

(Map p354; ☎087 810 7257; www.geckolipe.com; 61 Mu 7, Walking St; r small 800-1200B, large 1630-2530B; 📶) Here is a wonderful hilltop collection of fan-cooled bamboo bungalows in two sizes nestled among trees. The smaller white-washed variety offers blonde floors and colourful-walled, cold-water bathrooms. The larger, thatch-topped golden-bamboo edition has stylish hot-water bathrooms and thicker mattresses. Good low-season discounts.

Blue Tribes BUNGALOW $$

(Map p354; ☎083 654 0316, 080 546 9464; www.bluetribeslipe.com; Hat Pattaya; bungalow 1400-2800B; ⏲Aug-May; 📶) Tucked into flower-filled gardens, Blue Tribes is one of Hat Pattaya's more attractive small resorts. The best choices are two-storey thatched wooden bungalows with downstairs living rooms and top-floor bedrooms fronted by sliding doors opening to sea views. Some rooms have minor wear and tear but all are comfy and most have breezy porches.

★Castaway Resort HOTEL $$$

(Map p354; ☎081 170 7605, 083 138 7472; www.castaway-resorts.com; Hat Sunrise; bungalow 3400-5400B; 📶) 🍃 Roomy dark-wood bungalows with hammock-laden terraces, cushions everywhere, overhead fans and fabulous, modern-meets-natural bathrooms embody Lipe at its barefoot-beach-chic best. This welcoming resort is also one of Lipe's most environmentally friendly, run on solar water heaters and lights (there's no AC). There's a super-chilled beachside cafe, plus high-season yoga classes (450B) and a good dive school (p355).

Mali Resort RESORT $$$

(Map p354; ☎091 979 4600; www.maliresortkohlipe.com; Hat Pattaya; bungalow incl breakfast 3700-9945B; ❄📶) Chic, laid-back and Bali-inspired, the gorgeous new bungalows at this American-owned resort offer dark-wood floors, thatched beamed ceilings, built-in day beds, carved-wood elephant lamps, colourful wall art and giant outdoor bathrooms with dual shower heads. All rooms offer access to the stunning, sophisticated beach bar and an ideal slab of Pattaya beachfront. Best deals online.

There are also older, more affordable garden cottages done up in plush linens.

Serendipity BUNGALOW $$$

(Map p354; ☎088 395 5158; www.serendipityresort-kohlipe.com; Hat Sunrise; r 7800-19,000B; ❄📶🏊) An exquisitely designed orange-themed spot, delightfully isolated by draping itself up above the boulder-strewn southern point of Hat Sunrise and accessed via a wooden boardwalk. Spacious dark-wood thatched bungalows feature private patios, seating areas inside and out, brass-bowl sinks, tea and coffee sets and air-con. The two penthouse suites include private pools with swoon-worthy views. The Thai/international **bar-restaurant** (mains 165-375B; ⏲noon-9.30pm; 📶) clings to the cliffside.

Eating

Find cheap eats at the roti stands and small Thai cafes along Walking St. Please take advantage of the waste-reducing water refill points at many resorts and eateries.

★Nee Papaya THAI $

(Map p354; mains 80-150B; ⏲9am-9.30pm) Delightful Nee offers an affordable fish grill nightly, all the standard curries (including a dynamite beef *pá·naang*), noodles and stir fries (beef, chicken, seafood or vegie), along with a tremendous array of fiery Isan dishes. She'll tone down the chilli quotient on request, but her food is best when spiced for the local palate, which is why she attracts droves of in-the-know Thai tourists.

Papaya Mom THAI $

(Map p354; Walking St; mains 90-200B; ⏲9am-10pm; ✎) A cute Isan food stall notable for its authentic eats and especially succulent meat dishes popular with local Thais (grilled spicy pork neck, *lâhp*). Vegetarians can raid the luscious fruit stand and thoughtful veg menu featuring a delicious bean-curd-and-bean-sprouts stir-fry.

The Box SPANISH, MEDITERRANEAN $$

(Map p354; ☎086 957 2480; www.theboxlipresort.com; Walking St; tapas 170-235B, mains 300-380B; ⏲7am-10.30pm; 📶) If you fancy a break from flaming-hot curries and seafood grills (it happens), rustle up a *tinto de verano* (red wine with lemonade) and a parade of authentically good Spanish tapas specials at this casually elegant, modern, wood-clad space. Top of the list are Spanish potato omelette, garlic prawns, Iberian ham, brie-and-caramelised-onion toast and some highly recommended (not-so-Spanish) burgers.

Daya's SEAFOOD, THAI $$

(Map p354; Hat Pattaya; mains 150-300B; ⏲7am-10pm) One of few places still locally run, Daya's is arguably the best of the fresh seafood barbecues put on nightly by Hat Pattaya's resorts.

Elephant Coffee House INTERNATIONAL $$

(Map p354; www.facebook.com/ElephantKohLipe; Walking St; dishes 180-440B; ⏲8am-1am) The bar is a long-tail, secondhand books are for sale and black-and-white local-life photos are plastered across varnished-concrete walls. Pop into this contemporary cafe for fabulous all-day breakfasts of thick French toast, excellent coffee and homemade muesli loaded with tropical fruit. Otherwise choose from fresh salads, sandwiches, burgers and the like. Also hosts live music.

Drinking & Nightlife

Good espresso-based coffee has become Lipe's thing. Coffee shops are sprinkled all over the island, particularly on Walking St.

Thankfully, driftwood-clad Rasta bars can still be found on all beaches. At least some things never change.

Maya Bar BAR

(Map p354; Walking St; ⏲6pm-late) A forever-packed, open-air cocktail bar that feels sultrily modern-rustic thanks to faded log stools, chunky-wood tables, flickering candles and a bamboo 'wall'. DJs spin dance/electronic beats after dark.

Pooh's Bar BAR

(Map p354; ☎074 750345, 089 463 5099; www.poohlipe.com; Walking St; ⏲10am-10.30pm; 📶) This expansive complex (which includes bungalows, a dive shop and several restaurants) was built by a Lipe pioneer and remains a popular local expat hang-out. Nightly films and sports are projected onto the big screen and there's often live music.

Getting There & Away

From 21 October to mid-May, speedboats run from Pak Bara to Ko Lipe via Ko Tarutao or Ko Bulon Leh at 9.30am, 10.30am, 11.30am, 2pm and 3pm (650B, 1½ hours). Boats return to Pak Bara at 9am, 9.30am, 12.15pm, 1pm, 1.30pm and 4pm. Low-season transport is weather dependent, but there's usually a direct daily boat from Pak Bara to Lipe at 11.30am, returning at 9.30am.

From November to late April, the high-speed **Tigerline** (☎081 358 0808, 089 737 0552; www.tigerlinetravel.com) ferry departs Ko Lipe at 10am for Phuket (2400B, eight hours), via Ko Phi-Phi (1950B, seven hours), Ko Lanta (1700B, five hours), Ko Muk (1600B, 3½ hours), Ko Kradan (1800B, 3½ hours) and Ko Ngai (1600B, 4½ hours).

From mid-November to late March, **Bundhaya Speedboat** (☎081 678 2826, 074 7503889; www.bundhayaspeedboat.com) and **Satun Pak Bara Speedboat Club** (Map p354; ☎099 404 0409, 099 414 4994; www.tarutaolipeisland.com) leave Ko Lipe at 9am for Ko Lanta (1900B, three hours), via Ko Bulon Leh (600B, one hour), Ko Kradan (1400B, two hours), Ko Muk (1400B, two hours) and Ko Ngai (1600B, 2½ hours). Speedboats return from Lanta at 10.30am.

Boats also run from Ko Lipe to Pulau Langkawi (p347) in Malaysia, mid-October to mid-April.

No matter which boat you end up using, you'll have to take a 50B long-tail shuttle to/from the **floating ferry jetty** (Map p354) off Hat Pattaya, and pay a 20B 'entrance fee'. It's part of a local agreement to share the flow. Speedboats *may* drop you directly on Hat Pattaya.

Ko Adang & Ko Rawi เกาะอาดัง/เกาะราวี

Ko Adang, the 30-sq-km island immediately north of Ko Lipe, has brooding, densely forested hills, white-sand beaches and healthy coral reefs. Lots of snorkelling tours make a stop here. Inland are a few short jungle trails and tumbling waterfalls, including **Pirate's Falls** (Map p350; Ko Adang), which is rumoured to have been a freshwater source for pirates (more of a cascading river than a waterfall). There are great views from **Chado Cliff** (Map p350; Ko Adang), a half-hour hike above the main beach; apparently pirates plotted attacks on commercial ships from this viewpoint.

Ko Rawi, a rocky, 29-sq-km jungled ellipse 1km west of Ko Adang, has first-rate beaches and large coral reefs offshore. Excellent snorkelling spots include north **Ko Yang** (Map p350), 1km south of Ko Rawi's south-eastern end, and tiny **Ko Hin Ngam** (Map p350), 3km further south, which has underwater fields of giant clams, vibrant anemones and striped pebble beaches. Legend has it that these stones are cursed: anyone who removes one will experience bad luck until the stone is returned.

Sleeping & Eating

Camping (site per person 30B) at Ao Lik on Ko Rawi is allowed, with park permission.

Ko Tarutao Marine National Park Accommodation BUNGALOW $
(Map p350; www.dnp.go.th; Ko Adang; d 600B, 6-person 1800B, camp site per person 30B, with tent hire 225B; Nov–mid-May) Ko Adang's park accommodation is near Laem Son ranger station in the island's southeast. There are attractive, fan-cooled doubles and six-person family bungalows, all with attached cold-water bathrooms, plus camping facilities. Book ahead, online or at the Pak Bara park visitors centre (p348). A small restaurant provides good Thai meals.

Getting There & Away

Long-tails from Ko Lipe take you to Ko Adang for around 200B or Ko Rawi for 500B, though you may have to bargain. Even a short stop on the islands will cost you the park entrance fee.

Understand Thailand's Islands & Beaches

Thailand's Islands & Beaches Today

These are troubled times for Thailand. With the military in charge again and no prospect of elections before 2017, the country remains divided politically between the rural poor and the traditional elite and the urban middle classes. A slowing economy and a poor human rights record have also tarnished Thailand's image as an oasis of relative stability in Southeast Asia. But visitors, especially from China, are still coming in droves.

Best in Print

Very Thai (Philip Cornwell-Smith) Colourful photos and essays on Thailand's quirks.

A Kingdom in Crisis: Thailand's Struggle for Democracy in the Twenty-First Century (Andrew MacGregor Marshall) Banned in Thailand, so read it before you go.

King Bhumibol Adulyadej: A Life's Work (Nicholas Grossman et al) Official biography of the king.

Best on Film

Tom-Yum-Goong (Prachya Pinkaew; 2005) Successful martial arts movie starring Tony Jaa, the Jackie Chan of Thailand.

Paradoxocracy (Pen-ek Ratanaruang; 2013) Traces the country's political history from the 1932 revolution on.

OK Baytong (2003) A drama about Buddhist–Muslim relations in the Deep South.

Top News Analysis Sites

The Diplomat (thediplomat.com) Current affairs magazine covering Asia Pacific.

New Mandala (asiapacific.anu.edu.au/newmandala) Commentary on news, society and culture in Southeast Asia.

Asia Times Online (atimes.com) Solid Southeast Asia reporting.

Another Day, Another Coup

On 22 May 2014, the Thai military under General Prayuth Chan-o-cha overthrew the elected Puea Thai government led by Yingluck Shinawatra. It was the 13th coup in Thailand since 1932 and brought to an end months of political crisis that saw parts of central Bangkok occupied by anti-government protestors. Prayuth said the coup was necessary to restore stability and end the risk of violence between the supporters of Yingluck and her exiled elder brother (also the former prime minister) Thaksin Shinawatra, and their opponents who regard Thaksin as the Lord Voldemort of Thailand. But while the coup was hailed by the urban middle classes and traditional elite, who accuse the Shinawatras of massive corruption, they are far outnumbered by the legions of rural poor who regard Thaksin as the only politician to have ever done anything for them.

Prayuth is now the head of the Orwellian-sounding National Council for Peace and Order (NCPO), the name the junta have given to their government. Since taking power the NCPO has repealed the 2007 constitution and ordered a new one to be drafted, muzzled the media and detained and imprisoned political opponents. Despite assurances that the NCPO would run the country only temporarily, there has been no announcement on when elections are likely to be held. What is certain is that they will not happen until the new constitution is finalised. With the first draft of the new version rejected in September 2015, few political commentators believe there will be an election until 2017 at the earliest. Even fewer are confident the revised constitution will end Thailand's bitter political divisions.

The NCPO is now under pressure for its failure to address Thailand's slumping economy. With foreign investment down since the coup and a deadly bomb attack in central Bangkok in August 2015 seemingly designed to hurt the crucial tourism sector, there is real concern over Thailand's economic future. Thailand's international image has also been damaged by increasing criticism of its human rights record, with human trafficking scandals and the alleged abuse of migrant workers highlighted by both the EU and Washington.

Southern Separatism

Thailand's south is mostly synonymous with golden beaches and swaying palm trees, but in the Deep South, abutting the Malaysian border, a long-running insurgency pits the Thai security forces against ethnic Malay Muslim separatists. Thailand's three southernmost provinces, Yala, Pattani and Narathiwat, and bits of neighbouring Songkhla Province, were once part of the sultanate of Pattani, which ruled the region from the 15th century until the turn of the 20th century when Buddhist Siam claimed the land. These areas have retained their culture and Muslim religion and speak their own language: Yawi, a Malay dialect. After 100-plus years of Thai rule, many of the area's 1.8 million residents want their own independent state or, at the very least, autonomy from Bangkok.

Resentment of the Thai authorities' heavy-handed rule of the region, which includes making the mostly Muslim, Yawi-speaking school population study in Thai and learn about Buddhism, has long festered. But the insurgency really kicked into life in 2004, after security forces crushed a demonstration in Tak Bai in Narathiwat Province, resulting in the deaths of 85 protesters. Now, an estimated 12,500 to 15,000 insurgents launch regular attacks. Almost 6000 people have been killed in the insurgency since 2004, making this Southeast Asia's most violent conflict, but foreigners have never been targeted.

Sporadic peace talks have taken place over the years, often hosted by Malaysia, but have foundered on the inability of either side to compromise or trust each other. The latest round began in August 2015 in Kuala Lumpur, with the different separatist groups uniting under the umbrella name Mara Patani and negotiating directly with the Thai government. But after a decade of violence, there is no end in sight to the insurgency, and many Thais are only dimly aware of why their army continues to fight in the Deep South.

POPULATION: **68.65 MILLION**

GDP: **US$373.8 BILLION**

GDP PER CAPITA: **US$5560**

UNEMPLOYMENT: **0.9%**

POPULATION BELOW THE POVERTY LINE: **13.2%**

if Thailand were 100 people

75 would be Thai
14 would be Chinese
11 would be Other

belief systems

(% of population)

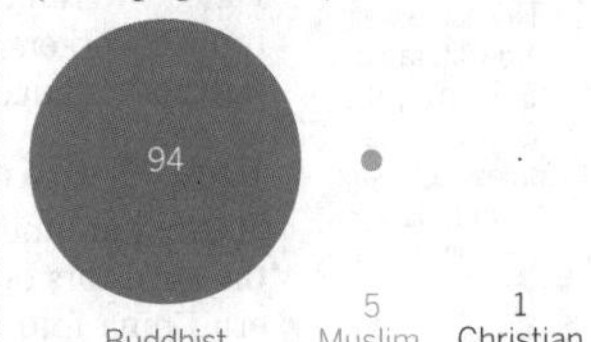

population per sq km

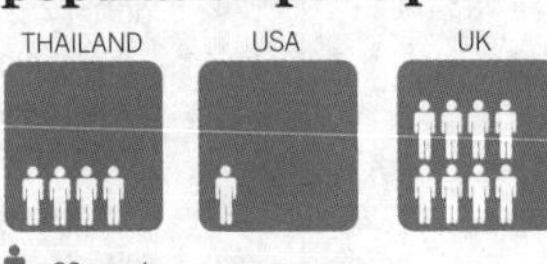

History & Politics

Thailand's history begins in neolithic times, moves through the dawn of Hindu and Buddhist civilisations and morphs into a time of great immigration, wars and various kingdoms. Since 1932 the country has been nominally a democracy, but frequent coups mean that in reality there have only been a few truly democratic governments since then.

History

Thai history began with immigrants from all directions exchanging dominance over the land. Eventually the country fused a national identity around language, religion and monarchy. While the kings resisted colonisation from the expansionist West, they ceded their absolute grip on the country when challenged by forces within. Since the transition to a constitutional monarchy in 1932, the military has predominantly ruled the country with a few democratic hiccups in between. Ongoing political tensions continue to fester.

Ancient History

Relief carvings at Angkor Wat depict Tai mercenaries serving in Khmer armies. The Khmer called them 'Syam'. The name was transliterated to 'Siam' by the English trader James Lancaster in 1592.

Little evidence remains of the cultures that existed in Thailand before the middle of the 1st millennium AD. *Homo erectus* fossils in Thailand's northern province of Lampang date back at least 500,000 years, and the country's most important archaeological site is Ban Chiang, outside Udon Thani, which provides evidence of one of the world's oldest agrarian societies. It is believed that the Mekong River Valley and Khorat Plateau were inhabited as far back as 10,000 years ago by farmers and bronze-workers. Cave paintings in Pha Taem National Park near Ubon Ratchathani date back some 3000 years.

Early Empires

Starting around the 10th century, the 'Tai' people, who are considered the ancestors of the contemporary Thais, began emigrating from southern China into present-day Southeast Asia. These immigrants came in consecutive waves and spoke Tai-Kadai, a family of monosyllabic and

TIMELINE

4000–2500 BC

Prehistoric Neolithic people develop pottery, rice and cereal cultivation, cattle and pig farming, and bronze metallurgy in northern Thailand.

6th–11th centuries AD

The Buddhist and Hindu, Indian-influenced Dvaravati, thought to be predominantly of the Mon ethnicity, establish city-states in central Thailand.

9th–13th centuries

Angkor extends control across parts of Thailand. The region is still influenced by the extravagant architectural and sculptural style of this once-dominant Southeast Asian kingdom.

tonal languages said to be the most significant ethno-linguistic group in Southeast Asia. Some settled in the river valleys of modern-day Thailand, while others chose parts of modern-day Laos and the Shan state of Myanmar.

They settled in villages as farmers, hunters and traders and organised themselves into administrative units known as *meu·ang*, under the rule of a lord, which became the building block of the Tai state. Over time, the Tai expanded from the northern mountain valleys into the central plains and northeastern plateau, where there existed several important trading centres ruled by various indigenous and 'foreign' empires, including the Mon-Dvaravati, Khmer (Cambodia) and Srivijaya (Malay).

Prime Minister Phibul Songkhram changed the name of the country in 1939 from 'Siam' to 'Prathet Thai' (or 'Thailand' in English); it was considered an overt nationalistic gesture intended to unite all the Tai-speaking people.

Dvaravati

The Mon dominated parts of Burma (present-day Myanmar), western Thailand and the central plains. From the 6th to 9th centuries, the Dvaravati emerged as a distinct Buddhist and Hindu culture associated with the Mon people. Little is known about this period, but it is believed that Nakhon Pathom might have been the centre and that overland trade routes and trading outposts extended west to Burma, east to Cambodia, north to Chiang Mai and Laos, and towards the northeast, as evidenced by findings of distinctive Dvaravati Buddha images, temples and stone inscriptions in Mon language.

The Dvaravati was one of many Indian-influenced cultures that established themselves in Southeast Asia at the time, but scholars single out the Dvaravati because of its artistic legacy and the trade routes that might have provided an early framework for what would become the core of the modern-day Thai state.

Khmer

While the Dvaravati are a historical mystery, the Khmers were Southeast Asia's equivalent of the Roman Empire. This kingdom became famous for its extravagant sculpture and architecture and had a profound effect on the art and religion of the region. Established in the 9th century, the Khmer kingdom built its capital in Angkor (modern-day Cambodia) and expanded westward across present-day central and northeastern Thailand. Administrative centres anchored by Angkor-style temples were built in Lopburi (then known as Lavo), Sukhothai and Phimai (near Nakhon Ratchasima) and linked by road to the capital.

The Khmer's large-scale construction projects were a symbol of imperial power in its frontier regions and examples of the day's most advanced technologies. Khmer elements – Hinduism, Brahmanism, Theravada Buddhism and Mahayana Buddhism – mark the cultural products of this period in Thailand.

King Naresuan is portrayed as a national hero and became a cult figure, especially worshipped by the Thai army. His story inspired a high-budget, blockbuster film series, *King Naresuan*, by filmmaker Chatrichalerm Yukol, funded in part by the Thai government.

10th century
Arrival of Tai peoples in Thailand from Southern China in several waves. Settlements expand from the northern mountain valleys to the central plains and northeast plateau.

1240–1438
Approximate dates of Sukhothai kingdom, which the Thais consider the first real Thai kingdom. The period is marked by flourishing arts and culture.

1283
Early Thai script invented by King Ramkhamhaeng of Sukhothai. The script is based on Indian, Mon and Khmer scripts. Buddhism is established as the official religion.

1292
Chiang Mai becomes the capital of Lanna. King Mengrai, a skilled diplomat, creates ties that dispel outside threats and allow the culture to grow.

Srivijaya

While mainland Thailand was influenced by forces from the north and west, the Malay peninsula was economically and culturally fused to cultures further south. Between the 8th and 13th centuries, the Malay peninsula was under the sway of the confederation of the Srivijaya, which controlled maritime trade between the South China Sea and Indian Ocean. The Srivijaya capital is believed to have been in Palembang on Sumatra.

In 1868 King Mongkut (Rama IV) abolished a husband's right to sell his wife or her children without her permission. The older provision, it was said, treated the woman 'as if she were a water buffalo'.

Of the series of Srivijaya city-states that grew to prominence along the Malay peninsula, Tambralinga established its capital near present-day Nakhon Si Thammarat and adopted Buddhism in the 13th century, while the states further south fell under the influence of Islam, creating a religious boundary that persists to this day. Remains of Srivijaya culture can be seen around Chaiya and Nakhon Si Thammarat. Many art forms of the Srivijaya kingdom, such as *năng đà·lung* (shadow theatre) and *lá·kon* (classical dance-drama), persist today.

Emerging Tai Kingdoms

In the 13th century, the regional empires started to decline and prosperous Tai city-states emerged with localised power and military might. The competing city-states were ultimately united into various kingdoms that began to establish a Thai identity. Scholars recognise Lanna, Sukhothai and Ayuthaya as the unifying kingdoms of the period.

Lanna

The Lanna kingdom, based in northern Thailand, dates its formation to the upper Mekong River town of Chiang Saen in the middle of the 12th century by King Mengrai, who settled the bickering between neighbouring towns by conquering them. He then migrated south to Chiang Mai (meaning 'new city') in 1292 to establish his capital. The king was a skilled diplomat and forged important alliances with potential rivals, notably King Ngam Muang of Phayao and King Ramkhamhaeng of Sukhothai; a bronze statue commemorating this confederation stands in Chiang Mai today. King Mengrai is also credited for successfully repulsing Mongol invasions in the early 14th century and building diplomatic ties in lieu of future attacks.

The Lanna kingdom is also recognised for its royal patronage of the Sinhalese tradition of Theravada Buddhism, now widely practised in Thailand, and of the distinctive northern Thai culture that persists in the region. The Lanna kingdom never went through an extensive expansion period as it was plagued by dynastic intrigues and wars, especially against Sukhothai and Ayuthaya.

1351–1767

Reign of Ayuthaya, which at its height in the 1600s controls parts of Burma, Laos and Cambodia, making it the predominant power in Southeast Asia at the time.

1511

Portuguese Duarte Fernandes becomes the first European to establish diplomatic relations with Thailand when he founds a foreign mission in Ayuthaya; other European nations follow.

1688

Pro-foreign King Narai dies and is followed by the Palace Revolution and the expulsion of the French. As a result, Thailand's ties with the West are near-severed until the 1800s.

1700

Ayuthaya's population is estimated to have reached one million, making it probably the largest city in the world at the time.

Sukhothai

During the 13th century, several principalities in the central plains united and wrested control from the dying Khmer empire, making their new capital at Sukhothai (meaning 'Rising of Happiness'). Thais consider Sukhothai the first true Thai kingdom and the period is recognised as an artistic and cultural awakening.

The most revered of the Sukhothai kings was Ramkhamhaeng, who is credited for developing the modern Thai writing system, which is based on Indian, Mon and Khmer scripts. He also established Theravada Buddhism as the official religion.

In its prime the Sukhothai kingdom extended as far as Nakhon Si Thammarat in the south, to the upper Mekong River Valley in Laos and to Bago (Pegu) in southern Myanmar. For a short time (1448–86) the Sukhothai capital was moved to Phitsanulok, but by that time another star was rising in Thailand, the kingdom of Ayuthaya.

Ayuthaya

In the mid-14th century, the Ayuthaya kingdom began to dominate the Chao Phraya River basin during the twilight of the Khmer period. It survived for 416 years, defining itself as Siam's most important early kingdom. It had an expansive sphere of influence (including much of the former Khmer empire) and played a fundamental role in organising the modern Thai state and social structure.

With a strategic island location formed by encircling rivers, Ayuthaya grew wealthy through international trade during the 17th century's age of commerce and fortified itself with superior Portuguese-supplied firearms and mercenaries. The river system connected to the Gulf of Thailand and to the hinterlands as well.

During this period Western traders 'discovered' Southeast Asia and Ayuthaya hosted many foreign settlements. Accounts by foreign visitors mention Ayuthaya's cosmopolitan markets and court. In 1690 Londoner Engelbert Campfer proclaimed, 'Among the Asian nations, the kingdom of Siam is the greatest.'

Ayuthaya adopted Khmer court customs, honorific language and ideas of kingship. The monarch styled himself as a Khmer *devaraja* (divine king) rather than Sukhothai's *dhammaraja* (righteous king); Ayuthaya continued to pay tribute to the Chinese emperor, who rewarded this ritualistic submission with generous gifts and commercial privileges.

The glories of Ayuthaya were interrupted by the expansionist Burmese. In 1569 the city had fallen to the great Burmese king, Bayinnaung, but regained independence under the leadership of King Naresuan. Then, in 1765, Burma's ambitious and newly established Kongbaung dynasty pushed eastward to eliminate Ayuthaya as a political and commercial

Top History Reads

Thailand: A Short History (2003) by David K Wyatt

A History of Thailand (2009) by Chris Baker and Pasuk Phongpaichit

Chronicle of Thailand: Headlines Since 1946 (2010) by William Warren

1767 After a 14-month siege, the capital city of Ayuthaya is sacked by the Burmese, bringing an end to the kingdom.

1768 Thai-Chinese King Taksin founds a new capital in Thonburi and re-establishes Thai supremacy following the sack of Ayuthaya by the Burmese.

1782 Founding of the Chakri dynasty with Bangkok as the new capital. King Rama I is ruler and his lineage continues to hold the throne to this day.

1826 King Rama III signs a treaty with Britain to fight with it against the Burmese.

rival. Burmese troops laid siege to the capital for a year before destroying it in 1767. The city was devastated, its buildings and people wiped out. The surrounding areas were deserted. So chilling was this historic sacking and razing of Ayuthaya that the perception of the Burmese as ruthless foes and aggressors still persists in the minds of many Thais to this day.

The Bangkok Era

With Ayuthaya in ruins, the royal line of succession was broken and chaos ensued. A former general, Taksin, claimed his right to rule, handily defeating potential rivals, and established his new capital in Thonburi, a settlement downriver from Ayuthaya with better access to trade. Consolidating his power, King Taksin, the son of a Chinese father and Thai mother, strongly promoted trade with China.

The king was deposed in 1782 by the military. One of the coup organisers, Chao Phraya Chakri, assumed the throne as Phraphutthayotfa Chulalok (r 1782–1809; posthumously known as Rama I) and established the Chakri dynasty, which still rules today. The new monarch moved the capital across the Chao Phraya River to modern-day Bangkok.

The first century of Bangkok rule focused on rebuilding what had been lost when Ayuthaya was sacked. Surviving knowledge and practices were preserved or incorporated into new laws, manuals of government practice, religious and historical texts, and literature. At the same time, the new rulers transformed their defence activities into expansion by means of war, extending their influence in every direction. Destroying the capital cities of both Laos and Cambodia, Siam contained Burmese aggression and made a vassal of Chiang Mai. Defeated populations were resettled and played an important role in increasing the rice production of Siam, much of which was exported to China.

Unlike the Ayuthaya rulers, who identified with the Hindu god Vishnu, the Chakri kings positioned themselves as defenders of Buddhism. They undertook compilations and Thai translations of essential Buddhist texts and constructed many royal temples.

FRIENDS OF THE KING

In the 1680s many foreign emissaries were invited to Ayuthaya by King Narai, who was keen to acquire and adopt foreign goods, culture and ideas. His court placed orders for spyglasses, hourglasses, paper, walnut trees, cheese, wine and marble fountains. He joined the French Jesuits to observe the eclipse at his palace in Lopburi and received a gift of a globe from France's King Louis XIV.

In the 1680s, Narai recruited the services of the Greek adventurer Constantine Phaulkon, who was later accused of conspiring to overthrow the ailing king. Instead, the accusers led a coup and executed Constantine.

1851–68

Reign of King Mongkut (Rama IV) and a period of Western influence. The king moves to modernise the country and integrates it into the world market of the day.

1855

Bowring Treaty between Siam and Britain stimulates the Thai economy by granting extraterritorial rights to British subjects in Siam and liberalising trade rules and regulations.

1868–1910

Reign of King Chulalongkorn (Rama V), who continues replacing the old political order with the model of the nation state. Increase of European imperialism in neighbouring countries.

1874

Slavery and the state labour system that had been in place since the Ayuthaya period is abolished. A salaried bureaucracy, police force and army are created.

In the meantime, a new social order and market economy was taking shape in the mid-19th century. Siam turned to the West for modern scientific and technological ideas and reforms in education, infrastructure and legal systems. One of the great modernisers, King Mongkut (Rama IV) never expected to be king. Before his ascension he had spent 27 years in a monastery founding the Thammayut sect based on the strict disciplines of the Mon monks he had followed. During his monastic career, he became proficient in Pali, Sanskrit, Latin and English and studied Western sciences.

During Mongkut's reign, Siam concluded treaties with Western powers that integrated the kingdom into the world market system, ceded royal monopolies and granted extraterritorial rights to British subjects.

Mongkut's son, King Chulalongkorn (Rama V) was to take much greater steps in replacing the old political order with the model of the nation-state. He abolished slavery and the corvée system (state labour), which had lingered on ineffectively since the Ayuthaya period. Chulalongkorn's reign oversaw the creation of a salaried bureaucracy, a police force and a standing army. His reforms brought uniformity to the legal code, law courts and revenue offices. Siam's agricultural output was improved by advances in irrigation techniques and increasing peasant populations. Schools were established along European lines. Universal conscription and poll taxes made all men the king's men.

Landmarks of the Bangkok Era

- *Wat Arun*
- *Wat Phra Kaew and Grand Palace*
- *Dusit Palace Park*

In 'civilising' his country, Chulalongkorn relied greatly on foreign advisers, mostly British. Within the royal court, much of the centuries-old protocol was abandoned and replaced by Western forms. The architecture and visual art of state, like the new throne halls, were designed by Italian artists.

Like his father, Chulalongkorn was regarded as a skilful diplomat and is credited with successfully playing European powers off one another to avoid colonisation. In exchange for independence, Thailand ceded territory to French Indochina (Laos in 1893, Cambodia in 1907) and British Burma (three Malayan states in 1909). In 1902 the former Pattani kingdom was ceded to the British, who were then in control of Malaysia, but control reverted to Thailand seven years later. Many residents of the Deep South continue to regard Thailand as a colonial power occupying their land.

Siam was becoming a geographically defined country in a modern sense. By 1902 the country no longer called itself Siam but Prathet Thai (the country of the Thai) or Ratcha-anachak Thai (the kingdom of the Thai). By 1913, all those living within its borders were defined as 'Thai'.

Democracy vs Military

In 1932, a group of young military officers and bureaucrats calling themselves Khana Ratsadon (People's Party) mounted a successful, bloodless coup that marked the end of absolute monarchy and introduced a constitutional monarchy. The leaders of the group were inspired by

1890

Siam's first railway, run by the Royal State Railway of Siam, connects Bangkok with Ayuthaya. This is the beginning of what will become the Northern Line.

1893

French blockade the Chao Phraya River over disputed Indochina territory. Bangkok is forced to cede the territory to France, strengthening French influence in the region.

1909

Anglo–Siamese Treaty sets Siam's southern border, giving it Yala, Pattani and Narathiwat from the former Pattani sultanate. Lands further south later become part of the Unfederated Malay States.

1913

King Vajiravudh requires all citizens to adopt surnames. Before this time most Thais used only a first name. Each last name is required to be unique to the family.

the democratic ideology they had encountered during their studies in Europe.

In the years after the coup, rival factions (royalists, military, civilians) struggled for the upper hand in the new regime. Even the People's Party was not unified in its vision of a democratic Thailand, and before general elections were held the military wing of the party seized control of the government. The leader of the civilian wing of the People's Party, Pridi Phanomyong, a French-educated lawyer, was forced into exile in 1933 after introducing a socialist-leaning economic plan that angered the military generals. King Prajadhipok (Rama VII) abdicated in 1935 and retired to Britain. Thailand's first general election was held in 1937 for half of the seats in the People's Assembly, the newly instated legislative body. General Phibul Songkhram, one of the leaders of the military faction of the People's Party, became prime minister, a position he held from 1938 to 1944 and again from 1948 to 1957.

Thailand has had 19 constitutions, all rewritten following various military coups. Constitution number 20 was being drafted in late 2015. Each reincarnation seeks to allocate power within the branches of government with a bias for the ruling interest (military, royalist or civilian) and against its political foes.

Phibul's regime coincided with WWII and was characterised by strong nationalistic tendencies centring on 'nation' and 'Thai-ness'. He collaborated with the Japanese and allowed them to use Thailand as a staging ground for its invasion of other Southeast Asian nations. By siding with the Japanese, the Phibul government hoped to gain international leverage and reclaim historical territory lost during France's expansion of Indochina. Thailand intended to declare war on the US and Britain during WWII. But Seni Pramoj, the Thai ambassador in Washington and a member of Seri Thai (the Thai Liberation Movement), refused to deliver the formal declaration of war, and thus saved Thailand from bearing the consequences of defeated-nation status. Phibul was forced to resign in 1944 and was tried for war crimes.

In an effort to suppress pro-royalist sentiments, Ananda Mahidol, the nephew of the abdicated king, was crowned Rama VIII in 1935, though he was only 10 years old and spent much of his childhood studying abroad. After returning to Thailand, he was shot dead under mysterious circumstances in his bedroom in 1946. In the same year, his brother, His Majesty Bhumibol Adulyadej (pronounced *poomípon adunyádèt*) was appointed the ninth king of the Chakri dynasty, going on to become the longest-reigning king in Thai history, as well as the world's longest-reigning monarch.

For a brief period after the war, democracy flourished: full elections for the National People's Assembly were held, and the 1946 Constitution sought to reduce the role of the military and provide more democratic rights. It lasted until the death of King Ananda, the pretext the military used to return to power with Phibul at the helm.

1916

The first Thai university, Chulalongkorn University, is established by King Vajiravudh. Even today diplomas are handed out by members of the royal family.

1917

Siam sends troops to join the Allies in WWI in hopes of gaining popularity with the French and British, thus protecting the country's sovereignty.

1924

Don Mueang International Airport (opened as a military base in 1914) welcomes its first commercial flight, opening up the country to nonmilitary air travel.

1932

Bloodless coup ends absolute monarchy and puts in place a constitutional monarchy. Leaders of the coup are inspired by democratic ideology learned from studies in Europe.

Military Dictatorships

In 1957, Phibul's successor, General Sarit Thanarat, subjected the country to a military dictatorship: abolishing the constitution, dissolving the parliament and banning political parties. From the 1950s, the US directly involved itself in Southeast Asia to contain communist expansion in the region. During the Cold War the US government gave economic and military support to the Sarit government and continued that relationship with subsequent military dictators, Thanom Kittikachorn and Praphat Charusathien, who ruled from 1964 to 1973. They negotiated a package of economic deals with the USA in exchange for allowing the US military to establish bases in Thailand to support the Vietnam War.

In 1973, an opposition group of left-wing activists, mainly intellectuals and students, along with peasants, workers and portions of the middle class, organised political rallies demanding a constitution from the military government. On 14 October that year, the military suppressed a large demonstration in Bangkok, killing 77 people and wounding more than 800. The event is commemorated by a monument on Th Ratchadamnoen Klang in Bangkok, near the Democracy Monument. King Bhumibol stepped in and refused to support further bloodshed, forcing Thanom and Praphat to leave Thailand.

A brief period of unstable democracy followed the events of 1973, with the increasingly radical student movement creating fears of home-grown communism among many Thais. In 1976 Thanom returned to Thailand (ostensibly to become a monk) and was received warmly by the royal family. In

LIBERAL COUNTERWEIGHT

Pridi Phanomyong (1900–83) was a French-educated lawyer and a civilian leader in the 1932 revolution and the People's Party. His work on democratic reforms in Thailand was based on constitutional measures and attempts to restrict by law military involvement in Thai politics. He supported nationalisation of land and labour, state-led industrialisation and labour protection. In 1934 he founded Thammasat University. He also served as the figurehead of Seri Thai (the resistance movement against WWII Japanese occupation of Thailand) and was Thailand's prime minister (1946).

Though acknowledged as a senior statesman, Pridi Phanomyong was a controversial figure and a major foe of Phibul and the military regimes. He was accused of being a communist by his critics and forced out of the country under suspicion of regicide following the mysterious death of King Ananda Mahidol. Since the thawing of the Cold War, his legacy has been re-examined and recognised for its democratic efforts and the counterbalancing effects it had on military interests. He was named one of Unesco's great personalities of the 20th century in 2000.

1935

King Prajadhipok abdicates. The government chooses Prince Mahidol as his successor.

1939

The country's English name is officially changed from Siam to Thailand to align the name more closely with the majority ethnic group.

1941

Japanese forces enter Thailand during WWII, using the country for access to invade British Malaya and Burma. Japanese pressure leads to Thailand signing an alliance with Japan.

1945

WWII ends; Thailand cedes seized territory from Laos, Cambodia and Malaysia that it gained from the French and British during the war.

response, protestors organised demonstrations at Thammasat University against the perceived perpetrator of the 14 October massacre. Right-wing, anti-communist civilian groups clashed violently with students. In the aftermath, many students and intellectuals were forced underground and joined armed communist insurgents – known as the People's Liberation Army of Thailand (PLAT) – based in the northern and southern jungles.

Military control of the country continued through the 1980s. The government of the 'political soldier', General Prem Tinsulanonda, enjoyed a period of political and economic stability. Prem dismantled the communist insurgency through military action and amnesty programs. But the country's new economic success created challenging rivals: prominent business leaders who criticised the military's role in government and their now-dated Cold War mentality. Communists, they maintained, should be business partners, not enemies.

It's Just Business

In 1988 Prem was replaced in fair elections by Chatichai Choonhavan, leader of the Chat Thai Party, who created a government dominated by well-connected provincial business people. His government shifted power away from the bureaucrats and set about transforming Thailand into an 'Asian Tiger' economy. But the business of politics was often bought and sold like a commodity and Chatichai was overthrown by the military on grounds of extreme corruption. This coup marked an emerging trend in Thai politics: the Bangkok business community and educated classes siding with the military against Chatichai, his provincial business-politicians and their money politics approach to governance.

Chulalongkorn (Rama V) enjoys a cult-like devotion due in part to the endearing photographs of him in European dress, ordinary farmer garb or military pomp. He defied tradition by allowing himself to be seen in public by his subjects and having his image widely disseminated.

In 1992, after reinstating elections, an unelected military leader inserted himself as prime minister. This was met with popular resistance and the ensuing civilian–military clash was dubbed 'Black May'. Led by former Bangkok governor and major general, Chamlong Srimuang, around 200,000 protestors (called the 'mobile phone mob', representing their rising urban affluence) launched a mass demonstration against the military rulers in Bangkok that resulted in three nights of violence with armed soldiers. On the night of 20 May, King Bhumibol called an end to the violence.

After Black May a new wave of democracy activists advocated for constitutional reforms. For most of the 1990s the parliament was dominated by the Democrat Party, which represented the urban middle class and business interests. Its major base of support came from the southern Thai population centres. Formerly port towns, these were now dominated by tourism and exports (rubber, tin and fishing). On the other side of the spectrum were the former pro-military politicians based in the central plains and the people of the agrarian northeast in new provincial towns who focused on state-budget distribution to their provinces. These political lines exist today.

1946

King Bhumibol Adulyadej (Rama IX) ascends the throne and will become the longest reigning monarch in Thai history; Thailand joins the UN.

1957

Sarit Thanarat leads a coup that introduces military rule, which lasts until 1973. The constitution is abolished, parliament is dissolved and political parties are banned.

1959

Thailand's first tourism authority is created. The first overseas office opens in New York in 1965 and a regional office opens in Chiang Mai in 1968.

1965

Thailand hosts US military bases during the Vietnam War under a 'gentlemen's agreement'. Around 80% of US airstrikes in Northern Vietnam will originate from Thailand.

In 1997 the boom years went bust and the Asian economic crisis unfolded. The country's economy was plagued by foreign-debt burdens, an over-extension in the real estate sector and a devalued currency. Within months of the crisis, the Thai currency plunged from 25B to 56B per US$1. The International Monetary Fund (IMF) stepped in to impose financial and legal reforms and economic liberalisation programs in exchange for more than US$17 billion to stabilise the Thai currency.

In the aftermath of the crisis, the Democrats returned to power uncontested, but were viewed as ineffective as the economy worsened.

Thaksinocracy & Two Coups

The economic slump began to ease in 2000 and business interests eclipsed the military as the dominant political force in Thai politics. The telecommunications billionaire and former police officer, Thaksin Shinawatra, through his Thai Rak Thai (TRT or 'Thai Loving Thai') party, capitalised on this rising nationalism and won a majority in the elections of 2001. Self-styled as a CEO-politician, Thaksin swiftly delivered on his campaign promises for rural development, including agrarian debt relief, village capital funds and cheap health care.

Thanks to the 1997 constitutional reforms designed to strengthen the prime minister's position, Thaksin's government was one of the most stable in Thai history. The surging economy and his bold, if strong-arm, leadership won an outright majority in 2005, effectively introducing one-party rule. His popularity among the working class and rural voters was immense.

In 2006, Thaksin was accused of abusing his powers and of conflicts of interest, most notably in his family's sale of their Shin Corporation to the Singaporean government for 73 billion baht (US$1.88 billion), a tax-free gain thanks to telecommunications legislation that he had helped craft. Demonstrations in Bangkok called for him to be ousted, and on 19 September 2006 the military staged a bloodless coup that forced Thaksin into exile. The TRT party was dissolved by court order and party executives were barred from politics for five years. As promised, the interim government held general elections in December, returning the country to civilian rule, but the outcome was unsatisfactory to the military and

2004 TSUNAMI: A DECADE ON

On 26 December 2004 the deadliest tsunami in recorded history rolled across the Indian Ocean, killing an estimated 5000 people and injuring a further 9000 in Southern Thailand alone. More than 10 years on and the region has long since regained its equilibrium, with tsunami evacuation signs erected at beaches one of the few physical indicators of the tragedy that occurred here.

1968
Thailand is a founding member of the Association of Southeast Asian Nations (ASEAN), designed to promote regional economic growth, social progress, peace and stability.

1973
Thai students, workers and farmers force the military government led by Thanom Kittikachorn to step down.

1976
Violent suppression of student movement by the military ends a brief period of unstable democracy.

1979
After three years of military rule, elections and parliament are restored. Thai authorities give safe haven to Khmer Rouge fleeing the North Vietnamese invasion of Cambodia.

the Bangkok upper and middle classes when Thaksin's political allies won a majority and formed a government led by Samak Sundaravej.

Demonstrations against the Thaksin-aligned government were led by Chamlong Srimuang (Black May activist and former Bangkok governor) and Sondhi Limthongkul (a long-time business and political rival of Thaksin). Their group, the People's Alliance for Democracy (PAD), earned the nickname 'Yellow Shirts' because they wore yellow (the king's birthday colour) to express their royalist allegiances; it was believed that Thaksin was so successfully consolidating power during his tenure that he had designs on the throne or at least planned to interrupt the royal succession.

Samak Sundaravej was unseated by the Constitutional Court in September 2008 on a technicality: while in office, he hosted a TV cooking show that the court found to be a conflict of interest. Still not politically satisfied, the Yellow Shirts seized control of Thailand's main airports, Suvarnabhumi and Don Mueang, for a week in November 2008 until the military engineered a silent coup and another favourable court ruling that further weakened Thaksin's political proxies. Through last-minute coalition building, Democrat Abhisit Vejjajiva was elected in a parliamentary vote, becoming Thailand's 27th prime minister.

Thaksin supporters organised their own counter-movement, the United Front for Democracy Against Dictatorship, better known as the 'Red Shirts'. Supporters hail mostly from the north and northeast and include anti-coup, pro-democracy activists as well as die-hard Thaksin fans. There is a degree of class struggle, with some Red Shirts expressing animosity towards the aristocrats. The Red Shirts' most provocative demonstration came in 2010 when Thailand's Supreme Court ordered the seizure of US$46 billion of Thaksin's assets after finding him guilty of abusing his powers as prime minister. Red Shirts occupied Bangkok's central shopping district for two months and demanded the dissolution of the government and reinstatement of elections. Protest leaders and the government were unable to reach a compromise and in May 2010 the military used force to evict the protesters, resulting in bloody clashes (91 people were killed) and a smouldering central city, with damage estimated at US$15 billion.

A general election was held in 2011, and Thaksin's politically allied Puea Thai party won a parliamentary majority. Thaksin's sister, Yingluck Shinawatra, became Thailand's first female prime minister and the country's youngest-ever premier. Widely seen as a proxy for her brother, demonstrations against the government began to intensify, until by late 2013 parts of central Bangkok were occupied by protesters demanding that Yingluck step down.

In May 2014, following a series of violent clashes that left 28 people dead, Yingluck was forced to stand down. A caretaker government was appointed, only for the Thai military to declare martial law on 20 May.

1980

Prem Tinsulanonda's government works to undermine the communist insurgency movement with military action and amnesty programs and eventually ends it with a political solution.

1988

Chatichai Choonhavan becomes first elected PM since 1976 and creates a government dominated by well-connected provincial business people.

1991–92

General Suchinda attempts to seize power due to the extreme corruption of Chatichai's government; King Bhumibol intervenes to halt civil turmoil surrounding 'Black May' protests.

1997

Asian economic crisis; passage of historic 'people's constitution'. International Monetary Fund steps in to reform and stabilise the Thai currency.

Two days later the military seized control of the country in Thailand's 13th coup since 1932. General Prayuth Chan-o-cha became the leader of the National Council for Peace and Order (NCPO), the name the junta have given their government, and immediately ordered a new constitution – Thailand's 20th in the last 80-odd years – to be drafted. Despite assurances that the NCPO would rule only temporarily, elections are unlikely to be held until 2017 at the earliest.

Troubles in the Deep South

Since 2001 ethnic Malay Muslim separatists have been waging a low-level insurgency in Thailand's southernmost provinces of Pattani, Narathiwat and Yala. These three provinces once comprised the historic kingdom of Pattani until it was conquered by the Chakri kings. Under King Chulalongkorn, the traditional ruling elite were replaced with central government officials and bureaucrats from Bangkok. During WWII a policy of nation-building set out to transform the multi-ethnic society into a unified and homogenous Thai Buddhist nation. This policy was resisted in the Deep South and gave birth to a strong separatist movement fighting for the independence of Pattani. In the 1980s and 1990s, the assimilation policy was abandoned and then-prime minister Prem promised support for Muslim cultural rights and religious freedoms. He also offered amnesty to the armed insurgents and implemented an economic development plan for the historically impoverished region.

The Thaksin regime took another approach to the region. Greater central control was exerted; this was viewed as a thinly disguised attempt to break up the traditional stronghold of the Democrat Party. But the policy did not take into consideration the sensitive and tenacious Muslim culture of the Deep South. In 2002 the government dissolved the long-standing inspectorate and the army-run joint civilian–police–military border security office – a unit often lauded for maintaining peace and stability and providing a communication link between the Thai government and the southern Muslims. In its place the Thai provincial police assumed control

Sacred Landmarks of Note

Tham Phraya Nakhon, Khao Sam Roi Yot National Park

Sanctuary of Truth, Pattaya

Wat Phra Mahathat Woramahawihaan, Nakhon Si Thammarat

Khmer temples, Phetchaburi

Big Buddha, Phuket

CLEANING UP PHUKET

One of the junta's first actions after seizing power in the 2014 coup was to announce a crackdown on crime and vice in an effort to change Thailand's sometimes sleazy image overseas. In Phuket that resulted in deploying hundreds of soldiers to evict unlicensed food stands, massage joints and hawkers from Patong and the other main beaches. A year later there was less commercial activity on Phuket's beaches, but many vendors had quietly returned or just refused to abide by eviction orders. It takes more than the army to stop a Thai from renting out sun-loungers.

2001

Self-styled CEO-politician Thaksin Shinawatra is elected prime minister. Campaign promises of rural development, agrarian debt and cheaper healthcare are quickly delivered.

2003

Government stages a huge, controversial crackdown on drugs, during which some 2500 people are killed. Human-rights groups blame the government; the government blames gangs.

2004

Indian Ocean tsunami kills 5000 people and damages tourism and fishing industries; Muslim insurgency reignites in the Deep South after brewing steadily since 2001.

2006

King Bhumibol celebrates 60th year on the throne; Thaksin government overthrown in a coup and prime minister forced into exile. Thaksin's allies win the following elections.

Thaksin was the first prime minister in Thai history to complete a four-year term of office. His sister Yingluck managed three years before being deposed in a coup.

of security, though they lacked a perceived moral authority and the support of the local population. In 2004 the government responded harshly to demonstrations that resulted in the Krue Se Mosque and Tak Bai incidents, which together cost the lives of at least 180 Muslims, many of them unarmed civilians. In 2005 martial law was declared in the area.

After more than a decade of violence, there is no end in sight to the conflict. The latest round of peace talks began in Kuala Lumpur in August 2015, with the different insurgent groups unitiing under the title Mara Patani and negotiating directly with the Thai government. But with neither side apparently willing to compromise and a deep-seated lack of trust between them, few observers are optimistic. Some form of autonomy for the Deep South may be a way forward, but successive Thai governments have been unwilling to contemplate the prospect of loosening their grip over the region.

Politics

Government

Much of the political drama that has unfolded since the 2006 coup involves a long-standing debate about how to structure Thailand's legislative body and, ultimately, who gets greater control. The National Assembly (or parliament of Thailand) currently has 630 members divided into two chambers (House of Representatives and the Senate) with a mix of seats being popularly elected and elected by party vote. The ratio of seats being popularly elected changes with each replacement constitution. The 1997 constitution, dubbed the People's Constitution, called for both chambers to be fully elected by popular vote. This power to the people paved the way for Thaksin and his well-loved Thai Rak Thai party to gain nearly complete control. The military and the elites have since rescinded this structure, often arguing that full democratic representation doesn't work in Thailand.

When Thai voters go to the polls they cast a ballot for the constituency MP (member of parliament) and for their preferred party, the results of which are used to determine individual winners and proportional representation outcomes for the positions assigned by party vote.

The prime minister is the head of the government and is elected via legislative vote by the majority party. The NCPO, who took power in the 2014 coup, have suggested that in the future an unelected prime minister can be installed.

Voting in Thailand is compulsory for all eligible citizens (over the age of 18) but members of the clergy are not allowed to vote. Voter turnout for national elections has steadily increased since the new millennium, a reflection of the way the various Thaksin governments have succeeded in politicising the rural poor. Charges of vote-buying typically accompany every election. Anecdotally, local party leaders make their rounds through the villages handing out money for the promise of a vote. In

2008

Cambodia successfully petitions Unesco to list Phra Wihan (known as Phrea Vihear in Cambodia) as a World Heritage Site, reigniting border tensions with Thailand.

2008

Yellow Shirt, anti-Thaksin, pro-royalist activists seize Bangkok's international airports, causing week-long shut-down.

2010

Red Shirt, pro-Thaksin activists occupy central Bangkok for two months demanding dissolution of the government and reinstatement of elections; military crackdown results in 91 deaths.

2011

Puea Thai party wins general election; Yingluck Shinawatra (Thaksin's younger sister) becomes Thailand's first female prime minister on a platform of reconciliation.

some cases, villagers will accept money from competing parties and report that they have no loyalty at the ballot box.

The ballots include a 'no' vote if the voter wishes to choose 'none of the above'. It is also common to 'spoil' the ballot, or disqualify it, by writing on it or defacing it. During the 2005 general election a large number of ineligible ballots contained anti-Thaksin messages.

Media

Southeast Asian governments are not usually fond of uncensored media, but Thailand often bucked this trend during the 1990s, even ensuring press freedoms in its 1997 constitution, albeit with fairly broad loopholes. This ended with the ascension of Thaksin Shinawatra, a telecommunications billionaire, at the beginning of the 21st century. With Thaksin as prime minister and his party holding a controlling majority, the press encountered the kind of censorship and legal intimidation not seen since the 1970s era of military dictatorships. The government filed a litany of defamation lawsuits against individuals, publications and media groups who printed embarrassing revelations about the Thaksin regime.

After the 2006 ousting of Thaksin, the media managed to retain its guarantees of press freedoms in the new constitution, but this was a 'paper promise' that did little to rescue the press from intimidation, lawsuits and physical attacks. Sweeping powers to ensure national security, often invoked against the press, were added to the emergency powers laws that went into effect after the coup.

Following the 2014 coup, there has been a widespread crackdown on both the media and freedom of expression. In its immediate aftermath, 15 TV and radio stations were closed and 100 websites were blocked, while around 1000 people – academics, bloggers, journalists, students and opposition politicians – have been detained for various periods. The domestic media now self-censors its stories to avoid getting into trouble, and some websites, like the Thailand section of the Human Rights Watch website, remain blocked in Thailand.

There has also been a sharp rise in the number of people being prosecuted under the country's lèse-majesté laws – causing offence against the dignity of the monarchy – which are some of the strictest in the world. Critics accuse the army of using the laws to silence their political opponents. Recent cases have seen two university students jailed for appearing in a play said to have defamed the monarchy, while in August 2015 one man received a 30-year prison sentence for posting comments on his Facebook page that were claimed to have insulted the monarchy.

The Democrat Party (Phak Prachathipat), founded in 1946, is now the longest-surviving political party in Thailand.

2012
More Yellow Shirt protests, culminating with a 10,000-strong march against Prime Minister Yingluck, whom protestors see as a puppet of ousted Prime Minister Thaksin.

2013
The International Court of Justice rules that Phra Wihan is part of Cambodia, although the area surrounding it and another 100km of border are still disputed.

2014
In May, the military launches its 13th coup since 1932, ousting Yingluck Shinawatra's Puea Thai government.

2015
After a draft version of Thailand's latest constitution is rejected in September, elections are postponed to 2017.

People & Culture

Thailand's cohesive national identity provides a unifying patina for ethnic and regional differences that evolved through historical migrations and geographic kinships with ethnically diverse neighbours.

Ethnic Makeup

Some 75% of the citizens of Thailand are ethnic Thais, providing a superficial appearance of sameness, but subtle regional differences do exist. In the central plains (Chao Phraya delta), Siamese Thais united the country through historic kingdoms and promulgated its culture and language. Today the central Thai dialect is the national standard and Bangkok exports unified culture through media and standardised education.

Southern (ɓàk đâi; often spelt *pàk tâi*) Thais define the characteristics of the south. The dialect is a little faster than standard Thai, the curries are a lot spicier and there is more mixing of Muslim folk beliefs into the regional culture thanks to the geographic proximity to Malaysia and the historic Muslim population.

The second-largest ethnic minority are the Malays (4.6%), most of whom reside in the provinces of the Deep South. The remaining minority groups in the south include a smaller percentage of non-Thai-speaking Moken (*chow lair,* also spelt *chao leh;* people of the sea, or 'sea gypsies'). A small number of Europeans and other non-Asians reside in Bangkok and the provinces.

Thai Chinese

People of Chinese ancestry – second- or third-generation Hakka, Teochew, Hainanese or Cantonese – make up 14% of the population, the

INVISIBLE MIGRANTS

The people of Myanmar fled to Thailand in enormous numbers during the most oppressive years of the Myanmar state. Approximately 150,000 people have entered the kingdom as political and ethnic refugees, but the vast majority are economic migrants (estimated at two to three million, of which less than half are documented). They fill the low-level jobs – fish-processing, construction, and domestic and factory work – that used to employ unskilled northeastern Thai labourers. In the south, most of the hotel and restaurant staff you meet day to day will probably be from Myanmar. Many Thais believe Thailand needs this imported workforce as the population is ageing faster than it is reproducing.

However, the government has been slower to respond to this emerging immigration 'situation' than the private sector, and this has caused problems. Because many immigrants reside and work in Thailand illegally, they are subjected to exploitative relationships with employers; human-rights activists describe their working conditions as modern-day slavery. These people can't return home due to possible persecution by the Myanmar regime and they can't turn to the Thai authorities in cases of workplace abuse because they would risk deportation.

world's largest overseas Chinese population. Bangkok and the nearby coastal areas have a large population of immigrants from China who came for economic opportunities in the early to mid-20th century. Historically wealthy Chinese introduced their daughters to the royal court as consorts, developing royal connections and adding a Chinese bloodline that extends to the current king.

The mercantile centres of most Thai towns are run by Thai-Chinese families and many places in the country celebrate Chinese festivals such as the annual Vegetarian Festival.

Thai Muslims

At around 4% of the population, Muslims make up Thailand's largest religious minority, living side by side with the Buddhist majority. To this day, many of Thailand's Muslims reside in the south, but an ever greater number is scattered through the nation. Most of Thailand's southern Muslims are ethnically Malay and speak Malay or Yawi (a dialect of Malay written in the Arabic script) in addition to Thai. In northern Thailand there is also a substantial number of Chinese Muslims who emigrated from Yúnnán in the late 19th century.

Regional Identity

Religion, royalty and tradition are the defining characteristics of Thai society. Thailand is the only country in Southeast Asia never colonised by a foreign power and this has led to a profound sense of pride. However, the country is not homogenous, and in the south a strong cultural identity prevails that is more in tune with the Islamic culture of Malaysia across the border.

Before modern political boundaries divided the Malay peninsula into two countries, the city states, sultanates and villages were part of an Indonesian-based Srivijaya empire – with intermingled customs and language – all vying for local control over shipping routes. Many southern Thai towns and geographic names bear the hallmark of the Bahasa language, and some village traditions would be instantly recognised by a Sumatran but not by a northern Thai. Chinese culture is also prominent in southern Thailand, as seen in the numerous temples and clan houses along with the often widespread appearance of Chinese writing on shopfronts. It is this intermingling of domestic and 'foreign' culture that defines the south.

Lifestyle

The ordinary life of southern Thais can be divided into two categories: country and city.

Those in rural coastal areas are typically employed in rubber farming or fishing, though rice and livestock farming are also evident. Rubber farmers live in small, typically inland settlements identified by straight rows of trees and pale sheets of drying latex; many islands on the Andaman coast are dotted with these shady rubber forests. Traditional Muslim villages are built directly over the water in a series of connected stilt houses. Because the Andaman Sea had a history of tranquil behaviour, there was no fear of the ocean's wrath, a preconception painfully destroyed by the 2004 tsunami.

Within the cities, life looks a lot like the rest of the country (busy and modern), but the presence of Chinese and Indian merchants marks the uniqueness of southern Thai cities. The commercial centres are also the market towns, where the brightly coloured fishing boats ease into the harbour, unloading the catch and filling the marina with the aroma of fish.

Arts Reading

The Thai House: History and Evolution (2002; Ruethai Chaichongrak)

The Arts of Thailand (1998; Steve Van Beek)

Flavours: Thai Contemporary Art (2005; Steven Pettifor)

Bangkok Design: Thai Ideas in Textiles & Furniture (2006; Brian Mertens)

Buddhist Temples of Thailand: A Visual Journey Through Thailand's 40 Most Historic Wats (2010; Joe Cummings)

The Roots of Thai Art (2012; Piriya Krairiksh)

Economy

Due to tourism, fishing, prawn farming and rubber, the south is Thailand's wealthiest region. Most rubber tappers are born into the industry, inheriting the profession of their fathers and mothers. Prawn and fish farming, on the other hand, are relatively new industries, introduced as an economic development program for rural communities losing ground to commercial fishing operations. The venture proved profitable and Thailand is now one of the leading exporters of farm-raised prawns. However, fish farms have been largely unregulated until recently, leading to a host of environmental problems, such as water pollution and the destruction of mangrove forests.

There is no universally accepted method of transliterating from Thai to English, so some words and place names are spelt a variety of ways.

Tourism has undoubtedly had the most tangible impact on the economy of the area, transforming many small villages into bilingual enterprises. Women who would otherwise sell products at market have studied Thai traditional massage. Other do-it-yourself franchises, so prolific in Thai communities, have been tailored to tourists: shops along beach thoroughfares sell sunscreen and postcards instead of rice whisky and grilled fish, itinerant vendors hawk sarongs and henna tattoos instead of feather dusters and straw brooms, while fishermen sometimes abandon their nets for bigger catches – tourists on snorkelling trips.

Across Thailand, the size of the middle class is growing with successive decades, bridging the gap between rich and poor. Thailand doesn't suffer from poverty of sustenance; even the most destitute Thai citizens can have shelter and food. Rather, the lower rung of Thai society suffers from poverty of material: money isn't available for extensive education, material goods or health care. This is most obvious when you look at the numbers: the average Thai income stands at around US$4500 a year, but some in rural provinces earn as little as US$570 a year. Although nationwide poverty has been reduced from 67% in 1986 to 11% in 2014 as a result of rising incomes, poverty persists in some rural areas.

Religion

Buddhism

Approximately 95% of Thais follow Theravada Buddhism, also known as Hinayana or 'Lesser Vehicle' Buddhism to distinguish it from the Mahayana or 'Great Vehicle' school of Buddhism. The primary difference between the faiths is that Theravada Buddhists believe individuals are responsible for their own enlightenment, while Mahayana Buddhists believe in putting others' salvation over one's own.

The ultimate end of all forms of Buddhism is to reach *nibbana* (from Sanskrit, nirvana), which literally means the 'blowing out' or extinction

SAVING FACE

Thais believe strongly in the concept of saving face, ie avoiding confrontation and endeavouring not to embarrass themselves or other people (except when it's *sà·nùk* – or 'fun' – to do so). The ideal face-saver doesn't bring up negative topics in conversation, doesn't express firm convictions or opinions and doesn't claim to have an expertise. Agreement and harmony are considered to be the most important social graces.

While Westerners might find a heated discussion to be good sport, Thais avoid such confrontations and regard any instance where voices are raised as rude and potentially volatile. Losing your temper causes a loss of face for everyone present, and Thais who have been crossed often react in extreme ways.

Minor embarrassments, such as tripping or falling, might elicit giggles from a crowd of Thais. In this case they aren't taking delight in your mishap, but helping you save face by laughing it off.

of all desire and thus of all *dukkha* (suffering). Having achieved *nibbana,* an individual is freed from the cycle of rebirths and enters the spiritual plane. In reality, most Thai Buddhists aim for rebirth in a 'better' existence in the next life, rather than striving to attain *nibbana.* To work towards this goal, Buddhists carry out meritorious actions *(tam bun)* such as feeding monks, giving donations to temples and performing regular worship at the local wát (temple). The Buddhist theory of karma is well expressed in the Thai proverb *tam dee, dâi dee; tam chôo·a, dâi chôo·a* (do good and receive good; do evil and receive evil).

There is no specific day of worship in Thai Buddhism; instead the faithful go to temple on certain religious holidays, when it is convenient or to commemorate a special family event. Most temple visits occur on *wan prá* (excellent days), which occur four times a month, according to phases of the moon. Other activities include offering food to the temple *sangha* (community of monks and nuns), meditating, listening to monks chanting *suttas* (discourses of the Buddha) and attending talks on *dhamma* (right behaviour).

Thailand Demographics

Population: 67.9 million

Fertility rate: 1.6

Percentage of people over 65: 9.9%

Urbanisation rate: 3%

Life expectancy: 74.4 years

Monks & Nuns

There are about 32,000 monasteries in Thailand and 200,000 monks, many of whom are ordained for life. Traditionally, every Thai male is expected to spend time as a monk, usually between finishing school and marrying or starting a career. Even His Majesty King Bhumibol served as a novice at Wat Bowonniwet in Banglamphu, Bangkok. Traditionally boys would devote a year or more to monastic life, but these days most men enter the *sangha* for two weeks to three months during *pan·săh* (Buddhist Lent), which coincides with the rainy season.

Women can become *mâa chee* (eight-precept nuns), but this is held in slightly lower regard than the status of male monks, as most Thais believe that a woman can only achieve *nibbana* if she is reincarnated as a man. Both monks and nuns shave their heads and wear robes (orange for men, white for women), give up most of their personal belongings and live on charity. Thais donate generously to the local wát, so monks often live quite comfortable lives.

An increasing number of foreigners are coming to Thailand to be ordained as Buddhist monks or nuns. If you want to find out more, visit the website Buddha Net (www.buddhanet.net).

As long as you dress appropriately and observe the correct etiquette, you will be welcome at most monasteries. However, take care not to disturb monks while they are eating or meditating – nothing breaks the concentration quite like tourists snapping photographs!

Lifestyle Statistics

Average age of marriage for a Thai man/woman: 27/24 years

Minimum daily wage in Bangkok: 300B

Entry-level professional salary: 9000B to 12,000B per month

Islam

Thailand is home to 3.3 million Muslims (just under 5% of Thailand's population) concentrated in the south of the country. Most Thai Muslims are of Malay origin and generally follow a moderate version of the Sunni sect mixed with pre-Islamic animism.

A decade-long revival movement has cultivated stricter Islamic practices and suspicions of outside influences. Under this stricter interpretation of Islam, many folk practices have been squeezed out of daily devotions and local people see the mainly Buddhist government and education system as intolerant of their way of life. Schools and infrastructure in the Muslim-majority south are typically underfund ed, and frustration with the Bangkok government is sometimes defined as a religious rather than political struggle.

There are mosques throughout southern Thailand, but few are architecturally interesting and most are closed to women. If you do visit a mosque, remember to cover your head and remove your shoes.

Other Religions

Half a per cent of the population – primarily hill tribes converted by missionaries and Vietnamese immigrants – is Christian, while another half a per cent is made up of Confucians, Taoists, Mahayana Buddhists and Hindus. There is also a community of around 70,000 Sikhs. More primordial animist beliefs, which long predate Buddhism and Hinduism, survive most noticeably in 'spirit houses' – shrines that provide a residence for a plot of land's *prá poom* (guardian spirits) – but also in festivals such Loi Krathong, the origins of which reside in animist belief, honouring the spirit of the water.

Instead of a handshake, the traditional Thai greeting is the *wâi* – a prayerlike gesture with the palms placed together.

Arts

Much of Thailand's creative energy has traditionally gone into the production of religious and ceremonial art. Painting, sculpture, music and theatre still play a huge role in the ceremonial life of Thais, and religious art is very much a living art form.

Literature

The most pervasive and influential work of classical Thai literature is the *Ramakian,* based on the Hindu holy book, the *Ramayana,* which was brought to Southeast Asia by Indian traders and introduced to Thailand by the Khmer about 900 years ago. Although the main theme remains the same, the Thais elaborated on the *Ramayana* by providing much more biographical detail on arch-villain Ravana (Thotsakan in the *Ramakian*) and his wife Montho. The monkey-god, Hanuman, is also transformed into something of a playboy.

The epic poem *Phra Aphaimani* was composed by poet Sunthorn Phu (1786–1855) and is set on the island of Ko Samet. *Phra Aphaimani* is Thailand's most famous classical literary work, and tells a typically epic story of an exiled prince.

The leading postmodern writer is Prabda Yoon, whose short-story collection *Probability* won the 2002 SEA Write award. Although his works have yet to be translated, he wrote the screenplay for *Last Life in the Universe* and other Pen-ek Ratanaruang–directed films, and in 2004 was commissioned by Thailand's Ministry of Culture to write a piece on the 2004 tsunami. The result, *Where We Feel: A Tsunami Memoir by an Outsider,* was distributed free along the Andaman coast.

Thai literature is usually written in Thai, however, some modern works you may find translated include the following:

- *Pisat, Evil Spirits*, by Seni Saowaphong, deals with conflicts between the old and new generations.
- *Lai Chiwit* (Many Lives), by Kukrit Pramoj, is a collection of short stories.
- *Monsoon Country,* by Pira Sudham, brilliantly captures the northeast's struggles against nature and nurture.
- *The Judgement*, by Chart Korbjitti, is a drama about a young village man wrongly accused of a crime.
- *Jasmine Nights,* by SP Somtow, is an upbeat coming-of-age novel that fuses traditional ideas with modern Thai pop culture.
- *Married to the Demon King,* by Sri Doruang, adapts the Ramayana into modern Bangkok.

Several Thai novels and short stories translated by Marcel Barang, including stories by Chart Korbjitti and two-time SEA Write winner Win Lyovarin, can be downloaded as e-books at www.thaifiction.com.

Cinema

When it comes to Thai cinema, there are usually two concurrent streams: movies that are financially successful and films that are considered cinematically meritorious. Only rarely do they successfully overlap.

Popular Thai cinema ballooned in the 1960s and '70s, especially when the government levied a tax on Hollywood imports, which kick-started a home-grown industry. The majority of films were cheap action flicks that were typically dubbed *nám nôw* (stinking water), but the fantastic (even nonsensical) plots and rich colours left a lasting impression on modern-day Thai filmmakers.

Thai cinema graduated into international film circles in the late 1990s and early 2000s, thanks in part to the output of Pratt Institute–educated arthouse director and screenwriter Pen-Ek Ratanaruang and his gritty and engrossing oeuvre. Apichatpong Weerasethakul is Thailand's leading cinéma-vérité director and has garnered three Cannes accolades, including the Palme d'Or (the festival's highest prize) for his *Uncle Boonmee Who Can Recall His Past Lives* (2010).

International film festivals today play host to a new crop of experimental directors from Thailand. Nawapol Thamrongrattanrit gained acclaim for his modern-girl-in-the-city screenplay *Bangkok Traffic Love Story* (2009) and followed up with his directorial debut *36* (2012), which uses 36 static camera shots to explore lost love and lost memories. *Mary Is Happy, Mary Is Happy* (2013) is a film festival hit that adapted the Twitter feed of a Thai teen into a movie. His most recent work includes *Heart Attack* (2015) and the documentary *The Master* (2014).

Film-fest fare has been bolstered by independent film clubs and self-promotion through social media. This is how low-budget filmmakers bypass the big studios, the ever-vigilant cinema censors and the skittish, controversy-averse movie theatres. In 2009 the film board introduced a rating system with seven classifications (including banned). Being censored may seem like the kiss of death, but it often guarantees indie success and cult status. Two political documentaries of 2013 challenged the board's sensitivities: Pen-ek's historical *Paradoxocracy* had to mute objectionable dialogue while Nontawat Numbenchapol's *Boundary* was initially banned, though that was lifted after an appeal. The Thai horror *Arbat* was banned in 2015 because it depicted 'misconduct' by Thai monks, which was considered a slur against Buddhism.

The big studios like ghost stories, horror flicks, historic epics, sappy love stories and camp comedies. Elaborate historical movies and epics serve a dual purpose: they can be lucrative and they promote national identity. Criticised as a propaganda tool, the *Legend of King Naresuan* epic focuses on the Ayuthaya-era king who repelled an attempted Burmese invasion. Each chapter (six have been released so far) has been a box-office winner.

Music

Traditional Thai music may sound a little strange to visitors, as the eight-note Thai octave is broken in different places to the European octave. Thai scales were first transcribed by Thai-German composer Phra Chen Duriyanga (Peter Feit), who also composed Thailand's national anthem in 1932.

The classical Thai orchestra is called the Ъèe·pâht and can include anything from five to 20 musicians. The most popular stringed instrument is the *ja·kêh,* a slender guitarlike instrument played horizontally on the ground. Woodwind instruments include the *klòo·i,* a simple wooden flute, and the Ъèe, a recorderlike instrument with a reed mouthpiece. You'll hear the Ъèe being played if you go to a Thai boxing match. Perhaps the most familiar Thai instrument is the *khĭm* or hammer dulcimer, responsible for the plinking, plunking music you'll hear in Thai restaurants across the world.

The contemporary Thai music scene is strong and diverse. The most popular genre is undoubtedly *lôok tûng* (a style analogous to country and western in the USA), which tends to appeal most to working-class Thais. The 1970s ushered in a new style dubbed *pleng pêu·a chee·wít* (literally 'music for life'), inspired by the politically conscious folk rock of the USA and Europe. The three biggest modern Thai music icons are rock staple Carabao, pop star Thongchai 'Bird' MacIntyre, and *lôok tûng* queen Pumpuang Duangchan, who died tragically in 1995.

Today there are hundreds of youth-oriented Thai bands, from chirpy boy and girl bands to metal rockers, making music that is easy to sing along with and maddeningly hard to get out of your head.

Architecture

The most striking aspect of Thailand's architectural heritage is its frequently magnificent Buddhist temples (wát). As with many Chinese Buddhist temple pagodas, one of the most distinctive features of Buddhist temple architecture is the *chedi* (stupa), a mountain-shaped monument that pays tribute to the enduring stability of Buddhism. Many contain relics of important kings or the historical Buddha or the remains of notable monks or nuns. Thai temples freely mix different foreign influences, from the corn-shaped stupa inherited from the Khmer empire to the bell-shaped stupa of Sri Lanka.

Thai temples are replete with Hindu-Buddhist iconography. *Naga*, a mythical serpentlike creature who guarded Buddha during meditation, is often depicted in entrance railings and outlining roof gables. On the tip of the temple hall roof is the *chôr fáh*: a golden bird-shaped silhouette suggesting flight.

A venerated Buddhist symbol, the lotus bud is another sacred motif that often decorates the tops of temple gates, verandah columns and the spires of Sukhothai-era *chedi*. Images of the Buddha often depict him meditating on a lotus pedestal. It carries with it a reminder of the tenets

CHOW LAIR

Southern Thailand is home to one of Thailand's smallest ethnic groups, the *chow lair*, literally 'people of the sea' (also spelt *chao leh*). Also known as Moken *(mor·gaan)* or sea gypsies, the *chow lair* are an ethnic group of Malay origin who are found along coasts as far north as Myanmar and as far south as Borneo. The remaining traditional bands of *chow lair* are hunter-gatherers who are recognised as one of the few groups of humans that live primarily at sea, although in recent years many have turned to shanty-like settlements on various islands. Perhaps as a result of generations of this marine lifestyle, many *chow lair* can hold their breath for long periods of time and also have an uncanny ability to see underwater. Life at sea has also helped them in other ways; during the 2004 tsunami, virtually no *chow lair* were killed, as folk tales handed down from generation to generation alerted them to the dangers of the quickly receding tide and they were able to escape to higher ground.

The *chow lair* were mostly ignored until recently when their islands became valuable for tourism. Entrepreneurs bought up large tracts of beachfront land and the *chow lair* moved on to smaller, less valuable islands. With these pressures, it was perhaps inevitable that the *chow lair* culture would slowly disappear. Many sea gypsies now make a living ferrying tourists around the islands or harvesting fish for seafood buffets at tourist resorts. One vestige of traditional *chow lair* life you may see is the biannual 'boat floating' ceremony in May and November, in which an elaborate model boat is set adrift, carrying away bad luck.

of Buddhism. The lotus can bloom even from the mud of a rancid pond, illustrating the capacity for religious perfection in a defiled environment.

Thais began mixing traditional architecture with European forms in the late 19th and early 20th centuries. The port cities, including Bangkok and Phuket, acquired fine examples of Sino-Portuguese architecture – buildings of stuccoed brick decorated with an ornate facade – a style that followed the Portuguese sea traders during the colonial era. It is locally known as 'old Bangkok' or 'Ratanakosin'.

Painting

Except for the prehistoric and historic cave paintings found in the south of the country, not much ancient formal painting exists in Thailand, partly due to the devastating Burmese invasion of 1767. The vast majority of what exists is religious in nature, and typically takes the form of temple paintings illustrating the various lives of the Buddha.

Since the 1980s boom years, Thai secular sculpture and painting have enjoyed increased international recognition, with a handful of Impressionism-inspired artists among the initial few to have reached this vaunted status. Succeeding this was the 'Fireball' school of artists, such as Manit Sriwanichpoom, who specialise in politically motivated, mixed-media art installations. In recent years Thai artists have again moved away from both traditional influences and political commentary and towards contemporary art, focusing on more personal themes, such as those seen in the gender-exploring works of Pinaree Sanpitak, or Maitree Siriboon's identity-driven work.

Fiction

The Lioness in Bloom: Modern Thai Fiction about Women (translated by Susan Fulop Kepner)

Four Reigns (Kukrit Pramoj)

Bangkok 8 (John Burdett)

Fieldwork: A Novel (Mischa Berlinski)

Theatre & Dance

Traditional Thai theatre consists of four main dramatic forms: *kŏhn* is a formal masked dance-drama, traditionally reserved for royalty, depicting scenes from the *Ramakian; lá·kon* is dance-drama performed for common people; *lí·gair* is a partly improvised, often bawdy, folk play featuring dancing, comedy, melodrama and music; and *hùn lŏo·ang (lá·kon lék)* is traditional puppet theatre enacting religious legends or folk tales.

Most of these forms can be enjoyed in Bangkok, both at dinner shows for tourists and at formal theatrical performances. There are also some distinctively southern theatrical styles predating the arrival of Islam on the Malay peninsula. The most famous is *má·noh·rah,* the oldest surviving Thai dance-drama, which tells the story of Prince Suthon, who sets off to rescue the kidnapped Manohraa, a *gin·ná·ree* (woman-bird) princess. As in *lí·gair,* performers add extemporaneous, comic, rhymed commentary. Trang also has a distinctive form of *lí·gair,* with a storyline depicting Indian merchants taking their Thai wives back to India for a visit.

Another ancient theatrical style in the south is shadow-puppet theatre (also found in Indonesia and Malaysia), in which two-dimensional figures carved from buffalo hide are manipulated against an illuminated cloth screen. The capital of shadow puppetry today is Nakhon Si Thammarat, which has regular performances at its festivals. While, sadly, a dying art, puppets are popular souvenirs for tourists.

The Sex Industry in Thailand

Prostitution was widespread in Thailand centuries before the country gained its current reputation among international sex tourists. Throughout Thai history the practice was accepted and common, though it has not always been respected by society as a whole. Today, prostitution is technically illegal but anti-prostitution laws are ambiguous and often unenforced.

History & Cultural Attitudes

Prostitution was declared illegal in 1960 under pressure from the UN. But a separate law passed in 1966 allows for entertainment places (go-go bars, beer bars, massage parlours, karaoke bars and bathhouses) that can legally provide non-sexual services (such as dancing, massage, a drinking buddy); sexual services are brokered through these venues, but they are not technically the businesses' primary purpose.

The Empower Foundation National Museum in Bangkok documents the history and evolution of sex workers and their labour movement in Thailand.

With the arrival of the US military in Southeast Asia to fight the Vietnam War from the mid-1960s on, enterprising forces adapted the existing framework to a new clientele. The industry targeted at foreigners is very visible with multiple red-light districts in Bangkok alone, but there is also a more clandestine domestic sex industry and myriad informal sex-for-hire channels.

In 1998 the International Labour Organization, a UN agency, advised Southeast Asian countries, including Thailand, to recognise prostitution as an economic sector and income generator. It is estimated that one-third of the entertainment establishments are registered with the government and the majority pay an informal tax in the form of police bribes.

Some reports cite the Thai sex industry as being worth US$4.3 billion or around 3% of GDP, but others claim it contributes as much as 10% of GDP. Similarly, figures on the number of sex workers in Thailand vary dramatically. A 2013 report by the United Nations Office on Drugs and Crime stated there were 250,000 sex workers, basing its estimate on figures from Thailand's Ministry of Health. But a 2003 study conducted by Bangkok's Chulalongkorn University estimated 2.8 million sex workers,

PROS & CONS

Women's rights groups take contrasting approaches to the question of prostitution. Abolitionists see prostitution as exploitation and an infraction of basic human rights. Meanwhile, mitigators recognise that there is demand and supply at work and try to reduce the risks associated with the activity through HIV/AIDs prevention and education programs (especially for economic migrants). Sex-worker organisations, such as Bangkok-based Empower, argue that prostitution is a legitimate job and the best way to help women is to treat the issue from a worker's rights perspective, demanding fair pay and compensation, legal redress and mandatory sick and holiday entitlements time.

HIV/AIDS

Thailand was lauded for its rapid and effective response to the AIDS epidemic through an aggressive condom-use campaign in the 1990s. But HIV/AIDS remains the number one cause of premature death in the country, according to a 2013 study by the University of Washington. Some 490,000 people are living with HIV/AIDS in Thailand and there has been a sharp rise in new infections among the gay and transgender community and male sex workers. Those three groups accounted for 41% of all new HIV/AIDS cases in 2013 and some estimates state that 30% of men who have sex with men in Bangkok are HIV positive.

of which 1.98 million were adult women, 20,000 were adult men and 800,000 were children, defined as any person under the age of 18.

Economic Motivations

Almost all women in the sex industry are there for financial reasons. Many find that sex work is one of the highest-paying jobs for their level of education, and they have financial obligations (be it dependents or debts). Most female sex workers come from farming families in Isan, the northeast of Thailand and the country's poorest region, and most did not graduate from high school.

Suspicious behaviour involving child-sex tourism can be reported on a dedicated hotline (1300).

With few high-earning job options open to them, working in the sex industry is a short-term means of earning far more than they can in a factory or a shop. Accurate information on sex-worker salaries is near impossible to come by, but some probably make 25,000B a month or more; the average monthly wage for a new graduate in Bangkok is 15,000B. Those economic factors provide a strong incentive for rural, unskilled women (and to a lesser extent, men) to engage in sex work.

Like many people in Thai society, sex workers remit a large percentage of their wages back to their home villages to support their families (parents, siblings and children). Their wages go on household goods, such as washing machines and TVs, motorcycles and cars and are often used to build bigger homes. The relative wealth of sex worker families acts as an incentive for other women to follow in their footsteps.

Child Prostitution & Human Trafficking

According to Ecpat (End Child Prostitution & Trafficking), there are currently 30,000 to 40,000 children involved in prostitution in Thailand, though estimates are unreliable. A 2003 Chulalongkorn University report estimated the number of children is as high as 800,000, though this figure includes anyone under the age of 18. Many of these are the children of displaced and marginalised people such as migrant workers in urban centres. Children of these fractured families often turn to street begging, which can be an entryway into prostitution usually through low-level criminal gangs.

In 1996, Thailand passed a reform law to address the issue of child prostitution. Two categories were defined – children under 15 and those over 15 – with harsher penalties for those found guilty of sex with under-15s. Fines and jail time are assigned to customers, establishment owners and even parents involved in child prostitution. Many countries also have extraterritorial legislation that allows nationals to be prosecuted in their own country for such crimes committed in Thailand.

NGOs

Ecpat *(www.ecpat.net) Anti-child prostitution and trafficking group.*

Coalition Against Trafficking in Women *(CATW; www.catwinternational.org) Anti-trafficking NGO.*

Empower Foundation *(www.empowerfoundation.org) Sex-workers union.*

Food & Drink

There's an entire universe of amazing dishes once you get beyond 'pad Thai' and green curry, and for many visitors food is one of the main reasons for choosing Thailand as a destination. Even more remarkable, however, is the love for Thai food among the locals: Thais become just as excited as tourists when faced with a bowl of well-prepared noodles or when seated at a renowned hawker stall. This unabashed enthusiasm for eating, not to mention an abundance of fascinating ingredients and influences, has generated one of the most fun and diverse food scenes in the world.

Staples & Specialities

Rice

In Thailand, to eat is to eat rice, and for most of the country a meal is not acceptable without this staple. Thailand maintains the world's fifth-largest area of land dedicated to growing rice, an industry that employs more than half the country's arable land and a significant portion of its population. Rice is so central to Thai food culture that the most common term for 'eat' is *gin kôw* (literally, 'consume rice') and one of the most common greetings is *Gin kôw rĕu yang*? (Have you consumed rice yet?)

There are many varieties of rice in Thailand, and the country has been among the world leaders in rice exports since the 1960s. The highest grade is *kôw hŏrm má·lí* (jasmine rice), a fragrant long grain that is so coveted by neighbouring countries that there is allegedly a steady underground business in smuggling out fresh supplies. The grain is customarily served alongside main dishes such as curries, stir-fries or soups, which are lumped together as *gàp kôw* (with rice). When you order plain rice in a restaurant, you use the term *kôw Ƀlòw* (plain rice) or *kôw sŏo·ay* (beautiful rice). Residents of Thailand's north and northeast eat *kôw nĕe·o* (sticky rice), a glutinous short-grained rice that is cooked by steaming, not boiling. And in Chinese-style eateries, *kôw đôm* (boiled rice), a watery porridge sometimes employing brown or purple rice, is a common carb.

Thailand is the world's second-largest exporter of rice, and in 2014 exported approximately 10.8 million tonnes of the grain.

Curries & Soups

In Thai, *gaang* (it sounds somewhat similar to the English 'gang') is often translated as 'curry', but it actually describes any dish with a lot of liquid and can thus refer to soups (such as *gaang jèut*) as well as the classic chilli-paste-based curries for which Thai cuisine is famous. The preparation of the latter begins with a *krêu·ang gaang*, created by mashing, pounding and grinding an array of fresh ingredients with a stone mortar and pestle to form an aromatic, extremely pungent-tasting and rather thick paste. Typical ingredients in a *krêu·ang gaang* include dried chilli, galangal, lemon grass, Kaffir lime zest, shallots, garlic, shrimp paste and salt.

Another food celebrity that falls into the soupy category is *đôm yam*, the famous Thai spicy-and-sour soup. Fuelling the fire beneath *đôm yam*'s often velvety surface are fresh *prík kêe nŏo* (tiny chillies) or, alternatively, half a teaspoon of *nám prík pŏw* (a roasted chilli paste). Lemongrass, Kaffir lime leaf and lime juice give *đôm yam* its characteristic tang.

Stir-Fries & Deep-Fries

The simplest dishes in the Thai culinary repertoire are the various *pàt* (stir-fries) introduced to Thailand by the Chinese, who are world famous for being able to stir-fry a whole banquet in a single wok.

The list of *pàt* dishes seems endless. Many cling to their Chinese roots, such as the ubiquitous *pàt pàk bûng fai daang* (morning glory flash-fried with garlic and chilli), while some are Thai-Chinese hybrids, such as *pàt pèt* (literally 'spicy stir-fry'), in which the main ingredients, typically meat or fish, are quickly stir-fried with red curry paste.

Tôrt (deep-frying in oil) is mainly reserved for snacks such as *glôo·ay tôrt* (deep-fried bananas) or *Ƀò·Ƀée·a* (egg rolls). An exception is *Ƀlah tôrt* (deep-fried fish), which is a common way to prepare fish.

Bangkok's Top 50 Street Food Stalls, by Chawadee Nualkhair, also functions well as a general introduction and guide to Thai-style informal dining.

Hot & Tangy Salads

Standing right alongside curries in terms of Thai-ness is the ubiquitous *yam*, a hot and tangy 'salad' typically based around seafood, meat or vegetables.

Lime juice provides the tang, while the abundant use of chilli generates the heat. Most *yam* are served at room temperature or just slightly warmed by any cooked ingredients. The dish functions equally well as part of a meal or on its own as *gàp glâam* (snack food to accompany a night of boozing).

Nám Prík

Although they're more home than restaurant food, *nám prík* (spicy chilli-based 'dips') are, for the locals at least, among the most emblematic of all Thai dishes. Typically eaten with rice and steamed or fresh vegetables and herbs, they're also among the most regional of Thai dishes, and you could probably pinpoint the province you're in by simply looking at the *nám prík* on offer.

Fruits

Being a tropical country, Thailand excels in the fruit department. *Má·môo·ang* (mangoes) alone come in a dozen varieties that are eaten at different stages of ripeness. Other common fruit include *sàp·Ƀà·rót* (pineapple), *má·lá·gor* (papaya) and *đaang moh* (watermelon), all of which are sold from ubiquitous vendor carts and accompanied by a dipping mix of salt, sugar and ground chilli. Yet a highlight of visiting Thailand is sampling the huge variety of indigenous fruits of which you've probably never heard. Many are available year-round nowadays, but April and May is peak season for several of the most beloved varieties, including durian, mangoes and mangosteen.

Lonely Planet's *From the Source: Thailand*, written and photographed in part by the author of this chapter, features authentic recipes from Bangkok and southern Thailand.

- **Custard apple** Known in Thai as *nóy nàh*, this fruit has knobbly green skin that conceals hard black seeds and sweet, gloopy flesh with a granular texture.
- **Durian** Known in Thai as *tú·ree·an*, the king of fruit is also Thailand's most infamous due to its intense flavour and odour, which can suggest everything from custard to onions.
- **Guava** A native of South America, *fa·ràng* is a green, applelike ball containing a pink or white flesh that's sweet and crispy.
- **Jackfruit** The gigantic green pod of *kà·nŭn* – it's generally considered the world's largest fruit – conceals dozens of waxy yellow sections that taste like a blend of pineapple and bananas (it reminds us of Juicy Fruit chewing gum).
- **Langsat** Strip away the yellowish peel of this fruit, known in Thai as *long·gong*, to find a segmented, perfumed pearlescent flesh with a lychee-like flavour.
- **Longan** *Lam yai* takes the form of a tiny hard ball; it's like a mini lychee with sweet, perfumed flesh. Peel it, eat the flesh and spit out the hard seed.

THAI NOODLES 101

In Thailand, noodles are ubiquitous, cheap and tasty. But they're also extremely varied and somewhat complicated to order. So with this in mind, we've provided a crash course in Thai noodles.

The Noodles

You'll find four main kinds of noodle in Thailand. When ordering, it's generally necessary to specify which noodle you want.

➡ **Bà·mèe** Made from wheat flour and egg, this noodle is yellowish in colour and sold only in fresh bundles.

➡ **Kà·nŏm jeen** This noodle is produced by pushing a rice-based dough through a sieve into boiling water.

➡ **Sên gŏo·ay đĕe·o** The most common type of noodle in Thailand is made from rice flour mixed with water to form a paste, which is then steamed to form wide, flat sheets. The sheets are folded and sliced into various widths ranging from *sên lék* (thin) to *sên yài* (wide).

➡ **Wún·sên** Almost clear and made from mung-bean starch and water, this noodle features occasionally in noodle soups.

The Dishes

➡ **Bà·mèe** The eponymous Chinese-style wheat-and-egg noodles are typically served with slices of barbecued pork, a handful of greens and, if you like, wontons.

➡ **Gŏo·ay jáp** Rice noodles and pork offal served in a fragrant, peppery broth; a dish popular among the Thai-Chinese.

➡ **Gŏo·ay đĕe·o kaang** An Islamic-world-influenced Thai dish of rice noodles served with a curry broth, often including garnishes such as peanuts, hard-boiled egg and peanuts.

➡ **Gŏo·ay đĕe·o lôok chín** This dish combines rice noodles in a generally clear broth with pork- or fish-based (or, less commonly, beef or chicken) balls; one of the most common types of noodles across the country.

➡ **Gŏo·ay đĕe·o reu·a** Known as boat noodles because they were previously served from the canals of central Thailand, these intense pork- or beef-based bowls are among the most full-flavoured of Thai noodle dishes.

➡ **Kà·nŏm jeen** This dish, named after its noodle, combines thin rice threads and typically mild, currylike broth served topped with a self-selection of fresh and pickled vegetables and herbs. *Kà·nŏm jeen* varies immensely from region to region and also tends to be one of the cheapest noodle dishes in the country.

➡ **Yen đah foh** Combining a slightly crimson broth with a variety of meatballs, cubes of coagulated chicken or pork blood and crispy greens, this dish is probably the most intimidating and popular noodle dish in Bangkok.

The Seasoning

Thai noodle dishes are often served slightly underseasoned. In these cases, it's seen as the eater's job to season his or her bowl using four common condiments: *prík nám sôm* (sliced mild chillies in vinegar), *nám Ƀlah* (fish sauce), *prík Ƀòn* (dried red chilli, flaked or ground to a near powder) and *nám·đahn* (plain white sugar). In typically Thai fashion, these condiments offer three ways to make the soup hotter – hot and sour, hot and salty, and just plain hot – and one way to make it sweet. Many shops also include a shaker of white pepper and more obscure noodle dishes may be served with condiments such as ground peanuts, ground chilli fried in oil, or Chinese vinegar.

➡ **Lychee** The pink skin of *lín·jèe* conceals an addictive translucent flesh similar in flavour to a grape; it's generally only available between April and June.

➡ **Mangosteen** The hard purple shell of *mang·kút*, the queen of Thai fruit, conceals delightfully fragrant white segments, some containing a hard seed.

➡ **Pomelo** Like a grapefruit on steroids, *sôm oh* takes the form of a thick pithy green skin hiding sweet, tangy segments; cut into the skin, peel off the pith and then break open the segments and munch on the flesh inside.

➡ **Rambutan** People have different theories about what *ngó* look like, not all repeatable in polite company. Regardless, the hairy shell contains sweet translucent flesh that you scrape off the seed with your teeth.

➡ **Rose apple** Known in Thai as *chom·pôo*, rose apple is an elongated pink or red fruit with a smooth, shiny skin and pale, watery flesh; a good thirst quencher on a hot day.

➡ **Salak** Also known as snake fruit because of its scaly skin; the exterior of *sàlà* looks like a mutant strawberry and the soft flesh tastes like unripe bananas.

➡ **Starfruit** The star-shaped cross-section of *má·feu·ang* is the giveaway; the yellow flesh is sweet and tangy and believed by many to lower blood pressure.

The authors of Eating Thai Food (www.eatingthaifood.com) have put together an 88-page illustrated PDF guide to identifying and ordering Thai dishes for foreign visitors.

Sweets

English-language Thai menus often have a section called 'Desserts', but Thai-style sweets are generally consumed as breakfast or a sweet snack, not directly following a meal. Sweets also take two slightly different forms in Thailand. *Kŏrng wăhn*, which translates as 'sweet things', are small, rich sweets that often boast a slightly salty flavour. Prime ingredients for *kŏrng wăhn* include grated coconut, coconut milk, rice flour (from white rice or sticky rice), cooked sticky rice, tapioca, mung-bean starch, boiled taro and various fruits. Egg yolks are a popular ingredient for many *kŏrng wăhn*, including the ubiquitous *fŏy torng* (literally 'golden threads'), probably influenced by Portuguese desserts and pastries introduced during the early Ayuthaya era.

Thai sweets roughly similar to the European concept of pastries are called *kà·nŏm*. Probably the most popular type of *kà·nŏm* in Thailand are the bite-sized items wrapped in banana leaves, especially *kôw đôm gà·tí* and *kôw đôm mát*. Both consist of sticky rice grains steamed with *gà·tí* (coconut milk) inside a banana-leaf wrapper to form a solid, almost toffeelike, mass.

Regional Variations

One particularly unique aspect of Thai food is its regional diversity. Despite having evolved in a relatively small area, Thai cuisine is anything but a single entity and takes a slightly different form every time it crosses a provincial border.

Drinks

Coffee, Tea & Fruit Drinks

Thais are big coffee drinkers, and good-quality arabica and robusta are cultivated in the hilly areas of northern and southern Thailand. The traditional filtering system is nothing more than a narrow cloth bag attached to a steel handle. This type of coffee is served in a glass, mixed with sugar and sweetened with condensed milk – if you don't want either, be sure to specify *gah·faa dam* (black coffee) followed with *mâi sài nám·đahn* (without sugar).

Black tea, both local and imported, is available at the same places that serve real coffee. *Chah tai*, Thai-style tea, derives its characteristic orange-red colour from ground tamarind seed added after curing.

Pok Pok, by Andy Ricker with JJ Goode, features recipes of the rustic, regional Thai dishes served at Ricker's eponymous Portland, Oregon; New York City; and Los Angeles restaurants.

Fruit drinks appear all over Thailand and are an excellent way to rehydrate after water becomes unpalatable. Most *nám pŏn·lá·mái* (fruit juices) are served with a touch of sugar and salt and a whole lot of ice. Many foreigners object to the salt, but it serves a metabolic role in helping the body to cope with tropical temperatures.

Thai Food by David Thompson is widely considered the most authoritative English-language book on Thai cooking. Thompson's follow-up, *Thai Street Food*, focuses on more casual street cuisine.

Beer & Spirits

There are several brands of beer in Thailand, ranging from domestic brands (Singha, Chang, Leo) to foreign-licensed labels (Heineken, Asahi, San Miguel). They are all largely indistinguishable in terms of taste and quality.

Domestic rice whisky and rum are favourites of the working class, struggling students and family gatherings as they're more affordable than beer. Once spending money becomes a priority, Thais often upgrade to imported whiskies. These are usually drunk with lots of ice, soda water and a splash of coke. On a night out, buying a whole bottle is the norm in most of Thailand. If you don't finish it, it will simply be kept at the bar until your next visit.

Where to Eat & Drink

Appon's Thai Food (www.khiewchanta.com) features nearly 1000 authentic, well-organised Thai recipes – many with helpful audio recordings of their Thai names – written by a Thai.

Prepared food is available just about everywhere in Thailand, and it shouldn't come as a surprise that the locals do much of their eating outside the home. In this regard, as a visitor, you'll fit right in.

Open-air markets and food stalls are among the most popular places at which Thais eat. In the morning, stalls selling coffee and Chinese-style doughnuts spring up along busy commuter corridors. At lunchtime, midday eaters might grab a plastic chair at yet another stall for a simple stir-fry, or pick up a foam box of noodles to scoff down at the office. In most small towns, night markets often set up in the middle of town with a cluster of vendors, metal tables and chairs, and some shopping as an after-dinner mint.

There are, of course, restaurants (*ráhn ah·hăhn*) in Thailand that range from simple food stops to formal affairs. Lunchtime is the right time to point and eat at the *ráhn kôw gaang* (rice-and-curry shop), which sells a selection of premade curries and other dishes. Come dinner the ubiquitous *ráhn ah·hăhn đahm sàng* (food-to-order shop) can often be

COFFEE, SOUTHERN-STYLE

In virtually every town or city in southern Thailand, you'll find numerous old-world cafes known to locals as *ráhn goh·Ƀée*. The shops are almost exclusively owned by Thais of Chinese origin and often seem suspended in time, typically having sported the same decor and menu for decades. Characteristics of *ráhn goh·Ƀée* include marble-topped tables, antique mugs and dishes, and an almost exclusively male clientele that also seems not to have budged since opening day. Some of the most atmospheric *ráhn goh·Ƀée* in Thailand can be found in the town of Trang.

The beans used at *ráhn goh·Ƀée* are sometimes grown abroad, but are roasted domestically. Although the beans are as black as the night, the drink typically tends to lack body. This may be due to the brewing method, which involves pouring hot water through a windsock-like piece of cloth that holds the loose grounds. Typically, *ráhn goh·Ƀée* is served over a dollop of sweetened condensed milk and a tablespoon (or more) of sugar in small, handleless glasses. For those lacking a sweet tooth, try *goh·Ƀée* (black coffee), or just ask them to hold the sugar. All hot coffee drinks are served with a 'chaser' of weak green tea.

Ráhn goh·Ƀée are also a great place for a quick bite. Upon arriving at the more traditional ones, you'll be greeted by a tray of steamed Chinese buns, sweet snacks such as sticky rice wrapped in banana leaf, or baked goods.

recognised by a display of raw ingredients – Chinese kale, tomatoes, chopped pork, fresh or dried fish, noodles, eggplant, spring onions – and serves a standard repertoire of largely Chinese-influenced dishes. As the name implies, the cooks attempt to prepare any dish you can name, a slightly more difficult operation if you can't speak Thai.

Vegetarians & Vegans

Vegetarianism isn't widespread in Thailand, but many of the tourist-oriented restaurants cater to vegetarians, and there are also a handful of *ráhn ah·hăhn mang·sà·wí·rát* (vegetarian restaurants) in Bangkok where the food is served buffet-style and is very inexpensive. Dishes are almost always 100% vegan (ie no meat, poultry, fish or fish sauce, dairy or egg products).

During the Vegetarian Festival, celebrated by Chinese Buddhists in September/October, many restaurants and street stalls in Bangkok go meatless for one month.

The phrase 'I'm vegetarian' in Thai is *pŏm gin jair* (for men) or *dì·chăn gin jair* (for women). Loosely translated this means 'I eat only vegetarian food', which includes no eggs and no dairy products – in other words, total vegan.

Maintained by a Thai woman living in the US, She Simmers (www.shesimmers.com) is a good resource for those making Thai food outside Thailand.

Habits & Customs

Like most of Thai culture, eating conventions appear relaxed and informal but are orchestrated by many implied rules.

Whether at home or in a restaurant, Thai meals are always served 'family-style', that is, from common serving platters. And the plates appear in whatever order the kitchen can prepare them. When serving yourself from a common platter, put no more than one spoonful onto your plate at a time. Heaping your plate with all 'your' portions at once will look greedy to Thais unfamiliar with Western conventions. Another important factor in a Thai meal is achieving a balance of flavours and textures. Traditionally, the party orders a curry, a steamed or fried fish, a stir-fried vegetable dish and a soup, taking great care to balance cool and hot, sour and sweet, salty and plain.

Originally Thai food was eaten with the fingers, and it still is in certain regions of the kingdom. In the early 1900s, Thais began setting their tables with fork and spoon to affect a 'royal' setting, and it wasn't long before fork-and-spoon dining became the norm in Bangkok and later spread throughout the kingdom. To use these tools the Thai way, use a serving spoon, or alternatively your own, to take a single mouthful of food from a central dish and ladle it over a portion of your rice. The fork is then used to push the now food-soaked portion of rice back onto the spoon before entering the mouth.

If you're not offered chopsticks, don't ask for them. Chopsticks are reserved for eating Chinese-style food from bowls or for eating in all-Chinese restaurants. In either case you will be supplied with chopsticks without having to ask. Unlike their counterparts in many Western countries, restaurateurs in Thailand won't assume you don't know how to use them.

Food Spotter's Guide

Spanning four distinct regions, with influences from China to the Middle East, a multitude of ingredients and a reputation for spice, Thai food can be more than a bit overwhelming. So to point you in the direction of the good stuff, we've put together a shortlist of the country's must-eat dishes.

1. Yam

This family of Thai 'salads' combines meat or seafood with a tart and spicy dressing and fresh herbs.

2. Pàt tai

Thin rice noodles fried with egg, tofu and shrimp, and seasoned with fish sauce, tamarind and dried chilli have emerged as the poster boy for Thai food – and justifiably so.

3. Gaang kĕe·o wăhn

Known outside of Thailand as green curry, this intersection of a piquant, herbal spice paste and rich coconut milk is single-handedly emblematic of Thai cuisine's unique flavours and ingredients.

4. Đôm yam

The 'sour Thai soup' moniker featured on many English-language menus is a feeble description of this mouth-puckeringly tart and intensely spicy herbal broth.

5. Bà·mèe

Although Chinese in origin, these wheat-and-egg noodles, typically served with roast pork and/or crab, have become a Thai hawker-stall staple.

1

3

5

AUSTIN BUSH ©

AUSTIN BUSH ©

6. Lâhp

Minced meat seasoned with roasted rice powder, lime, fish sauce and fresh herbs is a one-dish crash course in the strong, rustic flavours of Thailand's northeast.

7. Kôw mòk

The Thai version of *biryani* couples golden rice and tender chicken with a sweet-and-sour dip and a savoury broth.

8. Sôm·đam

'Papaya salad' hardly does justice to this tear-inducingly spicy dish of strips of crunchy, unripe papaya pounded in a mortar and pestle with tomato, long beans, chilli, lime and fish sauce.

9. Kôw soy

Even outside of its home in Thailand's north, there's a cult following for this soup that combines flat egg-and-wheat noodles in a rich, spice-laden, coconut-milk-based broth.

10. Pàt pàk bûng fai daang

'Morning glory', a crunchy green vegetable, flash-fried with heaps of chilli and garlic is, despite the spice, Thai comfort food.

6

8

AUSTIN BUSH ©

AUSTIN BUSH ©

10

AUSTIN BUSH ©

Environment

Bound to the east by the Gulf of Thailand and to the west by the Andaman Sea, an extension of the Indian Ocean, Thailand possesses one of the most alluring coastlines in the world, with exquisitely carved limestone formations above water and tremendously rich coral reefs below. Hundreds of tropical islands of all shapes and sizes adorn the coast, from flat sandbars covered in mangroves to looming karst massifs licked by azure waters and ringed by white-sand beaches.

The Land

Thailand's odd shape – bulky and wide up north, with a long pendulous arm draping to the south – has often been compared to the head of an elephant. With an area of 517,000 sq km, which makes it slightly larger than Spain, Thailand stretches an astounding 1650km along a north–south axis and experiences an extremely diverse climate, including two distinct monsoons from both the southwest and northwest. The north of the country rises into high forested mountains, while the south consists of a long ridge of limestone hills covered in tropical rainforest.

If anyone in Thailand comes across a white elephant, it must be reported to the Bureau of the Royal Household, and the King will decide whether it meets the criteria to be a royal white elephant.

Both the Andaman and the Gulf Coasts have extensive coral reefs, particularly around the granitic Surin and Similan islands in the Andaman Sea. More reefs and Thailand's most dramatic limestone islands sit in Ao Phang-Nga near Phuket. The west coast is of particular interest to divers because the waters are stunningly clear and extremely rich in marine life.

Wildlife

With its diverse climate and topography, it should come as no surprise that Thailand is home to a remarkable diversity of flora and fauna. What is more surprising is that Thailand's environment is still in relatively good shape, particularly considering the relentless development going on all over the country. That said, there are certainly problems for some endangered species as well as marine environmental issues.

Animals

Animals that live on the coasts and islands of Thailand must adapt to shifting tides and the ever-changing mix of salt water and freshwater. Beyond larger animals, keep your eyes open for smaller creatures, such as the odd little mudskipper, a fish that leaves the water and walks around on the mudflats when the tide goes out, or the giant water monitor, a fearsome 350cm-long lizard that climbs and swims effortlessly in its hunt for small animals.

Without a doubt you will see some of the region's fabulous birdlife – Thailand is home to 10% of the world's bird species – especially sandpipers and plors on the mudflats, and herons and egrets in the swamps. Look overhead for the sharply attired, chocolate-and-white Brahminy kite, or scan low-lying branches for one of the region's many colourful kingfishers. You are likely to spot a troop of gregarious and noisy crab-eating macaques, and don't be surprised to see these monkeys swimming from shore. With luck you may glimpse a palm civet, a complexly marbled, catlike creature, or a serow, the reclusive 'goat-antelope', which bounds fearlessly among inaccessible limestone crags.

The oceans on either side of the Thai peninsula are home to hundreds of species of coral, and the reefs created by these tiny creatures provide the perfect living conditions for countless species of fish, crustaceans and tiny invertebrates. You can find one of the world's smallest fish (the 1cm-long dwarf pygmy goby) and the largest cartilaginous fish (the 12m-long whale shark), plus reef denizens such as clownfish, parrotfish, wrasse, angelfish, triggerfish and lionfish. Deeper waters are home to larger species such as groupers, barracudas, sharks, manta rays, marlin and tuna. You might also encounter turtles, whales and dolphins.

Endangered Species

Thailand is a signatory to the UN Convention on International Trade in Endangered Species of Wild Fauna and Flora (Cites), but the enforcement of these trade bans is notoriously lax – just walk around the animal section of Bangkok's Chatuchak Weekend Market to see how openly the rules are flouted. Due to habitat loss, pollution and poaching, a depressing number of Thailand's mammals, reptiles, fish and birds are endangered, and even populations of formerly common species are diminishing at an alarming rate. Rare mammals, birds, reptiles, insects, shells and tropical aquarium fish are routinely smuggled out to collectors around the world or slaughtered to make souvenirs for tourists.

Many of Thailand's marine animals are under threat, including whale sharks, although they have been seen more frequently in Thai waters recently, and sea turtles, which are being wiped out by hunting for their eggs, meat and shells. Many other species of shark are being hunted to extinction for their fins, which are used to make shark-fin soup.

The rare dugong (similar to the manatee and sometimes called a sea cow), once thought extinct in Thailand, is now known to survive in a few small pockets, mostly around Trang in southern Thailand, but is increasingly threatened by habitat loss and the lethal propellers of tourist boats.

The Thai government is slowly recognising the importance of conservation, perhaps in part due to the efforts and leadership of Queen Sirikit, and many of the kingdom's zoos now have active breeding and conservation programs. Wildlife organisations such as the Phuket Gibbon Rehabilitation Centre are working to educate the public about native wildlife and have initiated a number of wildlife rescue and rehabilitation projects.

> Fed on up to 540,000 metric tons of wild-caught trash fish, a staggering 250,000 to 300,000 metric tons of shrimp are harvested from fish farms each year in Thailand, according to the World Wild Fund for Nature.

Plants

Southern Thailand is chock-full of luxuriant vegetation, thanks to its two monsoon seasons. The majority of forests away from the coast are evergreen rainforests, while trees at the ocean edge and on limestone formations are stunted due to lack of freshwater and exposure to harsh minerals.

The most beautiful shoreline trees are the many species of palm trees occurring in Thailand, including some found nowhere else in the world. All have small tough leaves with characteristic fanlike or featherlike shapes that help dissipate heat and conserve water. Look for the elegant cycad palm on limestone cliffs, where it grows in cracks despite the complete absence of soil. Collected for its beauty, this common ornamental plant is disappearing from its wild habitat.

Thailand is also home to nearly 75 species of salt-tolerant mangroves – small trees highly adapted to living at the edge of salt water. Standing tiptoe-like on clumps of tall roots, mangroves perform a vital ecological function by trapping sediments and nutrients, and by buffering the coast from the fierce, erosive power of monsoons. This habitat serves as a secure nursery for the eggs and young of countless marine organisms, yet Thailand has destroyed at least 50% of its mangrove swamps to make way for prawn farms and big hotels. Mangrove restoration projects across Thailand are attempting to reverse these massive losses.

National Parks

The famous white sands of Thailand's beaches are actually tiny bits of coral that have been defecated by coral-eating fish.

National parks in Thailand are a huge draw. The popular island getaways of Ko Chang and Ko Samet sit just off the mainland along the eastern gulf coast. Ko Tarutao Marine National Park is remote and undeveloped for real back-to-nature vacations. Ao Phang-Nga, north of Phuket, is endlessly photogenic with its limestone cliffs jutting out of the aquamarine water while knotted mangrove roots cling to thick mudflats. Meanwhile the Similan Islands and Surin Islands Marine National Parks, in the waters of the Andaman Sea, have some of the world's best diving.

Approximately 13% of Thailand is covered by 127 national parks (including marine national parks) and 44 wildlife sanctuaries. Of Thailand's protected areas, 18 parks protect islands and mangrove environments. Thailand's parks and sanctuaries contain more than 850 resident and migratory species of birds and dwindling numbers of tigers, clouded leopards, koupreys, elephants, tapirs, gibbons and Asiatic black bears, among other species.

Despite promises, official designation as a national park or sanctuary does not always guarantee protection for habitats and wildlife. Local farmers, wealthy developers and other business interests will often prevail, either legally or illegally, over environmental protection in Thailand's national parks. Islands that are technically exempt from development may not adhere to the law and government doesn't always sufficiently enforce regulations.

Environmental Issues

Thailand is wealthier, better developed and more educated than its regional neighbours, so there is an awareness of environmental issues that barely exists in countries such as Cambodia and Myanmar. But that awareness is often limited in scope, and while this is slowly changing, it rarely develops into the sort of high-profile, widespread movements seen in Europe, North America or Australia.

As such most issues have a low profile, with only the most visible problems, such as pollution, over-development and a lack of adequate planning, registering with visitors. Look a little deeper, however, and it's evident that the environment has often been the victim in Thailand's rapid modernisation drive. Many Thais don't see a problem with cutting down mangroves to make prawn farms, or powering their development with energy from dams in Laos and dubious natural-gas concerns in Myanmar.

A raft of well-intentioned environmental laws may suggest Thailand is turning the corner towards greater ecological consciousness, but corruption and lack of political resolve have severely hampered efforts to enforce such laws, and the deep split within Thai politics means that this situation is unlikely to change in the short term. Ironically, however, this same lack of political stability has also scared off investment in environmentally damaging sectors.

The Land Environment

The main area in which Asia exceeds the West in terms of environmental damage is deforestation, though current estimates indicate Thailand still has about 25% of its forests remaining, which stands up favourably against the UK's more modest 13%. The government's National Forest Policy, introduced in 1985, recommended that 40% of the country should be forested, and a complete logging ban in 1989 was a big step in the right direction. By law Thailand must maintain 25% of its land area as 'conservation forests', but the logging ban has simply shifted the need for natural resources elsewhere. While illegal logging persists in Thailand on a relatively small scale, in neighbouring Cambodia, Laos and particularly Myanmar the scale has been huge since the 1989 ban. A large number of logs are illegally slipped over the border from these countries.

Despite Thailand being a signatory to Cites, all sorts of land species are still smuggled out of Thailand, either alive or as body parts for traditional Chinese medicines. Tigers may be protected by Thai law, but the kingdom remains the world's largest exporter of tiger parts to China (tiger penis and bone are believed to have medicinal effects and to increase libido). Other animal species are hunted (often illegally) to make souvenirs for tourists, including elephants, jungle spiders, giant insects and butterflies, and along the coast clams, shells and pufferfish.

The government has cracked down on restaurants serving *ah·hăhn Ъàh* (jungle food), which includes endangered wildlife species such as barking deer, bears, pangolins, gibbons, civets and gaurs. A big problem is that national-park officials are underpaid and undertrained, yet are expected to confront armed poachers and mercenary armies funded by rich and powerful godfathers.

The widely touted idea that ecotourism can act as a positive force for change has been extensively put to the test in Thailand. In some instances tourism has definitely had positive effects. The expansion of Thailand's national parks has largely been driven by tourism. In Khao Yai National Park, all hotel and golf-course facilities were removed to reduce damage to the park environment. As a result of government and private-sector pressure on the fishing industry, coral dynamiting has been all but eliminated in the Similan and Surin Islands to preserve the area for tourists.

However, tourism can be a poisoned chalice. Massive developments near and frequently within national parks have ridden roughshod over the local environment in their rush to provide bungalows, luxury hotels, beach bars and boat services for tourists. Ko Phi-Phi and Ko Samet are two national parks where business interests have definitely won out over the environment. In both cases the development began in areas set aside for *chow lair* (also spelt *chao leh;* sea gypsies, the semi-nomadic people who migrate up and down the coast). Ko Lipe in Ko Tarutao Marine National Park and Ko Muk in Hat Chao Mai National Park now seem to be heading the same way.

Rubbish and sewage are growing problems in all populated areas, even more so in heavily visited areas where an influx of tourists overtaxes the local infrastructure. One encouraging development was the passing of the 1992 Environmental Act, which set environmental quality standards, designated conservation and pollution-control areas, and doled out government clean-up funds. Pattaya built its first public wastewater treatment plant in 2000 and conditions have improved ever since.

While Thais generally remain reluctant to engage in broader environmental campaigns, people are increasingly aware of the issues, particularly when they will be affected. Local people have campaigned for years against the building of dams, though usually without success. With Thailand aiming to boost its production of renewable energy by a quarter by 2021, the Energy Generating Authority of Thailand (EGAT) is set to buy 90% of the US$3.5 billion Thai-built Xayaburi Dam's electrical output in northern Laos (one of 11 dams along the lower Mekong) when it becomes operational. Damming the Mekong for hydroelectric power may generate 'clean' electricity, but at great environmental cost, including contributing to the

SOUTHERN THAILAND'S NATIONAL PARKS

PARK	FEATURES	ACTIVITIES
Mu Ko Chang National Marine Park	archipelago marine park with virgin rainforests, waterfalls, beaches & coral reefs	snorkelling, diving, elephant interactions, hiking
Khao Laem Ya/Mu Ko Samet National Park	marine park with beaches, near-shore coral reefs	snorkelling, diving, boat trips, sailboarding
Kaeng Krachan National Park	mainland park with waterfalls & forests; plentiful birdlife & jungle mammals	bird-watching
Khao Sam Roi Yot National Park	coastal park with caves, mountains, cliffs & beaches; serow, Irrawaddy dolphins & 300 bird species	cave tours, bird-watching, kayaking
Ang Thong Marine National Park	40 scenic tropical islands with coral reefs, lagoons & limestone cliffs	sea kayaking, hiking, snorkelling
Khao Luang National Park	mainland park with forested mountain peaks, streams & waterfalls; jungle mammals, birds & orchids	hiking
Ao Phang-Nga National Marine Park	coastal bay with limestone cliffs, islands & caves; coral reefs & mangroves	sea kayaking, snorkelling, diving
Khao Lak/Lam Ru National Park	coastal park with cliffs & beaches; hornbills, monkeys & bears	hiking, boat trips
Khao Sok National Park	mainland park with thick rainforest, waterfalls & rivers; tigers, monkeys, *rafflesia* & 180 bird species	hiking, elephant interactions, tubing
Laem Son National Park	coastal & marine park with 100km of mangroves; jungle & migratory birds	bird-watching, boat trips

extinction of the endangered Mekong giant catfish and the disappearance of the Irrawaddy dolphin from Mekong waters.

A group of ecologically engaged Buddhist monks, popularly known as Thai Ecology Monks, uses peaceful activism to empower local communities in their fight against deforestation and other environmental exploitation.

The Marine Environment

Thailand's coral reef system, including the Andaman coast from Ranong to northern Phuket and the Surin and Similan Islands, is one of the world's most diverse. Some 600 species of coral reef fish, endangered marine turtles and other rare creatures call this coastline home.

The 2004 tsunami caused high-impact damage to about 13% of the Andaman coral reefs. However, damage from the tsunami was much less than first thought and relatively minor compared to the ongoing environmental degradation that accompanies an industrialised society. Coral reefs naturally recover, and this restoration process among the Andaman reefs was rapid, with corals showing regrowth just two to three years after the tsunami. It is estimated, however, that about 25% of Thailand's coral reefs have died as a result of industrial pollution and that the annual loss of healthy reefs will continue at a rapid rate. Even around the dive centre of Phuket, dead coral reefs are visible on the northern coast.

PARK	FEATURES	ACTIVITIES
Similan Islands Marine National Park	marine park with granite islands; coral reefs & seabirds; underwater caves	snorkelling, diving
Sirinat National Park	coastal park with casuarina-backed beaches; turtles & coral reefs	walking, snorkelling, diving
Surin Islands Marine National Park	granite islands; coral reefs, whale sharks & manta rays	snorkelling, diving
Hat Chao Mai National Park	coastal park with sandy beaches, mangroves, lagoons & coral islands; dugong & mangrove birds	sea kayaking, snorkelling, diving
Khao Phanom Bencha National Park	mainland mountain jungle with tumbling waterfalls; monkeys	hiking
Ko Phi-Phi Marine National Park	archipelago marine park with beaches, lagoons & sea cliffs; coral reefs & whale sharks	sea kayaking, snorkelling, diving
Ko Tarutao Marine National Park	archipelago marine park with remote jungle islands & tropical beaches; monkeys, jungle mammals & birds	snorkelling, hiking, diving
Mu Ko Lanta Marine National Park	archipelago marine park with scenic beaches; coral reefs & reef sharks	sea kayaking, elephant interactions, hiking, snorkelling, diving
Mu Ko Phetra Marine National Park	rarely visited archipelago marine park; dugong, birds & coral reefs	sea kayaking, snorkelling
Tharnbok Korannee National Park	coastal park with mangrove forests & limestone caves; monkeys, orchids & seabirds	sea kayaking

The biggest threat to corals is sedimentation from coastal development: new condos, hotels, roads and houses. High levels of sediment in the water stunts coral growth. Other common problems include pollution from anchored tour boats or other marine activities, rubbish and sewage dumped directly into the sea, and agricultural and industrial run-off. Even people urinating in the water as they swim creates by-products that can kill sensitive coral reefs.

The environmental wake-up call from the tsunami emphasised the importance of mangrove forests, which provide a buffer from storm surges. Previously mangroves were considered wastelands and were indiscriminately cut down. It is estimated that about 80% of the mangrove forests lining the gulf coast and 20% of those on the Andaman coast have been destroyed for conversion into fish and prawn farms, tourist development or to supply the charcoal industry. Prawn farms constitute the biggest threat because Thailand is the world's leading producer of black tiger prawns, and the short-lived, heavily polluting farms are built in pristine mangrove swamps at a terrific environmental and social cost.

Prawn farms are big business (annual production in Thailand has soared from 900 tonnes to 277,000 tonnes in the past 10 years), and the large prawn-farming businesses are often able to operate in spite of environmental protection laws. Protesting voices rarely get heard in the media.

Contributing to the deterioration of the overall health of the ocean are Thailand and its neighbours' large-scale fishing industries, frequently called the 'strip-miners of the sea'. Fish catches have declined by up to 33% in the Asia-Pacific region in the past 25 years and the upper portion of the Gulf of Thailand has almost been fished to death. Most of the commercial catches are sent to overseas markets and rarely see a Thai dinner table. The seafood sold in Thailand is typically from fish farms, another large coastal industry for the country.

According to a July 2014 report *Polishing off the Ivory: Surveys of Thailand's Ivory Market* from the wildlife-trade monitoring network TRAFFIC, the availability of ivory in Bangkok nearly tripled in the 18 months prior to the release of the report.

Making a Difference

It may seem that the range of environmental issues in Thailand is overwhelming, but there is actually much that travellers can do to minimise the impact of their visits or even to make a positive impact. The way you spend your money (and what you spend it on) has a profound influence on the kingdom's economy and on the profitability of individual businesses. Ask questions up front and take your money elsewhere if you don't like the answers. For instance, a number of large-scale resorts that lack road access transport clients across fragile mudflats on tractors (a wantonly destructive practice), so when booking a room inquire about transport to the hotel.

Of the region's countless dive shops, some are diligent about minimising the impact their clients have on the reefs; however, if a dive shop trains and certifies inexperienced divers over living reefs, then it may be damaging the local ecosystem. Ask up front if a dive operation is engaged in any projects to protect the environment. As a rule, do not touch or walk on coral, monitor your movements so that you avoid accidentally sweeping into coral, and do not harass marine life (responsible dive shops should make you aware of this).

If you're keen to get up close to elephants, opt for a low-impact interaction at a proper sanctuary rather than a ride or show, which carry animal-welfare issues.

Make a positive impact on Thailand by checking out one of the many environmental and social groups working in the kingdom. If you do some research and make arrangements before arriving, you may connect with an organisation that matches your values (p410).

Thai Massage

For many visitors, Thai massage is just another way to relax, or relieve aching muscles following a long bus or train ride. But this complex art is a major part of traditional Thai medicine and is the fruit of spiritual and medicinal roots that reach back to the time of the historical Buddha.

Spiritual & Philisophical Origins

The Thai form of massage can be traced to Tantric Buddhist Vajrayana teachings that originated in India and Tibet. Translated from the Sanskrit, Vajrayana means 'Diamond Vehicle' or 'Thunderbolt Vehicle', and marks a transition in Mahayana Buddhism when practices became more ritualised as opposed to primarily using abstract meditations to reach nirvana. Among other things, Vajrayana introduced the ideas of mantra (a symbol, word or group of words that can help spiritual transformation) and mandala (a symbol, often artistically depicted, that represents the universe). The school of thought flourished in India and Tibet between the 6th and 11th centuries, but its main influence on Thailand was its healing arts.

Practitioners recommend drinking lots of water or green tea after a massage to flush out any dislodged toxins.

Like Thai culture itself, influences on medicine came from many directions, including China, India and other Southeast Asian regions. Both Ayurvedic and traditional Chinese medicine are at the roots of Thai massage. Practitioners generally follow the 10 Sen lines, or channels, through the body with specific pressure points along them, which are similar to the Chinese meridians and Indian *nadis*. In Thai theory these lines carry several types of 'wind' (depending on the Sen line) from air that is inhaled through the lungs. When a line is blocked or unbalanced, illness or symptoms will ensue. At the same time, yoga *asana* stretches are used to open joints, aided by the loosening power of rocking, thumb pressure and rhythmic compression.

Thai massage is often called the 'expression of loving kindness' because at the heart of the practice is the compassionate intent of the healer. In its true form, the masseur will bond with the client in a meditative state and both parties will experience a deeper sense of awareness through humility and concentration.

History

Jivaka Komarabhacca, the physician to the historical Buddha himself, is said to be the father of Thai massage and Thai traditional medicine. Although he wasn't mentioned at length in Buddhist scriptures, Dr Jivaka holds extremely high status in Thai lore; there's a statue of him at the Grand Palace in Bangkok, and you'll often see his likeness next to statues of the Buddha, like a protector. It's said that the doctor spread the practice of massage to monasteries to help ease the monks' pain after long hours of meditation. Today's massage practitioners still practise *wâi kroo* (the Thai tradition of giving prayers and offerings to a teacher) devoted to the revered physician with chants that include his name.

King Rama V commissioned a textbook, completed in 1900, of traditional Thai medicine that included massage.

Massage techniques and knowledge were passed down through the generations by masters to their disciples within the monasteries. With the support of royalty and the devotion of the practitioners, techniques evolved for healing the sick and injured of the community. Everything was passed down orally until the 1830s when Wat Pho was built and included stone engravings and statues explaining and depicting Thai massage arts. It wasn't until the 1920s that Thai massage became a profession.

Getting a Massage

Where & How Much

Any tourist area in southern Thailand will have many massage options. Most places are air-conditioned shops with big reclining chairs for foot massages and manicures/pedicures and another area for a row or two of mattresses with curtained partitions for full body massages. Some shops also offer body scrubs and other spa services. Along busy beaches you'll find sheltered, elevated platforms with rows of mattresses where you can be pummelled in your swimsuit as you gaze at the sea. There may only be a masseuse or two in more remote areas, but these independent practitioners tend to be more skilled than those working in the big shops.

Massages are generally most expensive near posh resorts, but this isn't always the case. Sometimes just walking a minute or two off the main drag or further down the beach will yield lower prices. Expect to pay 200B to 500B for a one-hour Thai massage or foot massage. Prices go

THE 10 SEN

Thai massage is based on these 10 energy pathways, and the goal of a good practitioner will be to balance and/or unblock these channels.

SEN	LOCATION	MAIN INDICATIONS
Sen Sumana	Tip of the tongue to the solar plexus region	digestive system, asthma, heart disease, bronchitis
Sen Ittha	Left nostril, over the head, down the back to the left knee	headache, sinus problems, urinary tract, back pain
Sen Pingkhala	Same as Sen Ittha but on right side	same as Sen Ittha plus gallbladder and liver disease
Sen Kalathari	Two lines make an X across body from tips of toes to shoulders and down to fingertips	digestive system, hernia, arthritis, mental disorder
Sen Sahatsarangsi	Left eye, down left side around to back of left leg, under foot, up front of left leg to navel	toothache, eye function, depression, gastrointestinal disease
Sen Thawari	Same as Sen Sahatsarangsi but on the right side	same as Sen Sahatsarangsi plus appendicitis and jaundice
Sen Lawusang	Left ear to left nipple to mid solar plexus region	ear disorders, cough, toothache, gastrointestinal disorders
Sen Ulangwa	Same as Sen Lawusang but on the right side	same as Sen Lawusang plus itchy skin and insomnia
Sen Nanthakrawat	Two lines, each from the navel: one to urine passageway and other to the anus	infertility, impotence, diarrhoea, irregular menstruation
Sen Kitchanna	Navel to penis in men, navel to uterus in women	Same as Sen Nanthakrawat plus balances libido

up for additions like oil, aloe for sunburn, aromatherapy or hot herbal compresses.

A more upscale option is to get a deluxe massage at an independent or resort spa. Practitioners here tend to have more credentials than the street shop or beach masseuses, although that doesn't always mean that they're better. The real advantage here is the more luxurious surroundings, which may include beautiful views, trickling water and teak furniture, a relaxing soundtrack, lots of pleasant smells and more privacy. At a spa you'll also have a bevy of other services on offer from body wraps to flower baths and foot scrubs. Massage prices at spas tend to start at around 1000B.

A foot massage begins with a foot bath and moisturising treatment before the practitioner strongly works pressure points.

Check-In

On busier, sleazier beaches there may be a tout outside the salon hustling tourists by crooning 'meestaa, want massage?' In classier parts of town, services are announced by a spa menu outside the door or perhaps a group of giggling masseuses hanging out on the front step. If the practitioners are dressed professionally, usually in matching uniforms, the place will probably be a straightforward massage parlour. If the women are very young, scantily dressed or heavily made up, this is a red flag that other services may be on offer. Private massage rooms at the back of the salon in lieu of the more common curtained-off massage areas can be another clue that the salon may be geared towards less savoury practices. A man asking for an 'oil massage' may also sometimes lead to techniques not on the advertised menu, even at what appear to be classy establishments.

Once you're inside, take off your shoes and follow your masseuse. Sometimes, you'll be asked to leave your clothes on while at other places you'll be given a pair of Thai-style pajamas or a sarong. In the case of the latter, strip down to your underwear either behind your curtain or in a changing area and put on the supplied garments. On the beach you'll usually be massaged in your swimsuit, and a sarong is sometimes offered to women who wish to take off their bikini tops.

The Massage

Thai massage is not for wimps. The session usually begins with relaxing kneading of the back, arms and legs and the practitioner will often ask you if the pressure is light or strong enough. Then it gets gnarly. First there's the chiropractic-like popping of joints – mostly fingers and toes but sometimes whole legs and arms as well as the back and neck. Then, even the tiniest masseuses will muscle you into yoga contortions that

TRADITIONAL THAI MEDICINE

Much like other schools of Asian medicine, traditional Thai medicine (TTM) takes a holistic approach to health to include the physical body, heart, mind, spirit and flow of energy through the Sen. Much is based on the four elements fire, water, air and earth, with each element ruling body parts and functions – earth rules the organs, air rules the 'wind' (generally meaning respiration and digestion), water rules bodily fluid and fire rules four types of bodily heat (including circulation). Living in harmony with nature, eating well and being in tune with one's own natural cycles (from night and day to ageing) are the keys to health by TTM standards.

Tastes are important to Thais in a culinary sense, and this extends into the realm of medicine. How a herbal remedy tastes determines how it balances the elements and what ailment it can treat. For example, sweet treats fatigue, salty is good for constipation, and bitter helps fight infection. TTM treatments generally include herbal remedies, massage and lifestyle changes.

WAT PHO

Wat Pho next to the Royal Palace in Bangkok is the ground zero of Thai massage. Before the royal wát was built on this site by Rama I in the late 1800s, a centre for traditional Thai medicine was here. The future wát incorporated this history into its curriculum and eventually became home to the first official school of Thai massage; inscribed tablets of the Sen pathways grace the temple's interior walls. Today the school is still considered the best in the country and visitors can attend training programs or simply come in and have a massage. In 2008 Wat Pho was recognised by Unesco in its Memory of the World Program. The manager of the school, Khun Serat, is the founder's grandson and many of the instructors are descendents of the original faculty.

Check the website www.watphomassage.com for details on everything from 30-hour Thai massage or foot massage courses, to several month-long training programs. A five-day course starts at 9500B, or you can get a half hour or hour-long traditional massage at the wát for 260B to 420B.

arch the back, extend the legs and arms and so much more that it feels like you're being turned into a human pretzel. You'll start the session on your back, get moved to a prone position about midway and then end with your head in the practitioner's lap for a final head massage and a popping back stretch. Overall the treatment itself isn't very relaxing, but you'll feel incredible afterwards. Let your massage therapist know in advance if you have any injuries and don't be afraid to tell them to ease up on a stretch or joint pop. As with any good workout, know your limits.

That said, Thai massage has become very watered down in many tourist areas and you may end up with just a light rub down without being contorted or popped in the slightest. Older ladies tend to give the most violent yet rewarding massages, but even with younger ones, you won't know until your nose is hitting your knee what kind of torturous therapy they're capable of.

If this sounds too scary, Swedish and other types of massage are often available, but you'll be missing out on a big cultural and maybe even spiritual experience. A more simple reflexology foot massage (available at almost all salons) may be a good place to start if you've never had a professional massage or are wary of the practice in any way.

Survival Guide

Responsible Travel

CULTURAL ETIQUETTE

Monarchy and religion are treated with extreme deference in Thailand. Thais avoid criticising or disparaging the royal family for fear of offending someone or, worse, being charged under strict lèse-majesté laws, which carry a jail sentence.

Buddha images are sacred objects. Posing respectfully for a photo in front of a statue is fine (unless it's expressly prohibited); avoid climbing upon them (in the case of temple ruins) or doing anything that might be construed as disrespectful. As part of their ascetic vows, monks are not supposed to touch or be touched by women. If a woman wants to hand something to a monk, the object is placed within reach of the monk or on the monk's 'receiving cloth'.

From a spiritual viewpoint, Thais regard the head as the highest and most sacred part of the body and the feet as the dirtiest and lowest. Shoes are not worn inside private homes and temple buildings, as a sign of respect and for sanitary reasons. Thais also step over the threshold, which is where the spirit of the house is believed to reside.

Thais don't touch each other's head or ruffle their hair as a sign of affection. Occasionally you'll see young people touching each other's head, which is a teasing gesture, maybe even a slight insult, between friends.

Social Conventions & Gestures

The traditional Thai greeting is made with a prayerlike, palms-together gesture known as a *wâi*. The depth of the bow and the placement of the fingers in relation to the face is dependent on the status of the person receiving the *wâi*. Adults don't *wâi* children and in most cases service people (when they are doing their jobs) aren't *wâi-ed*, though this is a matter of personal discretion.

In the more traditional parts of the country, it's not proper for members of the opposite sex to touch one another, either as lovers or as friends. But same-sex touching is quite common and is typically a sign of friendship, not sexual attraction. Older Thai men might grab a younger man's thigh in the same way that buddies slap each other on the back. Thai women are especially affectionate with female friends, often sitting close to one another or linking arms.

Thais hold modesty in personal dress in high regard, though this is changing among the younger generation. The importance of modesty extends to the beach as well. Except for urbanites, most provincial Thais still swim in a T-shirt and shorts, or even jeans. For this reason, sunbathing nude or topless is not acceptable and in some cases is even illegal. Remember that swimsuits are not proper attire off the beach; wear a cover-up in between the sand and your hotel.

TOURISM

Most forms of tourism, despite the prevailing prejudices, have a positive economic effect on the local economy in Thailand by providing jobs for young workers and business opportunities for entrepreneurs. But in an effort to be more than just a consumer, many travellers look for opportunities to spend where their money might be needed, either on charitable causes or activities that preserve traditional ways of life.

Diving

The popularity of Thailand's diving industry (p41) places immense pressure on fragile coral sites. To help preserve the ecology, adhere to these simple rules.

- Avoid touching living marine organisms, standing on coral or dragging equipment (such as fins) across the reef. Coral polyps can be damaged by even the gentlest contact.
- When treading water in shallow reef areas, be careful not to kick up clouds of sand,

ESSENTIAL ETIQUETTE

Dos

Stand respectfully for the national anthem It is played on TV and radio stations and at public and government places at 8am and 6pm. If you're inside a building, you don't have to stand.

Rise for the royal anthem It is played in movie theatres before every screening.

Smile a lot It makes everything easier.

Bring a gift if you're invited to a Thai home Fruit, drinks or snacks would be acceptable; flowers are usually for merit-making purposes not home decor.

Take off your shoes When you enter a home or temple building, or wherever there are sandals piled up at the door.

Lower your head slightly When passing between two people having a conversation or when passing near a monk; it is a sign of respect.

Dress modestly for temple visits Cover to the elbows and ankles and always remove your shoes when entering any building containing a Buddha image.

Give and receive politely Extend the right hand out while the left hand gently grips the right elbow when handing an object to another person or receiving something – truly polite behaviour.

Respect all Buddha images and pictures of the monarchy Signs of disrespect can have serious consequences.

Sit in the 'mermaid' position inside temples Tuck your feet beside and behind you so that your feet aren't pointing at the Buddha image.

Don'ts

Don't get a tattoo of the Buddha It is considered sacrilegious.

Don't criticise the monarchy The monarchy is revered and protected by defamation laws.

Don't prop your feet on tables or chairs Feet are considered dirty and people have to sit there.

Don't step on a dropped bill to prevent it from blowing away Thai money bears a picture of the king. Feet + monarchy = grave offence.

Never step over someone or their personal belongings Aaah, attack of the feet.

Avoid tying your shoes to the outside of your backpack They might accidentally brush against someone, gross.

Don't touch a Thai person on the head It is considered rude, not chummy.

Women cannot touch monks or their belongings Step out of the way when passing a monk on the footpath, and do not sit next to them on public transport.

which can easily smother the delicate reef organisms.

- Take great care in underwater caves where your air bubbles can be caught within the roof and leave previously submerged organisms high and dry.
- Join a coral (or beach) clean-up campaign sponsored by a dive shop.
- Don't feed the fish or allow your dive operator to dispose of excess food in the water. The fish become dependent on this food source and don't tend to the algae on the coral, causing harm to the reef.

Elephant Encounters

Throughout Thai history, elephants have been revered for their strength, endurance and intelligence, working alongside their mahouts harvesting teak, transporting goods through mountainous terrain or fighting ancient wars. But many of the elephants' traditional roles have either been outsourced to machines or outlawed (logging was officially banned in 1989, although it still goes on along the Thai/Myanmar border), leaving the domesticated animals and their mahouts without work. Some mahouts turned to begging on the streets in Bangkok and other tourist centres, but most elephants find work in

Thailand's tourism industry; their jobs vary from circus-like shows to elephant camps giving rides to tourists to 'mahout-training' schools, while sanctuaries and rescue centres provide modest retirement homes to animals that are no longer financially profitable to their owners.

It costs about 30,000B (US$1000) per month to provide a comfortable living for an elephant; this amount is equivalent to the salary of Thailand's upper middle class. Welfare standards within the tourism industry are not standardised or subject to government regulations, so it's up to the conscientious consumer to encourage the industry to ensure safe conditions for elephants.

With more evidence available than ever to support claims by animal welfare experts that elephant rides and shows are harmful for these gentle giants, who are often abused to force them to perform for humans, a small but growing number of sanctuaries offer more sustainable interactions such as walking with and bathing retired and rescued elephants. If you're still bent on riding one, however, ask the right questions to ensure you choose a well-run operation.

- Does the camp employ a veterinarian?
- What is its policy on procuring new elephants? Some camps buy illegally caught wild elephants whose registration has been forged so that they appear to have been born in captivity.
- How many hours per day do the elephants work? A brisk-paced walk for about four hours per day (with breaks for eating and drinking in between) is considered adequate exercise.
- How many adults do the elephants carry? An elephant can carry a maximum of 150kg (330lb) of weight on its back, plus a mahout on its neck. Tally up you own and your partner's combined weight and request a separate elephant if you tip the scales.
- Are the elephants kept in a shady spot near fresh water and a food source? What do they eat? A balanced diet includes a mixture of fruit, grasses, bamboo and pineapple shoots. With bananas for dessert only.
- Do the elephants have noticeable wounds? This is often a sign of mistreatment.
- What kind of seat is used for elephant riding? Wooden seats, custom-made to fit the elephant's back, cause less irritation and stress on the animal.
- What is the camp's birth/death rate? Happy elephants have babies.

VOLUNTEERING

Thailand is still a developing country, lacking a tight-knit social safety net, an executed environmental protection program and equal labour protections. There are myriad volunteering organisations in Thailand, but be aware that so-called 'voluntourism' has become a big business and that not every organisation fulfils its promise of meaningful experiences. Lonely Planet does not endorse any organisations that we do not work with directly, so it is essential that you do thorough research before agreeing to volunteer with any organisation.

Environmental & Animal Welfare Work

At centres and sanctuaries that rely on volunteer labour, your hard work is often rewarded with meaningful interactions with the animals. There are also smaller organisations throughout the country.

Starfish Ventures (www.starfishvolunteers.com) Places volunteers in conservation, teaching and animal welfare programs, including working with elephants, throughout Thailand.

Wild Animal Rescue Foundation (WARF; ☎02 712 9715; www.warthai.org) Operates the Phuket Gibbon Rehabilitation Centre and a conservation education centre in Ranong Province on the Andaman coast. Job placements include assisting with the daily care of gibbons that are being rehabilitated for life in the wild or counting and monitoring turtle nests.

Wildlife Friends of Thailand Rescue Centre (☎032 458 135; www.wfft.org; Phetchaburi) Puts volunteers to work caring for sun bears, macaques and gibbons at its animal rescue centre.

Humanitarian & Educational Work

When looking for a volunteer placement, it is essential to investigate what your chosen organisation does and, more importantly, how it goes about it. If the focus is not primarily on your skills and how these can be applied to help local people, that should ring alarm bells. Any organisation that promises to let you do any kind of work, wherever you like, for as long as you like, is unlikely to be putting the needs of local people first. For any organisation working with children, child protection is a serious concern, and organisations that do not conduct background checks on volunteers should be regarded with extreme caution. Experts recommend a three-month commitment for volunteering with children. Visit www.thinkchildsafe.org for more information.

Open Mind Projects (☎088 564 0734; www.openmindprojects.org) Offers volunteer positions in IT, health care, education and community-based ecotourism throughout Thailand.

Volunthai (www.volunthai.com) A family-run operation that places volunteers in teaching positions at rural schools with homestay accommodation.

Directory A–Z

Accommodation

Thailand offers a wide variety of accommodation from cheap and basic to pricey and luxurious.

Guesthouses

Guesthouses are generally the cheapest accommodation in Thailand and can be found all along the backpacker trail. In more remote areas like the eastern seaboard, guesthouses (as well as tourists) are not as widespread.

Rates vary according to facilities and location. In provincial towns, the cheapest rooms range from 150B to 350B and usually have shared bathrooms and rickety fans. Private facilities, air-con and sometimes a TV can be had for 400B to 800B. But prices are much higher in the beach resorts, where a basic fan room can start at 600B to 800B. Many guesthouses make their bread and butter from on-site restaurants that serve classic backpacker fare (banana pancakes and fruit shakes). Although these restaurants are convenient and a good way to meet other travellers, don't judge Thai food based on these dishes.

Most guesthouses cultivate a travellers' ambience with friendly, knowledgeable staff and book exchanges. But there are also plenty of guesthouses with grumpy, disgruntled clerks.

Many guesthouses can be booked online, but due to inconsistent cleanliness and quality, it is advisable to look at a room in person before committing. In tourist centres there are usually alternatives nearby if your preferred place is full. Guesthouses require payment in cash normally.

Hostels

Hostels are less common in Thailand than elsewhere in Asia, mostly because guesthouses are so cheap, but there are a few around. All offer a mix of dorms and private rooms, as well as the usual traveller services. Most can be booked online.

Hotels

In provincial capitals and small towns, the only options are often older Thai-Chinese hotels, once the standard in Thailand. Most cater to Thai guests and English is usually limited. These are multi-storey buildings and might offer a range of rooms

SLEEPING PRICE RANGES

The following price ranges refer to a double room with bathroom in high season. Unless otherwise stated, tax is not included in the price, which only applies to larger hotels and high-end options.

$ less than 1000B

$$ 1000–3000B

$$$ more than 3000B

COMMISSION HASSLES

In the popular tourist spots you'll be approached, sometimes surrounded, by touts or transport drivers who get a commission from the guesthouse for bringing in potential guests. While it's annoying for the traveller, this is an acceptable form of advertising among small-scale businesses in Thailand. As long as you know the drill, everything should work out in your favour. Touts get paid for delivering you to a guesthouse or hotel (whether you check in or not). Some places refuse to pay commissions, so in return the touts will steer customers away from those places (by saying they are closed or burned down). In less scrupulous instances, they'll tell you that the commission-paying hotel is the one you requested. If you meet with resistance, call the guesthouse for a pick-up, as they are often aware of these aggressive business tactics.

Climate

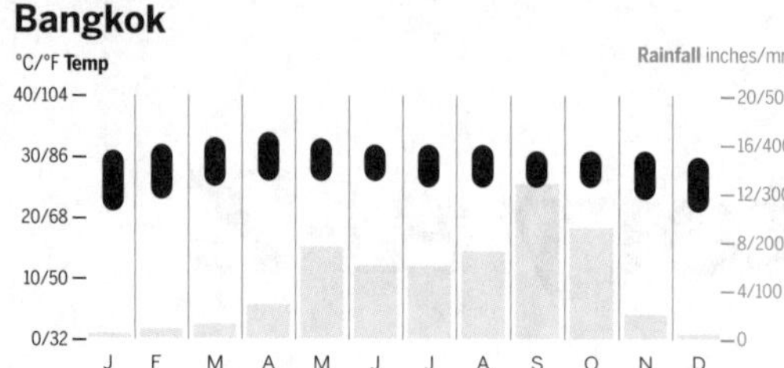

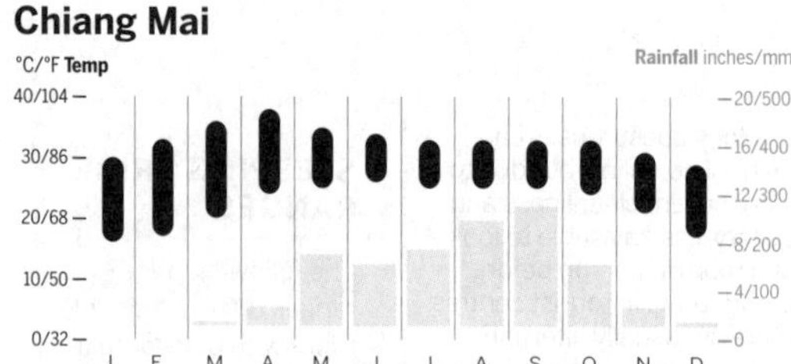

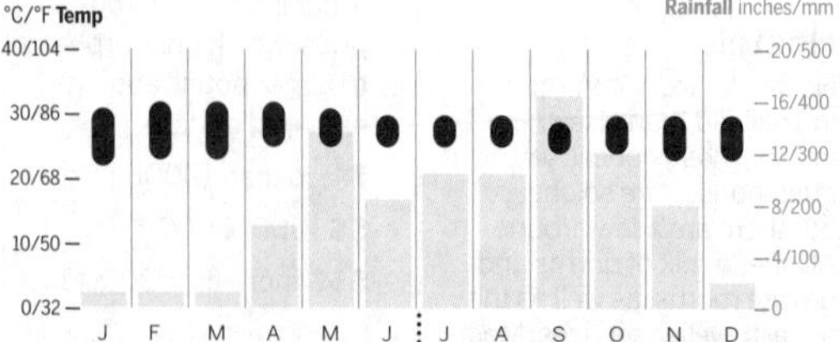

from midrange options with private bathrooms, air-con and TVs to cheaper ones with shared bathroom facilities and a fan. In a few of the really old places the toilets are squats and the 'shower' is a *klong* (large terracotta basin from which you scoop out water for bathing). Although these Thai-Chinese hotels have tonnes of accidental retro charm, we've found that, unless they've been recently refurbished, they are too old and worn to represent good value compared to guesthouses.

In recent years, there has been a push to fill the budget gap for older backpackers and young affluent travellers who want the ambience of a guesthouse with the comforts of a hotel. 'Flashpacker' hotels in major tourist towns have dressed up the utilitarian options of the past with stylish decor and more comfort.

International chain hotels can be found in Bangkok, Phuket and other high-end beach resorts. Many of these upscale resorts combine traditional Thai architecture and modern minimalism.

Most top-end hotels and some midrange hotels add a 7% government tax (VAT) and an additional 10% service charge. The additional charges are often referred to as 'plus plus'. A buffet breakfast will often be included in the room rate. If the hotel offers Western breakfast, it is usually referred to as 'ABF', meaning 'American breakfast'.

Midrange and chain hotels, especially in major tourist destinations, can be booked in advance and some offer internet discounts through their websites or online agents. They also accept most credit cards, but fewer places accept American Express.

National Parks Accommodation

Most national parks have bungalows or campsites available for overnight stays. Bungalows typically sleep as many as 10 people and rates range from 800B to 2000B, depending on the park and the size of the bungalow. These are popular with extended Thai families, who bring enough provisions to survive the apocalypse. A few parks also have *reu·an tăa·ou* (longhouses).

Camping is available at many parks for 60B to 90B per night. Some parks rent tents and other sleeping gear, but the condition of the equipment can be poor.

Reservations for all park accommodation must be made in advance through the **central booking system** (☎02 561 0777; www.dnp.go.th/parkreserve/nationalpark.asp?lg=2). Do note that reservations for campsites and bungalows are handled on different pages within the website.

> **BOOK YOUR STAY ONLINE**
>
> For more accommodation reviews by Lonely Planet authors, check out http://lonelyplanet.com/hotels/. You'll find independent reviews, as well as recommendations on the best places to stay. Best of all, you can book online.

Customs Regulations

The Customs Department (www.customs.go.th) maintains a helpful website with specific information about customs regulations. Thailand has the usual list of prohibited imports, such as illegal drugs, firearms and ammunition (unless registered in advance) and pornographic media. Items allowed include the following:

- a reasonable amount of personal effects (clothing and toiletries)
- professional instruments
- 200 cigarettes
- 1L of wine or spirits

When leaving Thailand, you must obtain an export licence for any antiques, reproductions or newly cast Buddha images (except personal amulets). Submit two front-view photos of the object(s) and a photocopy of your passport, along with the purchase receipt and the object(s) in question, to the **Department of Fine Arts** (☎02 628 5032; www.finearts.go.th). Allow four days for the application and inspection process to be completed.

Electricity

Thailand uses 220V AC electricity; power outlets most commonly feature two-prong round or flat sockets.

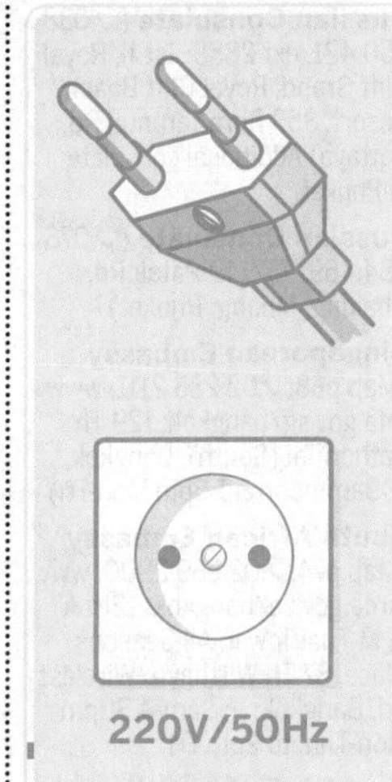

Embassies & Consulates

Foreign embassies are located in Bangkok.

Australian Embassy (Map p68; ☎02 344 6300; www.thailand.embassy.gov.au; 37 Th Sathon Tai/South, Bangkok; ⏰8.30am-4.30pm Mon-Fri; Ⓜ Lumphini exit 2)

Cambodian Embassy (Map p78; ☎02 957 5851; 518/4 Th Pracha Uthit/Soi Ramkhamhaeng 39, Bangkok; ⏰9am-noon Mon-Fri; Ⓜ Phra Ram 9 exit 3 & taxi)

Canadian Embassy (Map p68; ☎02 646 4300; www.thailand.gc.ca; 15th fl, Abdulrahim Pl, 990 Th Phra Ram IV, Bangkok; ⏰7.30am-12.15pm & 1-4.15pm Mon-Thu, to 1pm Fri; Ⓜ Si Lom exit 2, Ⓢ Sala Daeng exit 4)

Chinese Embassy (Map p78; ☎02 245 0888; www.chinaembassy.or.th/eng; 57 Th Ratchadaphisek, Bangkok; ⏰9am-noon & 3-4pm Mon-Fri)

Danish Embassy (Map p68; ☎02 343 1100; http://thailand.um.dk; 10 Soi 1, Th Sathon Tai, Bangkok; ⏰10am-noon & 1-3pm Mon-Thu)

Danish Consulate (☎076 388283; www.thailand.um.dk; 59/148 Moo 7, Sai Yuan Rd, Phuket; ⏰10am-1pm Tue-Thu)

French Embassy (Map p84; ☎02 657 5100; www.ambafrance-th.org; 35 Soi 36, Th Charoen Krung, Bangkok; ⏰8.30am-noon Mon-Fri; ⛴ Oriental Pier)

French Consulate (☎076 304 050; info@agenceconsulairephuket.fr; 96/15 Moo 1, Chalermprakiat Rama 9 Rd, the Royal Place, Phuket; ⏰10-11.30am Mon-Fri) Additional consulates in Chiang Mai, Chiang Rai, Ko Samui, Pattaya, and Surat Thani.

German Embassy (Map p68; ☎02 287 9000; www.bangkok.diplo.de; 9 Th Sathon Tai/South, Bangkok; ⏰8.30-11.30am Mon-Fri; Ⓜ Lumphini exit 2)

Indian Embassy (Map p70; ☎02 258 0300; www.indianembassy.in.th; 46 Soi 23, Th Sukhumvit, Bangkok; ⏰9am-noon & 3-4.30pm Mon-Fri)

Indian Visa Centre (Map p70; ☎02 664 1200; www.indiavisathai.com; IVS Global Services, 22nd fl, 253 Soi 21/Asoke, Th Sukhumvit, Bangkok; ⏰8.30am-2pm & 4.30-5.30pm Mon-Fri)

Indonesian Embassy (Map p74; ☎02 252 3135; www.kemlu.go.id/bangkok; 600-602 Th Phetchaburi, Bangkok; ⏰9am-noon & 2-4pm Mon-Fri)

Israeli Embassy (Map p70; ☎02 204 9200; http://embassies.gov.il/bangkok-en; 25th fl, Ocean Tower 2, 75 Soi 19, Th Sukhumvit, Bangkok; ⏰9am-noon)

Japanese Embassy (Map p68; ☎02 207 8500; www.th.emb-japan.go.jp; 177 Th Witthayu/Wireless Rd; ⏰8.30am-noon & 1.30-4pm Mon-Fri)

Laotian Embassy (Map p78; ☎02 539 6667; www.laoembassybkk.gov.la/index.php/en; 502/1-3 Soi Sahakarnpramoon, Th Pracha Uthit/Soi Ramkhamhaeng 39, Bangkok;

EATING PRICE RANGES

The following price ranges refer to a standard main-course meal.

$ less than 150B

$$ 150–350B

$$$ more than 350B

8am-noon & 1-4pm Mon-Fri; M Phra Ram 9 exit 3 & taxi)

Malaysian Embassy (Map p68; 02 629 6800; www.kln.gov.my/web/tha_bangkok/home; 33-35 Th Sathon Tai/South, Bangkok; 8am-4pm Mon-Fri; M Lumphini exit 2)

Malaysian Consulate (074 311062; 4 Th Sukhum, Songkhla; 8.15am-noon & 1-4pm Mon-Thu, 8.15am-noon & 2-4pm Fri)

Myanmar Embassy (Map p68; 02 233 7250; www.myanmarembassybkk.com; 132 Th Sathon Neua/North, Bangkok; 9am-noon & 1-3pm Mon-Fri; S Surasak exit 3)

Nepalese Embassy (Map p78; 02 391 7240; http://nepalembassybangkok.com; 189 Soi 71, Th Sukhumvit, Bangkok; 9am-noon Mon-Fri)

Netherlands Embassy (Map p74; 02 309 5200; http://thailand.nlembassy.org; 15 Soi Ton Son, Bangkok; 8.30-11.30am Mon-Thu; S Chit Lom exit 4)

New Zealand Embassy (Map p74; 02 254 2530; www.nzembassy.com/thailand; 14th fl, M Thai Tower, All Seasons Pl, 87 Th Witthayu/Wireless Rd, Bangkok; 8am-noon & 1-2.30pm Mon-Fri; S Phloen Chit exit 5)

Philippine Embassy (Map p70; 02 259 0139; www.bangkokpe.dfa.gov.ph; 760 Th Sukhumvit, Bangkok; 9am-noon & 1-6pm Mon-Fri)

Russian Embassy (Map p68; 02 234 2012; www.thailand.mid.ru; 78 Th Sap, Th Surawong, Bangkok; 9am-11.45am Mon, Tue, Thu & Fri)

Russian Consulate (038 250 421, ext 2888; 1st fl, Royal Cliff Grand, Royal Cliff Beach Resort, 353 Phra Tamnuk Rd, Pattaya) Additional consulate in Phuket.

Russian Consulate (076 384 469; 75/149 Patak Rd, Chalong, Muang, Phuket)

Singaporean Embassy (Map p68; 02 286 2111; www.mfa.gov.sg/bangkok; 129 Th Sathon Tai (South), Bangkok; 9am-noon & 1-5pm Mon-Fri)

South African Embassy (Map p74; 02 659 2900; www.dirco.gov.za/bangkok; 12th A fl, M Thai Tower, All Seasons Place, 87 Th Witthayu/Wireless Rd, Bangkok; 8am-4.30pm Mon-Thu, to 2pm Fri)

Spanish Embassy (Map p70; 02 661 8284; http://es.embassyinformation.com; 23 fl, Lake Ratchada Office Complex, 193 Th Ratchadaphisek, Bangkok; 8.30am-3.30pm Mon-Fri)

Swiss Embassy (Map p74; 02 674 6900; www.eda.admin.ch/bangkok; 35 Th Witthayu/Wireless Rd, Bangkok; 9-11.30am Mon-Fri)

UK Embassy (Map p74; 02 305 8333; www.gov.uk/government/world/organisations/british-embassy-bangkok; 14 Th Witthayu/Wireless Rd, Bangkok; 8am-4.30pm Mon-Thu, to 1pm Fri; S Phloen Chit exit 5) Additional consulates in Chiang Mai.

US Embassy (Map p74; 02 205 4000; http://bangkok.usembassy.gov; 120-122 Th Witthayu/Wireless Rd, Bangkok; 7am-4pm Mon-Fri; S Phloen Chit exit 5) Additional consulate in Chiang Mai.

Vietnamese Embassy (Map p74; 02 251 3552; www.vietnamembassy-thailand.org; 83/1 Th Witthayu/Wireless Rd, Bangkok; 9-11.30am & 2-4.30pm Mon-Fri)

Food

For in-depth information on Thailand's glorious cuisine, see p386.

LGBT Travellers

Thai culture is relatively tolerant of both male and female homosexuality. There is a fairly prominent LGBT scene in Bangkok, Pattaya and Phuket. With regard to dress or mannerism, the LGBT community are generally accepted without comment. However, public displays of affection – whether heterosexual or homosexual – are frowned upon.

It's worth noting that, perhaps because Thailand is still a relatively conservative place, lesbians generally adhere to rather strict gender roles. Overtly 'butch' lesbians, called tom (from 'tomboy'), typically have short hair, bind their breasts and wear men's clothing. Femme lesbians refer to themselves as dêe (from 'lady'). Visiting lesbians who don't fit into one of these categories may find themselves met with confusion.

Utopia (www.utopia-asia.com) posts lots of Thailand information for LGBT travellers and publishes a gay guidebook to the kingdom.

Insurance

A travel-insurance policy to cover theft, loss and medical problems is a sound idea. Policies offer differing medical-expense options and there is a wide variety of policies available, so check the small print. Be sure that the policy covers ambulances or an emergency flight home.

Some policies specifically exclude 'dangerous activities', which can include scuba diving, motorcycling or even trekking. A locally acquired motorcycle licence is not valid under some policies. Do not dive without diver's insurance.

You may prefer a policy that pays doctors or hospitals directly rather than you having to pay on the spot and claim later. If you have to claim later, make sure you keep all documentation.

Worldwide travel insurance is available at www.lonelyplanet.com/bookings. You can buy, extend and claim online any time – even if you're already on the road.

Thailand has been considering a new regulation requiring foreign visitors to be covered by health insurance before arrival. This measure aims to curb an annual bill of 200 million baht in unpaid hospital bills from foreign patients. So far, no new rules have been introduced but that may change.

Internet Access

You'll find plenty of internet cafes just about everywhere. The going rate is anywhere from 20B to 120B an hour. Connections tend to be pretty fast and the machines are usually well maintained. Wireless access (wi-fi) is available in most hotels and guesthouses, as well as in many cafes, restaurants and bars.

Legal Matters

In general, Thai police don't hassle foreigners, especially tourists. They generally go out of their way to avoid having to speak English with a foreigner, especially regarding minor traffic issues.

One major exception is drugs, which most Thai police view as either a social scourge against which it's their duty to enforce the letter of the law or, occasionally, an opportunity to make untaxed income via bribes.

If you are arrested for any offence, the police will allow you the opportunity to make a phone call to your embassy or consulate in Thailand, if you have one, or to a friend or relative if you don't. There's a whole set of legal codes governing the length of time and manner in which you can be detained before being charged or put on trial, but a lot of discretion is left to the police. In the case of foreigners the police are more likely to bend these codes in your favour. However, as with police worldwide, if you don't show respect you will make matters worse.

Thai law does not presume an indicted detainee to be either 'guilty' or 'innocent', but rather a 'suspect' whose guilt or innocence will be decided in court. Trials are usually speedy.

The **tourist police** (1155 24hr hotline) can be very helpful in cases of arrest. Although they typically have no jurisdiction over the kinds of cases handled by regular cops, they may be able to help with translations or with contacting your embassy. You can call the hotline number 24 hours a day to lodge complaints or request assistance with regard to personal safety.

Maps

ThinkNet (www.thinknet.co.th) produces high-quality, bilingual city and country maps, including interactive-map CDs. For GPS users in Thailand, most prefer the Garmin units and associated map products, which are accurate and fully routed.

Money

The basic unit of Thai currency is the baht. There are 100 satang in one baht; coins include 25-satang and 50-satang pieces and baht in 1B, 2B, 5B and 10B coins. Older coins have Thai numerals only, while newer coins have Thai and Arabic numerals. The 2B coin is similar in size to the 1B coin but it is gold in colour. The two satang coins are typically only issued at supermarkets where prices aren't rounded up to the nearest baht.

Paper currency is issued in the following denominations: 20B (green), 50B (blue), 100B (red), 500B (purple) and 1000B (beige).

ATMs & Credit/Debit Cards

Debit and ATM cards issued by a bank in your own country can be used at ATMs in Thailand to withdraw cash (in Thai baht only) directly from your account back home. ATMs are widespread throughout the country. You can also buy baht at foreign-exchange booths at some banks.

Thai ATMs charge a 180B foreign-transaction fee on top of whatever currency conversion and out-of-network fees your home bank charges. Before leaving home, shop around for a bank account that has free international ATM usage and reimburses fees incurred at other institutions' ATMs.

Aeon is the only Thai bank that we know of that doesn't charge the 180B usage fee on foreign accounts, but its ATM distribution is somewhat limited – many ATMs are located in Big C stores.

Credit cards, as well as debit cards, can be used for purchases at some shops, hotels and restaurants. The most commonly accepted cards are Visa and MasterCard. American Express is typically only accepted at high-end hotels and restaurants.

To report a lost or stolen credit/debit card, call your card's hotline in Bangkok.

American Express (02 273 5500)

MasterCard (001 800 11887 0663)

Visa (001 800 11535 0660)

Changing Money

Banks or the rarer private moneychangers offer the best foreign-exchange rates. When buying baht, US dollars are the most accepted currency, followed by British pounds and Euros. Most banks charge a commission and duty for each traveller's cheque cashed.

Current exchange rates are printed in the *Bangkok Post* and the *Nation* every day, or you can walk into any Thai bank to see a daily rate chart.

Foreign Exchange

Visitors must declare cash over US$20,000 when arriving or departing. There are also certain monetary requirements for foreigners entering Thailand; demonstration of adequate funds varies per visa type but typically does not exceed a traveller's estimated trip budget. It's rare that you'll be asked to produce such financial evidence, but be aware that these laws do exist. The **Ministry of Foreign Affairs** (☎02 203 5000; www.mfa.go.th) can provide more detailed information.

It's legal to open a foreign-currency account at any commercial bank in Thailand. As long as the funds originate from out of the country, there aren't any restrictions on maintenance or withdrawal.

Tipping

Tipping is not generally expected in Thailand. The exception is loose change from a large restaurant bill; if a meal costs 488B and you pay with a 500B note, some Thais will leave the 12B change. It's not so much a tip as a way of saying 'I'm not so money grubbing as to grab every last baht'.

At many hotel restaurants or other upmarket eateries, a 10% service charge will be added to your bill. When this is the case, tipping is not expected. Bangkok has adopted some standards of tipping, especially in restaurants frequented by foreigners.

Opening Hours

All government offices and banks are closed on public holidays.

Banks 9.30am to 3.30pm Monday to Friday; ATMs accessible 24 hours.

Bars 6pm to midnight (officially); closing times vary due to local enforcement of curfew laws; bars close during elections and certain religious public holidays.

Clubs (discos) 8pm to 2am; closing times vary due to local enforcement of curfew laws; clubs close during elections and certain religious public holidays.

Government offices 8.30am to 4.30pm Monday to Friday; some close for lunch (noon to 1pm), while others are open 9am to 3pm Saturday.

Live-music venues 6pm to 1am; closing times vary due to local enforcement of curfew laws; venues close during elections and certain religious public holidays.

Restaurants 10am to 10pm; some shops specialise in morning meals and close by 3pm.

Shops Local stores 9am to 6pm daily; department stores 10am to 10pm daily. In some small towns, local stores close on Sunday. 7-Elevens stay open 24 hours.

Photography

Memory cards for most digital cameras are generally widely available in the electronic sections of most shopping malls.

Be considerate when taking photographs of the locals. Learn how to ask politely in Thai and wait for an embarrassed nod. In some of the regularly visited hill-tribe areas, be prepared for the photographed subject to ask for money in exchange for a picture. Other hill tribes will not allow you to point a camera at them.

Post

- Thailand has a very efficient postal service and local postage is inexpensive. Typical provincial post offices are open between 8.30am and 4.30pm on weekdays and 9am and noon on Saturdays. Larger main post offices in provincial capitals may also be open for a half-day on Sundays.
- Most provincial post offices sell do-it-yourself packing boxes. Don't send cash or other valuables through the mail.
- Thailand's poste-restante service is generally very reliable. When you receive mail you must show your passport and fill out some paperwork.

Public Holidays

1 January New Year's Day

February (date varies) Makha Bucha Day, Buddhist holy day

6 April Chakri Day, commemorating the founder of the Chakri dynasty, Rama I

13–15 April Songkran Festival, traditional Thai New Year and water festival

1 May Labour Day

5 May Coronation Day, commemorating the 1946 coronation of HM the King and HM the Queen

May/June (date varies) Visakha Bucha, Buddhist holy day

July (date varies) Asanha Bucha, Buddhist holy day

12 August Queen's Birthday

23 October Chulalongkorn Day

October/November (date varies) Ork Phansaa, the end of Buddhist Lent

5 December King's Birthday

10 December Constitution Day

31 December New Year's Eve

Safe Travel

Although Thailand is not a dangerous country to visit, it is smart to exercise caution, especially when it comes to dealing with strangers (both Thai and foreigners) and travelling alone. In reality, you are more likely to be ripped off or have a personal possession surreptitiously stolen than you are to be physically harmed.

Assault

Assault of travellers is rare in Thailand, but it does happen. Causing a Thai to 'lose face' (feel public embarrassment or humiliation) can sometimes elicit an inexplicably strong and violent reaction. Often alcohol is the number one contributor to bad choices and worse outcomes.

Be aware that an innocent flirtation might convey firmer intentions to a recipient who does not share your culture's sexual norms.

Border Issues & Hot Spots

Thailand enjoys generally amicable relations with its neighbours, and most land borders are fully functional for both people and goods. However, the ongoing violence in the Deep South means Lonely Planet does not recommend the crossing at Sungai Kolok into Malaysia, while the entire Muslim-majority provinces (Yala, Pattani and Narathiwat) should be avoided by casual visitors.

Cross-border relations between Thailand and Myanmar have significantly normalised, with more land borders between the two countries scheduled to open in the near future. But Myanmar does occasionally close some crossings due to events at home. Check your government's foreign ministry for current travel warnings before you travel.

Drug Possession

It is illegal to buy, sell or possess opium, heroin, amphetamines, hallucinogenic mushrooms and marijuana in Thailand. Belying Thailand's anything-goes atmosphere are strict punishments for possession and trafficking that are not relaxed for foreigners. Possession of drugs can result in at least one year or more of prison time.

PRACTICALITIES

Newspapers

Bangkok Post (www.bangkokpost.com) and the *Nation* (www.nationmultimedia.com) are the daily English-language newspapers.

Radio

There are more than 400 AM and FM radio stations; short-wave radios can pick up BBC, VOA, Radio Australia, Deutsche Welle and Radio France International.

TV

Six VHF TV networks carry Thai programming; TrueVision cable provides international programming.

Weights & Measures

Thailand follows the international metric system. Gold and silver are weighed in *bàht* (15g).

Drug smuggling – defined as attempting to cross a border with drugs in your possession – carries considerably higher sanctions, including the death penalty.

Scams

Thais can be so friendly and laid-back that some visitors are lulled into a false sense of security, making them vulnerable to scams of all kinds. Bangkok is especially good at long, involved frauds that dupe travellers into thinking that they've made a friend and are getting a bargain on highly valuable gem stones (which are actually pretty, sparkling glass).

Follow the Tourism Authority of Thailand's suggestion: 'Disregard all offers of free shopping or sightseeing help from strangers.' They will invariably take a commission from your purchases.

Theft & Fraud

Exercise diligence when it comes to your personal belongings. Ensure that your room is securely locked and carry your most important effects (passport, money, credit cards) on your person. Take care when leaving valuables in hotel safes.

Follow the same practice when you're travelling. A locked bag will not prevent theft on a long-haul bus.

When using a credit card, don't let vendors take your credit card out of your sight to run it through the machine. Unscrupulous merchants have been known to rub off three or four or more receipts with one purchase. Sometimes they wait several weeks – even months – between submitting each charge receipt to the bank so that you can't remember whether you've been billed by the same vendor more than once.

To avoid losing all of your travel money in an instant, use a credit card that is not directly linked to your bank account back home so that the operator doesn't have access to immediate funds.

Contact the **tourist police** (☎1155 24hr hotline) if you have any problems with consumer fraud.

Touts & Commissions

Touting is a longtime tradition in Asia, and while Thailand doesn't have as many touts as, say, India, it has its share. In Bangkok, túk-túk drivers, hotel employees and bar girls often take new arrivals on city tours; these almost always end up in high-pressure sales situations at silk, jewellery or handicraft shops.

Touts also steer customers to certain guesthouses that pay a commission. Travel agencies are notorious for talking newly arrived tourists into staying at badly located, overpriced hotels.

Some travel agencies often masquerade as TAT, the government-funded tourist information office. They might put up agents wearing fake TAT badges or have signs that read TAT in big letters to entice travellers into their offices where they can sell them bus and train tickets for a commission. Be aware that the official TAT offices do not make hotel or transport bookings. If such a place offers to do this for you, then it is a travel agency not a tourist-information office.

When making transport arrangements, talk to several travel agencies to look for the best price, as the commission percentage varies greatly between agents. And resist high-intensity sales tactics from an agent trying to sign you up for everything: plane tickets, hotel, tours etc.

Shopping

Many bargains await you in Thailand, but don't go shopping in the company of touts, tour guides or friendly strangers, as they will inevitably take a commission on anything you buy, thus driving prices up beyond an acceptable value and creating a nuisance for future visitors.

Antiques

Genuine Thai antiques are increasingly rare. Today, most dealers sell antique reproductions or items from Myanmar. Bangkok is the centre of the antique and reproduction trade.

Real antiques cannot be taken out of Thailand without a permit. No Buddha image, new or old, may be exported without the permission of the Department of Fine Arts.

Clothing

Clothes tend to be inexpensive in Thailand but ready-made items are not usually cut to fit Westerners' body types. Increasingly, larger-sized clothing is available in metropolitan malls or tourist centres. Markets sell cheap everyday items and are handy for picking up something when everything else is dirty. For chic clothes, Bangkok and Ko Samui lead the country with design-minded fashions. The custom of returns is not widely accepted in Thailand, so be sure everything fits before you leave the store.

Thailand has a long sartorial tradition, practised mainly by Thai-Indian Sikh families, but this industry is filled with cut-rate operators and commission-paying scams. Be wary of the quickie 24-hour tailor shops; they often use inferior fabric and have poor workmanship. It's best to ask long-time foreign residents for a recommendation and then go for two or three fittings.

Fakes

In Bangkok and other tourist centres there's a thriving black-market street trade in fake designer goods. No one pretends they're the real deal, at least not the vendors. Technically it is illegal for these items to be produced and sold, and Thailand has often been pressured by intellectual-property enforcement agencies to close down the trade. Rarely does a crackdown by the police last and often the vendors develop more surreptitious means of distribution, further highlighting the contraband character of the goods. In Patpong market, for example, vendors might show you a picture of a knock-off watch, you pay for it and they go around the corner to fetch it. Usually, they come back, although you'll wait long enough to start wondering.

Furniture

Rattan and hardwood furniture items are often good purchases and can be made to order. Due to the ban on teak harvesting and the subsequent exhaustion of recycled teak, 70% of export furniture produced in Thailand is made from parawood, a processed wood from rubber trees that can no longer be used for latex production.

Gems & Jewellery

Thailand is a leading exporter of gems and ornaments, rivalled only by India and Sri Lanka. However, rough-stone sources in Thailand have

BARGAINING

If there isn't a sign stating the price for an item, then the price is negotiable. Bargaining for nonfood items is common in street markets and some mum-and-dad shops. Prices in department stores, minimarts and so forth are fixed.

Thais respect a good haggler, but remember that the point of bargaining is to achieve a mutually acceptable price and not to screw the vendor into the ground. Always let the vendor make the first offer, then ask 'Can you lower the price?' This usually results in a discount. Now it's your turn to make a counter-offer; always start low but don't bargain at all unless you're serious about buying.

It helps immeasurably to keep the negotiations relaxed and friendly. Smile a lot and avoid losing your temper or raising your voice.

decreased dramatically and stones are now imported from Myanmar, Sri Lanka and other countries to be cut, polished and traded.

Although there are a lot of gem and jewellery stores in Thailand, it has become so difficult to dodge the scammers that the country no longer represents a safe and enjoyable place to buy these goods, especially if you don't know a lot about gems. It is better just to window shop.

Lacquerware

Lacquerware furniture and decorative items were traditionally made from bamboo and teak but these days mango wood might be used as the base. From start to finish it can take five or six months to produce a high-quality piece of lacquerware, which may have as many as five colours. Flexibility is one characteristic of good lacquerware: a well-made bowl can have its rim squeezed together until the sides meet without suffering damage.

Textiles

At Bangkok's Chatuchak Weekend Market and at many of the popular tourist-friendly markets throughout the islands and beaches, you can find a slew of traditional textiles from all over the kingdom, including the culturally rich regions of the north.

Fairly nice bah·dé (batik) is available in the south in patterns that are more similar to the batik found in Malaysia than in Indonesia.

Telephone

The country code for Thailand is ☎66 and is used when calling the country from abroad. All Thai telephone numbers are preceded by a '0' if you're dialling domestically (the '0' is omitted when calling from overseas). After the initial '0', the next three numbers represent the provincial area code, which is now integral to the telephone number. If the initial '0' is followed by an '8' or a '9', then you're dialling a mobile phone.

International Calls

If you want to call an international number from a telephone in Thailand, you must first dial an international access code plus the country code followed by the subscriber number.

The standard international direct-dial prefix is 001. It is operated by the Communications Authority of Thailand (CAT) and is considered to have the best sound quality; it connects to the largest number of countries but is also the most expensive. The next best is 007, a prefix operated by the telecommunications company TOT, with reliable quality and slightly cheaper rates. If you have a Thai SIM card, the carrier will have its own direct-dial prefix, often very cheap.

Dial ☎100 for operator-assisted international calls or reverse-charges (collect) calls. Alternatively, contact your long-distance carrier for its overseas operator number, a toll-free call, or try ☎001 9991 2001 from a CAT phone and ☎1 800 000 120 from a TOT phone.

Mobile Phones

The easiest phone option in Thailand is to acquire a mobile phone equipped with a local SIM card.

Thailand is on the GSM network and mobile-phone providers include AIS, DTAC and True Move.

You have two phone options. You can buy a mobile phone in Thailand at one of the urban shopping malls or phone stores near the markets in provincial towns or you can use an imported phone that isn't SIM-locked (and supports the GSM network). To get started, buy a SIM card from one of the carriers (AIS and DTAC are most popular), which includes an assigned telephone number. You will need to show your passport when you buy a SIM card, under a new regulation that means all phone numbers must be registered. Once your phone is SIM-enabled you can buy minutes with prepaid phonecards. SIM cards and refill cards (usually sold in 50B to 500B denominations) can be bought from 7-Elevens throughout the country.

Thailand has a 3G network and DTAC and True Move offer 4G LTE coverage in Bangkok, although it's not as fast as 4G should be. Coverage and quality of the different carriers varies from year to year based on network upgrades and capacity. As of 2015, True was regarded as having the highest data connectivity. Carriers usually sell talk-data packages based on usage amounts.

There are various promotions, but rates typically hover at around 1B to 2B per minute anywhere in Thailand and between 5B and 9B for international calls. SMS is usually 3B per message, making it the cheapest 'talk' option. AIS offers a one-month unlimited-data-use deal for 800B, but all the companies have deals, so shop around.

Calling overseas through phones in most hotel rooms usually incurs additional surcharges (sometimes as much as 50% over and above the CAT rate); however, sometimes local calls are free or at standard rates. Some guesthouses will have a mobile phone or landline that customers can use for a per-minute fee for overseas calls.

Time

Thailand's time zone is seven hours ahead of GMT/UTC (London). At government offices and local cinemas, times are often expressed according to the 24-hour clock, eg 11pm is written '23.00'.

Toilets

The Asian-style squat toilet is becoming less common in Thailand. There are still specimens in rural places, provincial bus stations, older homes and modest restaurants, but the Western-style toilet is becoming more prevalent and appears wherever foreign tourists can be found.

If you encounter a squat, here's what you should know. You should straddle the two footpads and face the door. To flush, use the plastic bowl to scoop water out of the adjacent basin and pour into the toilet bowl. Some places supply a small pack of toilet paper at the entrance (5B), otherwise bring your own stash or wipe the old-fashioned way with water.

Even in places where sit-down toilets are installed, the septic system may not be designed to take toilet paper. In such cases there will be a waste basket where you're supposed to place used toilet paper and feminine hygiene products. Most modern toilets also come with a small spray hose – Thailand's version of the bidet.

Tourist Information

The government-operated tourist information and promotion service, **Tourism Authority of Thailand** (TAT; ☎1672; www.travelthailand.tourismthailand.org), produces excellent pamphlets on sightseeing, accommodation and transport. TAT's head office is in Bangkok and there are 22 regional offices throughout the country.

TAT also has a number of overseas information offices; check its website for contact information.

Travellers with Disabilities

Thailand presents one large, ongoing obstacle course for the mobility impaired. With its high curbs, uneven footpaths and nonstop traffic, Bangkok can be particularly difficult. Many streets must be crossed via pedestrian bridges flanked with steep stairways, while buses and boats don't stop long enough even for the fully mobile. Rarely are there any ramps or other access points for wheelchairs.

A number of more expensive top-end hotels make consistent design efforts to provide disabled access to their properties. Other deluxe hotels with high employee-to-guest ratios are usually good about accommodating the mobility impaired by providing staff help where building design fails. For the rest, you're pretty much left to your own resources.

Some organisations and publications that offer tips on international travel include the following:

Accessible Journeys (www.disabilitytravel.com)

Mobility International USA (www.miusa.org)

Society for Accessible Travel & Hospitality (www.sath.org)

Visas

The **Ministry of Foreign Affairs** (☎02 203 5000; www.mfa.go.th) oversees immigration and visa issues. Check the website or the nearest Thai embassy or consulate for application procedures and costs.

Tourist Visas & Exemptions

The Thai government allows tourist-visa exemptions for 61 different nations – including Australia, New Zealand, the USA and most of Europe – allowing entry to the country without a pre-arranged visa for 30 days. A further 19 countries, including China, can get a visa on arrival valid for 15 days.

For those arriving in the kingdom by air, a 30-day visa is issued without a fee. For those arriving via a land border, the visa is valid for 15 days. Some countries (including Brazil, South Korea, Argentina, Chile and Peru) receive a 90-day free visa at all borders.

Without proof of an onward ticket and sufficient funds for the projected stay any visitor can be denied entry, but in practice this is a formality that is rarely enforced.

If you plan to stay in Thailand longer than 30 days (or 15 days for land arrivals), you should apply for the 60-day tourist visa from a Thai consulate or embassy before your trip. Contact the nearest Thai embassy or consulate to obtain application procedures and determine fees for tourist visas.

By the time you read this, Thailand should be offering a new, six-month tourist visa for 5000B that allows multiple entries as long as you leave the country every 60 days (even if you only walk across a border, or fly out, and then come straight back).

Non-Immigrant Visas

The Non-Immigrant Visa is good for 90 days and is intended for foreigners entering the country for business, study, retirement or extended family visits. There are multiple-entry visas available in this visa class; you're more likely to be granted multiple entries if you apply at a Thai consulate in Europe, the US or Australia than elsewhere. If you plan to apply for a Thai work permit, you'll need to possess a Non-Immigrant Visa first.

Visa Extensions & Renewals

If you decide you want to stay longer than the allotted time, you can extend your visa by applying at any immigration office in Thailand. The usual fee for a visa extension is 1900B. Those issued with a standard stay of 15 or 30 days can extend their stay for seven to 10 days (depending on the immigration office) if the extension is handled before the visa expires. The 60-day tourist visa can be extended by up to 30 days at the discretion of Thai immigration authorities.

Another visa-renewal option is to cross a land border. A new 15-day visa will be issued upon your return and some short-term visitors make a day trip out of the 'visa run'.

If you overstay your visa, the usual penalty is a fine of 500B per day, with a 20,000B limit. Fines can be paid at the airport or in advance at an immigration office. If you've overstayed only one day, you don't have to pay. Children under 14 travelling with a parent do not have to pay the penalty.

Foreign residents in Thailand should arrange visa extensions at the immigration office closest to their in-country address.

Volunteering

For information about volunteering in Thailand, see p410.

Women Travellers

- Women travellers face relatively few problems in Thailand. With the great amount of respect afforded to women, an equal measure should be returned.
- Thai women, especially the younger generation, are showing more skin than in the recent past. You can wear spaghetti-strap tops and navel-bearing shirts without offending Thais' sense of modesty. But to be on the safe side, cover up if you're going deep into rural communities or to temples.
- Attacks and rapes are not common in Thailand, but incidents do occur, especially when an attacker observes a vulnerable target: a drunk or solo woman. If you return home from a bar alone, be sure to have your wits about you. Avoid accepting rides from strangers late at night or travelling around in isolated areas by yourself – common sense stuff that you might forget in a new environment filled with hospitable people.
- Be aware that frivolous flirting could unintentionally cause a Thai man to feel a loss of face, especially when the involved parties have different intentions. Always bear in mind that what may seem commonplace in your culture may be received very differently abroad.

Transport

GETTING THERE & AWAY

Flights, tours and rail tickets can be booked online at lonelyplanet.com/bookings.

Entering the Country

Entry procedures for Thailand, by air or by land, are straightforward: you'll have to show your passport and you'll need to present completed arrival and departure cards. Blank arrival and departure cards are usually distributed on the incoming flight or, if you're arriving by land, can be picked up at the immigration counter.

You do not have to fill in a customs form on arrival unless you have imported goods to declare. In that case, you can get the proper form from Thai customs officials at your point of entry. There can also be minimum funds requirements.

Air

Airports

Bangkok is Thailand's primary international and domestic gateway. There are also smaller airports throughout the country serving domestic and sometimes inter-regional routes.

Suvarnabhumi International Airport (☎02 132 1888; www.suvarnabhumiairport.com) Located 30km east of central Bangkok, Suvarnabhumi International Airport began commercial international and domestic service in 2006. The airport's name is pronounced *sù·wan·ná·poom*, and it inherited the airport code (BKK) previously held by the old airport at Don Mueang. The airport website has real-time details of arrivals and departures.

Don Mueang International Airport (☎02 535 1253; www.donmueangairportthai.com) Bangkok's other airport, Don Mueang International Airport, 25km north of central Bangkok, was retired from service in 2006 only to reopen later as Bangkok's de facto budget airline hub.

Phuket International Airport (☎076 327230; www.phuketairportthai.com) International destinations include Seoul, Hong Kong, Singapore, Dubai and Shanghai.

Ko Samui Airport (www.samuiairportonline.com) International Asian destinations include Hong Kong, Singapore and Kuala Lumpur.

Tickets

In some cases, eg when travelling to neighbouring countries or to domestic destinations, it is still convenient to use a travel agent in Thailand. The amount of commission an agent will charge often varies, so shop around to gauge the discrepancy in prices. Paying by credit card generally offers protection, because most card issuers provide refunds if you can prove you didn't get what you

CLIMATE CHANGE & TRAVEL

Every form of transport that relies on carbon-based fuel generates CO_2, the main cause of human-induced climate change. Modern travel is dependent on aeroplanes, which might use less fuel per kilometre per person than most cars but travel much greater distances. The altitude at which aircraft emit gases (including CO_2) and particles also contributes to their climate change impact. Many websites offer 'carbon calculators' that allow people to estimate the carbon emissions generated by their journey and, for those who wish to do so, to offset the impact of the greenhouse gases emitted with contributions to portfolios of climate-friendly initiatives throughout the world. Lonely Planet offsets the carbon footprint of all staff and author travel.

paid for. Agents who accept only cash should hand over the tickets straightaway and not tell you to 'come back tomorrow'. After you've made a booking or paid your deposit, call the airline and confirm that the booking was made.

Airfares during the high season (December to March) can be expensive.

ISLAND TRANSFER TICKETS

You may see air tickets on low-cost carriers (mostly Air Asia) that go to islands that don't have airports, such as Ko Phi Phi, Ko Lanta and Ko Ngai. These tickets fly to the nearest airport then include bus and boat transport to the island. If you don't mind being shuttled like cattle, this can be a good option since the cost is about the same as arranging the ground transport by yourself except you don't have the hassle that goes with it.

In other cases carriers may say they go to islands that have airports (like Ko Samui or Ko Pha-Ngan), but actually fly into a nearby airport and include ground and boat transportation in the cost. Make sure you check the details before booking. In these cases the ticket price is usually cheaper than flying to the island direct, although the travel time will be much longer.

Land

Thailand shares land borders with Laos, Malaysia, Cambodia and Myanmar. Travel between all of these countries can be done by land via sanctioned border crossings. With improved highways, it is also becoming easier to travel from Thailand to China.

Bus, Car & Motorcycle

Road connections exist between Thailand and all of its neighbours, and these routes can be travelled by bus, shared taxi and private car. In some cases you'll take a bus to the border point, pass through immigration and then pick up another bus or shared taxi on the other side. In other cases, especially when crossing the Malaysian border, the bus will stop for immigration formalities and then continue to its destination across the border.

Train

The state railways of Thailand and Malaysia meet at Butterworth (93km south of the Thai–Malaysian border), which is a transfer point to Penang (by boat) or to Kuala Lumpur and Singapore (by Malaysian train).

There are several border crossings for which you can take a train to the border and then switch to automobile transport on the other side. The Thai–Cambodian border crossing of Aranya Prathet to Poipet and the Thai–Laos crossing of Nong Khai to Vientiane are two examples.

Another rail line travels to the Malaysian east-coast border town of Sungai Kolok, but because of ongoing violence in Thailand's Deep South we don't recommend this route for travellers.

Border Crossings

Make sure you familiarise yourself with all relevant visa information (p420).

CAMBODIA

Cambodian tourist visas are available at the border for US$20, though some borders charge 1500B. Bring a passport photo and avoid the runner boys who want to issue a health certificate or other 'medical' paperwork for additional fees.

Aranya Prathet to Poipet The most direct land route between Bangkok and Angkor Wat.

Chong Sa to Ngam Choam Remote border crossing where you'll have to hire private transport (instead of a share taxi) on the Cambodian side of the border.

Hat Lek to Krong Koh Kong The coastal crossing for travellers heading to/from Ko Chang/Sihanoukville.

O Smach to Chong Chom Periodically closed due to fighting at Khao Phra Wihan. You'll have to hire private transport on the Cambodian side.

Pong Nam Ron to Pailin A backdoor route from Ko Chang (via Chanthaburi) to Battambang and Angkor Wat.

CHINA

Yunnan Province in southwest China is accessible via Laos. You'll need to arrange your Chinese visa prior to departure, ideally in Bangkok or Chiang Mai.

The main crossing in Laos is Boten to Mengla. You can reach Boten in five to six hours from Chiang Khong via Huay Xai.

LAOS

It is hassle-free to cross into Laos from northern and northeastern Thailand. Lao visas (US$35 to US$50) can be obtained on arrival, and applications require a passport photo.

Crossings include Chiang Khong to Huay Xai, Mukdahan to Savannakhet, Nakhon Phanom to Tha Khaek and Chong Mek to Vangtao. But the main crossing is at Nong Khai.

Nong Khai to Vientiane The main transport gateway to Laos via the first Thai–Lao Friendship Bridge.

MALAYSIA

Malaysia, especially the west coast, is easy to reach via bus, train and even boat.

As well as the crossings listed here, other crossings include Hat Yai to Padang

Besar and Sungai Kolok to Kota Bharu, but we don't recommend taking these routes due to the violence in the Deep South.

Hat Yai to Butterworth The western spur of the train line originating in Bangkok terminates at Butterworth, the mainland transfer point to Penang. Less popular these days due to unrest in the Deep South.

Ko Lipe to Pulau Langkawi Boats provide a convenient high-season link between these two Andaman islands.

Satun to Pulau Langkawi/ Kuala Perlis Boats shuttle from this mainland port to the island of Langkawi and the mainland town of Kuala Perlis.

MYANMAR

As part of the AEC (ASEAN Economic Community) integration goals, Myanmar has lifted travel restrictions at four of its borders with Thailand. The Singkhon Pass crossing close to Prachuap Khiri Khan should be open by the time you read this. Other open crossings include Mae Sot to Myawadi.

Ban Phu Nam Ron to Htee-Khee A new crossing requiring major infrastructure investment; the Thai government intends to develop this route as a link between Bangkok and Myanmar's Dawei port in the Andaman Sea.

Mae Sai to Tachileik This crossing is popular with travellers to renew their Thai visas, as it is convenient for Chiang Mai and Chiang Rai.

Ranong to Kawthoung This is a popular visa-renewal point in the southern part of Thailand.

GETTING AROUND

Air

Hopping around the country by air continues to be affordable. Most routes originate from Bangkok, but Ko Samui and Phuket have a few routes to other Thai towns.

Thai Airways International operates many domestic air routes from Bangkok to provincial capitals. Bangkok Air is another established domestic carrier. Air Asia and Nok Air are the domestic budget carriers.

Boat

Long-tail boats are a staple of transport on rivers and canals in Bangkok and in the south.

Between the mainland and islands in the Gulf of Thailand or the Andaman Sea, you may also see 8m- to 10m-long wooden boats with an inboard engine and a simple roof to shelter passengers and cargo. Faster, more expensive hovercraft or jetfoils are available in tourist areas.

BICYCLE TRAVEL IN THAILAND

For travelling just about anywhere outside Bangkok, bicycles are an ideal form of local transport – cheap, nonpolluting and slow-moving enough to allow travellers to see everything. Bicycles can be hired in many locations, especially guesthouses, for as little as 50B per day, though they aren't always high quality. A security deposit isn't usually required.

Bicycle touring is also a popular way to see the country; most roads are sealed and have roomy shoulders. With duties high on imported bikes, in most cases you'll do better to bring your own bike to Thailand rather than purchase one there. No special permits are needed to bring a bicycle into the country, although it may be registered by customs – which means if you don't leave the country with your bicycle you'll have to pay a customs duty. It's advisable to bring a well-stocked repair kit.

Bus & Minivan

The bus network in Thailand is prolific and reliable, and is a great way to see the countryside and sit among the locals. The Thai government subsidises the Transport Company *(bò·rí·sàt kŏn sòng)*, usually abbreviated to Baw Khaw Saw (BKS). Every city and town in Thailand linked by bus has a BKS station, even if it's just a patch of dirt by the side of the road.

By far the most reliable bus companies in Thailand are the ones that operate out of the government-run BKS stations. In some cases the companies are entirely state-owned, in others they are private concessions.

We do not recommend using bus companies that operate directly out of tourist centres, such as Bangkok's Th Khao San, because of repeated instances of theft and commission-seeking stops. Be aware of bus scams and problems.

Increasingly, though, minivans are the middle-class option. Minivans are run by private companies and because their vehicles are smaller they can depart from the market (instead of the out-of-town bus stations) and will deliver guests directly to their hotel.

Bus Classes

The cheapest and slowest are the *rót tam·má·dah* (ordinary fan buses), which stop in every little town and for every waving hand along the highway. Only a few of these ordinary buses, mostly in rural locations or for local destinations, still exist since most have been replaced by air-con buses.

The bulk of the bus service consists of faster, more comfortable air-con buses, called *rót aa* (air bus). Longer routes offer at least two classes of air-con buses: 2nd class and 1st class. The latter have toilets. 'VIP' and 'Super VIP' buses have fewer seats so that each seat reclines further; sometimes these are called *rót norn* (sleeper bus).

It is handy to bring along a jacket, especially for long-distance trips, as the air-con can turn the cabin into a deep freeze.

The service on these buses is usually quite good and on certain routes sometimes includes a beverage service and video.

On overnight journeys the buses usually stop somewhere en route for 'midnight *kôw đôm'* (rice soup), when passengers are awakened to get off the bus for a meal.

Reservations

You can book air-con BKS buses at any BKS terminal. Ordinary (fan) buses cannot be booked in advance. Privately run buses can be booked through most hotels or any travel agency, but it's best to book directly through a bus office to be sure that you get what you pay for.

Car & Motorcycle

Driving Licence

Short-term visitors who wish to drive vehicles (including motorcycles) in Thailand need an International Driving Permit, though this requirement is not always enforced.

Fuel

Modern petrol (gasoline) stations are in plentiful supply all over Thailand wherever there are paved roads. In more remote, off-road areas *ben·sin/nám·man rót yon* (petrol containing benzene) is usually available at small roadside or village stands. All fuel in Thailand is unleaded, and diesel is used by trucks and some passenger cars. Several alternative fuels, including gasohol (a blend of petrol and ethanol that comes in different octane levels, either 91% or 95%) and compressed natural gas, are used by taxis with bifuel capabilities. For news and updates about fuel options, and other car talk, see the website of BKK Auto (www.bkkautos.com).

Hire

Cars, jeeps and vans can be rented in most major cities and at airports from local companies as well as international chains. Local companies tend to have cheaper rates than the international chains, but their fleets of cars tend to be older and not as well maintained.

Motorcycles can be rented in major towns and from guesthouses and small mum-and-dad businesses in many smaller tourist centres for 200B a day and up. Renting a motorcycle in Thailand is relatively easy and a great way to tour the countryside. For daily rentals, most businesses will ask that you leave your passport as a deposit. Before renting a motorcycle, check the vehicle's condition and ask for a helmet (which is required by law).

Many tourists are injured riding motorcycles in Thailand because they don't know how to handle the vehicle and are unfamiliar with the road rules and conditions. Drive slowly, especially when roads are slick, to avoid damage to yourself and to the vehicle, and be sure to have adequate health insurance. If you've never ridden a motorcycle before, stick to the smaller 100cc step-through bikes with automatic clutches. Remember to distribute weight as evenly as possible across the frame of the bike to improve handling. Bear in mind that if you fall off, you will be paying both medical bills and for any damage to the bike.

Insurance

Thailand requires a minimum of liability insurance for all registered vehicles on the road. The better hire companies include comprehensive coverage for their vehicles. Always verify that a vehicle is insured for liability before signing a rental contract; you should also ask to see the dated insurance documents. If you have an accident while driving an uninsured vehicle, you're in for some major hassles.

Road Rules & Hazards

Thais drive on the left-hand side of the road (most of the time!). Other than that, just about anything goes, in spite of road signs and speed limits.

The main rule to be aware of is that right of way goes to the bigger vehicle; this is not what it says in the Thai traffic law, but it's the reality. Maximum speed limits are 50km/h on urban roads and 80km/h to 100km/h on most highways – but on any given stretch of highway you'll see various vehicles travelling as slowly as 30km/h and as fast as 150km/h.

Indicators are often used to warn passing drivers about oncoming traffic. A flashing left indicator means it's OK to pass, while a right indicator means that someone's approaching from the other direction. Horns are used to tell other vehicles that the driver plans to pass. When drivers flash their lights, they're telling you not to pass.

In Bangkok traffic is chaotic, roads are poorly signposted, and motorcycles and random contraflows mean you can suddenly find yourself facing a wall of cars coming the other way.

Outside the capital, the principal hazard when driving in Thailand, besides the general disregard for traffic laws, is having to contend

SĂHM·LÓR & TÚK-TÚK

Săhm·lór (also spelt săamláw) are three-wheeled pedicabs and are now found only in small towns where traffic is light and old-fashioned ways persist.

The modern era's version of the human-powered săhm·lór is the motorised túk-túk (pronounced *'đúk đúk'*). They're small utility vehicles powered by screaming engines (usually LPG-powered) and a lot of flash and sparkle.

With either form of transport the fare must be established by bargaining before departure. In tourist centres, túk-túk drivers often grossly overcharge foreigners, so it's useful to have a sense of how much the fare should be before soliciting a ride. Hotel staff are helpful in providing reasonable fare suggestions.

Readers interested in pedicab lore and design may want to have a look at Lonely Planet's hardcover pictorial book *Chasing Rickshaws*, by Lonely Planet founder Tony Wheeler.

with so many different types of vehicles on the same road: trucks, bicycles, túk-túk (pronounced *'đúk dúk'*) and motorcycles. This danger is often compounded by the lack of working lights. In village areas the vehicular traffic is lighter, but you have to deal with stray chickens, dogs and water buffaloes.

Hitching

Hitching is never entirely safe in any country and we don't recommend it. Travellers who hitch should understand that they are taking a small but potentially serious risk. Hitching is rare these days in Thailand, so most passing motorists might not realise the intentions of the foreigner standing on the side of the road with a thumb out. When Thais want a ride they wave their hand with the palm facing the ground. This is the same gesture used to flag a taxi or bus, which is why some drivers might stop and point to a bus stop if one is nearby.

In some of the national parks without public transport, Thais are often willing to pick up a passenger standing by the side of the road.

Local Transport

City Bus & Sŏrng·tăa·ou

Bangkok has the largest city-bus system in the country. The etiquette for riding public buses is to wait at a bus stop and hail the vehicle by waving your hand palm-side downward. You typically pay the fare once you've taken a seat or, in some cases, when you disembark.

Elsewhere public transport is provided by *sŏrng·tăa·ou* (a small pick-up truck outfitted with two facing rows of benches for passengers). They sometimes operate on fixed routes, just like buses, but they may also run a share-taxi service where they pick up passengers going in the same general direction. In tourist centres, *sŏrng·tăa·ou* can be chartered just like a regular taxi, but you'll need to negotiate the fare beforehand. You can usually hail a *sŏrng·tăa·ou* anywhere along its route and pay the fare when you disembark.

Depending on the region, *sŏrng·tăa·ou* might also run a fixed route from the centre of town to outlying areas or even points within the provinces. Sometimes these vehicles are larger six-wheeled vehicles (sometimes called *rót hòk lór*).

Mass Transit

Bangkok is the only city in Thailand to have an above-ground and an underground light-rail public-transport system. Known as the Skytrain and the Metro respectively, both systems have helped to alleviate the capital's notorious traffic jams, but are restricted to just three routes.

Motorcycle Taxi

Many cities in Thailand have *mor·đeu·sai ráp jâhng* (100cc to 125cc motorcycles) that can be hired, with a driver, for short distances. If you're empty-handed or travelling with a small bag, they can't be beaten for transport in a pinch.

In most cities you'll find motorcycle taxis clustered near street intersections. Usually they wear numbered vest-like jackets. Fares start at 10B for very short hops. Establish the price before you jump on the back.

Taxi

Bangkok has the most formal system of metered taxis. In other cities a taxi can be a private vehicle with negotiable rates. You can also travel between cities by taxi, but you'll need to negotiate a price as few taxi drivers will run a meter for intercity travel.

Train

Thailand's train system is most convenient as an alternative to buses for the long journey south. However, delays are common on many routes.

The 4500km rail network is operated by the State Railway of Thailand (www.railway.co.th) and covers four main lines: the northern, southern, northeastern and eastern lines. All long-distance trains originate from Bangkok's Hualamphong station.

Classes

The SRT operates passenger trains in three classes – 1st, 2nd and 3rd – but each class varies considerably depending on whether you're on an ordinary, rapid or express train.

1st class In 1st class, passengers have private cabins, which are available only on rapid, express and special-express trains.

2nd class The seating arrangements in a 2nd-class, non-sleeper carriage are similar to those on a bus, with padded seats facing towards the front of the train. On 2nd-class sleeper cars, pairs of seats face one another and convert into two fold-down berths. The lower berth has more headroom than the upper berth and this is reflected in a higher fare. Children are always assigned a lower berth. There are air-con and fan 2nd-class carriages. Second-class carriages are only found on rapid and express trains.

3rd class A typical 3rd-class carriage consists of two rows of bench seats divided into facing pairs. Each bench seat is designed to seat two or three passengers, but on a crowded rural line nobody seems to care.

Costs

Fares are determined by a base price with surcharges added for distance, class and train type (special-express, express, rapid, ordinary). Extra charges are added if the carriage has air-con and for sleeping berths (either upper or lower).

Reservations

Advance bookings can be made from one to 60 days before your intended date of departure. You can make bookings in person from any train station. Train tickets can also be purchased at travel agencies, which usually add a service charge to the ticket price. If you are planning long-distance train travel from outside the country, you should email the State Railway of Thailand (via the Contact Us page on its website) at least two weeks before your journey. You will receive an email confirming the booking. Pick up and pay for tickets an hour before leaving at the scheduled departure train station.

It is advisable to make advanced bookings for long-distance sleeper trains from Bangkok, especially around Songkran in April and the peak tourist-season months of December and January.

For short-distance trips you should purchase your ticket at least a day in advance for seats (rather than sleepers).

Partial refunds on tickets are available depending on the number of days prior to your departure you arrange for a cancellation. These arrangements can be handled at the train-station booking office.

Station Services

You'll find that all train stations in Thailand have baggage-storage services (or cloak rooms). Most stations have a ticket window that will open between 15 and 30 minutes before train arrivals. There are also newsagents and small snack vendors and cafes.

Most train stations have printed timetables in English, although this isn't always the case for smaller stations. Bangkok's Hualamphong station is a good spot to load up on timetables.

Health

Health risks and the quality of medical facilities vary depending on where and how you travel in Thailand. The majority of major cities and popular tourist areas are well developed with adequate and even excellent medical care. But travel to remote rural areas can expose you to some health risks and less adequate medical care.

Travellers tend to worry about contracting exotic infectious diseases when visiting the tropics, but such infections are far less common than problems with pre-existing medical conditions and accidental injury (especially as a result of traffic accidents).

Becoming ill in some way is common, however. Respiratory infections, diarrhoea and dengue fever are particular hazards in Thailand. Fortunately, most common illnesses can be prevented or are easily treated.

The advice we provide is a general guide and does not replace the advice of a doctor trained in travel medicine.

BEFORE YOU GO

Pack medications in clearly labelled original containers and obtain a signed and dated letter from your physician describing your medical conditions, medications and syringes or needles. If you have a heart condition, bring a copy of your electrocardiography (ECG) taken just prior to travelling.

If you take any regular medication bring double your needs. In Thailand you can buy many medications over the counter without a doctor's prescription, but it can be difficult to find the exact medication you are taking.

FURTHER READING

- **International Travel & Health** (www.who.int/ith) Health guide published by the World Health Organization (WHO).
- **Centers for Disease Control & Prevention** (www.cdc.gov) Country-specific advice.
- **Healthy Travel – Asia & India** (Lonely Planet) Includes pretrip planning, emergency first aid, and immunisation and disease information.
- **Traveller's Health: How to Stay Healthy Abroad** (Dr Richard Dawood) Considered the 'health bible' for international holidays.

Insurance

Don't travel without health insurance – accidents *do* happen. You may require extra cover for adventure activities such as rock climbing or diving, as well as scooter/motorcycle riding. If your health insurance doesn't cover you for medical expenses abroad, ensure you get specific travel insurance that does. Most hospitals require an upfront guarantee of payment (from yourself or your insurer) prior to admission. Inquire before your trip about payment of medical charges and retain all documentation (medical reports, invoices etc) for claim purposes.

Vaccinations

Specialised travel-medicine clinics are your best source of information on which vaccinations you should consider taking. The Centers for Disease Control (www.cdc.gov) has a travellers' health section that contains recommendations for vaccinations. The only vaccine required in Thailand by international regulations is yellow fever. Proof of vaccination will only be required if you have visited a country in the yellow-fever zone (in Africa and South America only) within the six days prior to entering Thailand.

IN TRANSIT

Deep Vein Thrombosis

Deep vein thrombosis (DVT) occurs when blood clots form in the legs during long trips such as flights, chiefly because of prolonged immobility. The longer the journey, the greater the risk. Though most blood clots are reabsorbed uneventfully, some may break off and travel through the blood vessels to the lungs, where they can cause life-threatening complications.

The chief symptom of DVT is swelling or pain of the foot, ankle or calf, usually, but not always, on one side. When a blood clot travels to the lungs, it may cause chest pain and difficulty breathing. Travellers with any of these symptoms should immediately seek medical attention.

To prevent the development of DVT on long flights you should walk about the cabin, perform isometric compressions of the leg muscles (ie contract the leg muscles while sitting) and drink plenty of fluids (nonalcoholic). Those at higher risk should speak with a doctor about extra preventative measures.

Jet Lag & Motion Sickness

Jet lag results in insomnia, fatigue, malaise or nausea. To avoid jet lag, drink plenty of fluids (nonalcoholic) and eat light meals. Upon arrival, seek exposure to natural sunlight and readjust your schedule.

Sedating antihistamines such as dimenhydrinate (Dramamine) and Prochlorperazine (Phenergan) are usually the first choice for treating motion sickness. Their main side effect is drowsiness. A herbal alternative is ginger. Scopolamine patches are considered the most effective prevention.

IN THAILAND

Availability & Cost of Health Care

Bangkok is considered the nearest centre of medical excellence for many countries in Southeast Asia. Private hospitals are more expensive than other medical facilities but offer a superior standard of care and English-speaking staff. The cost of health care is relatively cheap in Thailand compared to most Western countries.

Self-treatment may be appropriate if your problem is minor (eg traveller's diarrhoea), you are carrying the appropriate medication and you are unable to attend a recommended clinic or hospital.

Be careful buying medication over the counter because fake medications and poorly stored or out-of-date drugs are common, especially outside major cities.

MEDICAL CHECKLIST

Recommended items for a personal medical kit include the following:

- antifungal cream, eg Clotrimazole
- antibacterial cream, eg Muciprocin
- antibiotic for skin infections, eg Amoxicillin/Clavulanate or Cephalexin
- antibiotics for diarrhoea include Norfloxacin, Ciprofloxacin or Azithromycin for bacterial diarrhoea; for giardiasis or amoebic dysentery take Tinidazole
- antihistamine – there are many options, eg Cetrizine for daytime and Promethazine for night
- antiseptic, eg Betadine
- contraceptives
- decongestant
- DEET-based insect repellent
- oral rehydration solution for diarrhoea (eg Gastrolyte), diarrhoea 'stopper' (eg Loperamide) and antinausea medication (eg Prochlorperazine)
- first-aid items such as scissors, Elastoplasts, bandages, gauze, thermometer (but not one with mercury), sterile needles and syringes (with a doctor's letter), safety pins and tweezers
- hand gel or hand wipes (both alcohol based)
- ibuprofen or another anti-inflammatory
- laxative, eg Coloxyl
- paracetamol
- steroid cream for allergic or itchy rashes, eg 1% to 2% hydrocortisone
- thrush (vaginal yeast infection) treatment, eg Clotrimazole pessaries or Diflucan tablet
- Ural or equivalent if you are prone to urine infections

Infectious Diseases

Cutaneous Larva Migrans

This disease, caused by dog or cat hookworm, is particularly common on the beaches of Thailand. The rash starts as a small lump, and then slowly spreads like a winding line. It is intensely itchy, especially at night. It is easily treated with medications and should not be cut out or frozen.

Dengue Fever

This mosquito-borne disease is increasingly problematic throughout Southeast Asia, especially in cities. As there is no vaccine, it can only be prevented by avoiding mosquito bites. The mosquito that carries dengue is a daytime biter, so use insect-avoidance measures at all times. Symptoms include high fever, severe headache (especially behind the eyes), nausea and body aches (dengue was previously known as 'breakbone fever'). Some people develop a rash (which can be very itchy) and experience diarrhoea. The southern islands of Thailand are particularly high-risk areas. There is no specific treatment, just rest and paracetamol – do not take aspirin or ibuprofen as they increase the risk of haemorrhaging. See a doctor to be diagnosed and monitored.

Dengue can progress to the more severe and life-threatening dengue haemorrhagic fever; however, this is very uncommon in tourists. The risk of this increases substantially if you have previously been infected with dengue and are then infected with a different serotype.

Hepatitis A

The risk in Bangkok is decreasing but there is still significant risk in most of the country. This food- and water-borne virus infects the liver, causing jaundice (yellow skin and eyes), nausea and lethargy. There is no specific treatment for hepatitis A. In rare instances it can be fatal for those over the age of 40. All travellers to Thailand should be vaccinated against hepatitis A.

Hepatitis B

The only sexually transmitted disease (STD) that can be prevented by vaccination, hepatitis B is spread by body fluids, including sexual contact. In some parts of Thailand up to 20% of the population are carriers of hepatitis B, and usually are unaware of this. The long-term consequences can include liver cancer, cirrhosis and death.

HIV

HIV is now the most common cause of death for people under the age of 50 in Thailand. Always practise safe sex, and avoid getting tattoos or using unclean syringes.

Influenza

Present year-round in the tropics, flu is the most common vaccine-preventable disease contracted by travellers, so everyone should consider vaccination. There is no specific treatment, just rest and paracetamol.

RARE BUT BE AWARE

Avian Influenza Most of those infected have had close contact with sick or dead birds.

Filariasis A mosquito-borne disease that is common in the local population; practise mosquito-avoidance measures.

Hepatitis E Transmitted through contaminated food and water and has similar symptoms to hepatitis A; can be a severe problem in pregnant women. Follow safe eating and drinking guidelines.

Japanese B Encephalitis Viral disease transmitted by mosquitoes, typically occurring in rural areas; vaccination is recommended for travellers spending more than one month outside cities.

Meliodosis Contracted by skin contact with soil. The symptoms are very similar to tuberculosis (TB). There is no vaccine, but it can be treated with medications.

Strongyloides A parasite transmitted by skin contact with soil; common in local populations. It is characterised by an unusual skin rash – a linear rash on the trunk that comes and goes. An overwhelming infection can follow. It can be treated with medications.

Tuberculosis The main symptoms are fever, cough, weight loss, night sweats and tiredness. Treatment is available with long-term multi-drug regimens.

Typhus Murine typhus is spread by the bite of a flea; scrub typhus is spread via a mite. Symptoms include fever, muscle pains and a rash. Following general insect-avoidance measures and taking Doxycycline will also prevent them.

Leptospirosis

Leptospirosis is contracted from exposure to infected surface water – most commonly after river rafting or canyoning. Early symptoms are very similar to the flu and include headache and fever. It can vary from a very mild ailment to a fatal disease. Diagnosis is made through blood tests and it is easily treated with Doxycycline.

Malaria

Most parts of Thailand visited by tourists, particularly city and resort areas, have minimal to no risk of malaria, and the risk of side effects from taking antimalarial tablets is likely to outweigh the risk of getting the disease itself. If you are travelling to high-risk rural areas (unlikely for most visitors), seek medical advice on the right medication and dosage for you.

Malaria is caused by a parasite transmitted by the bite of an infected mosquito. The most significant symptom of malaria is fever, but general symptoms such as headache, diarrhoea, cough or chills may also occur – the same symptoms as many other infections. A diagnosis can only be made by taking a blood sample.

Measles

This highly contagious viral infection is spread through coughing and sneezing. Measles starts with a high fever and rash and can be complicated by pneumonia and brain disease. There is no specific treatment. Ensure you are fully vaccinated.

Rabies

This uniformly fatal disease is spread by the bite or lick of an infected animal – most commonly a dog or monkey. You should seek medical advice immediately after any animal bite and commence post-exposure treatment. Having a pre-travel vaccination means the post-bite treatment is greatly simplified.

If an animal bites you, gently wash the wound with soap and water and apply iodine-based antiseptic. If you are not pre-vaccinated, you will need to receive rabies immunoglobulin as soon as possible, followed by five shots of vaccine over 28 days. If pre-vaccinated, you need just two shots of vaccine given three days apart.

STDs

The sexually transmitted diseases most common in Thailand include herpes, warts, syphilis, gonorrhoea and chlamydia. People carrying these diseases often have no signs of infection. Condoms will prevent gonorrhoea and chlamydia but not warts or herpes. If after a sexual encounter you develop any rash, lumps, discharge or pain when passing urine, seek immediate medical attention. If you have been sexually active during your travels, have an STD check on your return home.

Typhoid

This serious bacterial infection is spread through food and water. It gives a high and slowly progressive fever, severe headache and may be accompanied by a dry cough and stomach pain. It is diagnosed by blood tests and treated with antibiotics. Vaccination is recommended for all travellers spending more than a week in Thailand or travelling outside the major cities. Be aware that vaccination is not 100% effective, so you must still be careful with what you eat and drink.

Traveller's Diarrhoea

Traveller's diarrhoea is by far the most common problem affecting travellers – up to 50% of people will suffer from some form of it within two weeks of starting their trip. In over 80% of cases, traveller's diarrhoea is caused by a bacteria (there are numerous potential culprits) and responds promptly to treatment with antibiotics.

Here we define traveller's diarrhoea as the passage of more than three watery bowel movements within 24 hours, plus at least one other symptom such as vomiting, fever, cramps, nausea or feeling generally unwell.

Treatment consists of staying well hydrated; rehydration solutions such as Gastrolyte are the best for this. Antibiotics such as Norfloxacin, Ciprofloxacin or Azithromycin will kill the bacteria quickly.

Loperamide is just a 'stopper' and doesn't get to the cause of the problem. It can be helpful, for example if you have to go on a long bus ride. Don't take Loperamide if you have a fever or blood in your stools. Seek medical attention quickly if you do not respond to an appropriate antibiotic.

Giardia lamblia is a parasite that is relatively common in travellers. Symptoms include nausea, bloating, excess gas, fatigue and intermittent diarrhoea. 'Eggy' burps are often attributed solely to giardiasis. The treatment of choice is Tinidazole, with Metronidazole being a second-line option.

Amoebic dysentery is very rare in travellers but may be misdiagnosed by poor-quality labs. Symptoms are similar to bacterial diarrhoea. You should always seek reliable medical care if you have blood in your diarrhoea. Treatment involves two drugs: Tinidazole or Metronidazole to kill the parasite in your gut and then a second drug to kill the cysts. If left untreated, complications such as liver abscesses can occur.

Environmental Hazards

Food

Eating in restaurants is the biggest risk factor for contracting traveller's diarrhoea. Ways to avoid it include eating only freshly cooked food and avoiding food that has been sitting around in buffets. Peel all fruit and cook vegetables. Eat in busy restaurants with a high turnover of customers.

Heat

Many parts of Thailand are hot and humid throughout the year. For most people it takes at least two weeks to adapt to the hot climate. Prevent swelling of the feet and ankles as well as muscle cramps caused by excessive sweating by avoiding dehydration and excessive activity in the hot hours of the day.

Heat stroke is a serious medical emergency and requires immediate medical treatment. Symptoms come on suddenly and include weakness, nausea, a hot dry body with a body temperature of over 41°C, dizziness, confusion, loss of coordination, fits and eventually collapse and loss of consciousness.

Insect Bites & Stings

Bedbugs live in the cracks of furniture and walls and then migrate to the bed at night to feed on you. You can treat the itch with an antihistamine. Lice inhabit various parts of your body but most commonly your head and pubic area. Transmission is via close contact with an infected person. They can be difficult to treat and you may need numerous applications of an anti-lice shampoo such as Permethrin. Pubic lice are usually contracted from sexual contact.

Ticks are contracted when walking in rural areas. They are commonly found behind the ears, on the belly and in armpits. If you have had a tick bite and experience symptoms such as a rash at the site of the bite or elsewhere, fever or muscle aches, you should see a doctor. Doxycycline prevents tick-borne diseases.

Leeches are found in humid rainforest areas. They do not transmit any disease, but their bites are often intensely itchy for weeks afterwards and can easily become infected. Apply an iodine-based antiseptic to any leech bite to help prevent infection.

Bee and wasp stings mainly cause problems for people who are allergic to them. Anyone with a serious allergy should carry an injection of adrenaline (eg an Epipen) for emergencies. For others, pain is the main problem – apply ice to the sting and take painkillers.

Parasites

The two rules to follow to avoid parasitic infections are to wear shoes and to avoid eating raw food, especially fish, pork and vegetables. A number of parasites are transmitted via the skin by walking barefoot, including strongyloides, hookworm and cutaneous *larva migrans*.

Skin Problems

Prickly heat is a common skin rash in the tropics, caused by sweat being trapped under the skin. Treat by taking cool showers and using powders.

Two fungal rashes commonly affect travellers. The first occurs in the groin, armpits and between the toes. It starts as a red patch that slowly spreads and is usually itchy. Treatment involves keeping the skin dry, avoiding chafing and using an antifungal cream

JELLYFISH STINGS

Box jellyfish stings range from minor to deadly. The jellyfish are generally found in the sea close to beaches and near river mouths and mangroves during the warmer months.

The initial sting can seem minor; however, severe symptoms such as back pain, nausea, vomiting, sweating, difficulty breathing and a feeling of impending doom can develop between five and 40 minutes later. Depending on the species of box jellyfish, stings are potentially fatal.

There are many other jellyfish in Thailand that cause irritating stings but no serious effects. The only way to prevent these stings is to wear protective clothing, which provides a barrier between human skin and the jellyfish.

First Aid for Severe Stings

Stay with the person, send someone to call for medical help, and start immediate CPR if they are unconscious. If the victim is conscious, douse the stung area liberally with vinegar – simple household vinegar is fine – for 30 seconds. Early application can make a huge difference. Some Thai beaches like Ko Kut and Ko Mak have installed vinegar stations on the beach. It is best to seek medical care quickly in case any other symptoms develop over the next 40 minutes.

such as Clotrimazole or Lamisil. The fungus *Tinea versicolor* causes small and light-coloured patches, most commonly on the back, chest and shoulders. Consult a doctor.

Cuts and scratches become easily infected in humid climates. Immediately wash all wounds in clean water and apply antiseptic. If you develop signs of infection, see a doctor. Coral cuts can easily become infected.

Snakes

Though snake bites are rare for travellers, there are over 85 species of venomous snakes in Thailand. Always wear boots and long pants if walking in an area that may have snakes. First aid in the event of a snake bite involves 'pressure immobilisation' using an elastic bandage firmly wrapped around the affected limb, starting at the hand or foot (depending on the limb bitten) and working up towards the chest. The bandage should not be so tight that the circulation is cut off, and the fingers or toes should be kept free so the circulation can be checked. Immobilise the limb with a splint and carry the victim to medical attention. It is very important that the victim stays immobile. Do not use tourniquets or try to suck the venom out.

The Thai Red Cross produces antivenom for many of the poisonous snakes in Thailand.

Sunburn

Even on a cloudy day sunburn can occur rapidly. Use a strong sunscreen (at least factor 30), making sure to reapply after a swim, and always wear a wide-brimmed hat and sunglasses outdoors. Avoid lying in the sun when the sun is at its highest in the sky (10am to 2pm). If you become sunburnt, stay out of the sun until you have recovered, apply cool compresses and take painkillers for the discomfort. One per cent hydrocortisone cream applied twice daily is also helpful.

Travelling with Children

Thailand is relatively safe for children from a health point of view. A medical kit designed specifically for children may include paracetamol or Tylenol syrup for fevers, an antihistamine, itch cream, first-aid supplies, nappy-rash treatment, sunscreen and insect repellent. It is a good idea to carry a general antibiotic (best used under medical supervision) – Azithromycin is an ideal paediatric formula used to treat bacterial diarrhoea as well as ear, chest and throat infections.

Good resources include the Lonely Planet publication *Travel with Children;* for those spending longer away, Jane Wilson-Howarth's book *Your Child's Health Abroad* is excellent.

Women's Health

Pregnant women should get specialist advice before travelling. The ideal time to travel is in the second trimester (16 and 28 weeks), when pregnancy-related risks are at their lowest. Most of all, ensure travel insurance covers all pregnancy-related possibilities, including premature labour.

Traveller's diarrhoea can quickly lead to dehydration and result in inadequate blood flow to the placenta. Many of the drugs used to treat various diarrhoea bugs are not recommended in pregnancy. Azithromycin is considered safe.

In Thailand's urban areas, supplies of sanitary products are readily available. Your personal birth-control option may not be available, so bring adequate supplies. Heat, humidity and antibiotics can all contribute to thrush. Treatment of thrush is with antifungal creams and pessaries such as Clotrimazole. A practical alternative is one tablet of fluconazole (Diflucan). Urinary-tract infections can be precipitated by dehydration or long bus journeys without toilet stops; bring suitable antibiotics for treatment.

Language

Thailand's official language is effectively the dialect spoken and written in central Thailand, which has successfully become the lingua franca of all Thai and non-Thai ethnic groups in the kingdom.

In Thai the meaning of a single syllable may be altered by means of different tones. In standard Thai there are five: low tone, mid tone, falling tone, high tone and rising tone. The range of all five tones is relative to each speaker's vocal range, so there is no fixed 'pitch' intrinsic to the language.

➡ **low tone** – 'Flat' like the mid tone, but pronounced at the relative bottom of one's vocal range. It is low, level and has no inflection, eg bàht (baht – the Thai currency).

➡ **mid tone** – Pronounced 'flat', at the relative middle of the speaker's vocal range, eg dee (good). No tone mark is used.

➡ **falling tone** – Starting high and falling sharply, this tone is similar to the change in pitch in English when you are emphasising a word, or calling someone's name from afar, eg mâi (no/not).

➡ **high tone** – Usually the most difficult for non-Thai speakers. It's pronounced near the relative top of the vocal range, as level as possible, eg máh (horse).

➡ **rising tone** – Starting low and gradually rising, sounds like the inflection used by English speakers to imply a question – 'Yes?', eg săhm (three).

WANT MORE?

For in-depth language information and handy phrases, check out Lonely Planet's *Thai Phrasebook*. You'll find it at **shop.lonelyplanet.com**, or you can buy Lonely Planet's iPhone phrasebooks at the Apple App Store.

The Thai government has instituted the Royal Thai General Transcription System (RTGS) as a standard method of writing Thai using the Roman alphabet. It's used in official documents, road signs and on maps. However, local variations crop up on signs, menus etc. Generally, names in this book follow the most common practice.

In our coloured pronunciation guides, the hyphens indicate syllable breaks within words, and some syllables are further divided with a dot to help you pronounce compound vowels, eg mêu·a-rai (when).

The vowel a is pronounced as in 'about', aa as the 'a' in 'bad', ah as the 'a' in 'father', ai as in 'aisle', air as in 'flair' (without the 'r'), eu as the 'er' in 'her' (without the 'r'), ew as in 'new' (with rounded lips), oh as the 'o' in 'toe', or as in 'torn' (without the 'r') and ow as in 'now'.

Most consonants correspond to their English counterparts. The exceptions are Ƅ (a hard 'p' sound, almost like a 'b', eg in 'hip-bag'); đ (a hard 't' sound, like a sharp 'd', eg in 'mid-tone'); ng (as in 'singing'; in Thai it can occur at the start of a word) and r (as in 'run' but flapped; in everyday speech it's often pronounced like 'l').

BASICS

The social structure of Thai society demands different registers of speech depending on who you're talking to. To make things simple we've chosen the correct form of speech appropriate to the context of each phrase.

When being polite, the speaker ends his or her sentence with kráp (for men) or kâ (for women). It is the gender of the speaker that is being expressed here; it is also the common way to answer 'yes' to a question or show agreement.

The masculine and feminine forms of phrases in this chapter are indicated where relevant with 'm/f'.

Hello.	สวัสดี	sà-wàt-dee
Goodbye.	ลาก่อน	lah gòrn
Yes./No.	ใช่/ไม่	châi/mâi
Please.	ขอ	kŏr
Thank you.	ขอบคุณ	kòrp kun
You're welcome.	ยินดี	yin dee
Excuse me.	ขออภัย	kŏr à-pai
Sorry.	ขอโทษ	kŏr tôht

How are you?
สบายดีไหม — sà-bai dee măi

Fine. And you?
สบายดีครับ/ค่า แล้วคุณล่ะ — sà-bai dee kráp/kâ láa·ou kun lâ (m/f)

What's your name?
คุณชื่ออะไร — kun chêu à-rai

My name is ...
ผม/ดิฉันชื่อ... — pŏm/dì-chăn chêu ... (m/f)

Do you speak English?
คุณพูดภาษาอังกฤษได้ไหม — kun pôot pah-săh ang-grìt dâi măi

I don't understand.
ผม/ดิฉันไม่เข้าใจ — pŏm/dì-chăn mâi kôw jai (m/f)

ACCOMMODATION

Where's a ...?	... อยู่ที่ไหน	... yòo têe năi
campsite	ค่ายพักแรม	kâi pák raam
guesthouse	บ้านพัก	bâhn pák
hotel	โรงแรม	rohng raam
youth hostel	บ้านเยาวชน	bâhn yow-wá-chon

Do you have a ... room?	มีห้อง ... ไหม	mee hôrng ... măi
single	เดี่ยว	dèe·o
double	เตียงคู่	đee·ang kôo
twin	สองเตียง	sŏrng đee·ang

air-con	แอร์	aa
bathroom	ห้องน้ำ	hôrng nám
laundry	ห้องซักผ้า	hôrng sák pâh
mosquito net	มุ้ง	múng
window	หน้าต่าง	nâh đàhng

Question Words

What?	อะไร	à-rai
When?	เมื่อไร	mêu·a-rai
Where?	ที่ไหน	têe năi
Who?	ใคร	krai
Why?	ทำไม	tam-mai

DIRECTIONS

Where's ...?
... อยู่ที่ไหน — ... yòo têe năi

What's the address?
ที่อยู่คืออะไร — têe yòo keu à-rai

Could you please write it down?
เขียนลงให้ได้ไหม — kĕe·an long hâi dâi măi

Can you show me (on the map)?
ให้ดู (ในแผนที่) ได้ไหม — hâi doo (nai păan têe) dâi măi

Turn left/right.
เลี้ยวซ้าย/ขวา — lée·o sái/kwăh

It's ...	อยู่ ...	yòo ...
behind	ที่หลัง	têe lăng
in front of	ตรงหน้า	đrong nâh
next to	ข้างๆ	kâhng kâhng
straight ahead	ตรงไป	đrong bai

EATING & DRINKING

I'd like (the menu), please.
ขอ (รายการอาหาร) หน่อย — kŏr (rai gahn ah-hăhn) nòy

What would you recommend?
คุณแนะนำอะไรบ้าง — kun náa-nam à-rai bâhng

That was delicious!
อร่อยมาก — à-ròy mâhk

Cheers!
ไชโย — chai-yoh

Please bring the bill.
ขอบิลหน่อย — kŏr bin nòy

I don't eat ...	ผม/ดิฉันไม่กิน ...	pŏm/dì-chăn mâi gin ... (m/f)
eggs	ไข่	kài
fish	ปลา	ɓlah
red meat	เนื้อแดง	néu·a daang
nuts	ถั่ว	tòo·a

Key Words

bar	บาร์	bah
bottle	ขวด	kòo·at
bowl	ชาม	chahm
breakfast	อาหารเช้า	ah-hăhn chów
cafe	ร้านกาแฟ	ráhn gah-faa
chopsticks	ไม้ตะเกียบ	mái đà-gèe·ap
cold	เย็น	yen
cup	ถ้วย	tôo·ay
dessert	ของหวาน	kŏrng wăhn
dinner	อาหารเย็น	ah-hăhn yen
drink list	รายการ เครื่องดื่ม	rai gahn krêu·ang dèum
fork	ส้อม	sôrm
glass	แก้ว	gâa·ou
hot	ร้อน	rórn
knife	มีด	mêet
lunch	อาหาร กลางวัน	ah-hăhn glahng wan
market	ตลาด	đà-làht
menu	รานการ อาหาร	rai gahn ah-hăhn
plate	จาน	jahn
restaurant	ร้านอาหาร	ráhn ah-hăhn
spicy	เผ็ด	pèt
spoon	ช้อน	chórn
vegetarian (person)	คนกินเจ	kon gin jair

Signs

ทางเข้า	Entrance
ทางออก	Exit
เปิด	Open
ปิด	Closed
ที่ติดต่อสอบถาม	Information
ห้าม	Prohibited
ห้องสุขา	Toilets
ชาย	Men
หญิง	Women

with	มี	mee
without	ไม่มี	mâi mee

Meat & Fish

beef	เนื้อ	néu·a
chicken	ไก่	gài
crab	ปู	ɓoo
duck	เป็ด	ɓèt
fish	ปลา	ɓlah
meat	เนื้อ	néu·a
pork	หมู	mŏo
seafood	อาหารทะเล	ah-hăhn tá-lair
squid	ปลาหมึก	ɓlah mèuk

Fruit & Vegetables

banana	กล้วย	glôo·ay
beans	ถั่ว	tòo·a
coconut	มะพร้าว	má-prów
eggplant	มะเขือ	má-kĕu·a
fruit	ผลไม้	pŏn-lá-mái
guava	ฝรั่ง	fa-ràng
lime	มะนาว	má-now
mango	มะม่วง	má-môo·ang
mangosteen	มังคุด	mang-kút
mushrooms	เห็ด	hèt
nuts	ถั่ว	tòo·a
papaya	มะละกอ	má-lá-gor
potatoes	มันฝรั่ง	man fa-ràng
rambutan	เงาะ	ngó
tamarind	มะขาม	má-kăhm
tomatoes	มะเขือเทศ	má-kĕu·a têt
vegetables	ผัก	pàk
watermelon	แตงโม	đaang moh

Other

chilli	พริก	prík
egg	ไข่	kài
fish sauce	น้ำปลา	nám ɓlah
ice	น้ำแข็ง	nám kăang

noodles	เส้น	sên
oil	น้ำมัน	nám man
pepper	พริกไทย	prík tai
rice	ข้าว	kôw
salad	ผักสด	pàk sòt
salt	เกลือ	gleu·a
soup	น้ำซุป	nám súp
soy sauce	น้ำซีอิ้ว	nám see-éw
sugar	น้ำตาล	nám đahn
tofu	เต้าหู้	đôw hôo

Drinks

beer	เบียร์	bee·a
coffee	กาแฟ	gah-faa
milk	นมจืด	nom jèut
orange juice	น้ำส้ม	nám sôm
soy milk	น้ำเต้าหู้	nám đôw hôo
sugarcane juice	น้ำอ้อย	nám ôy
tea	ชา	chah
water	น้ำดื่ม	nám dèum

EMERGENCIES

Help!	ช่วยด้วย	chôo·ay dôo·ay
Go away!	ไปให้พ้น	ɓai hâi pón

Call a doctor!
เรียกหมอหน่อย rêe·ak mŏr nòy

Call the police!
เรียกตำรวจหน่อย rêe·ak đam·ròo·at nòy

I'm ill.
ผม/ดิฉันป่วย pŏm/dì-chăn ɓòo·ay **(m/f)**

I'm lost.
ผม/ดิฉัน หลงทาง pŏm/dì-chăn lŏng tahng **(m/f)**

Where are the toilets?
ห้องน้ำอยู่ที่ไหน hôrng nám yòo têe năi

SHOPPING & SERVICES

I'd like to buy ...
อยากจะซื้อ ... yàhk jà séu ...

I'm just looking.
ดูเฉย ๆ doo chĕu·i chĕu·i

Can I look at it?
ขอดูได้ไหม kŏr doo dâi măi

How much is it?
เท่าไร tôw-rai

That's too expensive.
แพงไป paang ɓai

Can you lower the price?
ลดราคาได้ไหม lót rah-kah dâi măi

There's a mistake in the bill.
บิลใบนี้ผิด นะครับ/ค่ะ bin bai née pìt ná kráp/kâ **(m/f)**

TIME & DATES

What time is it?
กี่โมงแล้ว gèe mohng láa·ou

morning	เช้า	chów
afternoon	บ่าย	bài
evening	เย็น	yen
yesterday	เมื่อวาน	mêu·a wahn
today	วันนี้	wan née
tomorrow	พรุ่งนี้	prûng née
Monday	วันจันทร์	wan jan
Tuesday	วันอังคาร	wan ang-kahn
Wednesday	วันพุธ	wan pút
Thursday	วันพฤหัสฯ	wan pá-réu-hàt
Friday	วันศุกร	wan sùk
Saturday	วันเสาร์	wan sŏw
Sunday	วันอาทิตย์	wan ah-tít

TRANSPORT

Public Transport

bicycle rickshaw	สามล้อ	săhm lór
boat	เรือ	reu·a
bus	รถเมล์	rót mair
car	รถเก๋ง	rót gĕng
motorcycle taxi	มอร์เตอร์ไซค์รับจ้าง	mor-đeu-sai ráp jâhng
plane	เครื่องบิน	krêu·ang bin
train	รถไฟ	rót fai
túk-túk	ตุ๊ก ๆ	đúk đúk

Numbers

1	หนึ่ง	nèung
2	สอง	sŏrng
3	สาม	săhm
4	สี่	sèe
5	ห้า	hâh
6	หก	hòk
7	เจ็ด	jèt
8	แปด	bàat
9	เก้า	gôw
10	สิบ	sìp
11	สิบเอ็ด	sìp-èt
20	ยี่สิบ	yêe-sìp
21	ยี่สิบเอ็ด	yêe-sìp-èt
30	สามสิบ	săhm-sìp
40	สี่สิบ	sèe-sìp
50	ห้าสิบ	hâh-sìp
60	หกสิบ	hòk-sìp
70	เจ็ดสิบ	jèt-sìp
80	แปดสิบ	bàat-sìp
90	เก้าสิบ	gôw-sìp
100	หนึ่งร้อย	nèung róy
1000	หนึ่งพัน	nèung pan
10,000	หนึ่งหมื่น	nèung mèun
100,000	หนึ่งแสน	nèung săan
1,000,000	หนึ่งล้าน	nèung láhn

When's the ... bus?	รถเมล์คัน ... มาเมื่อไร	rót mair kan ... mah mêu·a rai
first	แรก	râak
last	สุดท้าย	sùt tái
next	ต่อไป	đòr bai

A ... ticket, please.	ขอตั๋ว ...	kŏr đŏo·a ...
one-way	เที่ยวเดียว	têe·o dee·o
return	ไปกลับ	bai glàp

I'd like a/an ... seat.	ต้องการ ที่นั่ง ...	đôrng gahn têe nâng ...
aisle	ติดทางเดิน	đìt tahng deun
window	ติดหน้าต่าง	đìt nâh đàhng

platform	ชานชาลา	chan-chah-lah
ticket window	ช่องขายตั๋ว	chôrng kăi đŏo·a
timetable	ตารางเวลา	đah-rahng wair-lah

What time does it get to (Chiang Mai)?
ถึง (เชียงใหม่) กี่โมง — tĕung (chee·ang mài) gèe mohng

Does it stop at (Saraburi)?
รถจอดที่ (สระบุรี) ไหม — rót jòrt têe (sà-rà-bù-ree) măi

Please tell me when we get to (Chiang Mai).
เมื่อถึง (เชียงใหม่) กรุณาบอกด้วย — mêu·a tĕung (chee·ang mài) gà-rú-nah bòrk dôo·ay

I'd like to get off at (Saraburi).
ขอลงที่(สระบุรี) — kŏr long têe (sà-rà-bù-ree)

Driving & Cycling

I'd like to hire a ...	อยากจะ เช่า ...	yàhk jà chôw ...
car	รถเก๋ง	rót gĕng
motorbike	รถ มอร์เตอร์ไซค์	rót mor-đeu-sai

I'd like ...	ต้องการ ...	đôrng gahn ...
my bicycle repaired	ซ่อมรถ จักรยาน	sôrm rót jàk-gà-yahn
to hire a bicycle	เช่ารถ จักรยาน	chôw rót jàk-gà-yahn

Is this the road to (Ban Bung Wai)?
ทางนี้ไป (บ้านบุ่งหวาย) ไหม — tahng née bai (bâhn bùng wăi) măi

Where's a petrol station?
ปั๊มน้ำมันอยู่ที่ไหน — bâm nám man yòo têe năi

Can I park here?
จอดที่นี่ได้ไหม — jòrt têe née dâi măi

How long can I park here?
จอดที่นี่ได้นานเท่าไร — jòrt têe née dâi nahn tôw-rai

I need a mechanic.
ต้องการช่างรถ — đôrng gahn châhng rót

I have a flat tyre.
ยางแบน — yahng baan

I've run out of petrol.
หมดน้ำมัน — mòt nám man

Do I need a helmet?
ต้องใช้หมวกกันน๊อกไหม — đôrng chái mòo·ak gan nórk măi

GLOSSARY

ah·hăhn – food
ao/ow – bay or gulf

bâhn/ban – house or village
bòht – central sanctuary or chapel in a Thai temple
BTS – Bangkok Mass Transit System (Skytrain)

chedi – stupa; monument erected to house a Buddha relic
chow lair/chao leh/chow nám – sea gypsies

dhamma – right behaviour and truth according to Buddhist doctrine

fa·ràng – foreigner of European descent; guava

ga·teu·i/kathoey – 'ladyboy'; transvestites and transsexuals
gò – see *ko*

hàht/hat – beach
hôrng/hong – room or chamber; island caves semisubmerged in the sea

Isan/ìsăhn – general term for northeastern Thailand

jataka – stories of the Buddha's previous lives
jeen – Chinese

kathoey – see *ga·teu·i*
khao/kŏw – hill or mountain
klorng/klong/khlong – canal
ko/koh/gò – island
Khun – honorific used before first name

laem/lăam – geographical cape

masjid/mátsàyít – mosque
meu·ang/muang – city
moo·ay tai/muay·thai – Thai boxing
MRT – Metropolitan Rapid Transit (Metro); the underground railway in Bangkok

nám – water or juice
nám đòk – waterfall
nibbana – nirvana; the 'blowing out' or extinction of all desire and thus of all suffering
nóy/noi – small

ow – see *ao*

pak tai/ɓàk đâi – southern Thailand
Pali – language derived from Sanskrit, in which the Buddhist scriptures are written
prá/phra – monk or Buddha image
prang/ɓrang – Khmer-style tower on temples

ɓàk đâi – southern Thailand
ɓèe·pâht/pìi-phâat – classical Thai orchestra
ɓrang – see *prang*

ráhn goh·ɓêe – coffee shops (southern Thailand)
Ramakian – Thai version of India's epic literary piece, the Ramayana
reu·an tăa·ou – a longhouse
rót aa – blue-and-white air-conditioned bus
rót tam·má·dah – ordinary bus (no air-con) or ordinary train (not rapid or express)

săh·lah/sala – open-sided, covered meeting hall or resting place
săhm·lór – three-wheeled pedicab
sangha – brotherhood of Buddhist monks; temple inhabitants (monks and nuns)
sà·nùk – fun
soi – lane or small street
Songkran – Thai New Year, held in mid-April
sŏrng·tăa·ou – small pickup truck with two benches in the back, used as bus/taxi
SRT – State Railway of Thailand
stupa/chedi – domed edifice housing Buddhist relics
suttas – discourses of the Buddha

talat – see *đa·làht*
TAT – Tourism Authority of Thailand
tha/tâh – pier, landing
tâm/tham – cave
thanŏn – street, road, avenue (we use the abbreviation 'Th' in this book)
túk-túk – motorised *săhm·lór*

vipassana – Buddhist insight meditation

wâi – palms-together Thai greeting
wan prá – Buddhist holy days which coincide with the main phases of the moon (full, new and half) each month
wang – palace
wát – temple, monastery
wí·hăhn/wihan – counterpart to *bòht* in Thai temples, containing Buddha images but not circumscribed by sema stones

yài – big

Behind the Scenes

SEND US YOUR FEEDBACK

We love to hear from travellers – your comments keep us on our toes and help make our books better. Our well-travelled team reads every word on what you loved or loathed about this book. Although we cannot reply individually to postal submissions, we always guarantee that your feedback goes straight to the appropriate authors, in time for the next edition. Each person who sends us information is thanked in the next edition – the most useful submissions are rewarded with a selection of digital PDF chapters.

Visit **lonelyplanet.com/contact** to submit your updates and suggestions or to ask for help. Our award-winning website also features inspirational travel stories, news and discussions.

Note: We may edit, reproduce and incorporate your comments in Lonely Planet products such as guidebooks, websites and digital products, so let us know if you don't want your comments reproduced or your name acknowledged. For a copy of our privacy policy visit lonelyplanet.com/privacy.

OUR READERS

Many thanks to the travellers who used the last edition and wrote to us with helpful hints, useful advice and interesting anecdotes: Danny Wongworawat, Dennis Vervlossen, Jamison Firestone, Jilly MacPherson, Kaori Hashimoto, Kerry Colmer, Virginia Scott

AUTHOR THANKS

Mark Beales

First, thanks to Sarah Reid for offering me the chance to return to this guide. In Bang Saen, Michiel and Mynd had some great tips and on Ko Kut, Seren was a star. On Ko Chang, thanks to Ian, Lisa and Olivier, who all helped immensely while Eric and Issac had some great ideas. The staff at TAT were as helpful as ever, especially K.Suladda and K.Kesorn. Lastly, thanks to Ann and Daniel.

Austin Bush

My thanks to the previous authors of this guide, Andrew Burke, Joe Cummings and China Williams – believe it or not, some of your words live on!; Destination Editor Sarah Reid; part-time research assistants Kathy MacLeod and Maher Sattar; and the rest of the kind folks on the ground in Bangkok.

David Eimer

Thanks to Sarah Reid and all the LP crew. As ever, much gratitude to everyone who passed on tips, whether knowingly or unwittingly.

Damian Harper

Many thanks to all who eased the way and came up with ideas, help and suggestions; most notably, gratitude to Neal Bambridge, Charoon Juntra, Brigitte Gomm, Matt Rubin, Jessica Meier, Eveline Fortuin, Amanda, Suwatchai Praesomboon, Stanley Chang and Mark Tewari. Loved the company of the charming family on the train from Hat Yai to Surat Thani, you are fine people and I wish you every good fortune. Cheers also to my brother and Thailand enthusiast, John. Thanks to Daisy, Tim and Emma, as always.

Isabella Noble

Thanks to everyone who helped out on the road, whether knowingly or not, particularly Jamie Monk and Lee Cobaj for the stellar Phuket intel. Cheers to Paul on Ko Phayam, elephant-expert John Roberts, the Gibbon Rehab Project crew and Ann for Thai language tips. Thanks to my hardworking co-authors, especially fellow island experts Mark Beales and Damian Harper. Extra special thanks to Andrew, Raquel and Papi for pitching in, and to my favourite research assistant, Jack Noble.

ACKNOWLEDGMENTS

Climate map data adapted from Peel MC, Finlayson BL & McMahon TA (2007) 'Updated World Map of the Köppen-Geiger Climate Classification', *Hydrology and Earth System Sciences*, 11, 1633–44.

Illustrations pp58–9 and pp64–5 by Michael Weldon.

Cover photograph: Ko Phi-Phi islands, Jack Malipan Travel Photography/Alamy ©.

THIS BOOK

This 10th edition of Lonely Planet's *Thailand's Islands & Beaches* guidebook was researched and written by Mark Beales, Austin Bush, David Eimer, Damian Harper and Isabella Noble. This guidebook was produced by the following:

Destination Editor Sarah Reid

Product Editors Joel Cotterell, Elin Berglund

Assisting Editors Susie Ashworth, Melanie Dankel, Bruce Evans, Simon Williamson

Regional Senior Cartographer Diana Von Holdt

Book Designer Cam Ashley, Jess Rose

Language Content Branislava Vladisavljevic

Cover Research Naomi Parker

Thanks to Joe Bindloss, Daniel Corbett, Andi Jones, Anne Mason, Wayne Murphy, Karyn Noble, Alison Ridgway, Luna Soo, Angela Tinson, Lauren Wellicome

Index

Map Pages **000**
Photo Pages **000**

Map Pages **000**
Photo Pages **000**

Map Legend

Sights

- Beach
- Bird Sanctuary
- Buddhist
- Castle/Palace
- Christian
- Confucian
- Hindu
- Islamic
- Jain
- Jewish
- Monument
- Museum/Gallery/Historic Building
- Ruin
- Shinto
- Sikh
- Taoist
- Winery/Vineyard
- Zoo/Wildlife Sanctuary
- Other Sight

Activities, Courses & Tours

- Bodysurfing
- Diving
- Canoeing/Kayaking
- Course/Tour
- Sento Hot Baths/Onsen
- Skiing
- Snorkelling
- Surfing
- Swimming/Pool
- Walking
- Windsurfing
- Other Activity

Sleeping

- Sleeping
- Camping

Eating

- Eating

Drinking & Nightlife

- Drinking & Nightlife
- Cafe

Entertainment

- Entertainment

Shopping

- Shopping

Information

- Bank
- Embassy/Consulate
- Hospital/Medical
- Internet
- Police
- Post Office
- Telephone
- Toilet
- Tourist Information
- Other Information

Geographic

- Beach
- Gate
- Hut/Shelter
- Lighthouse
- Lookout
- Mountain/Volcano
- Oasis
- Park
- Pass
- Picnic Area
- Waterfall

Population

- Capital (National)
- Capital (State/Province)
- City/Large Town
- Town/Village

Transport

- Airport
- Border crossing
- Bus
- Cable car/Funicular
- Cycling
- Ferry
- Metro/MRT/MTR station
- Monorail
- Parking
- Petrol station
- Skytrain/Subway station
- Taxi
- Train station/Railway
- Tram
- Underground station
- Other Transport

Note: Not all symbols displayed above appear on the maps in this book

Routes

- Tollway
- Freeway
- Primary
- Secondary
- Tertiary
- Lane
- Unsealed road
- Road under construction
- Plaza/Mall
- Steps
- Tunnel
- Pedestrian overpass
- Walking Tour
- Walking Tour detour
- Path/Walking Trail

Boundaries

- International
- State/Province
- Disputed
- Regional/Suburb
- Marine Park
- Cliff
- Wall

Hydrography

- River, Creek
- Intermittent River
- Canal
- Water
- Dry/Salt/Intermittent Lake
- Reef

Areas

- Airport/Runway
- Beach/Desert
- Cemetery (Christian)
- Cemetery (Other)
- Glacier
- Mudflat
- Park/Forest
- Sight (Building)
- Sportsground
- Swamp/Mangrove

OUR STORY

A beat-up old car, a few dollars in the pocket and a sense of adventure. In 1972 that's all Tony and Maureen Wheeler needed for the trip of a lifetime – across Europe and Asia overland to Australia. It took several months, and at the end – broke but inspired – they sat at their kitchen table writing and stapling together their first travel guide, *Across Asia on the Cheap*. Within a week they'd sold 1500 copies. Lonely Planet was born.

Today, Lonely Planet has offices in Franklin, London, Melbourne, Oakland, Beijing and Delhi, with more than 600 staff and writers. We share Tony's belief that 'a great guidebook should do three things: inform, educate and amuse'.

OUR WRITERS

Mark Beales

Need to Know, First Time, What's New, Ko Chang & Eastern Seaboard After working as a journalist for 13 years, Mark swapped the chilly shores of England for the sunnier coasts of Thailand. Since 2004 Mark has lived in Thailand, where he has contributed to around a dozen books for Lonely Planet, been a TV presenter and dragged his backpack to every country in Southeast Asia. Mark lives with his wife, Ann, and their son, Daniel. For more on Mark's work, visit www.markbeales.com.

Austin Bush

Bangkok, Eat Like a Local, Food & Drink, Food Spotter's Guide Austin Bush came to Thailand in 1999 as part of a language study programme hosted by Chiang Mai University. The lure of city life, employment and spicy food eventually led Austin to Bangkok. City life, employment and spicy food have managed to keep him there since. He is a native of Oregon and a writer and photographer who often focuses on food; samples of Austin's work can be seen at www.austinbushphotography.com.

David Eimer

Hua Hin & Upper Gulf, Deep South section of Ko Samui & Lower Gulf, Thai Massage, Responsible Travel, Directory, Transport, Health A decade of visiting Thailand in search of beaches and fine food prompted David to relocate to Bangkok in 2012. Since then, his work as a journalist for a variety of newspapers and magazines has taken him from the far south of Thailand to its northernmost extremities, with many stops in between. He also contributed to Lonely Planet's *Thailand*.

Damian Harper

Month by Month, Itineraries, Choose Your Beach, Diving & Snorkelling, Travel With Children, Ko Samui & Lower Gulf, People & Culture, Environment Damian traded a career in bookselling for a four-year degree in Chinese, a decision that propelled him towards the Far East and a sharp change of tack into travel journalism and guidebook writing. Since the late 1990s, Damian has worked on Lonely Planet guides to places as diverse as China, Malaysia, Singapore & Brunei, Vietnam, Hong Kong, Macau and Guangzhou, London and Ireland. You can find him at www.damianharper.com.

Isabella Noble

Welcome to Thailand's Islands & Beaches, Top 15, If You Like, Regions at a Glance, Phuket & Andaman Coast English-Australian-Spanish Isabella writes about Thailand, India, Spain and beyond for Lonely Planet, Telegraph Travel and others. A big fan of Phuket despite its touristy reputation (she also penned Lonely Planet's *Pocket Phuket*), Isabella first fell for the Andaman on a 2008 backpacking extravaganza. She lives in London and blogs at www.isabellanoble.blogspot.com. Find her on Twitter and Instagram (@isabellamnoble).

Published by Lonely Planet Publications Pty Ltd
ABN 36 005 607 983
10th edition – July 2016
ISBN 978 1 74321 873 0

10 9 8 7 6 5 4 3 2
Printed in China